CW00422129

TEXT, IMAGE, INTERPRETATION

Prof. Éamonn Ó Carragáin

STUDIES IN THE EARLY MIDDLE AGES

*Editorial Board under the auspices of the
Centre for Medieval Studies, University of York*

Elizabeth M. Tyler (University of York)
Julian D. Richards (University of York)
Ross Balzaretti (University of Nottingham)

VOLUME 18

TEXT, IMAGE, INTERPRETATION
Studies in Anglo-Saxon Literature and its Insular Context in Honour of Éamonn Ó Carragáin

Edited by

Alastair Minnis and Jane Roberts

BREPOLS

British Library Cataloguing in Publication Data

Text, image, interpretation : studies in Anglo-Saxon literature and its insular context in honour of Eamonn O Carragain. - (Studies in the early Middle Ages ; 18)
1. English literature - Old English, ca. 450-1100 - History and criticism 2. Literature, Medieval - History and criticism 3. Civilization, Anglo-Saxon 4. Sacred space - History - To 1500 5. Civilization, Medieval 6. Christian art and symbolism - Medieval, 500-1500
I. O Carragain, Eamonn II. Minnis, A. J. (Alastair J.) III. Roberts, Jane Annette
829'.09

ISBN-13: 9782503518190

© 2007, Brepols Publishers n.v., Turnhout, Belgium

All rights reserved. No part of this publication may be reproduced,
stored in a retrieval system, or transmitted, in any form or by any means,
electronic, mechanical, photocopying, recording, or otherwise,
without the prior permission of the publisher.

D/2007/0095/84
ISBN: 978-2-503-51819-0

Printed in the E.U. on acid-free paper

CONTENTS

I. Looking Outwards

II. Reading Texts

III. Reading Stones

ABBREVIATIONS

AASS   Johannes Bollandus, *Acta Sanctorum quotquot toto orbe colun-*
            tur (Antwerp, 1643–; repr. Brussels, 1965–)

Art B.   *The Art Bulletin*

CASSS   *Corpus of Anglo-Saxon Stone Sculpture* (Oxford, 1984–)

CCCA   Corpus Christianorum, Clavis Apocryphorum (Turnhout,
            1992–)

CCCM   Corpus Christianorum, Continuatio Mediaevalis (Turn-
            hout, 1966–)

CCSA   Corpus Christianorum, Series Apocryphorum (Turnhout,
            1983–)

CCSL   Corpus Christianorum, Series Latina (Turnhout, 1953–)

CLA   *Codices Latini Antiquiores: A Palaeographical Guide to Latin*
            Manuscripts prior to the Ninth Century, ed. by E. A. Lowe, 11
            vols and Supplement (Oxford, 1934–79); Addenda, *Mediae-*
            val Studies, 47 (1985), 317–66; Addenda II, *Mediaeval*
            Studies, 54 (1992), 286–87

CSA   Corpus della scultura altomedievale (Spoleto, 1959–)

CSEL   Corpus Scriptorum Ecclesiasticorum Latinorum (Vienna,
            1866–)

DAJ   *Derbyshire Archaeological Journal*

EETS	Early English Text Society (London, 1864–)
OS	Original Series
ES	Extra Series
SS	Supplementary Series

| JBAA | *Journal of the British Archaeological Association* |

| JEGP | *Journal of English and Germanic Philology* |

| JWCI | *Journal of the Warburg and Courtauld Institutes* |

| MANCASS | The Manchester Centre for Anglo-Saxon Studies, University of Manchester |

| MGH | Monumenta Germaniae Historica, cited by series and volume |

| NESAT | The North European Symposium on Archaeological Textiles |

| NQ | *Notes and Queries* |

| PG | *Patrologia cursus completus, Series Graeca*, ed. by J. P. Migne, 161 vols (Turnhout, 1857–66) |

| PL | *Patrologia cursus completus, Series Latina*, ed. by J. P. Migne, 221 vols (Turnhout, 1844–64) |

| PMLA | *Publications of the Modern Language Association of America* |

Carol A. Farr

Figure 6, p. 119. Virgin and child enthroned with angels, The Book of Kells. Dublin, Trinity College, MS 58, fol. 7ᵛ. By permission of The Board of Trinity College, Dublin.

Figure 7, p. 132. *Magnificat* initial, The Book of Kells. Dublin, Trinity College, MS 58, fol. 191ᵛ. By permission of The Board of Trinity College, Dublin.

Catherine E. Karkov

Figure 8, p. 138. Opening of the Order of the Mass. Cambridge, Corpus Christi College, MS 422, p. 51. By kind permission of Corpus Christi College.

Anna Maria Luiselli Fadda

Figure 9, p. 150. The Last Judgement. Ivory panel, London, Victoria and Albert Museum. By kind permission of the Victoria and Albert Museum.

Figure 10, p. 151. Clonmacnois, Co. Offaly, Cross of the Scriptures, west side. Photo: Peter Harbison, by kind permission.

Figure 11, p. 159. The *Ba* hovering above the dead body. From the Livre des Morts de Tchenena (Egypt, Nouvel Empire, XVIII dynasty), Paris, Musée du Louvre. Drawing by Luca Luiselli.

Figure 12, p. 163. Clonmacnois, Co. Offaly, Cross of the Scriptures, east side. Photo: Peter Harbison, by kind permission.

Figure 13, p. 166. Clonmacnois, Co. Offaly, Cross of the Scriptures, bottom panel of west side. Photo: Peter Harbison, by kind permission.

Charles D. Wright

Figure 14, p. 171. The Alfred Jewel (gold, rock crystal, enamel; length 6.2 cm). By kind permission of the Visitors of the Ashmolean Museum, Oxford.

Figure 15, p. 172. The Fuller Brooch (silver niello; diameter 11.4 cm). By kind permission of the Trustees of the British Museum.

Elizabeth Coatsworth

Figure 16, p. 194. St Gregory the Pope: detail from the maniple from the tomb of St Cuthbert, Durham Cathedral Treasury. Reproduced by kind permission of Durham Cathedral.

Figure 17, p. 197. Detail from the Bayeux Tapestry, 11th Century: Harold is offered the crown. Muséé de la Tapisserie de Bayeux, Centre Guillaume le Conquérant, Bayeux, France. By special permission of the City of Bayeux.

Figure 18, p. 201. Detail with inscription from the Cloth of St Ewald, from St Kunibert, Cologne. © Rheinisches Bildarchiv.

Andy Orchard

Figure 19, p. 340. Oxford, Bodleian Library, MS Junius 11, p. 10, lines 7–14. From *Genesis A*, lines 195–205. By kind permission of the Bodleian Library, Oxford.

Figure 20, p. 340. Oxford, Bodleian Library, MS Junius 11, p. 74, lines 10–14. From *Genesis A*, lines 1511–19. By kind permission of the Bodleian Library, Oxford.

Carol Neuman de Vegvar

Figure 21, p. 412. Shaft from Lowther, Cumbria (Lowther 1a–bC), London, British Museum. Photo: © British Museum, by permission.

Figure 22, p. 413. Shaft from Edlingham (Edlingham 1D). Church of St John the Baptist, Edlingham, Northumberland. Photo: © Department of Archaeology, Durham University; photographer T. Middlemass, by permission.

Figure 23, p. 425. Guiselle Vasi (1710–82): engraving of S. Maria del Rosario with Capella di S. Croce in the distance on Monte Mario; from his *Delle Magnificenze di Roma Antica e Moderna* (Rome, 1747–61), VII, 39. Photo: The Institute of Fine Arts, New York University, by permission.

Jane Hawkes

Figure 24, p. 432. Bakewell, Derbyshire: remains of cross-shaft and lower portion of cross-head: (a) west face, (b) east face, (c) south face, (d) north face. Photo: *Corpus of Anglo-Saxon Stone Sculpture*, Ken Jukes.

Richard N. Bailey

George Henderson

Niamh Whitfield

Michael Ryan

COLOUR PLATES

Michelle P. Brown

Plate 1, p. 553. Canon Table, Barberini Gospels. Vatican City, Biblioteca Apostolica Vaticana, MS Barb. lat. 570, fol. 1ʳ. © The Biblioteca Apostolica Vaticana. By kind permission of the Prefect of the Biblioteca Apostolica Vaticana.

Plate 2, p. 554. Incipit of St Luke's Gospel, Barberini Gospels. Vatican City, Biblioteca Apostolica Vaticana, MS Barb. lat. 570, fol. 80ʳ. © The Biblioteca Apostolica Vaticana. By kind permission of the Prefect of the Biblioteca Apostolica Vaticana.

Catherine E. Karkov

Plate 3, p. 555. Christ in majesty; opening of the Canon of the Mass. Cambridge, Corpus Christi College, MS 422, pp. 52–53. By kind permission of Corpus Christi College.

Elizabeth Coatsworth

Plate 4a, p. 556. End square 1 from the 'velamen' of St Harlindis, from St Catherine's Church, Maaseik.© IRPA-KIK, Brussels.

Plate 4b, p. 556. End square 2 from the 'velamen' of St Harlindis, from St Catherine's Church, Maaseik. © IRPA-KIK, Brussels.
The reverse of the woven braid is shown in both cases.

Plate 5, p. 557. The Alexander Flag. © Mainfränkisches Museum, Würzburg, Germany.

George Henderson

Niamh Whitfield

Michael Ryan

Éamonn Ó Carragáin's scholarship rests securely on a wide range of interdisciplinary interests, bringing together insights from fields as widely disparate as archaeology, art history, and liturgy to shed light on the literature and artefacts of Anglo-Saxon England. With equal ease he has reached out to write superbly well on topics as diverse as the High Crosses of Ireland and the Roman landscape in Botticelli's *Punishment of Korah*. When undertaking to draw together a Festschrift in his honour, therefore, we knew full well that the resultant essays could range very far afield and resist inclusion within a single, integrated volume. And so we asked the contributors to concentrate on issues relating to 'text, image, interpretation', with the aim of producing a volume that was both intellectually cohesive and celebratory of Éamonn's polymathic passions inasmuch as it transcended the established methods of the single discipline. The contributors, scattered about Canada, the United States, and Italy as well as Britain and Ireland, have risen to this challenge superbly well. We thank them for their industry and their enthusiasm.

The book's fundamental trajectory proceeds from the wider world to focus on insular culture, as inscribed in text and stone. Thus the first section looks out-wards to medieval Rome, more generally to western Europe, and backwards to the world-geography of the ancient world. It leads off with reference to Rome as a centre of pilgrimage, in a paper by Jennifer O'Reilly, a colleague of Éamonn's who has collaborated with him on several important studies. She explores why Bede is 'tantalizingly silent' on what pilgrims actually saw in Rome, examining the theme of pilgrimage in some of his exegetical works to explain such reticence. Then come two papers centred on different aspects of Rome and Italy: Alan Thacker explains the context within which the Roman cult of the martyrs, important for our understanding of the development of insular hagiography, emerges; and Malcolm

Parkes assesses the evidence for the presence of Italian books in Anglo-Saxon England. There follow three papers on manuscripts: Michelle Brown on the affiliations and symbolism of the Barberini Gospels; Carol Farr on the significance of 'Virgin and Child with Angels' illumination for the history of the Book of Kells; and Catherine Karkov on the unique combination of liturgical and computistical materials, illustrations, glosses, neumes, and vernacular texts that make up the Red Book of Darley. Next, the relation between Soul and Body in Anglo-Saxon literature and art is examined by Anna Maria Luiselli Fadda, who brings a wide range of evidence to the interpretation of one of Old English poetry's most compelling themes. This is followed by Charles Wright's intriguing and satisfying solution to the enigmatic iconography of the Alfred Jewel and the Fuller Brooch, which draws on a Latin apocryphal tradition to explain their presentation of Sight. Elizabeth Coatsworth then offers an analysis of the placing of inscriptions on hangings, clothing, and vestments extant from Anglo-Saxon England — a new synthesis, which has long been needed, from the undoubted expert in this area. The section closes with Diarmuid Scully's examination of Adomnán's account of Cormac Ua Liatháin's third oceanic voyage far into the North Atlantic, where he is attacked by unknown creatures and saved through Columba's intercession with God. It is quite fitting that the first section should end by looking outwards not just to classical literature but to the wider context of the ancient and early medieval understanding of sacred and secular world-geography, and that it is written by one of Éamonn's students who now is among his colleagues at University College, Cork.

A range of texts — Latin, English, and Scandinavian — is considered in the central section of the book. Very properly, pride of place is given to the most famous of Anglo-Saxon writers, the Venerable Bede. George Hardin Brown demonstrates Bede's mastery of register in the commentary *On 1 Samuel*, a detailed and nuanced analysis from the doyen of Bede scholars. Equally, the last paper within the section should serve as a reminder that much of Anglo-Saxon England must for a time have echoed to the sounds of Scandinavian traditions. In an extraordinary feat of detection, Richard North pieces together the fragments of a lost Old Norse poem to consider what evidence they offer for the knowledge of Christianity among late tenth-century Scandinavians and for their symbolic frameworks. Between these excursus, a sequence of papers deals with many aspects of the four major codices of Old English poetry. First, Elaine Treharne, following on from Éamonn's publications on the Vercelli Book, offers her own provocative interpretation as a contribution towards the debate on the reasons that lie behind its production. Paul Szarmach also chooses a topic related to the Vercelli Book. Beginning from consideration of intersections of the verbal and the visual in *The*

Dream of the Rood, he opens out his analysis to reflect more generally on art and its didactic function in the Middle Ages. Three papers have as their central concern poetry from the Exeter Book: Fred Biggs moves from an analysis of the presentation of Beccel and Pege in *Guthlac B* and Felix's *Vita sancti Guthlaci* to explain how Anglo-Saxon poets use characters to convey abstract ideas; Hugh Magennis discusses subjectivity as a key to understanding *The Seafarer*'s emphasis on the individual and the physical; and Eric Stanley examines how the word *frumstaþol* should be understood in the Riddle that precedes *The Husband's Message*. The last two of these papers look to the other two major codices that contain Old English poetry, to Oxford, Bodleian Library, MS Junius 11, and London, British Library, Cotton MS Vitellius A. XV. Andy Orchard reconsiders the possibility, once commonly entertained but now long out of vogue, that *Genesis A* may itself have served as a source and model for later poems still extant; and Jane Roberts, from an analysis of the second division of *Beowulf*, considers the function of reflective passages in the Old English poetic tradition.

Éamonn Ó Carragáin has, over the last few decades, demonstrated brilliantly how words and images work together powerfully to create complex meanings in that extraordinary cultural achievement which is the Ruthwell Cross. The third section deals with less vocalized sculpture, with buildings, and with the insular landscape. Here, the sculptured stonework of Northern Britain is juxtaposed with early Christian monuments and remains from Ireland, and European analogues and records are brought to bear on their interpretation. First, Carol Neuman de Vegvar reassesses the roles Anglo-Saxon carved stone crosses held in their original positions, in a highly original study which moves beyond the point of view of Church and political élites to speculate about the functions that the crosses served for the wider public. Next come three analyses of particular pieces of sculpture from early medieval Britain: Jane Hawkes offers a new reading of a group of pre-Viking Mercian crosses, examining them with reference to liturgical and exegetical writings then current in Anglo-Saxon England; Richard Bailey teases meaning out of the figural panels of the largely neglected Winwick Cross, relating the apocryphal death of Isaiah to the cult of St Oswald; and George Henderson explores the fragmentary standing figures at Tarbat, reassessing recent speculative study of the function of Anglo-Saxon apostle-groups. The last three papers look to Ireland, to what is different from, as well as comparable with, the artefacts and landscape of Britain. Looking to early Irish literature as well as to the landscape and what it can tell us, Niamh Whitfield explores the puzzling lack of evidence for self-standing baptisteries or even for fonts in early Medieval Ireland, arguing that in Ireland holy wells served as important centres at which baptismal ceremonies were performed. Michael Ryan reflects on the seemingly haphazard accumulations of buildings that are so distinctive of Irish ecclesiastical sites, pointing to the strong tendency of the early Irish church to continue to follow the Early Christian model of building complexes of structures for religious purposes ('sacred cities' indeed). Arguing that there was no need to expand individual churches to accommodate elaborate shrines and means of access to them for pilgrims, he suggests that there was little pressure to build large structures even if resources were available for that purpose. With great panache he concludes that open-air Eucharistic celebrations were the exception rather than the rule, reminding those of us who have been fortunate enough to visit Rome with Éamonn as our guide of many a sunny al fresco meal. Finally, Elisabeth Okasha demonstrates the importance of nineteenth-century antiquarian records for our knowledge of carved and inscribed stones at such sites as Gallarus, Kilfountan, Kilmalkedar, and Reask, providing a fascinating introduction to the Kerry travels and writings of Henry Pelham, Lady Chatterton, George Petrie. and John Windele. This is a quite appropriate way to end a volume in honour of a great present-day *peregrinus*.

It was our ambition, as editors, to bring together new readings of Anglo-Saxon literature, manuscript illumination, and iconography, to set them within their most immediate insular contexts, and to establish links with the larger world of early medieval learning. The bibliography of the honorand's writings, compiled by his colleague-son Tomás Ó Carragáin, provides a measure by which the contributors have set their sights, and we hope that their papers will be seen as making a significant contribution to the scholarship of Anglo-Saxon England in particular and, more generally, to the histories of ideas, of liturgy, of iconography, of literary forms.

We wish to thank the Isobel Thornley Bequest Fund for a generous grant that covered the cost of drafting the map of Rome on pp. 32–33 in Alan Thacker's essay. For help of various kinds we are grateful to Brenda Bolton, David Ellis, Anne FitzGerald, Jon Millington, Tomás Ó Carragáin, Alan Thacker, and Jean Verstraete, and to the anonymous readers for their comments. We owe a particular debt of gratitude to Simon Forde, Deborah A. Oosterhouse, and Elizabeth Tyler for all that they have done in the making of this book.

Alastair Minnis
Jane Roberts
September 2006

FOREWORD

Mary Clayton

Magistra betst: Éamonn Ó Carragáin

Éamonn Ó Carragáin was born in Clonmel, Co. Tipperary, on 28 May 1942. He was educated at the High School in Clonmel and then became a seminarian at St Patrick's College, Maynooth, where he studied English and History, gaining a First Class Honours degree in 1962. As a seminarian, Éamonn was immersed in the cycle of the Catholic liturgy, and this lived experience of the liturgy has been crucial to his life as a scholar. Having decided that the priesthood was not for him, Éamonn then moved to University College Dublin where, under the supervision of Alan Bliss, he completed (in 1965) an MA thesis on the sectional divisions and the structure of *Beowulf*. Éamonn had the unusual distinction of having a long paper based on his MA thesis published by the Royal Irish Academy in 1967.

While still studying in UCD, Éamonn was appointed an Assistant in English at Trinity College Dublin, and he taught there from 1964 to 1966. In September 1966, he moved to Queen's University, Belfast, where he lectured in English until 1972. Professor John Braidwood (himself an enthusiastic teacher of Old English literature and the history of the English Language) was head of the English Department at the time, and Seamus Heaney was a colleague; among Éamonn's students at Queen's were Alastair Minnis and Hugh Magennis. Here, under the supervision of John Braidwood, Éamonn began work on his PhD thesis, 'The Vercelli Book as an Ascetic Florilegium', which was completed in 1975. While he was at Queen's he met Malcolm Parkes, who frequently visited the university to lecture in palaeography. Malcolm has had an abiding influence on his work, becoming a lifelong mentor and friend.

In 1972, Éamonn was appointed as a Statutory Lecturer in English at University College Cork. He met Mary McCarthy that same year; they married in 1973, confirming Éamonn's status as Corkonian. They have three children, Tomás,

Caitríona, and Eoghan. Éamonn became Professor of Old and Middle English in UCC in 1975 and has also spent terms as a Visiting Professor in Konstanz and in Cornell. He has served as Chair of the Department of English in UCC many times, and throughout his career has been a constant advocate for UCC Library; he is also a leading force behind both the Munster Ecclesiastic and Monastic Libraries and the 'Transmissions and Transformations of the Ancient World' projects in UCC. Enabling the research of others has been as important to him as his own work. Éamonn's warm gift for friendship and his extraordinary intellectual generosity mean that he is in contact with scholars all over the world, and he has brought many of them to Cork. He was elected a Member of the Royal Irish Academy in 2005.

It was his PhD thesis on the Vercelli Book that first awoke Éamonn's interest in the Ruthwell Cross, which has dominated his publications ever since, culminating in 2005 in his magisterial *Ritual and the Rood: Liturgical Images and the Old English Poems of the 'Dream of the Rood' Tradition*. He has done more than anyone else to interpret the cross, drawing on his expertise in the liturgy, art, archaeology, iconography, theology, and literature of the late antique and early medieval worlds; the very air that Éamonn breathes is interdisciplinary and this approach is now, because of him, recognized as crucial to an understanding of the Ruthwell Cross. As all of his work demonstrates, Éamonn is a polymath and his intellectual passions extend far beyond the Middle Ages to include the Irish language, opera, film, World War II, and Rome — classical, medieval, Renaissance, romantic, and modern Rome. The city has been a presence in his life since he and Mary first visited it in the early 1980s, and he has been a constant visitor. Éamonn was Balsdon Senior Fellow at the British School at Rome in 1990 and European Teaching Fellow of the European Union at Roman Universities and at the British School at Rome in 1998. He is a Membro Corrispondente of the Istituto Nazionale Italiano di Studi Romani. His study tours to Rome, with groups of either 'adults' or 'medievalists', are legendary.

I was lucky enough to be in First Year English when Éamonn was appointed to UCC and was taught by him through to the MA. Like so many of his students, I still have vivid memories of his teaching — of his singing *Beowulf* to the tune of 'Sliabh na mBan', of the wealth of images he used to illuminate texts, of the intellectual excitement which characterized each class, of how he could open up a whole world through any one text. Undergraduates, postgraduate, and Adult Education students in UCC all testify to his prodigious learning and the exhilarating passion of his teaching. Éamonn's energy and enthusiasm are unabated; his retirement will, I know, offer him even more opportunities for intellectual adventuring.

I. Looking Outwards

BEDE ON SEEING THE GOD OF GODS IN ZION

Jennifer O'Reilly

In research papers spanning his academic career and brought to a remarkable synthesis in *Ritual and the Rood*, Éamonn Ó Carragáin has not only made a major contribution to the study of the Ruthwell Cross and the Old English poems of the *Dream of the Rood* tradition, but has enlivened our visualization of the city of Rome and its importance in the world of Bede.[1] *Ritual and the Rood* analyses creative Anglo-Saxon responses to aspects of papal Rome, especially its stational liturgy and cults of St Peter, the Virgin, and the Cross, and considers the art and inscriptions of some of the chief churches which are likely to have been seen by visiting monastic leaders and other pilgrims. Éamonn Ó Carragáin's own convivial study tours of Rome in recent years have illuminated such sites for many medievalists. Bede, however, our most important source on early Anglo-Saxon contacts with papal Rome, and well-placed to know a good deal about Roman liturgy and its architectural contexts, is tantalizingly silent on what pilgrims actually saw there. The following reflection on the theme of pilgrimage in some of Bede's exegetical works, which may help explain this reticence, is offered in tribute to a generous friend and colleague at University College Cork, with whom I have for many years had the pleasure of teaching and sharing research interests in Insular monastic culture and its inheritance from the Mediterranean world.

Bede was acutely aware of the propensity of religious people to worship idols. Splendid church buildings could aid and reflect true devotion, but they could also be accorded the veneration properly owed to what they represented. Bede drew on the whole range of biblical architectural images and accounts of the building of the

---

[1] Éamonn Ó Carragáin, *Ritual and the Rood: Liturgical Images and the Old English Poems of the 'Dream of the Rood' Tradition* (London, 2005).

Tabernacle and the Temple in his descriptions of the living *ecclesia*, which he empha-sized was not to be confused with any individual church building.[2] Similarly, in the tradition of the fathers, he used biblical accounts of the journey to the Promised Land and to Jerusalem to describe the inner pilgrimage of the faithful in his exe-gesis, but when he wrote of Anglo-Saxon pilgrims, he described their pious moti-vation and the spiritual significance of Rome rather than the external details of their journey and its destination, as two contrasting examples may illustrate.

Caedwalla, king of the West Saxons, who was still a savage pagan at the time of the late conversion of the Isle of Wight, gave up his throne to win an everlasting kingdom and went to Rome.[3] Bede explains that Caedwalla had learned that only through baptism could the human race enter the heavenly life; he wanted the special privilege of receiving it 'in the fountain of baptism within the threshold of the apostles'. Pope Sergius gave him the baptismal name Peter, 'that he might be united in name also with the blessed chief of the apostles, to whose most sacred body he had come from the ends of the earth, inspired by loving devotion'. He was baptized on Easter Saturday 689 and died days later, joining 'the bands of the blessed in heaven', and was buried in St Peter's.[4] Bede presents the pilgrimage of a barbarian king drawn from 'earth's remotest end' to Rome and passing from death to life, from earth to heaven at Easter, as a didactic tableau of the primary conversion of the Anglo-Saxon people and the role of Petrine, papal Rome as the source of baptism and the centre of faith for the universal Church.

Benedict Biscop, a more seasoned pilgrim, also died in 689 but was buried near the relics of St Peter in the monastic church at Wearmouth. Bede dissolved the physical distance between Rome and Northumbria by noting that Benedict's body in death 'was not far from the altar and relics of him whom he had always loved during his earthly life and who had opened for him the gates of heaven'.[5] Bede

---

[2] Arthur G. Holder, 'Allegory and History in Bede's Interpretation of Sacred Architecture', *American Benedictine Review*, 40 (1989 A), 115–31 (pp. 119–25); *Bede: On the Temple*, trans. by Seán Connolly (Liverpool, 1995), introduction, pp. xvii–lv.

[3] *Bede's Ecclesiastical History of the English People*, ed. and trans. by Bertram Colgrave and R. A. B. Mynors (Oxford, 1969), 4.15,16; 5.7. All citations of the *Historia ecclesiastica* are from this volume.

[4] 'Hoc sibi gloriae singularis desiderans adipsci, ut ad limina beatorum apostolorum fonte bap-tismatis ablueretur [...]. Cui etiam tempore baptismatis papa memoratus Petri nomen inposuerat, ut beatissimo apostolorum principi, ad cuius sacratissimum corpus a finibus terrae pio ductus amore uenerat, etiam nominis ipsius consortio iungeretur': *Historia ecclesiastica*, 5.7.

[5] 'ut quem degens in carne semper solebat amare, quo pandente ianuam regni caelestis intra-bat, ab huius reliquiis et altari post mortem nec corpore longius abesset': *Historia abbatum*, in

treats the first of Benedict's pilgrimages to Rome, *c.* 654, as an expression of devotion and ascetic exile from earthly preoccupations — the renunciation of country, home, and family for Christ's sake (Matthew 19. 29, Mark 10. 29) — but notes that the Pope himself had ordered Benedict to curtail one pilgrimage for the higher purpose of escorting Theodore, a teacher of truth, to his appointed task as archbishop in Britain, 668.[6] He records that in Theodore's day the journey to Rome was considered to be an act of great merit, but makes it clear that Benedict's primary and predestined role was to raise up spiritual sons for Christ; his subsequent pilgrimages, the last three undertaken from Britain, are shown to serve this purpose directly. They are seen not in terms of the fulfilment or indulgence of Benedict's personal devotional aims, but as his untiring efforts to bring back spiritual sustenance from Rome, enabling his monastic community to remain within the cloister of the monastery to serve Christ.[7]

In contrast to his omission of descriptions of the Roman shrines of Peter and Paul and other churches and images pilgrims saw, Bede lists the variety of spiritual treasures Benedict Biscop brought back from Rome, in particular the many holy pictures, both iconic and narrative, to be displayed in the churches dedicated to St Peter and St Paul in Wearmouth-Jarrow. The images recalled scripture at a variety of levels of understanding. In the church at Jarrow, the typological pairing of scenes from the Old Testament with the events of the passion they prefigured gave pictorial expression to one of the techniques of biblical exegesis.[8] Those in the church at Wearmouth functioned as affective aids to learning, devotion, and compunction. Bede describes them as bringing the face of Christ and his saints before the eyes, making beholders more intensely aware of the Lord's incarnation, while the scenes of judgement prompted the examination of conscience. This is very like Adamnán of Iona's report of the effect certain holy sites had on pilgrims in Jerusalem.[9]

Venerabilis Baedae: opera historica, ed. by Charles Plummer, 2 vols (Oxford, 1896), I, 379; trans. by D. F. Farmer in J. F. Webb, *The Age of Bede*, rev. edn (Harmondsworth, 1998), pp. 187–210 (p. 202). All citations to the *Historia abbatum* are to Plummer's edition.

[6] *Historia abbatum*, c. 3; *Homeliarum Evangelii libri II*, I.13, ed. by David Hurst, CCSL, 122 (Turnhout, 1955), pp. 92–93, trans. by Lawrence T. Martin and David Hurst in *Bede the Venerable: Homilies on the Gospels*, 2 vols (Kalamazoo, 1991), I, 129.

[7] *Homeliarum Evangelii*, I.13, trans. by Martin and Hurst, *Homilies on the Gospels*, I, 132. On Benedict's role, see Ó Carragáin, *Ritual and the Rood*, pp. 91–92, 223–24.

[8] *Historia abbatum*, c. 9. See George Henderson, *Bede and the Visual Arts* (Jarrow Lecture, 1980), pp. 13–17.

[9] *Historia abbatum*, c. 6; Adamnán, *De locis sanctis*, I, c. 23, 13, ed. and trans. by Denis Meehan (Dublin, 1958), p. 66, lines 35–39.

The only pilgrimage churches Bede visualizes are the holy places of Jerusalem and beyond. He refers to the written record of contemporaries who have been in Jerusalem, but does so in order to describe the enshrined sepulchre of Christ in the context of an Easter homily on the significance of the Resurrection for all peoples. His account includes material from Adamnán's *De locis sanctis*, and he also made his own version of Adamnán's whole work, which he regarded as 'useful to many and especially to those who live very far from the places where the patriarchs and apostles dwelt and only know about them what they have learned from books'.[10] The work is useful because the places described recall the events of scripture and the descriptions help clarify details of the literal text of scripture, which is an essential preparation for understanding its underlying spiritual meaning.[11] After acknowledging the pilgrim Arculf as a source of Adamnán's account, however, Bede dispenses with Adamnán's device of presenting much of the useful information through the eager eye-witness testimony of a pilgrim visiting the sites. He opens his own version of *De locis sanctis* by reference instead to the journey to the heavenly Jerusalem:

> Da Iesu, ut patriam semper tendamus ad illam,
> Quam beat aeternum uisio summa tui.

[Grant, O Jesus, that we may always press toward that homeland, which delights eternally in the highest vision of you.][12]

This was the subject of his life's work. The speed of Caedwalla's journey from baptism to the joys of the heavenly homeland, like that of two young princely victims of his early savagery, was dramatically satisfying but not typical.[13] Bede

---

[10] 'Fecitique opus [. . .] multis utile et maxime illis, qui longius ab eis locis, in quibus patriarchae uel apostoli erant, secreti ea tantum de his, quae lectione didicerint, norunt': *Historia ecclesiastica*, 5.15. The next two chapters quote extracts from Bede's version of Adomnán's *De locis sanctis* to describe the churches marking the sites of the nativity, crucifixion, resurrection, and ascension. See also *Homeliarum Evangelii*, II.10.

[11] Thomas O'Loughlin, 'The Exegetical Purpose of Adomnán's *De locis sanctis*', *Cambridge Medieval Celtic Studies*, 24 (1992), 37–53, and '*Res, tempus, locus, persona*: Adomnán's Exegetical Method', *Innes Review*, 48 (1997), 95–111.

[12] Bede, *De locis sanctis*, in *Itineraria et alia geographica*, ed. by J. Fraipont, CCSL, 175 (Turnhout, 1965), pp. 251–80 (p. 251, lines 9–10), trans. in W. Trent Foley and Arthur G. Holder, *Bede: A Biblical Miscellany* (Liverpool, 1999), pp. 5–25 (p. 5). The relationship between literal pilgrimage and the inner journey had often been debated in the late fourth and early fifth centuries, for example, in Jerome's Epistle 53 to Paulinus.

[13] *Historia ecclesiastica*, 4.16.

often warned that the baptized 'must first be trained by long struggles in the exercise of virtues, and then they will be granted the abiding gift of heavenly blessedness', just as, when the Israelites had been 'liberated from Egypt by the blood of the lamb and had been led through the Red Sea, the Lord first instructed them for forty years in the desert, and so led them into the land of promise'.[14]

The Forty-two Mansiones on the Desert Journey

Bede was concerned in his exegetical works to equip a native Anglo-Saxon pastorate with the intellectual resources for understanding the literal text of the Latin Bible, but also to feed them spiritually so that they might interiorize the hidden meaning of scripture and teach its precepts by example as well as words.[15] He was encouraged in this task by his friend Acca, Bishop of Hexham, 'a very learned theologian' who had been to Rome, and had built up 'a very large and most noble library'.[16] In a letter of c. 716 Bede replied to a scholarly query from Acca concerning the chronology of the Israelites' forty-two halting-places (mansiones) on the journey to the Promised Land.[17] At first sight it seems an unpromising subject.

Origen had long ago reported that the text in question, Numbers 33. 1–49, was often regarded as difficult and even unnecessary for Christians to read. He contended, however, that since all of scripture proceeds from the Holy Spirit, no part of it, not one iota, can possibly be useless or unnecessary. Moses, moreover, had been commanded by God to write down the names of the camping-places of the children of Israel who went out of Egypt (Numbers 3. 1–2). Origen recognized that scripture contains food for various spiritual appetites and that this

---

[14] 'Denique dominus liberatum sanguine agni populum de Aegypto et per rubrum mare eductam prius in deserto quadraginta annis instituit et sic in terram repromissionis induxit quia nimirum populus fidelium non statim post baptisma caelestis patriae potest gaudia subire sed primo longis uirtutum exercendus agonibus ac deinde perpetuis supernae beatitudinis est donandus muneribus': *Homeliarum Euangelii*, I.1, ed. by Hurst, p. 3, lines 48–55, trans. by Martin and Hurst, *Homilies on the Gospels*, I, 3; see further II.8 (p. 72).

[15] Alan Thacker, 'Bede's Ideal of Reform', in *Ideal and Reality in Frankish and Anglo-Saxon Society: Studies Presented to J. M. Wallace-Hadrill*, ed. by Patrick Wormald, Donald Bullough, and Roger Collins (Oxford, 1983), pp. 130–53.

[16] 'in litteris sanctis doctissimus [. . .] amplissimam ibi ac nobilissimam bibliothecam fecit': *Historia ecclesiastica*, 5.20.

[17] *De mansionibus filiorum Israel, PL*, 94, 699–702; trans. in Foley and Holder, *Bede: A Biblical Miscellany*, pp. 29–34.

particular text would be spat out by many, but argued that, if properly interpreted according to St Paul's example, it could reveal the way of salvation. The apostle, followed by the fathers of the Church, viewed the Israelites' divine deliverance from slavery in Egypt — their crossing of the Red Sea, their temptation and sin in the wilderness, and God's provision of manna and water from the rock to sustain them on their journey to the Promised Land — as a historical event but also as a figure of the Christian life and mysteries, written down for the instruction of present readers (I Corinthians 10. 1–11). Accordingly, Origen argued that the details of the forty-two campsites on the route could, for some readers, reveal particular insights about the way to the heavenly promised land and the new Jerusalem, like certain other apparently obscure or superfluous biblical listings of names and numbers concerning the twelve tribes of Israel and their encampments, which were to give rise to much ingenious exegesis.[18] He urged the reader to turn the eyes of the mind towards the divine author and earnestly ask the meaning of such texts.

Origen expounded the passage by revealing the spiritual significance concealed within the number forty-two and the very names of the campsites or resting places of the Israelites on their desert pilgrimage. The route-map of the ancient Israelites recorded by Moses was thereby decoded, at least for a readership whose spiritual capacity was advanced beyond the elementary or 'carnal' stage of understanding, as a divinely given guide for the journey of the soul and of the Church, the new Israel, advancing from camp to camp through the desert of this world, gradually ascending heavenwards. Origen's homily now survives only in Rufinus's translation but was influential, especially through its appropriation by Jerome in a letter to Oceanus in Rome. Jerome had thereby improved on the hesitant answer he confessed he had once given when Fabiola, another member of his circle and a zealous student of the scriptures, had asked him to explain the deep mysteries of the list of *mansiones* in the Numbers text.[19]

Bede's letter, therefore, concerns a passage which was an ancient *crux*; it cites Jerome's work, which it is likely Acca knew too, but does not simply summarize it. Bede affirmed that the Numbers text had been written down as a sign signifying a great mystery, but he did not copy the arcane etymologies of the names of the forty-two *mansiones* which were so important to Origen, Jerome, and Isidore and

---

[18] *In Numeros homilia XXVII*, *PG*, 12, 780–801; trans. by Rowan A. Greer, *Homily XXVII on Numbers*, in *Origen* (London, 1979), pp. 245–69 (pp. 245–47).

[19] Ep. 77, *Ad Oceanum*; Ep. 78, *Ad Fabiolam. De mansionibus filiorum Israhel*, *S. Jérôme Lettres*, ed. by J. LaBourt, 8 vols (Paris, 1949–63), IV, 39–52 (p. 47), 52–93.

which entirely occupy the commentary on the Book of Numbers in the Irish Reference Bible.[20] Nor did he feel it necessary to explain, as they had done, the Christological significance of the number forty-two, or the meaning of the name 'Israel' as 'seeing God'.[21] Rather, he focussed on Acca's technical question about the historical relationship between the number of resting-places or campsites and the number of years the Israelites spent meandering in the desert. He resolved the apparent contradictions and obscurities in the biblical account of the historical journey by a close reading of the literal text of Numbers 33 and a comparison with other Pentateuch passages, and then briefly expounded the story's spiritual meaning.

In his early commentary on the Acts of the Apostles, which had also been sent to Acca, Bede cited the patristic interpretation of the number forty as designating this temporal earthly life and then linked the forty years of the Exodus and the forty days between Christ's resurrection and ascension to provide an insight into the spiritual life. The forty days of Christ's post-resurrection appearances and *conversatio* with his disciples signified to them that after his Ascension he would, by his hidden presence, fulfill his promise to be with them always (Matthew 28. 20). Bede assures the reader that Christ's promise extends to his latter-day disciples, whose lifespans and spiritual lives are prefigured in the forty-year journey of the Israelites of old: 'For after we have been buried in death with Christ through baptism (Romans 6. 4), as though having passed over the path through the Red Sea (see I Corinthians 10. 1–2), it is necessary for us, in this wilderness, to have the Lord's guidance. May he lead us to the heavenly kingdom.'[22]

Bede's letter to Acca on Numbers 33 assumes knowledge of this interpretative tradition and succinctly develops the theme to provide an initiated reader with a highly allusive interpretation of the Exodus journey described in scripture, where

---

[20] *Pauca problesmata de enigmatibus ex tomis canonicis. Praefatio et libri de pentateucho Moysi*, ed. by Gerard MacGinty, CCCM, 173 (Turnhout, 2000), pp. 196–204.

[21] Christ's descent from heaven to earth at his incarnation, represented by the forty-two generations of his human ancestors (Matthew 1. 1–17), was linked with humanity's ascent to heaven from the Egypt of sin through the forty-two *mansiones*. The etymology of 'Israhel uir uidens deum' is included in Jerome's *Liber interpretationis hebraicorum nominum*, ed. by P. de Lagarde, CCSL, 72 (Turnhout, 1959), p. 139, line 22.

[22] 'Nam postquam consepulti fuerimus cum Christo per baptismum in mortem, quasi rubri maris calle transito, necessarium in hac solitudine domini habemus ducatum, qui nos ad caelestia regna perducat': *Expositio Actuum Apostolorum*, 1.3, ed. by M. L. W. Laistner, CCSL, 121 (Turnhout, 1983), pp. 6–7, lines 25–33, trans. by Lawrence T. Martin (Kalamazoo, 1989), p. 10.

it takes forty years — a lifetime — to progress at irregular intervals through the forty-two *mansiones*. The Israelites led by Moses through the Red Sea had sinned in the desert, wandered about for years, and eventually died there; it was the younger generation who, recapitulating their fathers' liberation from slavery in Egypt, had finally crossed the river Jordan under Joshua and defeated the Canaanite tribes in order to inherit the Promised Land. Bede expounds the familiar Old Testament account as a description not simply of primary conversion and baptism, but of the lifelong process of continuing conversion by which the soul aspires to fulfill the baptismal image of casting off the old self and putting on the new, created in the likeness of God (Ephesians 4. 22–24; Colossians 3. 9–10).[23]

Bede is here offering spiritual consolation to one already advanced on the journey. The purpose of the final section of the letter is no longer to instruct Acca on the literal text of Numbers but to sustain a fellow pilgrim with the spiritual meaning of God's word. He draws from the text divine reassurance that whenever, through sin, we turn aside from the path of truth, then, through penance, the soul is gradually brought back to higher things and so resumes the heavenward ascent. The soul grows to spiritual maturity in the desert of this life by learning and re-learning, with God's help, how to produce deeds worthy of repentance, to fortify the camp and ward off the demonic attacks of temptation, and, at last, to cross the river of death and enter the kingdom of heavenly promise.

De virtute in virtutem

In the hermeneutical tradition of commenting on a scriptural text through another scriptural text, Origen and Jerome had used words from Psalm 83. 8 to illuminate the image of spiritual progress figured in the *mansiones* of the Israelites' pilgrim journey through the desert: 'ibunt de virtute in virtutem: videbitur Deus deorum in Sion' ('they shall go from virtue to virtue: the God of gods shall be seen in Zion').[24] Bede used the same psalm verse in his letter to Acca:

---

[23] Foley and Holder, *Bede: A Biblical Miscellany*, pp. 33–34.

[24] 'et ita per singula quaeque tentamenta vitae ac fidei prosecuta, mansiones habere dicitur: in quibus per singula virtutum quaeruntur augmenta: et impletur in iis illud quod scriptum est: *Ibunt de virtute in virtutem*, usquequo perveniatur ad ultimum, imo ad summum gradum virtutum, et transeatur flumen Dei, ac promissa suscipiatur haereditas': Origen, *In Numeros homilia XXVII, PG*, 12, 786; trans. by Greer, *Origen*, p. 252. The Vulgate wording of the full psalm verse is 'Etenim benedictionem dabit legislator; ibunt de virtute in virtutem, videbitur Deus deorum in Sion' (Psalm 83. 8). For variants, see below, notes 29, 30. Ambrose briefly used the Origenist

incessu proficimus *de virtute in virtutem* quasi castra quaedam mansionesque, Deo duce, rectissimas Dei conspectu dignissimas per desertum mundi sitientis agamus.

[As long as we are advancing *from virtue to virtue* as if to certain camps and resting-places throughout the desert of [this] arid world, let us do whatever things are right and proper in the sight of God, secure in the progress of our good work with God as our leader.][25]

He pictured the Church and the faithful soul as yearning for heaven and hastening to climb the ascent out of slavery in Egypt in the hope of 'being set free from this vale of tears' in order, at last, to go up to the place prepared for the blessed, that is, to see the God of gods in Zion. For a reader familiar with the Psalter through the daily monastic office, the idea of the desert journey as a spiritual ascent is strengthened by Bede's use of Psalm 83. 8 and his allusion to the last words of the previous verse, 'ascensiones in corde suo disposuit, in valle lacrimarum, in loco quem posuit' ('In his heart he has disposed to ascend by steps, in the vale of tears').

The psalm describes the desire and longing of Hebrew pilgrims going up to Jerusalem to God's house. Like the Israelites' original Exodus journey to the Promised Land, the journey to Jerusalem was used by patristic writers as a figure of the inner pilgrimage from earth to heaven. The psalmist's words had been directly related by Cassiodorus to the faithful acquiring particular virtues by mounting each step to the Temple and gaining ascendancy over contrary vices with God's help. He quotes the opening phrase of Psalm 83. 8, 'Etenim benedictionem dabit legislator' ('For he who gave the law shall give a blessing'), when describing the movement from virtue which lies in the law to virtue which lies in grace; both merge in the person of Christ, the author of both the Old and the New Testaments. Cassiodorus urges that the soul, receiving forgiveness from the divine law-giver through grace, must not slacken, but always continue to advance heavenwards 'from virtue to virtue'.[26] Gregory the Great had quoted the same psalm verse, 'ambulabunt de virtute in virtutem', in relating the steps of the

---

spiritual interpretation of the names of the *mansiones* in his commentary on Psalm 118, *Beati immaculati in via*, which elaborates the metaphor of walking in the law of the Lord: *Expositio Psalmi CXVIII*, ed. by M. Petschenig, CSEL, 62 (Vienna, 1913), 5.5.

[25] *De mansionibus filiorum Israel, PL,* 94, 701; trans. in Foley and Holder, *Bede: A Biblical Miscellany,* p. 33.

[26] 'Sequitur *etenim benedictionem dabit qui legem dedit.* Cum prophetiae tempus esset sub lege Domini constitutum, nec adhuc uenisset gratiae donum, eumdem dicit *benedictionem daturum,* id est gratiam suam, *qui legem dedit* ante iustitiam: docens Dominum Christum utriusque testamenti euidenter auctorem, cum dicit, *benedictionem dabit qui legem dedit*': Cassiodorus, *Expositio psalmorum,* ed. by M. Adriaen, CCSL, 98 (Turnhout, 1958), p. 770, lines 146–52.

Temple in Ezekiel's vision to the soul's ascent through the seven gifts of the Holy
Spirit leading to the heavenly life.[27]

Both patristic works were familiar to Bede, who used lines from Psalm 83
repeatedly and with considerable variety of theological and spiritual inflection in
his own exegesis. The recitation of the psalms in the daily pilgrimage of the monastic life and the liturgical use of scriptural allusions to the Exodus journey and
Jerusalem pilgrimage, particularly in the season of Lent and Easter, made such
spiritual interpretations of the literal text deeply felt. Patristic commentators saw
Psalm 83. 8 as a resonant evocation of the spiritual journey which progresses
through stages to the heavenly city symbolized by the earthly Jerusalem. Variant
Latin translations offered commentators different nuances. The Gallican version
used in the Vulgate has 'ibunt de virtute in virtutem', where the verb in the third
person plural (often supplied with the subject *sancti*, meaning the blessed or the
elect) suggests their going forth or advancing, and *virtus* might be understood not
simply as virtue but as spiritual power, strength or fortitude, goodness or even perfection.[28] Indeed, the Hebrew Psalter text (the version contained in the Codex
Amiatinus) has 'ibunt de fortitudine in fortitudinem', wording which had prompted
Jerome and others to stress that the journey was not a progression from weakness
to strength, but from being strong to being stronger.[29] The Roman Psalter evokes
the image of advancing on foot, 'ambulabunt de virtute in virtutem'.[30]

Periphery and Centre

In 716, the year in which Acca consulted Bede about the Israelites' journey to the
Promised Land, Bede's abbot, Ceolfrith, set out on pilgrimage to Rome.[31] The

---

[27] Gregory the Great, *Homiliae in Hiezechielem prophetam*, 2.3.3, ed. by M. Adriaen, CCSL,
142 (Turnhout, 1971), pp. 238–39, lines 49–66.

[28] *Biblia sacra iuxta Vulgatam versionem*, ed. by Roger Gryson and others, 4th edn (Stuttgart,
1969), p. 876.

[29] *Biblia sacra*, p. 877.

[30] *Le Psautier Romain*, ed. by Robert Weber, Collectanea Biblica Latina, 10 (Vatican, 1953),
p. 208.

[31] Bede notes that work on his commentary on Samuel was interrupted by each of these
events: see the opening lines of his letter to Acca, *De mansionibus filiorum Israel*, trans. in Foley
and Holder, *Bede: A Biblical Miscellany*, p. 29, and the letter to Acca accompanying *In primam
partem Samuhelis libri IIII*, ed. by David Hurst, CCSL, 119 (Turnhout, 1962), p. 212.

liturgy of the early Anglo-Saxon Church used the Roman Psalter, and the phrase *ambulantes de virtute in virtutem* appropriately formed one of the antiphons chanted at Wearmouth the morning Ceolfrith left, when he led his community from Mass in solemn procession. As they walked they sang, 'The way of the just is right and the journey of the holy is prepared' (Isaiah 26. 7) and 'walking from strength to strength' (Psalm 83. 8), as well as Psalm 66, which prays for God's mercy and blessing and that his way may be known on earth.[32] The processional chants implicitly associated Ceolfrith's pilgrimage to the shrines of the holy apostles in Rome with pilgrimage to Jerusalem and the inner heavenward journey it represented.

The links between Rome and Jerusalem were well developed. Papal Rome had fostered the concept that Rome had been refounded from Jerusalem by St Peter and St Paul; it was the western extremity of their evangelizing mission from the biblical centre of the earth at Jerusalem and became the new centre from which their papal successors continued the apostolic mission to the ends of the earth. Like Jerusalem, Rome drew all peoples to itself. The veneration of Rome as the site of the martyrdom and tombs of the Princes of the Apostles was crucial to the recognition of papal Rome as the guardian of the faith they had received. Christ's unique commission to Peter (Matthew 16. 18–19), in which each of his papal successors shared, demonstrated the oneness of the universal Church, the brotherly concord of Peter and Paul its harmony and unity. These were important themes in the iconography of early Roman churches, but Rome also came to share symbolically in the spiritual associations of the pilgrim city of Jerusalem through the *imitatio* of its topography and cults. The architecture, iconography, and liturgy of Petrine Rome incorporated images of Jerusalem, the earthly symbol of the heavenly city. Rome itself came to function as a symbol of the New Jerusalem and the Church in heaven.[33]

The stational liturgy of Rome, for example, which involved the papal court in processing to basilicas in the city for the pope as bishop to celebrate Mass in each of these *stationes* on its own particular day in the liturgical calendar, included two

---

[32] 'Uia iustorum recta facta est, et iter sanctorum praeparatum est' and 'ambulantes de uirtute in uirtutem': *Vita Ceolfridi*, 25, ed. by Charles Plummer, *Historia abbatum auctore anonymo*, in *Baedae: opera historica*, I, 396–97, trans. by Farmer in Webb, *Age of Bede*, pp. 221–22. Discussed by Éamonn Ó Carragáin, *The City of Rome and the World of Bede* (Jarrow Lecture, 1994), pp. 8–14. All citations of the *Vita Ceolfridi* are to Plummer's edition.

[33] Jennifer O'Reilly, 'The Art of Authority', in *After Rome*, ed. by Thomas Charles-Edwards (Oxford, 2003), pp. 141–89 (pp. 148–51).

Lenten processions from the Lateran to the nearby basilica of *Hierusaleme* and its relic of the True Cross.[34] The first of these ceremonies enacted the Church's symbolic pilgrimage to Jerusalem in preparation for Holy Week; the second, on Good Friday, imitated the ancient Good Friday procession of the bishop and pilgrims in Jerusalem to venerate the Cross at Golgotha. The processions recalled Old Testament images of the Exodus journey and of pilgrims going up to Jerusalem for the Passover, which were evoked in the liturgy of Lent and Easter, but also had a strongly eschatological dimension as a figure of the pilgrim Church *in via*, journeying towards its completion in the heavenly Jerusalem at the end of time.

Éamonn Ó Carragáin has vividly suggested how the inspiration of the stational liturgy of papal Rome, expressing the unity of the churches of the city of Rome and of the universal Church under its bishop but also the community of all the saints on earth with those in heaven, is reflected in the anonymous biographer's account of Ceolfrith's ceremonial departure to Rome. He led his community from Mass and they processed with incense and chant around the Wearmouth altars of St Peter, St Mary, and St Lawrence, 'three of the greatest patrons of Rome'.[35] The antiphons and psalm were repeated as the monks processed towards the river, where Ceolfrith venerated the cross and set off on his final pilgrimage. Though he died on the way, before reaching Rome, his followers ardently believed he would reach his heavenly destination.[36]

Ceolfrith had enjoined the monks of St Peter's, Wearmouth, to preserve concord and unity with the brothers of St Paul's, Jarrow, as members of one monastery under one abbot. Bede described the brotherly love that would unite the two houses just as it had bound together the two chief apostles, Peter and Paul.[37] The close connection between the two houses and the shrine of St Peter in Rome was renewed by Ceolfrith's pilgrimage and expressed in the distribution of the three great pandect Bibles produced at Wearmouth-Jarrow during his abbacy: the anonymous biographer says that one remained in the church of St Peter at Wearmouth, one in the church of St Paul at Jarrow, and Ceolfrith took the third one (the Codex Amiatinus) as a gift to St Peter's shrine at Rome. The texts and images of the opening quire variously demonstrate the spiritual interpretation of

---

[34] See Ó Carragáin, *Ritual and the Rood*, pp. 148–50, 183–201, for a luminous account of these and other examples of the Roman stational liturgy and the veneration of the cross.

[35] *City of Rome*, pp. 8–14 (p. 13).

[36] Letter of Ceolfrith's successor Hwaetberht to Gregory II, *Vita Ceolfridi*, 30.

[37] *Historia abbatum*, c. 7.

God's word, in harmony with the universal Church.[38] Ceolfrith's dedication of the book is 'to the body of sublime Peter, justly venerated, whom ancient faith declares to be head of the Church' and seeks in return 'a memorial in heaven' for himself and his community.[39] The Pope wrote to the new abbot of Wearmouth-Jarrow, acknowledging Ceolfrith's gift to their common lord and patron, the blessed Peter, Prince of the Apostles, and prayed that 'this most approved teacher of the holy precepts of the rule might show the way in God's sight to worthy disciples'. He again acknowledged the late abbot's spiritual leadership when he called on divine grace to perfect Ceolfrith's merits 'like those of Aaron and Moses, the holy leaders of the chosen people who were called away before they reached the Promised Land'.[40]

The theme of the Exodus journey runs through the prefatory texts and diagrams of the Codex Amiatinus. Cryptic allusions to Christ, his Church, and the Temple of the heavenly Jerusalem are contained within the double-page depiction of the Tabernacle surrounded by the encampments of the twelve tribes, and their leaders, Aaron and Moses (Numbers 2. 1–31). Both the prologue of the book on fol. 4 and the *titulus* of the diagram on fol. 6, which sets out the arrangement of the books of the Bible according to the Septuagint, refer to the seventy palm trees at one of the forty-two campsites, *in mansione Helim*, as a figure of the constituent books of scripture. The diagram of the Pentateuch on fol. 7ᵛ, citing the spiritual interpretation of each of the five books of Moses from Jerome's Epistle 53, sharpens his allusion to the significant numerology of the book of Numbers: 'are not its very figures and *mensurae terrae* and the forty-two *mansiones* in the wilderness so many mysteries?'[41]

---

[38] Florence, Biblioteca Medicea Laurenziana, MS Amiatino I.

[39] *Vita Ceolfridi*, 37, records the dedication: 'Corpus ad eximii merito uenerabile Petri | Dedicat aecclesiae quem caput alta fides | Ceolfridus Anglorum extremis de finibus abbas [...]. In caelis memorem semper habere locum.'

[40] 'fidem eius in muneris conlatione probantes, dignum commemorationibus assiduis censuimus, ac probatissimum preceptorem in sanctis ac regularibus institutis dignis auditoribus praeuium ante Deum existere peroramus, ut illum, Aaron et Moysi sanctis diuinae plebis ducibus ad promissionis patriam tendentibus euocatis': *Vita Ceolfridi*, 39, trans. in Webb, *Age of Bede*, p. 228.

[41] In the Codex Amiatinus the phrase *mensurae terrae* replaces *prophetiae Balaam* used in Jerome's letter: 'Numeri uero nonne totius arithmeticae et prophetiae Balaam et quadraginta duarum per heremum mansionum mysteria continent?' *S. Jérôme Lettres*, 3, Ep. 53.8, ed. by LaBourt, p. 16, lines 24–26. For the illustrations of the Codex Amiatinus as visual exegesis, see Jennifer O'Reilly, 'The Library of Scripture: Views from Vivarium and Wearmouth-Jarrow', in *New Offerings, Ancient Treasures: Studies in Medieval Art for George Henderson*, ed. by Paul Binski and Will Noel (Stroud, 2001), pp. 3–39.

Bede, however, does not apply the biblical image of the Exodus to the details of Ceolfrith's arduous journey towards Rome. Rather, in a letter to Acca he mourned the passing of the leadership of Moses and Aaron in Ceolfrith's departure from his abbatial office.[42] Notwithstanding his own frequent exegetical use of Psalm 83. 8, Bede in the *Historia abbatum* does not mention that it was sung on the occasion of Ceolfrith's departure for Rome.[43] Ceolfrith's literal pilgrimage is not criticized, but neither is it presented as a model for all to follow.

The Prologue of the Rule of St Benedict, an important influence in the life of Wearmouth-Jarrow, uses Psalm 14 to describe the route of the virtuous life by which the Lord shows the faithful the way to his tabernacle and his holy mountain. The path becomes an image of the monastic life itself, narrow at the outset:

> Processu vero conversationis et fidei, dilatato corde inenarrabili dilectionis dulcedine curritur via mandatorum Dei, ut ab ipsius numquam magisterio descedentes, in eius doctrinam usque ad mortem in monasterio perseverantes, passionibus Christi per patientiam participemur, ut et regno eius mereamur esse consortes.
>
> [But as we progress in this way of life and faith, we shall run on the path of God's commandments [...]. Never swerving from his instructions, then, but faithfully observing his teaching in the monastery until death, we shall through patience share in the sufferings of Christ that we may also deserve to share in his kingdom.][44]

Bede's account of Ceolfrith's final pilgrimage chiefly commemorates his long and exemplary practice of the monastic life. Bede insists that the resignation from abbatial cares was prompted by Ceolfrith's concern that he could no longer in old age teach the community by the vigorous example necessary to provide the spiritual leadership required for the community's disciplined observance of the Rule, handed down by its father on the authority of traditional practice. The only details which Bede gives of the journey show Ceolfrith as frail and ill but faithfully continuing in the monastic life of prayer without ceasing and in celebration of the Eucharist.[45]

The new abbot in a letter to the Pope praised Ceolfrith for having fostered his monastery's 'spiritual peace and liberty in the calm of the cloister'. He honoured

---

[42] Bede, *In primam partem Samuhelis*, ed. by Hurst, p. 212.

[43] However, he earlier explains the appropriateness of the psalm (82), which was being sung by the monks in church at the moment that Benedict Biscop died in his monastic cell: *Historia abbatum*, c. 14.

[44] *The Rule of St Benedict*, ed. and trans. by Timothy Fry (Collegeville, MN, 1981), pp. 164, 166.

[45] *Historia abbatum*, c. 16, c. 22.

him as a future 'mighty patron and advocate for our transgressions before the throne of grace', though was resigned to the probability that Ceolfrith would die in Rome and his body remain there.[46] Bede applauded Hwaetberht's zeal in securing the privilege of bringing the bodies of two past saintly abbots, Eosterwine and Sigfrid, into the chapel of St Peter's at Wearmouth, to entomb them next to the monastery's founding father, Benedict Biscop, who was buried near the altar of St Peter.[47] These local lives of virtue were therefore memorialized not only in the liturgical calendar and literary *monumenta* of the *Vita Ceolfridi* and *Historia abbatum*, but in the fabric of the monastery, together with the imported relics of St Peter and other universally honoured saints, to guide future generations undertaking the daily round of their life-long pilgrimage within the monastic precincts.

Bede's exegetical works present this concept of the living *ecclesia* and the community of saints through combining the biblical metaphors of journeying to Jerusalem and of building the Temple. In *De templo* he explains that 'in the universal assembly of the elect various righteous persons succeed each other' and lesser ones are glad to follow faithfully in their footsteps, guided by the example of the life, sayings, and writings of the righteous: 'For we know that virtues beget virtues and saints *advance from virtue to virtue until the God of gods is seen in Zion*' (Psalm 83. 8).[48] The foundations of humility are laid in the individual soul by following the example of such teachers; the wall is built up by good works, by laying one upon another like courses of stones, and by *advancing from virtue to virtue*.[49] He pictures those of greatest virtue, who are closest to the Lord through their

---

[46] 'Commendamus autem tuae sanctae benignitati [...] uenerabiles patris nostri dilectissimi canos, Ceolfridi uidelicet abbatis, ac nutritoris tutorisque nostrae spiritalis in monastica quiete libertatis et pacis'; 'magnum pro nostris excessibus apud supernam pietatem intercessorem habemus et patronum': *Historia abbatum*, c. 19; *Vita Ceolfridi*, 30.

[47] *Historia abbatum*, c. 20.

[48] 'Scimus enim uirtutes de uirtutibus nasci et sanctos *ambulare de uirtute in uirtutem* donec *uideatur Deus deorum in Sion*': *De templo*, ed. by David Hurst, CCSL, 119A (Turnhout, 1969), pp. 203–04, lines 478–80; trans. by Connolly, *On the Temple*, p. 80.

[49] 'Post fundamentum uero talibus ac tantis lapidibus compositum aedificanda est domus praeparatis diligentius lignis ac lapidibus ac decenti ordine collacatis quae olim de prisco suo situ uel radice fuerant abstracta quia post prima fidei rudimenta post collocata in nobis iuxta exemplum sublimum uirorum fundamenta humilitatis addendus est in altum paries operum bonorum quasi superimpositis sibi inuicem ordinibus lapidum ambulando ac proficiendo *de uirtute in uirtutem*. Vel certe lapides fundamenti grandes pretiosi quadrati primi sunt ut supra dixeram ecclesiarum magistri': *De templo*, ed. by Hurst, p. 156, lines 356–70; trans. by Connolly, *On the Temple*, p. 16.

humility, as large, squared, precious stones forming the foundation of the house of the Lord. The courses of stones or timber laid upon them are the priests and teachers who followed, each in his own time, 'by whose ministry the fabric of the Church grows or by whose virtues it is shaped'.[50]

Ceolfrith had resolved to visit once more the shrines of the holy apostles in Rome, where he had gone with Benedict as a young man, but now with the intention of awaiting death there by giving himself to unhindered prayer and penance. Once he had secured his release from office, Ceolfrith left his own community and kindred 'to be a stranger in foreign lands so that he might with greater freedom and purity of heart devote himself to contemplation with the legions of angels in heaven'. Hwaetberht's letter of commendation to the Pope described Ceolfrith beginning once more, as though newly summoned to the heavenly life as a reward for his love of virtue, to set out as a pilgrim for Christ at the end of his days: 'thus the glowing fire of penance may more freely burn away the old thorns of earthly cares in the furnace of the Spirit'.[51]

On Seeing the God of Gods in Zion: The Ascent to Contemplation

Bede used the same penitential image, but of St Cuthbert, who had also laid aside the burden of pastoral care when he withdrew from Lindisfarne after many years in the monastery and journeyed, not to Rome but further out into the Ocean bounding the ends of the earth, to the tiny island of Farne.[52] Cuthbert gave himself undividedly to prayer and fasting and the rigours of the solitary life to prepare himself for death or, rather, eternal life, so that 'the flame of his old contrition

---

[50] *De templo*, ed. by Hurst, p. 156, lines 364–70. The image is applied to the ministry of Gregory the Great and to Augustine's successor, Lawrence. Gregory's care of souls is contrasted with popes who devoted themselves to building churches and adorning them with gold and silver; *Historia ecclesiastica*, 2.1. Lawrence 'strove to build up the foundations of the Church which had been so magnificently laid' (I Corinthians 3. 10–11) by 'frequent words of holy exhortation and by continually setting a pattern of good works' ('Laurentius archiepiscopi gradu potitus strenuissime fundamenta ecclesiae, quae nobiliter iacta uidit, augmentare atque ad profectum debiti culminis et crebra uoce sanctae exhortationis et continuis piae operationis exemplis prouehere curauit': *Historia ecclesiastica*, 2.4).

[51] 'rursus incipit peregrinari pro Christo, quo liberius prisca sollicitudinum secularium spineta, camino spiritali feruens compunctionis ignis absumat': *Historia abbatum*, c. 19.

[52] *Historia ecclesiastica*, 4.28; *Vita Sancti Cuthberti*, c. 17, ed. and trans. by Bertram Colgrave, *Two Lives of Saint Cuthbert* (Cambridge, 1940), pp. 215–17.

might consume more easily the implanted thorns of worldly cares'.[53] He too had first secured the support of his community:

> Gaudebat namque quia de longa perfectione conuersationis actiuae, ad otium diuinae speculationis iam mereretur ascendere. Laetabatur ad eorum sortem se pertingere de quibus canitur in psalmo, *Ambulabunt de uirtute in uirtutem, uidebitur Deus deorum in Syon.*

> [He rejoiced because, after a long and blameless active life, he was now held worthy to rise to the repose of divine contemplation. He rejoiced to attain to the lot of those concerning whom the Psalmist sings: 'the saints shall go forth from strength to strength; the God of gods shall be seen in Zion'.] [54]

Origen's interpretation of the *mansiones* in the desert had described how, before arriving at perfection, the soul dwells in the wilderness, where it is trained in the commandments and tested by temptations and demons, overcoming them by increasing in virtues one by one and fulfilling what is written, 'They shall go from virtue to virtue'.[55] As in some other Insular works of hagiography, such as the lives of Fursa and Guthlac, Psalm 83. 8 is associated in the *Vita Cuthberti* with the anchoritic life of spiritual warfare in desolate places.[56] Cuthbert had progressed from learning the rudiments of the solitary life, in temporary withdrawals on the outer precincts of the Lindisfarne monastery, to the more remote battlefield of Farne where, armed with virtues, he engaged in combat against demonic attack, overcoming temptations (Ephesians 6. 16–17). The fortification of the

---

[53] 'Abiecit pondus curae pastoralis, atque ad dilectum heremiticae conuersationis agonem quamtotius remeare curauit, quatinus inolita sibi sollicitudinis mundanae spineta liberior priscae compunctionis flamma consumeret': *Vita Sancti Cuthberti*, c. 36, ed. and trans. by Colgrave, pp. 266–67.

[54] *Vita Sancti Cuthberti*, c. 17.

[55] Trans. by Greer, *Origen*, pp. 252, 257.

[56] Wanting to live the life of a pilgrim, Fursa constructs a monastery in a Roman camp in the kingdom of the East Angles and has visions of angels who sing, '*Ibunt sancti de uirtute in uirtutem, et iterum Videbitur Deus deorum in Sion*', and protect him from the onslaughts of evil spirits attempting to prevent his journey to heaven: *Historia ecclesiastica*, 3.19. When Guthlac is delivered from temptation and torment by evil spirits and returned to his island dwelling in the fens, he hears heavenly voices singing, '*Ibunt* sancti *de uirtute in uirtutem* et reliqua': *Felix's Life of Saint Guthlac*, 33, ed. and trans. by Bertram Colgrave (Cambridge, 1956), p. 108. St Brendan and his companions approach an island of anchorites where three choirs — of boys, youths, and elders — are continuously on the move except when each choir in turn stands in one place to chant Psalm 83. 8, so that the versicle is sung without ceasing, at all stages of the anchoritic life: *Navigatio Sancti Brendani abbatis, from Early Latin Manuscripts*, c. 17, ed. by Carl Selmer (Notre Dame, 1959), p. 49.

camp in the desert and the entry into the Promised Land are here located on an island in the North Sea.

With the help of angels Cuthbert built a dwelling place, at one point described as a *mansione*, at another as the *civitas* of his *imperium*. Unlike the great sites in Rome or the fine stone churches of Wearmouth-Jarrow, built in the Roman manner, it was constructed of turf and boulders, rough timber and straw; it is not the building but its inhabitant, Cuthbert, who is a dwelling place of the Holy Spirit. He is shown as already living very close to the angelic life, a citizen of the heavenly Jerusalem. His dwelling on Farne was surrounded by a rampart so high 'that he could see nothing else but the heavens which he longed to enter'; it 'lifted the whole bent of his mind to higher things', restraining the lust of the eyes and of the thoughts.[57] The image recalls Gregory the Great's teaching that, in order to contemplate the invisible Creator, it is necessary to cast out earthly and heavenly images from the mind's eye and thoughts arising from the bodily perceptions of the senses.[58] Bede records that Gregory too in his monastic seclusion 'used to think nothing but thoughts of heaven, so that, even though still imprisoned in the body, he was able to pass in contemplation beyond the barriers of the flesh'. The true holiness of Gregory and Cuthbert, however, was revealed in their surrender of such longed-for exile from earthly concerns and their submission again to the burden of office and pastoral care when it was required of them.[59]

In a homily on John 1. 43–51 where Christ, wanting to go to Galilee, summons Philip to follow him, Bede shows the nature of true discipleship through the patristic explanation of 'Galilee' as meaning both 'a passing over' and 'revelation'. In its first sense, the name denotes the passing of faithful disciples from vices to virtues, or their gradual daily progress from lesser to greater virtues so that, with the Lord's help, they journey on and pass over 'from this vale of tears to the height of heavenly gladness' (see Psalm 83. 6–7). In its second sense, 'revelation', it

---

[57] 'Nam intrinsecus uiuam cedendo rupem, multo illum fecit altiorem, quatinus ad cohibendam oculorum siue cogitationum lasciuiam, ad erigendam in superna desideria totam mentis intentionem, pius incola nil de sua mansione praetor coelum posset intueri': *Vita Sancti Cuthberti*, c. 17 (pp. 216–17); see also *Historia ecclesiastica*, 4.28.

[58] Gregory, *Homiliae in Hiezechielem prophetam*, 2.5.9, ed. by Adriaen, pp. 281–82.

[59] 'ut nulla nisi caelestia cogitare soleret, ut etiam retentus corpore ipsa iam carnis claustra contemplatione transiret': *Historia ecclesiastica*, 2.1; 4.28; *Vita Sancti Cuthberti*, c. 24, ed. and trans. by Colgrave, p. 239. See further Clare Stancliffe, 'Cuthbert and the Polarity Between Pastor and Solitary', in *St Cuthbert, his Cult and his Community to A.D. 1200*, ed. by Gerard Bonner, David Rollason, and Clare Stancliffe (Woodbridge, 1989), pp. 21–42 (pp. 36–42).

suggests the blessedness of eternal life for which the faithful labour in this present life. Bede emphasizes that the psalmist includes both interpretations of the name 'Galilee' in one verse, when he says: 'They will walk from virtue to virtue; the God of gods will be seen in Zion' (Psalm 83. 8). He identifies the psalmist's prophecy as the vision concerning which the apostle Paul says, 'We, with unveiled faces beholding the Lord's glory, are transformed from glory to glory, as by the Spirit of the Lord' (II Corinthians 3. 18). Bede makes it clear that the heavenward journey described by the psalmist in Psalm 83. 8 means following the Lord by imitating him: just as he suffered and was resurrected and entered into his glory, so he showed his followers how to grow in virtue and pass through transitory sufferings to the joy of eternal gifts.[60]

The same patristic etymologies of 'Galilee', and the same text from Corinthians, are combined in Bede's great Easter homily on the risen Christ's final appearance to his disciples on earth, which foreshadows their perpetual vision of him in heaven. Obeying the directive of the angel at the tomb, the disciples had gone to Galilee and, seeing Christ there, some adored him (Matthew 28. 7, 17). Bede explains that those who are Christ's follow him and they in their turn pass over from death into life; seeing him there 'they adore him whom they contemplate in his divine form, and praise him for ever'. With extreme economy Bede suggests the transformation of redeemed humanity: 'Then, indeed, "we, with unveiled face, beholding the glory of the Lord are changed into the same likeness" (II Corinthians 3. 18), all of us who now commit our way to him and follow his footsteps.'[61] In his homily on Pentecost, the liturgical completion of the Easter

---

[60] 'In eo autem quod reuelationem sonat ipsam uitae aeternae beatitudinem pro qua in praesenti laborant insinuans cuius utramque interpretationem nominis psalmista uno uersiculo conprehendit ubi ait: *Ambulabunt de uirtute in uirtutem, uidebitur Deus deorum in Sion.* Haec est namque uisio de qua dicit apostolus: *Nos autem reuelata facie gloriam domini speculantes in eandem imaginem transformamur a gloria in gloriam tamquam a domini spiritu.* Bene ergo uocaturus ad sequendum se discipulum Iesus uoluit exire in Galileam, id est in transmigrationem factam siue reuelationem, ut uidelicet sicut ipse teste euangelio *proficiebat sapientia et aetate et gratia apud Deum et homines* (Lk. 24:26) sicut passus est et resurrexit et ita intrauit in gloriam suam sic etiam suos sequaces ostenderet proficere uirtutibus ac per passiones transitorias ad aeternorum dona gaudiorum transmigrare debere': *Homeliarum Evangelii*, I.17, ed. by Hurst, pp. 120–21, lines 46–61; trans. by Martin and Hurst, *Homilies on the Gospels*, I, 167.

[61] 'Sequuntur hi qui sunt Christi et ipsi in suo ordine ad uitam transmigrant ibique eum uidentes adorant quem in specie suae diuinitatis contemplantes sine fine conlaudant. Cui uisioni congruit illud quod Galilaea etiam reuelatio interpretatur. Tunc etenim *reuelata facie* sicut apostolus testatur *gloriam domini speculantes in eandem imaginem transformamur* quicumque

season, Bede describes Christ's resurrection as the pattern for the faithful: 'We must believe that our bodies too, after their resurrection, will be endowed with heavenly glory.' The children of the resurrection will no longer require earthly sustenance; their joy will consist of none other 'than that which is chanted in the psalm, "Blessed are they who dwell in your house, O Lord, they will praise you for ever". And again, "The God of gods will be seen in Zion"' (Psalm 83. 5, 8). The mysteries of that age, 'when God will be all in all' (I Corinthians 15. 28), remain hidden.[62]

It can be seen from these examples that Bede does not use Psalm 83. 8 simply to describe moral progress. The active love of neighbour, itself the work of grace, is a condition of every stage of the heavenward journey he describes, but he further associates the psalm text with the ascent to contemplation, which for most is only completed in heaven.[63] Acca longed to 'see the good things of the Lord in the land of the living' (see Psalm 26. 13), and in *De templo* Bede once more offered his friend an aid to achieving a glimpse of that vision through the scriptures. He pictured Acca in the exile of this present life (and possibly in literal exile too) but solaced by the contemplation of 'the unfathomable mysteries of the heavenly mansions' (see John 14. 2), like the blessed John exiled on Patmos.[64] To describe that contemplative vision Bede repeatedly returned to Psalm 83, and especially its

---

modo reuelamus ad eum uiam nostram eiusque uestigia fide non ficta sequimur': *Homeliarum Evangelii*, II.8, ed. by Hurst, p. 234, lines 30–33; trans. by Martin and Hurst, *Homilies on the Gospels*, II, 69–70.

[62] 'Sed et nostra post resurrectionem corpora caelesti gloria praedita credendum est ad quicquid uoluerint agendum esse potentia ad ueniendum ubicumque libuerit esse promptissima; sed quia nulla tunc manducandi necessitas uel utilitas aliunde possit inferri nullatenus inmortale saeculum cibis mortalibus esse fruiturum ubi filiis resurrectionis non aliud esca et potus uita et salus gaudium pax et omnia bona quam illud nimirum sit quod in psalmo canit: *Beati qui habitant in domo tua domine in saecula saeculorum laudabunt te*; et iterum: *Videbitur Deus deorum in Sion*. Vnde et apostolus illius saeculi archana describens ait: *Quando erit Deus omnia in omnibus*': *Homeliarum Evangelii*, II.9, ed. by Hurst, p. 244, lines 178–89, trans. by Martin and Hurst, *Homilies on the Gospels*, II, 85.

[63] For other examples of Bede's exegesis on the active and contemplative life, and for discussion of the patristic background, see Scott DeGregorio, 'The Venerable Bede on Prayer and Contemplation', *Traditio*, 54 (1999), 1–39 (pp. 27–32).

[64] 'iuxta exemplum beati Iohannis qui ab imperatore nefando intra angustias unius paruissimae religatus insulae confestim a pio conditore per spiritum est ad contemplanda infinita illa caelestium mansionum archana introductus et ubi putatus est': *De templo*, ed. by Hurst, p. 144, lines 64–67; trans. by Connolly, *On the Temple*, p. 3. See further note 73 below.

image of seeing God, in various contexts and with a variety of theological as well as spiritual insights gained from reading it in the light of other scriptural texts.

The incarnation and resurrection of Christ are central to the vision. In an Advent homily on John 1. 15–18, for example, the psalm is evoked for him by the Gospel's declaration of the invisible God made known in Christ, the transcendent Word made flesh: 'No man has seen God at any time; the only begotten Son of God who is in the bosom of the Father, he has declared (*narrauit*) him.' He emphasizes there is one heavenly homeland for all the blessed, but they will experience it according to their varying spiritual merits. Bede affirms that Christ will, after the general judgement, reveal the glory of the invisible and indivisible Trinity by leading all the elect to the vision of his brightness. To those who had only understood him in his humanity he will reveal his divinity. Meanwhile, to some of the faithful who have already died, he has begun to fulfill his promise that 'He who loves me is loved by my Father, and I will manifest myself to him' (John 14. 21). This blessing is already being experienced by the apostles, martyrs, confessors, and others, though many righteous but less perfect people wait in the blessed rest of paradise for the general resurrection when they will appear before the face of the Lord, while others of the elect will first be chastised in purgatory. Bede says that the only begotten Son will tell all of them about God, but 'according to the capacity of each, when at the time of resurrection, *he who gave the law will give a blessing*, so that, journeying from the virtue of faith and hope to the virtue of contemplation, they may *see the God of gods in Zion*'.[65]

Bede's use of other scriptural texts about seeing God can extend our understanding of what might be meant by his use of the image as it occurs in Psalm 83. 8. In *De locis sanctis*, Adamnán, having closely questioned the pilgrim Arculf, describes the rock-hewn cave of Christ's sepulchre, which is clad in marble, adorned with gold, and enshrined within a great pilgrimage church in Jerusalem. Adamnán adds that doubtless the prophet was prophesying the burial and resurrection of Christ in this cave when he said, 'he shall dwell in a high cave of

---

[65] 'Qua autem ratione ad uisionem incommutabilis et aeterni luminis perueniri debeat euangelista consequenter exposuit dicens: *Vnigenitus filius qui est in sinu patris ipse narruit* [...]. Quibus tamen omnibus unigenitus filius qui est in sinu patris Deum iuxta modum cuiusque capacitatis narrabit cum tempore resurrectionis *benedictionem dederit qui legem dedit* ut *ambulantes de uirtute* fidei et spei in uirtutem contemplationis uideant *Deum deorum in Sion*, id est incommutabilis ueritatis cuius beneficiis et muneribus aeternis laus et gratiarum actio in omnia saecula saeculorum': *Homeliarum Evangelii*, I.2, ed. by Hurst, p. 11, lines 169–71; p. 13, lines 220–26; trans. by Martin and Hurst, *Homilies on the Gospels*, I, 15, 17.

the strongest rock' and 'you shall see the king with glory' (Isaiah 33. 16, 17). Bede, though fond of the Isaiah text, omits it from his own version of *De locis sanctis* and elsewhere in his exegesis expounds it as referring to Christ and members of his body, the Church.[66] *De templo* describes the eternal reward of those who observe the law by loving their neighbour, whom they can see, and God, whom they now do not see. In the next life they will 'see the king in his beauty' (Isaiah 33. 17), that is, God in the glory of his divinity, but will also see their neighbour glorified and beautified in God; human nature will be eternally united to God.[67] In his gospel homilies he warns that only the eyes of the just will see the king in all his beauty, meaning that only those who follow the example and teaching of Christ's human life will see his divinity, for 'Blessed are the pure in heart, for they shall see God' (Matthew 5. 8).[68] The *Letter on the death of Bede* by the deacon Cuthbert records

---

[66] Similarly, Gregory the Great noted that the Isaiah text describes the heights the faithful soul can ascend by the virtues of the active life and by fixing his thoughts on heavenly things, though he cannot in the flesh behold the land of the living as it really is: 'He shall dwell in high places [. . .]. His eyes shall see the king in his beauty, they shall behold the land afar off' (Isaiah 33. 16–17). At the Judgement the pure in heart will at last 'see the king in all his beauty', that is, in his divinity. 'Qui ambulat in iustitiis [. . .] et claudit oculos suos ne uideat malum (Isaiah 33. 15), ilico ab eiusdem actiuae uitae gradibus ad quae contemplationis culmina ascendatur adiunxit, dicens: "Iste in excelsis habitabit, munimenta saxorum sublimitas eius, panis ei datus est, aquae eius fideles sunt." *Regem in decore suo uidebunt oculi eius, cernent terram de longe.* [. . .]. *Regem in decore suo oculi* nostri conspiciunt, quia Redemptor noster in iudicio et a reprobis homo uidebitur, sed ad divinitatis eius intuendam celsitudinem soli qui electi sunt subleuantur': *Moralia in Iob*, III.51, ed. by M. Adriaen, 3 vols, CCSL, 143–143B (Turnhout, 1979–85), III, 1620, lines 26–29, 42–44.

[67] 'Qui ergo decalogum in Dei et proximi dilectione custodiunt iure mercedem huius custodiae in Dei simul et proximi uisione percipiunt quique in hac uita et proximum quem uident et Deum quem non uident diligunt hi in futura uita et Deum *regem in decore suo* et proximum in Deo glorificatum ac decoratum *uidebunt*': *De templo*, ed. by Hurst, p. 227, lines 1383–88; trans. by Connolly, *On the Temple*, pp. 108–09.

[68] 'Nam et reprobi in iudicio Christum uidebunt sed sicut scriptum est: *Videbunt in quem transfixerunt.* Soli autem *regem in decore suo uidebunt oculi* iustorum. *Beati* enim *mundo corde quoniam ipsi Deum uidebunt*': *Homeliarum Evangelii*, II.17, ed. by Hurst, p. 305, lines 170–73, trans. by Martin and Hurst, *Homilies on the Gospel*, II, 170. This homily is on John 14. 15–21, the last verse of which is also linked with Isaiah 33. 17 in Bede's homily on Luke 2. 45–52: '*Me ipsum*, inquit, *manifestabo* (John 14. 21), id est non qualem me omnes conspicere qualem etiam infideles uidere possunt et crucifigere sed qualem *in decore suo regem* saeculorum soli uidere possunt oculi mundi, sanctorum talem me ad rependendam uicem dilectionis his qui me diligunt ostendam' (*Homeliarum Evangelii*, I.19, ed. by Hurst, p. 135, lines 21–26 on Luke 2. 42–52; trans. by Martin and Hurst, *Homilies on the Gospels*, I, 188).

Bede's own yearning for the vision: 'The time of my departure is at hand, and my soul longs to see Christ my King in all his beauty' (Isaiah 33. 17).[69]

Augustine's psalm commentary, which Bede knew well, cites the opening of Psalm 83. 8, 'For he who gives the law will give a blessing', and asks its meaning, which he finds in the second part of the same verse: 'Grace shall come after the law; grace itself is the blessing. And what has that grace and blessing given us? *They shall go (ambulabunt) from virtue to virtue.*' Augustine explains that there is a diversity of virtues, which he describes under the form of the gifts of the Spirit and the cardinal virtues; they are acquired through grace and are necessary in this earthly vale of tears, but from these many virtues we go to one Virtue, namely, 'Christ, the power of God (*Dei virtutem*) and the wisdom of God' (I Corinthians 1. 24). He repeats the psalm verse, in variant form, *ibunt a virtutibus in virtutem*, and recasts his argument: what will that one virtue be, towards which we are going, but the virtue of contemplating God alone? He asks, 'What is contemplation?' and answers, 'the God of gods shall appear in Zion' ('Apparebit Deus deorum in Sion'). He shall appear as he is, 'God with God, the Word with the Father, by whom all things were made [see John 1. 3], and he shall appear to the pure in heart, because "Blessed are the pure in heart, for they shall see God"' (Matthew 5. 8).[70]

The blessing or beatitude to which Augustine refers (Matthew 5. 8) is itself a key text. It is used, for example, in Cassian's description of monastic perfection as attaining to complete purity of heart, which is love.[71] Cassian uses Psalm 83. 8 to describe phases in the longing for that state of blessedness as degrees of perfection, moving from fear to love:

---

[69] 'Tempus uero absolutionis meae prope est; etenim anima mea desiderat Regem meum Christum in decore suo uidere': Cuthbert, *Epistola de obitu Bedae*, ed. and trans. by Colgrave and Mynors in *Bede's Ecclesiastical History*, pp. 580–87 (pp. 584–85).

[70] 'sub lege gemuimus; quid restat, nisi ut benedictionem det qui legem dedit? Adueniet gratia post legem; ipsa est benedictio. Et quid nobis praestitit ista gratia et benedictio? *Ambulabunt a uirtutibus in uirtutem.* Hic enime per gratiam multae uirtutes dantur [. . .]. Multae uirtutes, sed hic necessariae; et ab his uirtutibus imus in uirtutem. Quam uirtutem? Christum, Dei uirtutem, et Dei sapientiam. Ipse dat diuersas uirtutes in loco hoc, qui pro omnibus uirtutibus necessariis in conualle plorationis et utilibus dabit unam uirtutem, seipsum': Augustine, *Enarrationes in psalmos*, ed. by D. E. Dekkers and J. Fraipont, 3 vols, CCSL, 38–40 (Turnhout, 1956), II, 1157, lines 7–11, 15–19.

[71] Cassian, *Conlationes*, 1. 1. 10, 14. 1. 9, in *Jean Cassien. Conférences*, ed. and trans. by E. Pichery, Sources chrétiennes, 42, 54, 64 (Paris, 1955–59), 42, p. 89; 54, p. 195.

Videtis ergo perfectionum gradus esse diuersos et de excelsis ad excelsiora nos a domino prouocari ita, ut is qui in timore dei beatus et perfectus extiterit, *ambulans* sicut scriptum est *de uirtute in uirtutem* et de perfectione ad aliam perfectionem, id est de timore ad spem mentis alacritate conscendens, ad beatiorem denuo statum, quod est caritas.

[We are called by the Lord from high things to still higher in such a way that he who has become blessed and perfect in the fear of God, going, as it is written, *from strength to strength*, and from one perfection to another [i.e. from fear of the Lord to hope], is summoned in the end to that still more blessed stage, which is love.][72]

He explains that all who fear the Lord will be blessed, though there is a great distinction between those who obtain mercy and those deemed worthy to enjoy the most glorious vision of God, 'for the Saviour says that in his Father's house are many mansions' (John 14. 2). Bede uses this image in a similar way.[73] Cassian adds that not all will reach the same measure of perfection of love. The disciplined experience of monastic practice, including knowing and learning the scriptures, prepares for insight into the hidden mysteries of scripture, where God is revealed; this transforming experience guides the ardent quest for greater purity of heart, leading to still deeper understanding of the divine word in scriptural texts which have long been known.[74]

---

[72] *Conlationes*, 11. 1. 12; ed. and trans. by Pichery, 54, p. 114.

[73] Bede similarly links John 14. 2 with fear and love and the image of 'star differing from star in glory' (I Corinthians 15. 41) in *De templo*. The many mansions of God's house will receive 'all those who fear him, and the Lord blesses those who love him, both little ones and great': *De templo*, ed. by Hurst, p. 144, lines 45–48; pp. 233–34, lines 1639–48; trans. by Connolly, *On the Temple*, p. 2. 'Nam et hoc in consolatione scripturarum inuenimus quia *benedixit omnes timentes se dominus pusillos cum maioribus* (Ps. 113. 21) multasque nobis in domo patris sui mansiones esse declaruit': *De templo*, ed. by Hurst, p. 144, lines 45–48; trans. by Connolly, p. 2. 'Sicut *stella a stella differt in claritate ita et resurrectio mortuorum* (I Cor. 15. 41–42). Quod utrumque iudex ipse ac distributor praemiorum dominus una sententia demonstrauit cum ait: *In domo patris mei multae sunt mansiones*. Vnam ergo domum domini fecit Salomon sed multos in ea thesauros ad recipienda uasa diuersi generis una tamen benedictione sanctificata parauit quia nimirum una est domus patris non manu facta aeterna in caelis sed multae in ea mansiones ac recipiendos omnes timentes se ac diligentes dominus benedicit pusillos cum maioribus. Amen': *De templo*, ed. by Hurst, pp. 233–34, lines 1639–48, trans. by Connolly, p. 117, and introduction, p. xxviii.

[74] See Columba Stewart, *Cassian the Monk* (Oxford, 1998), pp. 42–44, and his Introduction to *Purity of Heart in Early Ascetic and Monastic Literature*, ed. by H. Luckman and L. Kulzer (Collegeville, MN, 1999), pp. 8–15; Philip Rousseau, 'Cassian, Contemplation and the Coenobitic Life', *Journal of Ecclesiastical History*, 26 (1975), 113–26; Robert Markus, *The End of Ancient Christianity* (Cambridge, 1990), pp. 187–89; Martin Laird, 'Cassian's Conferences Nine and Ten: Some Observations Regarding Contemplation and Hermeneutics', *Récherches de théologie ancièrie et mediévale*, 62 (1995), 145–56.

Like Augustine and Cassian, Bede links the beatitude of Matthew 5. 8 with Psalm 83. 8, for instance in *De tabernaculo*, where he adds that the heavenly reward of the faithful — seeing God — is sometimes disclosed by divine grace even in this earthly life, to those who are pure in heart. Though God dwells in light inaccessible to earthly hearts, Bede cites Moses on the Exodus journey as an example of some spiritual teachers who 'have been permitted to ascend to the grace of divine contemplation once they have perfected the active life'. Such teachers do not then retire from the active life; they exemplify love of God and neighbour when they descend the mountain and by their word and example mediate something of the inner understanding of the divine word granted to them, assisting others to advance, according to their capacity, *from virtue to virtue* (Psalm 83. 8).[75] The precept is embodied in Bede's portrait of Cuthbert, who was fired with divine love and longing for the life of contemplation, yet summoned the people committed to his charge to heavenly things. He believed that 'to give the weak brethren help and advice was a fit substitute for prayer, for he knew that he who said, "Thou shalt love the Lord thy God", also said, "Thou shalt love thy neighbour"' (Matthew 22. 37, 39).[76]

There is an extraordinary spiritual and theological coherence in the multiplicity of contexts and ways in which Bede uses the psalm text to describe the heavenward journey, both in the life of the individual and of the Church through the ages. In a final example, he makes extensive use of Psalm 83, linked with the beatitude, Matthew 5. 8, in a rhapsodic description of the life of eternity which forms the climax of his vast exegesis on Easter, the mystical meaning of *computus*, and the sanctification of time in *De temporum ratione*.[77] Earlier in the work, he had related the term 'Passover' first to the passing over, in baptism, from 'the power of Satan to the portion allotted to the saints', then to the soul's daily

---

[75] 'Septimo autem die uocat ad altiora dominus Moysen quia post operum perfectionem requiem nobis lex promittit aeternum ut qui in altitudine rectae actionis domino assistere curauimus iam ad eius uisionem atque colloquium ascendere mereamur iuxta illud psalmistae: *Etenim benedictionem dabit qui legem dedit, ambulabunt de uirtute in uirtutem, uidebitur Deus deorum in Sion*': *De tabernaculo*, ed. by Hurst, CCSL, 119A, p. 8, lines 136–42; *Bede: On the Tabernacle*, trans. by Arthur Holder (Liverpool, 1994), pp. 3–6, also pp. 44, 91.

[76] 'Hoc ipsum quoque orationis loco ducens, si infirmis fratribus opem suae exhortationis tribueret, sciens quia, qui dixit "Diliges Dominum Deum tuum", dixit et "Diliges proximum"': *Historia ecclesiastica*, 4.28.

[77] *De tempore ratione*, c. 71, ed. by C. W. Jones and T. Mommsen, CCSL, 123B (Turnhout, 1977), p. 554, lines 73–91; trans. by Faith Wallis, *Bede: The Reckoning of Time* (Liverpool, 1999), p. 249, introduction, pp. lxxi, lxxxiii–lxxxiv.

passing over from vice to virtue and the love of God and neighbour throughout the pilgrimage of life, and then to the passage from death to resurrection.[78] He emphasizes that it is only through the mystery of Christ's resurrection — our Passover (I Corinthians 5. 7) — that we hope we shall 'return once more to that first realm of supernal joy from which we departed into a far-off land', but that in order to make a spiritual Passover it is necessary to 'pass over to better things by daily progress'.[79]

The *De temporum ratione* draws to a close with an evocation of the future resurrection of the faithful in the Eighth Age of the world, on the Eighth Day (the day of the Lord), which was prefigured in Christ's resurrection on the eighth day of the week. Bede comments that the psalmist was prophetically longing for the vision of that eternal Eighth Day when he said, 'Better is one day in thy courts than a thousand' (Psalm 83. 11). He adds that the Lord himself, who is 'the way, the truth, and the life' (John 14. 6), has declared who will be able to enter into the one unending day of light, the Eighth Day, and see this vision: 'Blessed are the pure in heart, for they shall see God' (Matthew 5. 8). The words of Psalm 83. 5 concerning pilgrims who worshipped God in the Temple in Jerusalem, 'Blessed are they that dwell in thy house: they shall praise thee for ever and ever', are interpreted as foretelling how the saints at the resurrection, when 'renewed in the blessed immortality of flesh and spirit', will eternally sing God's praises in heaven. Finally, Bede tells of their beatitude in the unending vision which shall delight them there, 'for he who gave the law will give a blessing and they will go from

---

[78] 'Et quia nos in baptismo, ut de potestate Satanae in partem sortis sanctorum transire queamus, sinceritatem ac veritatem tenere necesse est, itemque toto nostrae peregrinationis tempore, quod septenario dierum numero uoluitur, quotidiano profectu ad meliora transire praecipimur, quasi et in pascha azymis uesci, et in diebus azymorum pascha spiritaliter agere cognoscimur [...]. In nomine quidem paschae, ut de uitiis ad uirtutes transitum quotidie faciamus spiritalem': *De tempore ratione*, c. 63, ed. by Jones and Mommsen, pp. 455–56, lines 57–63; c. 64, p. 458, lines 89–91; trans. by Wallis, *Reckoning of Time*, pp. 150–51. Gregory's similar explanation warns that none comes to the day of the Lord save he who has kept the love of God and of his neighbour, *Homiliae in Hiezechielem prophetam*, 2.4.3, ed. by Adriaen, p. 259, lines 62–82.

[79] 'Quia per huius mysteria solemnitatis primam nos stolam recepturos, primum supernae beatitudinis regnum, a quo in longinquam regionem discessimus, nos repetituros esse speramus [. . .]. Nec minus etiam moralem nobis commendant paschalia tempora sensum': *De tempore ratione*, c. 64, ed. by Jones and Mommsen, p. 456, lines 14–17; p. 458, lines 88–91; trans. by Wallis, *Reckoning of Time*, pp. 151–52, 154. Ceolfrith's letter to Nechtan stresses the necessity of keeping the Passover with Christ by faith, hope, and love, *Historia ecclesiastica*, 5.21, p. 545. For the idea of *peregrinatio* as a return (*reditus*) to our true *patria*, see M. A. Claussen, '"Peregrinatio" and "Peregrini" in Augustine's *City of God*', *Traditio*, 46 (1991), 33–75 (pp. 71–73).

strength to strength and the God of gods will be seen in Zion' (Psalm 83. 8).[80] The vision of the invisible God is beyond mortal imagining. Through the words of the psalmist Bede evokes the contemplation of the divine, which is the recognition of who God is, in the revelatory act of seeing.

---

[80] 'sed nobis tunc incipiet cum ad eam uidendam meruerimus intrare, ubi quo actu occupentur sancti, perfecta spiritus et carnis inmortalitate renouati, testatur psalmista, qui Deo per laudem amoris canit: *Beati qui habitant in domo tua, in saeculum saeculi laudabunt te.* Quo uisu delectentur, idem consequenter exponit: etenim *benedictionem dabit,* qui *legem* dedit, *ambulabunt de uirtute in uirtutem, uidebitur Deus Deorum in Sion.* Quales ad hunc uenire possint, ipse qui est *uia, ueritas et uita,* testatur dominus, *Beati mundo corde, quoniam ipsi Deum* uidebunt': *De tempore ratione,* c. 71, ed. by Jones and Mommsen, p. 544, lines 81–91; trans. by Wallace, *Reckoning of Time,* p. 249.

Martyr Cult within the Walls: Saints and Relics in the Roman *Tituli* of the Fourth to Seventh Centuries

Alan Thacker

In its earliest phases, at the very least up to the mid-fifth century, martyr cult in Rome was undoubtedly associated primarily, if not exclusively, with extramural sites. It centred on the tombs (real or supposed) within the city's cemeteries and catacombs of those who had, or were believed to have, suffered for the faith.[1] The purpose of this paper is to look at the impact of this increasingly fundamental aspect of the city's spiritual and liturgical life upon the churches within the walls of Rome, in particular the *tituli*, in effect the parish churches of *abitato*. As we shall see, while never as central as the extramural holy sites, the *tituli*'s role in martyrial cult developed, especially through papal initiative in the first four centuries after the peace of the Church. The complex interplay between the varying attractions presented by the churches considered in this paper and the older cemeterial sites was an essential element in the experience of pilgrims such as the English grandees who travelled to the Eternal City from the 650s onwards, and whose activities and culture Éamonn Ó Carragáin has done so much to illumine.

I am very grateful to Julia Hilner and Richard Gem for reading and commenting on an earlier draft of this paper.

[1] For a recent review, see Alan Thacker, 'Rome of the Martyrs: Saints' Cults and Relics, 4th–7th Century', in *Roma Felix: Formation and Reflections of Medieval Rome*, ed. by Éamonn Ó Carragáin and Carol Neuman de Vegvar (Aldershot, forthcoming).

Intramural

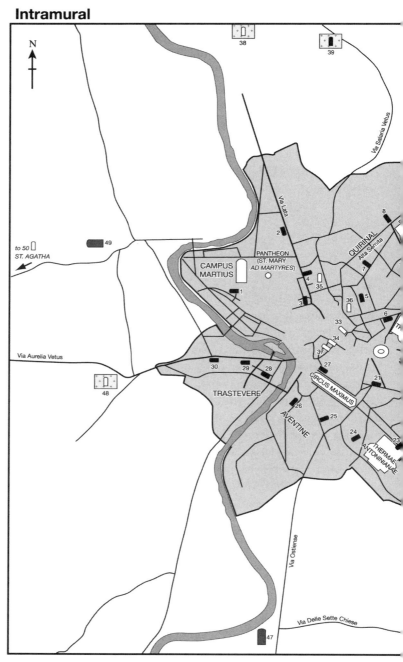

Map 1. Map of Rome showing *tituli* and main extramural churches.

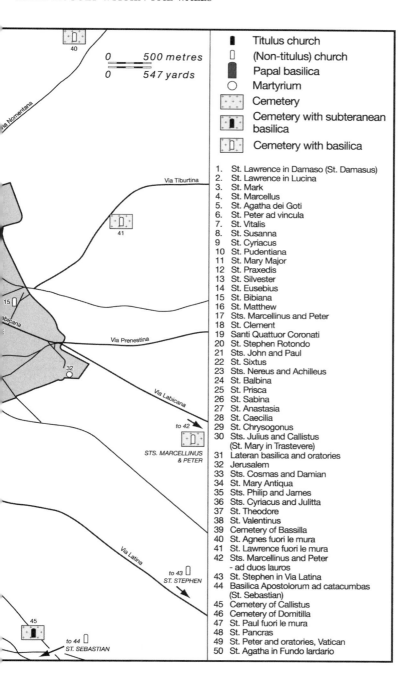

Legend:

- ▮ Titulus church
- ▯ (Non-titulus) church
- ▮ Papal basilica
- ○ Martyrium
- Cemetery
- Cemetery with subteranean basilica
- Cemetery with basilica

1. St. Lawrence in Damaso (St. Damasus)
2. St. Lawrence in Lucina
3. St. Mark
4. St. Marcellus
5. St. Agatha dei Goti
6. St. Peter ad vincula
7. St. Vitalis
8. St. Susanna
9. St. Cyriacus
10. St. Pudentiana
11. St. Mary Major
12. St. Praxedis
13. St. Silvester
14. St. Eusebius
15. St. Bibiana
16. St. Matthew
17. Sts. Marcellinus and Peter
18. St. Clement
19. Santi Quattuor Coronati
20. St. Stephen Rotondo
21. Sts. John and Paul
22. St. Sixtus
23. Sts. Nereus and Achilleus
24. St. Balbina
25. St. Prisca
26. St. Sabina
27. St. Anastasia
28. St. Caecilia
29. St. Chrysogonus
30. Sts. Julius and Callistus (St. Mary in Trastevere)
31. Lateran basilica and oratories
32. Jerusalem
33. Sts. Cosmas and Damian
34. St. Mary Antiqua
35. Sts. Philip and James
36. Sts. Cyriacus and Julitta
37. St. Theodore
38. St. Valentinus
39. Cemetery of Bassilla
40. St. Agnes fuori le mura
41. St. Lawrence fuori le mura
42. Sts. Marcellinus and Peter - ad duos lauros
43. St. Stephen in Via Latina
44. Basilica Apostolorum ad catacumbas (St. Sebastian)
45. Cemetery of Callistus
46. Cemetery of Domitilla
47. St. Paul fuori le mura
48. St. Pancras
49. St. Peter and oratories, Vatican
50. St. Agatha in Fundo Iardario

The *tituli* emerged in the fourth and fifth centuries.[2] They comprised a group of churches, which by 400 had come to be regarded as Rome's principal centres of pastoral care and as having an especial link with the pope. That link was most fully expressed in the distribution of the *fermentum*. Defined by Pope Innocent I in a letter dated 417, this comprised a particle of the bread consecrated at the papal Mass and dispatched on the same day to the priests of the urban churches for inclusion in their chalices at their own celebration of the liturgy. Sent exclusively to the priests of the *tituli*, it was a sign of the close unity between the pope and his urban clergy.[3]

The origins of the *tituli* were various. Some developed from house churches (*domus ecclesiae*), domestic centres of Christian worship which might pre-date the peace of the Church. Others were new foundations. A few, such as the *titulus Damasi*, were established by a pope on his own patrimony, but many more were founded through private endowment, with the aid of rich patrons, albeit with papal participation. By the fifth century they formed an urban pastoral network, irregularly distributed throughout intramural Rome. Several were acquiring baptisteries.[4] Their number and function, as seen from a sixth-century perspective, were defined by the compiler of the surviving early biographies of the *Liber pontificalis*, in his account of Pope Marcellus (305/06–306/07). Marcellus, he says, organized the twenty-five *tituli* within Rome 'as dioceses for the baptism and repentance of many converts from paganism and for the burial of martyrs'.[5] These arrangements, or something very like them, were certainly in existence by 499

[2] For recent discussion, see Victor Saxer, 'La chiesa di Roma dal V al X secolo: administrazione centrale e organizzazione territoriale', in *Roma nell'alto medioevo*, 2 vols, Settimane di Studio del Centro Italiano di Studi sull'alto medioevo, 48 (Spoleto, 2001), pp. 493–632 (pp. 553–71); Julia Hilner, 'Families, Patronage and the Titular Churches of Rome', in *Dynasty, Patronage and Authority in a Christian Capital: Rome, 300–850*, ed. by K. Cooper and J. Hilner (Cambridge, forthcoming).

[3] *La lettre du pape Innocent Ier à Décentius de Gubbio*, ed. by R. Cabié, Bibliothèque de la Revue d'histoire ecclésiastique, 58 (Leuven, 1973), pp. 26–89, 50–53; quoted by Saxer, 'La chiesa di Roma', p. 508.

[4] Saxer, 'La chiesa di Roma', pp. 553–71; S. Tarquini, 'Pellegrinaggio e assetto urbano di Roma', *Bullettino dell'Istituto storico italiano per il medio evo*, 107 (2005), 1–133, esp. pp. 38–41; Hilner, 'Families, Patronage and Titular Churches'.

[5] 'quasi diocesis, propter baptismum et paenitentiam multorum qui convertebantur ex paganis et propter sepulturas martyrum': *Liber pontificalis*, ed. by L. Duchesne, 2 vols, Bibliothèque des Écoles françaises d'Athènes et de Rome, 2nd series, 3 (Paris, 1886–92), 2nd edn with third vol. (Paris, 1955–57), I, 164 [henceforth *LP*].

when a synod held by Pope Symmachus was attended by the priests of some twenty-nine *tituli*.[6]

The sixth-century compiler of the *Liber pontificalis* was clearly aware of an established link between the *tituli* and martyr cult. But what exactly was that relationship? Did it, as he suggested, go back to the origins of the *tituli* and if so, what were its implications for the development of such cult within Rome? There are several ways of approaching these questions. We need to look at the issue of dedications, how and when the *tituli* came to bear the names of specific saints, and whether this had implications for the cult of those whose names were so used. We also need to investigate the relationship of these urban churches with the extramural basilicas and catacombs. And lastly — and perhaps most crucially — we must re-examine the issue of relics, and in particular corporeal remains, within the walls.

The Naming and Dedication of Tituli

A church dedication is important because it implies (or has been held to imply) that the church in question had special involvement in the cult of its titular saint and may even have contained his or her relics. Let us then look at the naming patterns of the early *tituli*. The fullest evidence comes from two well-known early lists of titular priests attesting Roman assemblies held in 499 and 595 (see Table 1). Only a few of the *tituli* mentioned in 499 are referred to as if they were dedicated to saints. In 595, by contrast, such usage was the norm.[7] This evidence is in fact less clear-cut than it looks. The manuscript witnesses to the 499 synod are late and present conflicting evidence of the number of *tituli* with saintly patrons. It is, of course, easy to see how a copyist of the eighth or ninth century, well aware of the usage of his own times, might have added the epithet *sanctus* to the patronal name. Nevertheless, as Julia Hilner has pointed out, all the manuscripts for 499 identify some churches dedicated to saints; it seems clear therefore that the usage existed by then.[8] Nor can we be sure that the lack of the designation *sanctus* necessarily implied that the patron was not to be regarded as a saint. In the one absolutely certain instance of an intramural saint-dedication in 499, that of

---

[6] *Acta synhodorum habitarum Romae*, MGH, Auctores antiquissimi, 12 (1894), pp. 410–15, table 1.

[7] *Acta synhodorum*, pp. 410–15; Gregory the Great, *Registrum epistolarum. Libri I–VII*, V, 57A, ed. by P. Ewald, MGH Epistolae, 1 (1887), pp. 366–67, table 1.

[8] Julia Hilner, unpublished draft, generously made available to the author.

Table 1. *The tituli of 499 and 595*

499	595
Aequitius *nos 13, 34, 43*	S. Silvester
Aemiliana *nos 16, 38, 60*	SS Quattuor coronati?
Anastasia *nos 36, 50, 61*	
Apostoli *nos 39, 42, 49*	SS Apostoli/Apostoli
Caecilia *nos 3, 54*	S. Caecilia
Chrysogonus *nos 9, 14, 26*	S. Chrysogonus
S. Clemens *nos 5, 6, 24*	S. Clement
Crescentiana *nos 17, 29, 63*	S. Sixtus?
Cyriacus *nos 21, 22*	S. Cyriacus
Damasus *no 15*	S. Damasus
Eusebius *nos 18, 35, 66*	S. Eusebius
Fasciola *nos 40, 41, 53*	SS Nereus et Achilleus
Gaius *nos 44, 47*	S. Susanna
Julius *nos 7, 28, 51*	SS Julius et Calixtus
S. Laurentius* *nos 59, 67*	S. Laurentius
Lucina* *nos 57, 62*	
Marcellus *nos 48, 56, 65*	S. Marcellus
Marcus *nos 52, 64*	S. Marcus
S. Mattheus *no 23*	SS Marcellinus e Petrus?
Nicomedis *nos 20, 37*	
Pammachius** *nos 4, 19*	SS Johannes et Paulus
By[Vi]sans** *nos 32, 33*	
Praxida *nos 1, 55*	S. Praxedis
Prisca *no 45*	S. Prisca
Pudens *nos 11, 12*	S. Pudens
Romanus *no 31*	
S. Sabina *nos 8, 30, 58*	S. Sabina
Tigrida *nos 27, 46*	S. Balbina?
Vestina *nos 2, 10, 25*	S. Vitalis
Total: 27/29	24

NB: On the basis of their location within the appropriate ecclesiastical *regio* and their non-appearance in 595, several of the *tituli* of 499 have been identified, not always with certainty, with *tituli* bearing new saint-dedications in the 595 list.

*For the identification of *titulus S Laurentii* with *titulus Lucinae* see below, p. 51n.

** For the identification of *tituli Pamacchii* and *Byzantis* see below, pp. 56–57.

the church of the Apostles, the priests of 499 attest simply as of the *titulus aposto-lorum* — not, as we might expect, *sanctorum apostolorum*.[9] Others very likely to have been regarded as saints, even though they were probably not consistently referred to as such by the several attestors for each church, include Saints Lawrence and Clement and — rather less certainly — Saints Caecilia and Sabina. It is then reasonably clear that by 499 contemporaries were perfectly familiar with the idea of Roman *tituli* bearing saintly dedications. On the other hand the convention of referring to them as the '*titulus* of x or y', stemming from a nomenclature that privileged an honoured patron or founder not necessarily regarded as a saint, died hard. It was only by the end of the late sixth century that in an official source the conservative Romans of Rome bowed before the (by then) almost universal western practice of referring to churches by the names of their saintly titulars — and even then the older practice remained in use beside the new. All we can say then of these lists is that they show us that in origin most of the *tituli* were not thought of primarily as associated with martyr cult. How much significance we can attach to the change in naming practice between 499 and 595 is something that we will be examining in this paper.

Tituli *Associated with Saints from an Early Period*

In a very few instances, *tituli* were associated with saints from before 450. The *titulus Clementis* seems to have been regarded from an early date as under the patronage of St Clement, the pope placed second after Peter in the Liberian catalogue and third in the *Liber pontificalis*.[10] He is unlikely to be the Clement commemorated with three other martyrs on 11 November in the first Roman calendar, the mid-fourth-century *Depositio martyrum*,[11] and in fact appears on 23 November in the Hieronymian martyrology, probably in the initial (earlier fifth-century) recension. Significantly, the entry in the martyrology does not allude to Clement's martyrdom or *passio*, but simply commemorates his feast day, *dies natalis*, in Rome. Although its witness is thus uncertain, the Pope was explicitly described as a martyr in the roughly contemporaneous council held at

---

[9] *Acta synhodorum*, pp. 413–14 (nos 39 and 49). Compare Gregory the Great, *Registrum*, ed. by Ewald, p. 367, where both *titulus apostolorum* and *titulus sanctorum apostolorum* appear.

[10] *LP*, I, 2–3, 123–24.

[11] *LP*, I, 12.

Vaison-la-Romaine (Dép. Vaucluse, France) in 442.[12] In any case, whatever Clement's initial status, it is clear that by the late fourth century, the *titulus* near the Colosseum was identified with his cult. Jerome noted in *De viris illustribus* that a church had been built to guard his memory in Rome.[13] An inscription of Pope Siricius appears to refer to a martyr as titular,[14] and a letter of Pope Zosimus of 417 expressly mentions the basilica of *Saint* Clement.[15]

As author of a celebrated epistle, Clement attracted literary attention from an early period and became the subject of widespread and wholly fictitious legends, first set out in the Clementine Recognitions and later elaborated in a *passio* which places his martyrdom and burial in Greece, in the Chersonese. Whether any of this material originated in Rome is unclear, but none of it alludes to the basilica on the Celian. It is therefore unlikely that it was written to serve the interests of a cult based at the *titulus*. What it does make absolutely apparent is that Clement had no identifiable tomb in Rome. The Leonine sacramentary, which was probably compiled from Roman material in the mid-sixth century, borrows from some of these Clementine traditions. The four Masses in his honour, written for the annual solemnity of the saint's *nataliciae*, recognize him as a martyr. Two of the prefaces note his wanderings abroad and recall to the papal throne in Rome before concluding with his martyrdom, significantly unlocated.[16] The sixth-century compiler of the *Liber pontificalis* explicitly acknowledges Clement's death and burial far away in the Chersonese.[17]

---

[12] *Martyrologium Hieronymianum*, ed. by H. Delehaye and H. Quentin, *AA SS Novembris*, II.2 (Brussels, 1931), pp. 615–16 [henceforth *Mart. Hieron.*]; J. D. Mansi, *Sacrorum conciliorum nova et amplissima collectio*, 31 vols (repr. Paris, 1901), VI, 454.

[13] 'Obiit tertio Trajani anno. Nominis eius memoriam usque hodie Romae extructa est': Jerome, *De viris illustribus*, 15 (*PL*, 23, 666), quoted in F. Guidobaldi, *San Clemente: Gli edifici romani, la basilica paleocristiana, et le fasi altomedievali*, San Clemente Miscellany, 4.1 (Rome, 1992), pp. 279–80, 301–03.

[14] 'S(alvo) Sir(icio) (ep)isc(opo) eccl(esiae sanctae) Ga[. . .] praesbyter (sancto) martyr(i clementi h)oc vo(luit dedicatum).' For the problems posed by de Rossi's reconstruction, see Guidobaldi, *San Clemente*, pp. 280–81, 304–07.

[15] 'Die cognitionis resedimus in basilica S. Clementis': *Epistulae imperatorem pontificum aliorum (Collectio Avellana)*, ed. by O. Guenther, 2 vols, CSEL, 35 (Vienna, 1895–98), I, 99–100; Guidobaldi, *San Clemente*, p. 281. Compare Leo I's reference to a *presbyter tituli Sancti Clementis*: Guidobaldi, *San Clemente*, as quoted in note 14 above.

[16] *Sacramentarium Veronese*, ed. by L. C. Mohlberg and others, Rerum ecclesiasticarum documenta, series major, 1 (Rome, 1956), pp. 150–52, esp. nos 1190 and 1197.

[17] H. Delehaye, *Étude sur le légendier romain*, Subsidia hagiographica, 23 (Brussels, 1936), pp. 96–116.

It seems clear then that, while the Romans regarded Clement as in some sense one of their own martyrs, they did not know the whereabouts of the body. That did not prevent them from actively promoting the Pope's liturgical cult. At the end of the fifth century the Clementine basilica was clearly important, staffed by at least three priests.[18] Pope Gelasius I (492–96) allegedly granted an indulgence to all who visited, perhaps, it has been suggested, on the occasion of the deposition of relics there.[19] Pope John II (533–35), who as priest of the *titulus* had already adorned the church, magnificently renewed the liturgical choir.[20] By then, almost certainly, the basilica had been involved in the development of the Masses recorded in the Leonine sacramentary and was celebrating Clement's feast day with some elaboration. Another honour probably conferred at this time was Clement's inclusion among the early popes invoked in the *Communicantes* prayer of the canon of the Roman Mass.[21] In all this, however, there is nothing to imply a relic cult of any kind in Rome.

Another saint associated with a *titulus* from an early period is Anastasia. Although in origin very probably a Roman figure, the church's founder or an early benefactor, in the fifth century she seems to have been confounded with a Greek saint, whose supposed remains had recently been (or were about to be) translated from Sirmium in Pannonia to Constantinople (460/61).[22] Perhaps in 457 on the saint's feast day (25 December), Leo the Great (440–61) preached a sermon against Monophysitism in the church, chosen because it was located in the Velabro, the quarter near the Tiber which was home to Egyptian traders who favoured the heresy. Although an addition to the first collection of the Pope's sermons, it is authentic. The only mention of Anastasia is in the title, where she is expressly named as saint and titular, in wording which the editor considers in general to be early (although the possibility that the epithet *sanctus* was added later cannot be ruled out).[23] Most probably then, in Leo's time the Anastasia of the *titulus* had

---

[18] *Acta synhodorum*, nos 5–6, 24 (pp. 411–12).

[19] *Italia pontificia*, vol. I: *Roma*, ed. by P. F. Kehr (Berlin, 1906), p. 44; Guidobaldi, *San Clemente*, p. 282.

[20] Guidobaldi, *San Clemente*, p. 282; F. Guidobaldi and others, *San Clemente: La scultura del VI secolo*, San Clemente Miscellany, 5.2 (Rome, 1992).

[21] V. L. Kennedy, *The Saints of the Canon of the Mass*, Studi di antichità cristiana, 14 (Vatican City, 1938), p. 116.

[22] Delehaye, *Legendier*, pp. 151–71, 221–49 (text).

[23] 'Tractatus [...] datus ad populum in basilica Sanctae Anastasiae': Leo the Great, *Tractatus septem et nonaginta*, ed. by A. Chavasse, 2 vols, CCSL, 138–138A (Turnhout, 1973), no. 96, II, 591–95.

been identified with the saint of Sirmium. Although the evidence of the list of 499 is ambiguous, there was certainly a liturgical cult by the sixth century when Anastasia was included in the Leonine sacramentary and added to the female saints commemorated in the *Nobis quoque* prayer in the Roman canon.[24] Relics may have been obtained after the translation, but if so, no relic cult is known. The church was, however, among the intramural basilicas visited by pilgrims to the holy places in the seventh century, when it was esteemed as the place where the crosses used in the processions to the stational churches were kept.[25]

By the sixth century, Anastasia's cult evidently required explanation. At all events a *passio* was produced which both linked her with Rome and provided a context for the absence of relics in the Eternal City. The *passio* makes Anastasia a noble Roman lady who adopts Chrysogonus, then under arrest in Rome, as her Christian teacher. She follows him to Aquileia whither he is sent to be interrogated and martyred by Diocletian. After further adventures, she is eventually martyred on the island of Palmaria (Palmarola in the Tyrrhenian Sea). Her remains are collected by a Christian matron who buries them in her (unlocated) garden, and at considerable expense builds a basilica there to house them.[26]

The choice of Chrysogonus as Anastasia's teacher was clearly significant, for it afforded the author of the *passio* the chance to explain another otherwise wholly unknown patron of a *titulus*. Like Anastasia, Chrysogonus was said to have been buried in an unlocated grave in a house far away from Rome. Almost certainly, his cult developed at much the same time as Anastasia's. Although he was probably not termed *sanctus* by the three priests of the *titulus* who subscribed the Acts of 499, the epithet was undoubtedly applied to him in inscriptions some twenty years later. Indeed, in one of them Chrysogonus is expressly referred to as 'the blessed martyr', perhaps evidence that by then the *passio* was in circulation.[27] In the sixth century, if not before, the cult enjoyed considerable success. Chrysogonus appears in the Hieronymian martyrology in variable entries reflecting the

---

[24] *Acta synhodorum*, nos 36, 50, and 61 (pp. 413–14); *Sacramentarium Veronese*, ed. by Mohlberg and others, p. 157; D. M. Hope, *The Leonine Sacramentary* (Oxford, 1971), pp. 25, 37; Kennedy, *Saints of the Canon*, pp. 183–85.

[25] *Codice topografico della città di Roma*, ed. by R. Valentini and G. Zucchetti, 4 vols, Fonti per la Storia d'Italia, 81, 88, and 90–91 (Rome, 1940–53), II, 120–21.

[26] Delehaye, *Legendier*, pp. 151–71, 221–49.

[27] For example, G. B. de Rossi, *Inscriptiones christianae urbis Romae*, 2 vols (Rome, 1857–88), I, no. 975; also G. B. de Rossi, *Roma sotterranea cristiana*, 3 vols (Rome, 1864–77), III, 519–20, 522.

story told in the *passio*; in the Echternach version his *dies natalis* (24 November) is said to have been kept at Rome — evidently a reference to the church in Trastevere — while in the Codex Wissemburgensis he is described as martyred at Aquileia.[28] The saint was named in the *Communicantes* prayer not only in Roman canon but also in those of Ravenna and Milan, his inclusion probably dating from much the same time as Anastasia's, the mid-sixth century.[29] Considerable modifications were apparently made to the church in Trastevere at this time. There is, however, no evidence that the church contained relics at this period, although the later ring crypt, usually dated to the pontificate of Gregory III (731–41), suggests that later it did and that they were important.[30]

We should consider these churches, whose ultimately sanctified patrons were deemed to have been buried far away from Rome, alongside a second group: those whose patrons were identified as martyrs buried in the Eternal City itself. A particularly interesting example is St Susanna.[31] The entry in the Hieronymian martyrology indicates that by the time it was made the *dies natalis* of the saint was being celebrated 'ad duas domus iuxta duoclecinas' (i.e. Diocletianas), that is, at the intramural *titulus* on the Alta Semita not far from the baths of Diocletian.[32] If, as Delehaye supposes, this entry belongs to the earlier fifth-century stratum of the text, then it is excellent evidence for the early development of the liturgical celebration of martyr cult within the walls. On the other hand, the foundation is named as *titulus Gai(i)* at the synod of 499.[33] In any case, it is clear that the *titulus* did not claim the body. The early sixth-century *passio* alleges that the saint was buried next to the martyr Alexander in the cemetery of the Jordani on the Via Salaria Nova[34] and that the house where she had been killed was taken over by

---

[28] *Mart. Hieron.*, pp. 618–19. A fourth-century stone sarcophagus from San Canzian d'Isonzo inscribed 'beatissimo martyri Chrysogono' shows there was an early cult of a saint of this name in the diocese of Aquileia: *Patriarchi. Quindici secoli di civiltà fra l'Adriatico e l'Europa Centrale* (Milan, 2000), pp. 66–67.

[29] Kennedy, *Saints of the Canon*, pp. 129–30, 194.

[30] R. Krautheimer, *Corpus basilicarum christianarum Romae*, 5 vols (Vatican City, 1937–77), I, 144–64, esp. p. 159; *LP*, I, 418.

[31] A. Amore, 'Note hagiografiche sul calendario perpetuo della Chiesa universale', *Antonianum*, 39 (1964), 18–53 (pp. 37–42).

[32] *Mart. Hieron.*, p. 434.

[33] *Acta synhodorum*, nos 44, 47 (p. 413).

[34] The location of Susanna's tomb is debated. Amore, following J. P. Kirsch, has argued that the location on the Via Salaria represents a reinterpretation of the original text which placed the

Pope Gaius (283–96) who offered the Eucharist there 'to commemorate St Susanna to the people' ('pro commemoratione beatae Susannae populo'). Because that house adjoined that of Susanna's father, the priest Gabinius, the site became known as *ad duas domus*.[35] Here again we have evidence from around 500 of an interest in explaining intramural cult and justifying it in terms of a physical link — the house where the saint lived and where her blood was spilt.

We may compare St Susanna with St Caecilia. Like Susanna, Caecilia was unknown to the earliest Roman calendar, the *Depositio martyrum*, although she may be named in a late fourth-century inscription.[36] Her entry in the Hieronymian martyrology is complex; while she may occur in the earliest recension, none of the references is entirely satisfactory.[37] Nevertheless, by 499 it is likely that, as patron of the celebrated *titulus* in Trastevere, she was regarded as a saint, and by 545, when Pope Vigilius was arrested in the *ecclesia Sanctae Caeciliae* celebrating her feast day (22 November), her status was secure. She is among the saints for whom Masses (five sets) were recorded in the Leonine sacramentary, and she was included among the female martyrs in the *Nobis quoque* of the Roman canon.[38] Almost certainly the consolidation of her position is connected with the composition of her famous — and entirely fictitious — *passio*, a text perhaps composed in the late fifth century.[39] In particular, the formulae for her Masses in the Leonine sacramentary draw upon that work and were probably composed shortly before it was circulated in Rome.[40] The *passio* pays much attention to Caecilia's house, in which the saint is said to have been martyred and which she is said to have given to Pope Urban I (222–30) to be converted into a church (namely the *titulus*). Very significantly, however, the author makes it clear that the saint's remains were buried extramurally, alleging that they were interred by Pope Urban in the most famous of all the catacombs, that of Callistus on the Via Appia.[41] Here then, we

burial in the cemetery of Alexander *iuxta civitatem Figlinas* on the Via Nomentana: Amore, 'Note hagiografiche', pp. 39–41.

[35] *Mart. Hieron.*, pp. 434–35; *De Sancta Susanna*, ed. by J. B. Sollerius and others, *AA SS Augusti*, II (Antwerp, 1735), p. 632.

[36] Krautheimer, *Corpus*, I, 95; de Rossi, *Inscriptiones*, I, 359–60 (no. 816).

[37] Delehaye, *Legendier*, p. 87.

[38] Hope, *Leonine Sacramentary*, pp. 25, 36, 50; Kennedy, *Saints of the Canon*, pp. 178–82.

[39] Delehaye, *Legendier*, pp. 73–96, 194–220.

[40] Hope, *Leonine Sacramentary*, p. 50.

[41] Delehaye, *Legendier*, pp. 76–77, 219–20.

are witnessing the creation of an intramural cult. A *titulus* is sanctified by the closest possible association with a Roman martyr, short of actually holding the saint's remains. A cult site outside the city is identified and becomes a focus of pilgrimage — the tomb of St Caecilia is named in the seventh-century itineraries created for foreign pilgrims to Rome.[42] But the feast day is celebrated at the intramural church — by no lesser person than the pope himself. The body was only installed in the *titulus* in the time of Paschal I (817–24).[43]

The evidence of this group of *tituli* would therefore suggest that, although in origin they had no connection with martyr cult, by the late fifth or early sixth century, often with papal support, they were developing a strong interest in the liturgical commemoration of the saints and in particular of their own patrons, many of whom were in the process of being sanctified. The passion narratives relating to these patrons exhibit a strong interest in burial in domestic locations.[44] Although these *tituli* contained no relics, several were being viewed as martyrial sites, where the holy had lived and shed their blood for the faith. In a sense, *tituli* such as St Caecilia and St Susanna had become relics themselves.

Relics Within the Walls

Some intramural churches did, however, contain relics, almost all imported and originating in shrines far distant from Rome. The earliest relics housed within the walls were Christological, brought from the Holy Land and almost certainly installed in a church established by Constantine in the vast imperial palace known as the Sessorium, in the far south-east corner of the walled city. Their exact nature is uncertain. In particular, it may perhaps be doubted whether they included ab initio the relics of the True Cross, brought to Rome from the Holy Land immediately after the *inventio* attributed to the Emperor's mother Helena in 326.[45]

---

[42] *Codice topografico*, ed. by Valentini and Zucchetti, II, 87–88, 110.

[43] *LP*, II, 56–58. For new discussion of Pascal's development of the cult of St Caecilia, see C. Goodson, 'Material Memory: Rebuilding the Basilica of S. Cecilia in Trastevere, Rome', *Early Medieval Europe*, 15 (2007), 2–34.

[44] While we can no longer assume that many of the *Gesta martyrum* were written primarily to provide *tituli* with founding myths, nevertheless they do reveal much about contemporary attitudes to Rome's saints and patrons and their links with their eponymous churches.

[45] *LP*, I, 179–80. The earliest secure evidence for the association of Constantine with the diffusion of relics of the Cross seems to be a sermon of Cyril, Bishop of Jerusalem, 348–50:

Although the sixth-century compiler of the *Liber pontificalis* believed that Constantine had indeed been responsible for enshrining wood from the Cross in his new basilica, the fact that in the early Middle Ages it was known as Jerusalem and that it only later acquired the designation Santa Croce in Gerusalemme suggests otherwise. At all events, it remains significant that the relics in which Constantine and his mother invested within the walls were exotic and dominical — a counterpart to the Emperor's primary extramural investment in apostolic remains entombed locally in the cemeteries.[46] That emphasis, apparent also in the dedication of the Lateran to the Saviour, continued into the fifth century. The chapels established at the Lateran by Pope Hilary (461–68) at the baptistery provide another very early instance of the installation of relics at an intramural site. In the early sixth century the author of Hilary's biography in the *Liber pontificalis* named three such chapels, those of St John the Evangelist, St John the Baptist, and the Holy Cross. There may also have been a fourth dedicated to St Stephen, presumably replaced by the existing seventh-century chapel of St Venantius. The focal point of each chapel was a silver relic shrine or *confessio* beneath the altar, weighing at least 100 pounds, and there were numerous other precious ornaments honouring the relics. Hilary paid particular tribute to the Holy Cross: the oratory's adornments included a gold cross enriched with jewels weighing 20 pounds, perhaps to contain the relic itself; above the *confessio* rose a gold arch weighing 4 pounds, supported by columns of onyx and crowned by a gold image of the Lamb of God weighing a further 2 pounds; before the *confessio* hung a gold lamp in the form of a crown adorned with dolphins, weighing 5 pounds.[47]

The significance of these chapels has recently been discussed by Gillian Mackie.[48] Clearly they paid honour to the baptistery, the mother of all such in Rome and a richly endowed institution in its own right. But such an opulent display of relics drawn from outside Rome and from the primary figures of the faith — Christ himself, his forerunner, and his beloved apostle — is doing more than that. With the developing veneration of the extramural martyrial sites, often

---

H. Brandenburg, *Ancient Churches of Rome*, trans. from the original by A. Kropp (Turnhout, 2005), pp. 106–08. Avitus believed that Pope Symmachus (499–514) kept a relic of the Holy Cross in Rome: *Opera*, ed. by R. Peiper, MGH, Auctores antiquissimi, 6.2 (1883), Epistula no. 20; Krautheimer, *Corpus*, I, 165–94.

[46] S. De Blaauw, *Cultus et Decor: Liturgia e architettura nella Roma tardoantica e medievale*, Studi e Testi, 355 (Vatican City, 1994), pp. 139, 166–67; Thacker, 'Rome of the Martyrs'.

[47] *LP*, I, 242–43, 247.

[48] G. Mackie, *Early Christian Chapels in the West* (Toronto, 2003), pp. 195–211.

at a considerable distance from the pope's sphere of operations, the papacy perhaps felt the need to enhance the prestige of the Lateran itself, hitherto, it would
seem, without physical relics of any kind. Here at the heart of the papal cathedral,
where doubtless the great of the city received the rites of initiation, they were
associated with an iconographic programme which, it has been argued, ultimately
alluded to the pope as the new Melchizedech, high priest of the new covenant.
The relics set the seal on the statement.

Again, the nature of these relics is uncertain. Significantly, however, they were
all drawn from sources outside Rome, presumably partly at least because it was difficult to obtain suitable material from the local cemeteries. Wood from the Cross
may well have been brought from the church of Jerusalem nearby. Relics of the
Baptist almost certainly came from the East. By the 590s they took the form of
hair or a phial containing the saint's blood and ashes and a tooth, and were sent
by Gregory the Great to such important dignitaries as the Visigothic king Reccared
or the Lombard queen Theodelina.[49] Hilary's actions may well mark the beginnings of the great collection of sacred treasure later kept in the papal chapel at the
Lateran, by the eighth century dedicated to St Lawrence and eventually known as
the *sancta sanctorum*. Although most of these relics probably came into papal
hands after the mid-eighth century, it is significant that the earliest authenticating
tags — dating probably from the sixth or seventh century — name relics of Christ
or other biblical or angelic figures.[50] By the twelfth century the collection included
the Baptist's camel-hair garment and two major relics of the Evangelist: his tunic
and an ampulla filled with manna which had issued from his body in the grave.[51]

Following on from Hilary's installations at the Lateran itself, his successor
Simplicius (468–83) established the enormous circular church of Santo Stefano
Rotondo on the Celian Hill, clearly intended as a great martyrium.[52] Although
there is no good evidence that it ever held relics of Stephen, small pieces of bone
or of dust impregnated with the protomartyr's blood were widely available in the
West after the *inventio* of the early fifth century, and it is difficult to believe that

---

[49] Gregory the Great, *Registrum epistularum*, ed. by Dag Norberg, 2 vols, CCSL, 140–140A
(Turnhout, 1982), IX, 229 (II, 810); Mackie, *Early Christian Chapels*, pp. 200, 327–28.

[50] P. Lauer, *Le trésor du Sancta sanctorum*, Monuments et Mémoires publiés par l'Academie
des Inscriptions et Belles-Lettres, 15 (Paris, 1960); Thacker, 'Rome of the Martyrs'.

[51] *Codice topografico*, ed. by Valentini and Zucchetti, III, 337–38; Mackie, *Early Christian
Chapels*, pp. 200–01. Almost certainly, however, the tunic was acquired by Gregory the Great:
Registrum, III, 3 (ed. by Norberg, I, 148).

[52] *LP*, I, 249; Krautheimer, *Corpus*, IV, 201–02, 236.

some of these had not been brought to Rome and placed in the church. The action of Theodosius II's consort, the Empress Eudocia, in bringing back relics of Stephen from Jerusalem to Constantinople in 439 provides an obvious analogy.[53] Certainly, some such items were at the disposal of Gregory the Great in the 590s, when they were dispatched to churches at Messina and Rimini.[54] That Stephen's relics did become available in Rome in the mid-fifth century is also suggested by the earlier construction of the extramural basilica of St Stephen at the third milestone on the Via Latina in the time of Leo I (440–61).[55] That church, to which a baptistery was annexed, contained an altar with a reliquary compartment, placed over a crypt with which, according to its nineteenth-century excavator, the compartment itself was linked. We cannot be certain this arrangement dates from the mid-fifth century, but if it did then we have a local source from which the new rotunda could have been supplied.[56] Significantly, Masses for Stephen the protomartyr appear in the Leonine sacramentary in August rather than in December, his *dies natalis*. They were most probably placed there principally to mark the all-important feast of the *inventio* (3 August), the means by which the relics became available, although they may also commemorate Pope Stephen I (254–57), whose cult as a martyr was developing in the mid-sixth century in the church on the Via Latina and whose feast day was 2 August.[57]

Another church connected with the early import of relics was the *titulus Vestinae*, established beside the Quirinal on the Vicus Longus in the time of Pope Innocent I (401–17). The sixth-century compiler of the *Liber pontificalis* was well informed about this important foundation. He relates that it was endowed by Vestina, a rich woman of Rome, who directed that the basilica should be dedicated to the holy martyrs Saints Gervasius and Protasius. Innocent was said to

[53] A. Thacker, '*Loca sanctorum*: The Significance of Place in the Study of the Saints', in *Local Saints and Local Churches in the Early Medieval West*, ed. by A. Thacker and R. Sharpe (Oxford, 2002), pp. 1–43 (pp. 12–14); K. G. Holum, *Theodosian Empresses* (Berkeley, 1982), pp. 184–85, 189.

[54] Gregory the Great, *Registrum*, II, 6; VI, 45 (ed. by Norberg, I, 94, 418).

[55] *LP*, I, 238; Krautheimer, *Corpus*, IV, 241–42.

[56] Krautheimer, *Corpus*, IV, 249, 250–51. Significantly, Anicia Demetrias, the founder of the Via Latina church, sprang from a family in close contact with Augustine when the relics of Stephen were discovered: P. R. L. Brown, 'Augustine and a Crisis of Wealth in Late Antiquity' and C. Leyser, 'Homo pauper, de pauperibus natus: Augustine, Church Property, and the Cult of Stephen', both in *Augustinian Studies*, 36 (2005), 5–30, 229–37.

[57] Hope, *Leonine Sacramentary*, pp. 30, 42–43.

have established the *titulus* and dedicated the church in accordance with her wishes. Almost certainly these actions involved the installation in the church's main altar of relics of the Milanese martyrs widely distributed by the Bishop to members of his circle after the famous *inventio* of 386. Very probably Vestina had acquired them from Ambrose himself or one of his associates.[58] Interestingly, however, the church, recorded as the *titulus Vestinae* in 499, appears in 595 as San Vitale.[59] Now St Vitalis together with St Agricola was the subject of another of Ambrose's *inventiones*, at Bologna in 393.[60] It seems likely that Vestina had also obtained relics of those martyrs from the same source and that the choice of Vitalis as titular for the church in 595 was determined by the contemporary renown of the new church under his patronage at Ravenna. In Gregory's own time the church seems to have been known indifferently as St Vitalis or Saints Gervasius and Protasius.[61] Clearly, in stating that Innocent I dedicated the church to Gervasius and Protasius the compiler of the *Liber pontificalis* was reflecting the usages of his own day. Vestina's church had received no formal titular saint but was thought of as containing relics of Northern Italian martyrs. The instability of the nomenclature suggests that there was no single pre-eminent cult.

For a clear, if relatively late, case of the import of corporeal relics into Rome we can turn to the church of Saints Cyriacus and Julitta, a mother and son supposedly martyred in the East under Diocletian.[62] The church (to be distinguished from the existing *titulus Cyriaci*) was built *de novo* in the heart of Rome behind the Forum of Nerva by Pope Vigilius (537–55), presumably before his deportation from the city in 545. Its original altar survives, built of fine brickwork and enclosing a large rectangular reliquary cavity.[63] Discovered during the basilica's remodeling in the late sixteenth century by the Cardinal-titular Alessandro de' Medici, it was, as the Cardinal recorded, enriched with Vigilius's dedicatory

---

[58] For Ambrose's *inventiones* and relic-distribution, see Thacker, '*Loca sanctorum*', pp. 5–12, and Thacker, 'Rome of the Martyrs'.

[59] *Acta synhodorum*, nos 2, 10, 25 (pp. 411, 412); Gregory the Great, *Registrum*, ed. by Ewald, pp. 366–67.

[60] Ambrose, *Exhortatio virginitatis*, PL, 16, 351–54.

[61] *Ecclesia beati martyris Vitalis*: Gregory the Great, *Registrum*, Appendix IX, 52 (ed. by Norberg, II, 1104); *titulus Protasi et Gervasi*: *Registrum*, XI, 15, 9 (II, 881).

[62] A. Rimoldi, 'Quirico e Giulitta', in *Bibliotheca sanctorum*, ed. by Iosepho Vizzini and others, 12 vols plus index and appendix (Rome, 1961–87), X, 1326–27.

[63] Krautheimer, *Corpus*, IV, 45; *Acta synhodorum*, nos 21, 22 (p. 412); *Sanctus Qiriacus* in 595: Gregory the Great, *Registrum*, ed. by Ewald, p. 367.

inscription and relics from the arms of the two saints.[64] A similar introduction of foreign relics may have occurred a little earlier, when Pope Felix IV (526–30) converted Vespasian's temple-forum of peace into the church of Saints Cosmas and Damian. The cult of these eastern saints had already been established in Rome in the time of Symmachus (498–514), who had built an oratory in their honour at Santa Maria Maggiore.[65] Nevertheless, it was probably under Felix that it achieved the prominence which led to the saints' inclusion in the *Communicantes* prayer in the Roman canon.[66]

All the examples so far discussed were obtained from sources outside Rome — from the Holy Land, Milan, and the East. Less certain is the origin of a further class of relic, those which were non-corporeal. One of the most significant and earliest of intramural relic cults focussed upon the chains of St Peter. First heard of in a non-Roman context, at a church in Spoleto founded by Bishop Achilleus, they may have been obtained from Rome when Achilleus, a protégé of the Emperor Honorius, was sent there in 419 to celebrate Easter at the time of a disputed papal election.[67] It is curious, however, that there is no early reference to such famous objects being in the city at this time. Indeed a later (Carolingian) tradition viewed them as the chains from which Peter was miraculously freed during his imprisonment by Herod, brought to Rome from the Holy Land by the Empress Eudoxia, resident in the city with her husband Valentinian III in the earlier 450s.[68] While it is most unlikely that she obtained the relics personally from the Holy Land, Eudoxia did associate her father Theodosius II and her mother Eudocia with her work at the basilica in which they were enshrined, and it is at least possible that she had received the chains from her mother. Eudocia had after all returned with relics from Jerusalem in 439.[69] The existence of the Petrine chains in Rome is in fact first reliably recorded in the early sixth century. Among the items requested from Pope Hormisdas by his legates in Constantinople are relics derived from the chains of both apostles, Peter and Paul, each to be dispatched in separate reliquaries and evidently emanating from separate

---

[64] Krautheimer, *Corpus*, I, 38.

[65] *LP*, I, 262, 279–80.

[66] Kennedy, *Saints of the Canon*, pp. 137–40.

[67] H. Grisar, 'Della insigne tradizione romana intorno alla catena di san Pietro nella basilica Eudossiana', *Civiltà cattolica*, 47 (1898), 205–21 (pp. 211–13).

[68] Paul the Deacon, *Homeliae in sanctis*, 38, *PL*, 95, 1485–89.

[69] Krautheimer, *Corpus*, III, 181. Eudoxia's central role is implicit in the later naming of the basilica which housed the chains: see below.

sources.[70] The existence of separate chains of St Paul, implicit in the letter to Hormisdas, is confirmed by a letter of Gregory the Great to the Empress Constantina in which he denied her (amongst other items) the head of the apostle but promised to send instead relics in the form of filings from the chains which the apostle bore on his neck and hands and through which, he claimed, many miracles were displayed among the people.[71]

While we have no knowledge of where the Pauline chains were on show, those of St Peter were firmly located by 500, when we hear of a priest of the basilica of St Peter *ad vincula*, St Peter in Chains. This church was the *basilica apostolorum*, which, as inscriptions placed within it indicate, was rededicated and reconstructed by Sixtus III (432–40) and further remodelled by Valentinian's empress Eudoxia in the mid-fifth century.[72] Recorded as the *titulus apostolorum* in both 499 and 595, it was also known as the *titulus Eudoxiae* by the time of Gregory the Great, perhaps in memory of the Empress's gift of the crucial relic of the chains.[73] An apsidal mosaic inscription, described as having very old lettering in the sixteenth century and referring to the 'formerly unharmed' chains of St Peter preserved under the church's roof, places the identification of the *basilica apostolorum* with St Peter *ad vincula* beyond doubt.[74] The mysterious allusion to the formerly pristine state of the chains presumably stems from the fact that some had already been detached or filed down to provide relics and might well indicate an early but post-Sistine date.[75] The building itself appears to have attained its earliest form around 400 and to have been substantially reconstructed in the mid-fifth century (in a form which Krautheimer believed was definitely post-Sistine).[76] The seventh-century sacramentary of the church apparently included an unusual feast of all the apostles (*in natale omnium apostolorum*) and a commemoration of the octave of the two

---

[70] *Collectio Avellana*, ed. by Guenther, no. 218 (pp. 670–80).

[71] Gregory the Great, *Registrum*, IV, 30 (ed. by Norberg, I, 250). Compare *Registrum*, XIII, 43 (II, 1049).

[72] Krautheimer, *Corpus*, III, 179–82, 226–27.

[73] *Acta synhodorum*, nos 39, 42, 49 (pp. 413–14); Gregory the Great, *Registrum*, ed. by Ewald, p. 367; Gregory the Great, *Registrum*, XI, 15 (ed. by Norberg, II, 881).

[74] 'Inlesas olim servant haec tecta cathenas | vincla sacrata Petri ferrum pretiosius auro' ('These roofs shelter the formerly unharmed chains, bonds of St Peter, iron more precious than gold'): Krautheimer, *Corpus*, III, 180, 226–27. First recorded in the eighth-century Sylloge of Verdun: de Rossi, *Inscriptiones*, II.1, 133, 134 (no. 1).

[75] Compare Grisar, 'Della insigne tradizione', p. 210.

[76] Krautheimer, *Corpus*, III, 180–82, 194–230, esp. pp. 228–30.

Roman apostles Peter and Paul. Another important day was 1 August, the feast of the Maccabees and later of the dedication of the church and the Petrine chains.[77] A plausible hypothesis, taking account of all this, might be as follows. An early church, dedicated to all the apostles, was rededicated primarily to the apostles Peter and Paul on the occasion of some rebuilding by Sixtus which has not been identified or does not survive. Further work was undertaken shortly afterwards in the mid-fifth century by the Empress Eudoxia, perhaps related to the installation of the chains, the placing of the dedicatory inscription *Inlesas olim* in the apse, and the subsequent emergence of the church as the cult site of St Peter *ad vincula*.[78]

At all events, from the early sixth century both chains and church occur quite frequently in the record. An inscription of 533 records a votive offering by the priest Severus in honour of the relic.[79] In 544 after presenting Pope Vigilius with a copy of his work on the Acts of the Apostles before the *confessio* of St Peter at the Vatican, Arator read the poem over four separate days to a great crowd of notables and others gathered in the church of St Peter 'quod vocatur ad vincula'.[80] In the seventh century, the church with its precious relics was one of those mentioned in a list of intramural churches appended to *De locis sanctis*, one of the pilgrim aides-memoires brought back from Rome.[81]

The cult of St Lawrence within the walls may have had special éclat for similar reasons. St Lawrence had enjoyed particular favour in Rome ever since his

---

[77] *Mart. Hieron.*, p. 408. The church possessed relics of the Maccabees, perhaps installed there in the later sixth century by Pope Pelagius I or II: G. B. de Rossi, 'Scoperto d'un sarcofago colle reliquie dei Maccabei nella basilica di San Pietro in Vincoli', *Bullettino di Archaeologia Cristiana*, 3rd series, 2 (1876), 73–76; O. Marucchi, *Éléments d'archéologie chrétienne*, 3 vols (Rome, 1899–1902), III, 317. I am grateful to Julia Hilner for these references.

[78] A. Chavasse, *Le sacramentaire Gélasien (Vaticanus Reginensis 316) sacramentaire presbytéral en usage dans les titres romains au VII* siècle*, Bibliothèque de théologie, série 4, Histoire de la théologie, 1 (Tournai, 1958), pp. 332–35. Compare G. Bartolozzi Casti, 'Nuove osservazione sulle basiliche di S. Pietro in Vincoli e dei SS. Giovanni e Paolo', in *Ecclesiae urbis: Atti del Congresso internazionale di studi sulle chiese di Roma, IV–IX secolo*, ed. by F. Guidobaldi and A. G. Guidobaldi, 3 vols (Vatican City, 2002), II, 953–77 (pp. 953–56). An undated inscription, now lost, but almost certainly known by the twelfth century to the author of the *Mirabilia*, commemorates restorations of the church by Sixtus III, Eudoxia, and Pope Pelagius, together with Eudoxia's deposition of the chains brought from Jerusalem, and Pelagius's of the relics of the Maccabees: Marucchi, *Éléments*, III, 313–18; *Codice topografico*, ed. by Valentini and Zucchetti, III, 41–42; Krautheimer, *Corpus*, III, 182.

[79] *LP*, I, 285.

[80] Arator, *De actibus Apostolorum*, ed. by A. P. McKinlay, CSEL, 72 (Vienna, 1951), p. xxviii.

[81] *Codice topografico*, ed. by Valentini and Zucchetti, II, 125–26.

association with a great imperial complex on the Via Tiburtina in the mid-fourth century.[82] According to the *Liber pontificalis*, Pope Damasus founded a *titulus* in honour of St Lawrence *iuxta theatrum*, that is, close to the Theatre of Pompey (in the Campus Martius), which he endowed with his own patrimony.[83] Here again, however, the *Liber pontificalis* was probably reflecting the usages of its own time rather than arrangements of Damasus himself. The *titulus* appears as the *titulus Damasi* in 499 and the *titulus Sancti Damasi* in 595; clearly there was no firm tradition about its dedication in this period.[84] On the other hand there was equally clearly an important link with the saint from a very early date. The eighth-century compiler of the *Sylloge Verdunensis*, who referred to the church as *S. Laurentius in Damaso* or *in Prasino*,[85] recorded that he saw an inscription *in illo throno*, in the apse, in which Damasus claimed to have dedicated this new building to Christ with the aid of St Lawrence.[86]

The major intramural dedication to Lawrence was not, however, the *titulus Damasi* but another early foundation in the Campus Martius: St Lawrence *in Lucina*. According to the compiler of the *Liber pontificalis*, this church was built by Sixtus III in honour of St Lawrence, whose tomb and *confessio* the Pope had already enriched and adorned.[87] That church appears as both the *titulus Lucinae* and the *titulus Sancti Laurentii* in the synod of 499 and simply as the *titulus Sancti Laurentii* in that of 595. Located at the ceremonial heart of the Campus Martius, by the altar of peace and the great sundial of Augustus, it lay in what was becoming the most densely inhabited part of Rome, and in 499 it had more attesting priests than any other: four all told (two as of the *titulus Lucinae*, two as of the *titulus Sancti Laurentii*).[88] Its role as a focus for the cult of the martyr was

---

[82] Thacker, 'Rome of the Martyrs'.

[83] *LP*, I, 212–13.

[84] *Acta synhodorum*, p. 411; Gregory the Great, *Registrum*, ed. by Ewald, p. 367.

[85] That is, 'in the property of Damasus' or 'in the property of the Greens' (the circus party).

[86] 'Haec Damasus tibi, Christe Deus, nova tecta dicavi | Laurenti saeptus martyris auxilio': *LP*, I, 214; de Rossi, *Inscriptiones*, II.1, 133–41, esp. p. 134 (no. 5).

[87] *LP*, I, 233–34.

[88] The *titulus S. Laurentii* of 499 is often identified as S. Lorenzo in Damaso (for example, Krautheimer, *Corpus*, II, 147–48; K. Blair-Dixon, 'Damasus and the Fiction of Unity: The Urban Shrines of St Lawrence', in *Ecclesiae urbis*, ed. by Guidobaldi and Guidobaldi, I, 331–52). It is more plausible, however, to identify it with the *titulus Lucinae*, S. Lorenzo in Lucina, since the *titulus Damasi* appears in 595 as S. Damaso. Compare Gregory the Great, *Registrum*, App. IV (ed. by Norberg, II, 1096). The fact that only one priest attests for S. Lorenzo in Lucina in 595 as

undoubtedly strengthened by its possession of an all-important relic, the gridiron (*craticula*) on which he had allegedly been roasted alive. The relic was certainly in the church in the seventh century, since it is recorded there in the list of intramural basilicas in *De locis sanctis*, placed immediately before the entry relating to the basilica of St Peter *ad vincula*.[89] Together with two ampullae of the martyr's blood, in 1112 it had been transferred by the Bishop of Ostia from an ancient altar to a new *confessio* beneath the main altar of the church. Perhaps it was already similarly displayed beneath an altar in the seventh century.[90]

From early times, then, relics were imported from the East to significant locations within the walls. The papacy in particular sought to enhance its power base in the south-east of the city in and around the Lateran by such means. At first, relics related to Christ himself, but later they derived from other eastern saints (the only western exception being the Milanese martyrs). In the early sixth century, eastern saints such as Cyriacus and Julitta and Cosmas and Damian were housed in new foundations which marked the beginning of a new enterprise to sanctify the area around the Fora, the ceremonial heart of ancient Rome.[91] Complementing these new cults, all probably focussed upon some kind of corporeal relic, were the cults of non-corporeal relics — the chains and the gridiron — also developing in intramural basilicas in the sixth century. While the gridiron was clearly indigenous, the provenance of the chains remains a mystery. They were, however, of crucial importance since in the sixth century, and especially under Gregory the Great, they provided the majority of the relics distributed by the popes to important petitioners.

Intramural Tomb-Cults

Although several of the relic cults discussed above appear to have involved corporeal remains, none was a fully fledged tomb-cult. The latter, of course, depended on the presence of bodies, either buried in situ or brought from elsewhere.

---

opposed to the four postulated for 499 may simply mark a change in the pattern of attestation rather than a reduction in numbers: *Acta synhodorum*, pp. 414–15; Gregory the Great, *Registrum*, ed. by Ewald, p. 367.

[89] *Codice topografico*, ed. by Valentini and Zucchetti, II, 124–25.

[90] F. Grossi Gondi, 'La confessio dell' altare maggiore e la cattedra papale a S. Lorenzo in Lucina', *Studi Romani: Rivista di archeologia e storia*, 1 (1913), 53–62.

[91] Richard Krautheimer, *Rome: Profile of a City, 312–1308* (Princeton, 1980), pp. 74–75.

Their development in intramural churches was inhibited by long-standing and deeply entrenched Roman traditions, prohibiting burial within the walls and interference with the dead. Recent archeological work is relevant here. It has shown that by the late fifth century the taboo against intramural burial was breaking down and that graveyards were being established in various places within the *disabitato*.[92] Such changes eased the way for the once unimaginable claim that an intramural church might house a holy tomb. Interference with the dead, in particular the translation of the holy dead, remained, however, more problematic. While the practice had long been known in the East and was well under way in Gaul, it has long been held that it was strongly resisted in Rome.[93] Yet, there too ancient attitudes may have been breaking down. One of the most interesting developments in this sphere was not strictly intramural but located at the Vatican during a period of schism, when it served as Pope Symmachus's principal base, in effect the equivalent of the intramural cathedral, the Lateran, then (502–06) occupied by a rival. To underline the Vatican's new role, Symmachus established there relic displays similar to those at the Lateran. In direct imitation of Hilary, he installed chapels of the Holy Cross, St John the Evangelist, and St John the Baptist at the baptistery. In addition, he used the eastern of the two rotundas attached to the south side of St Peter's to found what has been termed a 'collective martyrium', with at least four chapels dedicated to some six saints in addition to Andrew himself.[94] Clearly, relics were an essential element in this new foundation; five silver *confessiones* are mentioned in the *Liber pontificalis*: those of the apostles Andrew and Thomas, Saints Cassian (of Imola) and the Roman martyrs Protus and Hyacinthus, Apollinaris (Bishop of Ravenna), and Sossius (deacon of Miseno in Campania).[95] A somewhat heterogeneous group, they suggest a certain despera-

---

[92] M. Costambeys, 'Burial Topography and the Power of the Church in Fifth-and Sixth-Century Rome', *Papers of the British School at Rome*, 69 (2001), 169–89.

[93] See, for example, A. Thacker, 'In Search of Saints: The English Church and the Cult of Roman Apostles and Martyrs in the Seventh and Eighth Centuries', in *Early Medieval Rome and the Christian West: Essays in Honour of Donald Bullough*, ed. by J. M. H. Smith (Leiden, 2000), pp. 247–77 (pp. 248–64).

[94] *LP*, I, 44, 261–62, and 265–66; Mackie, *Early Christian Chapels*, pp. 72, 257–58; R. Gem, 'The Vatican Rotunda: A Severan Monument and its Early History', *JBAA*, 158 (2005), 1–45; J. Richards, *The Popes and the Papacy in the Early Middle Ages, 476–752* (London, 1979), pp. 89–90.

[95] S. Orienti, 'Apollinare di Ravenna', in *Bibliotheca sanctorum*, ed. by Vizzini and others, II, 239–48; A. M. Raggi, 'Cassiano di Imola', in ibid., II, 909–11; R. Calvino, 'Sosso', in ibid., IX, 1319–23; *Depositio martyrum*, ed. by Duchesne, *LP*, I, 12.

tion in Symmachus's attempt to enhance St Peter's as an alternative to the Lateran. We may wonder how he came by his treasures. In one case only do we have any indication. As Margharita Cecchelli has recently pointed out, Symmachus unambiguously recorded in an inscription now lost that he had reburied the bodies of Protus and Hyacinthus with fresh honour. The inscription is generally believed to have been located in the Vatican rotunda, and hence to record the saint's translation from the cemetery of Bassilla on the Via Salaria Vetus to rest beneath Symmachus's altar in his new martyrium. That ties in with later evidence of the presence of the bodies within the walls, despite the discovery of the apparently unopened *loculus* of Hyacinthus in situ in the cemetery of Bassilla in the mid-nineteenth century.[96] While this translation, if such there was, would represent a bold violation of tradition and suggest that ancient attitudes were eroding, interestingly the precedent which it set was not followed for over a century and a half. It might be thought that the terrible destruction wrought by the Gothic Wars on the suburbs of the Eternal City would have facilitated the removal of more bodies from the ruined catacombs. That it did not may have been because there were vested interests highly resistant to such changes. The whole process may have been more complex than has sometimes been supposed and will be considered later in this paper.

First, however, we need to examine the most famous and debated intramural tomb-cult, that of the martyrs John and Paul. By the seventh century the remains of the two saints were apparently on display at the eponymous basilica on the Celian Hill, where they were noted in contemporary pilgrim itineraries. Indeed, the most comprehensive and best organized of these texts opens with this church, expressly singling it out as an intramural tomb site before moving on to the Via

---

[96] 'Martyribus sanctis Proto pariterque Hyacintho | Symmachus hoc parvo veneratus honore patronos | exornavit opus sub quo pia corpora rursus | condidit; his aevo laus et perennis in omni' ('To the holy martyrs Protus and Hyancinthus: Symmachus having venerated the patrons with this small honour, adorned the work under which he reburied the holy corpses. To them be perpetual praise throughout all ages'): de Rossi, *Inscriptiones*, II, 42, 207; *LP*, I, 266, n. 18; M. Cecchelli, 'Sulla translazione dei martiri Proto e Giacinto da S. Ermete al Vaticano', in *Ecclesiae urbis*, ed. by Guidobaldi and Guidobaldi, I, 645–59. I have followed Duchesne and Cecchelli in their location of the inscription, although, as Richard Gem has pointed out to me in a personal communication, there is no secure evidence for this. Gem himself believes it could have been placed in the *spelunca* in the cemetery of Bassilla, where seventh-century pilgrim guides still locate the two saints: *Codice topografico*, ed. by Valentini and Zucchetti, II, 75, 117, 143–44. If so, the principal remains may have been reburied at the extramural site and only minor relics installed in the Vatican *confessio*.

Flaminia.[97] According to their legend, confected in the early sixth century, John and Paul were two brothers, traditionally *praepositus* and *primicerius* of Constantia daughter of Constantine, who suffered for their faith under Julian the Apostate and were executed and secretly buried in their own house on the Celian.[98] We may suspect that the changes in attitude to intramural burial just referred to come into play here. While a random burial (particularly one made in secret) is of course possible at any time, a publicly acknowledged and institutionalized interment of the kind implicit in a tomb cult is quite another matter. By the late fifth century an intramural tomb-cult evidently seemed permissible — if in fact extremely unusual. In the fourth and earlier fifth century, however, it would have seemed revolutionary indeed.

There is no doubt of the vigour of the cult of John and Paul in sixth-century Rome or of the existence of a *titulus* in their honour by *c.* 500. According to the compiler of the life of Symmachus in the *Liber pontificalis*, who in this matter should be considered a near-contemporary source, priests of the *titulus*, supporters of Symmachus, were slain in the riots of 502 stirred up by the disputed election of 498; later (probably) the Pope built steps behind the apse of the *titulus* ('fecit grados post absidam').[99] Sixth-century inscriptions refer unambiguously to the *titulus* of Saints John and Paul from as early as 535, and it is among those mentioned in the record of the synod of 595.[100] In one of the early itineraries, that recorded by William of Malmesbury, the gist of the legend is clearly set out. John and Paul were martyrs, buried *intra urbem* on the Celian Hill, in their own house which was made into a church after their martyrdom.[101] There are obvious echoes here of the cult of St Caecilia.

By the mid-sixth century the saints had entered the Roman liturgy. The Leonine sacramentary records eight Mass sets for their feast although their two names are mentioned only in one of them. The preface of one of these Masses

---

[97] *Codice topografico*, ed. by Valentini and Zucchetti, II, 72–73. Compare the list of intramural churches, where the two martyrs are said to rest in one tomb: ibid., p. 124.

[98] *Passio Sancti Johannis et Pauli*, ed. G. Henschenius and others, *AA SS Junii* V (Antwerp, 1709), pp. 37, 158–63.

[99] *LP*, I, 262.

[100] Krautheimer, *Corpus*, I, 271; A. Silvagni, A. Ferrua, D. Mazzolini, and C. Carletti, *Inscriptiones christianae urbis Romae septimo saeculo antiquiores, nova series*, 10 vols (Rome, 1922–92) [henceforth *ICUR*], II, no. 5178; de Rossi, *Inscriptiones*, I, 514 (no. 1123); Gregory the Great, *Registrum*, ed. by Ewald, p. 367.

[101] *Codice topografico*, ed. by Valentini and Zucchetti, II, 152.

clearly refers to the relics of the brothers being within the city itself and assumes that the celebrant on their feast day in June will be in Rome and at a church dedicated to the martyrs.[102] By the later sixth century they were sufficiently venerated to be invoked in the *Communicantes* prayer of the canon of the Mass at Rome, Ravenna, and Milan.[103]

Remarkably, despite all this, nothing at all is known of Saints John and Paul before the sixth century. They do not occur in the *Depositio martyrum* and the entry in the Hieronymian martyrology seems to depend on the *passio* and is therefore probably late.[104] The ascription of the dedication of the monastery founded by Leo I at the Vatican to the two saints depends upon a late insertion in the *Liber pontificalis*.[105] An inscription preserved in fragmentary form in the *Sylloge Leidensis* has been attributed to Damasus, but is now considered to be of uncertain date.[106] Nor can any reference to the church either under the denomination of the later titulars or of Pammachius, the supposed founder, be securely dated before 499.

That, on the whole, recent scholarship has tended to the view there was an early cult reflects the influence of the archaeological evidence.[107] Beneath the present church lay a luxurious house built over abandoned apartments and shops, the owner of which had converted to Christianity in the fourth century. In the fifth century, the then owner built a grand three-aisled basilica over the site and is presumed to have given his name to the new *titulus*, first mentioned as the *titulus Pammachii* in 499 and probably still known primarily by that designation when the riots already mentioned took place in 502.[108] The crucial physical evidence underpinning the view that the saints were enshrined from an early period in this intramural site was a minuscule structure which in its Christian phase was approached from an open courtyard by a flight of fourteen steps and which had

---

[102] Hope, *Leonine Sacramentary*, pp. 23–24, 39, 136, and 139; *Sacramentarium Veronese*, ed. by Mohlberg and others, pp. 34–37, esp. no. 271.

[103] Kennedy, *Saints of Canon*, pp. 131–36, 194.

[104] In particular the evidence of two key manuscripts (Berne and Codex Wissemburgensis) that the entry was in the form 'passio sanctorum martyrum Johannis et Pauli fratrum': *Mart. Hieron.*, pp. 336–37.

[105] *LP*, I, 239, 241.

[106] A. Ferrua, *Epigrammata damasiana* (Rome, 1942), p. 229.

[107] Krautheimer, *Corpus*, I, 267–303.

[108] An inscription from the time of Innocent I (401–17) suggests that it was also known as the *titulus V(B)izantis*, a title which remained in use until 499: *ICUR*, new series, V, no. 13122. Presumably Byzans was also involved in the foundation or endowment of the church.

a rectangular opening at eye level. This structure was adorned with paintings showing saints and martyrs, including a scene in which two men and a woman are killed. It was later cut off by the pavement of the basilica. A deep shaft descended from the painted area to the ground floor of the house. There, cut out of the rock, were three small pits which have been regarded as graves. As a whole, the arrangements have been interpreted as a *confessio* giving access to a sacred tomb or tombs below.

Recently, however, that interpretation has been challenged. Beat Brenk has suggested that the pits are not tombs at all and that the so-called *confessio* is in fact a tiny private oratory. He argues that the opening long interpreted as a *fenestella* had originally been filled with a reliquary housing the owners' collection of relics. It was only after the composition of the *passio* had engendered a new interest in the cult that the structure was remodelled to resemble a *confessio*.[109] The results of the recent reappraisal of the structures under Saints John and Paul will throw more light on this question. In the meantime, it is perhaps worth noting that the investigations have disclosed no martyrial tombs.[110] Indeed, the *passio* is remarkably vague about the whereabouts of the saints' burial place, which would seem odd if it was composed around a cult site where saints had been venerated for the previous two hundred years. It has in fact all the appearance of a text compiled to endow an existing *titulus* with an appropriate cultic tradition. Its inclusion of the superogatory and patently fictitious Crispin, Crispinianus, and Benedicta was almost certainly inspired by the paintings in the oratory; the fact that those responsible for finding the bodies and establishing a church in the house are said to be the Senator Vizantius and his son Pammachius clearly derives from the patronal names associated with the fifth-century *titulus*;[111] and as Brenk suggests, the transformation of the oratory by the construction of the shaft and associated staircase may have been a response to the story put about by the *passio* that there were saints buried within the *titulus*.[112] The *passio* thus constitutes a fascinating example of the interdependence and interaction of text and physical evidence. The passion

---

[109] B. Brenk, 'Microstoria sotto la chiesa di Santi Giovanni e Paolo: la cristianizziane di una casa privata', *Rivista dell' Istituto nazionale d'archeologia e storia dell' arte*, 3rd series, 18 (1995), 169–205. See now also Brandenburg, *Ancient Churches of Rome*, pp. 155–62.

[110] Brandenburg, *Ancient Churches of Rome*, p. 159.

[111] Priests of *tituli* of Pammachius and V(B)izans subscribe in 499 but not in 595. It has been plausibly supposed that the two foundations were either intimately connected, presumably adjacent, or even the same, and replaced by the *titulus* of John and Paul in 595. See above, note 108.

[112] Brenk, 'Microstoria sotto la chiesa', esp. pp. 192–97, 205.

narrative was in part constructed around the surviving late antique pictorial programme while the structure itself was reconfigured to add verisimilitude to the text. The outcome was a full-blown and highly successful sixth-century cult. The hitherto unknown John and Paul rose from almost total obscurity in the fifth century (perhaps just names in a martyrology in some way associated with the site on the Celian) to remarkable prominence in the sixth. Almost certainly the belief that they were buried within the house on the Celian is part of that reinvention.

The cult of St Bibiana provides an interesting analogy to that of Saints John and Paul. According to the *Liber pontificalis*, Pope Simplicius (468–83) dedicated a basilica on the Esquiline to the saint at the place where her body rested.[113] Clearly, to the sixth-century compiler there was nothing strange about a publicly acknowledged intramural burial. Nothing is known about St Bibiana herself. She occurs only in a late version of the Hieronymian martyrology (2 December) and is not mentioned in the Leonine or Gregorian sacramentaries or in the pilgrim itineraries; a *passio*, composed in the seventh century, which forms a kind of appendix to the the *passio* of Saints John and Paul, claims that she was buried in the family home with other martyred relatives.[114] St Bibiana was not a *titulus* and the cult was evidently a minor one. Nevertheless, the discovery near the church of sixth-century interments, including three sarcophagi at its very threshold, suggests that there may then have been at least some burials if not a cemetery *ad sanctam* and that the cult may for a while have enjoyed modest success.[115] It is perhaps significant that Leo II (682–83) chose a site immediately next to St Bibiana for the deposition of the corporeal remains of Saints Simplicius, Faustinus, and Beatrice, one of the earliest of Roman translations.[116] All this provides both a context for the developments at Saints John and Paul, although there is no evidence of burials *ad sanctos* on the Celian. In particular, the fact that the hagiography of the cult of St Bibiana is very closely linked with that of John and Paul suggests that they set the standard for such intramural cults. The notion of saints being secretly buried in their houses provided a convenient means of explaining intramural cults in a period when burial practice was being relaxed while allowing the known conventions to be apparently observed.

---

[113] *LP*, I, 249: 'basilicam intra urbe Roma, iuxta palatium Licinianum, beatae martyris Bibianae, ubi corpus eis requiescit'.

[114] G. D. Gordini, 'Bibiana', in *Bibliotheca sanctorum*, ed. by Vizzini and others, III, cols 177–81; *Mart. Hieron.*, pp. 631–32; Delehaye, *Legendier*, pp. 124–43.

[115] Costambeys, 'Burial Topography', pp. 175–82.

[116] *LP*, I, 360.

It was a natural extension to the contemporary preoccupation — evident in the *Gesta* — with *tituli* as originating in houses where the saints had lived and died.

Links Between Tituli *and the Cults in the Catacombs*

The late fifth century, then, sees tentative moves towards establishing tomb cults in intramural churches. These developments occurred in churches with which the popes were closely associated. As we have seen, St Bibiana was a papal foundation, while Saints John and Paul, which lay on the Celian, very close to the Lateran, first occurs in the record in connexion with Pope Symmachus's building activity there. In the early sixth century, before the catastrophe of the Gothic wars, popes such as Symmachus, John I, and Felix IV also did what they could in the cemeteries, and as a result, as we have seen, one translation apparently occurred. Such activity, allied with the enhancement of martyrial cult in the *tituli*, raises the issue of the relationship between the intramural churches and the extramural individuals or communities responsible for the martyrial tombs.

As has already been stressed, martyrial cult was originally focussed primarily on the cemeterial basilicas. But how was that cult serviced? The most important apostolic and martyrial shrines, those of Saints Peter, Paul, Lawrence, and Agnes, were located within or near large and well-endowed basilicas, all founded by Constantine or by members of his family in the first half of the fourth century. Although the matter is debated, it seems likely that in the fourth century most if not all of these grand foundations and the martyrial shrines with which they were associated had their own administrators, even if they were dependent on urban clergy for liturgical celebration. We know, for example, of a guardian (*custos*) at St Peter's in the time of Liberius (352–66).[117] Indeed the degree to which the extramural imperial basilicas were under papal control at all in this period is difficult to determine. St Peter's, for example, was certainly defying papal authority in the matter of funeral feasts in honour of the martyrs in the 390s. Others, however, may have been more responsive. At St Lawrence on the Verano, Pope Damasus (366–84) was able to intervene and establish — or at least enrich — the martyrial shrine; and at St Agnes on the Via Nomentana, as we shall see, the basilica was brought directly under papal control in the early fifth century.[118]

---

[117] Athanasius, *Historia Arianorum ad Monachos*, XXXVII (*PG*, 25, 735); Thacker, 'Rome of the Martyrs'. See also De Blauuw, *Cultus et Decor*, pp. 44–46.

[118] Thacker, 'Rome of the Martyrs'.

Whatever the arrangements for the great extramural basilicas, the position in the lesser cemeterial churches is clear. Innocent I's letter of 417 establishes beyond all doubt that priests had been assigned to be installed in them. In defining the rules governing the distribution of the *fermentum*, he decreed that it should not be sent to priests established in the cemeteries, because of the problems of transporting the sacrament over longer distances.[119] The fact that the extramural churches were excluded is a sign that they were less integrated than the *tituli* into the papal system. It is clear too that in this early period the main focus for the liturgy on the feast day of the martyr was an appropriate basilica at or near the tomb. Even on days on which the pope celebrated Mass, services were also conducted in the cemeterial basilicas by a local priest without the addition of the *fermentum*.[120] Most martyrial tombs, however, were located in the cramped spaces of the catacombs where it would not have been possible to hold a major liturgical celebration. Crucial here is Prudentius's description of the arrangements relating to the cult of Hippolytus at both his burial-place and in the great basilica of St Lawrence, in the cemeteries in the Verano beside the Via Tiburtina. Prudentius makes it clear that the sacrament was offered on a regular basis in the confined *cubiculo* which housed the richly adorned altar-shrine (*ara, mensa*) containing the bones of the martyr, but that on the saint's feast day (13 August) the press of worshippers made it necessary to transfer the celebratory Mass to the neighbouring basilica. Even on that high day Prudentius does not seem to have envisaged the pope as necessarily present; he describes the celebrant simply as *antistes*, a designation meaning priest or bishop.[121]

The crucial evidence of links between the intramural *tituli* and the extramural basilicas is the account in the *Liber pontificalis* of the foundation of the *titulus Vestinae* during the pontificate of Innocent I (401–17). According to the early sixth-century compiler, the church was endowed by Vestina through the labours of the priests Ursicinus and Leopardus and the deacon Livanus. As we have seen, at Vestina's behest the Pope established the church, which also included a baptistery, as a *titulus* in honour of Saints Gervasius and Protasius. The compiler then adds that Innocent caused the church of St Agnes to be delivered to the care of the priests Leopardus (presumably to be identified with the agent of Vestina) and

---

[119] *La Lettre du pape Innocent*, ed. by Cabié, pp. 26–28.

[120] Saxer, 'La chiesa di Roma', pp. 572–74.

[121] Prudentius, *Peristephanon liber*, ed. and trans. by H. J. Thompson, 2 vols (Cambridge, MA, 1949–53), XI, lines 153–236.

Paulinus to be roofed and decorated. With their assignment (*depositio*), he says, authority over St Agnes was granted to the *titulus Vestinae*.[122] The *titulus* on the Vicus Longus was reasonably well sited for such oversight, although St Susanna by the Alta Semita, on the Quirinal, would clearly have been even better placed, if in existence by then.[123] The continuance of the link is confirmed by an inscription commemorating a seventh-century acolyte of the *titulus Vestinae* found at St Agnes.[124]

By the early sixth century, it is clear that there was also a close institutional connection between the *titulus* of St Chrysogonus and the cemeterial basilica of St Pancras, physically connected by the Via Aurelia and its intramural continuation in Trastevere. The priests of the *titulus*, sometimes but not always together with the *praepositius* of San Pancras, sold burial places in the cemetery, over which we may therefore presume they exercised some kind of authority.[125] Part of their responsibilities was undoubtedly to ensure that Mass was said every Sunday at the cemeterial basilica. Such arrangements appear to have ceased only in 594, when Gregory the Great, complaining that the priests to whom St Pancras had been committed were neglecting their duties, removed them and established in their place a monastery whose abbot was to ensure that a *presbyter peregrinus* resided with him and undertook to celebrate the holy mysteries.[126]

We should be cautious, however, in assuming that such control by *titulus* and ultimately pope was the norm at the cemeterial churches. In particular, as Victor Saxer has pointed out, the fact that a *titulus* might bury its clergy in a specific cemetery is not necessarily evidence that it exercised powers similar to the priests of St Chrysogonus over St Pancras.[127] The control of St Agnes and St Pancras by intramural *tituli* may simply have arisen from the fact that (as their interventions at the sites themselves imply) the popes had authority over these particular cemeterial basilicas and could arrange their staffing as they wished.

Attempts were apparently made to build on such exemplars in the sixth century. By then we have instances of the establishment of intramural churches

---

[122] *LP*, I, 220–22.

[123] For uncertainty about the dating of the Christian community there, see Krautheimer, *Corpus*, IV, 275.

[124] Krautheimer, *Corpus*, I, 314; de Rossi, *Inscriptiones*, I, 536 (no. 1185).

[125] De Rossi, *Roma Sotterranea*, III, 518–22; de Rossi, *Inscriptiones*, I, no. 975.

[126] Gregory the Great, *Registrum*, IV, 18 (ed. by Norberg, I, 236–37).

[127] Saxer, 'La chiesa di Roma', pp. 556–58.

bearing the same dedication as an extramural cult-centre. One such was the little-known *titulus* of Marcellinus and Peter, whose priests first attest at the synod of 595.[128] Located very near the Lateran, on a site first dedicated by Pope Siricius, it seems likely that this was a new dedication developed in the sixth century, perhaps in response to the disruption of the Gothic Wars.[129] Interestingly, Marcellinus and Peter are absent from the Leonine sacramentary, even though they were soon to rise to such prominence that they were included in the *Nobis quoque* prayer of the Roman canon.[130] That would point to a mid- to late sixth-century date for the *titulus*. It has been suggested that the *Passio Sanctorum Marcellini et Petri*, almost certainly a sixth-century work, and one undoubtedly focussed upon the cult in the cemeterial basilica, was produced in response to the establishment of the intra-mural *titulus*.[131] That suggests that there was a serious possibility of the intramural church becoming the principal cult centre, where the feast day was celebrated and from which the cult centre was administered. The disappearance of the *titulus* after 595 is evidence that any such initiative came to nothing. The pull of the ancient centre in the catacombs attached to the great imperial mausoleum-church of Santa Helena was too great.

Very near the *titulus* of Marcellinus and Peter, but a little further to the west and on the Celian Hill itself, lay another intramural cult-centre: the basilica of the *Quattuor coronati*. The sources for this cult are very complicated and confusing, and its origins have been much discussed. Although attempts have been made to argue that it was established at the church on the Celian from a very early date, the entry in the Hieronymian martyrology which localizes the cult there is highly unusual and occurs only in two of the early manuscripts of the text, those from Berne and Dublin. Almost certainly, therefore, despite the assertion of Delehaye to the contrary, that entry does not belong to the text's original stratum, which reflects the Roman calendar before *c.* 450.[132] While it is possible that the *Quattuor*

[128] Gregory the Great, *Registrum*, ed. by Ewald, p. 367.

[129] J. Guyon, *Le cimetière aux deux lauriers: Recherches sur les catacombes romaines*, Bibliothèque des Écoles françaises d'Athènes et de Rome, 264 (Rome, 1987), pp. 432–33; R. Coates-Stevens, 'Dark Age Architecture in Rome', *Papers of the British School at Rome*, 65 (1997), 177–232 (pp. 193–95).

[130] Kennedy, *Saints of the Canon*, pp. 158–61.

[131] Guyon, *Le cimetière*, pp. 438–39; *Acta Sanctorum Marcellini et Petri*, ed. by G. Henschenius and others, *AA SS Junii* I (Antwerp, 1695), pp. 171–73.

[132] *Mart. Hieron.*, pp. 590–91. Against this, see the highly convincing arguments of A. Amore, 'I Santi Quattro Coronati', *Antonianum*, 40 (1965), 177–243 (pp. 188–91), followed by J. Guyon,

coronati may have been anciently associated with the basilica in some way, it seems much more likely in fact that the main development of the cult took place in the sixth century. It should be noted that the priests of the basilica attest the synod of 499 as of the *titulus Aemilianae* and only appear in 595 as of the *Quattuor coronati*.[133]

The designation is mysterious. Whatever its origins, the literature which gave it content gained currency only in the sixth century. The crucial text is the famous *passio*, which purports to give an account of not four but *five* martyred masons, done to death and buried in unknown graves in Pannonia, and which initially presumably had nothing to do with the *Quattuor coronati*. It has been claimed that it is reliable text — in short that the Pannonian martyrs had a genuine existence — but there is nothing whatsoever to verify this.[134] The *passio* moreover concludes with a particularly blatant fiction (often regarded as an addition), patently an attempt to adapt the story to a Roman audience. This final section asserts that Pope Miltiades (311–14) together with St Sebastian had retrieved the bodies of four Roman soldiers whose names were unknown and buried them on the Via Labicana; the Pope had further decreed that they were to be honoured under the Pannonians' names because they had been martyred on the latters' *dies natalis*, which is given as 8 November.[135] The sources of this bizarre confection appear to have been twofold. First, the names of the four principal Pannonians occur in the early fifth-century *Acta Sancti Sebastiani*, applied to martyrs with whose fate Sebastian is involved and who perish at sea.[136] Secondly, three of these names, together with an unknown Clement, appear in the *Depositio martyrum*, with a commemoration on 9 November and a resting place, *in comitatum*, identified (to

---

'Les Quatres Couronnés et l'histoire de leur culte des origines à la fin du IXᵉ siècle', *Mélanges d'archéologie et d'histoire de l'École française de Rome (Antiquité)*, 87 (1975), 505–61 (p. 515).

[133] *Acta synhodorum*, nos 16, 38, 60 (pp. 412–14); Gregory the Great, *Registrum*, ed. by Ewald, p. 367.

[134] Guyon's suggestion that they are evoked in the five churches of Sopianae, a town near Sirmium, whose medieval name was *Quinque Ecclesiae* or *Ad V Basilicas* seems to this author at least more sustained by hope than conviction; 'Les Quatres Couronnés', pp. 528–30.

[135] *De SS Quattuor Coronati*, ed. by C. de Smedt and others, *AA SS Novembris* III (Brussels, 1910), pp. 743–84, esp. pp. 778–79. Arguments have raged about the authenticity of the main body of the text, but no one is in doubt that the concluding section which distinguishes the five Pannonians from the four Romans is late.

[136] *Acta S Sebastiani*, ed. by G. Henschenius, *AA SS Januarii* II (Antwerp, 1643), pp. 265–78, esp. p. 276; Guyon, 'Les Quatres Couronnés', p. 521.

my mind plausibly) with a burial site connected to the imperial palace complex on the Via Labicana.[137]

The Leonine sacramentary gives two sets of Masses for the *Quattuor coronati*, described in one of the prefaces as patrons (*patroni*) of the place where the celebration took place. That would seem to be fairly clear evidence that by the time of its compilation in the mid-sixth century the church on the Celian Hill was the site of a liturgical commemoration of the eponymous Four.[138] The day on which the feast associated with the basilica is entered in the Hieronymian martyrology is 8 November, the day before the entry in the *Depositio martyrum*, and presumably the date fixed for the celebration of the dedication of the basilica in honour of the Four. It is also, significantly, the date which the author of the final section of the *passio* regarded as the *dies natalis* of the *Quattuor coronati*.[139]

In the last resort it is impossible to resolve all the problems posed by these sources. It would seem that the patronal feast of the *titulus* on the Celian, held on 8 November, gained prestige in the sixth century from the association of the *Quattuor coronati* with the Pannonian masons made fashionable by the new *passio* and with a group of Roman martyrs, long commemorated in a grave on the Via Labicana. There is no mention of the basilica in the *passio* so there is no need to assume that this link was initially promoted by the priests of the *titulus*. By the seventh century, however, the connecting of intramural and extramural sites had unquestionably succeeded. A new intramural basilica was established by Honorius I (625–38), and the extramural tomb on the Via Labicana was in all the pilgrim aides-memoires.[140] Indeed, so successful was the cult that it was one of those promoted in Canterbury by the Roman missionaries.[141]

One other example of this trend, though less fully evidenced, is the cult of Nereus and Achilleus, well-established Roman saints who occur in the earliest

---

[137] *LP*, I, 12; Amore, 'I Santi Quattro Coronati', pp. 226–34, summarized in Amore, 'Quattro Coronati', in *Bibliotheca sanctorum*, ed. by Vizzini and others, X, 1276–86.

[138] *Sacramentarium Veronese*, ed. by Mohlberg and others, p. 147; Hope, *Leonine Sacramentary*, p. 35.

[139] *Mart. Hieron.*, pp. 590–91; *De SS Quattuor Coronati*, ed. by de Smedt and others, pp. 778–79.

[140] *Codice topografico*, ed. by Valentini and Zucchetti, II, 83, 113, and 146; Krautheimer, *Corpus*, IV, 28–29, 32–34, and 35.

[141] *Bede's Ecclesiastical History of the English People*, ed. and trans. by Bertram Colgrave and R. A. B. Mynors, repr. with corrections (Oxford, 1991), 2.8.

stratum of the Hieronymian martyrology.[142] The martyrial tombs lay in a basilica *ad corpus* within the cemetery of Domitilla to the south of the city on what is now the Via delle Sette Chiese. The complex was said to have been rebuilt (*refecit*) by John I (523–26).[143] By 595 the intramural *titulus Fasciolae*, which may have had a long association with the cemetery,[144] was dedicated to Saints Nereus and Achilleus.[145] Like Saints Marcellinus and Peter and the *Quattuor coronati*, the bodies were never removed. They were still being venerated in the catacomb of Domitilla in the seventh century.[146]

We have seen that there is some evidence that a number of *tituli* identified their titulars as saints from an early period — including St Clement, St Anastasia, and (probably) St Susanna. That probably implies liturgical commemoration of their *dies natales*, although we have no conclusive evidence of this. What we do know is that as the Roman liturgy developed in the sixth century, a number of saints were certainly being celebrated liturgically in intramural churches and in several instances attempts appear to have been made to refocus martyrial cult on urban *tituli* in the late fifth and earlier sixth centuries. In the case of Caecilia, the Pope was clearly directly involved in the intramural celebration of a saint who was by then unquestionably believed to be buried extramurally in one of the most famous of catacombs. The churches on and around the Celian Hill, an area close the Lateran and an important theatre of papal activity, form a particularly striking group. At Saints John and Paul a full-blown intramural tomb-cult was promoted, while at the Quattuor coronati and at Saints Marcellinus and Peter attempts were made (in one case with permanent success) to take over cult sites at the catacombs. At St Clement the long-established identification of the titular with the martyred Pope was boosted by well-developed liturgical celebration. Such developments, which were fresh at the time that the *Liber pontificalis* was being put together, surely underlie the compiler's well-known remark, already referred to, that *tituli* had responsibility for the burial of the martyrs.[147] By the end of the century

---

[142] *Mart. Hieron.*, p. 249.

[143] *LP*, I, 276, 277.

[144] A late fourth- or early fifth-century inscription found at the cemetery names a lector of the *titulus*: de Rossi, *Inscriptiones*, I, 124, n. 262.

[145] *Acta synhodorum*, nos 40–41, 53 (pp. 413–14); Gregory the Great, *Registrum*, ed. by Ewald, p. 367. Compare Gregory the Great, *Registrum*, XI, 15 (ed. by Norberg, II, 881).

[146] *Codice topografico*, ed. by Valentini and Zucchetti, II, 89, 110, and 149.

[147] Above at note 5.

(despite the ruin of the cemeteries in the Gothic Wars and the subsequent threat from the Lombards) the impetus had clearly stalled. Popes such as Pelagius II and Gregory the Great were stressing that saints could on no account be moved. And, as we shall see, in the seventh century the great majority of the cult sites remained obstinately cemeterial and extramural.

The Papacy, Intramural Cults, and Relic Distribution in the Sixth and Seventh Centuries

The growing importance of intramural cults for the papacy is evident above all in the shaping of the central prayer of the Mass, the canon, and especially in the composition of two prayers to which we have already referred on several occasions: the *Communicantes* and the *Nobis quoque*. These prayers, which associate the offering of the Mass with the whole company of apostles and martyrs, were probably added to the canon in their original form by Pope Gelasius I (492–96), but the order and number of the saints in both was subject to restructuring throughout the sixth century until it was fixed by Gregory the Great.[148] If we take the saints of the *Communicantes* first, the list begins with the Virgin, Peter and Paul, and the rest of the apostles; it then moves on to early popes, starting with Peter's immediate successors up to and including Clement, then Sixtus II (257–58) and Cornelius (251–53); and it concludes with Cyprian, Lawrence, Chrysogonus, John and Paul, and Cosmas and Damian. We may detect two special categories, neither the subject of local cult in Rome: the non-Roman apostles, in whom the popes were undoubtedly developing an interest in the sixth century, in tandem with their claims to be the pre-eminent apostolic see; and Linus and Cletus, presumably added to bridge the gap between Peter and Clement.[149] If we except these two groups, it becomes apparent that intramural cults, often relatively recently introduced, were disproportionately represented in the *Communicantes*. After the apostles and the earliest popes we have Clement, the subject of liturgical cult at the intramural basilica on the Celian, followed by a group of three figures, two of them martyred popes, all culted in the cemetery of Callistus on the Via Appia, the site of the early papal pantheon (the so-called crypt of the popes) and always very closely associated with the papacy. The other saints of the *Communicantes* were all venerated in intramural *tituli*. Lawrence of

[148] Kennedy, *Saints of the Canon*, esp. pp. 189–99.

[149] See the arguments of Kennedy to this effect: *Saints of the Canon*, pp. 102–13.

course was buried on the Via Tiburtina — but his cult was very much under papal control by the late sixth century when Pelagius II built his beautiful basilica, and in any case he was the dedicatee of at least one urban *titulus*. John and Paul, as we have seen, were the focus of the only enduring intramural tomb-cult; Chrysogonus was culted liturgically within the walls; Cosmas and Damian were in a new intramural church established by Felix IV.

The *Nobis quoque* saints begin with John the Baptist, whose relics were one of the principal treasures of the Lateran, and Stephen, venerated at the great martyrium on the Celian. The list then includes two apostles omitted from the *Communicantes* (Matthias and Barnabas) and Ignatius of Antioch (probably added quite late because of his letter to the Romans)[150] before moving on to three Roman saints: Alexander, the martyr whose tomb in the catacomb of the Jordani on the Via Salaria Nova had been renovated by Pope Symmachus,[151] and Marcellinus and Peter, whose cult was introduced into an intramural *titulus* in the sixth century. The list concludes with a group of female saints:[152] Felicity (originally perhaps the martyr of Rome, but later probably identified with her more famous African namesake), Perpetua (also African, commemorated together with the African Felicity in the earliest Roman calendar),[153] Agatha (a Sicilian martyr favoured by Symmachus, who founded a basilica in her honour on the Via Aurelia, and above all by Gregory the Great, who placed her in the canon, having established her as titular of a former Arian church within the walls),[154] Lucy (another Sicilian whom Gregory added to the canon), Agnes (whose cult site was extramural but as we have seen papally controlled), Caecilia (whose cult was primarily intramural in the sixth century), and Anastasia (whose cult was also intramural). Although here the picture is perhaps slightly less clear-cut, it is evident that intramural cults were again disproportionately over-represented.

Another gauge of the importance of intramural cults to the popes of the sixth and seventh centuries is their role as source of the relics sent to petitioners. Except for one or two very special cases, the papacy seems to have embarked on relic distribution only in the late fifth and early sixth centuries; the few glimpses we get

---

[150] Kennedy, *Saints of the Canon*, pp. 149–51, 197–98.

[151] *LP*, I, 263. Compare *Depositio martyrum*, ed. by Duchesne, *LP*, I, 11; Kennedy, *Saints of the Canon*, pp. 151–58.

[152] For what follows unless otherwise indicated, see Kennedy, *Saints of the Canon*, pp. 168–77.

[153] *Depositio martyrum*, ed. by Duchesne, *LP*, I, 11.

[154] Krautheimer, *Corpus*, I, 2–12; *LP*, I, 312.

at this early stage suggest that their gifts principally comprised contact relics or perhaps oil and dust from the tomb of St Peter and filings from the apostolic chains or from the grid-iron of St Lawrence.[155] When, later, we get a more complete picture from the letters of Gregory the Great, we find that, as Conrad Leyser has observed, the relics which the Pope sent out to petitioners were derived from a surprisingly restricted group of martyrs.[156] Significantly, besides the apostles Peter and Paul, they included several saints venerated at intramural churches: Stephen, Agatha, Lawrence, John and Paul, and Cyriacus. Two, Agnes and Pancras, were culted at centres which appear to have long been under the control of intramural *tituli* and ultimately of the popes themselves. That control was soon to be effectively expressed by Honorius I's new buildings at both saints' extramural tombs. Of the remainder, Hermes, the most favoured with four distributions, was venerated in an extramural basilica in the cemetery of Bassilla, remodelled by Pelagius II;[157] Hyacinthus, whose original tomb was also in the cemetery of Bassilla, seems to have been translated by Symmachus and perhaps lay in the latter's church of St Andrew at the Vatican.[158] St Sebastian lay at the former apostolic site *ad duas catacumbas* on the Via Appia, long under papal control.[159] There is an interesting correlation with relics sent by Pope Vitalian to Oswiu, king of the Northumbrians, in 667. They derived from Peter and Paul, Lawrence, John and Paul, the martyr Gregory (included presumably because of Pope Gregory's role as evangelist of England), and Pancras. The dedications of the missionaries' early churches at Canterbury, which presumably give some indication of the relics they brought with them, yield a similar picture: Saints Peter and Paul, the *Quattuor coronati*, and St Pancras.

The papacy's activity in setting up fresh cult sites in the seventh century fits into this pattern. While they were active in the major extramural centres under their control, such as St Lawrence on the Via Tiburtina, St Agnes on the Via Nomentana, and St Pancras on the Via Aurelia, they made few additions to the established pattern within the walls. It is true that, as early as 608, Boniface IV

---

[155] Thacker, 'Rome of the Martyrs'; Avitus, *Opera*, Epistulae nos 8, 29; *Collectio Avellana*, ed. by Guenther, no. 218 (pp. 670–80).

[156] C. Leyser, 'The Temptations of Cult: Roman Martyr Piety in the Age of Gregory the Great', *Early Medieval Europe*, 9 (2000), 289–307 (pp. 300–01).

[157] *LP*, I, 309; Krautheimer, *Corpus*, I, 196–209.

[158] *Codice topografico*, ed. by Valentini and Zucchetti, II, 74–75.

[159] Krautheimer, *Corpus*, IV, 99–147.

(608–15) sought to provide an intramural focus of martyr cult by establishing the Pantheon as the church of St Mary and the Martyrs (*S. Maria ad Martyres*).[160] But this most certainly did not involve (as was once believed) the wholesale import of martyrial relics from the cemeteries into Rome. As earlier, most seventh-century translations to intramural sites were from outside the city itself. The Dalmatian pope John IV imported Venantius, Anastasius, and Maurus from his native land and established them in the Lateran baptistery (640–42), while the Greek Theodore (642–49) installed Primus and Felicianus, the martyrs of Nomentum, hitherto enshrined at the fourteenth milestone on the Via Nomentana, in Santo Stefano Rotondo. Leo II brought Saints Simplicianus and Faustinus and others from a site nearer Rome — the fifth milestone on the Via Portuensis — but still outside the cemeterial zone, in a church or oratory next to St Bibiana's.[161] Such evidence suggests that while the seventh-century popes felt an increasing need to surround themselves with relics within easy reach of their principal spheres of action, they experienced considerable difficulty in achieving their aims. Symmachus's presumed translation of Protus and Hyacinthus remained exceptional. The main cemeterial sites appear to have been resistant to interference with their holy dead, and the popes were forced to look further afield.

The popes, then, were clearly interested in establishing intramural cult sites. They even imported relics to this end. But very rarely did they move Roman martyrs within the walls. Indeed, under Pelagius II, Gregory the Great, and Honorius I they made every effort to leave them in situ. In part, Gregory's famous letter to the Empress Constantina, detailing Lawrence's revenge on the diggers who had inadvertently disturbed his body, was special pleading to excuse himself for not handing over major relics and thus diminishing Rome's precious deposit of sanctity. But we may suspect that Roman conservatism about interfering with the dead remained a factor and that, even more importantly, there were vested interests represented by the guardians of the cemeterial sites — the *custodes* or *praepositi* of the Roman sources, the *electi viri* mentioned by Bishop Wilfrid's biographer[162] — whom the popes did not wish to alienate. In the end, the links which had been established in the mid-sixth century between intramural *tituli* and important extramural sites did not continue to develop or developed only slowly. In one instance indeed, that of Marcellinus and Peter, the pull of the extramural

---

[160] *LP*, I, 317. Compare Bede, *Ecclesiastical History*, 2.4.

[161] *LP*, I, 330, 332, 334, 360, and 361.

[162] *Vita S. Wilfridi*, ed. by B. Colgrave (Cambridge, 1927), cap. 33.

site was so strong that the *titulus* itself seems to have lost much of its significance. Papal relic distributions remained restricted to a relatively small group of saints and derived mostly from intramural relic deposits or a few papally controlled tombs in the cemeteries. Yet in the seventh century the pilgrims themselves were apparently fascinated by the martyrs in the catacombs. The so-called itineraries and the activities of Wilfrid establish clearly that it was the number and variety of holy tombs that impressed.[163] The relics which her agent obtained for the Lombard queen Theodelinda were drawn from an extremely wide range of sacred deposits.[164] While the main urban basilicas were listed in a text such as *De locis sanctis*, it was the extramural sites to which it was mainly devoted. The popes guarded the most revered remains and distributed the most coveted relics, but over Rome's martyr cult as a whole they appear to have exercised little direct control.

[163] Thacker, 'Rome of the Martyrs'.

[164] *Codice topografico*, ed. by Valentini and Zucchetti, II, 36–47.

History in Books' Clothing:
Books as Evidence for Cultural Relations between England and the Continent in the Seventh and Eighth Centuries

M. B. Parkes

Bede recorded in his *Historia ecclesiastica gentis anglorum* that Pope Gregory the Great sent gifts to Augustine at Canterbury of all things necessary for the worship and ministry of the church in England, and many manuscripts ('necnon et codices plurimos').[1] Two early surviving gospel books produced in Italy have been associated with St Augustine: Cambridge, Corpus Christi College, MS 286 was produced in Rome in the second half of the sixth century;[2] the other, Oxford, Bodleian Library, MS Auct. D. 2. 14, was copied in the mid-seventh century somewhere in Southern Italy.[3] The text in both manuscripts is the version used at Rome in the time of Gregory the Great: an Italian version of the Old Latin text with some Vulgate readings.[4]

The Corpus manuscript was in England *c.* 700, when the text was corrected by a scribe who used English Uncial script with a 'display' form of Insular **N**. Subsequently, further corrections by another scribe were entered in a small Insular

---

[1] *Bede's Ecclesiastical History of the English People*, 1.29, ed. and trans. by Bertram Colgrave and R. A. B. Mynors (Oxford, 1969), pp. 104–05.

[2] *CLA*, II, 126. See A. Petrucci, 'L'onciale Romana: origini, sviluppo e diffusione di una stilizzazione grafica altomedievale (*s.* VI–IX)', *Studia medievale*, 3rd series, 12 (1971), 75–134 (pp. 108, 110–11, and 124).

[3] *CLA*, II, 230.

[4] The text in the Corpus manuscript is cited by editors as X, and the (better) text in the Bodleian manuscript is cited as O.

Minuscule.[5] Early in the fifteenth century Dom Thomas Elmham, a monk of St Augustine's, Canterbury, described books in the abbey, which he believed to be the earliest books of the entire English church.[6] Some of these have been identified from Elmham's detailed descriptions, but the books which fit these descriptions were copied in Canterbury during the eighth century.[7] Elmham's list included a 'Textus Evangeliorum', also known as the 'Textus Sanctæ Mildredae' (St Mildthryth, abbess of Minster-in-Thanet *c.* 691–*c.* 738), which was kept in the vestry. The only codicological detail described by Elmham was a table of the Eusebian Canons at the beginning of the book. This book could be the Corpus manuscript, which now lacks its first leaves (the text begins in the list of capitula preceding Matthew's Gospel), but the Eusebian sections according to the table were entered in the margins of the text by an Italian scribe.[8] The Corpus manuscript was certainly at St Augustine's by the tenth century, when two grants of land to the abbey were copied on blank pages in the text (fols 74[v] and 77[v]).[9] Early in the eleventh century a list of saints whose relics were kept in the abbey was added on a flyleaf (fol. 1[v]) and includes St Mildretha.[10]

The Bodleian manuscript (Auct. D. 2. 14) was adapted for use as a gospel lectionary soon after it was copied, since the original scribe subsequently indicated pericopes for certain feasts in the margins. Others were entered by a second Italian

---

[5] See the corrections in the bottom margin of the page illustrated in E. A. Lowe, *English Uncial* (Oxford, 1960), pl. IIa, where the second stroke of the letter **N** begins near the bottom of the first. The Insular Minuscule of another corrector is illustrated in *CLA*, II, 126, 'muliere' between the columns of the text.

[6] *Historia monasterii S. Augustini Cantuariensis by Thomas Elmham*, ed. by C. Hardwick, Rolls Series, [8] (London, 1858), pp. 96–98: 'haec sunt primitiae librorum totius ecclesiae Anglicanae'.

[7] For example, the 'Biblia Gregoriana' with inserted purple leaves is probably London, British Library, Royal MS 1. E. VI (*CLA*, II, 214), and the Psalter kept on the high altar is now the Vespasian Psalter, London, British Library, Cotton MS Vespasian A. I (*CLA*, II, 193). See J. J. G. Alexander, *Insular Manuscripts, 6th to the 9th Century*, Survey of Manuscripts Illuminated in the British Isles, 1 (London, 1978), nos 32 and 29 with plates.

[8] The Eusebian Canons are tables of parallel passages in all four Gospels prefixed to gospel books. Eusebian sections were inserted in the margins of the text in each Gospel, and list the parallel passages in the other Gospels.

[9] N. R. Ker, *Catalogue of Manuscripts Containing Anglo-Saxon* (Oxford, 1957), no. 55.

[10] This would suggest that the Corpus manuscript had been at Minster-in-Thanet before it reached St Augustine's.

scribe.[11] The book reached England during the eighth century, where a scribe corrected the text from an Irish version.[12] This scribe used the ligature **tio**, which appears in English manuscripts from the beginning of the eighth century.[13] Some passages in the text marked for lections were punctuated with *positurae*, probably in the ninth or tenth century.[14] An entry written upside down in the bottom margin of fol. 149[v] by one of the eighth-century scribes provides a clue to the provenance of the manuscript in England. The scribe's skills were limited, but he attempted to write in a formal, Insular Minuscule hand, approximately the same size as the handwriting of the text.[15] This entry is most likely a collect for the feast of St Chad (Ceadda) on 2 March: 'Eligite do*minus* sacerdote sibi et sacrificand⟨*um digni* ?⟩ laudis Ic [*for* Hic] est sacerdos magnos qui in diebus suis placuit deo confersor [*for* confessor] s*anct*i *et* sacerdos magni beati s*ancte* ceadda.' The text on this page is John 9. 11–20, the only gospel account of the gift of sight to a blind man at the pool of Siloa. This lection would seem to be appropriate for the

---

[11] David Ganz, 'The Annotations in Oxford, Bodleian Library, Auct. D. II. 14', in *Belief and Culture in the Middle Ages: Studies Presented to Henry Mayr-Harting*, ed. by Richard Gameson and Henrietta Leyser (Oxford, 2001), pp. 35–44. Lists of entries by Italian scribes are on pp. 37–39.

[12] The Irish version appears in L (Lichfield Gospels: Lichfield Cathedral, s.n.), Q (Book of Kells: Dublin, Trinity College, MS A. I. 6 [58]) and R (Rushworth Gospels: Oxford, Bodleian Library, MS Auct. D. 2. 19).

[13] The ligature **tio** is illustrated in *CLA*, II, 230, col. b line 6 'pretio'. For the earliest datable example (*c.* 704 x 705) see the plate in Pierre Chaplais, 'The Letter from Bishop Wealdhere of London to Archbishop Brihtwold of Canterbury: The Earliest Original "Letter Close" Extant in the West', in *Medieval Scribes, Manuscripts and Libraries: Essays presented to N. R. Ker*, ed. by M. B. Parkes and Andrew G. Watson (London, 1978), pp. 3–23. Other examples include: Paris, Bibliothèque nationale de France, fonds latin, 10349, top line of *CLA*, V, 595, *s.* viii (probably in the south of England judging from other letter forms); Düsseldorf, Staatsarchiv HS Z. 4 nr. 2, last word in *CLA*, Supplement, 1687, *s.* viii[2], probably Mercia; hand of second glossator from Southern England in 'Codex Fuldensis': see M. B. Parkes, *Scribes, Scripts and Readers: Studies in the Communication, Presentation and Dissemination of Medieval Texts* (London, 1991), pl. 23 (5) *s.* viii[2]. Lowe also records the appearance of the ligature in Würzburg, Universitätsbibliothek, M. P. Th. f. 43 (*CLA*, IX, 1411, Mercia or Southern England), *s.* viii, and London, British Library, Cotton MS Tiberius A. XV, fols 175–80 (*CLA*, II, 189, not visible on plate; Southern England), *s.* viii. The ligature appears in ninth-century charters, for example, *Facsimiles of Ancient Charters in the British Museum*, ed. by E. A. Bond, 4 vols (London, 1873–78), II, nos 18 (passim) and 28.

[14] On *positurae*, see M. B. Parkes, *Pause and Effect: An Introduction to the History of Punctuation in the West* (London, 1992; Berkeley, 1993), pp. 35–40. For the lections, see Ganz, 'Annotations in Oxford, Bodleian Library, Auct. D. II. 14', pp. 41–43.

[15] Lowe, *English Uncial*, pl. IV.

feast of St Chad. When Chad became Bishop of Mercia he established a small community near a spring close to the church of St Mary at Stowe (half a mile from the present cathedral at Lichfield). He was buried near this church, and the spring became a place of healing, known as 'St Chad's Well'. Springs in other places associated with Chad were also named after him.[16] Eventually Chad was regarded as a tutelary saint of healing springs, and the tradition spread to other parts of the country where there was no other obvious connection with him.[17] The later history of the manuscript is obscure. By the first half of the twelfth century the book was in a monastic community somewhere in the West Midlands.[18] The book was given to Sir Thomas Bodley by Sir Robert Cotton in 1603.[19]

The medieval history of these two books relies partly on legends, but the earliest hint of an existing tradition that connects these manuscripts with St Augustine appears in a letter from Humfrey Wanley to Narcissus Marsh in 1700. Wanley referred to a reading in the text 'which I have observed in an antient Copy of the 4 Evangelists in the Bodleian Library, that I take to be one of the 2 Copies of the Gospels which Gregory the Great sent to St Augustine of Canterbury upon his conversion of K. Ethelbert'.[20] The Bodleian manuscript can only be Auct. D. 2. 14, and the other manuscript referred to is almost certainly Corpus 286 in Cambridge.

During the seventh century Northumbria and parts of Mercia were dominated by the Irish culture from Iona and Dál Riada in Argyll. Under the patronage of

---

[16] *Bede's Ecclesiastical History*, ed. and trans. by Colgrave and Mynors, pp. 336–39, 344–45. Other springs named after Chad: one close to the monastery at Barrow-on-Humber (Lindsey) founded by him (ibid., pp. 336–37), another at Lastingham (North Yorkshire), where he had been abbot (ibid., pp. 316–17).

[17] For example: at Wilne (Derbyshire); the spring between Chadwell and Chatwell (on the border of Shropshire and Staffordshire); in London at King's Cross (where the site is commemorated by the name 'St Chad's Place'); at Chadwell-St-Mary (Essex); and at Bedhampton (Hampshire).

[18] Ganz, 'Annotations in Oxford, Bodleian Library, Auct. D. II. 14', p. 44, suggests that the manuscript survived at Lichfield Cathedral; but other possibilities could include the community at the church of St Mary at Stowe (the source of the tradition) or a community of secular priests like that at St Chad's Church, Shrewsbury, founded in 779.

[19] A single leaf from a Service Book, including a list of books at the monastery of Bury St Edmunds (*s.* xi[2]) was added at the end of the book. It has no obvious codicological connection with the original manuscript — see Ker, *Catalogue*, no. 290 — and was perhaps bound into the book when it was owned by Sir Robert Cotton.

[20] *Letters of Humfrey Wanley, Palaeographer, Anglo-Saxonist, Librarian 1672–1726*, ed. by P. L. Heyworth (Oxford, 1989), no. 69, pp. 143–45 (p. 144).

King Oswald (634–42), who had been baptized there when he was in exile, missionaries led by Bishop Aidan from Iona began the conversion of the Northumbrian peoples. Aidan established his see at Lindisfarne near the royal seat at Bamburgh, and by the end of the century ten new monasteries had been founded north of Flamborough Head.[21] The impact of Irish spirituality encouraged some converts to go to Ireland and lead a more ascetic life, or to further their studies.[22] The earliest surviving gospel books were copied by Irish scribes, or scribes trained by the Irish.[23] The impact of Irish learning is reflected in a copy of the Pseudo-Isidore *De ordine creaturarum* by an anonymous Irish author.[24] Early Northumbrian manuscripts of other texts by Irish authors have not survived, but Bede used the Pseudo-Hilary on the Pauline Epistles when preparing his own commentary on the seven canonical epistles, and he revised calculations in Irish computistic texts for his own works on chronology.[25] The extent of Irish influence in the eighth century is represented in a copy of a commentary on the psalms produced by Edilberict, an English scribe. The emphasis on the exposition of the literal sense of the text is characteristic of the Irish tradition, and some glosses are in Irish and the Northumbrian dialect of Old English.[26]

[21] *Bede's Ecclesiastical History*, chapters 3, 5, 15, 17, ed. and trans. by Colgrave and Mynors. The monasteries were Hartlepool (640), Melrose (before 651), Ad Caprae Caput (Gateshead, 653), Lastingham (654), Ingaetlingham (Collingham, *c.* 654), Whitby (*c.* 657). Ripon (*c.* 654–60), Coldingham (before 672), Hackness (before 680), and Paegnaleach (unidentified).

[22] Among them Æthelwine (subsequently Bishop of Lindsey *c.* 680–92), Chad (Bishop of Lichfield 669–72), Tuta (Bishop of Lindisfarne 664), and Willibrord (leader of the mission to Frisia in 690, founder of the monastery at Echternach in 698).

[23] Durham, Cathedral Library, MS A. II. 10 (*CLA*, II, 247); R. A. B. Mynors, *Durham Cathedral Manuscripts to the End of the Twelfth Century* (Durham, 1939), no. 6, pl. 4. The most informative illustration is in *The Making of England: Anglo-Saxon Art and Culture AD 600–900*, ed. by Leslie Webster and Janet Backhouse, British Museum Exhibition Catalogue (London, 1991), no. 79.

[24] On the Irish origin of this text, see M. C. Diaz y Diaz, 'Isidoriana, I. Sobre el Liber de Ordine Creaturarum', *Sacris erudiri*, 5 (1958), 147–66. The Northumbrian manuscript (*s.* viii[1]) is now Basel, Universitätsbibliothek, MS F. III b (*CLA*, VII, 844).

[25] The earliest surviving manuscript of Pseudo-Hilary is Karlsruhe, Badische Landesbibliothek, Cod. Augiensis CCXXXIII, produced probably at Reichenau (*s.* ix *in.*). On this copy, and comparison with Bede's text, see *Scriptores Hiberniae minores*, vol. I, ed. by Robert E. McNally, CCSL, 108B (Turnhout, 1973), pp. vii–xv. On Bede's revision of computistic texts, see *Bedæ opera de temporis*, ed. by C. W. Jones (Cambridge, MA, 1943), pp. 105–13.

[26] Vatican City, Biblioteca Apostolica Vaticana, MS Palatinus lat. 68, *s.* viii (*CLA*, I, 78). See *Glossa in psalmos*, ed. by M. McNamara, Studi e testi, 310 (Vatican City, 1986).

Ireland also played a significant role in the early transmission of Isidore's works.[27] The earliest surviving copy of his *Etymologiae sive origines* in England was produced by an Irish scribe at the turn of the seventh and eighth centuries. Remnants of this copy survived in south-west England in the binding of a volume containing records of the monastery at Glastonbury and were there before 1189, when the bifolium was used as a wrapper.[28] The early history of this monastery has been obscured by the legends promoted by monks later in the Middle Ages, but it was probably a community of Celtic monks in the seventh century when it certainly had Irish connections.[29] Further evidence for the existence of copies of Isidore in southern England appears in the works of Aldhelm. Twelve of the subjects of his *aenigmata* were derived from the *Etymologiae*, and later he quoted from the *De ortu et obitu patrum* and the *De officiis*. Aldhelm probably encountered these texts during his studies at Malmesbury under Abbot Maeldubh.[30] A generation later Bede only quoted Isidore to correct him, but the earliest surviving copies of Isidore's *Etymologiae* from Northumbria were produced later in the eighth century.[31]

The influence of the Roman Church had reached Northumbria before the synod of Whitby in 664, but the blending of Continental and Irish cultures began to emerge after Benedict Biscop finally established the double monastery of Wearmouth-Jarrow in 682. Bede records that Benedict Biscop on his fifth journey to Gaul and Rome, this time with Ceolfrith, brought back not only numerous books but also pictures, relics of the martyrs, and John the archchantor to teach

---

[27] See Bernhard Bischoff, 'Die europäische Verbreitung der Werke Isidors von Sevilla', in his *Mittelalterliche Studien*, vol. I (Stuttgart, 1966), pp. 171–94 (pp. 180–87). The earliest surviving copy of the *Etymologiae* was produced by an Irish scribe, *s.* vi$^{2/4}$, now St Gall, Stiftsbibliothek, MS 1399 a. 1 (*CLA*, VII, 985); see Parkes, *Scribes, Scripts and Readers*, pl. 1.

[28] Longleat House (Wiltshire), NMR 10589 (*CLA*, Addenda II, 1873).

[29] See also the extracts from the earliest life of St Dunstan, trans. by Dorothy Whitelock, *English Historical Documents c. 500–1042* (London, 1955), p. 826, no. 234.

[30] See the notes on pp. 347–54 in *Aldhelm: The Poetic Works*, trans. by Michael Lapidge and James L. Rosier (Cambridge, 1985). Aldhelm quoted from the *De ortu et obitu patrum* and the *De officiis* in the prose version of his *De laudibus virginitate*.

[31] For Bede and Isidore, see Paul Meyvaert, 'Bede the Scholar', in *Famulus Christi: Essays in Commemoration of the Thirteenth Centenary of the Birth of the Venerable Bede*, ed. by Gerald Bonner (London, 1976), pp. 40–69 (p. 58). The earliest surviving copy of Isidore's *Etymologiae* produced in Northumbria is now Düsseldorf, Staatsarchiv, Fragment 28 + HS Z. 4 nr 3 (*CLA*, VIII, 1189), *s.* viii^2.

the Roman mode of chanting in the *opus dei*. Biscop finally visited Rome in 684 when he brought further treasures for the monastery.[32]

Among these books from Rome were copies of the 'new' translation of the Bible (the Vulgate version) and one of the Old Latin version.[33] The fragment of a sixth-century copy of Maccabees, now in Durham,[34] is almost certainly a remnant of one of these copies, which were used to establish the text during the production of three Bibles *c.* 690–716: the 'Codex Amiatinus' intended as a present for St Peter at Rome,[35] and a copy for each of the two houses of the monastery at Wearmouth and Jarrow.[36] Leaves from a gospel book also written there have been preserved with the Utrecht Psalter.[37] A Wearmouth-Jarrow scribe replaced a bifolium in another copy of the Gospels produced at Rome in the sixth century. The bifolium contains Luke 2. 8 – 3. 10 copied from an exemplar closely related to the Codex Amiatinus.[38]

---

[32] For Biscop's fifth journey to Rome, see *Venerabilis Baedae opera historica*, ed. by Charles Plummer, 2 vols (Oxford, 1896), *Historia abbatum*, § 6, I, 368–69 (trans. in J. A. Giles, *The Biographical Writings of Venerable Bede* (London, 1845), pp. 83–102); *Historia abbatum auctore anonymo, Vita sanctissimi Ceolfridi abbatis*, § 9, ed. by Plummer, I, 391, states that Ceolfrid went with him on this journey (trans. in Whitelock, *English Historical Documents*, no. 155, p. 699). On Biscop's final visit to Rome see *Historia abbatum*, § 9, ed. by Plummer, I, 373.

[33] See Bede, *Historia abbatum*, § 15, ed. by Plummer, I, 379; *Historia abbatum auctore anonymo*, § 20, ed. by Plummer, I, 395 (trans. by Whitelock, *English Historical Documents*, no. 155, p. 702, § 20).

[34] Durham, Cathedral Library, MS B. IV. 6, fol. 169* (*CLA*, II, 153; Mynors, *Durham Cathedral Manuscripts*, no. 1, pl. 1; Lowe, *English Uncial*, pl. IIb); see also Parkes, *Scribes, Scripts and Readers*, pp. 117–18.

[35] Codex Amiatinus: Florence, Biblioteca Medicea Laurenziana, MS Amiatino 1 (*CLA*, III, 299); Lowe, *English Uncial*, pls VIII and IX.

[36] Leaves from the Bibles at Wearmouth and Jarrow are preserved in London, British Library, Additional MSS 37777 and 45025, and British Library, Loan MS 81 (*CLA*, II, 177 + Addenda I, p. 351); Lowe, *English Uncial*, pl. X, and see the second reference in note 33 above.

[37] Utrecht, Universiteitsbibliotheek, MS 32, fols 93–104 (*CLA*, X, 1587); Lowe, *English Uncial*, pls XI and XII.

[38] Würzburg, Universitätsbibliothek, M. P. Th. f. 68 (*CLA*, IX, 1423). On the manuscript, see Bernhard Bischoff and Josef Hofmann, *Libri Sancti Kyliani: Die Würzburger Schreibschule und die Dombibliothek im VIII und IX Jahrhundert*, Quellen und Forschungen zur Geschichte des Bistums und Hochstifts Würzburg, 6 (Würzburg, 1952), pp. 93–94. On the text of Luke in the bifolium (Lowe, *English Uncial*, pl. VI), see Bonifatius Fischer, *Lateinische Bibelhandschriften im frühen Mittelalter* (Freiburg-im-Breisgau, 1985), p. 173. The book was probably taken to

The assumption that other books imported by Benedict Biscop and Ceolfrith may be identified from the texts cited in the works of Bede is not reliable. Bede may have borrowed books from elsewhere: for example, from the 'ecclesiastica uolumina' accumulated at Hexham by Bishop Acca (709–31), to whom Bede addressed several of his commentaries on biblical texts and other works.[39] Moreover, Bede may have used quotations in the works of other authors, when a complete text of the author he was citing was not available to him.[40] Other surviving books produced at Wearmouth-Jarrow (apart from gospel books and a fragment of a Psalter) are a fragment from a copy of Gregory's *Moralia*, copies of Bede's works,[41] and a fragment of a copy of Justinus's Epitome of the lost 'Historiae Philippicae' by Pompeius Trogus.[42] The handwriting of the scribe in this manuscript is very close to that of 'Scribe D' in the 'Leningrad Bede', produced in Bede's lifetime.[43] The exemplar of this copy of Justinus was at least accessible in Wearmouth-Jarrow.

The blending of Irish culture and the Roman culture introduced at Wearmouth-Jarrow appears in the gospel book copied by Eadfrith at Lindisfarne, a monastery with a strong Irish tradition.[44] It was written in Insular Half-uncial,

---

Germany by missionaries in the eighth century, and since the beginning of the nineteenth century it has been associated with Burchard (an Anglo-Saxon), the first Bishop of Würzburg (742–53).

[39] *Bede's Ecclesiastical History*, 5.20, ed. and trans. by Colgrave and Mynors, pp. 530–33. Acca probably acquired books during his travels with Wilfrid: see *The Life of Bishop Wilfrid by Eddius Stephanus*, text, translation, and notes by Bertram Colgrave (Cambridge, 1927; repr. 1985), p. 150. Acca also contributed information for the *Historia ecclesiastica*; see Colgrave and Mynors, pp. 376–77.

[40] Peter Hunter Blair, 'From Bede to Alcuin', in *Famulus Christi*, ed. by Bonner, pp. 239–60 (pp. 247–50). Blair's argument about Bede's knowledge of Virgil has been challenged, but it may well apply to quotations in Bede's other works.

[41] Parkes, *Scribes, Scripts and Readers*, pp. 94–100, 106–08.

[42] Fragment (formerly in Weinheim [private collection], present whereabouts unknown), *CLA*, IX, 1370 + London, British Library, Harley MS 5915, fol. 10 (among a collection of fragments assembled by John Bagford, 1650–71), *CLA*, Addenda II, p. 303. (On Bagford, shoemaker and antiquary, see *The Diary of Humfrey Wanley 1715–1726*, ed. by C. E. Wright and Ruth C. Wright, 2 vols (London, 1966), II, 440.)

[43] See the facsimile edition by O. Arngart, *The Leningrad Bede*, Early English Manuscripts in Facsimile, 2 (Copenhagen, 1952), discussed in Parkes, *Scribes, Scripts and Readers*, pp. 97–106. The manuscript is now cited as St Petersburg, Russian National Library, Q. v. I. 18.

[44] Lindisfarne Gospels: London, British Library, Cotton MS Nero D. IV (*CLA*, II, 187). Facsimile edition by T. D. Kendrick, *Evangeliorum quattuor Codex Lindisfarnensis* (Oltun, 1960), with comprehensive introduction by T. J. Brown, R. L. S. Bruce Mitford, A. S. C. Ross, and E. G. Stanley. This manuscript was later regarded as an adjunct to the relics of St Cuthbert, Bishop of

but laid out on the pages *per cola et commata* in double columns as in Italian books. The text belongs to the Northumbrian Vulgate version (closely related to that in the Codex Amiatinus), and the Lindisfarne Gospels is one of the earliest copies to contain the Eusebian Canon Tables and what became the standard prefatory material. It also contains lections for Neapolitan feasts.[45]

When Benedict Biscop visited Rome for the third time in 667, the Pope asked him to accompany Theodore of Tarsus as a guide and interpreter on his journey to England. Theodore, a Greek monk, had been consecrated as Archbishop of Canterbury, after Wigheard, the archbishop elect, died in Rome.[46] Theodore was also accompanied by Hadrian, abbot of Hiridianum (near Naples), to support the new Archbishop in England. Theodore was Archbishop from 669 to 690, and in 671 Hadrian became abbot of the monastery of Saints Peter and Paul (subsequently known as St Augustine's) in Canterbury, which he ruled until his death, *c.* 709.[47]

Theodore and Hadrian established a school at Canterbury and attracted students from different parts of England. Among them were Oftfor and John (who had been educated in Hild's monastery at Whitby), Tobias, Albinus, and Aldhelm who had received his previous education at Malmesbury.[48] The

---

Lindisfarne 685–87. Éamonn Ó Carragáin, *Ritual and the Rood: Liturgical Images and the Old English Poems of the 'Dream of the Rood' Tradition* (London, 2005), discusses the relationship between Wearmouth-Jarrow and Lindisfarne briefly on pp. 56–57, in the much wider context of the culture in Northumbria.

[45] Prefatory matter: Jerome's letter to Pope Damasus (beginning 'Novum opus') on his own revision of the text, and how to use the Canon Tables; Jerome's other preface (beginning 'Plures fuisse') commenting on the four evangelists; Canon Tables preceded by the explanatory letter from Eusebius to Carpianus. On the list of pericopes for Neapolitan feasts, see Brown's introduction in the facsimile edition. The text in another Northumbrian gospel book (London, British Library, Royal MS 1. B. VII; *CLA*, II, 213) is very close to that of the Lindisfarne Gospels and also contains the same prefatory matter and the lists of Neapolitan feasts.

[46] On Biscop's journey with Theodore, see Bede, *Historia abbatum*, § 3, ed. by Plummer, I, 366–67.

[47] Hadrian's arrival in England was delayed, and Benedict Biscop was abbot of the monastery from 669 to 671. Biscop then went back to Northumbria, where he founded the monastery at Wearmouth in 674. From 978 the abbey at Canterbury was dedicated to St Augustine of Canterbury. See further Bernhard Bischoff and Michael Lapidge, *Biblical Commentaries from the Canterbury School of Theodore and Hadrian* (Cambridge, 1994), p. xxx.

[48] Oftfor became Bishop of Worcester in 691; John became Bishop of Hexham in 687, and Bishop of York in 705 (thereafter he was known as John of Beverley); Tobias became Bishop of Rochester *c.* 716–26; Albinus succeeded Hadrian as abbot of the monastery at Canterbury; Aldhelm became abbot of Malmesbury, and the first Bishop of Sherborne *c.* 705–09.

curriculum at the school was described by Aldhelm in a letter to Leutharius, bishop of the West Saxons, written in or about 671. It included courses on Roman law, the hundred different types of poetic metres, music (the mode of chanting), computation (especially the reckonings which calculate how the heavens revolve in times and seasons), and the study of the scriptures.[49] Theodore's teaching on the scriptures was based on the Antiochene approach to exegesis, which emphasized the literal sense of the text and expounded the history, geography, and flora and fauna of the Holy Land.[50]

Theodore and Hadrian must have brought some books with them, but none have been identified.[51] However, a copy of Arator's *De actibus apostolorum* produced in Italy during the sixth century could have been imported by Hadrian. The remnants of this copy survive as offsets on the inner sides of the wooden boards of an early fifteenth-century binding on a twelfth-century manuscript from St Augustine's Abbey, Canterbury, where Hadrian had been abbot.[52]

Two students who had studied under Theodore and Hadrian at Canterbury subsequently went to Rome. Oftfor went to pursue his studies further, and when he returned to England he went to the kingdom of the Hwicce, where eventually in 691 he was consecrated as bishop of the see located at Worcester. He most likely brought back from Italy a fifth-century copy of Jerome on Ecclesiastes. Afterwards this book was in the possession of Cuthswitha, abbess and founder of the monastery at Inkberrow in eastern Worcestershire (693–?709). A number of

---

[49] *Aldhelmi opera*, ed. by Rudolfus Ehwald, MGH, Auctores antiquissimi, 15 (1919), pp. 475–78. Parts of the curriculum had more practical uses than Aldhelm's letter may suggest, although he indicated that the modulation of melodies was determined by the syllables in the text of the Canticles to emphasize the sense; the computation of the heavens enabled monks to calculate the date of Easter and the appropriate times for the night offices.

[50] Examples of Theodore's exposition of the scriptures survive in later manuscripts: Würzburg, Universitätsbibliothek, M. P. Th. f. 38 (*s.* ix), and Milan, Biblioteca Ambrosiana, M. 79 supra (*s.* xi) under the heading 'Hec Theodorus tradedit': see Bischoff, *Mittelalterliche Studien*, I, 207–09. Theodore's so-called Penitential is a series of answers to questions posed by a priest named Eoda, which is preserved in Cambridge, Corpus Christi College, MS 320, part II (*s.* x^{4/4}).

[51] There is no evidence to support the suggestion that Theodore imported the bilingual copy of the Acts of the Apostles (now Oxford, Bodleian Library, MS Laud Greek 35). Likewise there is no evidence to link Hadrian with the list of Neapolitan feasts in some gospel books produced in the North of England.

[52] Offsets of the copy of Arator are in Oxford, Bodleian Library, MS e Mus. 66, copied in St Augustine's, Canterbury (*s.* xii¹). For a complete facsimile of the offsets, see E. A. Lowe, *Palæographical Papers*, ed. by L. Bieler, 2 vols (Oxford, 1972), I, pls 59–60 (*CLA*, Supplement, 1740).

leaves were replaced in England, but later in the eighth century it was taken, or sent, to missionaries in Germany.[53]

In 688 Aldhelm, by then abbot of Malmesbury, also visited Rome. He brought back to England an altar and a chasuble (which he gave to King Ine, who placed it in the church at Bruton, Somerset), and probably books as well.[54] It is likely that he acquired in Rome a copy of the *Breviarum Alarici*, a compilation of excerpts from early Roman law codes with a continuous gloss or *interpretatio* and commentaries. The manuscript has not survived but was copied by William of Malmesbury in the 1130s.[55] Since Aldhelm was interested in riddles, and had been composing *aenigmata* for some time, he probably acquired a copy of the riddles composed by Symphosius, a pagan author in North Africa in the late fourth and early fifth centuries. It is more likely that Aldhelm could have acquired a copy at Rome than elsewhere at this time. He quoted verses from thirteen of these riddles in his treatise on poetic metres illustrated by his own *aenigmata*, which he sent to 'Acircius' (Aldfrith, King of Northumbria 686–705), with whom he had had a close spiritual relationship for a long time.[56]

In the last quarter of the seventh century Athilwald (a former pupil of Aldhelm) composed four poems including one about three pilgrims who brought back books from Rome.[57] These poems have survived in only one manuscript, copied at Mainz in the first half of the ninth century, and are incorporated in the correspondence of Boniface and Lull.[58] The poem about the pilgrims is addressed

---

[53] Patrick Sims-Williams, 'Cuthswith, Seventh-century Abbess of Inkberrow near Worcester, and the Würzburg Manuscript of Jerome on Ecclesiastes', *Anglo-Saxon England*, 5 (1976), 1–21 (pp. 14–15); the manuscript is Würzburg, Universitätsbibliothek, M. P. Th. q. 2; *CLA*, IX, 1430.

[54] *Willelmi Malmesbiriensis monachi de gestis pontificum Anglorum*, ed. by N. E. S. A. Hamilton, Rolls Series, [52] (London, 1870), p. 364, § 218; p. 371, § 222.

[55] William's copy is in Oxford, Bodleian Library, MS Arch. Selden. B. 16, fols 140ᵛ–222ᵛ. On the influence of Roman law in England, see Eric John, *Land Tenure in Early England* (Leicester, 1960), pp. 11–23.

[56] Aldhelm, *De metris et aenigmatibus ac pedum regulis*, in *Aldhelmi opera*, ed. by Ehwald, pp. 59–204. See also *Aldhelm: The Prose Works*, trans. by Michael Lapidge and Michael Herren (Cambridge, 1979), pp. 31–47; *Poetic Works*, trans. by Lapidge and Rosier, pp. 61–94.

[57] Athilwald's poem: *Aldhelmi opera*, ed. by Ehwald, pp. 528–33. The books are described in lines 107–16.

[58] Vienna, Österreichische Nationalbibliothek, MS 751 (s. ix¹). The arrangement of the letters in the manuscript is haphazard: see *Die Briefe des heiligen Bonifatius und Lullus*, ed. by Michael Tangl, MGH, Scriptores rerum Germanicorum, New Series, 1 (1955), pp. xii–xiii, who rearranged the letters in a hypothetical chronological order. The exemplars for this manuscript

'ad Wihtfridum', but given the context in which it has survived, it is tempting to correct this address to 'ad Wynfridum', and to identify the recipient as Wynfrid (later given the name Boniface by Pope Gregory II), who was a monk at Nutschelle until 716.[59] Later, before setting out on his mission to Germany in 719, Boniface acquired relics and probably books in Rome. Among the books used by Boniface was the 'Codex Fuldensis', a copy of a Harmony of the Gospels followed by the rest of the New Testament, which had belonged to Victor, Bishop of Capua 541–54, whose handwriting appears in the manuscript.[60] Later glosses were added by Boniface and by another Anglo-Saxon scribe (perhaps Lull).[61] Chests containing books were broken open by the Frisian mob who killed him and his companions in 754.[62] About the time when Boniface first set out on his mission to Germany, Cuthwine, bishop of the East Angles (*c.* 716–30) acquired two illustrated books in Rome, which have not survived. But Bede saw one of them in which the sufferings and labours of the apostle Paul were depicted on the appropriate pages of the text. The other manuscript, containing the *Carmen paschale* of Sedulius, was copied on the Continent in the early ninth century before it too was lost.[63]

---

may have been first drafts and original letters at Mainz, the seat of the see occupied by both Boniface and Lull: see Wilhelm Levison, *England and the Continent in the Eighth Century* (Oxford, 1946), pp. 280–90.

[59] *Vita sancti Bonifatii archiepiscopi Moguntini auctore Willibaldo*, § 3, ed. by W. Levison, MGH, Scriptores rerum Germanicarum in usum scholarum, 57 (1905), pp. 11–13; trans. by C. H. Talbot, *The Anglo-Saxon Missionaries in Germany* (London, 1954), pp. 31–33. Nutschelle (now called Nursling) is between Southampton and Winchester.

[60] Codex Fuldensis: Fulda, Landesbibliothek, MS Bonifatius 1 (*CLA*, VIII, 1196). There is no evidence that this manuscript had ever been in England. The 'Anglo-Saxon' binding was made for the book when it was retrieved after Bonifatius's death. The format of the book suggested to Bernhard Bischoff that the original covers may have been an ivory diptych which was stripped off the book by the Frisians who murdered him: see Parkes, *Scribes, Scripts and Readers*, p. 135, n. 48.

[61] For these glosses, see Parkes, *Scribes, Scripts and Readers*, pp. 121–42.

[62] Boniface's correspondence reveals that he sought and acquired books from England as well (*Die Briefe des heiligen Bonifatius und Lullus*, ed. by Tangl, nos 30, 34–35, 63, 75–76, and 91). A list of books used by Boniface is constructed by Hermann Schüling, 'Die Handbibliothek des Bonifatius', in *Börsenblatt für den Deutschen Buchhandel*, Frankfurter Ausgabe, no. 77a (September, 1961), pp. 1687–1719 (p. 1709, section II).

[63] Description of the first manuscript in Bede's *De octo quaestionibus*, PL, 93, 456. Dorothy Whitelock wondered if Abbot Esi (who provided Bede with information about the early East Anglian church) had brought this manuscript to Northumbria: 'Bede and his Teachers and

At York in 735 Æthelbert took over the direction of the cathedral school founded by his brother Bishop Ecgberht. Æthelbert was master of the school for over thirty years and assembled a good collection of books for his students. Like Benedict Biscop he travelled several times on the Continent, and visited Rome with his pupil Alcuin, searching for new books to take back to York and for new developments in scholarship.[64] In 766 Æthelbert succeeded Ecgberht as Archbishop of York, and Alcuin became master of the school. Alcuin, like Æthelbert, was a good teacher, and the renown of his school attracted students, including some of the converts from the mission field on the Continent.[65] Later in his life Alcuin incorporated in his poem on York a list of authors (but not their texts) whose works were available in the library. The list is dominated by the Fathers of the Church, Christian poets, and grammarians, but records only three classical poets.[66] Alcuin composed this poem not long after he had left England for the court of Charlemagne in 782, and one of the reasons why Alcuin omits the texts of authors is that the list is part of a nostalgic reconstruction of the church at York as he remembered it.

During the late seventh and eighth centuries Anglo-Saxon readers took a keen interest in the classical Latin poets. Aldhelm, Bede, and other Anglo-Saxon poets were familiar with the works of Virgil, and the earliest surviving copy of Servius's commentary on the *Aeneid* was produced in south-west England during the first half of the eighth century.[67] Judging from quotations Aldhelm knew a wider range of classical Latin poets than Bede (notably Juvenal, Lucan, Lucretius, Ovid, Persius, and Proba), but Bede preferred Christian poets and drew on the poetry

Friends', in *Famulus Christi*, ed. by Bonner, pp. 19–39 (p. 30). On Bede's response to this manuscript, see George Henderson, *Bede and the Visual Arts* (Jarrow Lecture, 1980), p. 7. The ninth-century copy of the Sedulius manuscript (Antwerp, Museum Plantin-Moretus, MS M. 17. 4) was identified by Ludwig Traube, *Vorlesungen und Abhandlungen*, 3 vols (Munich, 1909–20), III, 239–41. On the illustrations, see Alexander, *Insular Manuscripts*, no. 65, pls 285–301.

[64] Alcuin, *Versus de patribus, regibus et sanctis Euboricensis ecclesie*, ed. by P. Godman (Oxford, 1982), lines 1454–63.

[65] See below, note 86.

[66] Alcuin, *Versus Euboricensis ecclesie*, lines 1521–37. The list includes authors not apparently known to Aldhelm and Bede: Hilary (of Poitiers), Leo, Aristotle, Boethius (presumably his translations of Aristotelian texts, or his philosophical works, since the *De consolatione philosophiae* was not in circulation before the ninth century, when the earliest copies contain only the metres); 'Tullius rhetor' (perhaps the anonymous *Rhetorica ad Herennium*). The three classical poets listed are Virgil, Lucan. and Statius.

[67] On the commentary of Servius on the *Aeneid*, see below, note 81.

of Venantius Fortunatus, Prosper of Aquitaine, Prudentius, and Sedulius.[68] Aldhelm composed *carmina ecclesiastica* and the *Carmen de virginitate* (with a prologue in acrostics) as well as the *aenigmata* in the treatise on metre.[69] Bede composed a metrical life of St Cuthbert and two collections of poetry which have not survived: a 'Liber hymnorum diverso metro sive rhythmo' and a 'Liber epigrammatum heroico metro sive elegiaco'. *Aenigmata* were composed by contemporaries of Bede: Hwætberht, abbot of Wearmouth-Jarrow (but circulated under the pseudonym 'Eusebius'); others were composed by Tatwine from the monastery of Breedon-on-the-Hill in Mercia.[70] Boniface probably composed the acrostic poem 'Iohannes celsi rimans mysteria celi', since the text in the earliest surviving copy is in his handwriting, almost certainly produced at Nutschelle before he went to Frisia in 716.[71]

Boniface also composed a *carmen figuratum* (figure poem) accompanied by a commentary, which he inserted as a frontispiece to his treatise on grammar.[72] *Carmina figurata* seem to have fascinated Anglo-Saxon writers. They encountered these poems in a copy of Publius Optatianus Porfyrius, a fourth-century poet at the court of the Emperor Constantine.[73] Bede knew these poems, but rejected

---

[68] The choice of poets is suggested by the authors quoted in their own works.

[69] *Carmina ecclesiastica*, see *Aldhelmi opera*, ed. by Ehwald, pp. 11–32, *Carmen de virginitate*, in ibid., pp. 350–71.

[70] The *aenigmata* of Hwætberht and Tatwine appear in London, British Library, Royal MS 12. C. XXIII and Cambridge, University Library, MS Gg. 5. 35 (both copied *s.* xi[1]).

[71] The acrostic poem appears in St Petersburg, Russian National Library, Q. v. I. 15. See Parkes, *Scribes, Scripts and Readers*, p. 122; Michael Lapidge, 'Autographs of Insular Authors of the Early Middle Ages', in *Gli autografi medievali: probleme paleografici e filologici*, ed. by P. Chiesa and L. Pinelli, Quaderni di cultura mediolatina, 5 (Spoleto, 1994), pp. 103–36, esp. pp. 109–15 with plate and translation of the text.

[72] Boniface's figure poem illustrated from Würzburg, Universitätsbibliothek, M. P. Th. f. 29, fol. 44, in Jeremy Adler and Ulrich Ernst, *Text als Figur: Visuelle Poesie der Antike bis zur Moderno*, Exhibition Catalogue Herzog August Bibliothek, Wolfenbüttel, no. 56 (1997–98), Abbildung 11, p. 34. On the manuscript, see Bischoff and Hofmann, *Libri Sancti Kyliani*, pp. 135–36, no. 136. The earliest surviving copy of Boniface's *Ars grammatica* is the bifolium in Oberkaufungen, Archiv der Ritterschaftlichen Stifts, Kaufungen, s.n. (*CLA*, Supplement, 1803): see W. A. Eckhardt, 'Die Kaufunger Fragment der Bonifatius-Grammatik', *Scriptorium*, 23 (1969), 280–97, pl. 99. Handwriting and provenance indicate that the manuscript was copied in the south of England (probably Nutschelle), *s.* viii *med.*, and during the Middle Ages was in the monastery founded by Boniface at Fulda.

[73] See Ulrich Ernst, *Carmen figuratum: Geschichte des Figurengedichts von den antiken Ursprüngen bis zum Ausgang der Mittelalters* (Cologne, 1991).

Porfyrius's metres because he was a pagan poet.[74] Lull (who was educated at Malmesbury) had a keen interest in poetry. In a letter to an unidentified abbess and a nun in *c.* 738, he described the complexity of an acrostic poem.[75] In a postscript to a letter addressed to Lull in 754, Milred, Bishop of Worcester, regretted that he was unable to send a copy of Porfyrius's *carmina figurata*, because it was on loan to Archbishop Cuthbert, who had not yet returned it.[76] Later, Alcuin composed *carmina figurata* and introduced Porfyrius's work to the court of Charlemagne.[77] A few figure poems composed by Alcuin, his pupil Joseph, and Theodulf, Bishop of Orléans, appear on four leaves from a manuscript produced in north-east France at the beginning of the ninth century.[78] The most elaborate collection of *carmina figurata* was composed by Hrabanus Maurus, a monk of Fulda, who had been sent to Tours to study under Alcuin, before returning to the monastery at Fulda, where he produced his *De laudibus sancte Crucis*.[79]

Books imported into England were copied, and some of these copies are the earliest surviving witnesses to their texts. The commentary on the Apocalypse by Primasius, Bishop of Hadrumentum in North Africa, was copied in south-west England at the end of the seventh century.[80] Servius's commentary on the *Aeneid* was also copied there in the first half of the eighth century.[81] The copy of Justinus's Epitome of the lost 'Historiae Philippicae' of Pompeius Trogus is the earliest witness not only to the text but to the best text, and is the only English manuscript which generated a transalpine tradition on the Continent.[82] The copy of Pliny the Elder's *Naturalis historia* produced probably in Northumbria in the first

---

[74] Bede, *De arte metrica*, in *Bedae venerabilis opera didascalia*, ed. by Charles W. Jones, CCSL, 123A (Turnhout, 1975), p. 138.

[75] *Die Briefe des heiligen Bonifatius und Lullus*, ed. by Tangl, no. 95.

[76] *Die Briefe des heiligen Bonifatius und Lullus*, ed. by Tangl, no. 112.

[77] For Alcuin's *carmina figurata*, see *Poetae latini medii aevi Carolini*, ed. by E. Duemmler, MGH, Antiquitates, 1 (1881, repr. 1964), pp. 224–27, nos 6 and 7.

[78] Bern, Burgerbibliothek, MS 212 II, fols 123–26 (*s. ix in.*); see Bischoff's remarks in *Karl der Grosse: Werk und Wirkung*, [Exhibition Catalogue] (Aachen, 1965), p. 201, no. 362.

[79] Facsimile edition by K. Holter, *Codices selecti phototypice impressi*, 33 (Graz, 1972).

[80] Oxford, Bodleian Library, MS Douce 140 (*CLA*, II, 234); glosses in the margins in Boniface's handwriting suggest that the book was at Nutschelle during the first quarter of the eighth century.

[81] Marburg, Hessisches Staatsarchiv, 319 Pfarrei Spangenberg, Hr Nr 1.

[82] See above, note 42; *Texts and Transmission: A Survey of the Latin Classics*, ed. by L. D. Reynolds (Oxford, 1983), p. 197, entry on Justinus.

half of the eighth century is the earliest surviving copy from North of the Alps.[83] The earliest surviving copy of the Rule of Benedict (but with Gallic interpolations) was produced in Kent at the end of the eighth century.[84] The sixth-century Italian copy of Arator preserved in a later binding at Canterbury is the earliest surviving witness to the text. Although there is no evidence that it was copied in England, the text was known to Aldhelm and Bede.[85]

Many of the books copied in Anglo-Saxon England were sent to the Continent, or taken there by missionaries. Liudger, a young Frisian, was sent twice to York to study under Alcuin, and he took back home numerous books copied from those in the library at York.[86] The destinations of some books copied by Anglo-Saxon scribes, especially fragments, have been suggested by their present locations in libraries which hold collections of surviving books from monasteries founded in Germany in the eighth century, Those which were probably at Fulda include the remnants of Isidore's *Differentiae* and *De natura rerum*, Jerome on Ecclesiastes and on Daniel, the commentary on the *Aeneid* by Servius, and the earliest copy of Boniface's Grammar.[87] A copy of Paulinus of Nola's poems and Edelberict's copy of a commentary on the psalms were at Lorsch.[88] Books probably at Werden (founded by Liudger, when Bishop of Utrecht) include fragments of copies of an abbreviated version of Cassiodorus on the psalms, Chrysostom, *De reparatione*

---

[83] Leiden, Bibliotheek te Rijksuniversiteit, Vossianus, MS Lat. F. 4 (*CLA*, X, 1578).

[84] Oxford, Bodleian Library, MS Hatton 48 (*CLA*, II, 240; Lowe, *Palæographical Papers*, I, pls 31–36; Lowe, *English Uncial*, pl. XX). From the late twelfth century the manuscript was at Worcester.

[85] For the copy of Arator see above, note 52.

[86] For Liudger, see Altfrid's *Vita Liudgeri*, ed. by G. H. Pertz, MGH, Scriptores, 2 (1829), pp. 403–19. Relevant chapters (9–13) are trans. by Whitelock, *English Historical Documents*, no. 160, pp. 724–26. Later Liudger became Bishop of Utrecht and founded the monastery at Werden.

[87] Fulda: Basel, Universitätsbibliothek: Pseudo-Isidore, *De ordine creaturarum*, MS F. III. b, fols 1–19 (*CLA*, VII, 844), *s.* viii[1], Northumbria; Isidore, *De natura rerum*, MS F. III. 15 f (*CLA*, VII, 848), *s.* viii; Isidore, *Differentiae*, MS F. III. 15.1 (*CLA*, VII, 849), *s.* viii; Jerome on Ecclesiastes, Kassel, Landesbibliothek, MS Theol. Fol. 21 (*CLA*, VIII, 1134), *s.* viii; Jerome on Daniel, Kassel, Gesamthochschulbibliothek, MS 2° Theol. 269 + Marburg, Hessisches Staatsarchiv, MS HR 2. 17 (*CLA*, VIII, 1145 + *CLA*, Addenda I, p. 357), *s.* viii *ex.*; Servius, Commentary on *Aeneid* (see above, note 81). See also note 72 above.

[88] Lorsch: Vatican City, Biblioteca Apostolica Vaticana: Commentary on psalms, MS Palatinus lat. 68 (*CLA*, I, 78), *s.* viii, Northumbria; Paulinus of Nola, MS Palatinus lat. 235 (*CLA*, I, 87), *s.* viii, Northumbria. See Bernhard Bischoff, *Lorsch im Spiegel seiner Handschriften*, Münchener Beiträge zur Mediävistik und Renaissance-Forschung, Beiheft (Munich, 1974), pp. 104 and 108.

lapsi, and of a book which contained Isidore's *Etymologiae* and Orosius's *Historiarum adversum paganos*, all produced in Northumbria during the eighth century.[89] Two books survive at Würzburg: a copy of the *Synonyma* of Isidore produced probably in Mercia, and a copy of Gregory's Homilies on Ezechiel in the south of England — both in the eighth century.[90]

Copies of works by Anglo-Saxon authors were also sent or taken to the Continent. Fragments of the earliest known copies of works by Aldhelm and Bede, produced in England in the first half of the eighth century, survive in libraries on the Continent: a bifolium of Aldhelm's treatise on poetic metres copied in Southern England, and a leaf from a manuscript of Bede's *De temporum ratione* copied at Wearmouth-Jarrow.[91] The earliest surviving copies containing complete texts of Aldhelm's works were also produced on the Continent. The treatise on poetic metres was copied in the monastery at Lorsch at the turn of the eighth and ninth centuries, where it was corrected by an Anglo-Saxon scribe; and about the same time, the *Carmen de virginitate* was copied at Murbach.[92] The earliest complete copy of the *De laudibus virginitate* was produced at Würzburg at the instigation of Bishop Gozbald (841–52).[93]

---

[89] Werden: Chrysostom, *De reparatione lapsi &c*, Düsseldorf, Landes- und Staatsbibliothek, MS B. 215 + C. 118 (*CLA*, VIII, 1187), *s.* viii *med.*, Northumbria; Düsseldorf, Staatsarchiv: Orosius, HS Z. 4 nr 2 (*CLA*, Supplement, no. 1687), *s.* viii[2]; Isidore, *Etymologiae*, Fragment 28 + HS Z. 4 nr 3, 1 + Gerleve (near Coesfeld) Stiftsbibliothek, s. n. (*CLA*, VIII, 1189 + Supplement, p. 6), *s.* viii[2]; Cassiodorus on psalms (Staatsarchiv) s.n. (*CLA*, Supplement, 1786), *s.* viii[1], Northumbria.

[90] Würzburg, Universitätsbibliothek: Gregory, Homilies on Ezechiel, M. P. Th. f. 43 (*CLA*, IX, 1411), *s.* viii[2], probably in South of England; Isidore, *Synonyma*, M. P. Th. f. 39 (*CLA*, IX, 1426), *s.* viii *ex.*, probably Mercia, with some Old English stylus glosses (noted in Ker, *Catalogue*, no. 400). See Bischoff and Hofmann, *Libri Sancti Kyliani*, pp. 95–97, nos 9 and 11.

[91] Aldhelm's *De metris*: Miscolc (Hungary), Lévay József Library, s.n. (*CLA*, Supplement, 1792; Addenda II, p. 307). Bede, *De temporum ratione*: Darmstadt, Hessische Landes- und Hochschulbibliothek, MS 4262 (*CLA*, Addenda I, 1822). On the dissemination of Bede's works, see D. Whitelock, *After Bede* (Jarrow Lecture, 1960). On early copies of works by Boniface, see above, notes 71 and 72.

[92] Aldhelm's *De metris*: Vatican City, Biblioteca Apostolica Vaticana, MS Palatinus lat. 1753: see Bischoff, *Lorsch im Spiegel seiner Handschriften*, pl. 7, and pp. 23 and 118–19. *Carmen de virginitate* at Murbach, Gotha, Landesbibliothek, Mbr I. 75 (*CLA*, VIII, 1207), plate in *Aldhelmi opera*, ed. by Ehwald, between pp. 544 and 545.

[93] Würzburg, Universitätsbibliothek, M. P. Th. f. 21: Bischoff and Hofmann, *Libri Sancti Kyliani*, pp. 31–32; plate in Ehwald, between pp. 544 and 545.

The synchronizing of Irish and Roman cultures in England during the seventh and eighth centuries produced an intellectual *renovatio*: manuscripts and fragments of books contain the sources that created it and sustained it. Alongside gospel books adorned by splendid initials and images, liturgical books, and the commentaries of the Fathers of the Church, other surviving books reveal a range of Christian and pagan literature, both in prose and in verse that indicate the diversity of this synchronic culture. It includes Christian poets such as Arator, Paulinus of Nola, and Sedulius; pagan poets such as Virgil, Juvenal, Lucretius, and Persius, and the elaborate techniques in the poems of Porfyrius and Symphosius; prose works of historians such as Justinus and Orosius, and Isidore, Pseudo-Isidore, and Pliny who described the nature of things and creatures. The trails left by the wanderings of manuscripts document the dissemination of English manuscripts on the continent of Europe in the eighth century — not only to the monasteries founded by the missionaries but also to the court of Charlemagne (the copy of Justinus). Anglo-Saxon culture contributed substantially to the Carolingian renaissance.

THE BARBERINI GOSPELS:
CONTEXT AND INTERTEXTUAL RELATIONSHIPS

Michelle P. Brown

O f all the great Insular Gospelbooks one that has attracted comparatively little study to date is the Barberini Gospels (Vatican City, Biblioteca Apostolica Vaticana, MS Barb. lat. 570).[1] The heady mix of cultural and stylistic references in the Barberini Gospels is, like that of the Lindisfarne Gospels, a complex and consciously synthetic one, designed to express a depth and breadth of international contacts within a Church that, ecumenically, stretched from the western coast of Ireland to the Middle East, and from Germany to parts of Africa. This international perspective is expressed gloriously in Barberini in the form of the miniatures depicting the evangelists that precede each of their Gospels. Eschewing their symbolic representation as the man, the lion, the bull, and the eagle — which nonetheless do feature in Barberini's opening Canon Table — and the complex schematic and exegetical approach of the Lindisfarne Gospels' evangelist miniatures,[2] the main artist of the Barberini Gospels depicts them in stately,

---

[1] See *CLA*, I, no. 63; J. J. G. Alexander, *Insular Manuscripts, 6th to the 9th Century*, Survey of Manuscripts Illuminated in the British Isles, 1 (London, 1978), no. 36; Patrick McGurk, *Latin Gospel Books from AD 400 to AD 800*, Les Publications de Scriptorium, 5 (Paris, 1961), no. *137; *The Making of England: Anglo-Saxon Art and Culture AD 600–900*, ed. by Leslie Webster and Janet M. Backhouse, British Museum Exhibition Catalogue (London, 1991), no. 160 and p. 195; for its context in relation to the 'Tiberius Group' of Southumbrian manuscripts, see Michelle P. Brown, 'Mercian Manuscripts? The "Tiberius" Group', in *Mercia: An Anglo-Saxon Kingdom in Europe*, ed. by Michelle P. Brown and Carol A. Farr (London, 2001), pp. 278–91. See also N. Bishop, 'The Barberini Gospels' (unpublished doctoral dissertation, University of Iowa, 2005).

[2] See Michelle P. Brown, *The Lindisfarne Gospels: Society, Spirituality and the Scribe* (London, 2003), pp. 346–69.

Byzantine fashion, as bearded figures engaged in the act of writing and seated within a balustraded landscape. The veil of iconoclasm that had shrouded the light of art in Byzantium during much of the seventh and eighth centuries had been lifted in the 780s, allowing its influence to be celebrated anew in the West.

The painterly, modelled figure style fuses with the Insular decorative vocabulary in the opening Canon Table (fol. 1ʳ; see Plate 1), where the evangelist symbols are joined by a hauntingly vivid male head, elegantly moustached, and an intriguing naked man who protects his beard and genitals from the hungry creatures that surround him. Likewise, the incipit page of St Mark's Gospel features two beautifully observed human heads with elaborate headdresses. These, and other details of the ornament, may have been imbued with deep symbolic significance, as we shall see.

Such Byzantine and eastern visual references were also a feature of art produced in the orbit of the court of Emperor Charlemagne in the late eighth and early ninth centuries — a court with which the English royalty, nobility, and Church had many contacts. Insular influence was also a contributory ingredient in Carolingian culture. The cultural cross-currents are rich and resonant, and the Barberini Gospelbook, with its surprising and engaging mix of elegant frigidity and anarchic exuberance, is a vibrant witness to its age. It would probably have been owned by a leading monastery or cathedral, and the text is marked so that the gospel readings could be read from it in church services on the greatest Christian festivals celebrating the birth, resurrection, and ascension of Christ. It would have made an imposing visual impact, reinforcing the import of the message it conveyed. At other times it may have served in the instruction of members of the religious community and have been shown proudly to visiting dignitaries and displayed on the high altar, where it might be seen by a broad cross-sector of the community, from kings to humble pilgrims.[3]

We cannot know for sure where it was made, or for whom, but at the very end of the book on fol. 153ʳ, at the end of his work on John's Gospel, the principal scribe concludes with the colophon 'Oro pro uuigbaldo', 'Pray for Wigbald'. What was his role? Perhaps he was the master-scribe who coordinated and planned the project and did much of the work on it and who wrote the colophon. Alternatively, he may have been its patron — the person who commissioned this splendid

---

[3] For a discussion of the use and context of such Insular Gospelbooks, see, for example, George Henderson, *From Durrow to Kells: The Insular Gospel-books 650–800* (London, 1987), and two of my own studies: '"In the Beginning was the Word": Books and Faith in the Age of Bede' (Jarrow Lecture, 2000), and *Lindisfarne Gospels*.

Gospelbook and may have donated it to the high altar of one of the great churches of the day.

The Barberini Gospelbook was written by four scribes, whom I have termed A–D, all of whom are responsible for some artwork within their sections, of varying degrees of artistic aptitude. They were joined by an artist of exceptional calibre, here termed the 'Artist', who was entrusted with the major components of the illumination: the opening page of the Canon Tables, the evangelist portraits, and a number of the decorated incipits.

The details of script and decoration point to a date within the early ninth century and to a southern English background for at least two of the four scribes:[4] C (the scribe who penned the colophon, perhaps Wigbald himself) and D. Its minor decoration and display script are related to those of later members of what is known as the 'Tiberius' group of manuscripts from Southumbria, notably the Tiberius Bede from which the group takes its name (London, British Library, Cotton MS Tiberius C. II) which is attributed to Canterbury, c. 810–25, and the Book of Cerne (Cambridge, University Library, MS Ll. 1. 10), attributed to western Mercia, c. 820–40.[5] The display script, with its linking mechanism of biting beast heads and human elements (see Fig. 1), stems ultimately from a Northumbrian background and can be paralleled in the terminals to some of the display lettering in the Gospel incipit pages of the Lindisfarne Gospels, made around 715–20. It is echoed on the Continent in subsequent eighth-century works such as the Cutbercht Gospels (Vienna, Österreichische Nationalbibliothek, Codex 1224), perhaps made in Salzburg but showing English input and a marked, up-to-date southern English influence. It is also developed further in a Columban milieu in the Book of Kells (Dublin, Trinity College Library, MS 58) and in other Irish contexts, such as the Book of Armagh (Dublin, Trinity College Library, MS 52; made in Armagh c. 807). However, it was in Southumbria that this generic strand of ornament evolved into a distinctive form of lacertine display script featuring brontosaurus-like biting beast-heads as a means of achieving ligature and comic anthropomorphic or grotesque elements. Zoomorphic or grotesque line-fillers and run-over symbols also evolved within the 'Tiberius' group

---

[4] I am preparing a full study of the manuscript's palaeography and the division of hands for script and artwork.

[5] For these attributions and those of other members of the Tiberius group, see Michelle P. Brown, *The Book of Cerne: Prayer, Patronage and Power in Ninth-Century England* (London, 1996), pp. 164–77, and 'Mercian Manuscripts?'.

Figure 1. The 'In principio' opening of St John's Gospel, with lacertine display script of 'Tiberius group' style, Barberini Gospels. Vatican City, Biblioteca Apostolica Vaticana, MS Barb. lat. 570, fol. 125ʳ. © The Biblioteca Apostolica Vaticana. By kind permission of the Prefect of the Biblioteca Apostolica Vaticana.

during the late eighth and early ninth centuries.[6] Scribes C and D are well-versed in this characteristic late 'Tiberius' repertoire. Barberini may provide a slightly earlier background to the fully developed 'Tiberius' style as seen in the Tiberius Bede and the Book of Cerne, and in a copy of saints' lives (Paris, Bibliothèque nationale de France, fonds latin, 10861) the script of which is closely related to Canterbury charters of c. 802–25.[7] The Book of Cerne and the Royal Bible, which are thought to date to c. 820–40, seem to be moving away from the rather nebulous hybrid creatures seen in Barberini, the Tiberius Bede, and the Paris saint's lives and may be slightly later, which would suggest a date for the Barberini Gospels at the end of the eighth or the beginning of the ninth century.

The 'Artist' was well-versed in the general Insular repertoire of ornament, his style of interlace and of zoomorphic decoration exhibiting affiliations with an ultimately Northumbrian background, the analogies for his animal ornament including an eighth-century cross-shaft from Abercorn (a bishopric near Edinburgh under Lindisfarne's control) which offers an extremely close parallel for the panel of opposed bipeds in the upper frame of Barberini's Matthew miniature (fol. 11ᵛ; see Fig. 2). For his plant ornament an intriguing parallel is to be found on the Bewcastle Cross in the distinctive bat-wing shaped leaf in its sundial panel which resembles that in Barberini's St Matthew miniature (just to the right of the evangelist's writing board). Such shared references may have derived, of course, from similar source materials rather than through direct relationships. Aside from these details and a generic background within the 'Hiberno-Saxon' style, the more modern aspects of his ornament, and that of the scribes with whom he worked — interlace, vine-scroll, animal, and foliate — exhibit close stylistic relationships with works such as the Gandersheim Casket, the Ormside Bowl, and the Rupertus Cross (the casket and bowl now thought to have been made in Southumbria and the cross in a Carolingian centre under English influence)[8] and with a group of sculptures stretching across central Mercia from Peterborough to Breedon-on-the-hill (Leics.). In recent discussion of the Gandersheim Casket, Farr, Webster, and Bailey have convincingly advanced a series of detailed manuscript, metalwork,

---

[6] See Brown, *Book of Cerne*, pp. 173–78, and 'Echoes: The Book of Kells and Southern English Manuscript Production', in *The Book of Kells: Proceedings of a Conference at Trinity College Dublin 6–9 September 1992*, ed. by Felicity O'Mahony (Aldershot, 1994), pp. 333–43.

[7] See Michelle P. Brown, 'Paris, Bibliothèque Nationale, lat. 10861 and the Scriptorium of Christ Church, Canterbury', *Anglo-Saxon England*, 15 (1987), 119–37, and Brown, 'Mercian Manuscripts?'.

[8] *Making of England*, ed. by Webster and Backhouse, nos 138, 134, and 133.

Figure 2. St Matthew miniature, Barberini Gospels. Vatican City, Biblioteca
Apostolica Vaticana, MS Barb. lat. 570, fol. 11ᵛ. © The Biblioteca Apostolica
Vaticana. By kind permission of the Prefect of the Biblioteca Apostolica Vaticana.

and sculptural comparanda, with the Barberini Gospels emerging as the closest parallel in book form.[9] The concentration of sculptures and of archaeological find-spots all support an origin within Mercia during the late eighth to early ninth centuries, and within the East Midlands focussing upon Peterborough in particular.

The skilled, painterly nature of the 'Artist's' work, with its Byzantine figure-style, has led some authors to suggest that it must have been produced on the Continent, possibly within an early Carolingian milieu. An interest in early Christian, Italian, and Byzantine art was certainly in evidence in Charlemagne's circle, but similar interests and references have also been discerned in late eighth- and early ninth-century Southumbria. The sculptures of Lichfield (with its recently discovered angel sculpture of c. 800, perhaps from St Chad's shrine), Breedon-on-the-hill, Peterborough (the Hedda Stone), Castor, and Fletton all exhibit an interest in similarly exotic stylistic references. They feature an eastern menagerie that incorporates fanciful hybrid beasts, for example, the cat-like creatures frequenting both the pages of Barberini and the sculptural friezes of Breedon and Fletton, probably modelled on eastern depictions of lions (for Insular artists a 'big cat' was, literally, a big cat), and a classicizing figure-style with a preponderance of bearded apostles of Byzantine fashion.[10] Likewise, the Royal Bible, the latest of the 'Tiberius' manuscripts, thought to have been made in Canterbury on the eve of the Viking invasions, combines features from Italo-Byzantine, Carolingian, and Southumbrian art in its remaining decorated incipit page. It would originally have been a splendid single-volume Bible, containing full-page miniatures and decorated incipits on purple pages. Its display script is, nonetheless, of contemporary 'Tiberius' fashion and incorporates features related to ninth-century 'Trewhiddle-style' metalwork, exhibiting a taste for cultural synthesis akin to that found in the

---

[9] For their respective discussions, see *Das Gandersheimer Runenkästchen: Internationales Kolloquium, Braunschweig, 24–26 März 1999*, ed. by Regine Marth (Braunschweig, 2000).

[10] Richard Jewell was the first to suggest Peterborough as a focus for this style. See his studies, 'The PreConquest Sculpture at Breedon on the Hill, Leicestershire' (unpublished doctoral dissertation, University of London, 1982), ch. 3, n. 30 and ch. 6, n. 27; 'The Anglo-Saxon Friezes at Breedon on the Hill, Leicestershire', *Archaeologia*, 108 (1986), 95–115; and 'Classicism of Southumbrian Sculpture', in *Mercia*, ed. by Brown and Farr, pp. 246–62. See also Rosemary J. Cramp, 'Schools of Mercian Sculpture', in *Mercian Studies*, ed. by Ann Dornier (Leicester, 1977), pp. 191–233; Richard Bailey, *The Meaning of Mercian Sculpture*, Vaughan Papers, 34 (Leicester, 1990); Brown, *Book of Cerne*, esp. pp. 76–80.

Barberini Gospels.[11] The influence of Carolingian palaeography and codicology has likewise been discerned in later manuscripts of the 'Tiberius' group.[12]

Such cultural cross-references would accord with the political and ecclesiastical climate of Mercia during this period in which Kings of Mercia, Offa and Coenwulf, went to some lengths to pursue their aspirations of parity with Charlemagne, and in which the Mercian episcopacy sought Carolingian analogies and support for their attempts to stave off lay encroachment of their property and privileges.[13] Diplomatic gifts, such as the Coptic textiles and Avar treasure sent by Charlemagne to Offa, would have led to an increase in shared access to artistic models and motifs. Superficial similarities between the figures in the Barberini Gospels and those in early Carolingian works such as the Godescalc Evangelistary could equally as well be attributed to a shared Carolingian/Mercian appropriation of cultural styles and visual metaphors, as to any more specific relationship. The advanced painting technique of the Barberini Gospels finds its context within the Insular tradition just as easily as within a Carolingian or Italian one.[14] Proficiency of painting technique and command of a naturalistic figure style do not necessarily indicate Continental production — something that de Rossi effectively demonstrated in the case of the Codex Amiatinus, thought until the late nineteenth century to have been the work of Italo-Byzantine craftsmen rather than of the Monkwearmouth/Jarrow scriptorium, by virtue of the Mediterranean style of its painting and script.[15] 'Good' does not necessarily mean classicizing, and classicizing does not necessarily mean Continental.

The name 'Wigbald' in the colophon of the Barberini Gospels might help to locate its master scribe or patron. Laurence Nees has proposed identification with

---

[11] See M. O. Budny, 'London, British Library, MS Royal 1.E.vi: The Anatomy of an Anglo-Saxon Bible Fragment' (unpublished doctoral dissertation, University of London, 1985), and Brown, 'Mercian Manuscripts?'.

[12] See Michelle P. Brown, 'Continental Symptoms in Insular Codicology: Historical Perspectives', in *Pergament*, ed. by P. Rück (Sigmaringen, 1991), pp. 57–62; *Book of Cerne*, pp. 47–48, 56; and 'Mercian Manuscripts?'.

[13] See Nicholas Brooks, *The Early History of the Church of Canterbury: Christ Church from 597 to 1066*, Studies in the Early History of Britain (Leicester, 1984), pp. 111–54; Catherine Cubitt, *Anglo-Saxon Church Councils 650–850* (London, 1995); Brown, *Book of Cerne*, pp. 164–65, 182–83. See also the introduction to *Mercia*, ed. by Brown and Farr.

[14] On which see the analysis of the painting technique and materials used in the Lindisfarne Gospels, in Brown, *Lindisfarne Gospels*, pp. 275–98, 430–51.

[15] See G. B. de Rossi, *La Bibbia offerta da Ceolfrido Abbate al Sepolchro di S. Pietro: Al Sommo Pontefice Leone XIII omaggio giubilare della Biblioteca Vaticana* (Vatican City, 1888).

a Wigbald who served in Charlemagne's early chancery, at the time that the Godescalc Evangelistary was being made in the 780s.[16] If this were the case, it is extremely surprising that there are so few signs of Continental influence in the script of the four scribes who penned the Barberini Gospels. To argue successfully for its production on the Continent one would have to postulate the existence of an early ninth-century Continental scriptorium, its output as yet otherwise unrepresented in the surviving record, staffed entirely by recent English recruits adhering to their indigenous scribal customs. Other than their common tendency to favour uncial 'a', which must be a scriptorium preference, and the habit of Scribe A, and occasionally Scribe C, of intruding a hooked 'T', there are no overtly Continental palaeographical features — certainly none consistent with the involvement of a Carolingian chancery scribe. The preparation of the membrane is inconsistent and may indicate experimentation with late antique/Continental practices, or just lack of scriptorium experience, but it does not indicate full familiarity with Continental manufacturing techniques. Such experiments may be observed in other Mercian books of the period.[17]

An ultimate debt to the fully fledged Insular style and painting technique of the Lindisfarne Gospels likewise led Françoise Henry to associate the colophon of the Barberini Gospels with Hygebeald, Bishop of Lindisfarne in the late eighth century.[18] However, the name Wigbald is not such an unusual one as she and Nees might suggest. It occurs within several documented English contexts from the period: Wigbeald, monk, in the Durham *Liber uitae* (London, British Library, Cotton MS Domitian A. VII), copied around 840 probably by the Lindisfarne community on Holy Island or Norham-upon-Tweed, whose floruit could have been any time before *c.* 840; Wigbeald or Vibald, count, who witnessed a West Saxon charter in around 670 (preserved in a copy of *c.* 795); Wigbeald or Wibald, a Mercian nobleman around 850, mentioned in the Evesham Chronicle. The Northumbrian monk and the Mercian nobleman cannot be entirely ruled out as

---

[16] See L. Nees, 'Godescalc's Career and the Problems of "Influence"', in *Under the Influence: The Concept of Influence in the Study of Illuminated Manuscripts*, ed. by Alixe Bovey (Turnhout, 2005). In a personal communication, Florentine Mütherich has expressed her scepticism concerning the suggestion of Continental manufacture for the Barberini Gospels and for the identification of the Wigbald in the Barberini Gospels' colophon as a Carolingian figure. She also kindly drew my attention to the reference to the Carolingian Wigbald, a member of the Carolingian royal chancery, in Josef Fleckenstein, *Die Hofkapelle der deutschen Könige*, 2 vols (Stuttgart, 1959), I, 94.

[17] See Brown, 'Continental Symptoms in Insular Codicology'.

[18] *The Book of Kells* (London, 1974), pp. 163, 215, and 220.

recipients of the prayers besought for 'Uuigbaldo' in the Barberini Gospels' colophon and indeed the person commemorated may not now be identifiable from other sources. Nonetheless, the most pertinent of these known individuals is perhaps Wigbeald or Wigbald (the latter representing the closest orthographical parallel for the name-form as it actually occurs in the Barberini Gospels), who is mentioned in a charter of 786 x 796 in which Abbot Beonna of Medeshamstede granted land at Swineshead, Lincs., to Cuthbert *princeps*.[19] Wigbald is cited in that charter as priest (*presbyter*) and 'arc'. If this reading is correct, he may have been an archdeacon (an office which the abbreviation 'arc' often denotes in inscriptions) or, less likely, an archcantor of Peterborough (then known as Medeshamstede), an important monastery and minster in eastern Mercia which provides a good stylistic context for the illumination of the Barberini Gospels, at around the time that it is likely to have been made. However, another proposed reading is 'an'c', which would suggest that he may have been a priest and hermit (anchorite). Peterborough possessed several anchorages, such as Thorney, during the early Middle Ages.[20] The latter form occurs in the older copy but remains inconclusive as its scribe has mistaken some earlier Anglo-Saxon letter forms (confusing 'v' and 'b', 't' and 'c', and perhaps in this case 'r' and 'n'). The involvement of anchorites in Insular book production is parallelled, however, by St Canice who copied the Gospels single handedly and Billfrith whose metalwork adorned the Lindisfarne Gospels.

Peterborough was a seventh-century Mercian royal foundation, subject to influence from Augustine's mission in Canterbury, to Frankish missionary activity in East Anglia, to Northumbrian control under Oswy and the influence of

[19] For details of this charter, see P. H. Sawyer, *Anglo-Saxon Charters, an Annotated List and Bibliography* (London, 1968), no. 1412. It survives only in copies of mid-twelfth-century date (London, Society of Antiquaries, MS 60, fol. 41) and thirteenth-century date (Peterborough, D.C., 1, fol. 131) but has been accepted by Sawyer and Whitelock as genuine. It is printed in W. de Grey Birch, *Cartularium Saxonicum*, 3 vols and index (London, 1885–99; repr. 1964), no. 271. This form of the personal name Wigbald was cited by W. G. Searle, *Onomasticon Anglosaxonicum: A List of Anglo-saxon Proper Names From the Time of Bede to That of King John* (Cambridge, 1897), p. 487, along with the other occurrences of the name in its various forms, as rehearsed above. The Prosopography of Anglo-Saxon England Database (<http://eagle.cch.kcl. ac.uk:8080/pase/index.jsp>) is being compiled, but to date the only Wigbald listed is the scribe mentioned in the colophon of the Barberini Gospels. No Wigbealds or variant name-forms appear.

[20] See also comments by S. Kelly, S. Keynes, and S. Miller on the British Academy and Royal Historical Society Database of Anglo-Saxon Charters, for which see <http://www.trin.cam.ac.uk/ chartwww/>. Allowance has to be made, however, for the twelfth- and thirteenth-century dates of the extant copies of the charter and for corruptions of both the personal name and the role during the process of transmission.

Northumbrian missionaries such as Chad and Cedd, and of Irishmen such as Diuma, first bishop of the Mercians.[21] It was an important centre of royal administration, frequently visited by Offa and other rulers, and maintained close ties with the Mercian heartland and West Midlands. Breedon-on-the-hill was one of its daughter houses, founded in the late seventh century, and they retained a close affiliation. This would account for the shared exoticism, technique, and motifs of their sculptural traditions. The sculptures from Peterborough and the nearby houses of Castor (a convent founded for Mercian royal women) and Fletton are made from stone quarried at nearby Barnack — the same stone used for some of the Breedon sculptures on the other side of Mercia.

If one were to seek an appropriate candidate for the person who instigated the production of the Barberini Gospels amongst those known from documentary sources to have borne the name mentioned in the colophon, then the Wigbald who was a priest and archdeacon or anchorite of Peterborough, or perhaps one of its anchorites, around 800 is surely the favourite. The record is known to be so fragmentary that this cannot be conclusive, but such a scenario would align particularly well with the evidence of stylistic affiliations and textual background which point to production within early ninth-century Southumbria, in a Mercian centre with Northumbrian, Irish, early Frankish, and Carolingian affiliations. Peterborough was still actively represented in the documentary field in the mid-ninth century, but was destroyed by Viking forces around 870, being refounded as a Benedictine house in the tenth century by St Æthelwold.[22] If the Barberini Gospels were a Peterborough book, it can be assumed to have left before or during the Viking raid, travelling to another, safer part of England or the Continent, or to have been seized as Viking loot and subsequently redeemed. The next substantial evidence for its provenance would point to it being in Italy, perhaps as early as the twelfth century.[23] There are no other internal indications of the manuscript's whereabouts, until a number of inscriptions and *probationes pennae* (trials

[21] On the history of Peterborough at this period, see Pauline Stafford, *The East Midlands in the Early Middle Ages* (Leicester, 1985), and F. M. Stenton, 'Medeshamstede and its Colonies', in *Preparatory to Anglo-Saxon England, being the Collected Papers of Frank Merry Stenton*, ed. by F. M. Stenton (Oxford, 1970), pp. 179–92.

[22] See Stafford, *The East Midlands*.

[23] See D. H. Wright on the Barberini Gospels, forthcoming, although the specific relationship he proposes between the display script of the Barberini Gospels and that of a twelfth-century Italian manuscript, the Mantua Missal, are not close enough to demonstrate that it was this specific Insular Gospelbook, rather than another volume containing the distinctive lacertine 'Tiberius' group display script, that was available as a model.

of the pen-nib) were added by an Italian hand during the late fourteenth or fifteenth century. The next annotations were added once the volume had entered the collection of Cardinal Francesco Barberini (1597–1679).[24] It was purchased for the Biblioteca Apostolica Vaticana by Pope Leo XIII in 1902.

It is noteworthy that the Barberini Gospels manuscript is one of only a few de luxe Insular Gospelbooks to mark lections — that is, the gospel readings appropriate to particular liturgical feast-days, confirming active use within the liturgy — as one might expect if its manufacture was undertaken partly by, and/or for, a cleric occupying a major liturgical role in an important cathedral.[25] When discussing lection marks and layout in the Barberini Gospels and the Book of Kells, Carol Farr notes that 'The Barberini Gospels, therefore, combine a paragraph or section division with the archaic Irish block layout […] common in Insular gospel manuscripts created after the mid-eighth century and can be seen on many pages in the Book of Kells'; but notes that although Barberini marks the non-Roman lection for Holy Thursday ('prima autem die azemorum', fol. 112ᵛ) it does not follow Kells and other books from the Irish tradition in their other emphases upon Old Latin Gospel divisions.[26] This would tend to imply that, like the minor decoration and display script of the 'Tiberius' group manuscripts, which also shares a generic similarity and some ancestral roots with the repertoire of the Book of Kells and other late eighth-/early ninth-century Irish books,[27] the Barberini Gospels had inherited some features that were also current in other books of around 800 which were more conservative in their adherence to the Insular tradition (such as

---

[24] For further discussion of the book's provenance, see the forthcoming studies by D. H. Wright and myself.

[25] On liturgical lections, see A. Chavasse, *Le sacramentaire Gélasien (Vaticanus Reginensis 316) sacramentaire presbytéral en usage dans les titres romains au VIIᵉ siècle*, Bibliothèque de théologie, 4, Histoire de la théologie, 1 (Tournai, 1958) and *Les Lectionnaires Romains de la Messe au VIIᵉ et au VIIIᵉ Siècle: Sources et derivés*, 2 vols, Spicilegii Friburgensis, Subsidia, 22 (Fribourg-en-Suisse, 1993). On aspects of lections within Insular manuscripts, see Carol Farr, *The Book of Kells: Its Function and Audience* (London, 1997), pp. 42–43. On lections in Insular manuscripts, see also Éamonn Ó Carragáin, *Ritual and the Rood: Liturgical Images and the Old English Poems of the 'Dream of the Rood' Tradition* (London, 2005). On relationships with Continental and Insular lections, see Farr, *Book of Kells*, Appendix I. A codicological note and discussion of the lection marks in the Barberini Gospels is included in my forthcoming study.

[26] On which see Carol Farr, 'Commas and Columba, Power and Patrick: Restating the Archaic in the Book of Kells', in *Omnia Disce: Medieval Studies in Memory of Leonard Boyle, O.P.*, ed. by Anne J. Duggan and others (Aldershot, 2005), pp. 129–54 (pp. 132–33, 135–36).

[27] On which see Brown, 'Echoes'.

the Book of Kells and the Macregol Gospels) and shared some of their evolu-
tionary traits and contemporary trends, but was not directly related to them.

The archdeacon, or archcantor, would have been responsible for reading, or
singing, passages from the Gospels on high days and holy days, bearing the Gospelbook before him in liturgical procession and using the decoration and layout to
help him to navigate the text during readings.[28] It is tempting to think of Wigbald
of Peterborough either serving as a priest and hermit, like St Cuthbert, and
likewise inspiring the manufacture of a splendid illuminated copy of the Gospels,
or, as archdeacon or archcantor, perhaps personally overseeing the production of
the impressive Gospelbook that he would carry to the high altar of the cathedral,
and probably functioning as the master-scribe himself — thereby combining the
meditative, prayerful role of the scribe with that of the liturgical lector. As the
early monastic founder Cassiodorus exhorted scribes in his commentary on Psalm
44/45. 1–2 (a work known in Insular circles) and in his *Institutiones*, Wigbald's
role in respect of the Barberini Gospels would have been to preach with the
fingers, and to unleash the tongue (Cassiodorus, *De institutione divinarum
litterarum*, ch. 30).[29]

Symbolic Meaning and Exegetical References in the Decoration of the Barberini Gospels

The realistic figural style of the evangelist portraits, with their stately Byzantine-
style author portraits, initially conceals the layers of symbolic meaning that wait

---

[28] On the role of the deacon and its reflection in Insular art, including a possible depiction of
a deacon at the head of the Matthew incipit page, fol. 29ʳ, of the Book of Kells, see Carol Farr,
'Liturgical Influences on the Decoration of the Book of Kells', in *Studies in Insular Art and
Archaeology*, ed. by R. T. Farrell and Catherine E. Karkov, American Early Medieval Studies, 1
(Oxford, OH, 1991), pp. 127–41, and 'Textual Structure, Decoration and Interpretative Images
in the Book of Kells', in *The Book of Kells*, ed. by O'Mahony, pp. 437–49 (p. 449). See also R. Reynolds, *The Ordinals of Christ from their Origins to the Twelfth Century*, Beiträge zur Geschichte
und Quellenkunde des Mittelaltersm, 7 (Berlin, 1978), pp. 56–68; Isidore, *De ecclesiasticis officiis*,
2.7, ed. by C. Lawson, CCSL, 113 (Turnhout, 1989), pp. 64–69; and Bede, *In Ezram et
Neemiam*, I, ed. by D. Hurst, CCSL, 119A (Turnhout, 1969), pp. 235–392, 277, lines 14446–63.

[29] For the *Institutiones*, see *PL*, 70, 1144–45. For discussion of the spirituality underlying the
work of Insular scribes, see, for example, Brown, '"In the Beginning was the Word"' and *Lindisfarne Gospels*, esp. pp. 397–99, and Jennifer O'Reilly, 'The Library of Scripture: Views from the
Vivarium and Wearmouth-Jarrow', in *New Offerings, Ancient Treasures: Studies in Medieval Art
for George Henderson*, ed. by Paul Binski and William Noel (Stroud, 2001), pp. 3–39.

to be unearthed by the visually and textually literate reader, in true Insular exegetical fashion. The Chi-rho page (fol. 18ʳ; see Fig. 3) is a highly symbolic component of the Barberini Gospels' decorative programme. As in the other Insular books in which such a page occurs, it was probably accorded this special dignity by virtue of the importance of the sacred name, representing Christ himself and serving as a potent symbol of his Incarnation (coupled with a liturgical function). In Barberini this symbolism is emphasized by the inhabited vine-scroll that springs from the 'Chi' itself, the birds and beasts that occupy its fronds and partake of the grapes — the Eucharistic sacrifice of Christ's redeeming blood.[30]

Immediately above the vine-scroll, forming part of a decorative escutcheon of Celtic La Tène spiralwork which terminates the upper left-hand stroke of the 'X', is the stylized head of a bull, seen in plan (from above) in classic La Tène fashion and imbued with an ornamental ambiguity, its horns transforming into bird heads.[31] This may be an intentional reference to the evangelist symbol of St Luke, one of the two Gospel writers who symbolize the human aspect of Christ's nature — the calf or bull representing the sacrificial victim of the Crucifixion.[32] Similar decorative allusions to the evangelist symbols are to be found in the decorated incipit pages of the Lindisfarne Gospels.[33] Other features of note here include a visual emphasis upon roundels containing quadruple spirals and the frequent quadruplets of whirling bird heads, recalling the use of four whirling devices in the carpet pages of the Lindisfarne Gospels that have been compared to the imagery of the evangelists as four flaming wheels in the Apocalypse.[34] The frequent pairing of beasts on this page, and elsewhere in the volume, for example the frame of the

---

[30] For a discussion of the possible significance of the stylized diamond-shaped human head at the foot of the 'Chi', see Carol Farr, 'Sign at the Crossroads', in *Shaping Understanding: Form and Order in the Anglo-Saxon World, 400–1100: A Conference held at the British Museum, 7–9 March 2002*, ed. by L. Webster (forthcoming).

[31] For a similar motif in the Lindisfarne Gospels' Mark incipit page, see Brown, *Lindisfarne Gospels*, p. 337.

[32] On the Insular tradition of depicting the evangelists and their symbols, see Brown, *Book of Cerne*, pp. 87–114, and 'Embodying Exegesis: Depictions of the Evangelists in Insular Manuscripts', in *Le Isole Britanniche e Roma in Età Romanobarbarica*, ed. by Anna Maria Luiselli Fadda and Éamonn Ó Carragáin, Biblioteca di Cultura Romanobarbarica, 1 (Rome, 1998), pp. 109–28, and *Lindisfarne Gospels*, pp. 346–63; see also O'Reilly, 'The Library of Scripture'. I am greatly indebted to Éamonn Ó Carragáin for first encouraging me to contemplate this theme and for pointing me in the right direction when I was studying the miniatures in the Book of Cerne.

[33] See Brown, *Lindisfarne Gospels*, pp. 333, 338–39, and 343–44.

[34] See Brown, *Lindisfarne Gospels*, pp. 328–29.

Figure 3. Chi-rho page, Barberini Gospels. Vatican City, Biblioteca Apostolica Vaticana, MS Barb. lat. 570, fol. 18ʳ. © The Biblioteca Apostolica Vaticana. By kind permission of the Prefect of the Biblioteca Apostolica Vaticana.

Matthew miniature (see Fig. 2), might also be related to the sort of number symbolism encountered in the Lindisfarne Gospels and on other monuments, such as the Bewcastle Cross, in which Christ is recognized between two beasts, in fulfilment of Habakkuk 3. 3 (Old Latin version), 'between two living creatures shall you know him'.[35] The curious human-headed winged bipeds at the foot of the 'I' seem to sniff the scent of the plants they hold to their faces (recalling a similar motif at the head of one of the Canon Tables in the Cutbercht Gospels, fol. 18ʳ), whilst the two beasts at the curves of the feet of the 'P' and 'I' bow, as if in homage, their tongues licking the words below. Perhaps an allusion is intended to the five senses, an iconography expressed more fully in a late ninth-century piece of Southumbrian metalwork, the Fuller Brooch.[36] The crossing of the strokes of the 'X' is formed of a diamond-shaped panel (similar to that in the Book of Kells, which may in turn be a visual echo of the star-motif — heralding Christ's birth — behind the crossing of the 'X' in the Lindisfarne Gospels). It contains a lively little figure — a winged quadruped with a grotesque human head, looking back over its shoulder at the sacred monogram. It is reminiscent of another mythical grotesque, occupying the bow of the 'E' that introduces the Passion narrative from St Matthew's Gospel in the Book of Cerne (fol. 3ʳ). The latter has been interpreted as a manticore, the human-headed lion which was the mythical harbinger of death, according to the *Physiologus* and the *Marvels of the East*, and which here presages the Crucifixion.[37] The Barberini beast seems to be a hybrid of the manticore and the winged senmurv — a hybrid creature from Persian mythology consisting of a winged biped with a fish or serpent tail, which represents the symbolic union of earth, air, and sea, and which features in another 'Tiberius' group manuscript of early ninth-century date, the Royal Prayerbook (London, British Library, Royal MS 2. A. XX, fol. 17ʳ). The meaning of this curious denizen of Barberini's menagerie may be to serve as a reminder of Christ's impending sacrifice at the moment at which his birth is first announced in the Gospels, and to celebrate the reconciliation and harmonization of Creation that these events secured.

---

[35] Pointed out by Éamonn Ó Carragáin in Éamonn Ó Carragáin, Jane Hawkes, and Ross Trench-Jellicoe, 'John the Baptist and the *Agnus Dei*: Ruthwell (and Bewcastle) Revisited', *Antiquaries Journal*, 81 (2001), 131–53; discussed in relation to the Lindisfarne Gospels by Brown, *Lindisfarne Gospels*, p. 328.

[36] See *Making of England*, ed. by Webster and Backhouse, no. 257. See also Charles Wright, 'Why Sight Holds Flowers: An Apocryphal Source for the Iconography of the Alfred Jewel and Fuller Brooch', in this volume, and Figure 15 there.

[37] See Brown, *Book of Cerne*, p. 118.

Similarly, the *Physiologus* may help with the interpretation of the decorated initial introducing Jerome's 'Novum Opus' — his letter to Pope Damasus in which he explained his temerity in attempting a new translation in the vulgar language of the day, Latin (the resulting edition being known accordingly as the 'Vulgate'). In Barberini the letter begins with an initial 'B' (giving prominence to part of the text which is usually treated as an introductory rubric) followed by a string of black-ribbon lettering with biting beast-head (fol. 7ʳ; see Fig. 4). The bow of the 'B', which is formed of panels of interlace on a black background (resembling the silver-niello metalwork favoured in Southumbria at this time) capped with a Celtic spiralwork terminal, ends

Figure 4. Incipit of Jerome's 'Nouum Opus', Barberini Gospels. Vatican City, Biblioteca Apostolica Vaticana, MS Barb. lat. 570, fol. 7ʳ. © The Biblioteca Apostolica Vaticana. By kind permission of the Prefect of the Biblioteca Apostolica Vaticana.

in a frontal beast-head. This looks rather like a cat, an impression reinforced by the small quadruped that is clutched, limp, in its mouth. Beneath this quadruped, which resembles a mouse, are three trefoil foliate lobes — perhaps with Trinitarian implications. These sprout from the head of a grotesque mask, which is bearded and sports four volutes or horns on its crown, the uppermost with foliate terminals, like small trees, and the lower flowing and curved, like rivers. The eyes of this creature peer above the lower part of the bow of the 'B', which obscures its mouth. Henderson has interpreted this caricature as a satyr, muzzled and rendered dumb by the Word, and perhaps even intended to represent the detractors whom Jerome anticipated would decry his work and whom he relied upon Pope Damasus, recipient of the letter, to silence.[38]

But what of the cat and mouse? A cat features in the border of the 'Quoniam' page in the Lindisfarne Gospels (fol. 139ʳ) and has been interpreted as the threat

---

[38] See George Henderson, 'The Barberini Gospels (Rome, Vatican, Biblioteca Apostolica. Barberini Lat. 570) as a Paradigm of Insular Art', in *Pattern and Purpose in Insular Art: Proceedings of the Fourth International Conference on Insular Art held at the National Museum & Galley, Cardiff 3–6 September 1998*, ed. by Mark Redknap and others (Oxford, 2001), pp. 157–69 (pp. 160–61).

of evil, waiting to pounce on the unwary, in the form of the solemn procession of birds who march towards it, several of which it has already eaten, or as Cruithne, the Celtic equivalent of Cerberus, guardian of the entrance to the underworld.[39] Cats also feature in the Book of Kells, notably in one detail on the Chi-rho page where two cats pin down two mice who are consuming a disc (the Eucharistic bread), with two more mice seated on the cats' backs, an ambiguous iconography, interpreted by Meehan as an image of peaceful co-existence.[40] I would tend to favour an interpretation for the Kells image as the faithful (the mice) partaking of the Eucharist which protects them from the threat of evil (the cats) through fellowship with other believers in the form of the communion of saints, represented by other mice overcoming the cats upon whose backs they perch. It should always be remembered, however, that multivalence can be the key when contemplating the Insular mindset: why have only one literal interpretation when you can also simultaneously have several symbolic ones?

The threat of evil would certainly also work as an interpretation for this motif in the Barberini context. Alternatively, perhaps this is not a cat and mouse at all, but a bear. The familiarity of western artists with the depiction of exotic fauna was sketchy to say the least, and the characteristics of more local creatures were often intruded. According to the *Physiologus*, the bear licks its young into shape.[41] The 'mouse' might therefore represent the unformed young — in this context the plethora of partially formed textual rescensions of the Gospels in circulation, which Jerome sought to 'lick into shape' by his work on the Vulgate, partaking during his work of the threefold sustenance of the Trinity in the form of the trilobate plant. The Physiologan imagery relates to God's act of Creation, shaping Man from dust and placing him within a garden in which trees grew from the ground and a river issued into four 'headstreams' (Genesis 2. 4–14). The 'satyr' mask might likewise represent God's creation of land and sea from the formless face of the earth, trees and four rivers (horns) issuing from it. The tiny, partially formed creature eating the trilobate plants might furthermore illustrate Genesis 1. 29–30, 'I give you every seed-bearing plant on the face of the earth [. . .]. And to [. . .] everything that has the breath of life in it — I give every green plant for

[39] See Brown, *Lindisfarne Gospels*, pp. 341 and 391 n. 163. On Christian cat imagery in general, see S. Lewis, 'Sacred Calligraphy: The Chi Rho Page in the Book of Kells', *Traditio*, 36 (1980), 139–58.

[40] See Bernard Meehan, *The Book of Kells* (London, 1994), p. 45, pl. 49; but for other, less benign, interpretations, see Lewis, 'Sacred Calligraphy'.

[41] See Florence McCulloch, *Medieval Latin and French Bestiaries* (Chapel Hill, 1962).

food'. The bow of the 'B' noticeably bisects the mask into two parts, perhaps explicable in relation to Genesis 1. 6–10 in which God divides the land, bearing vegetation, and the seas by the sky, the movement of air and the celestial bodies of the heavens being evocatively portrayed by the swirl of the letter itself and the whirling spirals at its head. Thus Jerome's work in shaping the Word of God into the Vulgate with the account of Christ's life-giving sacrifice, for the sustenance of God's Creation, may here be intended to be related symbolically to God's own initial, life-giving act of Creation — for 'In the beginning was the Word, and the Word was with God, and the Word was God' (John 1. 1).

One of the most complex pieces of symbolic decoration in the Barberini Gospels occurs at the very start of the book, on the opening page of the Canon Tables (fol. 1ʳ; see Plate 1). The numbers which embody the Word of God contained in the Gospels and which trace their concordance — where they agree and disagree — are contained on this page within an architectural arcade. In early medieval art the Canon Tables were often represented thus, perhaps symbolizing the entrance to the Holy of Holies, the chancel, wherein were enshrined the sacred numbers of the Gospel passages — the embodiment of Christ himself, the Word.[42] In the tympana of the arcades, surmounting the four columns of numbers, are half-length busts of the four evangelist symbols with attributes — haloes, wings, and books.[43] They are labelled underneath, in uncials by Scribe A, who also penned the numbers, but these labels do not accord with the depictions. Matthew is correctly symbolized by a bearded man and John by an eagle, but the symbols for Mark and Luke are reversed, with Luke's calf or bull above Mark's caption and Mark's lion above that for Luke. This mislabeling may have arisen in copying from an exemplar, for the symbols are paired, each couple facing one another in dialogue, as in the 'beast canon tables' of the Book of Kells or those in the first of the two Maasaik Gospels,[44] which arrange the symbols in differing groupings to accord with the varied agreements signalled by the concordance numbers below, an Insular tradition associated with the Irish sage, Ailerán the Wise.[45] If an artistic

---

[42] See Carl Nordenfalk, *Die Spatantiken Kanontafeln*, 2 vols, Göteborgs Kungl. Vetenskaps- och Vitterhets-Samhälles handligar (Göteborg, 1938), and Brown, *Lindisfarne Gospels*, pp. 166–67, 179–82, and 301.

[43] On Insular evangelist imagery, see Brown, *Book of Cerne*, pp. 87–114, and *Lindisfarne Gospels*, pp. 346–63, and O'Reilly, 'The Library of Scripture'.

[44] Alexander, *Insular Manuscripts*, no. 22.

[45] See P. McGurk's discussion of the Canon Tables in *The Book of Kells, MS 58, Trinity College Library Dublin*, facsimile and commentary, ed. by Peter Fox and others, 2 vols (Lucerne,

model had depicted Luke facing leftwards and Mark to the right, the 'Artist' may have retained this formula in order to preserve the effect of colloquy between the gospel writers. However, it surely would not have been beyond so gifted an artist to have reversed the direction of the two heads in question. Other explanations have included reference to an alternative ordering of the symbols by Iranaeus, but this ascribed the lion to Matthew and the man with Mark, a different transposition to that seen in Barberini's evangelist symbols.[46]

More plausible, perhaps, is the possibility that the pairings were intentionally designed in order to emphasize the two complementary and indivisible aspects of the nature of Christ, symbolized by the four Gospels and the evangelist symbols. Matthew's man and Luke's calf signified the humanity of Christ, his incarnation and sacrifice; Mark's lion and John's eagle signified his divinity, his resurrection, kingship, and Second Coming as Judge. This interpretation was based upon the visions of Ezekiel (chs 1 and 10) and the Apocalypse or Book of Revelation (ch. 4) and was a theme explored in exegetical works by Gregory the Great (*Homily on Ezekiel*, Book I, Homily 8, chs 20–21)[47] and by Bede in his *Explanatio Apocalypsis* (Bk I, ch. 4) and his *De tabernaculo* (Bk I, ch. 4). The theological implications were explored visually throughout the Insular world, and with particular complexity and subtlety in the Lindisfarne Gospels, the Book of Kells, the Book of Armagh, and the Book of Cerne.[48] A similar pairing is observed in the Lindisfarne Gospels, where Matthew and Luke, symbols of Christ's vulnerability, are depicted as bearded and ageing in mortal fashion, whilst Mark and John, symbols of Christ's triumph and immortality, are shown youthful and clean-shaven.[49] The captions do not in fact refer to the individual evangelists, but are part of one continuous inscription, spread across the four columns: 'Canon Primus in quo Quatt(uor), Matheus, Marcus, Lucas, Iohannis.' The names are placed in relation to the columns of numbers below and signify the Gospels to which they belong.

1990), pp. 52–57. See also N. Netzer, 'The Origin of the Beast Canon Tables Reconsidered', in *The Book of Kells*, ed. by O'Mahony, pp. 322–32.

[46] On Iranaeus's possible influence on Bede in this respect, see Brown, *Lindisfarne Gospels*, p. 363.

[47] See *PL*, 76, 815.

[48] See, for example, Brown, *Book of Cerne*, pp. 87–114, 'Embodying Exegesis', and *Lindisfarne Gospels*, pp. 346–63; also Carol Farr, 'Lection and Interpretation: The Liturgical and Exegetical Background of the Illustrations in the Book of Kells' (unpublished doctoral dissertation, University of Texas at Austin, 1989) and *The Book of Kells*; and O'Reilly, 'Library of Scripture'.

[49] See Brown, *Lindisfarne Gospels*, pp. 49–350.

Above, the four symbols are engaged in their own eternal colloquy and introduce the Tables as a whole, rather than relating specifically to the contents of Canon I on the first page.

Perhaps the most remarkable detail of this page is the naked male priapic figure who crouches further down the central column of the first Canon Table (see Plate 1). This shivering soul clutches his beard and touches his genitals (an ancient protective gesture), defending them from the beasts which advance from the forest of interlace to attack his head and bare buttocks. Henderson has interpreted him as a denizen of Hell or the arch-heretic Arius, citing some interesting iconographic parallels: wrestlers pulling one another's beards in the 'Quoniam' page of the Book of Kells (others that might usefully be added in the same book are the naked, tattooed, and possibly Pictish warrior who is attacked by a lion at the head of the Mark incipit page, fol. 51^r, perhaps signifying the triumph over secular power of the celestial kingship of the lion of Judah, the resurrected Christ, symbolized by Mark's lion; and the male figure entwined with beasts at the head of the Lucan genealogy on fol. 63^r — a living, inhabited family tree); a squatting figure on a broken cross-arm from Strathmartine (Angus); wrestlers, their buttocks attacked by serpents, on the Pittensorn panel from Perthshire; and a figure in Hell at the base of the Rothbury Cross in Northumbria.[50] Other interpretations also present themselves. The beard is a well-known symbol of masculinity. In contemporary Welsh law-codes a man could divorce his wife for casting aspersions on his beard (she, in turn, could divorce him for obesity), and beard-pullers are to be found in early medieval art, from the pages of the Book of Kells and the carved panels of Irish high crosses to Viking metalwork.[51] An apotropaic function may have been intended — as in protecting itself, the figure also protects the volume from evil and theft, in the manner of the anathemas that are often inscribed into medieval books.

In an age when the conversion to Christianity was an active force and paganism lingered on, the parameters of old and new faiths often becoming blurred, the protective role of ancient fertility gods, such as the Germanic Frikko/Old Norse Freyr would have been well known and ripe for conversion into a Christian context. The phallus had performed an ancient, amuletic function in the Greek and Roman world and in northern European prehistory. In a Christian context it

[50] See Henderson, 'Barberini Gospels', pp. 163–65.

[51] For a discussion of the iconography of the beard, see P. Gjaedar, 'The Beard as an Iconographical Feature in the Viking Period and the Early Middle Ages', *Acta Archaeologica*, 35 (1964), 95–114.

could also function in connection with the cults of saints, such as that of Saints Cosmas and Damian (whose church, adjacent to the forum, would have been much frequented by Anglo-Saxon pilgrims), with waxen phalli being sold to pilgrims in Isernia as ex-voto offerings to the physician-saints.[52] The figure might also signify the ever-present threat of evil, the forces of chaos waiting to engulf humanity and kept at bay by the Word of God — encapsulated in the sacred numbers of the Canon Tables which themselves embodied that Word.[53] As Weir and Jerman pointed out in their discussion of such sexually charged iconography, it was not erotic in function, 'but rather the reverse, that these extraordinarily frank carvings were more probably an element in the medieval Church's campaign against immorality, and that they were not intended to inflame the passions but rather to allay them'.[54] Such a figure reminds the reader to abandon temptations of the flesh in the face of the Gospels and the promise of salvation they contain, and provides protection against such temptation, rather like the sheelagh-na-gigs which adorned many a Romanesque church in Britain and Ireland (such as Kilpeck). Our modern tunnel vision and inverted prudery in respect of sexual imagery was not shared by the medieval world.

Above this figure is an elegant, bearded male head, with penetrating eyes and facial features carefully modelled by the 'Artist', serving as the capital to the central column (see Plate 1). How he is to be interpreted is uncertain, but Henderson has suggested that he represents Christ, based upon analogy with the Continental Flavigny Gospels and the early eleventh-century Anglo-Saxon Eadui Codex.[55] Another possibility is that he represents an apostle, as do the human busts in roundels set above the arcades in the two Insular-style Gospelbooks in Maasaik,[56] or in the Trier Gospels from Echternach (Trier, Domschatz, Cod. 61).[57] Like that of the crouching figure below, his beard is threatened by two biting beasts. Human-headed masks are known in just such an architectural context from the ancient Egyptian period onward. Henderson cites an interesting example of grotesque masks, like those in the Book of Cerne, on a roman entablature from

---

[52] See Ruth Mellinkoff, *The Search for Powerful Protection* (forthcoming), ch. 6, for this and other sexual and scatological motifs and themes.

[53] See Brown, *Lindisfarne Gospels*, pp. 166–67, 179–82, and 301.

[54] Anthony Weir and James Jerman, *Images of Lust: Sexual Carvings on Medieval Churches* (London, 1986).

[55] See Henderson, 'Barberini Gospels', p. 163.

[56] Alexander, *Insular Manuscripts*, no. 22, pls 88–95, and no. 23, pls 96–103.

[57] Alexander, *Insular Manuscripts*, no. 26, pl. 108.

Neumagen, near to the Insular foundation of Echternach,[58] and lion-masks some-times feature amongst the Canon Tables of Carolingian Court School manu-scripts and in those of the Royal Bible from Canterbury. In an Insular context, human and animal heads are found at the heads of the architectural columns of the Canon Tables in London, British Library, Royal MS 1. B. VII (which is part of the Italo-Northumbrian textual family but which may have been made in Southumbria and which exhibits Merovingian influence in its display script), and in the Maaseik Gospels (Maaseik, Church of St Catherine, s.n., fols 5ʳ–5ᵛ; prob-ably made on the Continent in the eighth century, under Northumbrian influ-ence).[59] These offer the best parallels for the sketchy heads and masks with which Scribe A sought to adorn some of the other Canon Tables in Barberini. There are also grotesque anthropomorphic masks at the heads of the columns flanking the image of St John in the Book of Cerne (fol. 31ᵛ) and biting the corners of the display panel on fol. 32ʳ. A clean-shaven androgenous mask is found at the head of the initial 'I' opening St Mark's Gospel (his roaring lion symbol forming the foot of the 'I') in a Gospelbook thought to have been made in Northumbria in the mid-eighth century, Durham, Cathedral Library, MS A. II. 16, fol. 37ʳ.[60] A Continental parallel for this feature can be found in the Codex Millenarius (Krems-münster, Stiftsbibliothek, MS Cim.1), with a human head, representing St Mat-thew's symbol, capping the head of the 'L' of his gospel's 'Liber' incipit (fol. 19ʳ).[61]

In its details and function Durham MS A. II. 16 initial offers an even closer parallel to the two heads that surmount the first and second 'I' of 'Initium' at the incipit of St Mark's Gospel in the Barberini Gospels (fol. 51ʳ; see Fig. 5).[62] Here, the roaring lion symbol of St Mark (the lion of Judah, symbol of kingship and of the triumphant resurrected Christ) has become the cross-stroke of the intervening 'N' and has sprouted wings (an attribute often found in early medieval depictions of evangelist symbols).[63] These faces are also beautifully modelled by the 'Artist'

---

[58] See Henderson, 'Barberini Gospels', p. 163, fig. 14.5.

[59] Alexander, *Insular Manuscripts*, no. 22.

[60] See C. D. Verey, 'Lindisfarne or Rath Maelsigi? The Evidence of the Texts', in *Northumbria's Golden Age*, ed. by Jane Hawkes and Susan Mills (Stroud, 1999), pp. 327–35, and Michelle P. Brown, 'House Style in the Scriptorium: Scribal Reality and Scholarly Myth', in *Anglo-Saxon Styles*, ed. by Catherine E. Karkov and George Hardin Brown (Albany, 2003), pp. 131–50.

[61] See D. H. Wright, 'The Codex Millenarius and its Model', *Münchner Jahrbuch der Bildenden Kunst*, 3rd series, 15 (1964), 37–54 (pp. 38–45, pls 1–8).

[62] See Henderson, 'Barberini Gospels', p. 158.

[63] See Brown, 'Embodying Exegesis', and O'Reilly, 'Library of Scripture'.

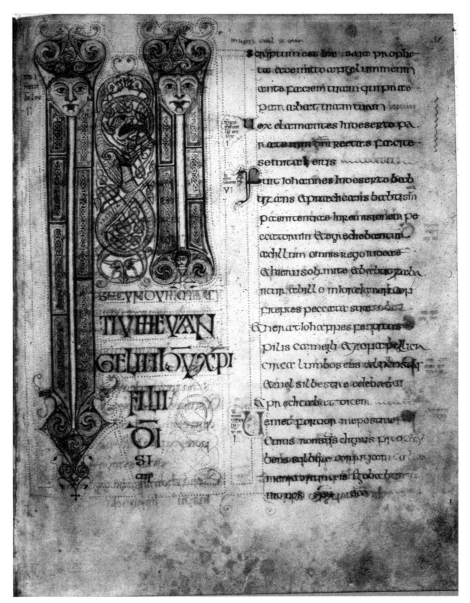

Figure 5. Incipit of St Mark's Gospel, Barberini Gospels. Vatican City, Biblioteca Apostolica Vaticana, MS Barb. lat. 570, fol. 51ʳ. © The Biblioteca Apostolica Vaticana. By kind permission of the Prefect of the Biblioteca Apostolica Vaticana.

and, as in Durham MS A. II. 16, their horned headdresses evolve into the sort of La Tène spiralwork which often serves as the terminal for the letter-strokes of major decorated initials. Effectively forming, as they do, two architectural columns and capitals, they may have been intended to call to mind the two columns of the Law: the Old and New Testaments. In the *Physiologus* the ibex, or wild goat, was supported, should it fall, by its two horns, symbolizing learned men supported by the harmony of the two Testaments, a theme encountered in the decoration of the Irish late eighth-century Derrynaflan Paten.[64] Henderson has also proposed an association of the masks with the phrase 'ante faciem tuam' (Mark 1. 2) and of the angel at the foot of the monogram with 'Ecce mitto angelum meum' (Mark 1. 2), proposing that Barberini is a rare early example of the medieval phenomenon of word illustration.[65] Such a reading need not preclude other levels of meaning.[66] At the foot of the second 'I' is a winged human bust, presumably St Matthew's symbol depicted as a winged angel, as in the Lindisfarne Gospels and the Book of Cerne, and in details within the Book of Kells. The harmony of the Gospels is being explored here, and the combination of the symbols of Saints Mark and Matthew would indicate a theme of Incarnation (symbolized by Matthew) and Resurrection (symbolized by Mark) and of the reconciliation of the two Testaments through Christ's humanity and sacrifice and through his divinity and resurrection. A simple, stylized, and seemingly aniconic page thus becomes a complex *figura* of the dual yet integral nature of Christ — a subject of great concern to the early Church and the crux of much of the debate concerning orthodoxy and heresy.

A magnificent dragon at the foot of the 'Q' of 'Quoniam', the incipit to St Luke's Gospel, in Barberini (fol. 80ʳ; see Plate 2), is attacked by a small black serpent, which descends from the dragon's own crested lappet to strike its nose. Henderson equates it with the 'magnus draco, serpens antiquus' of the Book of Revelation, and the dragon trampled by Christ in Psalm 90, and goes on to link the serpent attack to the words 'If Satan also be divided against Satan, how shall his

---

[64] See McCulloch, *Medieval Latin and French Bestiaries*, p. 132; Michelle P. Brown, 'Paten and Purpose: The Derrynaflan Paten Inscriptions', in *The Age of Migrating Ideas: Early Medieval Art in Northern Britain and Ireland, Proceedings of the Second International Conference on Insular Art held in the National Museums of Scotland in Edinburgh, 36 January 1991*, ed. by R. Michael Spearman and John Higgitt (Edinburgh, 1993), pp. 162–67 (p. 164).

[65] See Henderson, 'Barberini Gospels', pp. 158–59.

[66] For an example of such multivalent reading, see the discussion of the evangelist miniatures in the Lindisfarne Gospels in Brown, *Lindisfarne Gospels*, pp. 346, 353, and 361.

kingdom stand?' (Luke 11. 18). Bede, in his exegesis on Luke's Gospel, commented upon this part of the Gospel text — the 'Quoniam quidem' preface — which warns against pseudo-evangelists and false witnesses posing as apostles and against the 'multifariae diversitate' of heresy (Bede, *Expositio in Lucam*, where Bede borrows Jerome's words 'How can they have concordance between them, whose works are divisive?'),[67] relating it to the 'Quoniam' page in the Book of Kells (fol. 188ʳ) which may incorporate a depiction of the torments of the damned, in the form of the tiny human and animal figures surrounding the lettering.[68] In Barberini's Quoniam page, the two male heads which form the infills to the bows of 'O' in the adjacent panel of display lettering, which sprouts a host of writhing, biting beasts, might likewise represent souls in torment — the false apostles (prefiguring the tenth-century Anglo-Saxon imagery of Arius and Satan in torment beneath the Trinity in the Aelfwine Prayerbook from Winchester; London, British Library, Cotton MS Titus D. XXVII). Once again, heresy and its rejection emerge as preoccupations of the makers of the Barberini Gospels. In the climate of Church Councils and interaction with the wider Christian oecumen which characterized the Mercian Church during the late eighth and early ninth centuries, such concerns were of great import.[69]

Similar human heads can be found as letter-infills in earlier Italian manuscripts and, closer to home, in an early ninth-century Irish copy of Theodore of Mopsuestia's *Commentary on the Psalms* (Milan, Biblioteca Ambrosiana, C. 301. inf., fol. 2ʳ).[70] Another such head occurs in the first line of display lettering on Barberini's 'In principio' page (fol. 125ʳ; see Fig. 1), as the infill to the bow of the final 'O' of 'Principio'. It parallels the sole instance of a human-headed letter in the Lindisfarne Gospels, at the foot of the 'C' in the same word and context (fol. 211ʳ). In Lindisfarne the human head may be intended to signify St Matthew's symbol, emphasizing the harmony of the Gospels and the connection between Christ's Incarnation (symbolized by Matthew's Gospel) and his Second Coming (symbolized by John's Gospel), or it may have played upon the 'Prince of Peace' nomenclature for Christ, a word play on 'princeps'/'principio'.[71] A human head

---

[67] Bede, *In Lucae evengelium expositio*, ed. by David Hurst, CCSL, 120 (Turnhout, 1983), pp. 19–20, 232–34.

[68] See Henderson, 'Barberini Gospels', p. 159.

[69] See Cubitt, *Anglo-Saxon Church Councils*; introduction to *Mercia*, ed. by Brown and Farr, and Joanna Story, *Carolingian Connections, Anglo-Saxon England and Carolingian Francia, c. 750–870* (Aldershot, 2003).

[70] See Alexander, *Insular Manuscripts*, no. 62, pl. 316.

[71] See Brown, *Lindisfarne Gospels*, pp. 343–44, fig. 147.

also features as part of an abbreviation of the sacred name 'ihesus' on fol. 179[v] of the Book of Kells and as the terminal of a 'd' introducing a Psalm extract on fol. 91[v] of the Book of Cerne.[72] A human-headed initial also features in the display script of Barberini's 'Liber' page (fol. 12[r]), where it may reinforce a link between the two Gospels — the incipit and explicit of Christ's mission, Alpha and Omega.

In other respects the 'Liber' and 'In Principio' incipit pages are relatively straightforward. They were the work of Scribes B and C, respectively. Evidently it was the 'Artist' who was the member of the team who was well versed in the intellectual intricacies of visually embodying exegesis and other ideas. In content, as well as in technique and artistry, he was much more sophisticated than the other members of the team, and it is easy to see why they should have sought his participation for most of the major components of the decorative programme. If Wigbald/Scribe C was masterminding the project, the 'Artist' was conceiving and implementing most of its visual and symbolic content. His decorative style points to an origin in Southumbria, like other members of the team, but he may have been more widely travelled, absorbing further intellectual, theological, and stylistic influences en route. The sense of his growing familiarity with the modern, fashionable Mercian decorative repertoire of the 'Tiberius' group, especially through the 'Artist's' collaboration with Scribe C (Wigbald) who exerted an influence upon his work in the Luke incipit page, suggests that he may have been recruited into the scriptorium because of his reputation and was gradually integrated within it.

His fellow team-members made their own distinctive contribution to other aspects of the decorative repertoire, however, and these were not without meaning. The exotic, hybrid beasts which adorn the incipit pages and enliven the line-endings of the Barberini Gospels might have served a similarly apotropaic function, some also imbued with the symbolism of Christian morality derived from the *Physiologus*. Their very ambiguity may have been intended to refer to the union of the creatures of earth, air, and water, created by God and entrusted to the care of humanity (Genesis 1. 20–28), the harmonious *tria genera* of Creation (a theme detected in the decoration of the Gandersheim Casket).[73] Their descendants are encountered in the margins of later medieval manuscripts, nowhere more so than lurking amongst the nightmarish species that inhabit the Luttrell Psalter, made for the lord of the manor of Irnham, near Peterborough, in the

---

[72] See Brown, *Lindisfarne Gospels*, pp. 343–44, figs 148–49.

[73] See *Das Gandersheimer Runenkästchen*, ed. by Marth, esp. Leslie Webster, 'Style and Function of the Gandersheim Casket', pp. 63–72 (pp. 64–65); for the Lindisfarne Gospels, see Brown, *Lindisfarne Gospels*, p. 383.

1330s–1340s.[74] Its pages are full of such grotesques, fusions of humans, animals, birds, and reptiles or fish, who threaten the stability of God's universe, which is guaranteed in the manorial environment by the royally (and implicitly divinely) appointed local vice-regent, Sir Geoffrey Luttrell.

The Fens and East Anglia were the *fons* of the European visionary genre of marvellous creatures and demons which developed in response to the eastern hagiography relating to St Anthony and other desert fathers. This began with the visions of the early seventh-century Irish missionary, Fursey, and of the eighth-century Anglo-Saxon prince turned hermit, Guthlac, later culminating in the fantasies of Hieronymus Bosch and the 'Monty Python' team. It is not surprising that the exoticism favoured by Offa and his court should have merged with a local visionary fascination with fantasy fauna and have culminated in the fossilized stone menagerie of the sculptures of Peterborough, Fletton, and Breedon-on-the-hill and in the carvings of the Gandersheim Casket. They find their most vivacious forms in the lively penwork of books such as the Tiberius Bede, the Book of Cerne, and the Barberini Gospels, the probable products of three great and interconnected religious houses of the day — Christ Church Canterbury, Lichfield Cathedral, and Peterborough Cathedral respectively — which formed the territorial lynchpins of Greater Mercia, including its client kingdom of Kent. In the Barberini Gospels they cohabit with elegant Byzantinizing figures dwelling in a neo-classical environment that both contrasts with and complements the desert wilderness of the Fenlands. The taste it evinces is both local and international, courtly and feral — the embodiment of the Mercia of Kings Offa and Coenwulf. Its symbolism is complex, coded, and highly literate, imbued with a knowledge of exegesis and a predisposition towards intertextuality, of the sort that might be conceived by a senior churchman of the day — perhaps Wigbald of Peterborough.

---

[74] London, British Library, Additional MS 42130; see Janet M. Backhouse, *The Luttrell Psalter* (London, 1989); Michael Camille, *Image on the Edge: The Margins of Medieval Art* (London, 1992) and *Mirror in Parchment: The Luttrell Psalter and the Making of Medieval England* (London, 1998); Michelle P. Brown, *The Luttrell Psalter, Facsimile and Commentary* (London, 2006).

BIS PER CHORUM HINC ET INDE: The 'Virgin and Child with Angels' in the Book of Kells

Carol A. Farr

Cú Chuimne, a monk of Iona who died in 741, revealed in his hymn praising the Virgin how the Columban community sang during offices:

> Cantemus in omni die
> concinentes varie
> conclamantes deo dignum
> ymnum sanctae Mariae
>
> Bis per chorum hinc et inde
> collaudemus Mariam
> ut vox pulset omnem aurem
> per laudem vicariam.
>
> [Let us sing every day,
> harmonising in turns,
> together proclaiming to God
> a hymn worthy of holy Mary.
>
> In two-fold chorus, from side to side,
> let us praise Mary,
> so that the voice strikes every ear
> with alternating praise.][1]

---

[1] Cú Chuimne, *Cantemus in omni die*, ed. and trans. by Thomas Owen Clancy and Gilbert Márkus, *Iona: The Earliest Poetry of a Celtic Community* (Edinburgh, 1995), pp. 181–85 (pp. 182, 183).

It tells of the singing back and forth between two choirs unified as a human community in the body of the Church, a unity with God.[2] This hymn is often cited as early evidence of Marian devotion at Iona, where over the next century images of her were carved upon two surviving stone crosses and painted upon a folio in the Book of Kells (Dublin, Trinity College Library, MS 58, fol. 7ᵛ; Fig. 6). The hymn and the picture present for me a confluence of imagery and religious practice within early medieval society, a pool of evidence and meaning from the depths of which emerge the voice and reflection of Professor Éamonn Ó Carragáin, a scholarly and entertaining guide for anyone exploring the religious culture of early medieval Western Europe. Over the twenty years I have known him, he has been a bountiful source of help professionally and in matters of scholarship, not to mention a great well of humour and fun. I hope that this paper may pay proper tribute to him and express my appreciation for his generosity as a scholar and friend.

Professor Ó Carragáin has spoken eloquently of the participation of sculpted stone crosses and manuscript images in the world of words and ritual action which surrounded them in daily religious life, emphasizing their reference to and enactment of the unity of heavenly and earthly liturgy.[3] Inspired by him, this essay will suggest that the picture of the Virgin and Child may be seen as evoking the heavenly and earthly liturgy, perhaps even referring to the community — one within the *familia* of St Columba and most likely at Iona — for which the Book of Kells was made, probably in the late eighth century.

Depicting the enthroned Virgin holding the Christ Child across her lap with four attendant angels, the picture is readily understood as a devotional icon located in a book. Nonetheless, it presents features and details which link it to its context in a gospel book and the devotional and liturgical experience of its likely audience, an early medieval monastic community, possibly an elite portion of that

---

[2] Clancy and Markus, *Iona*, pp. 177, 179, and 186; David Howlett, 'Five Experiments in Textual Reconstruction and Analysis', *Peritia*, 9 (1995), 1–50 (p. 27). Cú Chuimne may have been an oblate or had some status in the community of Iona other than that of monk; see Douglas Mac Lean, 'Scribe as Artist, Not Monk: The Canon Tables of Ailerán "the Wise" and the Book of Kells', *Peritia*, 17–18 (2003–04), 433–70 (pp. 466–69).

[3] Éamonn Ó Carragáin, *Ritual and the Rood: Liturgical Images and the Old English Poems of the 'Dream of the Rood' Tradition* (London, 2005), pp. 79–354; Ó Carragáin, *The City of Rome and the World of Bede* (Jarrow Lecture, 1994), pp. 4–5, 9–15; Ó Carragáin, '*Traditio Evangeliorum* and *Sustenatio*: The Relevance of Liturgical Ceremonies to the Book of Kells', in *The Book of Kells: Proceedings of a Conference at Trinity College Dublin 6–9 September 1992*, ed. by Felicity O'Mahony (Aldershot, 1994), pp. 398–436 (pp. 398–400); Ó Carragáin, 'The Ruthwell Crucifixion Poem in its Iconographic and Liturgical Contexts', *Peritia*, 6–7 (1987–88), 1–71.

Figure 6. Virgin and child enthroned with angels,
The Book of Kells. Dublin, Trinity College, MS 58, fol. 7ᵛ.
By permission of The Board of Trinity College, Dublin.

community. The picture presents an excellent demonstration of the Insular skill in creating cruciform designs.[4] Two superimposed crosses structure its composition. Three golden yellow half-circles centred at sides and top edge set the viewer's eye on two paths through the halo, face, body, and throne of the Virgin to create a pair of intersecting horizontal and vertical lines, while the wings of the four angels initiate diagonals through the lines of the figures creating an X (*Chi*)-shape. Within this larger scheme, the two shapes appear repeatedly. Three crosses decorate the Virgin's halo, themselves setting up a cross pattern in the picture's visual centre. Her brooch suggests a cross-shape and bears a pattern of interwoven, merging cross- and *Chi*-shapes.[5] Crosses appear in the decoration of the terminals of the rods held by the two uppermost angels, and yet more emerge in the multicoloured shapes on the lower part of the throne, including crosses within circles inscribed in pale brown at its corners. In the two half-circles of the large cross's transom, even the limbs of the interlaced human figures weave together in X-shapes.

The base of the Virgin's throne appears to have a gilt surface inlaid with polychrome enamel. Its back terminates in a lion's head, positioned next to the Virgin's halo. The animal's tongue extends beyond its jaws to form interlace around the throne's back, while an extravagant decorative form with a trumpet

[4] Suzanne Lewis, 'Sacred Calligraphy: The Chi Rho Page in the Book of Kells', *Traditio*, 36 (1980), 139–58 (pp. 155–56); see also Michelle P. Brown, *The Lindisfarne Gospels: Society, Spirituality and the Scribe* (London, 2003), pp. 312–31; Emmanuelle Pirotte, 'Hidden Order, Order Revealed: New Light on Carpet-Pages', in *Pattern and Purpose in Insular Art: Proceedings of the Fourth International Conference on Insular Art held at the National Museum & Galley, Cardiff 3–6 September 1998*, ed. by Mark Redknap and others (Oxford, 2001), pp. 203–07; Éamonn Ó Carragáin, 'The Necessary Distance: *Imitatio Romae* and the Ruthwell Cross', in *Northumbria's Golden Age*, ed. by Jane Hawkes and Susan Mills (Stroud, 1999), pp. 191–203 (p. 202); Jennifer O'Reilly, 'Gospel Harmony and the Names of Christ: Insular Images of a Patristic Theme', in *The Bible as Book: The Manuscript Tradition*, ed. by John L. Sharpe III and Kimberly van Kampen (London, 1998), pp. 73–88 (p. 82); Bernard Meehan, *The Book of Durrow: A Medieval Masterpiece at Trinity College Dublin* (Dublin, 1996), pp. 45–50; Catherine Karkov, 'The Chalice and Cross in Insular Art', in *The Age of Migrating Ideas: Early Medieval Art in Northern Britain and Ireland, Proceedings of the Second International Conference on Insular Art held in the National Museums of Scotland in Edinburgh, 36 January 1991*, ed. by R. Michael Spearman and John Higgitt (Edinburgh, 1993), pp. 237–44; Éamonn Ó Carragáin, 'The Meeting of St. Paul and St. Anthony: Visual and Literary Uses of a Eucharistic Motif', in *Keimelia: Studies in Archaeology and History in Honour of Tom Delaney*, ed. by Gearóid MacNiocaill and Patrick Wallace (Galway, 1988), pp. 1–58 (pp. 17–18, 24).

[5] Niamh Whitfield, 'The Waterford Kite-Brooch and its Place in Irish Metalwork', in *Late Viking Age and Medieval Waterford Excavations 1986–1992*, ed. by Maurice F. Hurley, Orla M. B. Scully, and Sarah W. J. McCutcheon (Waterford, 1997), pp. 490–517 (pp. 498–99).

spiral arises behind its jaw, presenting an elaborate version of conventional Irish stylization of animals' manes and birds' combs. Simpler versions bedeck animals lurking on numerous folios (33^r, 40^v, 201^v, 253^v, 254^r, and 290^v) and are seen in the upright ear-lappets in Irish prestige metalwork and wooden objects.[6] Besides glorifying the figures seated upon the throne, the extremely grand lion head probably also would have been seen by the picture's viewers as a reference to the lion of Judah, signifying the royal house of David. The lion would remind the viewer of the prophets' words which would have been interpreted throughout the Church as telling of the incarnation and Christ's kingship.[7] Lions flank the Virgin and Child on the head of St Martin's Cross, Iona, where their references to David are clear.[8]

The central figures are linked visually and thematically to the figures and decoration surrounding them. The cross- and X-shape of the composition's framework create strong visually unifying elements which are reinforced by details such as the way the wings of the two upper angels show through the wine-coloured area of the Virgin's halo, doing double-duty as part of the pattern created by the three crosses within it. Distribution of the rich colours over the composition further unifies it and accents its structure. While deep red, rose, and brilliant green are most outstanding in the picture's present condition, shades of yellow, ranging from bright to dull, serve an important visual role of highlighting the design, standing in for gold leaf or powdered gold pigment, both of which are rare in Insular manuscripts associated with Ireland.[9]

Shades of yellow are used to represent things which would have been embellished with or made of yellow metal such as gold or bronze: the throne with its polychrome inlay, the Virgin's brooch, her veil, the edge and crosses of her halo,

---

[6] Susan Youngs, *'The Work of Angels': Masterpieces of Celtic Metalwork, 6th–9th Centuries AD* (Austin, 1990), pp. 91–92 (Hunterston brooch), 92 (Westness brooch-pin), 99–100 (Killamery brooch); Niamh Whitfield, 'Motifs and Techniques of Celtic Filigree: Are They Original?', in *Irish and Insular Art, 500–1200: Proceedings of a Conference at University College Cork, 31 October–3 November 1985*, ed. by Michael Ryan (Dublin, 1987), pp 75–84 (p. 76 figs. 1a, 1b); James Lang, 'Eleventh-Century Style in Decorated Wood From Dublin', in ibid., pp. 174–78 (pp. 177–78). I am grateful to Dr Niamh Whitfield for her personal comments.

[7] See, for example, Augustine, Commentary on Psalm 76. 1, ed. and trans. by Philip Schaff, *Early Church Fathers*, vol. VIII (New York, 1886), p. 355; Augustine, *De consensu evangelistarum*, ed. by F. Weihrich, CSEL, 43 (Vienna, 1904), I.6.9.

[8] Ian Fisher, *Early Medieval Sculpture in the West Highlands and Islands*, Royal Commission on the Ancient and Historical Monuments of Scotland and the Society of Antiquaries of Scotland, Monograph Series, 1 (Edinburgh, 2001), p. 133.

[9] Brown, *Lindisfarne Gospels*, pp. 277–80.

the sceptres held by the two angels at the top, and the objects held by the angels in the lower corners. The narrow yellow borders of the half-circles and around the edge of the picture evoke the gold of altar crosses, as well as book covers and reliquary boxes (which often bore cross-shaped decoration), objects to which the page's cruciform design makes reference. Further liturgical furnishings may be seen in the hands of the angels in the lower corners. The angel on the left holds what appears to be a liturgical fan or flabellum, symbolizing purity because it was used to whisk flies from the altar and the Eucharist.[10] Opposite this angel, another holds what resembles a branch with leaves, but it has a handle or ferrule from which a pair of symmetrically curling cords or tubes extend and terminate in identical tri-lobed leaves. Vines with trefoil leaves are a convention of Insular decoration, deriving from earlier and contemporary art traditions of the Mediterranean, and in both regions they appear in abstracted, symmetrical designs, similar to that of the object in the picture.[11] The object the angel holds could represent the 'rod from the root of Jesse', signifying the incarnation as prophesied in the Old Testament (Isaiah 7. 14; 11. 1–16), although the leafy or flowering shoot becomes a usual attribute of the Virgin — held by her, not by accompanying figures — around 1000.[12] The way in which the angel holds the object downward, the articulation of a ferrule, its symmetry and dull-yellow colour suggest that it could represent a liturgical sprinkler, called an aspergillum, which is used in place of a bough of the plant called hyssop in the Bible, in the ceremony of asperges or the blessing and sprinkling of holy water.

The priest performs asperges before any ceremony preceding Mass, such as the blessing of the paschal candle or water and salt. Sometimes it is performed in place of the penitential rite. A purification of the altar, assistants, and congregation, it is known to have been performed in papal liturgy, in which the pope used an actual sprig of hyssop, as early as Leo IV (847–55). In medieval western liturgy,

[10] Françoise Henry, *The Book of Kells* (London, 1974), p. 188; Martin Werner, 'The Madonna and Child Miniature in the Book of Kells', *Art B.*, 54 (1972), 1–23, 129–39 (pp. 11–12); Hilary Richardson, 'Remarks on the Liturgical Fan, Flabellum or Rhipidion', in *Age of Migrating Ideas*, ed. by Spearman and Higgitt, pp. 27–34.

[11] Douglas Mac Lean, 'Northumbrian Vine-scroll Ornament and the *Book of Kells*', in *Northumbria's Golden Age*, ed. by Hawkes and Mills, pp. 178–90 (pp. 186–90).

[12] Mary Clayton, *The Cult of the Virgin Mary in Anglo-Saxon England* (Cambridge, 1990), pp. 148, 171; Jonathan J. G. Alexander, 'The Illumination', in *The Book of Kells, MS 58, Trinity College Library Dublin: Commentary*, ed. by Peter Fox (Lucerne, 1990), pp. 263–314 (p. 307); Martin Werner, 'Crucifixi, Sepulti, Suscitati: Remarks on the Decoration of the Book of Kells', in *The Book of Kells*, ed. by O'Mahony, pp. 450–88 (p. 485).

chanting during the asperges included antiphons based on either Psalm 50. 9 ('Asperges me, Domine') or, during Easter time, Psalm 118. 1 ('Vidi aquam'), meant to lead worshippers into penitential thoughts and contemplation in their role in the sacrifice.[13] The ceremony is based upon the ritual sprinkling mentioned at several points in the Old Testament in cleansing rituals (Leviticus 14. 47, 49–51; Numbers 19. 8; Numbers 19. 6). Bidden to the elders by Moses for sprinkling the blood of the sacrifice upon their doors in Egypt (Exodus 12. 22; 24. 8) and used again by him to sprinkle the blood of victims upon the Hebrews after the giving of the commandments (Exodus 24. 8), hyssop has further associations with divine covenant and protection. These associations of ritual sprinkling with hyssop are elaborated upon in Hebrews 9. 18–22, which concerns the priesthood and the earthly and heavenly church. It concludes with a statement evoking Christ's sacrifice and intercession on behalf of mankind: 'Et omnia pene in sanguine secundum legem mundantur: et sine sanguinis effusione non fit remissio.'[14] These connections are reinforced by the account of Christ's crucifixion, in John 19. 29, in which hyssop was used to raise the sponge filled with vinegar to his lips just before his death. For Augustine hyssop, 'a lowly herb', became in this passage a sign of Christ's humility by which he cleansed mankind of sin:

> Unde est illud in psalmo, *Asperges me hyssopo, et mundabor*. Christi namque humilitate mundamur; quia nisi humiliasset semetipsum, factus obediens usque ad mortem crucis, non utique sanguis ejus in peccatorum remissionem, hoc est, in nostram mundationem fuisset effusus.[15]

> [Hence we have it said in the psalm, 'Thou shalt purge me with hyssop, and I shall be cleansed' (Psalm 50. 9). For it is by Christ's humility that we are cleansed; because, had He not humbled Himself, and became obedient unto the death of the cross, His blood certainly would not have been shed for the remission of sins, or, in other words, for our cleansing.]

The humility of Christ and his mother is emphasized in scripture and patristic exegesis as requisite to the incarnation and redemption. The Virgin Mary referred to herself as the handmaid of God, accepting her role, and Christ took the form of

---

[13] Andrew Hughes, *Medieval Manuscripts for Mass and Office: A Guide to their Organization and Terminology* (Toronto, 1982), pp. 34, 82–83; John J. Wynne, 'Asperges', in *The Catholic Encyclopedia*, vol. I (New York, 1907), p. 793.

[14] 'Indeed according to the Law, it might almost be said, everything is cleansed by blood and without the shedding of blood there is no forgiveness' (Hebrews 9. 22).

[15] Augustine, *In Ioannis Evangelium tractatus*, 119.4, ed. by Radbod Willems, CCSL, 36 (Turnhout, 1954), pp. 658–60 (p. 660).

a human being, obediently accepting death on the cross and simultaneously raised up to the heights and recognized as the Lord 'by all the tongues in heaven, on earth and in the depths'.[16] The plant on which the function of the aspergillum was based was a symbol of purification and forgiveness which further signified Christ's purging of mankind's sin and his covenant of salvation, enacted in the liturgy of the Mass.

Furthermore, *hyssopum* (or *ysopum*) is the word used for *aspergillum* in early church dedication liturgies from Francia and Rome recorded in *ordos* of the eighth and ninth centuries. In these ceremonies, a branch of hyssop is dipped in lustral water and used to asperse the church's interior and altar.[17] In a ninth-century commentary on a church dedication ordo, 'Quid significent duodecim candelae', the aspersion ceremony is compared with baptism, in which the living stones of the church, symbolically the community of believers, are sprinkled, signifying the bestowing of the Holy Spirit's presence within it. The branch of hyssop signifies 'the humility of Christ, which shattered the hardness of our obstinacy and knows how to heal interior sufferings and impurity'.[18]

The object which the angel holds, however, resembles neither of the two known sprinklers which survive in contexts from the seventh through the ninth century and are believed to be of Irish or Northumbrian manufacture. These are of slightly flattened, spherical shape, made of two hemispheres of beaten metal, the upper with a short, hollow tube which served as a handle. Besides not looking like the angel's object, their originally intended context of use is uncertain because both were found in 'foreign' female graves. Whether they were ecclesiastical objects or used for domestic ritual cleansing is undecided.[19] They are, however, unique objects. One wonders if high-status, ecclesiastical *aspergilla* may have been of more elaborate design, imitating a plant-like shape to evoke the hyssop of scripture and the antiphons chanted during the liturgy. Moreover, a liturgical sprinkler with a foliate form could unify references to the incarnation as a reminder of the rod of Jesse and as the hyssop of sacrifice, covenant, and forgiveness. Together with the flabellum and angels, who participate in the heavenly liturgy, the depicted foliate object could have served to cue the viewers' recognition of a liturgical context, so that the Virgin and Child may have been understood to be shown

---

[16] Luke 1. 38; Philippians 2. 5–11.

[17] Ordo XLI, *Les Ordines romani du haut moyen âge*, ed. by Michel Andrieu, 5 vols (Leuven, 1931, 1948–51, 1956–61), IV, 338–49 (p. 342). See also Brian Repsher, *The Rite of Church Dedication in the Early Medieval Era* (Lampeter, 1998), pp. 51–53.

[18] Repsher, *Rite of Church Dedication*, pp. 89, 124–26.

[19] Youngs, 'Work of Angels', pp. 56, 122.

within a church. In turn, such a context would evoke recognition of the Child as Eucharist, the Virgin as the Church or Temple which holds the Incarnate Word, instigating contemplation of the multivalent significance of the image, a feature of the manuscript's other decorated pages and pictures.[20]

The four angels are usually understood by us as iconographic elements that 'belong to' images of the enthroned Virgin. The picture in the Book of Kells is tied by a network of similarities with early depictions of the Virgin and Child, but its particular combination of iconographic features is unmatched in surviving images thought to have been made before the early ninth century in areas outside of Ireland and Britain. Occurrence of these features in Insular stone sculpture has recently been connected with the influence of Iona's Columban community, recognizing that the needs of particular situations, not just available models, determined choices of poses and accompanying figures.[21] For the ninth-century viewer the angels would have intensified a sense of contiguousness with the holy figures. They point to the Way and the Word, affirming the holiness of the central figures in unison with several other elements of the picture, and the viewer would have been reminded of their role as heavenly messengers who played a part in the incarnation as well as being co-worshippers with human believers. They would have reminded the viewer of two of the most beautiful hymns of the Mass, the Gloria and the Sanctus, both of which derive from biblical texts sung by angels.[22] By the late eighth century, these two ancient prayers certainly would have been heard and sung by important Irish monastic communities such as that at Iona.[23] Both appear in the Stowe Missal (Dublin, Royal Irish Academy, MS D. II. 3, fols 13[v] and 23[v]), a contemporary of the Book of Kells, probably made at Tallaght around 800.[24] The Gloria, beginning with verses sung by the angels at

---

[20] Jennifer O'Reilly, 'The Book of Kells, Folio 114r: A Mystery Concealed Yet Revealed', in *Age of Migrating Ideas*, ed. by Spearman and Higgitt, pp. 106–14; O'Reilly, 'Gospel Harmony'.

[21] Jane Hawkes, 'Columban Virgins: Iconic Images of the Virgin and Child in Insular Sculpture', in *Studies in the Cult of Saint Columba*, ed. by Cormac Bourke (Dublin, 1997), pp. 107–35; Jane Hawkes, *The Sandbach Crosses: Sign and Significance in Anglo-Saxon Sculpture* (Dublin, 2002), pp. 141–45; see also Ernst Kitzinger, 'The Coffin Reliquary', in *The Relics of Ssintt Cuthbert*, ed. by C. F. Battiscombe (Oxford, 1956), pp. 202–304 (pp. 249–65).

[22] Luke 2. 14; Isaiah 6. 3.

[23] Josef A. Jungmann, *The Early Liturgy to the Time of Gregory the Great*, trans. by Francis A. Brunner (Notre Dame, 1959), pp. 71, 295–96, and 302–03.

[24] J. J. G. Alexander, *Insular Manuscripts, 6th to the 9th Century*, Survey of Manuscripts Illuminated in the British Isles, 1 (London, 1978), pp. 70–71.

Christ's birth, stands in this manuscript among the opening prayers of the Mass, as it had from the sixth century.[25] It had always been a hymn sung by the people themselves, so that its presence at the beginning helps to express the idea that the Mass is of the community.[26] In the Stowe Missal, a tenth-century inscription designates it 'The Angelic Hymn'.[27] The Sanctus, a prayer for intercession which concludes the Preface, also has nearly always been sung by the people or the choir, enacting the seraphs' antiphonal chanting of the text in the Book of Isaiah.[28] In the Stowe Missal, the Sanctus is introduced by a prayer calling upon orders of angels who worship God in heaven together with all the voices of the Church on earth, a feature typical of early Eucharistic prayers of the Preface.[29] The prayer is actually based on two texts, the second being the greeting of triumph proclaiming Christ's entry into Jerusalem (Matthew 21. 9), but the Stowe Missal extends it further with statements of Christ's incarnation and role as saviour through his passion.[30] Memory of angelic voices heard through the hymns of the liturgy and referred to in prayers would bring the picture to life, making vivid the sense of being one with the body of Christ, the Church.

The 'metallic' yellow colour borders the three half-circles at the centre top and sides of the picture. What significance the animal and human interlace within them could have had for the early medieval viewer is difficult to determine. On one level, elaborate interlace signified high-status decoration, but because the half circles define a cross-pattern, a figure full of meaning in the context of a Virgin and Child image, they may have had a significance related to the themes of incarnation, passion, and salvation. The pair of animals in the upper half-circle might have reminded the viewers of the Canticle of Habakkuk (3. 1–19, from the Old

---

[25] *The Stowe Missal, MS. D. II. 3 in the Library of the Royal Irish Academy, Dublin*, ed. by George F. Warner, 2 vols, Henry Bradshaw Society, 31–32 (London, 1906; repr. Woodbridge, 1989), II, 4; Adrian Fortescu, 'Gloria in Excelsis Deo', in *The Catholic Encyclopedia*, vol. VI (New York, 1913), pp. 583–85.

[26] Jungmann, *Early Liturgy*, p. 295.

[27] *Stowe Missal*, ed. by Warner, II, 4. I thank Michelle Brown for her personal comments on the date.

[28] Jungmann, *Early Liturgy*, II, 302–03; Hughes, *Medieval Manuscripts*, p. 88.

[29] Adrian Fortescue, 'Sanctus', in *The Catholic Encyclopedia*, vol. XIII (New York, 1913), pp. 432–34; Ó Carragáin, '*Traditio Evangeliorum*', p. 399.

[30] 'Osanna in excelsis benedictus qui venit de celís ut conversaretur in terris homo factus est ut dilicta carnis deleret hostia factus est ut per passionem suam vitam aeternam credentibus daret': *Stowe Missal*, ed. by Warner, II, 10.

Latin version of the Bible), a liturgical text to which Professor Ó Carragáin has related several other iconographic elements in Insular art.[31] The body of the Christ Child lies directly below them, recognized as the incarnate God: 'In medio duorum animalium innotesceris' ('you will be known in the midst of two animals'). Along with the lion's head of the throne, they underscore the mystery of God become human according to Old Testament prophecy. Moreover, they top the vertical axis of the cross-pattern, providing further reminder of the canticle sung at lauds on Friday and the Adoration of the Cross on Good Friday, with its richly multivalent references to the incarnation, passion, resurrection, and ascension.[32]

The pairs of interlaced human figures in the half-circles creating the terminals of the cross's horizontal element are unusual accompaniments to the Virgin, but a similarity exists with the square terminals of the cross-page (late eighth to early ninth century) from Ireland which is bound with St Gall, Stiftsbibliothek, cod. 1395 (fol. 422).[33] Like the three half-circles of the picture's cruciform shape, the terminals of the St Gall cross are decorated with human and animal interlace, a combination occurring in other cross-shapes or quadripartite designs in the Book of Kells. Several scholars have connected designs such as the panels of the carpet page and the rhombus at the centre of the *Chi* of the *nomen sacrum* at Matthew 1. 18 (fols 33ʳ and 34ʳ) with cosmological diagrams, basing their interpretations on patristic and Insular writings on the cross-shaped frame of heaven and four-sided cosmic structure. Many of these texts interpret the quadripartite shapes as Christological figures, signifying multivalently and simultaneously the incarnation of the Word, the Church on earth as the dwelling-place of God, and the heavenly Church.[34]

---

[31] Éamonn Ó Carragáin, 'Christ over the Beasts and the *Agnus Dei*: Two Multivalent Panels on the Ruthwell and Bewcastle Crosses', in *Sources of Anglo-Saxon Culture*, ed. by Paul E. Szarmach, Studies in Medieval Culture, 20 (Kalamazoo, 1986), pp. 377–403 (pp. 383–86, 388–89); Ó Carragáin, 'The Ruthwell Cross and Irish High Crosses: Some Points of Comparison and Contrast', in *Ireland and Insular Art*, ed. by Ryan, pp. 118–28 (pp. 118–19); Ó Carragáin, 'Meeting of St Paul and St Anthony', pp. 4–12, 19–22, 27–31, and 38–44; Ó Carragáin, '*Traditio Evangeliorum*', pp. 422–32.

[32] Ó Carragáin, '*Traditio Evangeliorum*', pp. 422–23.

[33] Alexander, *Insular Manuscripts*, p. 79 fig. 282.

[34] O. K. Werckmeister, *Irische-Northumbrische Buchmalerei des 8 Jh. und monastische Spritualität* (Berlin, 1967), pp. 147–73; Lewis, 'Sacred Calligraphy'; O'Reilly, 'Gospel Harmony', pp. 73–88; Jennifer O'Reilly, 'Patristic and Insular Traditions of the Evangelists: Exegesis and

The multivalent image of Christ, Church, and cosmos is believed to relate also to the pictures on folios 114[r] and 202[v] as well as the four symbols pages in the Book of Kells.[35] In this respect the panel set into the border to the right of the picture may have some significance. Several art historians have noticed that the profile heads in the panel probably were meant to be 'looking at' or at least to link the picture visually to the beginning words of the Matthean *breves causae*, *Nativitas Christi*, on the facing page.[36] While it is not absolutely certain that the picture, which is on a single folium or stub, originally faced the summaries of the Nativity, its present position is taken to be original by many scholars, and the facing page presents textual and visual contents that seem compatible with the picture of the Virgin and Child.[37]

Whether the picture originally faced the present folio 8[r] or was paired somehow with another picture or decorated page, the six profile heads probably would have had multiple meanings for early medieval viewers. Groups of profiles on folios 124[r] (who, it is believed, gazed across to an image of the Crucifixion on fol. 123[v]) and 202[v] (who watch the Temptation of Christ and fill the Temple below) refer to a typological sense of Christian history which binds together Old Testament past, the Church on earth in the present, and the future events of Apocalypse and Second Coming.[38] Viewers may have seen the six profiles as the

Iconography', in *Le Isole Britanniche e Roma in Età Romanobarbarica*, ed. by Anna Maria Luiselli Fadda and Éamonn Ó Carragáin, Biblioteca di Cultura Romanobarbarica, 1 (Rome, 1998), pp. 49–94 (pp. 66–94); Carol Farr, 'History and Mnemonic in Insular Gospel Book Decoration', in *From the Isles of the North: Early Medieval Art in Ireland and Britain*, ed. by C. Bourke (Belfast, 1995), pp. 137–46.

[35] O'Reilly, 'Book of Kells, Folio 114r'; O'Reilly, 'Patristic and Insular Traditions', pp. 87–91; Carol Farr, *The Book of Kells: Its Function and Audience* (London, 1997), pp. 51–75, 104–16, 134, and 156–58.

[36] Heather Pulliam, 'The Book of Kells: Demarcating the Sacred Environment', *Cosmos*, 12 (1996), 203–22 (pp. 207–08); Heather Pulliam, *Word and Image in the Book of Kells* (Dublin, 2006); Werner, 'Madonna and Child Miniature', p. 11; Alexander, 'The Illumination', p. 307; George Henderson, *From Durrow to Kells: The Insular Gospel-books 650–800* (London, 1987), p. 155; O'Reilly, 'Gospel Harmony', p. 82; Henry, *Book of Kells*, p. 188.

[37] The 'charters' on folios 6[v] and 7[r], often cited as evidence of the original position, were written at the earliest in the late eleventh century, and the last one ends on folio 7[r], the next one beginning folio 27[r]. See Gearóid Mac Niocaill, 'The Irish "Charters"', in *The Book of Kells*, ed. by Fox, pp. 153–65; Máire Herbert, 'Charter Material from Kells', in *The Book of Kells*, ed. by O'Mahony, pp. 60–77.

[38] Henry, *Book of Kells*, p. 173; Lewis, 'Sacred Calligraphy', pp. 156–57; Henderson, *From Durrow to Kells*, pp. 163–64; Jennifer O'Reilly, 'Text and Image: The Wounded and Exalted

ancestors of Christ, another reference to Christ's royalty and to the incarnation as fulfilment of Old Testament prophecy.[39] On another level, members of the Columban *familia* may have understood them to signify the perfection of Christ's salvation through the patristic interpretation of the number six, famously by Augustine, Isidore of Seville, and Bede. The lowest number equal to the sum of its factors $(1 + 2 + 3 = 6)$, it was the common denominator of temporal perfection. God created the world in six days 'because the perfection of the works was signified by the number six'.[40] By analogy there were six ages of man and six ages of the world. On the sixth day, 'man was created in the image of God [...] and in the sixth age of the human race, the Son of God came and was made the Son of Man, that he might reshape us into the image of God'.[41] Henderson and O'Reilly have suggested that the six busts represent the Christian community contemplating the page opposite.[42] The picture's audience would thus have been looking at a representation of themselves in present time inset like an enamel-work panel into the incarnation and the Gospels.[43] The panel underscored the connection of the picture's audience — members of the community of Christians, the Church on earth — with the image of the Virgin and Child, depicting them within the perfect history of salvation.

Signs of the incarnation — the X or Greek letter *Chi*, cross and body of Christ — subsume the Church in heaven as well as that on earth, the past as well as present and future: these are temporally multivalent signs that reveal the nontemporal existence of the divine. Some of the most remarkable references in the Book of Kells to the body of Christ are made in the depiction of the Temptation

---

Christ', *Peritia*, 6–7 (1987–88), 99–100; Cormac Bourke, 'The Book of Kells: New Light on the Temptation Scene', in *From Ireland Coming: Irish Art From the Early Christian to the Late Gothic Period and its European Context*, ed. by Colum Hourihane (Princeton, 2001), pp. 49–59; Jennifer O'Reilly, 'Exegesis and the Book of Kells: The Lucan Genealogy', in *The Book of Kells*, ed. by O'Mahony, pp. 344–97 (pp. 359–61); Farr, *Book of Kells*, pp. 51–75.

[39] Alexander, 'The Illumination', p. 307.

[40] Augustine, *De civitate Dei*, 11.30, ed. by Bernhard Dombart and Alfons Kalb, CCSL, 48 (Turnhout, 1955), p. 350.

[41] Augustine, *De trinitate*, 4.4, ed. by William John Mountain and François Glorie, CCSL, 50 (Turnhout, 1968), pp. 169–70 and 171–72; *Bede: The Reckoning of Time*, trans. by Faith Wallis (Liverpool, 1999), pp. 32, 108–09, and 356–59; Isidore of Seville, *Chronica maiora*, ed. by T. Mommsen, MGH, Auctores antiquissimi, 11 (1894).

[42] Henderson, *From Durrow to Kells*, pp. 154, 163–64; O'Reilly, 'Text and Image', p. 99. O'Reilly emphasizes fulfilment of Old Testament prophecy (Zacharias 12. 10).

[43] Pulliam, 'Book of Kells', p. 207; Pulliam, *Word and Image*.

of Christ, where the Temple in Jerusalem is depicted as the body of Christ, the heavenly and earthly Church, its ground level built of busts resembling those on folio 7[v], while beside it a similar group observes Christ's refutation of Satan.[44] This multivalent image represents the *Communio sanctorum*, which appears as the central theme of the prayers of the Book of Cerne and in later Anglo-Saxon images of the choirs of saints.[45] References to the *Communio sanctorum* appear in prayers and liturgy of the Mass and divine office as preserved in early manuscripts from Ireland and Britain, such as the Stowe Missal and Book of Cerne, as well as in the Irish martyrologies.[46] Made up of choirs of saints including all the orders of angels, prophets, the Virgin, saints in heaven, and the living, it expresses the idea that all the groups of living and dead, heaven and earth participate spiritually and liturgically in one body of Christ, exchanging prayers through each other. The angels and cosmic cross- and *Chi*-forms overlaying the Virgin and Child folio construct an image of the body of saints in heaven and on earth, and the panel of six profiles puts the viewers into the picture. Perhaps the vines which grow from vases in the upper and lower right corners also refer to the *communio sanctorum*, whose members are connected by the true vine, the figure Christ uses in John 15, which has Eucharistic references as well.

The Virgin as the mother of God also merges with this figure of the body of the church and the cross signs. In patristic writings, the Virgin was a member of the body of the Church and also she was the *typos* of it, an idea which developed alongside the figure of the Church as the body of Christ made up of the stones of the believers.[47] The Virgin as a figure of the Church appears prominently in patristic writing, and the idea continued to be developed through the Middle Ages. The *Liber de ortu et obitu patrum* of the Irish Pseudo-Isidore gives a litany of her titles, which include 'daughter of King David', 'rod of Jesse', 'bedchamber

---

[44] Farr, *Book of Kells*, pp. 51–75; O'Reilly, 'Exegesis', pp. 359–61, 391–97.

[45] Michelle P. Brown, *The Book of Cerne: Prayer, Patronage and Power in Ninth-Century England* (London, 1996), pp. 108–09; 113–15, 147–51, and 183–84; Robert Deshman, 'The Galba Psalter: Pictures, Texts and Context in an Early Medieval Prayerbook', *Anglo-Saxon England*, 26 (1997), 109–39 (pp. 113–28, 134–36).

[46] John Hennig, 'Studies in Early Western Devotion to the Choirs of Saints', *Studia patristica*, 8 (1963), 239–47.

[47] Sr Isabell Naumann, 'Aspects of Mary and the Church Through the Centuries', *The Mary Page* <http://campus.udayton.edu/mary/resources/maryandchurch.htm>; H. Fries, 'Wandel des Kirchenbildes und dogmengeschichtliche Entfaltung', in *Mysterium Salutis*, ed. by J. Feiner and M. Löhrer, 5 vols and suppl. vol. (Einsiedeln, 1965–76), IV.1, 223–79 (p. 236).

of the Trinity', 'Temple of God', and 'shrine of the Holy Spirit'.[48] Her titles suggest the semiosis which could be applied to the figure of the Virgin in liturgical and devotional contexts, and these include the image of the Church, especially in the Temple, the dwelling place of God on earth and image of heaven. The picture in the Book of Kells was made and viewed against this rich interpretative background, its elements such as the angels, flabellum, branch of hyssop, and inset of profiles facilitating its viewers' understanding of her as the vessel of the incarnation and the means by which they might enter into the salvation which was its point.[49] Moreover, the large cross and the *Chi* which overlay the figure of the Virgin evoke her significance in salvation history and for the community of individuals to which the Book of Kells belonged. Their perception of this would surely have been powerfully shaped by developments of Marian feasts and devotions in Roman liturgy over the course of the seventh and eighth centuries.[50]

As a gospel book, the Book of Kells includes texts from which liturgical hymns were taken. Some of these have special decoration, while others receive virtually none. The beginning of the *Gloria* (fol. 194ᵛ) is not decorated at all. Quite prominent decoration and enlargement, however, are bestowed upon the initials of the Lord's Prayer (fol. 45ʳ) and the canticles *Magnificat* and *Benedictus* (fols 191ᵛ, 193ʳ). The gospel canticles pertain to the Virgin, and at least the first two canticles in Luke, as well as the Lord's Prayer, would have been sung on a daily basis by many Insular monastic communities of the late eighth century. The Lord's Prayer, *Magnificat*, and *Benedictus* appear in the offices in the Book of Mulling and *Liber Hymnorum*, while the *Visio Adomnán* II has the two canticles.[51] Folio 191ᵛ (Fig. 7) was carefully written so that Elizabeth's words, *Benedicta tu inter mulieris* (Luke 1.42),

---

[48] *Liber de ortu et obitu patriarcharum*, 41.1, ed. by J. Carracedo Fraga, CCSL, 108E (Turnhout, 1996), p. 44. See also Robert E. McNally, *The Bible in the Early Middle Ages* (Westminster, MD, 1959; repr. Atlanta, 1986), p. 67.

[49] Michael O'Carroll, 'Our Lady in Early Medieval Ireland', in *Seanchas: Studies in Early and Medieval Irish Archaeology, History and Literature in Honour of Francis J. Byrne*, ed. by Alfred P. Smyth (Dublin, 2000), pp. 178–81 (pp. 180–81).

[50] Éamonn Ó Carragáin, 'Crucifixion as Annunciation: The Relation of *The Dream of the Rood* to the Liturgy Reconsidered', *English Studies*, 63 (1982), 487–505 (pp. 491–96, 501–05); Ó Carragáin, *City of Rome*, pp. 4, 19–23; Ó Carragáin, *Ritual and the Rood*, pp. 97–99, 107–08, 237–47, 308–11, 315, 338, and 332.

[51] H. J. Lawlor, *Chapters on the Book of Mulling* (Edinburgh, 1897), pp. 145–66; R. Atkinson and J. H. Bernard, *The Irish Liber Hymnorum*, 2 vols, Henry Bradshaw Society, 13–14 (London, 1897–98), I, p. xxiii. The *Magnificat* does not appear in the offices of the Antiphonary of Bangor; Michael Curran, *The Antiphonary of Bangor* (Dublin, 1984), pp. 169–91.

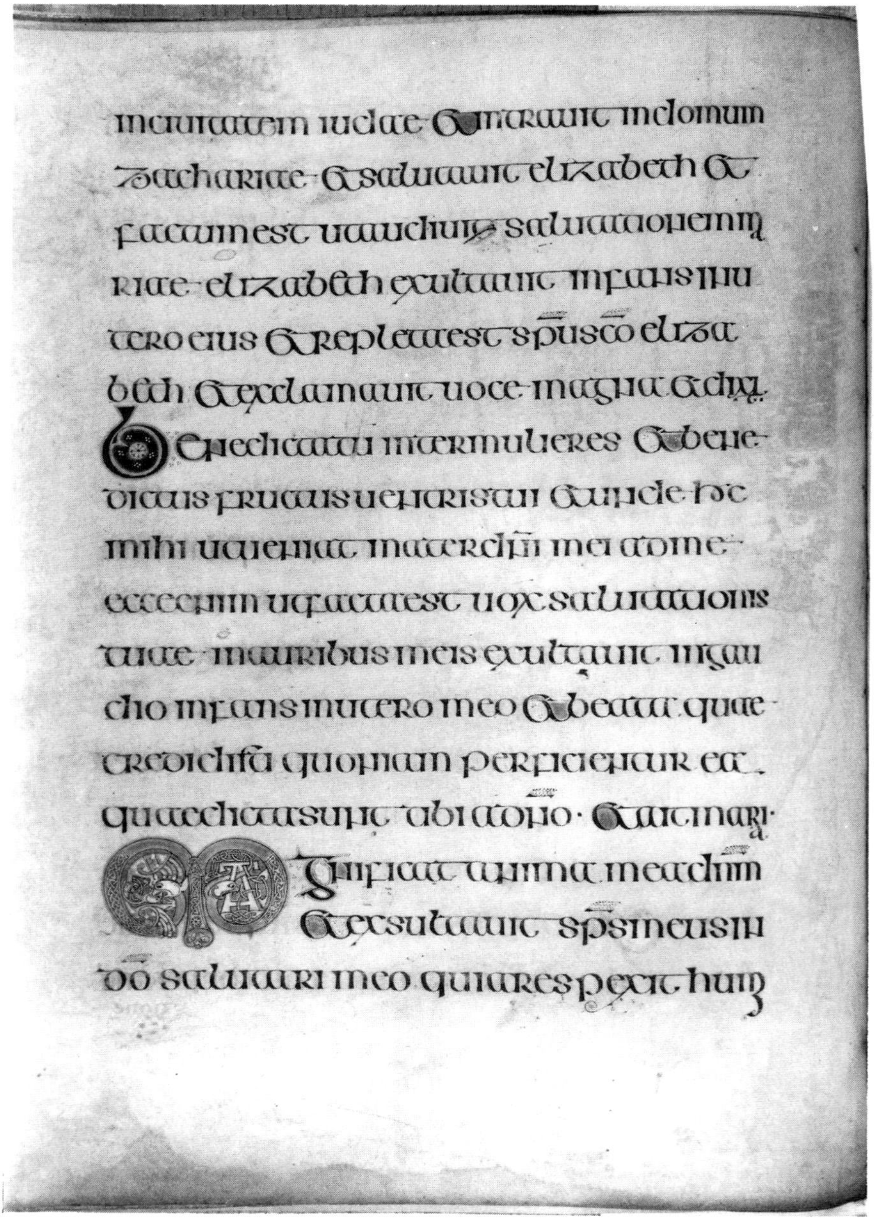

Figure 7. *Magnificat* initial, The Book of Kells. Dublin, Trinity College, MS 58, fol. 191ᵛ. By permission of The Board of Trinity College, Dublin.

which appear in the liturgy of the feast of the Annunciation, and Mary's canticle begin lines of text.[52] In Insular gospel books the *Magnificat* initial is typically enlarged and drawn as a pair of arcs, but in the Book of Kells it is large enough to enclose the following A, a square display capital. Coloured in yellow and green, its arcs terminate with, on the right, a lion's head which grips the letter A in its jaws, and, left, a swirling triad of birds. The triad repeats in a triangle of interlace, a triquetra, and the capital A's shape. Would the triads refer to the Virgin's significance as the Church, the 'bedchamber of the Trinity', as expressed in the litany of the *De ortu et obitu patrum* and alluded to in the depiction of the Virgin as Church? The animal head, also, is a plainer version of the lion head on the back of the throne, perhaps referring to God's promise to Abraham for the elevation of Israel and to Old Testament prophecy of the incarnation through the house of Judah. In the picture, the richly decorated throne, heavenly court of angels, hyssop sprinkler, inset of present-day believers, and visual references to cross and Eucharist evoke in multiple senses the canticle's promises of elevation of the humble.

Like the *Magnificat*, the hymn of Cú Chuimne belonged to the picture's liturgical context. The hymn repeatedly alludes to biblical texts and doctrine that have been seen in the picture. In stanza 3, Cú Chuimne refers to Mary's royal descent and fulfilment of the promise of salvation ('Mary of the Tribe of Judah, Mother of the Most High Lord').[53] The hymn and the picture use the Old Testament references to the royal house and thus emphasize her role as loving universal mother in the incarnation rather than bestowing her with the crown of the Queen of Heaven, as two of the surviving Roman pictures of the Enthroned Virgin with Angels depict her.[54] The following stanzas speak of her reception of the word, announced by the archangel Gabriel, and contemplate this mystery using riddle-like figures of speech and inversions. Stanza 7 proclaims:

> Per mulierem et lignum
> Mundus prius periit
> Per mulieris virtutem
> Ad salutem rediit.

---

[52] On the Annunciation lection, see Ó Carragáin, *Ritual and the Rood*, pp. 97, 101–03, and 357.

[53] 'Maria de tribu Iudae | Summi mater Domini | Oportunam dedit curam | Egrotanti homini.' Ed. and trans. by Clancy and Márkus in *Iona*, p. 182.

[54] Icon of the Virgin and Child, Santa Maria in Trastevere, Rome (early eighth century) and fragments of wall-painting of Maria Regina, Santa Maria Antiqua, Rome (mid-sixth); for illustrations, see Lawrence Nees, *Early Medieval Art* (Oxford, 2002), fig. 84; D. Russo, 'Maria', in *Enciclopedia dell'arte medievale* (Rome, 1997), VIII, 210.

> [By a woman and a tree
> the world first perished;
> by the power of a woman
> it has returned to salvation.][55]

Cú Chuimne refers to the patristic typology of Eve and the tree in the Garden of Eden/Mary and the Cross, made from the tree from which Satan tempted Eve, and to the liturgical merging of Annunciation and Crucifixion.[56] The same figure can be seen in the picture of the Virgin and Child, where the figure of the enthroned Virgin merges with the forms of the cross and *Chi*, which in turn are figures of the world with further salvation and Eucharistic themes imbued by the vines, hyssop, and flabellum. Three more stanzas draw beautiful images of the mystery of the incarnation through 'Maria mater miranda'.

The final three stanzas call upon her spiritual protection, to 'be perfected by God, taken up by Mary', and to be spared the ensnaring flame of the 'dread fire' of damnation. It ends with the voice of the *communio sanctorum*:

> Christi nomen invocemus
> Angelis sub testibus
> Ut fruamur et scripamur
> Litteris celestibus.
>
> [Let us call on the name of Christ,
> below the angel witnesses,
> that we may delight and be inscribed
> in letters in the heavens.][57]

The angels at the top of the picture point to the Virgin and Child: they and the Virgin call upon the name of Christ together with the members of the community depicted in the inset panel in the liturgy in which heaven and earth participate. All are set within signs of incarnation and salvation. Perhaps the profiles look toward the gospel book itself, as their way to being 'written in letters in the heavens'. The final stanza also looks back to the beginning of the hymn, the invocation to a community, not an individual, to sing every day of the Virgin's great accomplishment and help to mankind, along with and in the manner of the angels 'in twofold chorus'. If we listen carefully to Cú Chuimne's hymn and what is left to us of the early liturgy in Ireland, we can gain some insight into how the picture was understood by its early medieval audience.

---

[55] Ed. and trans. by Clancy and Márkus in *Iona*, pp. 182–83.

[56] Ó Carragáin, 'Crucifixion as Annunciation', pp. 491–98.

[57] Ed. and trans. by Clancy and Márkus in *Iona*, pp. 184–85.

TEXT AND IMAGE IN THE RED BOOK OF DARLEY

Catherine E. Karkov

The inspiration for this paper came in reading Éamonn Ó Carragáin's explanation of the way in which the runic poem carved around the vine-scroll on the narrow sides of the Ruthwell Cross demands to be read.[1] Éamonn demonstrated that the arrangement of the inscription in the borders forces the viewer to move his or her eyes down, up, and across the vine-scroll, uniting the image and the text in an unusual and powerful way. The union of object and viewer is made even more powerful by the fact that the inscribed verses are spoken in the voice of the cross of the crucifixion, which is itself symbolized by the vine-scroll. Yet in reading the poem and looking at the imagery, the viewer also becomes joined to the monument. We assume the voice of the cross, and we see ourselves in the animals that inhabit the vine-scroll. While the exact merging of word and image seen on the Ruthwell Cross is unique, complex interactions of the visual and verbal elements of Anglo-Saxon works of art, and the conscious effort to unite the reader or viewer with the text or object, remained characteristic of Anglo-Saxon culture. Ruthwell is one of the earliest manifestations of this phenomenon; the Red Book of Darley, the focus of this paper, is one of the latest.

The Red Book of Darley (Cambridge, Corpus Christi College, MS 422) now consists of two parts which have been joined together from at least the twelfth century:[2] Part I (pp. 1–26) containing a tenth-century copy of the *Dialogues of*

---

[1] Éamonn Ó Carragáin, 'The Ruthwell Crucifixion Poem in its Iconographic and Liturgical Contexts', *Peritia*, 6–7 (1987–88), 1–71 (pp. 34–35).

[2] Additions to both parts were made by a single twelfth-century hand. Mildred Budny, *Insular, Anglo-Saxon, and Early Anglo-Norman Manuscript Art at Corpus Christi College, Cambridge: An Illustrated Catalogue* (Kalamazoo, 1997), p. 647.

Solomon and Saturn in prose and verse, and Part II (pp. 27–586),[3] a manual which combines elements of a sacramentary, missal, and breviary. Part II was produced *c.* 1061 either at Sherborne or at the New Minster, Winchester, for use at Sherborne.[4] The combination of texts in Part II is unusual and makes the book a significant witness to the development of the service book in Anglo-Saxon England, as well as to the development of medieval service books in general.[5] The liturgical readings are prefaced by a calendar and a series of computistical texts and tables (pp. 27–49), and by two pages of prayers and lections added in the twelfth century (pp. 49–50) to the blank pages at the end of the third quire. The liturgical texts begin with the Order of the Mass introduced by two images (Plate 3): a miniature of Christ in majesty which is part of the Preface of the Mass on p. 52, and a historiated initial containing a depiction of the crucifixion in the *T* that begins the Canon of the Mass on the facing page.[6] The basic subject matter is in no way unusual. By the mid-eleventh century there was a tradition of illustrating the Preface with an image of Christ in majesty, and the first prayer of the Canon with one of the crucifixion;[7] however, the way in which text and image are brought together in these two drawings is highly unusual, if not unprecedented. The iconography of both images has no exact parallel, an aspect of the pages that has been discussed at some length by Barbara Raw and Jennifer O'Reilly.[8] Neither scholar, however, was concerned with the way in which the opening lines of text

[3] Pages 571–86 were added in the twelfth century.

[4] Budny, *Catalogue*, pp. 645, 647.

[5] Helmut Gneuss, 'Liturgical Books in Anglo-Saxon England and their Old English Terminology', in *Learning and Literature in Anglo-Saxon England: Studies Presented to Peter Clemoes on the Occasion of his Sixty-fifth Birthday*, ed. by Michael Lapidge and Helmut Gneuss (Cambridge, 1985), pp. 91–141 (p. 101); Budny, *Catalogue*, p. 645.

[6] For a full list of the manuscript's contents, see Budny, *Catalogue*, no. 44.

[7] See Elizabeth Parker McLachlan, 'The Bury Missal in Laon and its Crucifixion Miniature', *Gesta*, 17 (1978), 27–35. The 'basic idea' of the design can be traced back to the eighth-century Sacramentary of Gellone (Paris, Bibliothèque nationale de France, fonds latin, 12048): see Richard Gameson, *The Role of Art in the Late Anglo-Saxon Church* (Oxford, 1995), p. 233; Eric Palazzo, *A History of Liturgical Books from the Beginning to the Thirteenth Century*, trans. by Madeleine Beaumont (Collegeville, MN, 1998), p. 57.

[8] Barbara C. Raw, *Anglo-Saxon Crucifixion Iconography and the Art of the Monastic Revival* (Cambridge, 1990); Jennifer O'Reilly, 'The Rough-hewn Cross in Anglo-Saxon Art', in *Ireland and Insular Art, A.D. 500–1200: Proceedings of a Conference at University College Cork, 31 October–3 November 1985*, ed. by Michael Ryan (Dublin, 1987), pp. 153–58.

function as a part of the images, an aspect of the manuscript that is every bit as unusual as its combination of texts or the iconography of its drawings.

The opening sequence of pages, pp. 51–53, is designed conventionally enough to draw the reader into the text and unite him[9] visually with the body of Christ, in a manner parallel to that in which he would be united physically with Christ in the Eucharist. The imagery does not illustrate the Mass, rather it illuminates its ultimate meaning; it 'makes Christ's death present [. . .] by sharing in the perpetual offering of Christ to his Father in the eternal present of heaven'.[10] The words of the text are themselves meant to accomplish the same thing, but the illustrations take the process further by allowing the viewer to experience visually, indeed sensually, the vision they convey. The text begins with the opening of the Order on p. 51, marked by a full-page initial *P* (Fig. 8).[11] The lines, written in display capitals, were recited alternately by the priest and the congregation.

> Per omnia secula seculorum
> Amen
> Dominus vobiscum
> Et cum spiritu tuo
> Sursum corda
> Habemus ad dominum

---

[9] I use the masculine pronoun throughout my discussion of the manuscript as the book was originally made for a priest, though we have no way of knowing exactly who. Christopher Hohler believed that the book was prepared by the original owner for his own personal use while travelling, and that the absence of the Masses for the principal feasts indicated that he expected to be back at his home base for these: Hohler, 'The Red Book of Darley', in *Nordiskt Kollokvium II I latinsk Liturgiforskning* (Stockholm, 1972), pp. 39–47 (p. 41). The presence of both Wulfsige's and Aldhelm's names in the calendar suggest that the manuscript was in Sherborne in the eleventh century. Wulfsige III was Bishop of Sherborne *c.* 993–1002, and Aldhelm was Bishop of Sherborne from 705. The manuscript may have been made at Sherborne, though its script is close to that of Winchester manuscripts of the late tenth century. Interestingly, a woman, the Empress Helena, became a focus for the book in the twelfth century, at which time a Mass for St Helen, lections for the Invention of the Cross, and antiphons including some addressed to St Helen were added to it. A sixteenth-century inscription on p. 586 identifies the manuscript as the Red Book of Darley, and indicates that it was owned by the church of St Helen at Darley Dale. It may well have been there as early as the twelfth century. The book may have been owned in the sixteenth century by Margaret Rollysley, who signed her name six times in the margins of pp. 130–31. The inscription on p. 586 also records that the manuscript eventually came into the possession of Richard Wendesley, who gave it to Matthew Parker. See further, Budny, *Catalogue*, pp. 648–50.

[10] Raw, *Anglo-Saxon Crucifixion Iconography*, p. 67.

[11] Page 50, the last verso of a quire, was originally blank.

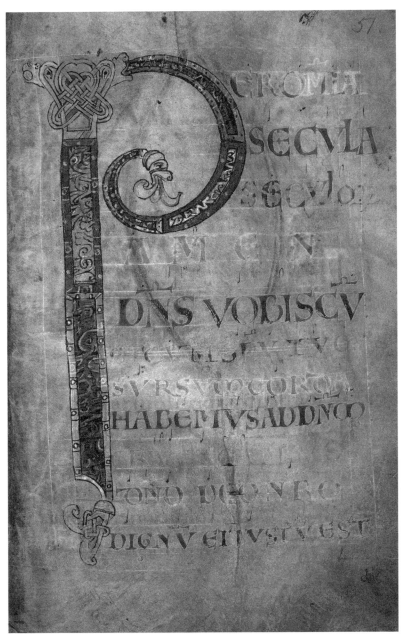

Figure 8. Opening of the Order of the Mass. Cambridge, Corpus Christi College, MS 422, p. 51. By kind permission of Corpus Christi College.

Gratias agamus domino deo nostro
Dignum et iustum est.

[Forever and ever.
Amen.
May the Lord be with you.
And with your spirit.
Lift up your hearts.
We have lifted up our hearts to the Lord.
Let us give thanks to the Lord our God.
It is right and just.][12]

These lines bring heaven and earth together by directing our hearts and prayers to God and expressing the hope that God will be with us. The body of the initial *P* is divided into panels filled with stylized acanthus ornament. While generally viewed as a purely decorative element of Anglo-Saxon art, acanthus scrolls traditionally symbolized redemption and/or paradise.[13] As such, it is possible to relate acanthus ornament, at least in some instances, to the vine-scrolls of the earlier sculpted stone crosses, like the cross at Ruthwell. The biting animal heads that make up the terminals of the upper stem and loop of the *P* might provide further evidence that a meaning of this sort may have been intended on this page. At the very least, the combination of animal and foliate ornament brings the letter to life and conveys a sense of organic, upward motion that both balances the motion of our eyes as we read down the lines of the page and visually suggests the raising up of hearts and voices described in the lines.

That sense of upward motion — visual, verbal, and spiritual — is continued when we turn the page and read the Preface.

Vere dignum et iustum est equum et salutare nos tibi semper et ubique gratios agere domine sancte pater omnipotens. Per christum dominum nostrum. Per quem majestatem tuam laudant angeli adorant dominationes tremunt potestates, coeli, coelorumque virtutes, ac beata seraphim socia exultatione concelebrant. Cum quibus et nostras voces ut admitti jubeas deprecamur supplici confessione dicentes. [Sanctus, sanctus, sanctus ...].[14]

---

[12] Punctuation of the Latin follows that of the manuscript throughout. Abbreviations have been silently expanded.

[13] See, for example, Catherine E. Karkov, *The Ruler Portraits of Anglo-Saxon England* (Woodbridge, 2004), p. 90; Herbert L. Kessler, *Seeing Medieval Art*, Rethinking the Middle Ages, 1 (Peterborough, 2004), pp. 29, 33.

[14] The *sanctus* is not included in CCCC 422.

[It is indeed just and right, our duty and our salvation, always and everywhere to give thanks to You, Lord, Holy Father, almighty and eternal. Through Christ our Lord. Through whom the angels praise Your majesty, the dominations worship it, the powers stand in awe. The heavens and the heavenly hosts together with the blessed seraphim in triumphant chorus unite to celebrate it. Together with them we entreat You that You may bid our voices also to be admitted, while we say in Holy praise. [Holy, Holy, Holy . . .].]

Here the arrangement of the text and illustration quite literally joins our words with those of the angels surrounding Christ. The union of the heavenly chorus with the voices of those participating in the Mass was made even clearer when neumes were added to the text, probably in the twelfth century.[15] The miniature itself does not simply accompany the text of the Preface, but is literally incorporated into it. It depicts Christ enthroned in a mandorla, one hand raised in blessing, suggesting that he has heard and received our words. In the other hand he holds a book representing, amongst other things, the eternal Word. Two angels carrying rods or sceptres support the mandorla, their wings crossed just above Christ's head. The words 'vere dignum et iustum est equum et salutare' are written in small capitals within the mandorla, physically surrounding Christ with words of praise, words which open with an echo of those that were lifted up to Christ on the previous page. Beginning with the word *nos*, they spread out around the lower bodies of the angels and flow seamlessly into the regular lines of text written at the bottom of the page. The result is both a revelation of our voices joining the angels in praise and the creation of a visionary space in which we are moved through voice, word, and eye first to a vision of Christ in heaven, a vision of the future in which we along with our words will be admitted into His presence, and then out again to the here and now of the text written on the page and the ecclesiastical setting in which it was recited.

The Canon of the Mass opens on the facing page with the *Te igitur*, a prayer of intercession.

TE IGITUR CLEMENTISSIME PATER PER JESUM CHRISTUM FILIUM TUUM DOMINUM NOSTRUM. Supplices rogamus ac petimus uti accepta habeas et benedicas. Haec dona. Haec sacrificia illibata. In primus quae tibi affermius pro ecclesia tua sancta catholica quam pacificare, custodire, adunare et regere digneris toto orbe terrarum una cum beatissimo famulo tuo.

[Therefore, most gracious Father, we humbly beg of You and entreat You through Jesus Christ Your Son, Our Lord. Hold acceptable and bless these gifts, these offerings, these holy and unspotted oblations which in the first place, we offer You for Your holy catholic

---

[15] Budny, *Catalogue*, p. 646.

church. Grant her peace and protection, unity and guidance throughout the worlds, together with Your blessed servant.]

On the previous page we saw the divine nature of Christ already in existence before his incarnation. On this page the eternal Word is made manifest in the human flesh of Christ crucified. The fact that the composition takes the form of a historiated initial helps not only to convey that symbolism, but again to unite the reader as he reads or recites these words with the body of Christ. Christ himself is represented as alive, and gazing with compassion at the figure of Mary who stands to his right; however, while his eyes are open, blood flows dramatically from the wound in his side. Above him are the dove of the Holy Spirit and the Hand of God.

As on the previous page our eyes are focussed on the central figure of Christ, who is surrounded and picked out visually by the dark green of the mandorla and the cross. Green is a colour that symbolizes life, the fertility of the earth and paradise.[16] It is used more specifically in the crucifixion miniature to identify the *tau* cross as a tree of life cross.[17] Plant motifs — the acanthus ornament of the initial *P* on p. 51, the sprig of a plant beneath the feet of Christ in majesty, the acanthus-like foliage that grows from and beside the cross — are also used to suggest the sequential and symbolic relationship of these three opening pages: the way in which they move us closer to union with Christ's body through participation in the Eucharist, and the salvation that such participation will bring. The two figural drawings also relate to each other compositionally through the way in which Christ is flanked by supporting figures: two angels on the one page, and the dove and Hand of God plus the Virgin and a column of text on the other. The 'interpenetration of the infinite and the finite' that is expressed in the performance of the liturgy is mirrored in the combined images of Christ, which together signify that it is through Christ's life and death that God, 'who is infinite and outside time, entered the finite world of human history'.[18] Reading the two images together, then, is every bit as important as reading them in relation to the prayers they introduce, and the artist has used specific details of iconography and composition to suggest the multivalent ways in which they relate to each other.

---

[16] Ananya J. Kabir, *Paradise, Death and Doomsday in Anglo-Saxon Literature* (Cambridge, 2001), pp. 142–47.

[17] On the *tau* cross in general, and this miniature's relation to other depictions of the *tau* cross in Anglo-Saxon crucifixion imagery, see O'Reilly, 'Rough-hewn Cross'.

[18] Raw, *Anglo-Saxon Crucifixion Iconography*, p. 67.

There are, however, also important differences between the compositions on the two facing pages. Christ in majesty is still and iconic, as is appropriate to the vision of eternity it depicts. The angels look directly out at us, helping our minds and eyes to negotiate the space between the world in which we stand and the as yet unattainable kingdom of heaven. The crucifixion, on the other hand, takes place in history. It is full of activity, and almost narrative in form, despite the fact that the event depicted is not narrated in the accompanying prayer. The dove with its wreath and the Hand of God enter the picture at dynamic angles; blood spurts from the wound in Christ's side and is echoed by the tendril growing from the side of the cross. The latter may be intended to symbolize the water that came from Christ's side at the crucifixion and is reminiscent of *The Dream of the Rood*, in which the visionary sees the cross begin 'swætan on þa swiðran healfe' ('to sweat on the right side').[19] The Virgin weeps emotionally into a fold of her robe as she gestures upwards toward the wound. Like the angels on the previous page, she is an intercessor, but a much more active and accessible one who not only looks out to meet our eyes, but whose gesture serves also to direct our eyes and our prayers (this is a prayer of intercession) to her Son. The open eyes of the living Christ help to suggest that our prayers have been heard and received with favour.

On its own the crucifixion is an almost frustratingly complex image. It is, first of all, not just a crucifixion but also a depiction of the Trinity with Mary.[20] As an image of the Trinity it figures the words of the absent *Sanctus* with their Trinitarian focus:

> Sanctus, sanctus, sanctus, dominus deus sabaoth. Pleni sunt coeli et terra gloria tua. Hosanna in excelsis. Benedictus qui venit in nomine domini. Hosanna in excelsis.
>
> [Holy, Holy, Holy. Lord God of Hosts. Heaven and earth are filled with your glory. Hosanna in the highest. Blessed is He Who comes in the Name of the Lord. Hosanna in the highest.][21]

---

[19] See Éamonn Ó Carragáin, '*Vidi Aquam*: The Liturgical Context of *The Dream of the Rood* 20a: "Swætan on þa swiðran healfe"', *NQ*, n.s., 30 (1983), 8–15.

[20] Surprisingly, it is not included in Barbara C. Raw, *Trinity and Incarnation in Anglo-Saxon Art and Thought* (Cambridge, 1997), even though it is somewhat contradictorily identified as an image of the Trinity in Raw, *Anglo-Saxon Crucifixion Iconography*, p. 155.

[21] For a different pictorial invocation of the *sanctus*, see the *Te igitur* page of the *c.* 790 Gellone Sacramentary (Paris, Bibliothèque nationale de France, fonds latin, 12048, fol. 143ʳ) in which the angels swoop down from heaven as if singing the hymn. See Lawrence Nees, *Early Medieval Art* (Oxford, 2002), pp. 169–70.

The movement from the Preface to the Canon of the Mass is thus effected on both a visual and a verbal level. The drawing of the crucifixion itself is a rare and very successful evocation of the inseparability of the two natures of Christ, and of the moment of Christ's death as the point at which that inseparability is most clearly demonstrated. The artist has used the diagonal line that runs between the hand of Mary and the Hand of God — their hands are almost mirror images of each other — to help convey that idea visually. The Hand of God the Father appears in the heavens, appropriately enough directly above the words 'Te igitur clementissime pater'. Christ's human mother stands on earth, and this is highlighted by the placing of a rocky groundline beneath her feet. Christ's wound, a sign of both his death and the eternal life that springs from it, rests approximately half way between the hands of God and Mary. While Mary may stand on earth, the location of the dove of the Holy Spirit over her head indicates that she is the mother not just of Christ incarnate, but of God,[22] and serves further to establish a link between the crucifixion and the annunciation. Barbara Raw has suggested that the complexity of the iconography may reveal a connection between this page and John of Fécamp's prayer *Summe sacerdotos*, in section 8 of which 'the bread and wine of the eucharist are linked to the flesh taken from Mary, who conceived through the Holy Spirit, and to the fountain which flowed from the wound in Christ's side'.[23] While such a connection remains uncertain, it would clearly be appropriate for the liturgical context of this particular text and image. The *Summe sacerdotos* and the *Te igitur*, like the sacrament of the Eucharist itself, are about transformation, as is virtually every aspect of this drawing. The theme of transformation can be extended to the *tau* cross on which Christ's body is suspended. It is not just a cross, but the sign of deliverance marked with the blood of the Paschal lamb in Exodus 12, the sign of the just in Ezekiel 9. 4, the sign of the Son of Man in Matthew 24. 30, and a sign of the Logos.[24] Its symbolism thus also serves to highlight the relationship between this image and that of Christ in majesty.

---

[22] See further the discussion of Mary in this iconography in Raw, *Trinity and Incarnation*, p. 180.

[23] Raw, *Anglo-Saxon Crucifixion Iconography*, p. 155.

[24] O'Reilly, 'Rough-hewn Cross', p. 154; Rudolf Suntrup, '*Te igitur*-Initialen und Kanon-bilder in mittlealterlichen Sakramentarhandschriften', in *Text und Bild, Aspekte des Zusammen-wirkens zweier Künste in Mittelalter und füher Neuzeit*, ed. by Christel Meier and Une Ruberg (Wiesbaden, 1980), pp. 278–382 (pp. 282–83, 289–303).

The presence of Mary without John is very unusual in an Anglo-Saxon crucifixion scene, as is the extreme emotion that she displays here.[25] As noted above,
she is present both as a guarantee of Christ's humanity and as an intercessor, and
it was in this last role that she was particularly popular in Anglo-Saxon England.
She was the focus of prayer from as early as the eighth century, and by the late
Anglo-Saxon period she had come to appear alongside Saints Michael and Peter
in prayers, homilies, and charters, many associated with centres of the monastic
reform such as Winchester and Worcester.[26] The ultimate source of these texts
was the apocryphal *Apocalypse of Mary* in which Mary, Michael, and apostles plead
for the souls of the damned.[27] In the CCCC 422 miniature, however, she also
appears as witness, a role with which she was traditionally, if less popularly, associated.[28] Gestures similar to the gesture towards the body of Christ that Mary
makes in this manuscript appear in a number of late Anglo-Saxon crucifixion
scenes.[29] She sees and she directs us to see. Her other gesture, raising her robe to
wipe away her tears, focuses our attention on her grief and on her role as mourner.
It is with these two roles, witness and mourner, that the owner of this manuscript
might have associated himself most closely. In his commentary on Psalm 21,
Augustine portrays Mary and John as role models of faith triumphing over the
Jews who mocked Christ, and he places the priest celebrating Mass with them at
the foot of the cross.[30] In looking at this image and reading this text, that is exactly
where the reader of this manuscript would be placed, both through his action as
he gazes, along with Mary, at the body of Christ, and through the arrangement of

[25] Other examples of the grieving Mary in Anglo-Saxon art are Cambridge, Fitzwilliam
Museum, no. M24–1938 (an ivory panel); Saint-Omer, Musée Sandelin, no. 2822 (an ivory
figure); London, British Library, Harley MS 2904, fol. 3ʳ (the Ramsey Psalter); Rouen,
Bibliothèque municipale, MS Y.6[274], fol. 71ᵛ (the Sacramentary of Robert of Jumièges).

[26] See further, Catherine E. Karkov, 'Judgement and Salvation in the New Minster Liber
Vitae', in *Apocryphal Texts and Traditions in Anglo-Saxon England*, ed. by Kathryn Powell and
Donald Scragg, Publications of the Manchester Centre for Anglo-Saxon Studies, 2 (Manchester,
2003), pp. 151–63.

[27] Mary Clayton, 'Delivering the Damned: A Motif in Old English Homiletic Prose', *Medium
Ævum*, 55 (1986), 92–102; Mary Clayton, *The Cult of the Virgin Mary in Anglo-Saxon England*
(Cambridge, 1990), p. 255.

[28] Clayton, *Cult of the Virgin*, p. 173.

[29] Paris, Musée Cluny (portable altar); Cambridge, University Library, MS Ff. 1. 23, fol. 88ʳ
(the Winchcombe Psalter); New York, Pierpont Morgan Library, MS 709, fol. 1ᵛ (the Judith of
Flanders Gospels).

[30] Raw, *Anglo-Saxon Crucifixion Iconography*, p. 81.

words on the page, which places the words 'supplices rogamus' ('we humbly pray') directly beneath the feet of Mary and Christ. It might be significant in this regard that the bishopric of Sherborne was dedicated to Mary, as this manuscript is thought to have been produced either at or for use at Sherborne Cathedral Priory.

The most unusual aspect of the CCCC 422 crucifixion is the absence of John, whose role as witness was one of the major themes of late Anglo-Saxon cruci-fixions.[31] In the crucifixion miniature in the late tenth-century Ramsey Psalter (London, British Library, Harley MS 2904, fol. 3ᵛ) John looks intently at the body of Christ as he writes on a scroll 'hic est discipulus qui testimonium perhibit' ('this is the disciple who bears witness to these things', John 21. 24); while in the mid-eleventh-century Winchcombe Psalter (Cambridge, University Library, MS Ff. 1. 23, fol. 88ʳ), a very sombre looking John inscribes on a tablet the words 'et ego vidi et testimonium' ('and I saw and gave testimony', John 19. 35).[32] In no other surviving Anglo-Saxon crucifixion scene does Mary appear beside the cross without John; nor, to the best of my knowledge, does she appear alone in early illuminated or historiated *Te igitur* initials.[33] Formally, the opening words of the *Te igitur* prayer are used in the Red Book of Darley to balance the figure of the Virgin and to complete the overall symmetry of the composition, as the figure of John would have done, which leads one to wonder: might this column of display capitals have been understood by the Anglo-Saxon artist and patron as substitut-ing for the figure of St John, witness to both the crucifixion and the water of life? Although its overall meaning is very different, one could cite as a slightly later parallel for a similar use of text the upper part of the miniature depicting Christ and Ecclesia in the Rupertsberg Codex of Hildegard von Bingen's *Scivias*, illus-trated in the third quarter of the twelfth century, in which a scroll with the words 'May she, O Son, be your Bride for the restoration of My people; may she be a mother to them, regenerating their souls through the salvation of the Spirit and the water' appears beneath Christ's left arm in place of the usual John. The words

---

[31] See especially, Jennifer O'Reilly, 'St John as a Figure of the Contemplative Life: Text and Image in the Art of the Anglo-Saxon Benedictine Reform', in *St Dunstan: His Life, Times and Cult*, ed. by Nigel Ramsay, Margaret Sparks, and Tim Tatton-Brown (Woodbridge, 1992), pp. 165–85.

[32] For illustrations of these images, see Raw, *Anglo-Saxon Crucifixion Iconography*, pls. X, XIV. Both manuscripts were produced at or for Ramsey. See Helmut Gneuss, *Handlist of Anglo-Saxon Manuscripts: A List of Manuscripts and Manuscript Fragments Written or Owned in England up to 1100* (Tempe, 2001), pp. 76, 123.

[33] For surveys of the material, see McLachlan, 'Bury Missal'; Suntrup, '*Te igitur*-Initialen'.

are those of God speaking directly to Hildegard in the text of the vision the image prefaces.[34]

There is nothing to connect the specific words of the CCCC 422 prayer with the writings of St John, but there are aspects of exegesis on John, as well as aspects of the iconography of these two pages, that suggest that this might have been the case. John was a model of virginity for anyone in the monastic life and was held up as an exemplary figure by monastic writers such as Aldhelm (Bishop of Sherborne from 705 to 710) and Ælfric.[35] As the apostle who wrote about Christ as the Word and image of God, he was also a model for the individual, specifically as scribe, and more generally as interpreter of scripture. Augustine instructed his readers to 'Raise yourself up to the evangelist, rise to his meaning'.[36] Ambrose too exhorted his readers to imitate John specifically by praying in front of a crucifix, placing themselves in his role as witness:

> Eris filius tonitrui, si fueris filius ecclesiae. Dicat et tibi de patibulo crucis Christus: ecce mater tua, dicat et ecclesiae: ecce filius tuus; tunc enim incipies esse filius ecclesiae, cum in cruce victorem videris Christum.

> [You will be a son of thunder if you have been a son of the church. May Christ say to you from the gibbet of the cross: 'Behold your mother' and may he say to the church, 'Behold your son'; then, truly, you will begin to be a son of the church when you see Christ victorious on the cross.][37]

What is crucial about this passage is that the reader/viewer actively takes part in the crucifixion. He does not just imitate John, but becomes John, beholding his mother Mary/Ecclesia. Barbara Raw notes that Christ's words to Mary and John are written next to their figures in the crucifixion miniature accompanying the *Te igitur* in a sacramentary from the second half of the tenth century from Verdun Cathedral (Munich, Bayerische Staatsbibliothek, Clm 10077, fol. 4ᵛ), drawing attention to the meaning of this particular moment and its significance for the reader as he participates in the Mass and is invited to participate symbolically in

---

[34] The original Rupertsberg manuscript was destroyed in World War II, but a facsimile had been produced between 1927 and 1933, and is now Eibingen, Abtei St Hildegard, cod. 1. The miniature illustrates Book 2, vision 6.

[35] Aldhelm: see Michael Lapidge and Michael Herren, *The Prose Works of Aldhelm* (Ipswich, 1979), p. 64; Ælfric: see *The Homilies of the Anglo-Saxon Church*, ed. by Benjamin Thorpe, 2 vols (London, 1844–46), I, 438, 458. See also Raw, *Anglo-Saxon Crucifixion Iconogrpahy*, p. 99.

[36] *In Johannis evangelium*, quoted in O'Reilly, 'St John', p. 171. See also Augustine, above p. 141.

[37] Quoted and translated in Raw, *Anglo-Saxon Crucifixion Iconography*, p. 100.

the crucifixion.[38] This is exactly what the reader of the Red Book of Darley is encouraged to do by the use of the text as part of the image in the crucifixion miniature. The arrangement of the opening words of the *Vere dignum* preface visualized the reader's voice surrounding Christ with words of praise; the arrangement of the words of the *Te igitur* place him alongside Mary at the foot of the cross as a son, and in this case a priest, of the Church. It is possible that this identification of the priest with John may have been furthered by the artist's depiction of Mary in a way that invites us to see her also as Ecclesia. Later representations of Ecclesia at the foot of the cross portray her holding out a chalice to catch the blood that flows from the wound in Christ's side, but, as Barbara Raw has pointed out, the gesture that the grieving woman makes towards the wound in this drawing may indicate her role as 'the guardian of the sacraments'.[39] Raw opts for an either/or interpretation of the figure,[40] but there is no reason that she could not have been intended to represent both Mary and Ecclesia.[41] The two had been identified with each other by the Anglo-Saxons since at least the tenth century,[42] and, as Éamonn Ó Carragáin reminds us, the life-giving water that flows from the cross in *The Dream of the Rood*, suggested here by the green leaf that grows from the cross, 'is a symbol of the salvation won by Christ and proclaimed by the Church'.[43]

The link between the viewer/reader and John would also have been encouraged visually in this drawing by the use of specific iconographic details which have their ultimate source in his writings. Perhaps most obviously, it was only in the account of the crucifixion in John's Gospel that Mary and the evangelist were described as present at the foot of the cross, and only John described the piercing of Christ's side, the making of the wound that figures so prominently in this drawing. John was also responsible for uniting the images of Christ and the tree of life.[44] In the Apocalypse, believed for much of the Middle Ages to have been written by the evangelist, John has a vision of the tree of life and of Christ in Majesty, in which he is told by Christ 'Blessed are they that wash their robes in the

---

[38] Raw, *Anglo-Saxon Crucifixion Iconography*, p. 81.

[39] Raw, *Anglo-Saxon Crucifixion Iconography*, p. 152.

[40] Raw, *Anglo-Saxon Crucifixion Iconography*, pp. 89, 151–52.

[41] Clayton (*Cult of the Virgin*, p. 169) identifies the figure in the initial to Psalm 51 in the Bury Psalter as either Mary or Ecclesia, noting that the one does not exclude the other.

[42] Clayton, *Cult of the Virgin*, chap. 4.

[43] Ó Carragáin, '*Vidi Aquam*', p. 14.

[44] See Revelation 22. 12–14; see also Ó Carragáin, '*Vidi Aquam*'.

blood of the Lamb: that they may have a right to the tree of life, and may enter in
by the gates into the city of heaven' (Revelation 22. 14). By including the detail
of the blood literally watering the leaf that grows from the cross and the acanthus-
like plant that has sprung up beneath it, the artist of the CCCC 422 drawing has
added a reference to this vision to the traditional *Te igitur* crucifixion scene.[45] The
tree of life cross is a feature of other Anglo-Saxon depictions of the crucifixion,[46]
but it is particularly appropriate here at the opening of the Canon of the Mass in
which the faithful will feed on the body and blood of Christ. Here too, the vision
of the tree of life is placed side by side with one of Christ in majesty,[47] and the two
are united further by the use of the colour green, the colour of the tree of life and
of paradise.[48]

It is impossible now to establish exactly for whom or by whom the Red Book
of Darley was produced, or the exact setting in which its texts would have been
read and its miniatures viewed.[49] We can, however, say that its complex integration of text and image, and its bringing together of the physical celebration of the
Mass with the act of reading and seeing, would have made it an especially personal
book, one that established a particularly sensual relationship between book and
reader. Just like the Ruthwell Cross, the opening pages of the Order of the Mass
demand the union of reader, word, and image. In the case of the Ruthwell Cross,
the reader/viewer is asked to identify with the voice and imagery of the monument, to touch the body of Christ as did the cross and the various figures, both
human and animal, depicted on it. The Red Book of Darley uses text and image
to unite the reader/viewer with the body of Christ in a different way, one that,
consciously or not, tropes the very act of integrating word and image: in drawing
the reader to Christ, the Word made flesh, it asks him to picture himself as text,
the flesh made word.

---

[45] The Lamb and a priest celebrating Mass at the altar are depicted in the terminals of the *V*
on the *Vere dignum* page in the mid-ninth-century Drogo Sacramentary (Paris, Bibliothèque
nationale de France, fonds latin, 9428, fol. 14ʳ). For an illustration, see Robert G. Calkins,
Illuminated Books of the Middle Ages (Ithaca, NY, 1983), pl. 86.

[46] See O'Reilly, 'Rough-hewn Cross'.

[47] Jennifer O'Reilly ('St John', p. 173) has put forward a similar interpretation of the combination of crucifixion and Christ in majesty illustrations in the contemporary Winchcombe
Psalter.

[48] On paradise see above, pp. 139, 141.

[49] See note 9 above.

The Mysterious Moment of Resurrection in Early Anglo-Saxon and Irish Iconography

Anna Maria Luiselli Fadda

C aroline Walker Bynum has recently pointed out that 'depictions of the general resurrection of humankind begin to appear only in the eighth century and only as part of other scenes (chiefly the crucifixion and Last Judgment); the mysterious moment of the resurrection of Christ was not directly depicted in art before the twelfth century'.[1] Amongst the earliest of such representations,[2] Bynum draws attention to an ivory panel, probably of Northumbrian origin, depicting the Last Judgement with a scene of the resurrection of the dead before the figure of Christ in majesty (Fig. 9: London, Victoria and Albert Museum, eighth–ninth centuries).[3] Another representation, portraying the crucifixion together with the moment of Christ's resurrection, is shown on the west side of the High Cross of Clonmacnois, Co. Offaly, Ireland (Fig. 10: Clonmacnois, Co. Offaly, second half of the ninth century).[4] The first scene above the base,

---

[1] Caroline Walker Bynum, *The Resurrection of the Body in Western Christianity, 200–1336*, Lectures on the History of Religion, 15 (New York, 1995), pp. 197–98.

[2] Bynum, *Resurrection*, p. 191. Amongst the earliest artistic representations of the general resurrection Bynum also includes the mid-ninth-century ivory used on the cover of the Book of Pericopes of the German emperor Henry II, which portrays the Crucifixion in a central position (Narbonne, Cathedral Treasury, mid-ninth century). This panel is, however, not of significance to the outcome of my argument.

[3] See C. R. Dodwell, *Anglo-Saxon Art: A New Perspective* (Manchester, 1982), pp. 88–89 and pl. 17b.

[4] For a description of the complete iconographic programme and the relevant representations, see, amongst others, Jacqueline O'Brien and Peter Harbison, *Ancient Ireland from Prehistory to the Middle Ages* (London, 1996), pp. 82–85; Roger Stalley, *Irish High Crosses* (Dublin, 1996).

Figure 9. The Last Judgement. Ivory panel, London, Victoria and Albert Museum. By kind permission of the Victoria and Albert Museum.

Bynum emphasizes, is to be understood as depicting the moment of Christ's reanimation and resuscitation, and she states that it is not, to her knowledge, found on the Continent.[5]

The significance of these two iconographic images is immediately clear. In the first place, their earliness offers precious evidence enabling us to recognize not only the characteristics, features, and forms by which the mystery of the resurrection was rendered *per figuras* as proclaimed in I Corinthians 15. 51, 'We shall all indeed rise again: but we shall not all be changed',[6] but also the ideas which were circulating in lands subject to the Christian mission on the margins of Europe and were connected with problems of the relationship between body and soul, as indicated in I Corinthians 15. 35, 'But some man will say: How do the dead rise again? Or with what manner of body shall they come?'. Furthermore, this evidence of Anglo-Saxon and Irish iconography is important because, whilst it involved new and different means of catechizing, it also availed itself of the attractive force and influence of images in order to present the moment of salvation in a form immediately recognizable to the faithful. The reasons for this choice are very clear. The mystery of life after death lay beyond the limits of the rational capacity of mankind. It was difficult to render linguistically the eschatological truth of the Pauline words in I Corinthians 15. 42–43, where the perishable body is raised imperishable, the dishonoured body is raised in glory, the weak body is raised in power, and the physical body is raised a spiritual body.

[5] Bynum, *Resurrection*, p. 198, n. 137.

[6] All English biblical quotations are taken from the Douay-Rheims version (in Richard Challoner's revision, 1749–52) as being close to the Latin Vulgate.

Figure 10. Clonmacnois, Co. Offaly, Cross of the Scriptures, west side.
Photo: Peter Harbison, by kind permission.

In the following pages, I seek to shed light on the 'language' which the two anonymous artists used to depict their understanding of the resurrection of the body after death. To begin with, I will pose certain reflections of a general nature on the typology of the two iconographic representations under discussion.

First, I wish to underline the exceptionally early development with which, in substantially peripheral areas such as England and Ireland, the iconography of the resurrection abandoned the traditional model of iconic symbolism (no doubt, under the stimulus of eastern monasticism or possibly because of a perceived danger to the faith in the lands of missionary activity), moving instead in the direction of a realistic representation of the central event of Christian salvation. Sensitive to these practical demands, our two artists depicted the theme of salvation not only as truth and divine reality but also truth and human reality. Whatever might be the quantity and quality of their personal devotion, the motivation underlying the iconographical choices of our two artists appears to have been the wish to present *in its totality* God's plan of redemption for man — formed from soul and body, the first immortal, the second ephemeral.

In both depictions, the resurrection is represented as neither a single scene nor an isolated image, but as part of complex and highly articulate dramatic compositions which develop the central theme of salvation through the sequence of historical events, arranged not according to the human experience of time — that is, the one first, the others following — but rather according to the sacral dimension of time. Therefore, these events could be considered as stopping places in God's design, each one with its own particular significance.

In the London ivory, we move from the central image of Christ as Judge within the mandorla, 'upon the seat of his majesty' (Matthew 25. 31), first towards the scene of humanity rising from the tomb (the event which precedes the Parousia, the advent of Christ at the Second Coming), and then towards that of the Last Judgement. Here the theme is entirely imagined and developed in eschatological time, as a vision of that which is known only through the word of God (Matthew 26. 64; Acts 7. 55); nonetheless, the 'day of the Lord', when Christ is in his glory, is seen as an actual reality.

In the Cross of Clonmacnois, the iconographic programme places Christ on the cross within the mandorla, depicted in the final act of his mission on earth. In two lower panels are depicted some earlier scenes of the passion which therefore, according to the human experience of time, precede the event in the mandorla. Finally, in the last panel, showing the very moment in which Christ rises from the sepulchre (this moment obviously comes in human chronology after the crucifixion), the artist projects his conception of the timelessness of the spirit in the theological significance of the redemption. However, here the iconography moves in perfect agreement with the canonical teaching of the Church: redemption involves not only the work which Christ completed on Calvary and his personal resurrection (Romans 3. 24; Colossians 1. 14; Ephesians 1. 7), but also the work which he will carry out at the end of time, at the moment of Parousia and the glorious resurrection of the just after the Day of Judgement (Luke 21. 28; Romans 8. 23; Ephesians 1. 14; 4. 30).

Despite the centrality of salvation in Christian doctrine, the chronological delay with which the resurrection (in the terms indicated by Bynum) had been iconographically imagined in the Middle Ages is by no means what we might have expected. This paradox may be explained by the great christological controversies occurring between the fifth and seventh centuries and the iconoclasm of the eighth to ninth centuries, both with their intense theological repercussions. Apostolic preachers and the activities of successive missionaries had accompanied their message with the hope of safe salvation, granted to all mankind by means of the crucifixion and resurrection of the Son and, with it, the resurrection of bodies on the Day of Judgement, coming at the end of time. The same great theological-philosophical diatribes of successive centuries, together with apocalyptic or eschatological writings both canonical and apocryphal, theological tracts, exegetical commentaries, homilies and sermons, and in general all the religious literature of the early Middle Ages, had placed at the centre of their discussion the bodily resurrection which implied the problematic passage from death to new life, from the decomposition of the body to its reconstitution, thus indicating that the matter in I Corinthians 15 was a key question.

The post-Apostolic Fathers had confronted the problem by making use of ancient metaphors for the resurrection. These were naturalistic images that transmitted the sense of material continuity or of repetition — for example, we may think of the famous legend of the phoenix[7] — but interpreted the eschatological event which, because of its nature, transcends the normal conditions of earthly life, according to the same mental and expressive categories in use in normal com-

---

[7] For the Old English poem about this mythical bird (the first 380 lines of which is based on the *De ave phoenice* usually ascribed to Lactantius), see the edition by N. F. Blake, *The Phoenix* (Manchester, 1964). See further Margaret Clare Sharp, 'A Historical and Literary Commentary on the *Phoenix* poem ascribed to Lactantius' (unpublished doctoral dissertation, University of Oxford, 1986), and Daniel O'Donnell, 'Fish and Fowl: Generic Expectations and the Relationship between the Old English *Phoenix* Poem and Lactantius's *De ave phoenice*', in *Germanic Texts and Latin Models: Medieval Reconstructions*, ed. by K. E. Olsen and others (Leuven, 2001), pp. 157–71.

munication. However, the change connected with the resurrection — that which is corruptible must clothe itself with immortality (I Corinthians 15), that which is mortal ought to be swallowed up in life (II Corinthians 5. 4) — demanded a different solution from what had been suggested up to that time: a theological solution to the unequivocal question posed in I Corinthians 15. 35, 'How do the dead rise again? Or with what manner of body shall they come?'.

It is true that from the end of the fourth century and beyond, more and more frequently 'the basic sense of bodily resurrection [was intended] not as transformation [or flux], but as reunion of scattered particles, which, once assembled, will shine with glory and never again undergo alteration'.[8] According to Bynum, 'relic cult and the doctrine of bodily resurrection were complementary ways of emphasizing the triumph of integrity over partition, of stasis and incorruption over decay'.[9] The truth is that the words of the Lord in Luke 21. 18, 'But a hair of your head shall not perish', guaranteed the structural integrity and the material continuity of bodies in the resurrection.[10]

It is also true that II Maccabees 7. 9–23 had made very clear that it is God, *rex mundi*, who will raise the dead to eternal life at the end of time, and through his mercy will render to each one spirit and life. The scriptures had also made clear that when man dies, the soul departs (Genesis 35. 18); on being raised from the dead, the soul returns into the body (I Kings 17. 21) and transforms the mortal body, once returned to dust (Genesis 3. 19) as 'a living soul' (Genesis 2. 7). Without any doubt, therefore, the scriptures were transmitting the idea that man would be raised from the dead in his totality, in his integrity of soul and of body (I Corinthians 15. 45; Genesis 2. 7). But the moment of resurrection — how the body relates with the soul, *how the dead are brought back to life* — remained nevertheless an ineffable truth, an inexpressible reality, beyond description in human language.

From the eighth century, iconography began to confront the theme of general resurrection, connecting it now both to the Last Judgement and to the crucifixion, with the purpose of instructing and edifying the Christian peoples. The

---

[8] Bynum, *Resurrection*, p. 158.

[9] Bynum, *Resurrection*, p. 108.

[10] The Fourth Lateran Council of 1215 was the first to confirm in a solemn and official manner the integrity and continuity of the resurrected body. See the *Conciliorum oecumenicorum decreta*, ed. by G. Alberigo and others (Bologna, 1972), Lateran IV, 1215, Canon 1, *de fide catholica*, pp. 230–31 (p. 230, lines 30–33: 'all of them will rise with their own bodies, which they now wear'). See also the Second Council of Lyons of 1274, *Conciliorum*, ed. by Alberigo and others, p. 314, and Bynum, *Resurrection*, p. 155 and n. 136.

patristic foundation of this practice is most authoritative. According to Augustine in his *De doctrina christiana*,[11] indoctrination, knowledge of the scriptures, and communication between men could occur, inter alia, whether mediated through 'signs' (*signa*) which address the 'eyes' (in a way, 'visible words': *uerba uisibilia*), or whether mediated through 'signs' which address the 'ears' and transmit sounds full of meaning (*significantem sonum*).[12] From his stance, Gregory the Great, in taking up Augustine's view, recognized and underlined the usefulness of images as instruments of indoctrination for the unlettered:[13] images were vested with a special importance in catechesis because they clarify immediately and lucidly the realities which are difficult to express and communicate with language.

If one considers the extraordinary influence of Gregory's pastoral teaching on Anglo-Saxon and Irish missionary practice,[14] it is not surprising that this use of iconographic representations in a didactic and liturgical function should have been fully confirmed and precisely documented in both England and Ireland. Here iconography is in fact a Bible in images and offers to the faithful a teaching and a fount of fertile meditation. It will suffice to consider, for example, the Irish crosses of the scriptures, to give an account of how these impressive iconographic monuments, 'unique documents in the history of Western Art'[15] and justly defined as 'sermons in stone',[16] were able to offer to Christians the concrete opportunity for continual learning and for constant meditation. In Anglo-Saxon lands, also, evidence in this sense is numerous and of extreme relevance.[17] Thus,

[11] Augustine, *De doctrina christiana libri quattuor*, ed. by Josef Martin, CCSL, 32 (Turnhout, 1962).

[12] *De doctrina christiana*, II.3.4, ed. by Martin, pp. 33–34.

[13] Gregory the Great, *Epistula* 9.209, in Gregory the Great, *Registrum epistularum*, ed. by Dag Norberg, CCSL, 140A (Turnhout, 1982), p. 768; *Epistula* 11.10, in ibid., pp. 873–76.

[14] See R. A. Markus, 'Augustine and Gregory the Great', in *St Augustine and the Conversion of England*, ed. by Richard Gameson (Stroud, 1999), pp. 41–49; Anton Scharer, 'The Gregorian Tradition in Early England', in ibid., pp. 187–201.

[15] See Hilary Richardson, 'The Concept of the High Cross', in *Irland und Europa: Die Kirche im Frühmittelater*, ed. by P. Ní Chatháin and M. Richter (Stuttgart, 1984), pp. 127–34.

[16] See Stalley, *Irish High Crosses*, p. 15.

[17] Catherine E. Karkov, Sarah Larratt Keefer, and Karen Louise Jolly, *The Place of the Cross in Anglo-Saxon England* (Woodbridge, 2006); for an exhaustive discussion of the argument, see now Éamonn Ó Carragáin, *Ritual and the Rood: Liturgical Images and the Old English Poems of the 'Dream of the Rood' Tradition* (London, 2005). See also Anna Maria Luiselli Fadda, 'La Croce nella tradizione poetica anglosassone (secc. VIII–X)', *Romanobarbarica*, 17 (2000–02), 333–59.

it is clear that in the field of content, the iconographic treatment does not stray from the canonical teaching of the Church, its practical utility being directed towards the promotion of religious instruction and to the spiritual elevation of Christians. But that which is characteristic and innovative is the use of the explanatory representations of the scriptures, based on texts and commentaries not necessarily canonical.

We should reflect above all on the extraordinary iconographical compositions of 'the things that shall befall you in the last days' (Genesis 49. 1), preserved in the London ivory (Fig. 9) which, as I mentioned earlier, depicts the last events which await for man 'from the foundation of the world' (Matthew 25. 34) — the bodily death, the resurrection of the body on the last day, the individual and general judgement. The complex iconographic programme of the panel develops in three levels. In the upper part, the scene reproduces faithfully the account of Matthew 25. 31–34. In the centre of the mandorla the Son of man is portrayed, seated 'upon the seat of his majesty' (Matthew 25. 31), whilst he unrolls a scroll on which are written the words of Matthew 25. 34, 'Venite, benedicti Patris mei, possidete paratum vobis regnum a constitutione mundi' ('Come, ye blessed of my Father, possess you the kingdom prepared for you from the foundation of the world'). On either side of Christ, two ranks of angels, arranged symmetrically, line up — three on each side — sounding their trumpets to summon and gather the souls (Matthew 24. 31; Ezekiel 7. 14; I Corinthians 15. 52).

The iconography of the central part of the panel also draws on the stock of written biblical sources. The whole scene, which is dominated by an angel who extends his arms towards the dead imploring them to rise, reproduces the Pauline account (I Corinthians 15. 52 or I Thessalonians 4. 16). The problem of how to represent the mysterious moment of the resurrection of the body on the day on which all humanity becomes liberated from the laws of the dead leads the artist to enrich the scene with many new details. By lingering over these realistic additions, by dwelling on the misery of the bodies, and tentatively even by representing their movements, he tries to render in the best possible way the reality of what was being recounted. The solution alighted upon is at once original and bold. While some bodies still lie inert, completely wrapped up in their shrouds, others are struggling to release themselves from the bandages which continue to envelop them. In the meantime, the souls, here represented in the form of doves, circle in flight to identify their own bodies, in order to gather up and reanimate their scattered bones (Ezekiel 37. 7). On the right-hand side, some figures await the arrival of their soul in the form of a dove. To the left, in an image of great appeal and sensitivity, a corpse with his mouth half-open turns his face towards his soul/dove in order to receive from it the vital breath and be empowered to rise up (Psalm 104. 29–30).

It is evident that the central idea of reference is the soul as 'the breath of life' (Genesis 2. 7). This idea, certainly, does not belong to Christianity alone. All the ancient religions share the belief in a force which rules life, which is precisely identified as wind, sigh, breath. In biblical language, some terms specifically designate the breath that is the beginning of earthly life, that is the human soul (Hebrew, *nefeš*, Greek, *psyché*, Latin, *anima*). The Latin *anima* alludes therefore to the blowing of breath, fragile and uncertain, which comes from God (Genesis 2. 7) and is made to return to him with death (Psalm 104. 29–30). Other terms signify the divine breath, the Spirit of God, which is the unique source of life (Hebrew *rûah*, Greek *pnèuma*, Latin *spiritus*). But the breath is inseparable from the body which it animates: it is the sign by which physical life manifests itself in man.

In the Middle Ages this concept finds its significant expression in the formulation of Isidore of Seville: 'The life of the body is the soul, and the life of the soul is God. And just as the body is dead without the soul, so the soul is dead without God.'[18] It is taken up in almost identical terms by Alcuin of York, Charlemagne's prestigious Anglo-Saxon advisor ('Just as the life of the body is the soul, so the life of the soul is God. When the soul leaves the body, the body dies'),[19] and it continues to be found, in the early years of the eleventh century, in Ælfric of Eynsham, the greatest of Anglo-Saxon homilists, who accompanies it with an impressive commentary:

> [. . .] ne gesihð nan man his saule on þisum life; Heo is úngesewenlic. ac þeahhwæðre heo wissað þone gesewenlican lichaman; Se lichama þe is gesewenlic· hæfð lif of ðære saule. þe is ungesewenlic; Gewite þ ungesewenlice út· þonne fylð adune þ gesewenlice. for ðan ðe hit ne stod na ær þurh hit sylf; Þæs lichoman lif is seo sawul· ꞇ þære saule líf is god; Gewite seo sawul ut· ne mæig se muð clypian. þeah ðe he gynige· ne eage geseon. þeah þe hit open si· ne nan lim ne deð nan ðing gif se lichama bið sawulleas.[20]

> [[. . .] no man sees his soul in this life. It is invisible, but, nevertheless, it guides the visible body. The body, which is visible, has life from the soul, which is invisible. If that which is visible depart, then will the visible fall down; because it before stood not of itself. The life

---

[18] Isidore, *Sententiarum libri tres*, cap. xii: de anima coeterisque sensibus, in *PL*, 83, 562a. The English translation is mine. See the full treatment of evidence for *anima* and *spiritus* by Beatrice La Farge in *'Leben' und 'Seele' in den altgermanischen Sprachen* (Heidelberg, 1990).

[19] Alcuin, *De animae ratione liber ad Eulaliam virginem*, *PL*, 101, 643b. The English translation is mine.

[20] *Ælfric's Catholic Homilies: The First Series: Text*, ed. by Peter Clemoes, EETS, SS, 17 (Oxford, 1997), p. 262, lines 120–28.

of the body is the soul, and the life of the soul is God. If the soul depart, the mouth cannot cry, though it gape; nor the eye see, though it be open; nor will any limb do anything, if the body be soulless.][21]

Nor is the image of the soul in the form of a dove original. It is well known that bird-imagery is frequently attested in patristic exegesis to represent the activities of the mind ranging in thought across sea and land.[22] The image of the bird/mind appears, to give one well-known example, in Boethius, *De consolatio philosophiae* (IV, prose I and metrum I).[23] In the eighth-century *Life of Gregory the Great* written by an anonymous monk of Whitby, it is related that when Bishop Paulinus died, 'his soul journeyed to heaven in the form of an exceedingly beautiful great white bird, like a swan'.[24] In Gregory the Great's *Dialogues*,[25] to give a more particular example, the soul is likened to a dove departing from the body at the time of death: St Benedict witnesses the soul of his sister Scholastica departing from her body 'in the form of a dove' (*in columbae specie*);[26] and when a priest named Spes dies, his brothers see a dove issuing 'from his mouth' (*ex ore eius*).[27]

This detail 'from his mouth' — which is not, to my knowledge, present until that moment — indicates a posture which recalls both the opening of the mouth in the funerary ceremonies of Ancient Egypt,[28] and the reuniting of *Ba*, the

---

[21] The translation is Thorpe's, from *The Homilies of the Anglo-Saxon Church: The First Part Containing the 'Sermones Catholici' of Ælfric*, ed. by Benjamin Thorpe (London, 1844–46; repr. New York, 1971), *dominica in quinquagesima*, pp. 152–65.

[22] See Peter Godman, *Poetry of the Carolingian Renaissance* (London, 1985), pp. 69–70. On the image of the soul in Western Art, see Ave Appiano, *Anima e forma: Studi sulle rappresentazioni dell'invisibile* (Torino, 2006).

[23] *La Consolazione della filosofia di Severino Boezio*, ed. by Claudio Moreschini (Turin, 1994), pp. 248–49.

[24] *The Earliest Life of Gregory the Great*, ed. by Bertram Colgrave (Cambridge, 1968; repr. 1985), p. 101; other evidence at p. 150, n. 68.

[25] Gregory the Great, *Dialogues*, ed. by Adalbert de Vogüé, 3 vols (Paris, 1979).

[26] *Dialogues*, 2.34.1, ed. by de Vogüé, II, 235.

[27] *Dialogues*, 4.11.4, ed. by de Vogüé, III, 49.

[28] See Jan Assmann, *Images et rites de la mort dans l'Égypte ancienne* (Paris, 2000), pp. 40–41; Jan Assmann, *Death and Salvation in Ancient Egypt* (Ithaca, NY, 2005), especially pp. 90–112; 310–17; Martin Bommas, *Heiligtum und Mysterium: Griechenland und seine ägyptischen Gottheiten* (Mainz, 2005), esp. pp. 11–13 (illustration at p. 11). The ritual for the opening of the mouth is the fundamental process for the preparation of the corpse for his 'second life' in the world to come. The collection of internal organs during the process of mummification lasting seventy days separated the body into its constitutive parts, being then ritually reconstituted. The

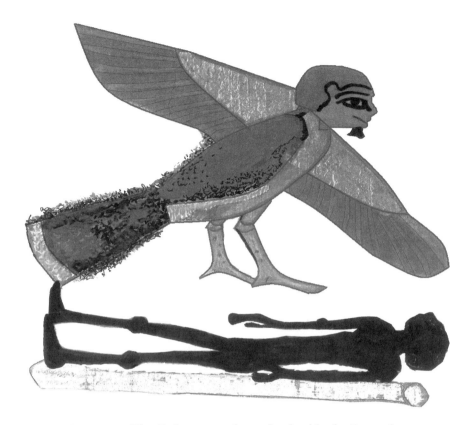

Figure 11. The *Ba* hovering above the dead body. From the
Livre des Morts de Tchenena (Egypt, Nouvel Empire, XVIII dynasty),
Paris, Musée du Louvre. Drawing by Luca Luiselli.

bird/soul, with its body (Fig. 11). (The *Ba*, one of the five constituent elements
of the human person, appears frequently in the form of a bird with a human head,
sometimes with human arms as well, in Egyptian sources and in papyri, where it
is often placed near its body. The *Ba* was closely connected to the physical body,
with which it shared the most natural demands and physical pleasures, such as

restoration of the heart through the mouth gave back to the dead person his own memory and
his personal identity and determined his personal continuity beyond death. (I am most grateful
to Dr Martin Bommas, University of Birmingham, for providing me with invaluable clarification
on funerary rites in Ancient Egypt.)

food, drink, and sexual activity. In order for the deceased to survive in the afterlife, the body had to be reunited with the *Ba* every night, thus reconstituting itself as an entity; and in the funerary ritual came 'the cancellation' of the separation of the *Ba* from his body first of all.)[29] We cannot be certain that this iconographic detail is a revival from Egypt, but much evidence appears to confirm it.[30] Egyptian religion considered death (following Jan Assmann's words) as 'la plus grande manifestation du divin et du sacré'; it promised to man 'une proximité de dieu après la mort'.[31] And again: 'La mort est la source et l'accomplissement du sacré,

[29] For essential bibliography, see Assmann, *Images et rites*, pp. 35, 83–86, and throughout; Ian Shaw and Paul Richardson, *British Museum Dictionary of Ancient Egypt* (Cairo, 1996), s.v. *Ba*, p. 47; Martin Bommas, 'The Ancient Egyptian Concept of Personal Constituents as Manifestation of Power and Knowledge', in *Anima e corpo: Lessico, idee, figurazioni letterarie e iconografiche nell'Antichità e nell'Alto Medioevo*, ed. by Anna Maria Luiselli Fadda, Atti del Convegno Internazionale, 12–13 marzo, 2004, Roma (forthcoming). See also H. P. Hasenfratz, 'Tod und Seele im alten Aegypten', in *Tod und Jenseits im Altertum*, ed. by G. Binder and B. Effe (Trier, 1991), pp. 88–102.

[30] It is well known that Egyptian religion exercised an enormous influence not only in the Hellenistic and Roman eras but also throughout the whole Middle Ages, above all through the mediation of Egyptian (Coptic) monasticism (the Coptic monks of the Egyptian desert lived amongst such important personalities of early Christianity as John Chrysostom, Rufinus, Palladius, Basil the Great, and Cassian). Michelle P. Brown, in *The Lindisfarne Gospels: Society, Spirituality and the Scribe* (London, 2003), p. 28, has pointed out that 'Eastern influences have long been recognised in Insular religion' and that 'there are also intriguing artistic influences, and perhaps transmission of techniques, such as the eastern "Coptic" form of sewing and binding preserved in the form of the St Cuthbert Gospel (British Library, Loan MS 74) which is suggestive of an actual learning/teaching process'. In literature, the most widely diffused theme in the Middle Ages, that of the 'Dialogue of the soul and the body', has long been related to the famous 'Dispute of a man with his *Ba*' from the period of the Middle Kingdom, which allows us to establish more securely connections with the Egyptian tradition: see Louise Dudley, *The Egyptian Elements in the Legend of the Body and Soul*, Bryn Mawr College Monographs, 8 (Baltimore, 1911); *The Report about the Dispute of a Man with his Ba: Papyrus Berlin 3024*, ed. by Hans Gredicke (Baltimore, 1970). In iconography, the certain influence of Egyptian funerary ritual is already indicated in the Muiredach Cross of Monasterboice, Co. Louth, Ireland (see Stalley, *Irish High Crosses*, p. 35 and pl. 9); the same older decoration of the manuscripts, for example in the *Cathach* of St Columba (Colum Cille), now at Dublin, Royal Irish Academy, and dated to the first years of the seventh century, has been attributed to Egyptian influence (see Michael Richter, 'Irland und Europa: die Kirche im Fruehmittelalter', in *Irland und Europa*, ed. by Ní Chatháin and Richter, pp. 409–32 (p. 431)), although with some reservations (see Julian Brown, 'The Oldest Irish Manuscripts and their Late Antique Background', in *Irland und Europa*, ed. by Ní Chatháin and Richter, pp. 311–27 (p. 326)).

[31] Assmann, *Images et rites*, p. 27.

la forme originelle du divin [...]. Elle est l'origine et la destination de la vie, *Alpha* et *Omega*, la réalité ultime.'[32] Also in our panel death re-enters into the sphere of the sacred, reabsorbed in the life of the soul. The separation of the soul from the body at the moment of death, its subsistence remote and independent of the body, the compulsory nature of its reconnection with the body at the time of the end, its ultimate destination towards the eternal life, after the divine judgement and the individual retribution, are all certainties that the London ivory shares in large measure with Egyptian religion. But the point I want to make is that here, for the first time in Christian areas, the soul-body problem assumed an iconographical form in which the corporeal could intelligibly be said to associate with the incorporeal, indicating that this was a key question.

Finally, in the lower part of our panel, the theme of the Last Judgement is depicted, which will close the time of history and will open the eternal kingdom of the Son of man (Daniel 7. 13–14). The iconography unfailingly illustrates Matthew 25. 31–46 with the addition of some details not described in the gospel text, but of great significance for the exegesis of I Corinthians 15. 35. All the dead are now gathered before the Highest Judge seated on the throne of his glory, separated the one from the other, the good on the right hand and the wicked on the left (Matthew 25. 32). To the right of Christ, an angel with open arms welcomes the just to introduce them transformed into their new life, according to I Corinthians 15. 52, 'the dead shall rise again incorruptible. And we shall be changed': they put on sumptuous clothing, the clothes of feast days. In fact, as returning 'living souls' (Genesis 2. 7), the elect wait until the manifestation of God is completed, so that the promise of the glory of paradise will be fulfilled. The symbolism of the clothes is very clear. According to Matthew 17. 2, just as the flesh of Christ had shown itself glorious in the splendour of the clothing at the moment of transfiguration, so now, at the hour of the Great Judgement, the bodies of the just bear, in the sumptuousness of clothing, the sign of the incorruptible glory of their spiritual condition. To the left of Christ, in contrast, a crowd of reprobates waits to be cast down in a second death, and in the meantime they crowd together, naked and terrified, before the Adversary of God, who is depicted according to biblical symbolism as an enormous beast with its jaws open: the Beast par excellence — the dragon, the serpent, Rahab, or Leviathan of Isaiah 27. 1; 51. 9; Job 7. 12, 41; Revelation 13. 1–11 — which avidly swallows and devours them.[33] Nudity and

---

[32] Assmann, *Images et rites*, p. 27.

[33] On the iconography of the resurrection of the dead, see particularly Bynum, *Resurrection*, especially pp. 186–99. The principal depictions of the Last Judgement (fourth–fourteenth

terror signal spectacularly the spiritual condition of those who have lived in guilt and now fear divine anger and punishment: 'I was afraid, because I was naked', says Adam to the Lord in Genesis 3. 10. In fact, it is the spoliation of clothes on Judgement Day which affirms the indignity of fallen man and his exclusion from everlasting glory.

It is hardly necessary to underline that the need to render recognizable an invisible nature, that of the spirit — not less real than perceptible nature — and hence to give a rational and pragmatic reply to the problem of man's destiny, assumes a material form in the iconography of our panel. From the corporality of the condition which attends the reprobates at the end of time (that is, ingestion, mastication, and the physical annihilation of the body) to the corporality of the individual soul (the dove), the incorporeal here becomes actual fact by means of images found and confined within the horizon of human experience. Nevertheless the basic ideology of our artist is apocalyptic: he believes in the celestial life which awaits all mankind 'in the time of the end' (Daniel 8. 17), when God's plan, having reached its conclusion, will carry out, together with judgement, the punishment of sinners and the salvation of the just. His message is in fact essentially established by making the distinction between a transitory period, which involves the experience of the soul after death until the Judgement Day, and a period, definitive and eternal, following the resurrection of the dead down to the Last Judgement. Thus, the artist directs the iconographic scheme of the panel towards the figurative description of this design by God for humanity.

On the west side of the High Cross of Clonmacnois (Fig. 10),[34] the iconography is also articulated as a function of God's design for salvation. Whilst in the London ivory the resurrection is related to the Parousia, as occurs in the first preaching of the mystery of salvation (for example, I Peter 1. 3; I Thessalonians 1. 10), at Clonmacnois the passion and resurrection of Christ are not only clearly connected one to the other (for example, Philippians 2. 9), but they constitute an indissoluble unity. Thus, while the whole east side of the cross (Fig. 12) is dedicated to the glorification of Christ, the west side, which interests us here, confronts in a global way the christological event, making use of a mise en scène of great dramatic force.

---

centuries) are discussed by Alison Morgan in *Dante and the Medieval Other World*, Cambridge Studies in Medieval Literature, 8 (Cambridge, 1990). On the motif of the Mouth of Hell and its connections with Leviathan, see especially Robert Hughes, *Heaven and Hell in Western Art* (New York, 1968).

[34] See O'Brien and Harbison, *Ancient Ireland*, pp. 82–85.

Figure 12. Clonmacnois, Co. Offaly, Cross of the Scriptures, east side.
Photo: Peter Harbison, by kind permission.

In the mandorla, Jesus, crowned with thorns, is nailed to the cross: it is the ninth hour, the last moment before his death. To the right, a figure armed with a long stick, a sponge at its tip, gives the dying Christ something to drink (Matthew 27. 46), and to the left, a soldier with a lance awaits His death in order to pierce His side (John 19. 34). St John, in his Gospel, had expressed in an emotionally charged and incisive form the Son of God's death (19. 30): 'And bowing his head, he gave up the ghost.' Our artist conforms to the image given by John and represents visually the invisible divine spirit, by means of its well-known symbol, the dove. Therefore, in one of the four small decorative medallions — the one which is set into the ring under the 'footstool' (*scabellum*: for example, I Chronicles 28. 2; Matthew 22. 44; Acts 2. 35) for Jesus's feet on the cross — we glimpse a dove with open wings flying towards the lower part: it is the spirit of Christ leaving his lifeless body.

It is possible that this representation may not be an original idea of our artist. In the canonical Gospels, the presence of the Spirit of God in Jesus shows itself on one occasion only, at the baptism in the River Jordan, when it descends from the sky in the form of a dove and rests on Christ's head (Matthew 3. 16–17; Mark 1. 10; Luke 3. 21–22; John 1. 32–34). But a widely diffused apocryphal text (*The Odes of Solomon*),[35] composed at the dawn of Christianity (*c*. A.D. 70) by an anonymous poet of Judaeo-Christian origin, preserves for us an image very close to that of Clonmacnois. In following the canonical scene of baptism, the poet imagines that the dove, symbol of the Holy Spirit, settles itself on Christ's head after he had breathed his last, whilst previously, at his baptism, it had entered into him:

> The dove flew above the head of Christ,
> because he was its lord.
> The bird sang above him
> and its voice resounded.[36]

That this text was the ultimate source for the Irish artist seems to be fairly likely. The circumstances are the same: also on the Cross of Clonmacnois the Holy Spirit in the form of a dove is present beside Christ in the moment of His death

---

[35] *Gli apocrifi del Nuovo Testamento*, ed. by Mario Erbetta, 3 vols (Torino, 1975), I.1–2 'Vangeli', I.1 Appendice, pp. 608–58. See also *The Odes of Solomon*, ed. by James Hamilton Charlesworth (Oxford, 1973), and *Oden Salomos: Text, Übersetzung, Kommentar*, ed. by Michael Lattke, 3 vols, Novum testamentum et orbis antiquus, 41 (Freiburg, 1999–2005).

[36] Ode 24: see *Gli apocrifi*, ed. by Erbetta, I.1–2 'Vangeli', I.1 Appendice, pp. 642–43; bibliography, synthesis of opinions, transmission, origins, and theology at pp. 608–18. The English translation is mine.

(in the image of the medallion). But the dove is close to Christ also in the moment of his resuscitation. This scene, portrayed in the lowest panel of the shaft of the west side of the cross (see Fig. 13), follows Matthew 27. 59–60 closely. Jesus, by now inert, is wrapped in a shroud, lying within the tomb sealed by a heavy sepulchral stone, on which sit two guards armed with lances, deeply asleep; other figures, presumably the pious women, are watching close to the guards. But here the artist adds a detail that the gospel account ignores. Jesus is portrayed with his mouth open, according to the typical Egyptian cliché, in the same posture as the dead on the London ivory, while the Holy Spirit, close by in the form of a dove, is restoring to him the breath of life. It is not necessary to search for any possibility of further sources to explain this detail. In all of this, there is a logical connection. Death is a departure, the separation of the soul from the body; but the body, closed in the tomb with its mouth open, presupposes the eventual return and resumption of an interrupted relationship.

It is evident that our artist aims to give here an organic and rational explanation of the fact of the resuscitation, implementing *per figuras* the silence of the evangelists. As has already been noted, the evangelists do not describe the event. They are silent both on the moment and on the way in which Christ recovered his spirit which, by his death, he had given up to God. They refer solely to the prodigious signs that follow the event (thus Matthew 28. 2 and following). It is also evident that our artist wishes to offer a theological explanation of it, in line with Christian thought. Two messages are transmitted with particular clarity. The first is not only that death and resurrection are strictly related one to the other, but that they constitute two indissoluble aspects of the unique mystery of salvation. The soul which leaves the mortal body of Christ and which seems circumscribed in the limits of its human individuality is the same Spirit which revives Jesus and makes of him 'a life-giving spirit' (I Corinthians 15. 45). The second message concerns the interpretation of the God-Man mystery in line with the official thought of the Church. As in the human person, there is here a unity of soul and body; so, as a Christian with strong theological interests, he sees this unity being repeated in the person of Christ, 'perfect God, perfect man', endowed with two natures, the divine nature as God, the human nature as human.[37] Christ is joined to his own mortal body just as the soul is united to the body: this iconographic presentation strongly supports the idea that the wholeness is associated with

---

[37] Council of Calcedon, A.D. 451: *Acta conciliorum oecumenicorum*, ed. by E. Schwartz, vol. II (Berlin, 1922–30), pp. 1932–38.

Figure 13. Clonmacnois, Co. Offaly, Cross of the Scriptures,
bottom panel of west side. Photo: Peter Harbison, by kind permission.

salvation and that in the moment of corporeal resurrection incorrupt bodies with their souls will be fully alive again.

But this iconography of salvation involves far more than the idea of an artist with strong theological interests whose spirituality is firmly anchored to the scriptures. It expresses a strong preoccupation, shared by the London ivory, on the mystery of life beyond death, on the body and on the soul, on the real significance of resurrection. Most of all, there is the problem of the relationship between the material and the immaterial, between the two processes of decomposition and reconstitution. The images indicate this type and this degree of speculation, and they betray the fears and the hopes about that which awaits man, the human being, after death.

Beyond doubt, the very fact that visibility was given to the crucial problem of the identity of man after death, as well as that an explanation of it was presented in such a concrete and rational way, constituted a remarkable legacy for all scholars, poets, mystics, religious, artists — not only in Anglo-Saxon England and Ireland but throughout western Christendom — who, in successive periods, would demonstrate afresh these same anxieties over the Christian promise of corporeal resurrection.

WHY SIGHT HOLDS FLOWERS:
AN APOCRYPHAL SOURCE FOR THE ICONOGRAPHY
OF THE ALFRED JEWEL AND FULLER BROOCH

Charles D. Wright

The enigmatic cloisonné enamel figure on the front of the Alfred Jewel (Fig. 14), a half-length portrait of a wide-eyed man seated and holding what appear to be flowers in each hand, has inspired many efforts at identification.[1] Only two proposed solutions, however, are still regularly cited as more or less equally plausible: Egil Bakka's that it is a personification of Sight,[2] and D. R. Howlett's that it is Christ as Wisdom.[3] Both identifications have much to commend them. Howlett draws attention to similar representations in early Insular manuscript illumination and sculpture of a figure holding floriate rods. The most impressive parallel is a roundel within the Temptation of Christ page in the Book of Kells (Dublin, Trinity College Library, MS 58, fol. 202ᵛ), which shows a bust of a nimbed man holding floriate rods (or labara?) in either hand.[4]

---

[1] For detailed descriptions of the Alfred Jewel, see David A. Hinton, *A Catalogue of the Anglo-Saxon Ornamental Metalwork 700–1100 in the Department of Antiquities Ashmolean Museum* (Oxford, 1974), no. 23, pp. 29–48, and Joan R. Clarke and David A. Hinton, *The Alfred and Minster Lovell Jewels*, 2nd edn (Oxford, 1979). It has generally been dated to the late ninth century. For an account of its discovery in 1693 near Athelney, Somerset, a site closely associated with Alfred, see Simon Keynes, 'The Discovery and First Publication of the Alfred Jewel', *Somerset Archaeology and Natural History*, 136 (1992), 1–8.

[2] Bakka, 'The Alfred Jewel and Sight', *Antiquaries Journal*, 46 (1966), 277–82. Hinton endorses Bakka's interpretation (*Catalogue*, p. 44).

[3] Howlett, 'The Iconography of the Alfred Jewel', *Oxoniensia*, 39 (1974), 44–52.

[4] This page has often been reproduced; for a readily accessible colour reproduction, see Bernard Meehan, *The Book of Kells* (London, 1994), p. 11. The parallel was first noted by O. M.

Howlett's interpretation of these rods as the flowering rod of Aaron is cogent for those representations (the great majority) in which Christ holds a floriate rod in one hand and a different object (usually a cross or a book, but in other cases a sword or keys) in the other. For those such as the Book of Kells, in which Christ (?) holds *two* such rods, it is rather less satisfactory, and Howlett's attempt to associate them with the Old Testament urim and thurimm is unconvincing.

Still, figures in the so-called 'Osiris pose' that hold flowers or floriate rods in both hands do afford striking parallels for the Alfred Jewel. As its name suggests, however, the 'Osiris pose' is not associated exclusively with the iconography of Christ, even in Christian art; similar depictions of evangelists, saints, angels, and other personages or personifications are found in early medieval works of art.[5] Indeed, in one of the most striking (and temporally and geographically proximate) parallels for the Alfred Jewel, the Anglo-Saxon silver niello disc-brooch known as the Fuller Brooch (Fig. 15),[6] the figure is a personification of Sight, part of a

Dalton, 'A Note on the Alfred Jewel', *Proceedings of the Society of Antiquaries*, 2nd series, 20 (1904), 71–77 (p. 71). As Hinton notes (*Catalogue*, p. 37), 'Designs of Christ holding two sceptres, some floral-headed, have a long ancestry, but not of Christ holding two flowers'. It is not certain, in any case, that the bust represents Christ; the figure is unbearded, whereas the much larger figure of Christ atop the Temple is bearded. Maidie Hilmo argues that the bust represents Christ's human nature, the larger figure his divine nature: *Medieval Images, Icons, and Illustrated English Literary Texts: From the Ruthwell Cross to the Ellesmere Chaucer* (Aldershot, 2004), p. 67.

[5] Many examples are cited by David Pratt, 'Persuasion and Invention at the Court of King Alfred the Great', in *Court Culture in the Early Middle Ages: The Proceedings of the First Alcuin Conference*, ed. by Catherine E. Cubitt, Studies in the Early Middle Ages, 3 (Turnhout, 2003), pp. 189–221 (pp. 216–20); see also Hinton, *Catalogue*, pp. 37–38. Martin Warner, 'The Madonna and Child Miniature in the Book of Kells: Part I', *Art B.*, 54 (1972), 1–23 (pp. 11–12), would identify some foliate rods in Insular art as palms; see also note 22 below.

[6] For detailed discussions of the brooch, see R. L. S. Bruce-Mitford, *Aspects of Anglo-Saxon Archaeology: Stutton Hoo and Other Discoveries* (New York, 1974), pp. 303–45; David M. Wilson, *Anglo-Saxon Ornamental Metalwork 700–1100 in the British Museum*, Catalogue of Antiquities of the Later Saxon Period, 1 (London, 1964), pp. 91–98, 211–14. Bruce-Mitford (p. 317) dates the brooch on stylistic grounds to 'the second quarter of the ninth century, or perhaps *c.* 850'. The Trewhiddle style, however, is predominantly mid- to late ninth century (see David M. Wilson, *Anglo-Saxon Art from the Seventh Century to the Norman Conquest* (London, 1984), p. 96; Leslie Webster in *The Making of England: Anglo-Saxon Art and Culture AD 600–900*, ed. by Webster and Janet Backhouse, British Museum Exhibition Catalogue (London, 1991), p. 268), and more recent scholarship has preferred a date for the Fuller Brooch in the second half of the ninth century to the early tenth century; cf. Hinton, *Catalogue*, p. 38. Webster (p. 280) and Pratt ('Persuasion', pp. 208–09) both date the brooch to the end of the ninth century. It is therefore probably roughly contemporary with the Alfred Jewel, but unfortunately its provenance is unknown.

Figure 14. The Alfred Jewel (gold, rock crystal, enamel; length 6.2 cm).
By kind permission of the Visitors of the Ashmolean Museum, Oxford.

Figure 15. The Fuller Brooch (silver niello; diameter 11.4 cm).
By kind permission of the Trustees of the British Museum.

programmatic representation of the Five Senses. Sight, the central figure, is surrounded by four lentoid panels containing smaller figures whose gestures clearly
show that they represent (clockwise from upper right) the other four senses of
Smell, Touch, Hearing, and Taste.[7] Sight holds what Robert Bruce-Mitford terms
'cornucopia',[8] from which emerge stylized plants of some kind.

It was on the strength of the formal correspondence with the Fuller Brooch
that Bakka argued the figure on the Alfred Jewel is also Sight. Howlett downplays

---

[7] See Bruce-Mitford's discussion of the iconography, *Aspects of Anglo-Saxon Archaeology*, pp.
317–25.

[8] Bruce-Mitford, *Aspects of Anglo-Saxon Archaeology*, p. 324.

the similarities between the two by stressing the different treatment of the common elements: 'the heads tilt in opposite directions, the eyes and facial features are distinct, and the flowers, vestments, colours, and media are all dissimilar'.[9] Yet these variations are no greater than those between the Alfred Jewel figure and the images of Christ that Howlett finds compelling, and the overall similarity of design is striking. If, as many scholars (including Howlett) have thought, the Alfred Jewel is an *æstel* intended for use as a book pointer,[10] an image of Christ figured as Wisdom would accord with the jewel's putative function in a general way; but an image of Sight would be even more specifically appropriate to an object that would, in Howlett's words, 'guide the eye and [...] aid copyists by preventing eye-skip'.[11]

Matthew Kempshall and David Pratt have independently associated the iconography of the Fuller Brooch and Alfred Jewel with the image of the 'mind's eyes', the *oculi mentis*, a Neoplatonic and patristic commonplace that Asser, drawing on Gregory's *Regula pastoralis*, applied to Alfred, and that Alfred himself rendered

---

[9] Howlett, 'Iconography', p. 50.

[10] In his Prologue to the translation of Gregory's *Pastoral Care*, Alfred says that he is sending to each of his bishops a copy of the book with an *æstel* worth 50 mancuses: *King Alfred's West-Saxon Version of Gregory's Pastoral Care*, ed. and trans. by Henry Sweet, EETS, OS, 45 and 50 (London, 1871), pp. 6–8. The meaning of the word *æstel* has been disputed, but it most likely refers to a 'pointer' for a book, and the Alfred Jewel, which has a flat back and a fitting designed to hold a short wooden or ivory rod, would serve such a function admirably. The similarly configured but less elaborate Minster Lovell jewel, as well as the more recently discovered fittings from Bowleaze Cove and Cley Hill, may have served the same function. See Pratt, 'Persuasion', pp. 196–98, with figs 29–31, and Leslie Webster, '*Aedificia nova*: Treasures of Alfred's Reign', in *Alfred the Great: Papers from the Eleventh-Centenary Conferences*, ed. by Timothy Reuter (Aldershot, 2003), pp. 79–103 (pp. 83–86, with figs 2–4). For detailed presentation of the linguistic evidence, see D. R. Howlett, 'Alfred's *Æstel*', *English Philological Studies*, 14 (1975), 65–74. The *æstel* theory has been supported as the most convincing one by, among others, Bakka ('Alfred Jewel', p. 282), Hinton (*Catalogue*, pp. 46–47), Pratt ('Persuasion', pp. 198–99), and Webster ('*Aedificia nova*', p. 82; 'Alfred Jewel', in *The Blackwell Encyclopaedia of Anglo-Saxon England*, ed. by Michael Lapidge and others (Oxford, 1999), pp. 28–29). According to an alternative view, the jewel may have been part of a crown or sceptre. Simon Keynes and Michael Lapidge, *Alfred the Great: Asser's Life of King Alfred and Other Contemporary Sources* (Harmondsworth, 1983), p. 205, characterize the *æstel* theory as 'undeniably attractive' but would not rule out the possibility that the jewel was part of 'a symbol of office'; Webster, '*Aedificia nova*', p. 82, characterizes the *æstel* theory as 'extremely plausible, and very probably correct [...] but not the only possible interpretation', and thinks that 'the most convincing alternative proposal' is that the jewel is part of a staff or wand.

[11] Howlett, 'Alfred's *Æstel*', p. 73.

as *modes eagan* in his translations both of Gregory's work and of Augustine's *Soliloquia*.[12] Neither Bakka, Kempshall, nor Pratt, however, suggests a compelling explanation for the objects held by the figures. Bakka and Kempshall do not venture one;[13] Pratt asks whether the 'plants' might symbolize 'salvation', or alternatively 'the undesired power and wealth that should accompany the pursuit of wisdom', but concludes that 'The precise meaning of the twin plant stems on the Fuller brooch and the Alfred Jewel [...] remains a very open question'.[14] One might dismiss these 'plant stems' as iconographically inert formal reflexes of the 'Osiris pose' model, yet their prominence suggests they are symbolic attributes of the figures who hold them. In his thorough analysis of the Fuller Brooch, Bruce-Mitford concluded that 'Since we have seen how carefully every detail of the iconography is worked out, we must suppose that the branches held by Sight are more than mere foliage'.[15] The artists of both jewel and brooch, then, probably chose the 'Osiris pose' model because the foliate or floriate objects such figures regularly hold were thought to have some literal or figural relevance to the faculty or organs of Sight.

There is little doubt that these objects are plants of some variety, and those on the Alfred Jewel are generally agreed to be flowers (or floriate rods). The jewel's designer seems to have gone out of his way to depict flowers in an anatomically precise (albeit simplified) way. According to Bakka,

---

[12] Kempshall, 'No Bishop, No King: The Ministerial Ideology of Kingship and Asser's *Res Gestae Aelfredi*', in *Belief and Culture in the Middle Ages: Studies Presented to Henry Mayr-Harting*, ed. by Richard Gameson and Henrietta Leyser (Oxford, 2001), pp. 106–27 (p. 125); and, in much greater detail, Pratt, 'Persuasion', pp. 212–16. Pratt urges the interpretation for the Fuller Brooch, but is non-committal regarding its application to the Alfred Jewel. Kempshall applies the interpretation to both artefacts, as does Webster, citing Pratt, in '*Aedificia nova*', p. 87, and 'Encrypted Visions: Style and Sense in the Anglo-Saxon Minor Arts, A.D. 400–900', in *Anglo-Saxon Styles*, ed. by Catherine E. Karkov and George Hardin Brown (Albany, 2003), pp. 11–30 (p. 20).

[13] Kempshall, 'No Bishop', p. 125, following Howlett, associates the incised plant motif on the back plate of the Alfred Jewel with the fruit-bearing tree of life in the Bible (Proverbs 3. 18, Psalm 52. 8, and Revelation 22. 2), but also with the images of the fruitfulness of just rulership in Irish mirrors for princes; but he does not specifically address the symbolism of the plants held by the main figures in either artefact.

[14] Pratt, 'Persuasion', p. 102. Hilmo, who interprets the figure as the Wisdom of God, suggests that they 'conjure up the idea of *þa blostma* "blossoms" of learning referred to in some of the incipits and explicits of Alfred's version of Augustine's *Soliloquies*' (*Medieval Images*, p. 68).

[15] Bruce-Mitford, *Aspects of Anglo-Saxon Archaeology*, p. 324. Bruce-Mitford suggests that Sight is 'probably intended to be shown possessing the fruits of the earth — in other words, these are *cornucopia*'.

The tops of the stems [. . .] can be fully explained in botanical terms as flowers, greatly simplified, but with the most important botanical elements present. In the centre is a round ovary, in one case surmounted by a dot, the stigma. The ovary is flanked by two stamens, which spring from below the ovary and consist of a long filament and a globular anther. At the base of the filaments are a pair of more or less reflexed petals, with narrow base and rounded tip. The usually green and inconspicuous sepals have been omitted in this simplified schematic representation.[16]

A botanist consulted by Bakka agreed that (in Bakka's words) 'it would be a correct stylization of a hypogenous flower, made with a real knowledge of the structure of the flower'.[17]

Simon Keynes and Michael Lapidge have described the 'cornucopias' held by Sight in the Fuller Brooch as 'overflowing with *flowers* and representing the fruits of the earth' (emphasis mine),[18] while Howlett, in the quotation above regarding the common design elements, also seems to assume they are flowers. If so, they are of a completely different variety than those depicted on the Alfred Jewel, and other commentators have identified them more vaguely as plants or foliate stems.[19] From each 'cornucopia' emerge four stems, double-nicked to indicate their rounded form. The outermost stem terminates as a leaf, while the inner three terminate as rounded knobs; Bruce-Mitford describes them as 'three drooping bud-like lobes'

[16] Bakka, 'Alfred Jewel', p. 281; the following quotation is from the same page. Hinton (*Catalogue*, pp. 33, 36, and 39) supports the interpretation of the objects as flowers, and the great majority of scholars have agreed that they are either flowers or floral-headed rods.

[17] The 'Tree of Life' on the back plate of the jewel has a central stem or bole and two branches, each of which, in Howlett's words, 'bears a flower of two petals and a centre' ('Iconography', p. 46). According to Hinton (*Catalogue*, p. 41), the back plate is possibly a later addition to the jewel, and in any case 'not considered an important part of the jewel'. I am therefore inclined to agree with Genevra Kornbluth, who considers both the back plate and animal-head socket 'iconographically insignificant'; 'Alfred and Minster Lovell Jewels', in *Medieval England: An Encyclopedia*, ed. by Paul E. Szarmach, M. T. Tavormina, and Joel T. Rosenthal (New York, 1998), pp. 17–18 (p. 17).

[18] Keynes and Lapidge, *Alfred the Great*, p. 204.

[19] They have variously been described as 'branches' (Bruce-Mitford, *Aspects of Anglo-Saxon Archaeology*, p. 324); 'stylized plants' (Howlett, 'Iconography', p. 50); 'cornucopias' (Hinton, *Catalogue*, p. 38, who also speaks of 'floral attributes'; it is unclear whether his reference to 'lobed pelta leaves' refers to these or to the plant-forms in other parts of the brooch, or both); 'leafy cornucopias' (Webster, in *Making of England*, p. 280); 'drooping foliate spray' (Webster, 'Metalwork', in *The Golden Age of Anglo-Saxon Art 966–1066*, ed. by Janet Backhouse, D. H. Turner, and Leslie Webster (London, 1984), p. 31); 'plant stems' (Pratt, 'Persuasion', pp. 208–09); 'foliate branches, sceptres, or cornucopias' (Catherine Karkov, 'Fuller Brooch', in *Medieval England*, ed. by Szarmach and others, p. 308); and 'cornucopias (or sprouting vegetal forms)' (Hilmo, *Medieval Images*, p. 66, n. 19).

and 'heavy leaves with bud-like ends'.[20] Two shorter lobes rise upward from behind the figure's shoulders and along either side of his face below the ears, and in some of the smaller roundels along the outer circumference there are similar vegetal lobes, sometimes threefold, sometimes twofold, but often consisting of a nested pair of v-shaped double lobes. The contrast between leaf- and lobe-shapes is clearly maintained in two of the smaller images, those of Smell and Hearing.

It is hazardous, to be sure, to attempt to classify ornamental plants in medieval art, since even when particular species are intended they may not be drawn from nature but from pattern. Indeed, these 'bud-like lobes' seem to have been part of a conventional vocabulary of stylized vegetal forms that artists could employ to represent different kinds of plants or parts of plants. Both in Irish art[21] and in other Anglo-Saxon Trewhiddle-style artefacts similar lobe shapes recur in con-figurations that may be foliate or floriate.[22] Taking my cue from Bakka, however, I consulted a plant physiologist, Professor Mosbah M. Kushad of the University of Illinois. With reference to the objects held by Sight in the Fuller Brooch, and specifically to the three drooping lobes adjacent to the upper leaf-shaped stem, Professor Kushad felt 'quite certain that the organs [...] are floral, assuming that

[20] Bruce-Mitford, *Aspects of Anglo-Saxon Archaeology*, pp. 309 and 315 respectively. Imme-diately above these plants, and framing Sight's face, are two triquetras or triskeles with leaf-like terminals; for a possible iconographic model, see note 46 below.

[21] Compare the lobed buds or leaves (?) in representations of 'sprouting vines' in the Book of Kells, discussed by Meehan, *Book of Kells*, pp. 57–64, with the accompanying illustrations. These lobes are usually shorter and stubbier than those in the Fuller Brooch, but are sometimes elongated and cigar-shaped. Paul Meyvaert, 'The Book of Kells and Iona', *Art B.*, 71 (1989), 6–19 (pp. 15–17), would derive these shapes from the floriated *coronis* or paragraph mark in Coptic manuscripts.

[22] Compare Hinton's discussion of the plant forms on the back plate of the Alfred Jewel, *Catalogue*, pp. 41–42. Bruce-Mitford describes some of the vegetal patterns in the background of the smaller figures on the Fuller Brooch as 'developing into leaves or flowers' (*Aspects of Anglo-Saxon Archaeology*, p. 310). Webster, '*Aedificia nova*', p. 90, compares the 'fleshy plant ornament' on the Abingdon sword-hilt to the Fuller Brooch and to the 'leaf forms' on the back plate of the Alfred Jewel, which Howlett describes as 'flowers'. In *Treasure Annual Reports 2000*, Part II (De-partment for Culture, Media and Sport: Cultural Property, Archive 2002 <http://www.culture. gov.uk/Reference_library/Publications/archive_2002/Treasure_Annual_Report_2000.htm>), p. 33, no. 41, and p. 36, no. 47, Webster describes two recently discovered Anglo-Saxon silver artefacts with 'lobed leaves' that he compares to the plant ornament on the Fuller Brooch. Reginald A. Smith, 'The Beeston Tor Hoard', *Antiquaries Journal*, 5 (1925), 135–40, refers to v-shaped nested lobes in several artefacts as 'clearly a simplified or degraded palmette' (p. 137, with reference to a silver brooch reproduced as his fig. 1).

they represent living tissue', though he did not think it was possible to identify any particular variety. The 'cornucopias' might, in his view, have been intended to represent calyxes.[23]

The point of this horticultural excursus is not to insist that the objects held by Sight in the Fuller Brooch — which virtually all commentators have agreed are plants of some kind — can only be described as flowers, but to confirm that they can plausibly be described as flowers, as some scholars have (perhaps casually) assumed them to be. The distinctively floral objects held by the figure on the Alfred Jewel, moreover, support the presumption that both Anglo-Saxon artists thought flowers (together with large, wide-open eyes) were the appropriate attribute for Sight.

Why should Sight hold flowers? According to an early medieval tradition attested in Anglo-Saxon England, God created Adam's eyes from flowers. The apocryphal legend known as *homo octipartitus* or Adam Octipartite, which recounts how God created Adam from eight (or in some cases seven) parts (*partes*) or 'pounds' (*pondera*), has been the subject of detailed investigation by Anglo-Saxonists, including Max Förster, J. M. Evans, Leslie Whitbread, Hildegard L. C. Tristram, and J. E. Cross and Thomas D. Hill.[24] Its ultimate source has been sought in the Book of the Secrets of Enoch (II Enoch), which survives only in Old Church Slavonic but was probably originally composed in Greek:

> On the sixth day I commanded my wisdom to create man from seven consistencies: one, his flesh from the earth; two, his blood from the dew; three, his eyes from the sun; four, his bones from stone; five, his intelligence from the swiftness of the angels and from cloud; six, his veins and his hair from the grass of the earth; seven, his soul from my breath and from the wind.[25]

---

[23] Interview of 13 January 2006; the quotation is from an e-mail message of the same date.

[24] Förster, 'Adams Erschaffung und Namengebung: Ein lateinisches Fragment des s.g. slawischen Henoch', *Archiv für Religionswissenschaft*, 11 (1907–08), 477–529. Evans, 'Microcosmic Adam', *Medium Ævum*, 35 (1966), 38–42. Whitbread, 'Adam's Pound of Flesh: A Note on Old English Verse *Solomon and Saturn (II)*, 336–339', *Neophilologus*, 59 (1975), 622–26. Tristram, 'Der "homo octipartitus" in der irischen und altenglischen Literatur', *Zeitschrift für celtische Philologie*, 34 (1975), 119–53. *The Prose Solomon and Saturn and Adrian and Ritheus*, ed. by James E. Cross and Thomas D. Hill (Toronto, 1982), pp. 68–70. See also Cross, 'The Literate Anglo-Saxon – On Sources and Disseminations', *Proceedings of the British Academy*, 58 (1972), 67–100 (pp. 72–73), and Hill, '*VIII Genitus Homo* as a Nomen Sacrum in a Twelfth-Century Anglo-Latin Fever Charm', *NQ*, n.s., 30 (1983), 487–88.

[25] II Enoch 30. 8A, trans. R. H. Charles, *The Apocrypha and Pseudepigrapha of the Old Testament*, 2 vols (Oxford, 1913), II, 448–49. In the recension translated by F. I. Andersen in *The Old Testament Pseudepigrapha*, vol. I: *Apocalyptic Literature and Testaments*, ed. by J. H. Charlesworth

The date of II Enoch has not been determined, with estimates 'ranging all the way from pre-Christian times to the late Middle Ages',[26] though two of the most recent authorities date the work towards the end of the first century A.D.[27] According to Jean-Claude Haelewyck, however, the passage in question — which occurs only in the longer recension — is an interpolation from an apocryphal tract *De Adami compositione et nomine* or *De plasmatione Adam*, which combines the Adam Octipartite motif with another apocryphal motif according to which Adam's name was devised as an anagram of the Greek names of the four stars or cardinal points.[28] Lorenzo DiTommaso agrees that this tract 'is not a fragment of 2 Enoch 30; rather, it is part of [a] tradition found throughout medieval literature and that has 2 Enoch 30 as it[s] most important parallel'.[29] Whether as source or parallel, the passage in II Enoch is obviously closely related to the Adam Octipartite motif, but most medieval versions enumerate eight parts or 'pounds', and also differ from II Enoch in some of the substances specified or parts of the body with which each is identified.[30]

(Garden City, 1983), p. 150, the relevant verse reads 'his eyes from the bottomless sea', but the editor notes (p. 151, note h) that two manuscripts 'derive man's eyes from the sun'. See also Émile Turdeanu, 'Dieu créa l'homme de huit éléments et tira son nom des quatre coins du monde', *Revue des études roumaines*, 13/14 (1974), 163–94; repr. in Turdeanu, *Apocryphes slaves et roumains de l'Ancien Testament*, Studia in Veteris Testamenti Pseudepigrapha, 5 (Leiden, 1981), pp. 404–35.

[26] Andersen, '2 Enoch', p. 95. My summary of the scholarship relies heavily on Frederick M. Biggs's *Sources of Anglo-Saxon Literary Culture* entries '2 Enoch' and 'De plasmatione Adam', in *The Apocrypha*, ed. by Biggs (Kalamazoo, 2007), pp. 10 and 4–5.

[27] Christfried Böttrich, 'The Melchizedek Story of *2 (Slavonic) Enoch*: A Reaction to A. Orlov', *Journal for the Study of Judaism in the Persian, Hellenistic and Roman Period*, 32 (2001), 445–70 (p. 451), and Andrei A. Orlov, 'On the Polemical Nature of *2 (Slavonic) Enoch*: A Reply to C. Böttrich', *Journal for the Study of Judaism in the Persian, Hellenistic and Roman Period*, 34 (2003), 274–303 (p. 302).

[28] *Clavis Apocryphorum Veteris Testamenti*, ed. by Jean-Claude Haelewyck, CCCA (Turnhout, 1998), p. 45 (no. 66), citing A. Vaillant, *Le livres des secrets d'Hénoch: Texte slave et traduction française* (Paris, 1976), p. 100; for the *De Adami compositione et nomine*, see pp. 14–15 (no. 10); C. Wright, 'Additions to the Bobbio Missal: *De dies malus* and *Joca monachorum* (fols. 6r–8v)', in *The Bobbio Missal: Liturgy and Religious Culture in Merovingian Gaul*, ed. by Yitzhak Hen and Rob Meens (Cambridge, 2003), pp. 79–139 (p. 86); and Biggs, 'De plasmatione Adam'.

[29] DiTommaso, *A Bibliography of Pseudepigrapha Research 1850–1999*, Journal for the Study of the Pseudepigrapha, Supplement Series, 39 (Sheffield, 2001), p. 448, as quoted by Biggs, 'De plasmatione Adam', p. 5.

[30] Evans, 'Microcosmic Adam', p. 39, would derive the 'blossoms' from the substance grass in II Enoch, but there it forms veins and hair, not the eyes.

Now in one group of Adam Octipartite texts, including two Old English versions, the eyes — specifically their 'variety' (i.e. of colouration) — are said to have been created not from the sun, as in II Enoch, but from a pound of flower(s). The earliest surviving text that associates the eyes with flowers is a question-and-answer dialogue from an eighth-century Italian manuscript, Sélestat, Bibliothèque Humaniste, 1 (1093),[31] which Förster edited as the earliest medieval Latin *Gesprächbüchlein*. This text enumerates seven *pondera*, the sixth of which is 'Pondus floris: inde est uarietas oculorum'.[32] A ninth-century Vatican manuscript of this dialogue, however, reads 'pondus solis',[33] and that this was the original form of the motif is suggested both by the parallel in II Enoch and by the self-explanatory rationale linking the organs of sight and sunlight. As Förster surmised, *floris* must be an early scribal error, one that characterizes the variant textual tradition Förster designated Version E. Once the scribal error had established itself, some explanation was called for, so *uarietas* was added (with the attendant change of *oculi* to *oculorum*) to link the *pondus floris* with the diverse colouration of the iris in different individuals. The scribe of the Vatican manuscript was probably familiar with other versions of the tradition and restored *solis*, but let *uarietas* stand.[34] This 'explanation' in turn induced some later scribes to alter the singular *pondus floris* to plural *pondus florum*, or simply to replace the phrase with *flores*.

The original 'solar' reading (without the *uarietas* explanation) remained the most widespread; it is retained in Förster's Latin Versions A–D, including an Anglo-Saxon manuscript of Version A, Cambridge, Corpus Christi College, MS 326 ('pars de sole, inde sunt oculi eius').[35] The 'floral' variant, however, occurs in

---

[31] *CLA*, VI, no. 829. On the manuscript, see also Wright, 'Additions to the Bobbio Missal,' p. 86.

[32] Max Förster, 'Das älteste mittellateinische Gesprächbüchlein', *Romanische Forschungen*, 27 (1910), 342–48 (p. 345); for a more recent edition, see Charles Munier, 'La chronique pseudo-hiéronymienne de Sélestat', *Revue Bénédictine*, 104 (1994), 106–22 (p. 111). Förster ('Adams Erschaffung', p. 494, n. 3) dated the *Gesprächbüchlein* to the sixth century, but his seventh-century date for the Sélestat manuscript was too early.

[33] The manuscript is Vatican City, Biblioteca Apostolica Vaticana, MS Reg. lat. 846 (first quarter of the ninth century). See Wright, 'Additions to the Bobbio Missal', p. 86.

[34] Förster, 'Adams Erschaffung', pp. 495–96. Förster leaves open the question as to whether the Vatican manuscript has preserved or restored the original reading, but its retention of *uarietas*, an explanation that makes sense with *floris* but is a non sequitur after *solis*, suggests *solis* is a scribal restoration.

[35] The text is printed from CCCC 326 (*c.* 1000), with variants from five other manuscripts ranging in date from the ninth to the fifteenth century, by Förster, 'Adams Erschaffung', pp.

other manuscripts unknown to Förster[36] and seems to have been popular among Insular (Anglo-Saxon and Celtic) authors, for it is also attested in an eighth-century Hiberno-Latin compilation, the *Liber de numeris* ('flores in varietate oculorum');[37] a florilegium known as the *Catechesis celtica* ('pondus florum unde est uarietas oculorum'),[38] which survives in a tenth-century Breton manuscript that transmits much Hiberno-Latin material; and in two Anglo-Saxon texts, the Durham Collectar (Durham, Cathedral Library, MS A. IV. 19, late ninth to early tenth century) and the *Prose Solomon and Saturn*.[39]

479–81; here the reading is 'IIIa pars de sole, inde sunt oculi eius' (p. 479). For the manuscript, see Helmut Gneuss, *Handlist of Anglo-Saxon Manuscripts: A List of Manuscripts and Manuscript Fragments Written or Owned in England up to 1100* (Tempe, 2001), no. 93.

[36] I can add three unpublished examples: St Gall, Stiftsbibliothek, cod. 230, p. 325 ('pondus florum inde uarietas oculorum') (on this manuscript, written probably at St Gall in the second half of the eighth century, see *CLA*, VII, no. 933); Venice, Biblioteca Marciana, II.46 (2400), fol. 135ᵛ ('pondus floris inde est uarietas oculorum') (on this manuscript, see Wright, 'Additions to the Bobbio Missal', pp. 83–87, with discussion of the Adam Octipartite text at p. 86; for Irish symptoms in the manuscript's contents, see p. 87); and London, British Library, Additional MS 37785, fols ii–v (additions in an Irish hand to a twelfth-century English manuscript), fol. ii ('pondus florum inde facta est varietas oculorum') (on this manuscript see *Catalogue of the Additions to the Manuscripts in the British Musuem in the Years MDCCCCVI–MDCCCCX* (London, 1912), pp. 138–39).

[37] *Liber de numeris*, 2.2, *PL*, 83, 1295; see R. E. McNally, 'Der irische Liber de numeris: Eine Quellenanalyse des pseudo-isidorischen Liber de numeris' (unpublished doctoral dissertation, Munich, 1957), p. 31.

[38] 'Catéchèses celtiques', in *Analecta Reginensia*, ed. by André Wilmart, Studi e Testi, 59 (Vatican City, 1933), p. 111; this passage is also printed by Robert E. McNally, *Scriptores Hiberniae minores*, CCSL, 108B (Turnhout, 1973), p. 185. On the Hiberno-Latin contents of the florilegium, see Martin McNamara, 'The Irish Affiliations of the *Catechesis Celtica*', *Celtica*, 21 (1990), 291–334; 'Sources and Affiliations of the *Catechesis Celtica* (MS. Vat. Reg. lat. 49)', *Sacris erudiri*, 34 (1994), 185–237; and 'The Affiliations and Origins of the *Catechesis Celtica*: An Ongoing Quest', in *The Scriptures and Early Medieval Ireland*, ed. by Thomas O'Loughlin, Instrumenta Patristica, 31 (Turnhout, 1999), pp. 179–203; Jean Ritmueller, 'MS Vat. Reg. Lat. 49 Reviewed: A New Description and a Table of Textual Parallels with the *Liber questionum in euangeliis*', *Sacris erudiri*, 33 (1992–93), 259–305.

[39] Förster, in my view mistakenly, regards the *Prose Solomon and Saturn* as a translation of the very same Latin text as in the Durham Collectar ('Adams Erschaffung', pp. 493–94). It is certainly closely similar (as are most texts within each version distinguished by Förster), and it certainly belongs with Förster's Version A; but the plural *blosmena* already differentiates it from the other Version A texts' reading *floris/blostmes*. See J. E. Cross's criticism of Förster's views, 'Literate Anglo-Saxon', pp. 72–73.

In the Chester-le-Street additions to the Durham Collectar, copied and glossed by the scribe Aldred *c*. 970, the motif occurs in Latin with an interlinear Old English gloss:

> Octo pondera de quibus factus est adam. pondus limi. inde factus est caro. pondus ignis inde rubeus est sanguis et calidus. pondus salis inde sunt salsae lacrimae. pondus roris. inde factus est sudor. *pondus floris inde est uarietas oculorum* [glossed *pvnd blostmes of ðon is fagvng egena*] pondus nubis inde est instabilitas mentium. pondus uenti inde est anhela frigida. pondus gratiae inde est sensus hominis.[40]

> [The eight pounds from which Adam was created: a pound of earth, from which the flesh was made, a pound of fire whence blood is red and hot, a pound of salt from which are salt tears, a pound of dew from which sweat was made, *a pound of flower whence the variety of the eyes*, a pound of cloud whence the instability of mind, a pound of wind whence the cold breath, a pound of grace whence the intelligence of man.] (emphasis mine)

The Durham Collectar retains the singular (*pondus floris/pund blostmes*), in agreement with the *Gesprächbüchlein*, but the *Prose Solomon and Saturn* exemplifies the alteration to the plural (*blosmena pund*):[41]

> 8 Saga me þæt andworc þe adam wæs of geworht, se ærustan man.
>   Ic ðe secge, of viii punda gewihte.
> 9 Saga me hwæt hatton þage.
>   Ic ðe secge, þæt æroste wæs foldan pund of ðam him wæs flesc geworht. Oðer wæs fyres pund; þanon hym wæs þæt blod read and hat. Ðridde wæs windes pund; þanon hym

---

[40] Ed. by U. Lindelöf, *Rituale Ecclesiae Dunelmensis: The Durham Collectar*, Surtees Society, 140 (London, 1927), p. 192; facsimile ed. by A. H. Thompson and others, *The Durham Ritual*, Early English Manuscripts in Facsimile, 16 (Copenhagen, 1969), with the text of the passage at fol. 86^rb10–86^va16. On the Chester-le-Street additions, see Thompson and others, p. 51, and *The Durham Collectar*, ed. by Alicia Corrêa, Henry Bradshaw Society, 107 (London, 1992), pp. 76–80.

[41] A Middle English dialogue echoes the substitution of *flores* for *pondus florum* ('the sevent is of flowres, wheroff Adam hath his yeen'): C. Horstmann, 'Questions by-twene the Maister of Oxenford and his Clerke', *Englische Studien*, 8 (1885), 284–87 (p. 285). In vernacular Irish texts one finds both solar and floral variants, but those Irish texts that specify flowers usually associate them with the colouration not of the eyes, but of the face or cheeks. See the tables of correspondences in Tristram, 'Der "homo octipartitus"', pp. 125–31. In the commentary to his forthcoming edition of the first recension of the Irish *An Tenga Bithnúa* ('The Evernew Tongue'), John Carey concludes that its enumeration of the materials of the human body represents a hybrid of Förster's Versions A and E; according to the Irish text, the brightness and light of the eyes comes from the sun and stars, while the 'freckling and pallor of faces' come from flowers (§13; I am grateful to Professor Carey for allowing me to consult his edition and commentary). One manuscript of the Second Recension of the work, however, also retains E's equation of flowers with the varied colouration of the eyes (*ildatha i suilibh*): Úna Nic Énrí and G. Mac Niocaill, 'The Second Recension of the Evernew Tongue', *Celtica*, 9 (1971), 1–59 (p. 12, line 73, *var. lect.*, MS P).

wæs his seo æðung geseald; feorðe wæs wolcnes pund; þanon hym wæs his modes
unstaðelfæstnes geseald. Fifte was gyfe pund; þanon hym wæs geseald sefa and geðang.
Syxste wæs blosmena pund; þanon hym was eagana myssenlicnys geseald. Seofoðo wæs
deawes pund; ðanon him becom swat. Eahtoðe wæs sealtes pund; þanon him wæron þa
tearas sealte.

[8 Tell me the substance from which Adam, the first man, was made.
     I tell you, from eight pounds' weight.
9 Tell me what they are called.
     I tell you, the first was a pound of earth from which his flesh was made. The second
was a pound of fire; from this his blood was red and hot. The third was a pound of wind;
from this his breath was given; the fourth was a pound of cloud; from this his instability
of mind was given. The fifth was a pound of grace; from this was given his understanding
and thought. *The sixth was a pound of blossoms; from this was given the variety of his eyes.*
The seventh was a pound of dew; from this he got sweat. The eighth was a pound of salt;
from this his tears were salt.][42]

The *Prose Solomon and Saturn* survives in a mid-twelfth-century manuscript,
London, British Library, Cotton MS Vitellius A. XV (currently bound with the
Beowulf manuscript). To my knowledge this text has not been precisely dated,
though Förster believed it to be eleventh century.[43] The *Joca monachorum* genre
upon which it is based, however, has its origins in the early Middle Ages,[44] and as
we have seen, the 'floral' variant was established already by the eighth century. It
could easily have been known in England by the late ninth century,[45] when both
the Alfred Jewel and Fuller Brooch are thought to have been made.

     The Alfred Jewel and Fuller Brooch represent, I therefore suggest, a distinctively
Anglo-Saxon iconography of Sight that adapted the 'Osiris pose' model to exploit
the felicitous congruence of its characteristic floriate rods or plant-stems[46] with

---

[42] *The Prose Solomon and Saturn*, ed. and trans. by Cross and Hill, pp. 26 and 67–68
(emphasis mine). In their commentary (pp. 68–70), Cross and Hill cite a variety of parallels, but
do not specifically discuss the floral/solar variants.

[43] Förster, 'Adams Erschaffung', pp. 493–94, n. 3.

[44] See Walther Suchier, *Das mittellateinische Gespräch Adrian et Epictitus nebst verwandten
Texten (Joca Monachorum)* (Tübingen, 1955); Wright, 'Additions to the Bobbio Missal', pp.
104–10.

[45] Whitbread, 'Adam's Pound of Flesh', argues that the tradition is alluded to in the poetic
Solomon and Saturn II, which may date to the Alfredian period; Whitbread's argument, however,
requires an unconvincing emendation of line 339, of MS *niehtes wunde* to *of eahta pundum*.

[46] An additional possible model might be coins of the 'Triquetras' group, one series of which
Anna Gannon has recently argued represents the Five Senses: *The Iconography of Early Anglo-
Saxon Coinage* (Oxford, 2003), pp. 188–89, with fig. 6.1. The coin that may represent Sight

the apocryphal tradition whereby God is said to have created the eyes from a pound of flower(s).[47] The iconography (which is not necessarily original to either the Alfred Jewel or the Fuller Brooch) draws on the comparatively rare type of 'Osiris pose' in which the figure holds in *both* hands floriate rods,[48] and each Anglo-Saxon craftsman has rendered them as stylized but organically correct flowers.[49]

Implicit in this identification of the iconography of the Alfred Jewel is an essentially positive interpretation of the faculty and organs of sight as the physical means whereby human beings access and acquire wisdom through reading. As Pratt has suggested, the *æstel* that accompanied each copy of the *Pastoral Care* 'promoted the pursuit of wisdom by encouraging the act of reading'.[50] Focussing mainly on the Fuller Brooch, however, and in light of 'ambivalent' patristic traditions regarding the physical senses, Pratt interprets the figure of Sight as 'the eternal spiritual faculty of man's eternal soul, the "mind's eyes" [. . . which] should be

---

shows a bust of a male figure staring forward, and on either side of his head are wreath-ties that Gannon compares with 'the two triskeles at the side of Sight on the [Fuller] brooch' (p. 188, n. 53). Some other Anglo-Saxon coins discussed by Gannon show busts or figures standing or seated with 'vegetation motifs'; see Gannon, pp. 71–72, 93–95.

[47] The fact that Isidore includes *vigeo* 'to flourish, bloom' among his etymological derivations of *visus* adds an iconographical grace note: 'Visus dictus quod vivacior sit caeteris sensibus, ac praestantior, sive velocior, ampliusque *vigeat*, quantum memoria inter caetera mentis officia': *Isidori Hispalensis Episcopi Etymologiarum sive Originum libri XX*, ed. by W. M. Lindsay, 2 vols (Oxford, 1911), XI.i.21.

[48] The closest parallel to the Fuller Brooch is a tenth-century Beneventan manuscript of Virgil's *Aeneid*, in which an unidentified 'womanly figure' 'bears plant stems that are similarly lobed, nicked, and interconnected' (Pratt, 'Persuasion', p. 218 and fig. 34). As in the brooch, one of the stems terminates in a leaf-shape in contrast to the others, which form two lobes and a tendril; Pratt refers to them as 'palmettes'.

[49] As Hinton (*Catalogue*, p. 32) notes, the enamel in the Alfred Jewel has crackled in most cloisons, 'and it is difficult to determine which colours have faded, and what colour scheme was originally intended'. However, there appear to be blue patches in both the figure's left eye and in the 'ovary' of the flower in his right hand. One side of the right eye, according to Hinton, may also be 'blue or purple-brown', though he notes that the makers of the replica 'who had a better opportunity to judge the colours' chose a 'bright pinky brown' (in Hinton's description the right eye, cloison 8 according to his diagram on p. 30, is referred to as '9', evidently by typographical error). The main colour of both 'ovaries' is 'reddish brown'. In any case, blue appears in one flower and at least one, and perhaps both, of the eyes, and the eyes themselves are varicoloured. (I am grateful to Thomas D. Hill for pointing out to me that the eyes and flowers appear to share some colouration.)

[50] Pratt, 'Persuasion', p. 221.

carefully distinguished from the five "outer senses", which perform an analogous role in perceiving the material world alone'.[51] As Pratt demonstrates, in his translation of the *Soliloquies* Alfred does subordinate the eyes of the body to the 'eyes of the mind'; yet it is precisely in the reading of edifying spiritual texts that the eyes of the body are most in harmony with the eyes of the mind. According to a riddle popular in Insular sources, for example, the 'three mute things' (*trea muta*) that bring wisdom (*sapientia*) into a man's heart are 'mind', 'eye', and 'letter' (*mens, oculus, littera*).[52] With reference to the Alfred Jewel, Pratt himself argues that 'there could be no more appropriate tool in the task of spiritual edification than a pointer which directed the eyes physically to the divine wisdom of the written word'.[53] Kempshall, citing several passages from the *Pastoral Care* that link sight and wisdom, concludes: 'Far from Sight having little relevance to the text from which Alfred forbade his *æstel* to be removed, the contents of the *Regula Pastoralis* prove how sight and wisdom were, in fact, intimately connected and therefore how the jewel can be interpreted as *both* sight *and* wisdom within a single, coherent design.'[54]

If the Alfred Jewel was an *æstel* for use by bishops while reading Alfred's translation of Gregory's *Pastoral Care*, there is a further reason why an image of Sight

----

[51] Pratt, 'Persuasion', pp. 215–16; see his survey of the 'ambivalent view' of the physical senses in patristic texts at pp. 210–12.

[52] The motif occurs in the *Collectanea Pseudo-Bedae*, ed. by Martha Bayless and Michael Lapidge (Dublin, 1998), p. 142, and in the *Prebiarium de multorium exemplaribus*, ed. by McNally, in *Scriptores Hiberniae minores*, p. 167. It also occurs in the Irish *Cesta Grega* ('Greek Questions'), and a corrupt version occurs in the Old English *Adrian and Ritheus* (no. 38), ed. by Cross and Hill, in *The Prose Solomon and Saturn*, p. 39: 'Saga me feower stafas dumbe. Ic þe secge, an is mod, oðer geþanc, þridde is stef, feorðe is ægesa.' The analogues suggest that *ægesa* is a scribal error for *eagan*. See the commentary by Cross and Hill, p. 154, and in *Collectanea Pseudo-Bedae*, ed. by Bayless and Lapidge, pp. 238–39, who also cite Hrabanus Maurus's poem on writing, ed. and trans. by Peter Godman, *Poetry of the Carolingian Renaissance* (Norman, OK, 1985), pp. 248–49: 'Nam digiti scripto laetantur, lumina visu, | Mens volvet sensu mystica verba dei' ('For the fingers rejoice in writing, the eyes in seeing, and the mind at examining the meaning of God's mystical words').

[53] Pratt, 'Persuasion', p. 200.

[54] Kempshall, 'No Bishop', p. 125. Webster, '*Aedificia nova*', p. 86, referring to the reused crystal spolia in the Alfred and 'Wessex' jewels, adds that 'the translucency of crystal could in any case certainly link it to ideas about seeing clearly and understanding, with which Alfred was much concerned, and which would be entirely appropriate to a pointer designed to be used with an exemplary text such as the *Regula Pastoralis*'. Webster (p. 87) also raises the provocative question whether the central domed blue glass insets on the Bowleaze and 'Wessex' jewels could 'represent the *oculus* — specifically that inner eye with which Alfred was so concerned?'.

would be relevant. The very word *episcopus* means 'overseer', and according to Isidore of Seville, its Latin equivalent was *speculator*:

> Episcopi autem Graece, Latine speculatores interpretantur. Nam speculator est praepositus in Ecclesia; dictus eo quod speculatur, atque praespiciat populorum infra se positorum mores et vitam.

> [Now 'bishops' in Greek are in Latin interpreted as 'overseers'. For an overseer is an overseer in the Church, and is so called because he watches, and looks out over the morals and life of the people placed beneath him.][55]

The etymology is repeated in the eighth-century Anglo-Saxon Corpus Glossary,[56] and *speculator* (or its equivalent *inspector*) is translated into Old English with forms of the verb *-sceawian*, linked to *biscop*, in a gloss to the Durham Collectar[57] and in several works by Ælfric.[58] Though Gregory does not explicitly cite the etymology, in his commentary on Ezechiel he discusses at length the image of the *speculator* for one in a position of spiritual authority,[59] and as Kempshall has

---

[55] *Etymologiae*, VII.xii.12. For a discussion of this tradition, see Christine Mohrmann, 'Episkopos – Speculator', in Mohrmann, *Études sur la latin des chrétiens*, 4 vols (Rome, 1958–77), IV, 232–52; and M. H. Hoeflich, 'The *speculator* in the Governmental Theory of the Early Church', *Vigiliae Christianae*, 34 (1980), 120–29.

[56] *An Eighth-Century Latin-Anglo-Saxon Glossary*, ed. by J. H. Hessels (Cambridge, 1890), p. 5, line 254: *Episcopus speculator*. Elsewhere (p. 194, lines 11, 14) the glossary equates *episcopus* with *(super)inspector* and *superspector*.

[57] *Rituale Ecclesiae Dunelmensis*, ed. by Lindelöf, p. 194: 'Episcopus græcum est nomen operis non honoris inde dictum est epi super scopus inspector ideo episcopi superinspectores nominantur : bisc' crecisc is noma voerces no worðvnges of ðon acvoeden is ofer insceawre f ðon bisco' of insceawras genomado biðon.'

[58] 'Biscop sceal læran. his leoda symle. mid boclicere lare. and him bysnian wel. ðreagan ða ðwyran. and ða ðeawfæstan lufian. beon heora hyrde. hold under criste. *ealle ofersceawigende. swa swa his nama swegð*. and yfel ne forsuwige. ne unriht ne geðafige': *CHom* II.21, ed. by Malcolm Godden, *Ælfric's Catholic Homilies: The Second Series:Text*, EETS, SS, 5 (Oxford, 1979), p. 183 (emphasis mine). See also Ælfric's *First Pastoral Letter to Wulfstan*, ed. by Bernhard Fehr, *Die Hirtenbriefe Ælfrics*, Bibliothek der angelsächsischen Prosa, 9 (1914; repr. with supplement by Peter Clemoes, Darmstadt, 1966), p. 112 (§116), and *Old English Homilies, First Series*, ed. by Richard Morris, 2 vols, EETS, OS, 29 and 34 (London, 1868; repr. 1969), pp. 157, 254. An alternative etymology, *superintendens*, was also popular; see Thomas N. Hall, 'Wulfstan's Latin Sermons', in *Wulfstan, Archbishop of York: The Proceedings of the Second Alcuin Conference*, ed. by Matthew Townend, Studies in the Early Middle Ages, 10 (Turnhout, 2004), pp. 93–140 (p. 107, n. 35).

[59] *Homiliae in Hiezechielem prophetam* I.5–6, ed. by M. Adriaen, CCSL, 142 (Turnhout, 1971), pp. 170–72, cited by Conrad Leyser, 'Vulnerability and Power: The Early Christian

noted, in the *Regula pastoralis* Gregory repeatedly alludes to the 'eyes' of those who must watch over others: 'Those in the highest authority are like eyes, using the light of knowledge to see ahead (*providere*); they should have eyes everywhere (Revelation 4. 6), including within, so that they can be watchful over themselves but also detect what is in need of correction in others.'[60] In translating one of these passages, Alfred indicates that the duty of rulers, including the bishop, is to 'watch' (*sceawian*) the people: 'Ða recceras sceolon bion beforan ðæm folce sua sua monnes eage beforan his lichoman, his weg & his stæpas *to sceawianne*. [. . .] Hu gerades mæg ðonne *se biscep* brucan ðære hirdelican are, gif he self drohtað on ðam eorðlicum tielongum ðe he oðrum monnum lean sceolde?' ('The rulers ought to be before the people as a man's eye before his body, *to see* his paths and steps. [. . .] How, then, can *the bishop* properly enjoy the pastoral dignity, if he is himself engaged in those earthly occupations which he ought to blame in others?', emphasis mine).[61]

Reading Gregory's *Pastoral Care* while guiding their own eyes with a pointer representing the faculty of sight, then, Alfred's bishops would acquire the wisdom both to scrutinize themselves with the 'eyes of the mind' and to 'watch over' their flocks.[62] And since the figure of Sight on the Fuller Brooch appears to wear a pallium inscribed with a cross, it may not be too fanciful to suggest that the brooch was made for Plegmund, Alfred's Archbishop of Canterbury from 890 to 923, who was granted the pallium by Pope Formosus and who assisted Alfred in the preparation of his translation of the *Pastoral Care*.[63]

Rhetoric of Masculine Authority', *Bulletin of the John Rylands University Library of Manchester*, 80 (1998), 159–74.

[60] Kempshall, 'No Bishop', p. 124, with reference to several passages in the *Regula pastoralis* and the corresponding passages in Alfred's translation.

[61] *King Alfred's [. . .] Pastoral Care*, ed. and trans. by Sweet, p. 131, lines 20–21 and p. 133, lines 3–5 (Hatton version).

[62] For reflections on the 'panoptic' authority of bishops, the *episcopus-speculator* etymology, and Asser's representation of Alfred's royal authority, see Leyser, 'Vulnerability and Power'.

[63] The pallium was normally granted only to archbishops; see Michael Lapidge, 'Pallium', in *Blackwell Encyclopaedia*, ed. by Lapidge and others, p. 352, and on Plegmund, see Simon Keynes's entry, pp. 371–72. The Fuller Brooch must have been intended for a very prominent person living during the late ninth century, and it is difficult to imagine why a brooch decorated with the image of a man wearing the pallium would be made for someone other than an archbishop.

TEXT AND TEXTILE

Elizabeth Coatsworth

Embroideries with inscriptions form a surprisingly large proportion of surviving early medieval embroideries from Western Europe.[1] Woven inscriptions on narrow wares such as edgings and girdles have survived too. As inscriptions they have received little attention, only rarely being considered alongside contemporary inscriptions in other media.[2] This lack of interest can be explained partly by the small number of recognizable textile objects surviving from the early Middle Ages, but another factor may be that embroidery, especially, is seen today as primarily informal, domestic work, or as decoration for clothing: its loss of prestige is attested by the adoption of the term 'tapestry', strictly applicable only to woven hangings, for the huge embroidered work of the eleventh century in Bayeux.[3] All the surviving inscriptions, however, occur on objects which had at least a temporary public function.

Here I want to consider not so much the epigraphy of the inscriptions as their content in their immediate context of a textile object with a specific function.[4]

---

[1] See Elizabeth Coatsworth, 'Stitches in Time: Establishing a History of Anglo-Saxon Embroidery', *Medieval Clothing and Textiles*, 1 (2005), 1–27.

[2] I attempted to fill this gap for the Anglo-Saxon examples at a MANCASS conference on Anglo-Saxon writing held in Manchester in 2003: E. Coatsworth, 'Inscriptions on Textiles Associated with Anglo-Saxon England', in *Writing and Texts in Anglo-Saxon England*, ed. by A. R. Rumble, Publications of the Manchester Centre for Anglo-Saxon Studies, 5 (Cambridge, 2006), pp. 71-95.

[3] Nicole de Reyniès, 'Bayeux Tapestry or Bayeux Embroidery?', in *The Bayeux Tapestry: Embroidering the Facts of History*, ed. by Pierre Bouet, Brian Levy, and François Neveux (Caen, 2004), pp. 69–76.

[4] I have not attempted a full catalogue, although most published examples in western Europe are mentioned. Because the emphasis is on content and context instead of epigraphy, I have

There are four main groups of inscriptions: those which commemorate donors, commissioners, or possible makers, and the recipients of their generosity; those which identify something in or on the textile; those which tell a story (though not necessarily in a strictly narrative form); and those which make a statement, sometimes in the form of a quotation, which directs the viewer or user to the deeper meaning of the object or its iconography. Textiles can have more than one type of inscription, and one example falls into all four categories.

Donors and Dedicatees

Only one inscription in this group may be earlier than the ninth century. It is on a composite textile object from Maaseik, the 'velamen' of St Harlindis (Plate 4a and 4b), which convincingly forms a cloak or veil-like garment.[5] The garment is made of red and purple brocaded silk, with a probable seventh- to ninth-century date range. It has appliqués of purple and green silk of a similar date, forming two crosses and two squares. These are edged with silk tablet-woven braids brocaded with gold. The inscription is on a red and beige braid, edging two sides of one of the squares, and all four sides of the other. It has been dated to the eighth or ninth century on epigraphic grounds, but is said to be difficult to localize. The inscription reads: 'hoc parvum munus erluinus su___ sorore sua / [s]co petro offe[r]/re curavit pro / anime illiu[s]'.[6] Erluinus and his sister have not been identified, but the materials and skill level imply wealth and access to skilled weavers. The braids are not in their original position and may originally have decorated some other object. The inscriptions are visible in their present position, which implies that, at the time of their incorporation into this garment, the persons mentioned were still seen as of importance to the church in which they were kept.

indicated only breaks (/), partially reconstructed letters [A] and complete loss of letters or words (___). Types of script and abbreviation marks are not represented.

[5] Two important composite early medieval textiles, the *casula* and the *velamen* were preserved at the abbey church of Aldeneik, which was founded by the sister Anglo-Saxon saints Harlindis and Relindis in the early eighth century, until in 1571 they were moved to St Catherine's Church, Maaseik. Now in the Treasury of St Catherine's Church, Maaseik, Limburg, Belgium.

[6] 'Erluinus at his own [...] this small gift [...] by [*or* with] his sister took care to offer it to St Peter for his [*or* her] soul.' Marguerite Calberg, 'Tissus et Broderies Attribués aux Saintes Harlinde et Relinde', *Bulletin de Société Royale d'Archéologie de Bruxelles* (Oct. 1952), 1–26 (pp. 4–6 and figs 1 and 2); Mildred Budny and Dominic Tweddle, 'The Early Medieval Textiles at Maaseik, Belgium', *Antiquaries Journal*, 65 (1985), 353–89 (pp. 378–79 and pl. LXVIIb). The pieces are *c.* 1.4–1.6 cm in width. The total length is not given.

A fragment of braid believed to be Anglo-Saxon (on the basis of the lettering, the weaving technique, and the materials used) is attached to the 'casula' of Saints Harlindis and Relindis (see below, p. 199) but all that remains is the incomplete inscription '__iausu__'.[7]

A lengthier text from Reims, France, is on a cushion made from an imported Byzantine silk of the first half of the ninth century, found in the coffin of St Remigius when his tomb in the cathedral was opened in 1647.[8] The inscription is not part of the original fabric: it completely fills a border around the edge of the cushion and is embroidered in gold. It is now damaged but the full text was recorded in 1647:

> hoc opus exiguum praesul clarissimus Hincmar Alpheide jussit condere sicque dare. Ille quidem jussit sed et haec mos laeta peregit protulit et factum quomodo cernis opus. Quae sub honore novo pulvillum condidit ipsum quo sustentetur dulce sacrarumque caput Remigii meritis Alpheidis ubique juvetur ipsiusque preces hanc super astra ferant.

> [The famous bishop Hincmar ordered this little work to be donated and put together thus by Alpheide. He ordered it, but she carried it out in so joyful a manner, that she created the work just as you see. On the occasion of the new honours she finished this little cushion by which the sweet and most holy head of St Remigius is supported and everywhere assisted by the merit of Alpheide, and this carries her prayers beyond the stars.][9]

The occasion for which the pillow was ordered by Bishop Hincmar was the translation of the relics of St Remigius (d. 533) into a new church dedicated in his honour in 852. The 'maker' of the cushion can reasonably be identified as Alpheide (Alpaid), a half-sister of Charles the Bald, because of both the richness of the material and the importance of the occasion. It has been described as the earliest signed European embroidery, but the wording is ambiguous as to the extent of Alpaid's actual contribution. It is also hard to overlook the flattering tone in which her contribution is commemorated, which implies it was not she who composed it and laid it out for the embroiderer to follow. The work would have been seen on the important public occasion of the translation. On the other hand, after the translation, 'the work you see' would no longer be seen by human

---

[7] Budny and Tweddle, 'Early Medieval Textiles at Maaseik', pp. 365–66. Several lengths survive, all *c.* 10 mm in width.

[8] Now in the Cathedral Treasury, Reims. Made up from two panels, together measuring 63.5 cm x 26 cm. See W. F. Volbach, *Early Decorative Textiles* (London, 1969), pp. 106, 112, and pl. 68.

[9] The transcript of the 1647 text is in Adele La Barre Starensier, 'An Art Historical Study of the Byzantine Silk Industry', 3 vols (unpublished doctoral dissertation, Columbia University, 1982), II, 606–08.

eyes. The text witnesses to Alpheide's pious act both to her contemporaries and to God in the form of a prayer on her behalf.

Another royal lady, Hemma, wife of Louis the German (the king of the East Franks 817–76 and half-brother to Charles the Bald) commissioned a girdle woven in silk and gold thread for Witgar, Bishop of Augsburg *c.* 860–76.[10] It carries an inscription which runs along its whole length: 'Witgario tribuit sacro spiramine plenum hanc zonam nitens sanctissima Hemma' ('To Witgar, filled with the Holy Spirit, the most holy and radiant Hemma gives this girdle'). The richness of the materials and flattering description of the donor clearly come out of the same milieu as Remigius's cushion. If the piece was intended as the *cingulum* which girdled the alb, it would only have been visible when the Bishop was not in full Mass vestments.

The most famous Anglo-Saxon donor inscriptions are on Mass vestments from the tomb of St Cuthbert, Durham.[11] These are on the reverse of wedge-shaped terminals at both ends of a stole and a maniple (below, p. 193). Although there were slight variations in layout, the texts were originally identical. They would not have been invisible in wear since, as the ends of these garments hang free, the backs would sometimes be seen.

At one end of each piece is the text 'Ælfflæd fieri precepit' ('Ælfflaed had this made'), and on the other, 'pio episcopo friðestano' ('for the pious bishop Frithestan'). These are highly professional pieces of work which also relate in a number of ways to the developing 'Winchester style' of the time, and the formula makes clear that Ælfflæd was the commissioner, not the embroiderer. Frithestan was Bishop of Winchester from 909 to 931. Ælfflæd is reasonably identified as the second wife of Edward the Elder, who was banished to the nunnery of Wilton at some date before *c.* 917 or 918 when Edward the Elder married his third wife, Eadgifu.[12] Mechthild Gretsch has pointed to the strained relationship between Edward's son and successor, Æthelstan, and Bishop Frithestan in the early years of his reign.[13]

[10] Augsburg, Diözesanmuseums, DM III, 1. Leonie von Wilckens, *Die Textilen Künste: von der Spätantike bis um 1500* (Munich, 1991), pp. 82–83 and pl.

[11] Now in Durham Cathedral Treasury. The tomb of St Cuthbert (d. 687) was opened and the textiles and other objects then remaining were removed in 1827. His tomb is known to have been opened a number of times in the medieval period. See notes 19–21 below for dimensions and other details.

[12] Sheila Sharp, 'The West Saxon Tradition of Dynastic Marriage', in *Edward the Elder 899–924*, ed. by N. J. Higham and D. H. Hill (London, 2001), pp. 79–88 (p. 82).

[13] Mechthild Gretsch, 'The Junius Psalter Gloss', in *Edward the Elder*, ed. by Higham and Hill, pp. 280–91 (p. 290).

Neither Edward nor Æthelstan would have had any particular interest in honour-ing Ælfflæd's gift, and Æthelstan is said to have made a gift of a stole and maniple to St Cuthbert, *c.* 934.[14] The inscriptions were irrelevant to the donation, but not seen as a bar to it.

There is a group of major pieces with inscriptions associated with the court of the Emperor Henry II, now preserved mainly in the Treasury of the Cathedral at Bamberg.[15] Of these, the Star-Mantle of Emperor Henry II is a good example: this has inscriptions relating to the various motifs representing scenes from the life of Christ and signs of the zodiac, and also a border with a large-scale decorative inscription. The dedicatory inscription, in which some letters are out of place, perhaps as a result of the resetting, reads: 'O decus Europae Cesar Heinrice beare angeat [augeat] impreium [imperium] ibti [tibi] rex qui regna [regent] wne [in evum]' ('O glory of Europe Emperor Henry, may you be happy, may the king who reigns in eternity increase your empire').[16] In smaller capitals above this border are the words: 'Pax ismaheli qui hoc ordinavit' ('Peace to Ismahel who commissioned this'). Clearly this was intended originally as a secular garment, although perhaps one with spiritual significance for a king as a leader of a Christian people. The inscriptions record it was given to the Emperor by Duke Ismahel of Bari, who died in Bamberg in 1020. It is assumed it was given to Bamberg cathedral by Henry or his wife, St Kunigund, for use as a cope. In 1503 the embroideries, including the dedicatory inscription and an Alpha and Omega, were cut away from the original ground material and remounted as appliqués on blue Italian silk damask.

Identifying Inscriptions

Other inscriptions describe either what was wrapped in the textile or what was depicted on it. A piece from St Maurice, Switzerland, a red wool tabby weave, in two fragments, embroidered in white linen thread and light blue, green, and

---

[14] *Historia de sancto Cuthberto*, in *Symeonis monachi opera omnia*, ed. by Thomas Arnold, Rolls Series, 2 vols (London, 1882–85), I, 196–214 (ch. 26).

[15] Examples not further discussed here are the mantle and the cope of St Kunigund (wife of Henry II) and the mantle of St Stephen, King of Hungary: see Marie Schuette and Sigrid Müller-Christensen, *The Art of Embroidery*, trans. by Donald King (London, 1964), pp. 298–99 and pls. Several are fragmentary, and some have been reconstructed in the sixteenth century in the manner described for the Star-Mantle of Henry II.

[16] See Schuette and Müller-Christensen, *Art of Embroidery*, p. 298 and pls. The cope is 54 cm h., 297 cm in diam.

yellow wool thread, has an inscription framed within an embroidered border. On the larger fragment, it can be seen that the border forms one corner of a rectangle. The inscription reads 'Pria/na Gervatius prot [. . .] eaem', evidence that the piece was once a cover for relics of the named, early Christian, Milanese saints, Gervasius and Protasius. It has been dated to the seventh to eighth centuries, which is the same date as the script on manuscript labels with the names of the saints, which accompanied the find.[17] The saints were placed in the church of San Ambrogio in Milan by St Ambrose himself, but in the first half of the ninth century, St Ambrose, St Gervasius, and St Protasius were all 'translated' into a new sarcophagus by Archbishop Angilbert of Milan, a possible occasion for a distribution of relics, or perhaps a date after which donations of these particular relics would have ceased.

An embroidery from Tongres in Belgium, apparently found in a reliquary, dates to the ninth to tenth centuries.[18] It is linen, embroidered in silk and gold thread. Its two rows of figures are now very worn. The upper row is probably the Flight into Egypt, but an identification of the lower register as Lot and his daughters seems highly arguable. The surviving letters are laid out in rows, one above each register of figures; and also vertically, between the figures:

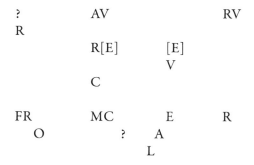

[17] Preserved in the Monastery of St Maurice. This was discovered in 1923, in an 'early medieval reliquary'. Two parchment labels accompanied the textile, one with text *sci nazari sci gervasi sci protasi*; the other with *sci gervuasi et sci prothasi*: both said to be in a 'Merovingian cursive' script of the seventh century. Dimensions of the textile fragments: a) H. 5.5 cm high, W. 13.5 cm; b) H. 3 cm, W. 4 cm. Brigitta Schmedding, *Mittelalterliche Textilen in Kirchen and Klostern der Schweiz: Katalog*. Schriften der Abegg-Stiftung, 3 (Bern, 1978), pp. 163–64 and fig.

[18] In the Cathedral Treasury. Found in 1866. H. 38.5 cm, W. 22 cm. *Tongeren Basiliek van O.-L.-Vrouw Geboorte: Clenodia Tungrensis*, vol. I: *Textiel van de vroege middeleuwen tot het Concilie van Trent*, ed. by C. Ceulemans, E. Deconinck, and J. Helsen (Leuven, 1988); von Wilckens, *Die Textilen Künste*, p. 173 and fig.

The loss of the full inscription has rendered some of the iconography indecipherable.

An example of iconography illuminated by inscriptions is on the two vestments from the tomb of St Cuthbert in Durham (see above, p. 190). One is a stole, of which eight fragments remain.[19] It is of red silk completely covered by embroidery in silk and gold thread. The inscriptions along the length of the stole identify figures representing prophets of the Old Testament and two apostles, one each on the front of the wedge-shaped terminals with the donor formulae. The centre panel of the stole has a representation of the *Agnus Dei*. The inscriptions read:

> Iacobvs apo / [break] / Aba[. . .] / Johel prpheta / Ose propheta / Esaias / Agnv Di / __mias prophet / Daniel propheta / Amos propheta / Ab[d]i[_] / [break] / Ionas prophea / Zacha__a __ / [break] / __ propeta: / Navvum propheta / [break] / Thomas apost.

> [James the Apostle / [break] / ?'Habbakuk' / Joel the Prophet / Hosea the Prophet / Isaiah / Lamb of God / [Jere]miah the Prophet / Daniel the Prophet / Amos the Prophet / Oba(d)i[ah]) / [break] / Jonas the Prophet / Zacha[ri]a[h] / [break] / prop(h)et (another prophet or possibly the remainder of the Zachariah panel) / Nahum the Prophet / [break] / Thomas the Apostle.][20]

The second piece, a maniple, is the same as the stole in materials and technique and similar in layout and style of design (Fig. 16).[21] At the centre is a depiction of the (Right) Hand of God; on either side are four figures in ecclesiastical dress. The wedge-shaped terminals have at one end a bust of St John the Evangelist and at the other of St John the Baptist. The inscriptions accompanying the figures read: Centre panel: 'Iohannes evg / Lavrentivs diacon[v]s / scs Syxtvs episc / Dextera Di / scs Gregorivs pap / Petrvs diaconus / Johannes b__' ('John the Evangelist / Laurence the Deacon / St Sixtus the bishop / the Right Hand of God / St Gregory the Pope / Peter the Deacon / John the B(aptist)').

---

[19] L. of seven fragments remaining in Durham: 196.9 cm., W. incl. edge braids 6 cm. Fragment at Ushaw College: L. 3.3 cm. See above, p. 190, for a discussion of date and provenance, and note 22 below for references.

[20] The detached Ushaw fragment has two letters ('ba') probably confirming the reading 'Habbakuk' for the first prophet at one end. See Richard N. Bailey, 'St Cuthbert's Relics: Some Neglected Evidence', in *St Cuthbert, his Cult and his Community to AD 1200*, ed. by Gerald Bonner, David Rollason, and Clare Stancliffe (Woodbridge, 1989), pp. 231–46 (pp. 237–38, 245 and fig.).

[21] L., exclusive of fringe, 82 cm, W. incl. edge braids 6 cm.

Figure 16. St Gregory the Pope: detail from the maniple
from the tomb of St Cuthbert, Durham Cathedral Treasury.
Reproduced by kind permission of Durham Cathedral.

The iconography of these pieces, and the significance of the figures, has been discussed very fully by Christopher Hohler.[22] My point is that speculation as to the iconography could not have been begun without the inscriptions: the prophets are simply figures facing alternately right and left, and some carry palms (though they are not martyrs) and some books; otherwise differences are minimal. Similarly on the maniple, the figures can be identified as ecclesiastics, but it is the inscriptions which allow us to speculate as to the aptness of the choice, for Mass vestments, of both the particular ecclesiastics and the saints on the terminals.

A fragment from Switzerland cut out and detached from its background has a figure of a saint in an architectural setting and identifiable as St Paul by his embroidered name. Another fragment originally from the same eleventh-century embroidery, a figure of Christ in Majesty, is identifiable by its iconography.[23]

Inscriptions Which Tell (Part of) a Story

Inscriptions which tell more of a story do not always leave less to speculation. A late tenth-century hanging called the 'Alexander Flag' (Plate 5), thought to have been made in south Germany, was preserved by being sewn onto the back of a banner of St Kilian, the patron saint of Wurzburg. This banner was made in 1266 to serve in the battle of the city against Herman I, Count of Henneberg.[24] It is embroidered in silk, in blue, red, and yellow with the background embroidered in interlace patterns in white. The border with a Latin inscription survives mainly on the right side though there is also a short section on the left. On the right there were clearly originally two lines of text separated by a band of decoration, and it is probable that this arrangement was originally followed on all sides. The scene

---

[22] Christopher Hohler, 'The Stole and Maniples (b) The Iconography', in *The Relics of Saint Cuthbert*, ed. by C. F. Battiscombe (Oxford, 1956), pp. 396–408; R. Freyhan, 'The Place of the Stole and Maniples in Anglo-Saxon Art', in ibid., pp. 409–32; Elizabeth Coatsworth, 'The Embroideries from the Tomb of St Cuthbert', in *Edward the Elder*, ed. by Higham and Hill, pp. 292–306 (pp. 295–96 and fig. 21.5).

[23] Christ fragment, now in the Schweizerischen Landesmusem, Zürich: Jenny Schneider, *Katalog der Sammlung des Schweizerischen Landesmus, Zürich* (Zürich, 1975), pp. 40, 132, and pl.; St Paul fragment now in Beromünster: Schmedding, *Mittelalterliche Textilen*, no. 24, pp. 39–41; von Wilckens, *Die Textilen Künste*, pp. 177–78.

[24] Now in the Mainfränkisches Museum, Inv. No. 5604 in Würzburg, Germany. 58 x 100 cm. Schuette and Muller-Christensen, *Art of Embroidery*, p. 299 and figs. The embroidery was removed from the banner between 1860 and 1875.

depicts the legendary flight of Alexander the Great. The origin of this story seems to go back to a Greek source of the third–fourth century A.D. In texts, it always occurs in the form of a letter from Alexander to his mother, Olympias. In it, Alexander travels through the air in a basket made of cattle hide, hanging from a yoke attached to the necks of two 'white birds', usually portrayed as griffins. He is stopped and sent back to earth by a bird in human form. It was translated into several languages and was known in the west in some form as early as the ninth century, although the Alexander Flag is the earliest western witness to the full story. The inscriptions read:

> (Right): '__m cvm pavcis promere versicvl__'; 'miracvla poli libvit prospir__'; and (Left): '__plvs c(?)elvm__'.
>
> [Right: '[. . .] to recount a few verses'; 'it pleased him to [. . .] the wonders'; Left: 'of heaven'.][25]

Schmidt suggests that although the story could be seen as an example of sinful pride, and was certainly used explicitly for this purpose in the later Middle Ages, in the Romanesque and earlier periods it may have been viewed more positively, as a tale of adventure, perhaps an expression of the power of majesty, or an expression of the interest shown in 'wonders' from the mysterious worlds outside Europe: if so, it would be an apt subject for a secular wall-hanging. In some of the Romanesque sculptured examples he cites, the scene is paired with Daniel in the Lion's Den, between two lions. The scenes are obviously comparable in layout — a human figure between two beasts — but it is not clear whether this means that the subjects were seen as parallels or as opposites. The similarity with the story of the flight of Wayland, which was sometimes, in Scandinavian England at least, portrayed on some otherwise Christian crosses, might also be a pointer to its interest for a contemporary audience.[26] Part of its ambiguity for us is that we do not know what original setting — ecclesiastical or secular — it was designed for. Its history before the thirteenth century is unknown.

The Bayeux Tapestry itself (now in the Muséé de la Tapisserie de Bayeux, Centre Guillaume le Conquérant, Bayeux, France) is too long for all its embroidered text to be included here (Fig. 17). It is a wall-hanging in nine joined pieces of linen

[25] See Victor Michael Schmidt, *A Legend and its Image: The Aerial Flight of Alexander the Great in Medieval Art* (Groningen, 1995), cat. 92, pp. 9–39, 207–08, and pl.

[26] See James T. Lang, 'Sigurd and Weland in Pre-Conquest Carving From Northern England', *Yorkshire Archaeological Journal*, 38 (1976), 83–94.

Figure 17. Detail from the Bayeux Tapestry, 11th Century: Harold is offered the crown. Muséé de la Tapisserie de Bayeux, Centre Guillaume le Conquérant, Bayeux, France. By special permission of the City of Bayeux.

embroidered in woollen thread; part of the end is missing.[27] It was thought that there were only eight sections; the eighth seam was discovered recently in a

[27] 68.38 m long x 45.7–53.6 cm high. Length of each section as follows, I: 13.70 m; II: 13.90 m; III: 8.19 m; IV: 7.725 m; V: 5.52 m; VI: 7.125 m; VII: 7.19 m; VIII: 2.8 mm, IX: 2.43 m.

thorough study of all aspects of the textile.[28] The lettering and the embroideries were worked as one, as can be seen where there are published photographs of both back and front.[29] It is not necessary to assume that the inscriptions and the full design were conceived together, however, even though they were executed together. The inscriptions are crowded together towards the beginning, and become sparser and more spaced out towards the end. That suggests that the topics covered were part of the original commission, but that when the design was worked out in relation to the dimensions of the space it was to occupy — a fascinating subject in itself — some of the scenes had to be drawn out at length, and the later inscriptions were drawn out with them, and, rather interestingly, not added to.[30]

Inscriptions As (Ambiguous) Statements

There are several inscriptions which seem to fulfil quite complex purposes. One is from Ravenna, from the tomb of a ninth-century but un-named archbishop in

---

[28] See Isabelle Bédat and Béatrice Girault-Kurtzeman, 'The Technical Study of the Bayeux Embroidery', in *Bayeux Tapestry*, ed. by Bouet, Levy, and Neveux, pp. 83–116, and other papers in this extremely useful book.

[29] See David J. Bernstein, *The Mystery of the Bayeux Tapestry* (London, 1986), p. 79 and pls. 44 and 46, and also n. 33, as this has been amply confirmed in the recent technical study.

[30] There is, unusually for a textile, a considerable literature on the relationship between text and images. In some places, the text serves only to identify key figures and sites, but generally a more extended text, though without commentary, is clearly intended to identify a whole scene. There is no agreement as to whether it was a cut down version of a longer text which has not survived, or was meant only as a guideline for 'guided tours' of the tapestry which could be extended or curtailed at any point as necessary: see Bernard Bachrach, 'Some Observations on the Bayeux Tapestry', *Cithara: Essays on the Judaeo-Christian Tradition*, 1 (1988), 5–28, and Richard Brilliant, 'The Bayeux Tapestry: A Stripped Narrative for their Eyes and Ears', *Word and Image*, 7 (April–June 1991), 98–126. An appealing idea is that the tapestry was deliberately neutral to support both pro-English and pro-Norman readings (and indeed variant Norman readings), 'a way of advancing the cause of reconciliation'; see Pierre Bouet, 'Is the Bayeux Tapestry Pre-English?', in *Bayeux Tapestry*, ed. by Bouet, Levy, and Neveux, pp. 197–215 (p. 215). Numerous other readings of the tapestry, from diverse points of view, have been put forward over the years. See Shirley Ann Brown, *The Bayeux Tapestry: History and Bibliography* (Woodbridge, 1988), pp. 23–44; Brown, 'The Bayeux Tapestry: A Critical Analysis of Publications 1988–99', in *Bayeux Tapestry*, ed. by Bouet, Levy, and Neveux, pp. 27–47. In this case, the choice of Latin as the language of the text may also have been seen as neutral in context.

Sant'Apollinare in Classe.[31] It is a tablet woven braid with soumak brocading, probably a girdle (the braid is reversible and was meant to be seen from both sides). The main weft was probably linen; the warp and brocading are in silk. There are seven surviving fragments, including fringes.[32]

The inscriptions (on three fragments) are based on verse 5 of Psalm 127(128):

(i): '__ lux + pax __'. (ii): 'Benedicat te Dns ex ion ut (et) videas quae bona __'. (iii): 'in Hierusalem omnibus diebus vita __'.

[i: '__Light + peace__'. ii: 'May the Lord bless you from Zion and may you see good things __'. iii: 'in Jerusalem all the days of your life'.]

An Anglo-Saxon origin has been suggested for these pieces, on the basis of the lettering and the soumak technique.[33] The words of the inscription are appropriate for a bishop to address to a congregation, when giving a solemn pre-communion blessing at Mass, when the girdle would have been hidden by the dalmatic; but they are also suitable on a gift from an unknown donor to the bishop in life, or as a commendation for a deceased ecclesiastic looking forward to the rewards of the spirit.[34]

Another Anglo-Saxon example is interesting in what it tells us about reliquary covers or perhaps church furnishings from the same broad date. This is from one

---

[31] Now in the Museo Arcivescovile, Ravenna. The fragments add up to *c.* 150 cm in length, width 1.5 cm.

[32] Mario Mazzotti, 'Antiche stoffe liturgiche ravennati', *Felix Ravenna*, 53 (1950), 40–45 and pl. p. 41; Mazzotti, *La Basilica di Sant'Apollinare in Classe*, Studi di Antichità Cristiana, 21 (Rome, 1954), fig. 77.

[33] Hero Granger-Taylor, 'The Weft-patterned Silks and their Braid: The Remains of an Anglo-Saxon Dalmatic of *c.* 800?', in *St Cuthbert, his Cult and his Community*, ed. by Bonner, Rollason, and Stancliffe, pp. 303–27 (pp. 308, 318–20, and pl. 56). Michelle Brown is cited in connection with the epigraphy. *The Making of England: Anglo-Saxon Art and Culture AD 600–900*, ed. by Leslie Webster and Janet Backhouse, British Museum Exhibition Catalogue (London, 1991), cat. no. 100d, pp. 135–36 and fig.

[34] This last was the meaning of the psalm as expounded by St Augustine in a sermon for the day dedicated to St Felix the Martyr. See *Expositions on the Book of Psalms by St Augustine, Bishop of Hippo*, trans. by A. Cleveland Cox, Select Library of the Nicene and post-Nicene Fathers of the Christian Church, 8 (Grand Rapids, MI, 1956), pp. 925–28. The same tomb in Ravenna produced a mappa, a forerunner of the maniple, and six other woven bands, four of them with inscriptions. Two apparently had extracts from Psalms 127(128) and 19(20), and two a dedication. These, because they were woven in silk, have been ascribed to Italy, and are regarded as evidence that silk weaving was being done at least in Italy at that date; they, together with the braids from Maaseik, show that the use of inscribed braids was widespread in the West, and that Psalm 127(128) may have been a popular subject for ecclesiastical vestments.

of the composite textiles from Maaseik, the so-called 'casula' of Saints Harlindis and Relindis (Plate 6).[35] This inscription consists of four openwork monograms, each an appliqué made of cloth cut and folded to shape, now placed one in each corner of the rectangular 'casula'. The backing material is painted linen, although the embroidered decoration covers the entire surface of each piece. Two are decorated with scrolls with undulating stems ending in trefoil leaves, the other two are decorated with embroidered frets with triquetra knots at the angles: all are edged with narrow borders which imitate the effect of beading.[36] They have been dated to Anglo-Saxon England of the early ninth century, like the better-known arcade and roundel strips of embroidery in the same group.[37] The term 'casula' implies a garment, but the composite forms a simple rectangle. Shown flat, the two monograms at the bottom appear reversed in relation to the two at the top. Like this they could represent M and A, or M and O, or Alpha and Omega, depending on which way up they are viewed. However, if the rectangle was draped over an altar or reliquary they would all have appeared the same way up to the observer: this to my mind is strong evidence that they represent Alpha and Omega, a very suitable subject for an altar cloth. The arcade and roundel embroidery strips on the same composite could also possibly have decorated an altar frontal originally.

An exceptionally interesting piece is from Cologne, from the church of St Kunibert: this is the Cloth of St Ewald (Hewald), from the shrine of two Anglo-Saxon martyrs (Fig. 18). Black Ewald (dark) and White Ewald (fair) were two Northumbrian missionaries to Saxony murdered by pagans *c.* 695. In the eleventh century their remains were translated to a position on either side of St Kunibert (a seventh-century Bishop of Cologne). At some stage the relics must have been moved to the thirteenth-century church dedicated to this saint.[38]

The complete piece consists of three joined panels of blue linen, with embroidery in silk thread, in shades of red, blue, brown, and grey, and a gilt-leather

[35] See also note 5 above.

[36] Each monogram measures *c.* 12 x 13.1 cm.

[37] Calberg, 'Tissus et Broderies Attribué aux Saintes Harlinde et Relinde', p. 12 and fig. 3; Mildred Budny and Dominic Tweddle, 'The Maaseik Embroideries', *Anglo-Saxon England*, 13 (1984), 65–96 (pp. 75–76 and pls. III, VIa, b); Budny and Tweddle, 'Early Medieval Textiles at Maaseik', p. 364 and pls LVIII, LXIIIb, LXIVa, b, and LXVa. There are other references to the Maaseik embroideries, but none which mention the monograms.

[38] *Bede's Ecclesiastical History of the English People*, ed. and trans. by Bertram Colgrave and R. A. B. Mynors (Oxford, 1969), 2.10 and p. 484 n.

Figure 18. Detail with inscription from the Cloth of St Ewald,
from St Kunibert, Cologne. © Rheinisches Bildarchiv.

strip couched with red silk.[39] The centre panel is purely ornamental. One end panel has figures carrying torches representing the sun and moon, and the signs of the zodiac within a decorative border. The opposite end panel has at its centre a personification of Annus with masks of Nox and Dies in his hands, surrounded again by signs of the zodiac, representations of the four seasons and the four elements, personifications of Oceanus and Terra, and Alpha and Omega representing Christ. The edge has an inscription which fills the framing borders, in which every letter is decorated with plant, animal, or interlace decoration. It reads: 'Populus qui conspicit omnis arte laboratum' ('all people who look on the work made by skill').

This is probably consciously ambiguous: it clearly refers to the work of God in Creation; but the created work immediately seen is the embroidery. Sight as a metaphor for spiritual insight, by which the inner meaning of texts and images could be discerned by the reader or viewer, has been noted before as a theme in early medieval art.[40] Monastic craftsmen could also show themselves to be highly conscious of the religious significance of their work. The monk Theophilus, for example, reminding goldsmiths of the high nature of their calling in providing rich decoration for churches, says their work gives viewers a glimpse of the paradise of God: 'quodque Creatorem Deum in creatura laudant et mirabilem in operibus suis praedicant, effecisti' ('thus you have caused them to praise God the Creator in his creation and to proclaim Him marvellous in all His works').[41] Theophilus is now generally identified with the early twelfth-century monk-goldsmith Roger of Helmarshausen, who worked in the area of north-west Germany centred on Cologne, where the earliest surviving manuscript of his work has also been found.[42] Theophilus uses words reminiscent of the embroidered inscription when speaking about the impact of the work on the observer, for example when he says:

> Quod si forte Dominicae passionis effigiem liniamentis expressam conspicatur fidelis anima, compungitur; si quanta sancti pertulerunt in suis corporibus cruciamina quantaque uitae eternae perceperunt praemia conspicit, uitae melioris obseruantium arripit.

---

[39] Overall L. 310 cm, W. 83 cm. The panel with the inscription is 90 cm long.

[40] For example, see the discussion of the Fuller Brooch in Rupert Bruce-Mitford, *Aspects of Anglo-Saxon Archaeology: Sutton Hoo and Other Discoveries* (London, 1974), pp. 303–25.

[41] *Theophilus: The Various Arts*, ed. and trans. by C. R. Dodwell (London, 1961), p. 63.

[42] *Theophilus*, ed. and trans. by Dodwell, pp. xviii–xliv.

[But if perchance the faithful soul observes the representations of the Lord's Passion represented in art, it is stung with compassion. If it sees how many torments the saints endured in their bodies and what rewards of eternal life they have received, it eagerly embraces the observance of a better life.][43]

Dodwell saw the Cloth of St Ewald as 'naïve and akin to folk art', but plumped for a tenth-century date because the inscription contained 'debased elements of Carolingian styles and anticipations of Ottonian ones'.[44] There is little disagreement with this date, but the rich materials and the complex subject matter, which find many echoes in the manuscript art of the period, preclude a 'folk art' origin. It has been more credibly suggested that the cloth was offered by Archbishop Bruno of Cologne (953–65) who in his will linked the two saints Ewald with St Kunibert, and the lettering and some details of the decoration have a considerable number of features in common with the decoration of the Gero Codex, also of the second half of the tenth century.[45] The embroidered letters are strikingly similar in form to those in the early eleventh-century Star-Mantle (above, p. 191), from the same courtly milieu, on which the subject matter shows a similar interest in the cosmos and its creator.[46]

It is therefore of the same date and probably associated with the same people for and by whom the Cologne 'Flag of War' was made (Plate 7).[47] This piece could

---

[43] *Theophilus*, ed. and trans. by Dodwell, pp. 63–64.

[44] C. R. Dodwell, *The Pictorial Arts of the West 800–1200* (New Haven, 1993), pp. 22–23.

[45] *Rhin-Meuse: Art et Civilisation 800–1400. Une exposition des Ministères belges de la Culture français et de la Culture néerlandaise et du Schnütgen-Museum de la ville Cologne* (Brussels, 1972), A10, pp. 167–68. See also A. Legner, *Ornamenta Ecclesiae. Kunst und Künstler der Romanik: Katalog zur Ausstellung des Schnütgen-Museum in der Josef-Haubrick-Kunsthalle* (Cologne, 1985), no. 1.8, pp. 62–63 and figs; von Wilckens, *Die Textilen Künste*, pp. 174–75.

[46] Another wall-hanging with inscriptions which plays on the same theme of Creation is the Gerona Tapestry, sometimes called the Genesis Tapestry of Creation. This, like the Bayeux Tapestry, is however an embroidery. It has at its centre Christ as Ruler of the World surrounded by scenes from the creation. The borders include a personification of Annus between the seasons, and there are also representations of the months. It dates to the late eleventh/early twelfth centuries. See P. de Palol, 'Une Broderie Catalane d'Epoque Romane: La Genese de Gerone', *Cahiers Archeologique*, 8 (1956), 175–214 and figs; Schuette and Muller-Christensen, *Art of Embroidery*, pp. 26–28, 299, figs 40–45; P. de Palol and M. Hirmer, *Early Medieval Art in Spain* (London, 1967), pp. 174, 483 and figs; von Wilckens, *Die Textilen Kunste*, pp. 175–76 and fig.

[47] Now in the Treasury of the Cathedral of Saints Peter and Mary. 33 x 33 cm. M. Backes and R. Dölling, *The Art of the Dark Ages* (New York, 1969), pp. 198–99; von Wilckens, *Die Textilen Kunste*, pp. 173–74; *Krone und Schleier: Kunst aus mittelalterlichen Frauenklöstern. Herausgegeben*

have been included in all four sections. Its inscriptions include the words 'Gerberga me fecit', prominently displayed. These words record the making (or probably only the commissioning and donation) of the 'flag' by Gerberga, widow of Louis IV king of the Franks (d. 957), and sister of the Emperor Otto I and of Archbishop Bruno of Cologne. It commemorates the defeat and exile of Count Reginar of Lotharingia, *c.* 958–60, achieved with the help of Bruno of Cologne. It is essentially a secular piece. To emphasize the narrow milieu from which these embroideries come, it may be noted that two daughters of Edward the Elder and Ælfflæd (the commissioner of the Durham vestments) were married to relatives of Gerberga: Eadgifu was married to Charles III (The Simple) of France, to whose son, Louis IV, Gerberga was married, while Edith was married to Gerberga's brother, the Emperor Otto I.

The 'flag' also has identifying inscriptions, but collectively they commemorate one historical event. It is of red silk embroidered in silk and gold thread. It is very worn and fragile so there are some gaps, also some places where attached letters have been distorted out of line or even turned upside down. The inscriptions identify Christ as Victor at the centre of the composition: 'IHS'/'XPS'. Above him is a damaged feature and letters which have been wrongly read as 'Rex terrae',[48] but the depiction is obviously the Hand of God, and the inscription, slightly out of alignment, reads 'dex/te/ra' — 'right hand'. The two archangels Michael and Gabriel are in the upper corners, left and right respectively, accompanied by '[sc]s Michael' and 'scs Gabriel'. In the lower corners are the figures of Saints Hilary, 'scs (I)larivs', and Baso, 'scs (B)aso'. St Hilary of Poitiers and St Baso, said to have been martyred at Laon, are a strong indication that the embroidery was commissioned and made locally. Between the archangels and saint and flanking the figure of Christ are encircled busts of 'S/o/l', the sun (left), and 'Lv/na', the moon (right). 'Reginar / comes' identifies Count Reginar who kneels at Christ's feet.

Another embroidered inscription runs around the edge of the textile, between framing lines. Starting from the top left corner it reads: '[B]enedictv(s) Dns Ds m/+evs qvi docet manvs mea/s ad prelivm e(t) dig/+itos meos ad be[llvm]' ('Blessed be the Lord my God who trains my hands for war and my fingers for

---

von der Kunst- und Ausstellungshalle der Bundesrepublik Deutschland, Bonn, und dem Ruhrland-museum Essen (Munich, 2005), cat. 176, p. 292.

   [48] Friedrich Wilelm Oediger, 'SCS LARIVS SCS BASO: Zur Kerkunft der Kriegsfahne im Kölner Domschatz', *Kölner Domblatt*, 12/13 (1957), 86–90 (p. 86). For a more accurate reading and a discussion of the iconography, see Anton von Euw, 'Zur Ikonographie der sog. Kriegsfahne im Kölner Domschatz', *Kölner Domblatt*, 21/22 (1963), 37–48.

battle', Psalm 143(144). 1). The inscription is obviously appropriate to the subject matter, as a thanksgiving for victory in war, but it, like the Cloth of Ewald (above, p. 200), could be an allusion to those whose contribution is through the work of their hands, made visible in the embroidered work. It belongs to a class of wall-hangings of which the Bayeux Tapestry (above, p. 196) is the supreme example, that is, of specially commissioned wall-hangings designed to commemorate victories in battle. There are accounts of other such hangings, such as one given to Ely by Ælfflæd, widow of Ealdorman Bryhtnoth (who was defeated and killed by Vikings at the Battle of Maldon in 991), recorded in the *Liber Eliensis* (*c.* 1170).[49] Both this and the 'Flag' at Cologne are associated with the women whose interests and relatives were involved in the deeds depicted.

Some Conclusions

There are a number of obvious points to make about all the surviving textile inscriptions discussed above. First, all are in forms of display script: those on the Cloth of St Ewald and the Star-Mantle of Henry II in elaborate capitals decorated with plant scroll and animal and abstract interlace, the rest in rustic or square capitals with occasional interspersed uncials, without distinction of initials. All are in Latin, except for the appliqués from Maaseik which represent the Greek letters Alpha and Omega. I have not found any in any vernacular language. This differentiates them from manuscripts, sculpture, and metalwork, on which inscriptions in a variety of scripts, including runic, and in vernacular languages are represented.

It seems clear that commissioning textile works for public display, for both secular and ecclesiastical use, was as important as commissioning costly works in any other medium, and the roles of Bishop Hincmar, Ismahel of Bari, and the unknown Erluinus (above, pp. 189, 191, and 188) tell us that this role was not confined to women. The existence in the West of Byzantine textiles, authenticated as gifts or tributes by their imperial inscriptions, possibly casts a light on the royal (if sometimes female) names attached to some of the embroideries discussed above, bearing in mind that coins with the validating names of moneyers and kings were also an emulation of Roman and Byzantine practice. One such example occurs on the so-called 'Nature Goddess' silk, a woven Byzantine silk of the late eighth to ninth centuries, one of the textiles removed from the grave of the Anglo-

---

[49] *Liber Eliensis*, ed. by E. O. Blake (London, 1962), Bk II, ch. 63.

Saxon saint Cuthbert.[50] Only a few letters survive, but other inscribed Byzantine silks of this quality, of which only six or so survive, have the names of emperors or of the officials under whom the silk was woven.[51] The inscriptions and the quality of the design of such pieces mark them out as important objects which were allowed to leave the Byzantine Empire only as diplomatic gifts or tributes.[52]

It is noticeable, however, that many of the examples of embroidery surviving before the eleventh century have female associations, and that a high proportion also have specifically royal connections. How narrow this milieu was is indicated by the relationships between the named females, which I have emphasized above. The significance of this seems to be that the world that could afford large-scale embroideries or those of rich materials was a small and perhaps exclusively courtly one, in which the practice of commissioning major textiles work for use in display would have spread with ease.

The preponderance in an admittedly small sample of female names may tell us, not that the great ladies involved were actively involved in the production of these works, but that embroidery and textiles were seen as an area of female expertise, in which they could be recognized as connoisseurs. The Reims cushion and the Witgar girdle with their flattering tributes to the royal ladies named in their dedications indicate recognition of their wealth, power, and importance as daughters and consorts of kings. At the same time, the history of the Durham stole and maniple shows how circumscribed was that power by loss of that status.

Most of the embroideries would have involved a very considerable time commitment, and some have been shown to demonstrate a very high level of design and professional skill. Helen Stevens demonstrated that the surviving Maaseik embroideries represent many months of work, and noted many features which suggested professional standards in design and practice.[53] The Durham embroideries demonstrate a high quality in design, materials, and execution: such tiny stitches on a very fine silk background would have taken at least as long, perhaps

---

[50] See note 11, above.

[51] No dimensions are given: the textile survives only as a number of decayed fragments. See Hero Granger-Taylor, 'The Inscription on the Nature Goddess Silk', in *St Cuthbert, his Cult and his Community*, ed. by Bonner, Rollason, and Stancliffe, pp. 339–41 and pls 50–51.

[52] R. S. Lopez, 'Silk Industry in the Byzantine Empire', *Speculum*, 20 (1945), 1–42 (pp. 4–8).

[53] H. M. Stevens, 'Maaseik Reconstructed: A Practical Investigation and Interpretation of 8th-century Embroidery Techniques', in *North European Symposium on Archaeological Textiles (NESAT)*, vol. III: *Textiles in Northern Archaeology Symposium in York 6–9 May 1987*, ed. by Penelope Walton and John-Peter Wild (London, 1990), pp. 57–60.

longer.[54] The Bayeux Tapestry was a huge undertaking by any standards, requiring the input of many workers and an overall design. Recent research has suggested that the full width of each section of the embroidered strip was embroidered in a single operation, and that this 'must have required precise indications or a tracing cartoon', probably a full drawing on the cloth itself. On the other hand, the skill levels of the embroiderers appear to have been diverse, with some areas very skilfully done with great economy of stitching, while others are 'positively disordered'.[55] This speaks, not of a lack of professionalism, but of the exceptional size of the commission, which must have scraped the barrel of the available talent. Only one piece is a small work in humble materials: this is the reliquary cover fragment from St Maurice in Switzerland (see above, p. 191).

The evidence suggests that embroidery was taken seriously as a medium for display, for decoration, for teaching, and indeed for propaganda, some of the functions fulfilled in later centuries by large and expensive tapestries. We do not think of them like this largely because so few have survived. The woven examples from this early period, all narrow wares from trimmings or girdles, are semi- rather than fully public objects, but as with the embroideries, the literate, high ecclesiastic and courtly milieu from which they come is still apparent in the materials from which they are made, the contexts in which they were found or can be assumed to have been used, their language, their script, and their content.

[54] See E. Plenderleith, 'The Stoles and Maniples. (a) The Technique', in *Relics of Saint Cuthbert*, ed. by Battiscombe, pp. 375–96.

[55] Bédat and Girault-Kurtzeman, 'Technical Study of the Bayeux Embroidery', pp. 96–97.

THE THIRD VOYAGE OF CORMAC IN ADOMNÁN'S
VITA COLUMBAE: ANALOGUES AND CONTEXT

Diarmuid Scully

In the *Vita Columbae*, Adomnán describes Cormac Ua Liatháin's three oceanic voyages in search of a spiritual retreat.[1] On his third voyage, Cormac sails far into the North Atlantic where he is attacked by unknown creatures and saved through Columba's intercession with God. This paper examines Adomnán's account of that voyage, comparing it with some analogous narratives in classical literature and viewing it in the context of the ancient and early medieval understanding of sacred and secular world-geography.

Cormac in Ocean: Adomnán's Narrative

Adomnán describes Cormac as a soldier of Christ (*V.Col.* 2.42) and monastic founder in Ireland (*V.Col.* 3.17). He was 'viro utique sancto, qui tribus non minus vicibus herimum in ociano laboriose quaesivit, nec tamen invenit' ('a holy man who sought with great labour not less than three times a desert in the ocean, and yet found none').[2] Adomnán says that his first voyage, launched into Ocean from

---

[1] *Vita Columbae*, ed. and trans. by A. O. Anderson and M. O. Anderson, *Adomnán's Life of Columba*, 2nd edn (Oxford, 1991) [henceforth *V.Col.*]. Research for the present article was funded by the Higher Education Authority's Programme for Research in Third Level Institutions as part of *Culture-Contact, Nation and State: Ireland in a Comparative Context*, a research project in the Department of History, University College Cork.

[2] *V.Col.* 1.6. Adomnán again uses the term *desertum* in *V.Col.* 2.42, where he also speaks of Cormac seeking a 'herimum in ociano' ('a spiritual retreat in Ocean'). For later Irish traditions concerning Cormac, see *Adomnán of Iona: Life of St Columba*, trans. by Richard Sharpe

north-western Ireland, failed because Cormac unwittingly took with him a monk who had left his community without abbatial consent (*V.Col.* 1.6).[3] Cormac's other two voyages appear to have been undertaken from Iona. His second voyage led him 'per infinitum ocianum' ('over limitless Ocean'), sailing 'in pilago intransmeabili' ('in the sea that cannot be crossed') before returning to Iona via the Orkneys (*V.Col.* 2.42). On his third voyage, which Adomnán also describes in *V.Col.* 2.42, Cormac sailed northwards for fourteen summer days and nights in a 'navigatio ultra humani excursus modum et inremeabilis videbatur' ('voyage beyond the range of human exploration, and one from which there could be no return'). Among other prodigies, he encountered unknown and terrifying seabeasts: 'Quaedam quippe usque in id temporis invisae mare obtegentes ocurrerant tetrae et infestae nimis bestiolae' ('loathsome and exceedingly dangerous small creatures covering the sea, such as had never been seen before that time').[4] These creatures, about the size of frogs, had the power to sting and seemed able to penetrate the ship's skin-covering. Cormac and his companions, 'valde turbati et pertimescentes, deum qui est in angustis pius et oportunus auxiliator inlacrimati precantur' ('in great alarm and terror, and with tears prayed to God, who is a true and ready helper in times of need'; Psalm 46. 1). Columba, 'quamlibet longe absens corpore spiritu tamen praesens in navi cum Cormaco erat' ('though far distant in body, was nevertheless in spirit present with Cormac in the ship'); he urged the Iona brothers to pray for Cormac, 'qui nunc humanae discursionis

---

(Harmondsworth, 1995), pp. 341–42. On early Irish monastic sea-voyage narratives and the vernacular *immrama* (voyage tales), see the collected articles in *The Otherworld Voyage in Early Irish Literature*, ed. by J. Wooding (Dublin, 2000); S. Mac Mathúna, 'The Structure and Transmission of Early Irish Voyage Literature', in *Text und zeittiefe*, ed. by H. L. C. Tristram (Tübingen, 1994), pp. 313–57; J. Borsje, *From Chaos to Enemy: Encounters with Monsters in Early Irish Texts* (Turnhout, 1996), pp. 93–175; M. Herbert, 'Literary Sea-voyages and Early Munster Hagiography', in *Celtic Connections: Proceedings of the Tenth International Conference of Celtic Studies*, ed. by R. Black and others (East Linton, 1999), pp. 182–89; G. S. Burgess and C. Strijbosch, *The Legend of St Brendan: A Critical Bibliography* (Dublin, 2000); J. Wooding, 'St Brendan's Boat: Dead Hides and the Living Sea in Columban and Related Hagiography', in *Studies in Irish Hagiography: Saints and Scholars*, ed. by J. Carey and others (Dublin, 2001), pp. 77–92.

[3] The relationship between this episode and later Irish voyage tales is discussed in W. F. Thrall, 'Clerical Sea-voyages and the *immrama*', in *The Manly Anniversary Studies in Language and Literature* (Chicago, 1923), pp. 276–83, repr. in *Otherworld Voyage*, ed. by Wooding, pp. 15–21 (pp. 17–18); J. Carney, 'Review of *Navagatio Sancti Brendani abbatis*', *Medium Ævum*, 32 (1963), 37–44, repr. in *Otherworld Voyage*, ed. by Wooding, pp. 42–51 (p. 48).

[4] Borsje, *From Chaos to Enemy*, pp. 160–64, discusses these creatures.

limitem immoderate navigando excessit' ('who now in his voyage has far exceeded the bounds of human travel'):

> Itaque nostris commembribus in periculo intollerabili constitutes mente conpati debemus fratribus, et dominum exorare cum eis.

> [In our minds, therefore, we must share the sufferings of our brothers, our fellow-members [compare Ephesians 4. 25; 5. 30], who are placed in unendurable danger; and we must pray to the Lord with them.]

Columba, who prophetically saw Cormac and his sailors imploring Christ's help, added his own prayers to 'omnipotentiam dei ventorum et cunctarum gubernaticem precatur rerum' ('the omnipotence of God, which controls the wind and all things'). His prayers were answered and a north wind blew Cormac's ship back to land and the saint. Adomnán concludes by urging the reader to consider Columba's greatness, who had such prophetic vision and the power to command the winds and Ocean in Christ's name (*V.Col.* 2.24; compare Matthew 8. 27).

Ideas of Ocean in Antiquity

The poets of antiquity view the invention of navigation as one of the developments ending the Golden Age when humanity and the gods lived in harmony and all nature was at peace; they regard sea-faring as an unnatural crime against the gods who separated the elements of sea and land.[5] Voyaging beyond the Pillars of Hercules is the ultimate marine transgression. Authorities locate the Pillars in various places, but their function is constant; they indicate the divinely ordained geographical boundaries within which mortals must live.[6] Ocean lies beyond the Pillars. The Ancients generally believe that Ocean surrounds the *orbis terrarum* ('the known, inhabited world') which comprises the continents of Europe, Asia, and Africa and their islands.[7] Poetically at least, they view Ocean as sacred,

---

[5] Catullus, 64; Virgil, *Georgics*, 1, 125–42; Horace, *Carm.* 1, 3; Ovid, *Metamorphoses*, 1, 89–112.

[6] See J. S. Romm's discussion of Pindar's understanding of the Pillars' significance in his *The Edges of the Earth in Ancient Thought* (Princeton, 1992), pp. 17–19.

[7] On Graeco-Roman conceptions of world-geography in a political and mythological as well as physical context, see J. O. Thomson, *History of Ancient Geography* (Cambridge, 1948); K. M. Barbour, 'The Geographical Knowledge of the Greeks and Romans', *Museum Africum*, 3 (1974), 57–76; J. Ramin, *Mythologie et géographie* (Paris, 1979); R. Moynihan, 'Geographical Mythology and Roman Imperial Ideology', in *The Age of Augustus*, ed. by R. Winkes (Providence, 1985), pp.

terrifying, and immeasurable. Homer describes it as the origin of the gods and begetter of all things, and Horace says that its British waters are 'beluosus' ('filled with monsters'); for Tacitus, Ocean is 'immensus' ('measureless'), and for Pomponius Mela it is an 'ingens infinitumque pelagus' ('a huge and boundless sea').[8]

Alexander the Great challenged nature and the gods when he marched to the eastern shores of Ocean in India. In Quintus Curtius Rufus's *Historiae Alexandri Magni*, he urges his men past 'Hercules et Liberi Patris terminus transituros illos' ('the limits of Hercules and Father Liber'). He tells them that they are capturing the limits of the world; 'ne Naturam quidem longius procedere; brevi incognita nisi immortalibus esse visuros' ('not even Nature could go farther; soon they would see what was unknown except to the immortals').[9] The troops are fearful of leaving the sun and stars behind for monster-haunted waters hidden from mortals by Nature.[10] But Alexander's ambitions drive him on; here at the ends of the earth he hopes to find a new Nature and new world beyond Ocean.[11] Alexander's projected expeditions, as envisaged in the sources, would have led him beyond western as well as eastern Ocean; Quintus Curtius reports that he planned to reach Gades (Cadiz), among other places in the West, 'ibi namque columnas Herculis esse fama vulgaverat' ('for the report had spread abroad that the Pillars of Hercules were there').[12] Alexander's ambitions and achievements were to have a profound influence on Roman imperialism, with the sources proclaiming that

149–62; C. Nicolet, *Space, Geography, and Politics in the Early Roman Empire* (Ann Arbor, 1991); Romm, *Edges of the Earth*; K. Clarke, *Between Geography and History: Hellenistic Constructions of the Roman World* (Oxford, 1999).

[8] Homer, *Illiad*, 14, 201, 206; Horace, *Carm.* 4.14, 48; Tacitus, *Germania*, 2.1; Pomponius Mela, *De Chorographia*, 3.1. Studies of Graeco-Roman views of Ocean include E. de Saint-Denis, *Le Rôle de la mer dans la poésie Latine* (Paris, 1935); A. Paulian, 'Le thème littéraire de l'Océan', *Caesarodonum*, 10 (1975), 53–58; A. Paulian, 'Paysages océaniques dans la litterature Latin', *Caesarodonum*, 13 (1978), 23–29; Paul Pédech, 'Le paysage marin dans la géographie Grec', *Caesarodonum*, 13 (1978), 30–39; Ramin, *Mythologie et géographie*, pp. 2–26; P. G. Dalché, 'Comment penser l'Océan? Modes de connaissances des *fines orbis terrarum* du nord-ouest (de l'Antiquité au XIIIᵉ siècle)', in *L'Europe et L'Océan au Moyen Age: Contribution à l'histoire de la navigation*, ed. by M. Balard (Nantes, 1988), pp. 217–33; Romm, *Edges of the Earth*, pp. 9–44.

[9] *Historiae Alexandri Magni*, ed. and trans. by J. C. Rolfe, *Quintus Curtius: History of Alexander* (Cambridge, MA, 1946), 9.4, 21; 9.9, 4.

[10] *Historiae Alexandri Magni*, 9.4, 18.

[11] *Historiae Alexandri Magni*, 9.6, 20. On classical ideas of new worlds beyond Ocean, see Romm, *Edges of the Earth*, pp. 124–42.

[12] *Historiae Alexandri Magni*, 10.1, 17.

Rome matches and surpasses his triumphs as a world-conqueror.[13] As James S. Romm observes, the seas around and beyond Britain and Germany became a significant theatre for Rome's attempts to realize its destiny as a global empire.[14]

Rome against Ocean: The Empire in the North Atlantic

Since Herodotus, many authorities like Quintus Curtius identified the Pillars of Hercules with the Straits of Gibraltar.[15] Accounts of voyages beyond the Straits emphasize the strangeness and perils of the Atlantic and its denizens on land and at sea.[16] The sources represent Britain as an *alter orbis* (another world) beyond Ocean; its inhabitants are, in Virgil's words, 'penitus toto divisos orbe Britannos' ('the Britons utterly divided from the whole world').[17] Poets and historians celebrating Britain's conquest display tremendous exhilaration at the unprecedented spectacle of Rome successfully leaving the Pillars behind and overcoming the horrors of Ocean — the sources often personify *Oceanus* around the island as a hostile deity — to capture this new world.[18] The Latin version of Josephus's

[13] R. Dion, *Aspects politiques de la géographie Antique* (Paris, 1977), pp. 247–50; Y. Roman, 'Auguste, l'Océan Atlantique et l'impérialisme Romain', *Ktema*, 8 (1983), 261–68 (p. 266, n. 55); Nicolet, *Space, Geography and Politics*, pp. 21–24, 85; Romm, *Edges of the Earth*, pp. 137–40; P. C. N. Stewart, 'Inventing Britain: The Roman Adaptation and Creation of an Image', *Britannia*, 26 (1995), 1–10 (p. 6).

[14] Romm, *Edges of the Earth*, pp. 140–49.

[15] Herodotus, *Histories*, 4.8, 2.

[16] See, for example, accounts of the early fifth-century B.C. voyages of the Carthaginians Hanno and, if Avienus may be relied upon, Himilco; *Le periple d'Hannon*, ed. and trans. by J. Ramin (Paris, 1976); *Rufus Festus Avienus, Ora maritima*, ed. and trans. by J. P. Murphy (Chicago, 1977).

[17] *Eclogues*, 1.66. A variety of sources from the time of Julius Caesar's British expeditions (55 and 54 B.C.) describe Britain as an *alter orbis* beyond Ocean; V. Santoro, 'Sul concetta di *Britannia* tra Antichità e Medioevo', *Romanobarbarica*, 11 (1992), 321–34 (p. 324, n. 5); J. A. (D.) Scully, 'The Atlantic Archipelago from Antiquity to Bede: The Transformation of an Image' (unpublished doctoral dissertation, University College Cork, National University of Ireland, 2000), p. 9, n. 28 and p. 13, n. 51; see pp. 278–92 for an anthology of classical and late antique Latin sources on Britain as an exotic island at the oceanic ends of the earth.

[18] On Britain's location in Ocean and Rome's struggle against Ocean in celebrations of the island's conquest, see D. R. Dudley, 'The Celebration of Claudius' British Victories', *University of Birmingham Historical Journal*, 11 (1959), 6–17; V. Tandoi, 'Il trionfo di Claudio sulla Britannia et il suo cantore', *Studi Italiani di Filologia Classica*, 34 (1962), 83–129; Roman,

Jewish Wars brings together the key themes found in celebrations of the conquest: Alexander took victory as far as Ocean, but the Romans have extended it beyond Ocean; Britain is a witness to this, located outside the world but brought into the world by Roman strength; Roman victory brought knowledge of those of whom an earlier age was unaware; it was a greater achievement to have crossed to the Britons than to have triumphed over them; how could the Britons resist since the elements themselves were subject to Roman power? Ocean taught them to endure slavery, once Ocean himself had learned unaccustomed servitude from the passage of Roman ships.[19]

In fact, Rome claimed that it dominated the entire Atlantic archipelago and its waters, with Juvenal declaring that Roman arms have reached beyond Ireland, the Orkneys, and Britain itself.[20] The Ancients knew of nothing certain west of Ireland except endless Ocean and usually regarded the Orkneys as the northern-most inhabited islands not only of the archipelago but the entire known world.[21] Roman power now extends to the furthest western and north-western reaches of the *orbis terrarum* and becomes an important element in the empire's claim to global dominion. The sources proceed to boast of victories over the whole inhab-

---

'Auguste, l'Océan Atlantique', pp. 266–68; F. Richard, 'Un thème impérial Romain: la victoire sur l'océan', in *L'idéologie du pouvoir monarchique dans l'Antiquité* (Paris, 1991), pp. 91–104; A. Ballard, 'Quelques aspects de l'imaginaire Romain de l'océan de César aux Flaviens', *Revue des Études Latines*, 76 (1998), 177–91; A. A. Barrett, 'Claudius' British Victory Arch in Rome', *Britannia*, 22 (1991), 1–19; D. Braund, *Ruling Roman Britain* (London, 1996); J. H. C. Williams, 'Septimus Severus and Sol, Carausius and Oceanus: Two New Roman Acquisitions at the British Museum', *Numismatic Chronicle*, 159 (1999), 307–13 and pl. 27; Scully, 'Atlantic Archipelago', pp. 7–21; K. Clarke, 'An Island Nation: Re-reading Tacitus' *Agricola*', *Journal of Roman Studies*, 91 (2001), 94–112. On Roman personifications of Ocean in treatments of Britain, see Scully, 'Atlantic Archipelago', pp. 16–20.

[19] 'Magnus virtus in Alexandro: quid mirum tamen? Ille usque ad oceanum victoriam extendit, Romani ultra oceanum. Testis est Britannia extra orbem posita [compare Virgil, *Ecl.* 1.66] sed Romanorum virtute in orbem redacta. Quos aetas ignoravit superior didicit Romanorum victoria [. . .] plus itaque fuit transisse ad Britannos quam triumphasse de Britannis. Quid facerent enim elementis iam Romano imperio subiectis? Docuit illos oceanus servitutis patientiam, postquam transfretantibus et ipse Romanorum navigiis insuetam sibi servitutem agnoverat': Pseudo-Hegesippus, *Historiae Libri V*, ed. by V. Ussani, CSEL, 66 (Vienna, 1932), 2.9, 1.

[20] *Satire* 2, 159–61.

[21] On Roman claims to power over Ireland, see C. Adams, '*Hibernia Romana*? Ireland and the Roman Empire', *History Ireland*, 4 (1996), 21–25, and Scully, 'Atlantic Archipelago', pp. 7–30, which discusses these claims and the empire's annexation of the Orkneys within the context of its poets' declarations of Roman dominion over the entire archipelago and Ocean around it.

ited earth from North to South and East to West.[22] Linking triumph over Britain with power over the other edges of the earth, Constantius's panegyrist declares:

> Nihil ex omni terrarum caelique regione non aut metu quietum est aut armis dormitum aut pietate devinctum. Et ex aliis quidem partibus aliqua restant, quae, si voluntas vel ratio rerum desiderent, possitis adquirere; ultra Oceanum vero quid erat praeter Britanniam? [...]. Nulla progrediendi causa superset nisi si, quod Natura vetuit, fines ipsius quaerantur Oceani.

> [There is nowhere in any region of heaven or earth which is not either at peace out of fear or subdued by arms or bound by gratitude. And indeed of other areas, some remain which you can acquire if you wish, or reasons of state require: but beyond Ocean what was there except Britain? [. . .]. No reason remains for advancing, unless one were to seek the boundaries of the Ocean itself, which Nature forbids.][23]

One Roman fleet glimpsed those forbidden boundaries beyond Britain. According to Tacitus's *Agricola*, the fleet that annexed the Orkneys saw but did not attempt to reach another island further north — Thule — and encountered a 'mare pigrum et grave' ('sluggish and almost motionless') sea in its vicinity.[24] For the Ancients, *Ultima Thule* ('Farthest Thule') was a real if uncertainly located place and a symbol of the utterly remote and unreachable.[25] Descriptions of the early Greek explorer Pytheas's voyage into the far North Atlantic variously report heavy seas around Thule (described as an island six days' sail north of Britain which experiences perpetual summer daylight and winter darkness), a frozen sea a day's sailing beyond it, and a region which is not sea, air, or earth but a substance — sea-lung — apparently fusing all three elements.[26] For Crates of Mallos, Pytheas's northernmost Atlantic is the entrance to the Homeric underworld,

---

[22] For instance, Claudian, *Panegyricus de quarto consulatu Honorii Augusti*, 24–40 (North–South imperial rule from Thule, Britain, Ireland, and the Orkneys to Africa); Pseudo-Hegesippus, *Historiae libri v*, 5.15 (East–West imperial rule from India to Britain).

[23] *Panegyrici Latini*, 8 (5).20, 3–5, trans. by C. E. V. Nixon and B. S. Rodgers in *In Praise of Later Roman Emperors. The Panegyrici Latini: Introduction, Translation and Historical Commentary with the Latin text of R. A. B. Mynors* (Berkeley, 1994), pp. 553 (Latin text) and 141 (English translation).

[24] *Agricola*, 10.5.

[25] L. G. De Anna, *Thule: Le fonti et le tradizioni* (Rimini, 1998).

[26] Romm, *Edges of the Earth*, pp. 22–23. For the surviving text of the voyage, see *Pytheas of Massalia, On the Ocean: Text, Translation and Commentary*, ed. and trans. by C. H. Roseman (Chicago, 1994). The Ancients regard the uttermost North and South of the planet as frozen and uninhabitable; thus Virgil, *Georgics*, 1, 235–36.

located in Cimmerian darkness at the bourne of Ocean.[27] This is indeed world's end, and the younger Seneca prophesies that any attempt at its penetration (which he links with the original crime of the invention of navigation) will cause a return to primeval chaos.[28]

Rome made no attempt to penetrate the uttermost oceanic north from Britain, but its ships did venture northwards from Germany. Expeditions into Ocean there began under Augustus (27 B.C. – A.D. 14), when Rome first asserted its claim to global rule.[29] Like Britain, Germany was another world severed from the *orbis terrarum* by Ocean.[30] Tacitus and others believed that Ocean beyond Germany also contained Pillars of Hercules; these Pillars were thought to connect north-eastern Ocean with the Caspian Sea or the Sea of Azov (the Maeotian swamps).[31] The search for these straits and the glory of extra-oceanic Germany's exploration and conquest provide the context for the Romans' voyages into the Atlantic around it.

Augustus announces Roman dominion over the world in the *Res gestae*. After declaring the pacification of all oceanic lands from Gades to the mouth of the Elbe, he states:

> cla[ssis m]ea p[er Oceanum] ab ostio Rheni ad solis orientis regionem usque ad fi[nes Cimbroru]m navigavit, quo neque terra neque mari quisquam Romanus ante id tempus adit, Cimbrique [. . .] per legatos amicitiam meam et populi Romanum petierunt.
>
> [My fleet sailed through Ocean eastwards to the territory of the Cimbri, a country which no Roman had ever visited before, either by land or sea, and the Cimbri [. . .] sent ambassadors and sought my friendship and that of the Roman people.] [32]

Augustus's comments recall Roman responses to the conquest of Britain emphasizing its people's previously unknown and unconquered status. This is unsurprising, for

[27] Geminus, 6.9 in *Pytheas*, ed. and trans by Roseman, F8; compare Homer, *Odyssey*, 11, 14–50.

[28] *Medea*, 329–79; Romm, *Edges of the Earth*, pp. 168–71.

[29] Nicolet, *Space, Geography and Politics*, pp. 15–56, discusses Augustus's claims; p. 87 and pp. 91–94 consider Roman voyages of exploration into Ocean beyond Germany under Augustus and Tiberius.

[30] *Germania*, 2.1.

[31] R. Dion, 'La géographie d'Homère inspiratrice de grands desseins impériaux', *Bulletin de l'Association Guillaume Budé*, 4 (1973), 463–85.

[32] *Res gestae*, ed. by V. Ehrenburg and A. H. M. Jones, *Documents Illustrating the Reigns of Augustus and Tiberius*, 2nd edn (Oxford, 1955), 26.4. On the Cimbri, see J. B. Rives, *Tacitus: Germania, Translated with an Introduction and Commentary* (Oxford, 1999), pp. 271–73. Translations of *Germania* passages in the present paper are taken from Rives; the Latin text is ed. by J. G. C. Anderson, *Cornelii Taciti de origine de situ Germanorum* (Oxford, 1938).

the land of the Cimbri — on the tip of the Jutland peninsula — is in effect the north-eastern equivalent of Britain, or more narrowly the Orkneys, in the north-west: the end-point of human oceanic exploration and expansion; hence Augustus's desire for Cimbrian recognition of Roman *imperium*. Pliny states that the Augustan fleet which reached the land of the Cimbri saw or learned of frozen regions beyond it.[33] He also says that the Scythian name for northern Ocean is the Amalchian, meaning 'Frozen', and that, according to the Greek geographer Philemon, the Cimbri themselves call part of these waters the Morimarusa — the Dead Sea — and another part the Cronian Sea, a name he himself elsewhere gives to the frozen sea beyond Thule.[34] Moreover, Tacitus's *Germania*, echoing his *Agricola*'s description of the seas around Thule, reports

> trans Suionas aliud mare, pigrum ac propre immotum, quo cingi claudique terrarum orbem [...] illuc usque et fame vera tantum natura.

> [a sluggish and almost immobile sea beyond the Suiones [who live on the verge of Ocean in the far reaches of the German world]; it is part of the sea that encircles and envelops the world [...]. Only so far, and the rumour seems true, does the natural world extend.][35]

Pomponius Mela, Pliny, and Tacitus himself report an unnatural world on its fringes: monstrous races of men with horses' hooves or ears big enough to cover their entire bodies, and peoples with human heads and animal bodies.[36]

Tacitus and others point out the impiety and consequences of venturing into Ocean here. In the *Annals*, Tacitus describes the fate of a Roman fleet led into northern Ocean by Germanicus, commander of the empire's forces in Germany, in A.D. 16. A storm drove the fleet into

> vasto et profundo ut credatur novissimum ac sine terris mare [...]. Ut quis ex longinquo revenerat, miraculo narrabant, vim turbinum et inauditas volucris, monstra maris, ambiguas hominum et beluraum formas, visa sive ex metu credita.

> [a tract so vast and profound that it is believed the last and landless deep [...]. Not a man returned from the distance without his tale of marvels — furious whirlwinds, unheard-of

---

[33] *Naturalis historia*, 2.167.

[34] *Naturalis historia*, 4.94–95; Pliny describes the seas beyond Thule as the *mare Cronium* in *Naturalis historia*, 4.104. Strabo's claim that the Cimbri are the ancestors of the Cimmerians (on the authority of Posidonius) in *Geography*, 7.2, 2 (see also 3.2, 12) may also have associated the former with the edges of the habitable world of mortals, since Homer locates the Cimmerians near the oceanic entrance to the underworld, *Odyssey*, 11, 14–19.

[35] *Germania*, 45.1.

[36] Pomponius Mela, *De Chorographia*, 3.56; Pliny, *Naturalis historia*, 4.95; Tacitus, *Germania*, 46.4 (sceptically).

birds, sea-monsters, enigmatic shapes half-human and half-bestial: things seen, or things believed in a moment of terror.][37]

Reading this passage in the light of the *Germania* and the elder Seneca's *Suasoriae*, it is evident that Germanicus's fleet was wrecked because it transgressed, albeit unwillingly, against the gods and Nature. Seneca rehearses the terrors of Ocean in language parallelling that of Quintus Curtius; he describes Alexander's counsellors warning against any attempt to enter Ocean: new and terrible creatures fill it; there is a heavy sea, darkness, and no stars or unknown ones; there is nothing beyond it.[38] Seneca proceeds to quote from a now lost poem by Albinovanus Pedo on the experiences of a Roman fleet in Ocean north of Germany, referring to either Germanicus's voyage in A.D. 16 or that of the elder Drusus, posthumously entitled Germanicus, some years earlier.[39] As the sailors find themselves becalmed in heavy seas filled with monsters, fog, and darkness, one exclaims:

> Anne alio positas ultra sub cardines gentes
> atque alium flabris intactum quaerimus orbem?
> Di revocant rerumque vetant cognoscere finem
> mortales oculos: aliena quid aequora remis
> et sacras violamus aquas divumque quietas
> turbamus sedes?

[Are we looking for races beyond, in another clime, a new world untouched by breezes? The gods call us back, forbid us to know the end of creation with mortal eyes. Why do our oars violate seas that are not ours, waters that are holy? Why do we disturb the quiet home of the gods?][40]

Rome has finally reached the spatial end of empire in Ocean. Tacitus spells out the message. Discussing the elder Drusus's naval explorations in the *Germania*, he says that Drusus led Rome's assault on Ocean but despite his daring never found the northern Pillars of Hercules:

---

[37] *An*. 2, 23–24, ed. and trans. by C. H. Moore and J. Jackson, *Tacitus, The Histories IV–V; The Annals I–III* (Cambridge, MA, 1931).

[38] *Suasoriae*, ed. and trans. by M. Winterbottom, *The Elder Seneca, Controversiae VII–X; Suasoriae* (Cambridge, MA, 1974), 1.1.

[39] On the Albinovanus Pedo fragment, its meaning and literary context, including discussion of Tacitean references to northern Ocean, see V. Tandoi, 'Albinovano Pedone e la retorica Giulio-Claudia delle conquista', *Studi Italiani di Filologia Classica*, 36 (1964), 129–68; 39 (1967), 5–66; E. Pianezzola, 'Au delà des frontières du monde: un topos rhétorique pour un rétablissement du texte d'Albinovanus Pédo', *Revue des Études Latines*, 62 (1984), 192–205; Romm, *Edges of the Earth*, pp. 142–49.

[40] *Suasoriae*, 1.15.

Nec defuit audentia Druso Germanico, sed obstitit Oceanus in se simul atque in Herculem inquiri. Mox nemo temptavit, sanctiusque ac reverentius visum de actis deorum credere quam scire.

[Ocean blocked any enquiry into its own secrets as well as those of Hercules, and after that no one made the attempt. Where the deeds of the gods were concerned, it seemed more devout and deferential to believe than to know.][41]

The Saints in Northern Ocean

Patristic and early Insular authorities follow the Ancients in viewing the Atlantic archipelago as an utterly remote world severed by Ocean from the *orbis terrarum*; Patrick, for example, announces that through his missionary work in Ireland the Gospel has been preached 'ubi nemo ultra est' ('at the limit beyond which no-one dwells').[42] Adomnán shares this understanding of the archipelago's location; Columba 'in hac parva et extrema ociani Britannici commoratus insula' ('dwelt in this little island [Iona] on the edge of Ocean').[43] Jennifer O'Reilly and other scholars have shown that the authorities' reading of scripture in the context of a Graeco-Roman geographical framework gives the Isles a position of immense significance in providential history. Undertaken in obedience to Christ's command to preach to all peoples (Matthew 28. 20) and fulfilling prophesies of the extension of salvation to the farthest gentiles in the last days, the conversion of

[41] *Germania*, 34.2.

[42] *Confessio*, ed. and trans. by D. Conneely, *The Letters of St Patrick* (Maynooth, 1993), p. 34; compare Acts 1. 8. On the late antique and early medieval understanding of world-geography, including the location of the Atlantic archipelago, see Y. Janvier, *La géographie d'Orose* (Paris, 1982); R. Baumgarten, 'The Geographical Orientation of Ireland in Isidore and Orosius', *Peritia*, 3 (1984), 189–203; Dalché, 'Comment penser l'Océan?'; T. O'Loughlin, 'The View from Iona: Adomnán's Mental Maps', *Peritia*, 10 (1996), 98–122; O'Loughlin, 'Living in the Ocean', in *Studies in the Cult of Saint Columba*, ed. by Cormac Bourke (Dublin, 1997), pp. 11–23; E. Edson, *Mapping Time and Space: How Medieval Mapmakers Viewed their World* (London, 1997); N. Lozovsky, *The Earth is our Book: Geographical Knowledge in the Latin West ca. 400–1000* (Ann Arbor, 2000); Scully, 'Atlantic Archipelago'; J. O'Reilly, 'Islands and Idols at the Ends of the Earth: Exegesis and Conversion in Bede's *Historia ecclesiastica*', in *Bède le Vénérable: Entre tradition et posterité*, ed. by S. Lebecq, M. Perrin, and O. Szerwiniack (Lille, 2005), pp. 119–45; A. H. Merrills, *History and Geography in Late Antiquity* (Cambridge, 2005).

[43] *V.Col.* 3.23. On Adomnán's sense of place and its significance, see O'Loughlin, 'View from Iona'; O'Loughlin, 'Living in the Ocean'; J. O'Reilly, 'Reading the Scriptures in the *Life* of Columba', in *Studies in the Cult of Saint Columba*, ed. by Bourke, pp. 80–106.

Britain and Ireland represents in microcosm the conversion of the whole world
and prepares the way for the Second Coming.[44] Adomnán shares this eschatological vision: the extra-oceanic Columba's birth 'in novissimis [. . .] saeculi
temporibus' ('in the last days of the world') and his fame that will 'novissimaque
orbis tempora clare inlustrabit' ('brightly illumine the latest years of the earth') is
foretold by Maucte, a disciple of Patrick who was himself the first Insular writer
to connect Ireland's conversion with the end of time.[45]

Responding to the archipelago's providential incorporation into the Christian
world, Insular sources emulate those Fathers who subvert the proclamations of
poets and historians on Roman universal dominion and victory over the oceanic
ends of the earth. Tertullian was one of the first patristic authorities to engage in
this assault on imperial pretensions. Writing in the early third century, he lists the
most prominent and distant of the innumerable peoples who have accepted Christianity; the faith has reached even Britain: 'et Britannorum inaccessa Romanis
loca Christo vero subdita' ('the haunts of the Britons, inaccessible to the Romans,
but subjugated to Christ'). The Romans, like Darius, Nebuchadnezzar, and
Alexander before them, have spatial limits to their empire, but

> Christi autem nomen ubique porrigitur, ubique creditur, ab omnibus gentibus supra
> enumeratis colitur, ubique regnat, ubique adoratur; omnibus ubique tribuitur aequaliter.

> [Christ's name is extending everywhere, believed everywhere, worshipped by all the above-
> enumerated nations, reigning everywhere, adored everywhere, conferred equally every-
> where upon all.][46]

Opening the *Historia ecclesiastica*'s narrative of archepelagic history with an
account of Julius Caesar's British expeditions in 55 and 54 B.C., Bede alludes to

---

[44] Jennifer O'Reilly, 'Introduction', in *Bede: On the Temple*, trans. by Seán Connolly (Liverpool, 1995), pp. xiii–lv (pp. xxxiii–li); O'Reilly, 'The Art of Authority', in *After Rome*, ed. by
Thomas M. Charles-Edwards (Oxford, 2003), pp. 141–89; O'Reilly, 'Islands and Idols'; see also
J. Davidse, 'The Sense of History in the Works of the Venerable Bede', *Studi medievali*, 23
(1983), 647–95 (pp. 664–68); G. Tugène, *L'idée de nation chez Bède le Vénérable* (Paris, 2001),
pp. 140–60.

[45] *V.Col.* 3.23. On Patrick's understanding of the end of time and its connection with the
edges of the earth, see T. O'Loughlin, *Saint Patrick, the Man and his Works* (London, 1999), pp.
42–47.

[46] *Adversus Iudaeos*, 7, 7–9, ed. by A. Kraymann, CCSL, 2 (Turnhout, 1954), pp. 1355–56.
Some patristic sources do, however, view the Roman empire and Christian community as coter-
minous and depict imperial triumph in oceanic Britain as proof of providentially ordained
universal rule; see, for example, Eusebius, *Vita Constantini*, 1.25; 4.50.

Tertullian's words on Christ's triumph over regions of the island unconquered by Rome.[47] Read in the context of his account of Roman Britain as a whole and of the archipelago's conversion to Christianity, this allusion establishes Christ as the islands' true and eternal ruler; it is clear from Bede that the Romans never subdued all Britain, let alone Ireland, and the ancestors of his own English people had lived beyond the empire's Continental frontiers.[48] For Bede and the Insular sources, following patristic tradition, papal and not imperial Rome is the centre of Christ's global spiritual empire.[49] Thus, Columbanus tells Pope Boniface IV that although the Irish are aware of Rome's imperial greatness, for them the city's true glory comes from its association with the Chair of Peter, the source of Irish Christianity (a reference to Palladius's mission, sent by Pope Celestine in the early 430s); speaking of Ireland's conversion in words reminiscent of Roman proclamations of imperial triumph over Ocean and world-rule from East to West, he depicts Peter and Paul drawing Christ's chariot across vast and raging Ocean ('in occidua transmundialis limitis loca'; 'to the western regions of earth's farthest strand').[50] He does not need to state the obvious to Boniface: no Roman emperor ever matched this achievement. The Pope's predecessor Leo I and the chronicler Prosper of Aquitaine, who recorded the Palladian mission, had already made that point in the fifth century. They describe the faith winning territories beyond the boundaries of the empire and declare that Rome's greatness lies in its apostolic primacy rather than earthly dominion.[51]

Pope Gregory I, with whom Columbanus corresponded, likewise represents the conversion of Britain as an achievement unmatched by Rome. In the last years

---

[47] *Historia ecclesiastica gentis Anglorum* (henceforth *HE*), ed. and trans. by Bertram Colgrave and R. A. B. Mynors, *Bede's Ecclesiastical History of the English People* (Oxford, 1969), 1.2.

[48] D. Scully, 'Bede, Orosius and Gildas on the Early History of Britain', in *Bède le Vénérable*, ed. by Lebecq and others, pp. 31–42.

[49] On Insular veneration for the apostolic see of Rome, see Éamonn Ó Carragáin, *The City of Rome and the World of Bede* (Jarrow Lecture, 1994); Ó Carragáin, *Ritual and the Rood: Liturgical Images and the Old English Poems of the 'Dream of the Rood' Tradition* (London, 2005); O'Reilly, 'Islands and Idols', pp. 122–24.

[50] *Ep.* 5, ed. and trans. by G. S. M. Walker, *Sancti Columbani opera*, Scriptores Latini Hiberniae, 2 (Dublin, 1957). See further D. Bracken, 'Authority and Duty: Columbanus and the Primacy of Rome', *Peritia*, 16 (2002), 168–213 (pp. 175–77).

[51] Leo, *Tractatus*, 82; Prosper, *De vocatione omnium gentium*, 2.16. For these ideas, see T. M. Charles-Edwards, 'Palladius, Prosper and Leo the Great: Mission and Primatial Authority', in *Saint Patrick, A.D. 493–1993*, ed. by D. Dumville (Woodbridge, 1993), pp. 1–12; Charles-Edwards, *Early Christian Ireland* (Cambridge, 2000), pp. 202–14; Bracken, 'Authority and Duty'.

of the western empire, the pagan Claudian's personification of Britannia, wearing a blue robe that swept around her feet like Ocean's flood, praised Rome for defending her seas against the barbarians.[52] But Gregory's Britannia never acknowledged Roman authority, and her own barbarism, symbolized by the violence of Ocean, was tamed by God alone:

> Ecce quondam tumidus, iam substratus sanctorum pedibus servit Oceanus; eiusque barbaros motus, quos terreni principes edomare ferro nequiuerant, hos pro divina formidine sacerdotum ora simplicibus verbis ligant.

> [See how proud Ocean has become a servant, lying low before the feet of the saints, and those barbarous motions, which earthly princes could not subdue with the sword, are now, through the fear of God, repressed with a single word from the lips of priests.][53]

Celebrating Gregory's decision to send the first Christian mission to the English, Bede quotes this passage and applies it specifically to their conversion.[54] Although keenly aware of classical *topoi* concerning Ocean's ferocity — he echoes Virgil on the 'tumida aequora' ('swelling main') when describing a storm beyond Farne Island — Bede remains silent on Roman and indeed any secular claims to power over its waters.[55] His account of Julius Caesar's British expeditions emphasizes the violence of the storms that assailed the invasion fleet and says nothing about the

---

[52] *De consulatu Stilichonis*, 2.247–55.

[53] *Moralia in Iob*, 27.11, 21, ed. by M. Adriaen, CCSL, 143–143B (Turnhout, 1979–85), p. 1346. G. Henderson points out Gregory's debt to classical and late antique *topoi* here and draws particular attention to Claudian; see *Bede and the Visual Arts* (Jarrow Lecture, 1980), pp. 9–11, repr. in *Bede and his World: The Jarrow Lectures 1958–1993*, ed. by M. Lapidge, 2 vols (Aldershot, 1994), II, 507–38 (pp. 15–17). Gregory's words may also be seen as a riposte to earlier Christian authors who described Roman emperors defeating Ocean around Britain. Firmicus Maternus, for example, in *De errore profanum religionum*, ed. by R. Turcan (Paris, 1982), 28.6, depicts Constans triumphing over rebellious Britain in mid-winter A.D. 342–43, scorning Ocean's rage and forcing the Britons, seas, and elements to obey him. Firmicus Maternus's imagery closely resembles that of secular or pagan celebrations of Constans's victory: *Panegyrici Latini*, 6 (7).5,4 and Libanius's *Oration* 49, 137.

[54] *HE* 2.1.

[55] *HE* 5.1; Virgil, *Aeneid*, 1, 142. Contrast Guy of Amiens's celebration of William the Conqueror as 'another Caesar [Iulius alter]' whose invasion of England is made possible when God calms the Channel just as he once gave St Peter a still sea for his feet to tread, *Carmen de Hastingae proelio*, ed. by C. Morton and H. Muntz (Oxford, 1972), lines 31–72. Bede uses imperial Roman *topoi* in his account of English kings whose dominion stretches across Britain (for example, Edwin in *HE* 2.16; O'Reilly, 'Islands and Idols', pp. 139–40), but nowhere depicts God subduing the elements on their behalf.

calm seas that later brought the Emperor Claudius to the island, but shows the saints exercising power over Ocean around Britain in the manner described by Gregory.[56] In an episode comparable to Columba's intervention to save Cormac, Aidan, leader of the Columban mission to the English, saved the life of the priest Utta from a storm at sea: 'Sicut factum est ut vir Dei et per prophetiae spiritum tempestatem praedixerit futuram, et per virtutem eiusdem spiritus hanc exortam, quamuis corporaliter absens, sopiuerit' ('the man of God foretold the storm by the spirit of prophesy and, by virtue of the same spirit, calmed it when it had arisen, though he was absent in body').[57] Bede's description of the storm echoes the gospel account of Christ calming the winds and waves on Lake Galilee in Matthew 8. 23–27. It also aligns Aidan with St Germanus of Auxerre, who long before the conversion of the English crossed Ocean from Gaul to combat the Pelagian heresy among the Britons. Quoting Constantius's life of Germanus, Bede tells how evil spirits raised a great storm at sea to prevent the saint from reaching and spiritually saving them; his desperate fellow-passengers awoke the sleeping Germanus (again an allusion to the Matthean Galilee episode), who called upon Christ's help, calmed the storm, and brought the ship quickly and quietly to the island.[58] Adomnán, who had read the *Vita Germani*, like Constantius and Bede places great emphasis on his protagonist's command of Ocean around the archipelago when he summarizes his miracles of power in *V.Col.* 1.1:

> Tumores quoque fluctuum instar montium aliquando in magna tempestate consurgentium ipso ocius orante sedati humiliati sunt. Navisque ipsius in qua et ipse cassu navigabat tunc temporis facta tranquilitate portum adpulsa est optatum. In regione Pictorum aliquantis diebus manens, inde reversus, ut magos confunderet contra flatus contraries venti erexit velum; et ita veloci cursu eius navicula enatans festinabat acsi secundum habuisset ventum. Aliis quoque temporibus venti navigantibus contrarii in secundos ipso orante converse sunt.

---

[56] On Julius Caesar's expeditions, see *HE* 1.2 (compare Orosius, *Historiarum adversum paganos libri vii*, 6.9; hereafter *Hist.*). Bede ignores pagan Roman boasts that Ocean around Britain calmed for Caesar on his triumphant return from Britain, e.g. Florus, *Epitome*, 1.45,17–19; compare Julius Caesar, *De bello Gallico*, 5.23. In *HE* 1.3 on Claudius's invasion, Bede also ignores Orosius's *Hist.* 7.6, which claims that God's favour for Rome in the era after Christ's birth is symbolized by the contrast between the storms that struck Caesar's ships and the calm seas at the time of Claudius's invasion in the A.D. 40s.

[57] *HE* 3.15.

[58] *HE* 1.17; *Vita Germani*, ed. by R. Borius, *Constance de Lyon: Vie de Saint Germain d'Auxerre*, Sources Chrétiennes, 112 (Paris, 1965), 3.13.

[Swelling waves also that once in a great storm rose like mountains, quickly subsided at his prayer, and were stilled [compare Matthew 8. 23–27]. And his ship, in which he himself chanced to be sailing, was at that time, when the calm fell, carried to the desired haven. On his return from a visit of some days to the district of the Picts, he raised his sail against the blast of contrary wind, in order to confound the magicians, and so his boat put out and sped on a rapid course as if it had had a following wind. At other times also, through his prayers, winds unfavourable to voyagers were changed to favourable ones.]

In *V.Col.* 2.34's more detailed account of the storm in Pictish territory, Adomnán relates that it was raised by pagan magicians with the aid of evil spirits and explicitly models his narrative on the *Vita Germani*. He points to the *Vita* as evidence that demons are sometimes allowed to raise storms by God's permission and compares Germanus, who came to Britain 'causa humanae salutis' ('in the cause of man's salvation') and overcame their tempest through prayer, with Columba who stilled the storm in the Picts' land and forced those pagans to recognize God's glory.[59] Elsewhere, Adomnán uses another of Columba's miracles to compare the saint to Elijah and Elisha, and to Peter, Paul, and John; he is revealed as 'homo profeticus et apostolicus' ('a man prophetic and apostolic') and is united 'cum Christo qui regnat cum patre in unitate spiritus sancit per omnia saecula saeculorum' ('with Christ, who reigns with the Father in the unity of the Holy Spirit, through all the ages of the ages').[60] Such explicit parallels between Columba's miracles and those of Christ, the prophets, and the saints in scriptural and Insular history affirm that Columba is a saint of the universal Church on earth and in heaven; they answer the doubts raised about him by Wilfrid in Bede's account of the Synod of Whitby, where supporters of the differing Columban and Roman paschal traditions met to resolve the controversy in 664.[61] Wilfrid, noting the Columbans' use of the saint's authority to justify their stance, had contrasted his limited authority with the plenitude of power given by Christ to Peter (Matthew 16. 18–19), representing the Roman and universal Easter. Wilfrid reduced the saint to 'ille Columba vester' ('that Columba of yours') and appeared to question his holiness and the value of his miracles (*HE* 3.25).

Adomnán's insistence on Columba's communion with Christ, the prophets, and the saints finds an echo in his account of Cormac's third voyage, where the saint is spiritually present with the monk in the farthest North because they are

---

[59] *V.Col.*2.34; *Vita Germani*, 3.13.

[60] *V.Col.* 2.33.

[61] See further Máire Herbert, *Iona, Kells and Derry* (Oxford, 1988), pp. 47–56, on the *V.Col.* as an attempt to defend and promote Columba's memory outside the Columban *familia* in the period of the Easter controversy.

'fellow-members', a reference to Paul's call to Christian unity in Ephesians 4. 25 and his statement in Ephesians 5. 30 that we are all members of Christ's body; a quiet but firm rebuke to those who would link the saint with those whom Christ will reject at the Last Judgement.[62] Furthermore, just as Adomnán says that Columba's Christlike calming of the Pictish storm led the pagans to acknowledge God's glory, he also writes that the saint's intervention to save Cormac should cause the reader to marvel and see in him the Christ of Galilee:

> Perpendat itaque lector quantus et qualis idem vir beatus, qui talem profeticam habens scientiam ventis et ociano Christi invocato nomine potuit imperare.

> [Let the reader therefore consider how great and of what nature was this blessed man, who had such prophetic knowledge, and by invoking the name of Christ was able to command the winds and the ocean [compare Matthew 8. 27].][63]

And it may be no coincidence that Bede presents Aidan performing a miracle reminiscent of Columba's intervention on Cormac's behalf. Before he wrote the *Historia ecclesiastica*, the Easter controversy led Northumbrian sources to suppress or misrepresent the Columban and wider Irish contribution to English Christianity.[64] Outside the Columban *familia*, it was Bede — and Bede alone — who restored Columba's good name and 'acclaimed this island [Iona] on the world's edge as a major centre of the Church's universal mission', not only to the English but to the Picts too.[65]

It is appropriate that the Insular saints who combat evil — whether in the form of paganism or heresy — should inherit and imitate Christ's power to subdue the wind and waves, for the restless sea in scripture represents the powers of chaos and evil that struggle in vain against God, whose command of the waters reveals him as ruler of the universe.[66] Their God-given victories over Ocean around

---

[62] *HE* 3.25; Matthew 7. 22–23.

[63] *V.Col.* 2.24.

[64] D. Scully, '*Gens innoxia*: The Irish in Bede's *Historia ecclesiastica gentis Anglorum*' (unpublished paper from the conference 'Mayo of the Saxons', Claremorris, Co. Mayo, 10–11 April 1996), pp. 1–16 (pp. 1–3).

[65] O'Reilly, 'Islands and Idols', p. 142. On Bede's view of the Columban mission and the Irish generally, see also O'Reilly, 'Introduction', pp. xxxv–xlvi; A. T. Thacker, 'Bede and the Irish', in *Beda Venerabilis: Historian, Monk and Northumbrian*, ed. by L. A. J. R Houwen and A. A. MacDonald (Groningen, 1996), pp. 31–59. See also T. Charles-Edwards, 'Bede, the Irish and the Britons', *Celtica*, 15 (1983), 42–52; Scully, 'Gens innoxia'; C. Stancliffe, *Bede, Wilfrid and the Irish* (Jarrow Lecture, 2003).

[66] On the meaning of the sea in scripture and patristic exegesis, see further Borsje, *From Chaos to Enemy*, pp. 93–175; O'Loughlin, 'Living in the Ocean', pp. 12–13.

Britain are all the more resonant given its waters' unholy pagan associations in some classical and late antique sources; Pomponius Mela, Plutarch, Claudian, and Procopius either locate or report traditions locating the entrance to the other-world in this region of the oceanic North-West.[67] If the seas around the archipelago were haunted by the old gods — demons — in the pagan past, then they are being cleansed of that pollution in the Christian present. Island monasteries like Iona are spiritual fortresses in Britannic Ocean where usurping evil spirits are vanquished and banished. Adomnán tells of Columba's victory on the island:

> Daemonque infestas ipse unus homo et innumeras contra se belligerantes cateruas occulis corporalibus visas et incipientes mortiferos super eius cenubialem coetum inferred morbos hac nostra de insula retrotrusas primaria deo auxiliante repulit.

> [He, one man alone, with God's aid repulsed innumerable hostile bands of demons making war against him, visible to his bodily eyes, and preparing to inflict deadly diseases upon his community of monks; and they were thrust back from this our principal island.][68]

Here, Iona becomes the oceanic counterpart of the Egyptian desert where the first monks went to fight Satan and his demons, and Adomnán later compares Columba with Anthony in that wilderness.[69] But if Columba could make Iona a sanctuary for his followers, why did Cormac fail to find his own oceanic desert retreat in the seas far north of the island?[70] A comparison of Adomnán's text with the analogous classical sources suggests that Cormac was frustrated in his search precisely because of those seas' extreme northern location. Sailing past the Orkneys, Cormac had left the world of men.[71] When attacked by the monstrous

---

[67] Pomponius Mela, *De chorographia* 3.48; Plutarch, *On the Obsolescence of the Oracles*, 419; Claudian, *In Rufinum*, 1, 123–33; Procopius, *De bello Gothico*, 8.20, 48–58. Discussion in S. Reinach, 'Les vierges de Sena', *Revue Celtique*, 18 (1897), 1–8; A. R. Burn, 'Procopius and the Island of Ghosts', *English Historical Review*, 70 (1955), 75–80; Scully, 'Atlantic Archipelago', pp. 34–37.

[68] *V.Col.* 1.1. Compare Bede on island monasteries and hermitages; see O'Reilly, 'Islands and Idols', pp. 142–44.

[69] As the editors note, *V.Col.* 3.23's description of Columba's fame spreading throughout the world and reaching Rome is modelled on Evagrius's translation of Athanasius, *Life* of Anthony, 93; the Evagrian *Life* appears in *PL*, 73, 125–70.

[70] *V.Col.* 1.6; 2.42.

[71] Adomnán may have regarded this as poetically rather than literally true; it is possible that Irish monks had discovered island retreats above the Orkneys in his time, and they certainly found such places in the course of the eighth and early ninth centuries, as Dicuil testifies; *Liber de mensura orbis terrae*, VII.6–15, ed. by J. J. Tierney with contributions by L. Bieler, Scriptores

creatures he was travelling in waters where no one had gone before him: this was no place for mortals to seek a dwelling or even to enter. Christian authorities shared the Ancients' sense that uttermost Ocean remained a zone beyond human exploration and knowledge. Describing the edges of the known world with particular emphasis on the Atlantic archipelago and the islands of far northern and north-eastern Ocean, Jordanes remarks:

> Oceani vero intranseabiles ulteriores fines non solum describere quis adgressus est, verum etiam nec cuiquam licuit transfretare, quia resistente, ulva et ventorum speramine quiescente impermeabilis esse sentitur et nulli cognita nisi ea qui eam constituit.

> [But the impassable farther bounds of Ocean not only has no-one attempted to describe, but no man has been allowed to reach; for by reason of obstructing seaweed and the failing of the winds it is plainly inaccessible and is unknown to any save to him who made it.][72]

The *Navagatio Brendani*'s account of the eponymous saint's experiences in the oceanic North adds to a sense of those waters as terrifying and forbidden. Sailing there, he encounters the conditions that Jordanes warns exist in uttermost Ocean — no wind and a coagulating sea — and subsequently finds a stinking, barren, and fiery island reverberating with a continuous wail, which he recognizes as the gates of hell.[73] The next day, on a mountainous island to the north, one of his monks is dragged away by demons, and seven days later Brendan encounters Judas on a barren rock, enjoying a temporary respite from hellish torments in the same island-mountain where the sinful monk now suffers; it is the dwelling of Leviathan and his followers.[74] It is hardly surprising that Brendan should encounter

---

Latini Hiberniae, 6 (Dublin, 1967), pp. 72–76. Nevertheless, even after the discovery of habitable islands to their north, the Orkneys continued to feature in the geographical imagination as the northern endpoint of habitable north-western Ocean. Several ninth- to thirteenth-century zonal maps of the Earth's climates, illustrating Macrobius's commentary on the *Dream of Scipio*, depict them immediately below the northern frozen zone; L. S. Chekin, *Northern Eurasia in Medieval Cartography* (Turnhout, 2006), pp. 95–107, pls VII.1–VII.2.3.

[72] *Getica*, ed. by T. Mommsen, MGH, Auctores antiquissimi, 5 (Berlin, 1882), 1.5; trans. by C. C. Mierow, 2nd edn (Cambridge, 1915), p. 52.

[73] *Navagatio Sancti Brendani abbatis, from Early Latin Manuscripts*, ed. by Carl Selmer (Notre Dame, 1959), c. 14, 23.

[74] *Navagatio Sancti Brendani abbatis*, ed. by Selmer, c. 23–25. On the far North as an infernal zone in the Irish sources, see further Borsje, *From Chaos to Enemy*, p. 164, where she comments that Adomnán's reference to the creatures attacking Cormac as having 'never been seen before' is used in Irish sources 'to characterise monsters from Hell'; see also J. Wooding, 'Monastic Voyaging and the Navagatio', in *Otherworld Voyage*, ed. by Wooding, pp. 226–45 (pp. 235–36).

such horrors there, for Lucifer boasts that 'I will exalt my throne above the stars of God, I will sit also upon the mount of the congregation, in the sides of the North' (Isaiah 14. 13–14).[75]

But Satan cannot overcome Brendan and his faithful monks. At the island-gates of hell, Brendan comforts them, urging them as soldiers of Christ to put on spiritual weapons and stand firm.[76] The theme of Christ's defence of the faithful even in farthest Ocean runs throughout the *Navagatio*. When the voyagers are attacked by a great sea-monster, Brendan saves them by calling on Christ's protection, assuring the monks that they have nothing to fear since the Lord who delivered Jonah from the belly of a whale will guard them.[77] Columba exercises the same power over the creatures of the sea, and his followers share his confidence that, under divine protection, these creatures will do them no harm. The monk Baithéne, advised by the saint that he will encounter a great whale, replies: 'Ego et illa bilua sub dei potestate sumus' ('I and that beast are in God's power').[78] Cormac too trusts in providence when attacked by the even more horrifying and entirely unknown monsters of the farthest North, calling on God, 'qui est in angustis pius et oportunus auxiliator' ('who is a true and ready helper in time of need'). The phrase comes from Psalm 46, which proclaims divine command of creation:

> God is our refuge and strength, a very present help in trouble. Therefore will we not fear, though the earth be removed, and though the mountains be carried into the midst of the sea; Though the waters thereof roar and be troubled, though the mountains shake with the swelling thereof. (Psalm 46. 1–3)

The contrast that the story of Cormac reveals between God's mercy towards his faithful in the farthest reaches of Ocean and the anger or indifference of the pagan deities who destroyed or abandoned the Romans in those waters is striking. The

---

[75] On the meaning of the North in scripture and patristic and Insular exegesis, see Scully, 'Atlantic Archipelago', pp. 160–75. On the medieval and Renaissance image of the North generally, see J. M. Alonso-Núñçz, 'Jordanes and Procopius on Northern Europe', *Nottingham Medieval Studies*, 31 (1987), 1–16; M. Spies, *Arctic Routes to Fabled Lands* (Amsterdam, 1997); S. C. Akbari, 'From Due East to True North: Orientalism and Orientation', in *The Postcolonial Middle Ages*, ed. by J. J. Cohen (London, 2000), pp. 19–34; Merills, *History and Geography*. P. Davison, *The Idea of North* (London, 2005), further considers the image of the North and its meaning in modern culture.

[76] *Navagatio Sancti Brendani abbatis*, ed. by Selmer, c. 14; compare Ephesians 6. 11–17.

[77] *Navagatio Sancti Brendani abbatis*, ed. by Selmer, c. 16.

[78] *V.Col.* 1.19.

episode also confirms Columba's enjoyment of extraordinary divine favour. In order to save Cormac, God allows the saint to project his spiritual power as far as the absolute limits of habitable reality in Ocean, far beyond the waters of the Atlantic archipelago calmed by other saints, which were themselves beyond the power of imperial Rome to control: an unparalleled achievement.[79]

Columba has truly conquered Ocean. Celebrating Claudius's invasion of Britain, a poet claimed that the Tiber once marked the limits of the Romans' kingdom, and their power was confined to the Continental limits of Ocean, but when they conquered the island, the boundaries of their empire were abolished and Ocean linked twin worlds.[80] In Adomnán's day, imperial Rome was one with Nineveh and Tyre and at the beginning and end of the *Vita Columbae* he reversed its boasts of power over the edges of the earth. Opening the *Vita*, Adomnán writes that, before the saint's birth, Maucte foretold that his fame would spread 'per omnes insularum ociani provincias' ('through all the provinces of Ocean's islands').[81] The archipelago's separation from the world is over, but in place of imperial Rome making its greatness known as far as the Isles through force, the *Vita*'s concluding words demonstrate that after his death, the fame of Columba by God's favour stretches across the *orbis terrarum* to petrine Rome:

> Et haec etiam eidem beatae memoriae viro a deo non mediocris est conlata gratia, qua nomen eius non tantum per totam nostram Scotiam, et omnium totius orbis insularum maximam Brittanniam, clare devulgari promeruit in hac parva et extrema ociani brittanici commoratus insula, sed etiam ad trigonam usque Hispaniam, et Gallias, et ultra Alpes pinias Italiam sitam pervenire, ipsam quqoue romanam civitatem, qaue caput est omnium civitatem, tantus et talis honor noscibilis eidem sancto inter cetera divinae donationis munera condonatus scitur a deo, qui se diligentes amat, et eos qui eum sapidis magnificent laudibus magis ac magis glorificans inmensis sublimate honoribus. Qui est benedictus in saecula. Amen.

> [And this great favour also was conferred by God on that man of blessed memory, that, although he lived in this small and remote island of the Britannic Ocean, he merited that

---

[79] There is a pleasing symmetry in one of the southernmost monks of Columba's *familia* (the Ua Liatháin belong to east Cork, between the harbour and the estuary of the Blackwater) finding safety in the northernmost reaches of the world under the saint's care; I owe this observation to Padraig Ó Riain, Emeritus Professor of Early and Medieval Irish, University College Cork.

[80] '[. . .] ultimam cingebat Thybris tua, Romule, regna: | hic tibi finis erat, religiose Numa. | et tua, Dive, tuo sacrata potentia caelo | extremum citra constit Oceanum. | at nunc Oceanus geminos interluit orbes; | pars est imperii, terminus ante fuit': *Anthologia Latina*, ed. by D. R. Shackleton-Bailey (Stuttgart, 1982), p. 324 (poem number 421).

[81] *V.Col.*, second preface.

his name should not only be illustriously renowned throughout our Ireland, and throughout Britain, the greatest of all islands of the whole world; but that it should also reach as far as three cornered Spain, and Gaul, and Italy situated beyond the Pennine Alps; also the Roman city itself, which is the chief of all cities [compare Athanasius's life of Anthony, 93]. So great and high honour of fame is known to have been bestowed upon that saint, among the other gifts of divine granting, by God, who loves those that love him, and, more and more glorifying those that magnify him with savoury praises, elevates them with boundless honours. And he is blessed through the ages. Amen.][82]

---

[82] *V.Col.* 3.23. On the spiritual significance of the phrase 'chief of cities' (and related terms) applied here to Rome, see Bracken, 'Authority and Duty', pp. 182–86. On patristic and Bedan ideas of Christianity abolishing the archipelago's geographical remoteness, see O'Reilly, 'Islands and Idols', pp. 121–22, 144.

II. Reading Texts

BEDE'S STYLE IN HIS COMMENTARY *ON I SAMUEL*

George Hardin Brown

From Alcuin in the early ninth century to Winthrop Wetherbee in the twentieth, Bede's style has been admired for its lucid clarity and efficient simplicity. Many concurred with the great editor of Bede's *Ecclesiastical History*, Charles Plummer, in his assertion: 'Bede's command of Latin is excellent, and his style is clear and limpid, and it is very seldom that we have to pause to think of the meaning of a sentence.'[1] However, medieval Latinists such as Richard Sharpe and Seán Connolly have now qualified that praise by showing that on closer inspection Bede's prose style is quite varied and, in his biblical commentaries at least, not so pellucid.[2] Actually, Bede's historical prose differs from his didactic prose, and his exegetical prose differs from both; and his exegetical style

I am pleased to offer this essay in tribute to my admired friend and fellow Bedan scholar, Éamonn Ó Carragáin, from whom I have learned much about Anglo-Saxon England and Rome. His great scholarship is only equaled by his affable generosity.

[1] *Venerabilis Baedae: opera historica*, ed. by Charles Plummer, 2 vols (Oxford, 1896), I, p. liii; see also p. liv.

[2] For an impressive survey of historic praise of Bede's style followed by a keen critical reassessment, see Richard Sharpe, 'The Varieties of Bede's Prose', being published in a Festschrift honouring Michael Winterbottom, titled *Aspects of Latin Prose*, edited by J. N. Adams and Michael Lapidge (London). Sharpe's analysis of Bede's prose style may serve as a companion piece to this essay; earlier versions of both were given at a Bede session at the Medieval Congress at Western Michigan University, 11 May 2003. For Wetherbee, see his 'Some Implications of Bede's Latin Style', in *Bede and Anglo-Saxon England: Papers in Honor of the 1300*[th] *Anniversary of the Birth of Bede, Given at Cornell University in 1973 and 1974*, ed. by Robert T. Farrell, British Archaeological Reports, 46 (Oxford, 1978), pp. 23–31. Seán Connolly's remarks appear in his notes to *Bede: On the Temple*, trans. by Seán Connolly with an introduction by Jennifer O'Reilly (Liverpool, 1997), p. 15.

in turn differs in its earlier and later format. So his earliest commentaries, such as those on the Apocalypse and Acts, proceed by a simple, brief phrase-by-phrase explanation, whereas his later commentaries, such as on the Tabernacle, on the Temple, and on Ezra, are more extensively discursive; into them he often interweaves patristic citations, adjusting them to his context by syntactic and grammatical changes. Within a biblical commentary such as the longest and the one Bede himself perceived as most difficult, *On I Samuel*, he changes the stylistic presentation according to the different structural registers of the commentary, so that within the commentary itself there exist very different styles.

Bede precedes the text with *capitula lectionum*, numbered short summaries of the historical sections.[3] These summaries, characteristically Bedan, are written, as Paul Meyvaert has pointed out, with a concision and a literary style uncommon for such headings.[4] In the manuscripts in the commentary itself the numbers of those *capitula* appear at the appropriate places, accompanied by parallel headings summarizing the allegorical interpretation in the section. Moreover, Bede divides the commentary into four main parts or books and furnishes prologues to each of the four parts. The prologues are stylistically more formal, hypotactic, and periodic than the ensuing commentaries on the verses. This essay will examine in some detail the structure and ideas of the first prologue and, after a summary of the other three prologues, will give two representative examples of the contrasting textual commentary.

Each of the four parts introduced by a prologue consists of about sixty pages in the CCSL edition.[5] The four divisions are not arbitrary; they represent

---

[3] Bede, *In primam partem Samvhelis libri IIII*, ed. by David Hurst, CCSL, 119 (Turnhout, 1962), pp. 5–8. Hurst, while furnishing at the head of the commentary the series of chapter headings that give the historical sections, annoyingly omits the parallel numbers of the *capitula* in the text, linking to the paired allegorical treatment, despite the fact that the numbers are in the manuscripts. The biblical chapter-and-verse divisions were not standardized until the twelfth century. Some earlier Bibles had chapter divisions for some books, and texts of the New Testament were provided with Eusebian canon tables for cross-referencing, but today's familiar chapter divisions were a result of Parisian scholastic consensus, often attributed to Stephen Langton. See Beryl Smalley, *The Study of the Bible in the Middle Ages*, 3rd edn (Oxford, 1983), ch. 5, and Margaret T. Gibson, *The Bible in the Latin West* (Notre Dame, 1993), pp. 10–11.

[4] See Paul Meyvaert's important 'Bede's *Capitula Lectionum* for the Old and New Testaments', *Revue Bénédictine*, 105 (1995), 348–80 (pp. 351, 373–75).

[5] Ed. by Hurst, pp. 5–272. The collection *Nomina locorum* (on pp. 273–87), excerpted from Jerome and Flavius Josephus, is not by Bede. Hurst's edition of Bede's works in CCSL has been justly criticized for its inaccuracies, lack of suitable punctuation, and poor editing; a better edition is therefore desirable.

thematic units, a confirmation for which is the fact that, although Bede's chapters differ somewhat from those of modern biblical editions, the modern Anchor Bible divides the first three parts in the same way.[6] Book I covers chapters 1–8, the story of Samuel, his birth, consecration, and career; Book II, comprising chapters 9–15, describes the advent of kingship, the choice of Saul, his troubled career, and his rejection; Book III, chapters 16–22, deals with the rise of David and his struggles with Saul; and Book IV, chapters 23–31, describes David's final ascendancy, the death of Samuel, and the death of Saul. Furnishing each of these books with a prologue is a unique phenomenon among Bede's commentaries. Although for the *De templo* he provides a tripartite initial prologue, I Samuel is the only commentary to which he appends a prologue for each major division, or book. Even though we might expect them to be like one another in content and format, that each prologue might summarize and introduce the following book, this is not the case. Each prologue is of a different length, in a different mode, and in a different style. Each prologue merits separate attention because of differing length, topic, and stylistic level. The fourth prologue is additionally important because of Bede's measured but poignant personal voice describing the shock to him caused by Abbot Ceolfrith's resignation, pilgrimage departure to Rome in 716, and subsequent death at Langres en route.[7]

The first prologue consists in the CCSL edition of 636 words in 65 lines. The most formal of the four prologues, it invites every reader to investigate the symbolic meaning of the specific text in order to apply it tropologically to ourselves and to our times. Halfway through the prologue, however, Bede changes from an address to the general reader to a more affective address to the prelate who encouraged him to create this commentary, Bishop Acca of Hexham, his learned and admired friend and diocesan to whom he dedicated a half dozen of his other commentaries and to whom he pays admiring tribute in *Historia ecclesiastica*, 5.20.

Studium nobis frequentiamque legendi ac meditandi litteras sanctas commendans apostolus ait : *Quaecumque enim scripta sunt ad nostram doctrinam scripta sunt ut per patientiam et consolationem scripturarum spem habeamus* (Romans 15. 4); et alibi : *Omnia in figura contingebant illis, scripta sunt autem ad correptionem nostram in quos fines saeculorum*

---

[6] I Samuel, ed. and trans. by P. Kyle McCarter, Jr, *The Anchor Bible*, vol. VIII (New York, 1980). McCarter, pp. 5–11, provides a summary of the complex history of the versions of the biblical text. Bede uses Jerome's Vulgate text, which is based on a proto-Masoretic version with emendations from the Septuagint.

[7] *Baedae: opera historica*, ed. by Plummer, I, pp. xiv–xv, with references to the *History of the Abbots of Wearmouth and Jarrow*.

deuenerunt (I Corinthians 10. 11). Sed et beatus apostolus Petrus dominicae incarnationis passionis et posterioris gloriae tempera commemorans dicit inter cetera : *Et omnes prophetae a Samuhel et deinceps qui locuti sunt et adnuntiarunt dies istos* (Acts 3. 24).[8]

The language and structure of this passage have the sanction of patristic tradition. In the fourth book of the *De doctrina christiana*, a work familiar to Bede, Augustine eloquently demonstrates that Paul, 'speaking with an amazing combination of wisdom and eloquence', uses numerous stylistic devices, such as *gradatio*, parallelism, balanced *cola* and *commata*, contrast, and periodic structure.[9] I see an analogously complex use of syntax and ornament in Bede's prologue. He begins by grounding his exegetical procedure on three aptly concatenated scriptural quotations: Romans 15. 4 specifies that all things written in scriptures are applicable to us; I Corinthians 10. 11 clarifies that for scripture to be understood rightly, it must be understood figurally, symbolically, typologically (Latin *in figura*, Greek *typikos*); and third, as St Peter in Acts 3. 24 tells us, the prophets, and specifically Samuel, predicted these days. Bede had used these texts before, but not artfully so linked. He introduced his commentary *On the Temple* with Romans 15. 4, and *On the Tabernacle* with I Corinthians 10. 11; but here he conjoins them and suitably adds the reference in Acts to Samuel. He introduces the texts with a present participial phrase ('commendans [...]') and closes by presenting the Petrine text with a similarly importunate participial phrase 'commemorans [. . .]'. The present participial phrases convey to the reader the idea of present relevance.

Having established the scriptural authority for the enterprise, he opens the prologue proper with a seventy-seven-word conditional sentence:

Si enim ad nostram correptionem doctrinam uel consolationem omnia scripta sunt nec soli Hieremias et Esaias ceterique tales qui uerbis futura signauerunt sed et Samuhel Ionas et Ezra eorumque consimiles qui praeterita uel sua uel aliorum gesta siue dicta conscripsere dies istos, hoc est nouae gratiae luce radiantes, insinuant, insistendum nobis

---

[8] Bede, *In primam partem Samuhelis*, ed. by Hurst, p. 9, lines 1–10. For my translation of this and the following text of the prologue, see the Appendix, no. 1.

[9] Augustine, *De doctrina christiana*, IV.34 (= VII.12), ed. and trans. by R. P. H. Green (Oxford, 1995), pp. 208–09. The whole of Book IV is a great *apologia* for the use of rhetoric in sacred writings; on his treatment of the tropes in scripture and in Christian authors, see also III.87 (= XXIX.40), pp. 170–71. For Bede's knowledge of the *De doctrina*, see M. L. W. Laistner, 'The Library of the Venerable Bede', in *Bede: His Life, Times, and Writings*, ed. by A. Hamilton Thompson (Oxford, 1935), pp. 237–66 (pp. 250, 263); *Bedae presbyteri exposito Apocalypseos*, ed. by Roger Gryson, CCSL, 121A (Turnhout, 2001), p. 588.

summopere est et pro suo cuique modulo Christi iuuante gratia nitendum ne ea quae propter nos scripta sunt nostro nos torpore uel incuria quasi aliena praetereant.[10]

The prodasis ('Si [...] scripta sunt [...] insinuant') contains contrastive members ('nec soli [...] sed et'), each affixed with relative clauses ('qui [...] signauerunt' and 'qui [...] conscripsere') and ending with the object of 'insinuant', 'dies istos', modified by an explanatory participial phrase. The apodasis ('insistendum [...] praetereant') is introduced with a double gerundive phrase of obligation ('insistendum [...] est' and 'nitendum'), to which is added an ablative phrase ('pro [...] modulo') and an ablative absolute ('Christi iuuante gratia'), before concluding with a negative purpose clause '(ne [...] praetereant'), which is in turn modified by a relative clause ('quae [...] scripta sunt') and an ablative of description ('nostro nos torpore uel incuria'). Note the insistence on 'us' ('nos') with 'propter nos' and 'nostro nos torpore'. In the last phrase Bede heightens this tropological thrust of the text by using his favourite figure of speech mentioned above, hyperbaton, separating 'nostro' from 'torpore' with the inserted 'nos'.

After that conditional sentence, Bede continues with a contrastive conjunction 'sed', leading into an indirect question:

Sed quo sensu in his correptionem qua ratione doctrinam quo intellectu consolationem nanciscamur qualiter omnia dies istos loquantur et adnuntient sollicite ac uigilanter intendamus imitantes pro captu nostri ingenioli scribam ilium doctum in regno caelorum qui profert de thesauro suo noua et uetera. Nam si uetera tantummodo de thesauro [...].[11]

The question is composed of three combined interrogative phrasals (' quo sensu', 'qua ratione', 'quo intellectu') followed by a subordinate clause ('qualiter [...] loquantur et adnuntient'), with the main clause properly in the subjunctive, modified by two adverbs ('sollicite ac uigilanter intendamus') — but we are not yet at the end of the sentence, because Bede adds on a participial phrase ('imitantes [...]') that cites Matthew 15. 32, modified by a qualifying phrase of modesty ('pro captu nostri ingenioli'). The end of that sentence performs a chiastic contrast with the beginning of the next, 'thesauro [...] uetera // uetera [...] thesauro'.

After this relatively brief indirect question (forty-three words), the next highly hypotactic sentence is more than double in length, containing eighty-eight words.

---

[10] Bede, *In primam partem Samuhelis*, ed. by Hurst, p. 9, lines 10–18. For my English translation of this sentence, see the Appendix, no. 1.

[11] Bede, *In primam partem Samuhelis*, ed. by Hurst, p. 9, lines 18–24. For my English translation, see the Appendix, no. 1.

> Nam si uetera tantummodo de thesauro scripturarum proferre, hoc est solas litterae figuras sequi ludaico more curamus, quid inter cotidiana peccata correptionis inter crebrescentes aerumnas saeculi consolationis inter innumeros uitae huius errores spiritalis doctrinae legentes uel audientes adquirimus dum aperto libro uerbi gratia beati Samuhelis Helcanam uirum unum duas uxores habuisse repperimus nos maxime quibus ecclesiasticae uitae consuetudine longe fieri ab uxorio complexu et caelibes manere propositum est, si non etiam de his et huiusmodi dictis allegoricum nouerimus exsculpere sensum qui nos uiuaciter interius castigando erudiendo consolando reficiat?[12]

It begins, after the conjunctive 'nam', with another condition, 'si [...] curamus', which involves a paronomasia on the word 'figuras', here meaning 'the forms of letters' that the literalist Jewish exegetes of the old dispensation follow rather than the *figura*, the symbolic meaning that the new Christian dispensation requires, according to the Pauline quote at the beginning. Bede then asks the question, how will we find spiritual help in the scriptures for our present threefold daily afflictions ('quid inter [...] inter [...] inter'). Note how the 'quid' is separated by an extraordinary hyperbaton from the partitive genitives it governs, 'correptionis', 'consolationis', and 'spiritualis doctrinae'. To this query Bede appends a concrete example, introduced by the temporal conjunction 'dum', which serves as an appendage to his sentence. Modern English sentence structure cannot bear such rhetorical syntactic weight; I have had to make it a separate sentence in my translation. The example Bede gives, fittingly taken from the opening sentence of the Samuel text, mentions the two wives of Eli, which, as he observes, are two women too many for any monk-reader seeking guidance from the text, so the scripture, if it is indeed for our profit, must be taken allegorically. Note the stylistic devices of the clause, how, for instance 'uirum unum' from I Samuel 1. 1 is juxtaposed with 'duas uxores', how the negative conditional 'si non' forces a positive response, and how the lightly metaphorical 'exsculpere' ('to carve out'), for an abstract sense of 'extract', is followed by a relative clause in which three gerunds are asyndetically embedded.

Addressing Acca, Bede explains that having completed his commentary on the evangelist Luke, he is now probing the text of another evangelist, this time an Old Testament seer, who also discloses the mysteries of Christ, but *in figura*.

> Vnde tuo crebro dilectissime ac desiderantissime omnium qui in terris morantur antistitum Acca prouocatus hortatu tuis fretus orationibus memorati prophetae qui tune uocabatur uidens scripta per lustrans, si quid donante illo qui ei multa spiritalia uidere

---

[12] Bede, *In primam partem Samuhelis*, ed. by Hurst, p. 9, lines 24–34. For my English translation, see the Appendix, no. 1.

dedit spiritale ac mysticum potuero contueri, litteris mandare curabo et post qualem-
cumque expositionem beati Lucae dictorum quibus euangelicos uel ipsius domini uel
apostolorum eius actus describit etiam hunc sanctissimum domino ex matris utero naza-
reum non minus suis in scriptis euangelistae quam historici functum officio probare
satagam quippe qui et ipse omnia mediatoris Dei et hominum hominis Iesu Christi
sacramenta figurato fidelis historiae sed plenissimo designarit eloquio. Denique ut de
ceteris taceam, si unius Dauid locum natiuitatis officium pastoris ruborem ac pulchritu-
dinem aspectus modum unctionis insigne uirtutum pondus tribulationum et promissi
olim regni gloriam recte consideras, quanta in his singulis fidei et ueritatis euangelicae
congesta mysteria cernis. Verum haec suo loco planius. Nunc ex ordine iniunctum opus
superno solum fidens auxilio et patrum uestigia sequens aggrediar. Et si quidem multorum
ut desidero meus sudor utilitati et commodo profuerit, multa me donandum mercede
cum illis a domino spero; sin autem, nec mihi tamen mea sollertia quae me tanto tempore
laboris huiusce otiosum esse superuacuisue rebus animum indulgere non sinit infructuosa
existere poterit. Ergo age uideamus prophetam Samuhelem qui locutus est et adnuntiauit
dies istos quod eiusdem locutionis et adnuntiationis suae fecerit initium et ex ordine
disserentes beati Petri apostolorum pnncipis adiutorio qui cuncta quibus diebus sint
aptanda perdocuit qualiter singula sint eisdem diebus aptanda quaeramus.[13]

In this appeal to Acca, the second word 'tuo' after the adverb 'unde' is separated
from its noun 'hortatu' by twelve words, but this hyperbaton causes no problem
for the reader because 'hortatu' is the only possible accompanying noun for 'tuo'.
In this sentence Bede plays on the meaning of prophet as 'seer', expressing the hope
that through Acca's prayers and encouragement he too by God's grace will be a
seer into the meaning of the text. As he had interpreted Luke's Gospel and the
Acts, Bede now will interpret Samuel, whom Bede boldly calls an 'evangelist', because
his speech and life prefigured ('figurato') the God-man Christ. Then by *praeteritio*
('ut de ceteris taceam'), Bede passes over further details of the text to point out
summarily the similarities between David and Christ. With a promise to take up
each of these topics in order, he says succinctly that he will now attack ('aggrediar') the text in an orderly fashion ('ex ordine') verse by verse, following his
guidelines, divine inspiration and, in his oft repeated phrase, patristic precedent
('patrum uestigia sequens'). His concluding sentence begins with an imperative
('age') and a hortatory subjunctive ('uideamus'), and fittingly ends by recalling the
words of the Petrine text with which he began the prologue, thus forming a structural envelope for the beautifully balanced introduction to his commentary.

One important thing remains to be noticed about the style of this prologue,
namely, Bede's use of the *cursus*. Gudrun Lindholm's study on medieval Latin

---

[13] Bede, *In primam partem Samuhelis*, ed. by Hurst, pp. 9–10, lines 34–64. For my English
translation, see the Appendix, no. 1.

prose rhythm records that Bede in his *Historia ecclesiastica* employed the *cursus*, the formal cadenced endings of clauses, rather sparingly in comparison with some Carolingian writers and later formalists such as Peter Damian.[14] We therefore might assume that in the rest of his works Bede, like Augustine, used the *cursus* only moderately. In the *De doctrina* Augustine, while admitting that 'the stylistic embellishment that derives from rhythmical clausulae is missing in the Latin scriptures', for himself says, 'I do not neglect clausular rhythm in my own speaking, but apply it in what I consider to be moderation'.[15] We might expect Bede to emulate Augustine's moderation; but an analysis of the clausal endings in this prologue indicates that Bede uses the *cursus* at the end of every sentence. Of the three types, *planus*, *tardus*, and *uelox*, Bede here favours the *tardus*, though he does include some *planus*, and in his other prologues we also find examples of *uelox*. Beginning with his own words after the three scriptural citations, we note 'aliena praetereant' (*tardus*), 'noua et uetera' (*tardus*), 'consolando reficiat' (*tardus*), 'mysteria cernis' (*planus*), 'sequens aggrediar' (*tardus*), 'existere poterit' (*tardus*), and 'aptanda quaeramus' (*planus*). Considering that there are twenty-five possible ways to end a clause in Latin, the fact that Bede uses only two — and these are two of the three formal *cursus* — indicates Bede's deliberate stylistic care in this prologue.

Before contrasting the style of the prologue with the simpler style in the commentary, some attention to the other three prologues is proper, because they too differ surprisingly in subject and style from the first. In the long prologue to Book II Bede declares that, instead of a proem, he is going to treat matters of chronology, since he is at the point of the history at which Samuel's leadership ends and Saul's rule begins.[16] Bede the historian and chronologist replaces Bede the stylist and allegorist. Still, although the prologue moves along at a business-like pace, it is not totally devoid of rhetorical devices, such as three anaphoric 'sunt qui'. In ninety-five lines he earnestly attempts to sort out the chronological reigns of Saul, David, and Solomon by reckoning the length of each rule from Moses through Judges on the basis of the few temporal markers in the scriptural text. This is a brave attempt by Bede, who never shirks a challenge when it comes to calendrical time reckoning. Modern biblical historians are still trying to figure out the chronology of these rulers. As the editors of the *New Oxford Annotated Bible* remark, 'The length of Saul's reign is not known; David and Solomon are each

---

[14] Gudrun Lindholm, *Studien sum mittelateinischen Prosrhythmus* (Stockholm, 1963), pp. 10–11.

[15] Augustine, *De doctrina christiana*, 115–17, ed. by Green, pp. 250–51.

[16] Bede, *In primam partem Samuhelis*, ed. by Hurst, p. 68, lines 1–8.

said to have ruled for forty years, which is often used as a general and somewhat indefinite number [. . .]', and the editors add: 'Problems of chronology of the kings of Israel and Judah permit no easy solution.'[17] After surveying various opinions and giving his own, Bede concludes his attempt with the sentence, 'But because this preface has proceeded at length, let us now proceed with the order of the scripture text that we are investigating' (II.94–95).

The third prologue is a brief twenty-five lines, in which Bede remarks to Bishop Acca (and the reader) that having explained 'non pauco sudore' ('with no little sweat') the meaning of Samuel's career in Book I and of Saul's in Book II, he will now undertake in the third to comment on the early activity of David, which he compares to the historical movement from Judaism to Christianity. The fourth prologue, again addressed to Bishop Acca, contains the famous autobiographical confession of his personal psychic stress:

> Tertio in beatum Samuhelem completo uolumine putabam me aliquamdiu reparata per quietem meditandi uel scribendi uoluptate sic demum ad inchoationem quarti manum esse missurum. Verum haec eadem mihi quies, si tamen quies est inopinata mentis anxietas, prolixior multo quam decreueram noua circumstantium rerum mutatione prouenit maxime discessu abbatis mei reuerendissimi qui post longam monasterialis curae obseruantiam subitus Romam adire atque inter loca beatorum apostolorum ac martyrum Christi corporibus sacra extremum senex halitum reddere disponendo non parua commissorum sibi animos et eo maiore quo improuisa conturbatione stupefecit. Sed qui Moysis longaeuo ab humanis rebus tollendo Iesum Naue in ducatum qui Eleazarum in sacerdotium Aaron patri substituit ipse prouecto aetate Ceolfrido ad beatorum apostolorum limina sancta properanti Huetberctum iuuenem cui amor studiumque pietatis iam olim Eusebii cognomen indidit ad regendas sacerdotio ducatuque spiritali fidelium animas abbatis uice substituit eiusdemque substitutionis gradum post electionem fraternam sua per tuum dilectissime antistes officium benedictione confirmauit. Redeunte temporum statu tranquilliore redit et mihi otium pariter ac delectatio mirabilia scripturae sacrae tota animae sollertis intentione scrutandi. Igitur quartum in Samuhelem allegoricae expositionis libellum a uictoria beati Dauid qua saluauit habitatores Ceilae atque ab oppugnantium Philisthinorum inruptione defendit cum tuis amantissime pontificum orationaibus incipiens quicquid illo reserante qui habet clauem Dauid potuero mysticum legentibus communicare curabo.[18]

> [Having completed the third book of the Commentary on Samuel, I thought that I would rest a while, and, after recovering in that way my delight in study and writing, proceed to take in hand the fourth. But that rest — if sudden anguish of mind can be called rest — has turned out much longer than I had intended owing to the sudden change of

---

[17] *The New Oxford Annotated Bible, New Revised Standard Version*, ed. by Bruce M. Metzger and Roland E. Murphy (New York, 1994), p. 338 OT.

[18] Bede, *In primam partem Samuhelis*, ed. by Hurst, p. 212.

circumstances brought about by the departure of my most reverend Abbot; who, after long devotion to the care of his monastery, suddenly determined to go to Rome, and to breathe his last breath amid the localities sanctified by the bodies of the blessed Apostles and Martyrs of Christ, thus causing no little consternation to those committed to his charge, the greater because it was unexpected. But just as God, when He removed the aged Moses, appointed Joshua to the leadership, and ordained Eleazar to the priesthood in place of his father Aaron, so in the room of the aged Ceolfrid, who was hastening to the sacred threshold of the Apostles, He ordained the younger Hwætbert who by his love and zeal for piety had long won for himself the name of Eusebius; and after election by the brethren, confirmed that appointment by His blessing conferred by thy ministry, dearest bishop. And now with the return of quieter times, there returns to me the leisure and delight for searching out the wondrous things of Holy Scripture carefully and with my whole soul. Therefore aided by thy prayers, most loving of prelates, I begin the fourth book of my allegorical Exposition on Samuel [from the victory of the blessed David by which he saved the inhabitants of Keilah and defended them from the assault of the attacking Philistines], and will endeavour to communicate to my readers all that I can of its mysteries, if He will but unlock them, Who holds the key of David.][19]

Even though the four prologues are distinct in style, content, and length, they each mark a major division of the commentary, with the first prefacing the whole work and two through four first reprising the preceding book before introducing the next one.

But now, by way of comparison and contrast to the formal prologues, let us look at Bede's exegetical prose as he comments on the verses of the Scriptural text, line by line. Bede's commentaries differ stylistically from modern biblical commentaries in that he not only explains the meaning of the text, providing historical, theological, etymological, and philological information, but he always contemporizes the text by applying it to our own personal Christian situation. In the allegorical mode, tropology is paramount. With this emphasis on personal morality, the commentaries take on a homiletic tone, a strongly suasive modality.

As a product of Bede's mature period the commentary on I Samuel exhibits a stylistic development.[20] In his commentary on the Apocalypse, verses of the text are typically glossed with only two or three lines of explanation, whereas the verses of I Samuel are provided with a much fuller, discursive commentary, anywhere

---

[19] This graceful translation of the prologue is by Plummer, *Baedae: opera historica*, I, pp. xv–xvi; but he omits lines 24–25 of the Latin, which I have translated within brackets in his text.

[20] Bede tells us in the prologue of Book IV that the Commentary on I Samuel was written after Ceolfrith's fateful departure for Rome in 716 (p. 212, lines 1–12). That means Bede was then forty-three years old or so, an age when a scholar of his abilities, who had been constantly writing since early youth, could only be considered 'mature', as his style in the work indeed demonstrates.

from a half dozen to two dozen or more lines, and sometimes more than a page in length. Still, if we compare the length of the *cola* and *commata* in the body of the commentary with that of the prologues, we observe a genuine stylistic difference: the phrases and clauses of the commentary are much more succinct.

Let us examine two thematically related examples from the commentary, one from Book I, commenting on I Samuel 2. 22–23, which deals with the aged Heli and his sons, and the other from Book II, chapter 8. 1–5, dealing with the aged Samuel and his sons. Throughout both of these passages the leitmotiv of age (*senex, senectus, senio, senesco*) is key.

> *Heli autem erat senex ualde*, et cetera usque ad id quod *puer Samuhel proficiebat atque cres-cebat et placebat tarn Deo quam hominibus.* In hac lectione mystice senescente et occasuro ludaismo Christi per euangelium fama crebrescit. Heli ergo senectus multa tempus prope finiendi sacerdotii legalis insinuat. *Quod enim antiquatur et senescit prope interitum est* (Hebrews 8. 13).
>
> *Et audiuit omnia quae faciebant filii sui uniuerso Israheli et quomodo dormiebant cum mulieribus quae obseruabant ad ostium tabernaculi.* Non parua nec uniformis filiorum Heli transgressio quae et diuinam religionem et dilectionem proximi maculare non timuit. Supra namque legitur quia de carnibus sanctis non quod statutum in lege sed quod sibi erat libitum praesumpserint quia prius quam Deo sacer adeps adoleretur partem sibi de hostia quam comederent praesumpserint quia crudam ab offerentibus carnem quam sibi accuratius pararent rapuerint quia populum domini transgredi fecerint et quod maxime horrendum est in contemptum creatoris cuncta quae diximus egerint. Sed et nunc quod fraternitatem laederet additur quia mulieres populi quae ad orandum confluebant pollu-erint et infra quod omnium malorum summa est adnectitur quia nec correpti a patre paenituerint. Haec enucleatius diximus ut per singula lector quid caueas memineris. Verum quod restat typica in parte complendum sacerdotum doctorumque est et uigilare in domino et ad uigilandum ceteros excitare dicentes: *Euigilate iusti et nolite peccare* (I Corinthians 15. 34). Sed doctores mali dormiunt et hoc cum mulieribus quae obseruant ad ostium tabernaculi quando pellicentes animas instabiles nec ipsi intrant neque eo qui uolunt uitae ostium intrare permittunt. Tale erat quondam periturae scelus Pharisaeae factionis, tale est et nunc in falsis professoribus christianae religionis.
>
> *Et dixit eis: Quare facitis res huiuscemodi quas ego audio res pessimas,* et cetera. Corri-puit delinquentes filios Heli, sed non audierunt. Et ipsa ueteris institutio sacerdotii suos ministros iubet esse perfectos, sed scribae Pharisaei et principes sacerdotum improbi paternam suae legis ac sacerdotii uocem perituri contemnebant. Verum iuxta litteram non neglegenter intuendum quod corripuit quidem filios Heli sed quia correptionem spernentes ut debuerat abicere supersedit una cum ipsis disperiit. Quid ergo nos miseri quid nostri similes merentur qui gaudent ad uitia qui emendare non audent qui consci-entiam sui metuunt et quod cunctus populus clamitat nescire se simulant.[21]

---

[21] Bede, *In primam partem Samuhelis*, cap. 6, I Samuel 2. 22–23; ed. by Hurst, pp. 29–30, lines 747–89. For my translation, see the Appendix, no. 2.

He begins the former by summarizing the meaning of the text of verses 22–26 symbolically ('mystice'): the priest Heli represents Judaism, growing old and fading ('senescente et occasuro') while the youthful Gospel of Christ grows and waxes strong ('crebrescit'). In the following powerful paragraph, in which Bede comments on the sins of Heli's priestly sons, note the fourfold epanalepsis of 'quia [...] quia [...] quia [...] quia [...]' and the sequential hypotactic units 'non quod [...] sed quod', 'prius quam [...] adoleretur', 'quam comederent', 'sibi [...] pararent', 'quod maxime horrendum est', and 'quae diximus'. All these elements are short and patent, if syntactically complex. Although the prose seems as hypotactic as that of the prologues, it is much briefer. In this passage Bede is explicit about the enormity of the sons' crimes to furnish a moral lesson for the reader. However, he adds in a final sentence to the exposition of this verse a symbolic interpretation that compares the corruption done by Heli's sons to that done now by false teachers and heretics. In verse 23, after pointing out that just as Heli, hearing the protests of the people, rebuked his sons but did not depose them and let them brazenly disregard him, so the scribes and Pharisees contemned the Father's law with the same disdain. Bede then applies the text tropologically, pointedly asking what we ourselves merit when we do not mend our ways, continue in our vices, and ignore the rebukes of the people.

Let us now turn to the passage in Book II, in which Bede discusses the text of chapter 8 by contrasting the old priest, this time not Heli but Samuel, and his feckless sons.

> *Factum est autem cum senuisset Samuhel posuit filios suos iudices Israhel*, et ceterausque ad id quod *ait Samuhel ad uiros Israhel, Vadat unusquisque in ciuitatem suam.* Haec lectio et ad litteram et typice intellecta arguit eos qui neglecto quod didicere sancto mandate suis potius concupiscentiis seruire desiderant. Quod et de omnibus falso fidelibus generaliter et de Iudaeis specialiter accipi potest qui uel post incarnationem saluatoris terreni regni amore praedicatores regni caelestis abiecerint uel quietissima olim regimina iudicum fastidientes contra domini consultum regalis sceptri gestierint stemmate sublimari.
>
> *Factum est autem*, inquit, *cum senuisset Samuhel posuit filios suos iudices Israhel.* Nomen senectutis in scripturis cum mystice ponitur aliquando maturitatem sapientiae et consilii grauitatem aliquando torporem mentis ab inchoatae uirtutis nouo feruore frigentem significat. Dictum est enim de iusto iudice cuius fallere sapientiam nulla conscientia praeualet, *Et antiquus dierum sedit* (Daniel 7. 9), dictum et de membris illius, *Gloria senum canities* (Proverbs 20. 29), id est sapientiae grauitas. Item in malam partem qui se a uirtutum studio tepescere senserat ait: *Inueteraui inter omnes inimicos meos* (Psalm 6. 8). Vtrique autem parti potest conuenire quod dicitur Samuhel senescens filios suos posuisse iudices Israhel. Cum enim fides et dilectio Christi senuisset apud Iudaeos quibusdam uidelicet ab ea quasi grandaeua senectute frigentibus quibusdam uero in ea quasi longa iam uiuendi consuetudine maturis posuit ipse dominus scribas et Pharisaeos eiusdem populi

iudices qui rectam uitae uiam discernere et subditis ostendere deberent qui filii Dei dicti sunt iuxta hoc quod ipse dixit in exodo: *Filius meus primogenitus Israhel* (Exodus 4. 22). Quod aeque ut dictum est et ad incarnationis dominicae et ad ea potest tempora referri cum primum in eodem populo sunt iudices a domino positi. Nam et tune propheta attestante iustus ex fide uiuebat (Hababbuk 2. 4) haud dubium quin ilia de qua Petrus ait: *Sed per gratiam domini Iesu credimus saluari quemadmodum et illi* (Acts 15. 11).

Fuitque nomen filii eius promogeniti Iohel et nomen secundi Abia iudicum in Bersabee, et non ambulauerunt filii illius in uiis eius. Iohel incipiens uel fuit Dei Abia pater fuit[22] Bersabee puteus iuramenti dicitur; est enim locus sicut ex nomine probatur ubi Abraham et Isaac foedus cum Abimelech pepigere iurantes significans fontem ilium salutarem qui circumcisionem et praeputium unius eiusdemque fidei pacto sociatos abluat in quo praefati fratres sunt iudices dati ut uitae uidelicet fontem et propinarent et biberent. Verum illi iuxta nomen suum incipientes quidem sed non perseuerantes usque in finem ut salui fierent et quondam ad Deum pertinentes patrumque populi uocabulo digni existentes nunc in contraria mutati suas traditiones et scelera legi pariter et gratiae praetulerunt. Sed et quisque nostrum cum a spiritali quam inchoauerat ardore tepescens infimos terrenosque cogitatus suae menti praeponit quasi degeneres filios senescens Samuhel Bersabee iudices statuit quia prauis sensibus baptismi mysterium subdit.

Congregati ergo uniuersi maiores natu Israhel uenerunt ad Samuhel in Ramatha dixeruntque ei: Ecce tu senuisti, et filii tui non ambulant in uiis tuis, constitue nobis regem ut iudicet nos sicut et uniuersae habent nationes. Congregati post ascensionem domini uniuersi maiores natu carnalis Israhel uenerunt aduersus eum miseruntque legationem post eum in Ramatha, id est in altitudinem caelorum[23] ubi omne quicquid terris agimus dicto citius patet, dicentes, Nolumus hunc regnare super nos (Luke 19. 14), et quasi ad eum quern latere nil potest uerba facientes, Ecce, inquiunt, tua in nobis fides et caritas senuit et filii quos enutristi et exaltasti ipsi spreuerunt te, malumus ergo instar gentium quae te non nouerunt et regnorum quae non inuocauerunt nomen tuum extranei a tuo ducatu manere quam tuae gratia fidei regno et patria priuari, si enim relicta pugnandi sollertia omnes tuae doctrinae simplicitatem sequimur *uenient Romani et tollent nostrum et locum et gentem* (John 11. 48). Haec quidem Iudaei quamuis non uoce mente tamen reproba et intentione aduersus dominum sunt et aduersus Christum eius locuti.[24]

Bede again gives an overview of the meaning of the entire chapter, in which the Israelites, justly dissatisfied with Samuel's sons as judges, demand a king to rule them. The effects of this rejection of theocracy that has been mediated by judges

---

[22] Compare Jerome, *Liber interpretationis hebraicorum nominum*, ed. by Paul de Lagarde, CCSL, 72 (Turnhout, 1959), 104.1, 'Iohel incipiens uel fuit dei'; 102.12–13, 'Abia pater dominus uel pater fuit'.

[23] Compare Jerome, *Liber interpretationis hebraicorum nominum*, 97.1, 'Ramath excelsa haec'; 104.17, 'Ramathaim excelsa eorum'.

[24] Bede, *In primam partem Samuhelis*, II, cap. 13, I Samuel 8. 1–5, ed. by Hurst, pp. 70–71, lines 96–164. For my translation, see the Appendix, no. 3.

in favour of a monarchy are both literally ('ad litteram') and symbolically ('typice') instructive. For verse 1 he makes a semantic distinction between the positive and negative Scriptural connotations of *senectus*, 'old age', the one indicating wisdom and the other decrepitude.

For verses 2–3 Bede resorts to a favourite stylistic process, etymology, whereby he draws on Jerome's explanation of the Hebrew meanings for the names Joel, Abijah, and Beersheba. Joel means 'beginning' and therefore not persevering, and Beersheba is 'the well of the oath', where Joel and Abijah as judges have desecrated it. Bede draws the moral conclusion that we too can become tepid in our faith and can desecrate our baptism.

For verses 4–5 Bede goes into the typological mode, comparing the actions of the Israelites in I Samuel to those of Jews who at the time of Christ preferred a terrestial king after the style of the Romans rather than the Lord's anointed, Jesus Christ.

Although this exegesis also proceeds with a style less formal than those of the prologues, it is by no means uncomplicated. Bede's style in his commentary is allusive, nuanced, layered with literal and symbolic, allegorical interpretations. The reader must concentrate to follow the thematic and syntactic connections. The Latin is often demanding. We have noted the complexity of the previous pages from Book II. Here too the syntax is rather exacting. For instance, at the end of his commentary on verse 1, he uses the difficult Latin construction 'haud dubium quin'. I wonder whether Bede's disciples poring over his text with all its stylistic complexity were as taxed as we are in the reading of it.

Within the commentary on I Samuel there is considerable variety in length of the individual passages and in styles of presentation. However, these two passages on the related topic of sad senescence and consequent loss of control in the parallel careers of Heli and his priestly successor Samuel serve as good examples of Bede's exegetical method in this commentary from his maturity. They also serve in stylistic contrast to the four divisional prologues. Although the stylistic registers of the prologues and the commentary differ, they are all representative of Bede's mature and later exegesis in their complexity and sophistication.

Appendix

English Translation by George Hardin Brown of Extracts from Bede, On I Samuel

1. The first prologue, CCSL, 119, pp. 9–10.

The Apostle [Paul], recommending to us zeal and frequency in the reading and meditating on the Holy Scriptures, says: 'For what things soever were written, were written for our learning: that through patience and the comfort of the scriptures, we might have hope' (Romans 15. 4, Douay-Rheims version). And elsewhere he writes: 'All these things happened to them in figure and they are written for our correction, upon whom the ends of the ages are come' (I Corinthians 10. 11). But also the blessed Apostle Peter, recalling the times of the Lord's incarnation, passion, and subsequent glory, says among other things: 'And all the prophets, from Samuel and afterwards, who have spoken, have told of these days' (Acts 3. 24).

For if all things are written for our correction, instruction, or consolation, not just Jeremiah, Isaiah, and such others, who indicated future events with their words, but also Samuel, Jonah, and Ezra, and their like, who wrote about their or others' past deeds and sayings, now make known these days, that is, the days shining with the light of new grace; we must be utterly intent and strive, each of us in his own way with the help of Christ's grace, lest those things which on our account have been written, may pass us by as irrelevant, because of our torpor or carelessness.

Rather, in what sense we should obtain correction from these, by what method instruction, by what understanding consolation, we should solicitously and vigilantly pay attention how all those writings speak to and announce these days. Thus we will imitate according to the capacity of our little talent that scribe instructed in the kingdom of heaven, 'who brings forth from his treasury new things and old' (Matthew 13. 52).

For if we only care to bring forth old things from the treasury of scriptures, that is, to follow only the outward appearances of the letter in the Jewish manner, what do we in our reading and listening get of correction among daily sins, what of consolation among increasing afflictions of the world, what of spiritual instruction among innumerable errors of this life? When in the book opened to Samuel, for example, we discover that the one man Elcana had two wives (I Samuel 1. 1), what does that mean for us especially, for whom the embrace of a wife is far removed from the custom of our ecclesiastical life, for us who have vowed to remain celibate? What is the meaning of this and similar texts if we do not know how to extract its allegorical sense, which vividly restores us interiorly by chastening, educating, and consoling?

Hence, having been challenged by your frequent exhortation, Acca, most beloved and desired of all bishops who dwell on earth, relying on your prayers, while scrutinizing the writings of the famous prophet who was then called Seer, if I will be able to behold anything spiritual and mystical (by his providing who allowed him to see many spiritual things) I will take care to set it down in writing. After my exposition, for what it is worth, of the sayings of blessed Luke, with which he describes the evangelical acts either of the Lord himself or of his apostles, I am engaged in investigating this Nazarean, very holy to the Lord from the womb, no less in his writings than as endowed with the office of historical evangelist, inasmuch as he designated by the figural but very full speech of a faithful historian all of the mysteries of the mediator of God and men, the man Jesus Christ. Finally, to pass over the rest in silence, if you rightly consider of the one David the place of his nativity, his office as pastor, the ruddiness and beauty of his countenance, the mode of his anointing, his distinctive virtues, the weight of his tribulations, and the glory of his once promised realm, you will discern among these how great are the accumulative mysteries of the one faith and evangelical truth. But all of these things will be explained more fully in their proper place.

Now I will set about the enjoined work in order, relying solely on divine aid and following the footsteps of the Fathers. And if indeed, as I desire, my effort will prove a benefit for the usefulness and comfort of many, I hope that many things will be given to me, along with them, as a reward by the Lord; but if not, my care will not be unfruitful which does not permit me to be idle in such a great time of labour or to indulge my spirit with vacuous things. Therefore carry on: let us see the prophet Samuel who has spoken and announced these days, what beginning of speech and pronouncement he will make and proceeding in order with the assistance of the blessed Peter, prince of the apostles, who has taught that all things are to be applied for these days, what sorts of specific things are to be adapted for these same days.

2. Book I, commentary on I Samuel 2. 22–23, CCSL, 119, pp. 29–30.

'Now Heli was very old', etc. up to the verse 'And the child Samuel advanced, and grew on, and pleased both the Lord and men' (I Samuel 2. 22–26). In this section, with Judaism in a mystical meaning growing old and failing, the fame of Christ increases through the Gospel. Therefore the great age of Heli indicates that the time of the priesthood of the Law is nearly at an end. 'For that which decays and grows old, is near its end' (Hebrews 8. 13).

'And he heard all that his sons did to all Israel: and how they lay with the women that waited at the door of the tabernacle.' That transgression of the sons of Heli, which did not fear to sully both divine religion and love of neighbour, was not slight nor was it limited to one form. For as it is said above, they presumed to take of the consecrated flesh not what was established in the Law but what was pleasing to themselves. For before the sacred fat was burnt for the Lord, they presumed to take a part of the offering for themselves, which they ate; and they robbed the raw flesh from those offering it and prepared it quite nicely for themselves; and they made the people of the Lord transgress; and, what is especially horrendous, they did all these things which we have spoken of in contempt of the Creator. But now is added that which violated brotherhood, in that they defiled the women of the people, who had come together to pray. And, as it is added below, they did what is the greatest of all evils, not repenting when corrected by their father. We have said these things more plainly so that you, reader, may remember what you should avoid. Now what remains is to be completed in typical meaning for priests and teachers to watch in the Lord, and to excite others to watch, saying: 'Awake, you just, and sin not' (I Corinthians 15. 34). But bad teachers sleep, and do so with women who watch before the door of the tabernacle, when they seduce unstable souls, and they themselves do not enter, nor allow those who wish to enter, the door of life. Such was once the crime of the Pharisaic faction that would pass away; such is the crime now among the false professors of the Christian religion.

And he said to them, 'Why do you do these kinds of things, which I hear about, very wicked things, from all the people?' He rebuked the misbehaving sons of Heli, but they did not listen. The institution itself of the old priesthood orders its ministers to be perfect, but the Scribes, Pharisees, and wicked leaders of the priests contemned the paternal voice of its Law and the priesthood that would perish. Indeed, according to the letter it should be observed not negligently that Heli indeed rebuked his sons but because he refrained from deposing them as he ought after they spurned correction he perished along with them. What about us wretches, what do we like them merit, who rejoice in vices, who dare not emend, who fear the consciousness of it, and pretend to be ignorant of what all the people clamour about?

3. Book II, commentary on I Samuel 8. 1–5, CCSL, 119, pp. 70–71.

'And it came to pass when Samuel was old, that he appointed his sons to be judges over Israel'; and so forth, up to that verse in which 'Samuel said to the men of Israel: Let every man go to his city' (v. 22). This reading both literally (*ad litteram*) and figuratively understood (*typice*) accuses those who, having neglected the sacred mandate that they learned, desire to serve instead their own concupiscences. That can be understood about all the unfaithful generally but particularly about the Jews who either after the incarnation of the Saviour disdaining the once tranquil rule of the judges, against the plan of the Lord have desired to be lifted up by the pedigree of the royal sceptre.

'And it came to pass when Samuel was old, that he appointed his sons to be judges over Israel' (I Samuel 8. 1). In the scriptures the noun 'old age' (*senectus*) when it is used in its symbolic sense sometimes signifies the maturity of wisdom and the gravity of counsel, but sometimes the torpor of a mind as it grows cold after the new fervour of inchoate virtue wanes. For it was said about the just judge whose wisdom no knowledge is able to impugn: 'And the Ancient of days sat' (Daniel 7. 9), and it was also said of his members: 'The dignity of the old is their gray hairs', that is, the gravity of wisdom. Likewise, he says it in the bad sense (*in malam partem*) who has perceived himself to grow tepid in the pursuit of virtues: 'I have grown old among all my enemies' (Psalm 6. 8). One can assign each sense, good and bad, to what is said about the elderly Samuel having appointed his sons as judges of Israel. For when the faith and love of Christ had grown old among the Jews — for some indeed grew cold from as it were such a great age, but some simply as mature from the custom of now living as it were so long — then the Lord himself appointed Scribes and Pharisees as judges of that same people, judges who were to decide the right way of life and to demonstrate it to the subjects who are said to be the children of God, according to what he himself said in Exodus, 'My son the firstborn Israel' (Exodus 4. 22). And likewise it can be said about the times of the Lord's incarnation and those events when judges were first appointed by the Lord among that same people. For, according to the witness of the prophet, the just man lived by faith (Habakkuk 2. 4); without doubt that is what Peter means, 'But by the grace of the Lord Jesus, we believe to be saved, in like manner as they also' (Acts 15. 11).

'Now the name of the firstborn son was Joel; and the name of the second was Abia, judges in Bersabee. And his sons did not walk in his ways' (I Samuel 8. 2–3). Joel means 'beginning' or 'he was of God'; Abia 'he was a father'; and Bersabee 'the well of the oath' (Genesis 21. 32), for it is the place as its name indicates where

Abraham and Isaac concluded a pact with Abimelech, signifying that salvific well which would cleanse the circumcision and the foreskin of one and the same faith, joined by covenant. There the aforesaid brothers were given as judges so that they might pour out and drink the well of life. But they, according to their name 'beginning' — but not persevering all the way to the end so that they might be saved — once belonged to God, and lived worthy of the name of the fathers and people, but now, changed to the opposite, they have preferred their traditions and crimes equally against the law and grace. But which one of us, when growing tepid from the spiritual ardor with which we began, prefers base and earthly thoughts for our mind growing old, as it were, like the degenerate sons of Samuel, judges of Bersabee, because he supplants the mystery of baptism with evil affections?

'Then all the ancients of Israel, being assembled, came to Samuel, to Ramatha. And they said to him: Behold you are old, and your sons walk not in your ways; make us a king to judge us, as all nations have' (I Samuel 8. 4–5). All the carnal elders of Israel assembled after the ascension of the Lord, they came against him, and they sent a legation after him into Ramatha, that is, in 'the heights' of the heavens where whatever we do in word on earth immediately is known, 'saying, We will not have this man to reign over us' (Luke 16. 14), and saying words as to him from whom nothing is able to lie hidden: 'Behold', they say, 'your faith and love have grown old in us and the sons whom you nourished and exalted they themselves have spurned you; we therefore prefer the counterpart of the gentiles who have not known you, and of their sovereignty which has not called upon your name, and to remain outside the bounds of your leadership, rather to be deprived of the grace of your faith, your sovereignty, and fatherland. For if we, with our cleverness left behind, all follow the simplicity of your doctrine, "the Romans will come and take our place and nation"' (John 11. 48). These things indeed have the Jews spoken, although not by voice but nonetheless by reprobate mind and intention, against the Lord and against his Christ.

The Form and Function of the Vercelli Book

Elaine Treharne

Determining the textual history, form, and function of the Vercelli Book has occupied some of our greatest Anglo-Saxon scholars for decades. Among these is Éamonn Ó Carragáin. Widely renowned for his erudite and engaging work on this manuscript, and particularly his visionary interpretations of *The Dream of the Rood*, it is a pleasure to offer my own brief interpretation of the Vercelli Book in gratitude for his work and his unfailing generosity to other scholars, and in the hope of contributing towards the debate on the possible reasons behind the production of the Vercelli Book.

The Vercelli Book has been variously dated, by Neil Ker to the second half of the tenth century and by Celia Sisam and Donald Scragg to the late tenth century.[1]

---

[1] Neil Ker, *Catalogue of Manuscripts Containing Anglo-Saxon* (Oxford, 1957; repr. 1991), item 394, p. 460; *The Vercelli Book (Vercelli Biblioteca Capitolaire CXVII)*, ed. by Celia Sisam, Early English Manuscripts in Facsimile, 19 (Copenhagen, 1976), p. 36; *The Vercelli Homilies and Related Texts*, ed. by D. G. Scragg, EETS, OS, 300 (Oxford, 1992), p. xxiii. The codex is dated to *c.* 975 by D. G. Scragg in 'The Compilation of the Vercelli Book', *Anglo-Saxon England*, 2 (1973), 189–207; repr. in *Anglo-Saxon Manuscripts: Basic Readings*, ed. by Mary P. Richards, Basic Readings in Anglo-Saxon England, 2 (New York, 1994), pp. 317–44 (p. 334). This date of compilation, as the latest possible, seems right from a palaeographical perspective at least. This distinction between the second half of the tenth century and the end of the tenth century may seem inconsequential, but as David N. Dumville crucially points out, 'I am not at all clear why, between 1957 and 1976, Ker's date of "x^2"[...] came to be subverted [to the last quarter of the tenth century]'; 'English Square Minuscule Script: The Mid-Century Phases', *Anglo-Saxon England*, 23 (1994), 133–64 (p. 140, n. 39). In terms of the cultural and intellectual context of the Vercelli Book, it seems likeliest that the codex, like the Exeter Book, is a product of the early Benedictine Reform era, if not of the movement itself.

Canonical Square Minuscule, Phase II,[2] it is likely to be datable a little before the mid-point of Ker's estimation, but no later; that is, up to about 975. Indeed, some of its letter forms together with its associations with other manuscripts suggest that the period of its production may be earlier rather than later in the period 950–75. Palaeographically, the key features[3] in such an assumption would be a combination of the following: the use of Square Minuscule *a*, where the cross-stroke creates a more pointed form of the letter; the use of **oc** *a*, especially in homilies XI, XIX, XX, and XXI;[4] the very frequent ligaturing of high *e*; the open-tailed Insular *g*; the use of tall *i* especially in initial position, when followed by *n* or *c*;[5] the *p*, with the bowl closed by a curl; the descender of thorn, which is often twice as long as the ascender;[6] the frequent use of all three forms of *y* (round-limbed, straight-limbed, and *f*-shaped) which indicates an earlier, rather than a later date in the second-half of the tenth century; and the hooked left lower limb of *x*. Of these features, some, such as the **oc** *a*, the long *i*, or the underslung *l*, occur irregularly such that one might propose their direct dependence on the earlier script of the varying exemplars.[7] Alternatively, the order in which the sections of the Vercelli Book were copied may not equate to the current sequence of texts.[8] Whether or not either of these scenarios is the case, however, there are sufficient

---

[2] For these, and related, classifications, see Dumville, 'English Square Minuscule Script'.

[3] For an immensely detailed and meticulous analysis of the development of tenth-century script, with an emphasis on the vernacular, see Patrick W. Conner, *Anglo-Saxon Exeter: A Tenth-Century Cultural History*, Studies in Anglo-Saxon History, 4 (Woodbridge, 1993), pp. 54–76. See also *The Vercelli Book*, ed. by Sisam, pp. 20–23.

[4] Where, however, it may represent a fossilized form derived from the exemplars.

[5] This mid-tenth-century feature is seen particularly in the poems *Andreas* and *Fates of the Apostles* at fols 29ᵛ–54ʳ. One might also note the rare and usually early use (that is, late ninth- to early tenth-century) of 'underslung' *l*, with its foot descending below the line and semi-ligatured to the following letter, which occurs with most frequency in Homily XIX and in the poem *Elene* (fols 106ᵛ–109ᵛ and 121ʳ–133ᵛ respectively), and which may say more about the date of the exemplars than the early date of the Vercelli Book itself.

[6] Ascender and descender become more equal in length by the second half of the tenth century. See Conner, *Anglo-Saxon Exeter*, p. 75.

[7] See also *The Vercelli Book*, ed. by Sisam, p. 20, n. 4.

[8] This, of course, would reinforce Scragg's theories on the compilation of the manuscript, and I shall be writing more extensively on this in a subsequent paper.

palaeographical grounds for claiming a date of compilation for the manuscript prior to 975.[9]

The Vercelli Book is of south-eastern origin, and probably originated at St Augustine's, Canterbury.[10] St Augustine's was the only monastic institution in the diocese of Canterbury[11] at the time when the Vercelli Book was written, quite possibly during the earliest years of the archiepiscopacy of Dunstan. Scragg proposes its origin at St Augustine's on the basis of linguistic and textual associations,[12] but it is possible to assign it to this monastery based also on palaeographical and contextual grounds. In the case of the first of these, Dumville has discussed the similarity of script between the Vercelli scribe and that of Cambridge, Corpus Christi College, MS 352, a mid-tenth-century St Augustine's manuscript;[13] codicologically, the rubrics, initials, and Insular method of quiring (hair facing flesh) are paralleled in other St Augustine's manuscripts of the mid-tenth century[14] and later in a combination with tendencies similar enough to indicate an origin at the abbey more convincingly than elsewhere.[15] It seems likely, therefore, that this

---

[9] Earlier by up to a quarter century than the Blickling Homilies. See Milton McC. Gatch, 'Eschatology in the Anonymous Old English Homilies', *Traditio*, 21 (1965), 117–65 (p. 136); repr. in his *Eschatology and Christian Nurture: Themes in Anglo-Saxon and Medieval Religious Life* (Aldershot, 2000), VII.

[10] *The Vercelli Homilies*, ed. by Scragg, p. lxxix, though Gatch, 'Eschatology in Anonymous Old English Homilies', p. 137, thinks it of possible Worcester origin.

[11] Tim Tatton-Brown, 'The City and Diocese of Canterbury in St Dunstan's Time', in *St Dunstan: His Life, Times and Cult*, ed. by Nigel Ramsey, Margaret Sparks, and Tim Tatton-Brown (Woodbridge, 1992), pp. 75–87 (p. 76).

[12] *The Vercelli Homilies*, ed. by Scragg, pp. lxxiv–lxxix.

[13] Dumville, 'English Square Minuscule Script', p. 140, n. 39.

[14] This quire arrangement was a conservative practice by this time. See Teresa Webber's description of the mid-tenth-century St Augustine's manuscript, Cambridge, Corpus Christi College, MS 369, in the recent catalogue, *The Cambridge Illuminations: Ten Centuries of Book Production in the Medieval West*, ed. by Paul Binski and Stella Panayotova (London, 2005), pp. 247–48, no. 112.

[15] See, for example, Elżbieta Temple, *Anglo-Saxon Manuscripts 900–1066*, Survey of Manuscripts Illuminated in the British Isles, 2 (London, 1976), where the major initials in the Vercelli Book (no. 28) are illustrated (pls. 97–99), and can be compared particularly with those of Cambridge, Trinity College, MS O. 3. 7 (no. 20; pls. 76–78) localized to *c.* 970, St Augustine's; or to pls. 96–109, which illustrate a variety of Wormald Type I and II initials from Canterbury manuscripts in the second half of the tenth century. A broadly similar initial *M* to those in the Vercelli Book at fols 106[v] and 112[r] is in the Trinity Amalarius — Cambridge, Trinity College, MS B. 11. 2

manuscript is a product of the abbey, and I should like to argue that it represents the compiler's attempts to meet the pastoral or devotional needs of the monks in the earliest years of the Reform period, though quite how far or in what ways the practices of the Reform movement had been adopted at St Augustine's is difficult to say.[16] In relation to the beginnings of the Reform movement, Gretsch comments that:

> We know from Æthelwold's own testimony, as well as from Wulfstan, that at that time Glastonbury was the only regular monastery anywhere in England. Since there must have been a monastic community of some sort at least at St Augustine's, Canterbury, Æthelwold's and Wulfstan's assertions can only be taken to mean that Glastonbury in the 940s was the only place where life was regulated in accordance with Benedictine observance and in a way similar to Continental monasteries.[17]

The manuscript evidence at St Augustine's in the mid-tenth century, though, seems to demand some qualification in our wholesale acceptance of Glastonbury's primacy in this period; it may well be that the glowing words of Æthelwold in his *Preface* to the Benedictine Rule[18] glorify Glastonbury to the detriment of other institutions, such as St Augustine's. It is certainly the case that the evidence from St Augustine's implies a vibrant intellectual community in these years, though whether it was regulated in the manner of Continental monasteries is impossible to say at present.

Those manuscripts that survive from St Augustine's in the mid-tenth century evince a dynamic and professional scriptorium that had a coherent programme of copying in this period. Among the manuscripts produced there are Cambridge, Trinity College, MS B. 11. 2, Amalarius's *De ecclesiasticis officiis*;[19] Cambridge,

---

— from St Augustine's, in the mid-tenth century. See <http://www.trin.cam.ac.uk/sdk13/MSS/TrinAmal/TrinAmalM1.jpg>.

[16] Mechthild Gretsch, in *The Intellectual Foundations of the Benedictine Reform*, Cambridge Studies in Anglo-Saxon England, 25 (Cambridge, 1999), demonstrates that the Benedictine Reform was underway in the latter part of the first half of the tenth century. At p. 251, for example, Gretsch examines how Dunstan's introduction of the *Regula S. Benedicti* to Glastonbury in 940 and Æthelwold's training there under Dunstan essentially indicate the beginnings of the Reform movement. However, that Dunstan became Archbishop of Canterbury in 959 must imply that reform was imminent in that diocese too, if it had not been established already.

[17] Gretsch, *Intellectual Foundations*, pp. 251–52.

[18] Cited in Gretsch, *Intellectual Foundations*, p. 252, n. 78.

[19] For a plate and a description, see Simon Keynes's invaluable *Anglo-Saxon Manuscripts in Trinity College*, Old English Newsletter, *Subsidia*, 18 (1992), no. 6, plate VI. The decorated initials in this manuscript are very similar to those in the Vercelli Book.

Trinity College, MS O. 2. 30, containing a version of the *Regula S. Benedicti*;[20] and, from the second half of the tenth century, Cambridge, Trinity College, MS O. 1. 18, containing Augustine's *Enchiridion ad Laurentium*.[21] It is firmly within this monastic context, I believe, that the Vercelli Book should be situated. It is a context that demonstrates the acceleration of a reforming movement, perhaps within the broader Benedictine reforms of Dunstan himself, or initially developing in parallel with it.[22]

The Vercelli Book is the production of one scribe, gathering his sources from a variety of exemplars available to him at the time.[23] It has been variously described as a homemade collection,[24] 'a book of personal devotional materials',[25] and 'a collection of pious reading'.[26] The scribe himself has been labelled as a mechanical and unintelligent copyist,[27] described as engaged in 'slavish copying',[28] 'working so haphazardly that he inadvertently repeated material'.[29] Some of these

---

[20] Keynes, *Anglo-Saxon Manuscripts*, no. 7, plate VII. The existence of this manuscript surely implies an adherence or major interest in the Benedictine Rule at this time.

[21] Keynes, *Anglo-Saxon Manuscripts*, no. 10. A second scribe in this manuscript also participated in copying other manuscripts that included texts such as Cassian's *De institutis coenobiorum* (for which see Keynes, p. 20).

[22] In the mid-tenth century, the St Augustine's scribes have not yet begun using Anglo-Caroline Minuscule; they use Square Minuscule up until approximately 970. This indicates the Benedictine Reform with its Continental influences may not yet have had a major impact on St Augustine's. Such an impact, one would imagine, was brought about with the arrival of Dunstan as Archbishop of Canterbury. However, see further below.

[23] As discussed in detail in Scragg, 'Compilation of the Vercelli Book'; *The Vercelli Book*, ed. by Sisam; and *The Vercelli Homilies*, ed. by Scragg.

[24] Éamonn Ó Carragáin, 'Rome, Ruthwell, Vercelli: *The Dream of the Rood* and the Italian Connection', in *Vercelli tra Oriente ed Occidente, tra tarda antichità e medioevo*, ed. by Vittoria Dolcetti Corazza (Alessandria, 1999), pp. 59–100 (p. 94).

[25] *The Vercelli Book*, ed. by Sisam, p. 44.

[26] *The Vercelli Homilies*, ed. by Scragg, p. xix.

[27] Scragg, 'Compilation of the Vercelli Book', p. 331: 'V [the Vercelli scribe] frequently copied mechanically and unintelligently, to the extent that he showed no grasp of the contextual meaning of words copied.' See also Paul E. Szarmach, 'The Scribe of the Vercelli Book', *Studia Neophilologica*, 51 (1979), 179–88, on the 'carelessness' of the scribe's errors.

[28] Mary Clayton, 'Homiliaries and Preaching in Anglo-Saxon England', *Peritia*, 4 (1985), 207–42; repr. in *Old English Prose: Basic Readings*, ed. by Paul E. Szarmach, Basic Readings in Anglo-Saxon England, 5 (New York, 2000), pp. 151–98 (p. 172).

[29] Scragg, 'Compilation of the Vercelli Book', p. 319. Gatch too, in 'Eschatology in the Anonymous Old English Homilies', p. 143, comments: 'The repetition of part of Homily II in

comments suggest a scribe who took little interest in what he was doing, rather than one committed to producing the best work that he could with the instructions given to him, and the resources, exemplars, and texts available to him. This is a scribe who seems to believe emphatically in the authority of the written word before him, or who has been told to copy exactly what is in the exemplar: a scribe who is not at ease working with Latin at all.[30] This is one of the reasons that make me think this scribe did not write this codex for his own personal use. Why would he copy material he did not fully understand if this were the case? It seems more likely that this scribe is writing under someone else's direction, a theory that will be developed later in this essay. The producer of the Vercelli Book, then, seems to be lacking the confidence one would expect from a scribe-compiler copying simply for themselves, which might explain why he depends on the exemplars for the linguistic forms, never mind some of the letter-shapes themselves.

Rather more contentious than the copying skills of this much-maligned scribe is the content itself. The Vercelli Book has been associated with Ælfric's derogation of the 'mycel gedwyld' that circulated in Anglo-Saxon England before the spiritual remedy provided by his own *Catholic Homilies*.[31] In the very well-known *Preface* to Ælfric's First Series of *Catholic Homilies*, he tells us that:

> Þa bearn me on mode, Ic truwige ðurh Godes gife, þæt Ic ðas boc of Ledenum gereorde to Engliscre spræce awende, na þurh gebylde micelre lare, ac for ðan ðe Ic geseah and gehyrde mycel gedwyld on manegum Engliscum bocum, ðe ungelærede menn ðurh heora bilewitnysse to micclum wisdome tealdon.[32]

XXI seems to indicate that the editor has used two sources containing some of the same materials and that he has carelessly allowed himself this repetition.' I shall comment in more detail on the repetition of homiletic texts below.

[30] Scragg states, 'it is worth observing that of thirteen homilies with brief quotations in Latin, only four are without error in the Latin, often so gross as to produce sheer nonsense': *The Vercelli Homilies*, ed. by Scragg, p. lxxiv. Szarmach refers to the scribe's 'careless transcription' of Latin; 'Scribe of the Vercelli Book', pp. 186–87.

[31] The crucial issue of heterodoxy versus orthodoxy, and the scholarly derogation of literary material labelled as 'heretical' or unorthodox, is analysed in the essays in *Apocryphal Texts and Traditions in Anglo-Saxon England*, ed. by Kathryn Powell and Donald Scragg, Publications of the Manchester Centre for Anglo-Saxon Studies, 2 (Manchester, 2003). Of particular note is Joyce Hill's summary, 'The Apocrypha in Anglo-Saxon England: The Challenge of Changing Distinctions', pp. 165–68.

[32] *Ælfric's Catholic Homilies: The First Series: Text*, ed. by Peter Clemoes, EETS, SS, 17 (Oxford, 1997), p. 174. My translation, with modern punctuation and capitalization added.

[Then it came into my mind, I believe through a gift of God, that I should translate this book from the language of Latin into English speech, not through the confidence of great learning, but because I saw and heard much heresy in many English books, which unlearned people through their simplicity esteemed as great wisdom.]

It has become commonplace to interpret this 'heresy in many English books' as referring directly to the Vercelli or Blickling Homilies,[33] an association that has, perhaps unintentionally, led to a damaging comparison between the anonymous religious texts and those of Ælfric himself. It is a marvellous irony that while Ælfric could not eradicate other vernacular writers' work as he might have wished, or prevent his own from being contaminated by contiguity with it, nevertheless modern scholarship has paid far less attention to the anonymous corpus than it has to the writings of Ælfric.[34]

In a sense, were it not for the poetry contained within the Vercelli Book, it might not have given rise to the amount of contemporary investigation that it has.[35] Even so, modern, positive analyses of the Vercelli Book have, to an extent, been perplexed by its 'lack' of specific, expected features. For example, the manuscript's lack of explicit organization — its texts are governed neither by the liturgical calendar nor by any obviously thematic development[36] — and its mixing of content — both prose and poetic texts intermingled without a clear rationale of contiguity — have led scholars to its being described as sui generis.[37] The failure

[33] As, for example, in Stanley B. Greenfield and Daniel G. Calder's influential *A New Critical History of Old English Literature* (New York, 1986), where they state that 'Ælfric was undoubtedly here referring to many of the apocryphal selections in the *Blickling* and *Vercelli Homilies*' (p. 77).

[34] On the issues of genre, authorship, audience, form, and scholarly responses to Old English religious prose, see Clare Lees's excellent *Tradition and Belief: Religious Writing in Late Anglo-Saxon England*, Medieval Cultures, 19 (Minneapolis, 1999), esp. pp. 22–35. There are also the obvious exceptions of scholars such as Charles D. Wright, who has worked extensively on the Vercelli Book, and whose findings are very different from mine. See, for example, his 'Vercelli Homilies XI–XIII and the Benedictine Reform: Tailored Sources and Implied Audiences', in *Preacher, Sermon and Audience in the Middle Ages*, ed. by Carolyn Muessig (Leiden, 2002), pp. 203–27. I am grateful to Charlie for discussing his views with me.

[35] See *The Vercelli Homilies*, ed. by Scragg, pp. xix–xxi.

[36] As Scragg points out, in his 'Compilation of the Vercelli Book', 'The first thing that can be said with some assurance is that the collection was not planned in its entirety before execution began, and the explanation for the confused order of items, with overlaps in content, is that a number of different exemplars were used for the material' (pp. 339–40).

[37] As by M. McC. Gatch, for example, in his *Preaching and Theology in Anglo-Saxon England: Ælfric and Wulfstan* (Toronto, 1977), p. 57.

of the Vercelli Book to meet the generic compliance of a book of religious prose as found within the Carolingian homiliary, or, more analogously, the structured vernacular codex, like the Blickling Homilies or Ælfric's two series of texts for the *Temporale*, has resulted, in many respects, in the relative isolation of the manuscript as a whole.[38]

In addition to the relative isolation of the volume by virtue of its generic individuation, there are also interesting physical idiosyncrasies. Paul E. Szarmach, who has worked extensively on this manuscript and its prose texts, points out in relation to its textual heritage, shared with Cambridge, Corpus Christi College, MSS 162 and 303, that

> The Vercelli Book is a compilation of booklets that easily betray at least three major origins, thanks in part to the use of different stylings in headings (for examples, titles in red or in black square capitals), whereas the two Corpus manuscripts indicate programmatic layout and design features through specific uniformity in the use of color and script.[39] Again, but now in the comparison of books as objects, Vercelli is an isolate, perhaps implying some form of personal book as opposed to a book with a public, liturgical function as a text for reading.[40]

Here, Szarmach is able to extrapolate from the physical appearance of the Vercelli Book its uniqueness in terms both of the method of compilation and of the intended function of the book. But such extrapolation presupposes that variable rubrication in manuscripts indicates the wholesale adoption of schemes from (non-extant) exemplars and that a lack of a programmatic layout precludes the

---

[38] It is isolated in terms of its genre, as much as anything else. While we cannot explain what the Vercelli Book is, we can decide what it isn't. Mary Clayton, for example, remarks that 'The Vercelli Book itself is not a homiliary: the manuscript as a whole is not arranged in the order of the liturgical year, which it makes no systematic attempt to cover, and it would, therefore, have been difficult to use for reading matter on liturgical occasions': 'Homiliaries and Preaching', p. 172.

[39] The two Corpus manuscripts referred to here are CCCC 162 and CCCC 303. It should be noted that while CCCC 303, of mid-twelfth-century Rochester origin, is consistent in its methods and colours of rubrication (all done by the least evident of the three scribes), the texts' punctuation and accenting, and, on occasion, language, vary considerably, demonstrating that the two main scribes often employed the practices of their varied exemplars.

[40] Paul E. Szarmach, 'The Recovery of Texts', in *Reading Old English Texts*, ed. by Katherine O'Brien O'Keeffe (Cambridge, 1997), pp. 124–45 (p. 131). This essay is of considerable importance for reminding scholars of the way in which assumptions are made about texts and manuscripts, and the different ways of interpreting the evidence that survives.

probability of public use.[41] These assumptions are not borne out by other manuscripts from Anglo-Saxon England.

The theory that manuscripts which could be, or which were, used for preaching ought to be compiled or organized in ways that adhere to a discernible structure, presumably reflecting the *Temporale*, is a reasonable one. This stricture applies to English collections of sermons and homilies for three reasons: the legacy of the earlier Continental models;[42] the shadow retrospectively cast upon the entire vernacular corpus by the methodology of Ælfric himself;[43] and the significant numbers of manuscripts that adhere to some such discernible system, such as the Blickling Homilies, Cambridge, Corpus Christi College, MSS 302 and 303, and so on.[44] It may be stating the obvious, but with the exception of the Blickling Homilies, many of the eleventh- and twelfth-century homiletic manuscripts utilize principally Ælfrician exemplars, and thus obviously follow the *Temporale*.[45] Yet if the Vercelli Book is unlike manuscripts that arrange religious texts in the order of the Church year, it could easily be described as presenting 'a wide variety of texts, written by a single scribe, who returned to add further elements [. . . with] differences in format, layout and decoration of the various texts [which] attest to

---

[41] This is, in some respects, confirmed by Scragg when he says, 'although the scribe mechanically copied rubrics to some of the items which specify their use liturgically, the material's practical use for preaching was not significant in the compilation and ordering of the collection': *The Vercelli Homilies*, ed. by Scragg, p. xix.

[42] For which see Clayton, 'Homiliaries and Preaching'.

[43] Particularly his statements in his Prefaces to the two series of *Catholic Homilies*, conveniently edited and discussed by Jonathan Wilcox in his edition of *Ælfric's Prefaces*, Durham Medieval Texts, 9 (Durham, 1994).

[44] For manuscript contents and relationships, see *Ælfric's Catholic Homilies: The Second Series: Text*, ed. by Malcolm Godden, EETS, SS, 5 (Oxford, 1979), and *Ælfric's Catholic Homilies: The First Series*, ed. by Clemoes. Clemoes makes a chronological distinction in the arrangement of these homiletic manuscripts. He states that 'Manuscripts carefully arranged in relation to the order of the church year (except those made up of saints' lives) are characteristic up to the middle of the eleventh century. After that miscellanies, including the substantial anthologies T, B, and C, are typical' (p. 162). This is not always the case, given that, for instance, CCCC 302 and 303 (both post-Conquest) are arranged according to the Church year, but the tenth-century Vercelli Book is not.

[45] This is true too of the *Sanctorale* where manuscripts also employ Ælfric's *Lives of Saints*. See, for example, J. Hill, 'The Dissemination of Ælfric's *Lives of Saints*: A Preliminary Study', in *Holy Men and Holy Women: Old English Prose Saints' Lives and their Contexts*, ed. by Paul E. Szarmach (Albany, 1996), pp. 235–59.

different exemplars'.[46] This is Mildred Budny's description of St Dunstan's Class-book, and I cite it not to suggest, of course, any direct link between Oxford, Bodleian Library, MS Auct. F. 4. 32 (the 'Classbook') and the Vercelli Book, but rather to problematize the strict expectations scholars have of particular 'types' of Anglo-Saxon manuscript compilation. More pertinently, as we shall see, the Ver-celli Book is very similar to other, later compilations of homilies and sermons — including the rare few that also incorporate poetry into the homiletic framework — in such a way as to completely undermine any sense of it being sui generis within the religious and intellectual context of the late Anglo-Saxon period. Indeed, simply because there is no contemporary book that is akin to Vercelli does not make Vercelli sui generis any more than the Exeter Book (Exeter, Cathedral Libary, MS 3501) or the Parker manuscript of the Anglo-Saxon Chronicle (Cam-bridge, Corpus Christi College, MS 173) might be. Extant extensive vernacular manuscripts prior to the late tenth century are not common enough for any indi-vidual codex of that date to be considered anomalous.

From the mid-eleventh century or slightly later, for example, there survive two companion volumes of religious prose: London, British Library, Cotton MS Cleo-patra B. XIII and London, Lambeth Palace Library, Lambeth MS 489. Although separate manuscripts now, these seem to have been compiled as a single volume for Bishop Leofric of Exeter in the earlier years of his episcopacy (1050–72).[47] Both contain a variety of sermons suitable for preaching at particular points in the Church year, and also a number of texts that have no specific function but would have been used *quando volueris*. As in the Vercelli Book, too, which illustrates the copying of the same text twice (in Homilies II and XXI), there is repetition of text within Cleopatra B. XIII and Lambeth 489, where part of the same Ælfric Second Series homily is copied twice, though at some physical remove.[48] Closely related to these compilations in terms of overall form and function are the volumes that are now Oxford, Bodleian Library, MSS Hatton 113 and 114. This extensive col-lection of homiletic texts and other religious prose pieces is datable to the second

---

[46] Mildred Budny, '"St Dunstan's Classbook" and its Frontispiece', in *St Dunstan: His Life, Times and Cult*, ed. by Ramsey, Sparks, and Tatton-Brown, pp. 103–42 (p. 114).

[47] See the invaluable work of T. A. M. Bishop, 'Notes on Cambridge Manuscripts Part III: MSS Connected with Exeter', *Transactions of the Cambridge Bibliographical Society*, 2 (1954–58), 192–200, where (p. 198) Bishop suggests these two manuscripts originally formed one volume. See also Elaine Treharne, 'Producing a Library in Late Anglo-Saxon England: Exeter 1050–1072', *Review of English Studies*, 53 (2003), 155–72.

[48] *Ælfric's Catholic Homilies: The Second Series*, ed. by Godden, Homily XL.

half of the eleventh century and is of Worcester origin. Rather like the Cleopatra B. XIII and Lambeth 489 collection, Hatton 113 and 114 together serve a variety of different purposes, providing texts for very specific occasions, such as Ascension Day and Pentecost, and non-specific items, used for preaching and teaching as and when the opportunity presented itself.[49]

Similarly, representing a broad codicological analogy to the Vercelli Book if only in its unselfconscious mixture of textual form is Cambridge, Corpus Christi College, MS 201, Part I, a manuscript of the first half of the eleventh century associable with Archbishop Wulfstan of York. This manuscript contains religious poetry, homilies, *Apollonius of Tyre*, and Wulfstanian political writings, legal tracts and lawcodes. It has been described as a 'unified devotional exercise connected with the sacrament of penance, and not a "hodge-podge" of isolated works'.[50] In his editorial and contextual work on this complex and intriguing manuscript, Caie suggests that the poems included in Part I are linked by their penitential and devotional nature, and that the 'key to the unity in subject matter in C[CCC 201] is undoubtedly to be found in the duties and interests of Wulfstan'.[51]

CCCC 201 is itself linked to Hatton 113 by the occurrence in the latter of a prose version of *Judgement Day II*, and by their shared homilies, composed by Wulfstan.[52] What these three eleventh-century comparanda of the Vercelli Book — CCCC 201, Cleopatra B. XIII + Lambeth 489, and Hatton 113 + 114 — have in common, apart from their erstwhile lack of discernible sustained structure and unity of textual configuration, is that each was almost certainly compiled for the

---

[49] For a fuller analysis, see Elaine Treharne, 'The Bishops' Books', forthcoming in *Early Medieval Europe*.

[50] Graham D. Caie, 'Text and Context in Editing Old English: The Case of the Poetry in Cambridge, Corpus Christi College 201', in *The Editing of Old English: Papers from the 1990 Manchester Conference*, ed. by D. G. Scragg and Paul E. Szarmach (Cambridge, 1994), pp. 155–62 (p. 162). See further *The Old English Poem 'Judgement Day II'*, ed. by Caie, Anglo-Saxon Texts, 2 (Cambridge, 2000), especially pp. 4–15; and also Caie, 'Codicological Clues: Reading Old English Christian Poetry in its Manuscript Context', in *The Christian Tradition in Anglo-Saxon England*, ed. by Paul Cavill (Cambridge, 2004), pp. 3–14 (p. 6).

[51] *The Old English Poem 'Judgement Day II'*, ed. by Caie, pp. 15–21 (p. 21). The poems are *Judgement Day II, An Exhortation to Christian Living, A Summons to Prayer, The Lord's Prayer II*, and *Gloria I*.

[52] On Wulfstan's homilies, see *The Homilies of Wulfstan*, ed. by Dorothy Bethurum (Oxford, 1957); *Wulfstan: Sammlung der ihm zugeschriebenen Homilien nebst Untersuchungen über ihre Echtheit*, ed. by A. S. Napier, Sammlung englischer Denkmäler in kritischen Ausgaben, 4 (Berlin, 1883); and the essays in *Wulfstan, Archbishop of York: The Proceedings of the Second Alcuin Conference*, ed. by Matthew Townend, Studies in the Early Middle Ages, 10 (Turnhout, 2004).

public and private use of one person, respectively, Wulfstan of York, Leofric of Exeter, and Wulfstan II of Worcester, all senior prelates, who took their pastoral duties very seriously throughout their careers. In the cases of all three, it is likely that they employed the homilies and other didactic texts in their manuscripts for public performance, especially in the case of the celebration of those solemn rites integrated into the liturgical calendar, such as the dedication of a church or baptismal ceremonies, where preaching, usually if not always by the bishop, was required.[53] The poems in CCCC 201, Caie suggests, together with the 'Benedictine Office' with which they are linked, 'might well have served a similar, didactic function for a lay audience: namely, providing non-liturgical meditations, based on the need for penance'.[54]

If such broad comparisons as exist between these eleventh-century manuscripts and the Vercelli Book are permissible, then interpreting the tenth-century poetic and prose compilation as a deliberately constructed set of pastoral and devotional texts for a prelate requires further exploration. Within the Vercelli Book, as outlined by Gatch, 'The Vercelli redactor seems to have been uncommonly interested in themes proper to seasons of the year'.[55] Thus, there are two homilies for Christmas, four for Epiphany, three for Lent, six for Rogationtide, and others for specific feasts, including that of St Martin. One might perceive *Elene* to be a text celebrating not only the Invention of the Cross, but also suitable as a hagiography for Helena herself. *The Dream of the Rood* is suitable for penitential purposes, for Lenten services, for the elucidation of the Good Friday liturgy, or for the Easter Vigil, among many other potential purposes.[56] The other poems in the Vercelli Book might similarly be seen as devotional in nature, urging, like *The Dream of the Rood*, a much greater focus on deliberate spiritual betterment through contrition, penance, and contemplation.[57] In terms of the prose homiletic texts, Gatch pro-

---

[53] As illustrated, for example, by the *Vita Wulfstani*, III.10.4. See *William of Malmesbury, Saints' Lives*, ed. and trans. by M. Winterbottom and R. M. Thomson, Oxford Medieval Texts (Oxford, 2002), pp. 120–24.

[54] *The Old English Poem 'Judgement Day II'*, ed. by Caie, p. 21.

[55] 'Eschatology in the Anonymous Old English Homilies', p. 143.

[56] See, for example, Earl R. Anderson, 'Liturgical Influences in "The Dream of the Rood"', *Neophilologus*, 73 (1989), 293–304; and, most importantly, Éamonn Ó Carragáin, *Ritual and the Rood: Liturgical Images and the Old English Poems of the 'Dream of the Rood' Tradition* (London, 2005).

[57] The other poems are, of course, *Andreas, The Fates of the Apostles, Soul and Body I*, and *Homiletic Fragment I*. All are edited by George Philip Krapp in *The Vercelli Book*, Anglo-Saxon Poetic Records, 2 (New York, 1932).

ceeds to analyse the possible thematic links between them,[58] and while these readings are convincing, one might also consider the pragmatic unity that emerges from multiple homilies for the same seasons, intermingled with single homilies for crucial feasts. This pragmatic unity is manifested by the functionality of the manuscript for someone present sporadically at major feasts in the Church year where a variety of materials were required for repeat performance. Such a figure, by analogy with the eleventh-century manuscripts discussed above, would be a bishop or (given the Vercelli Book's probable origin at St Augustine's) an abbot.[59]

At this point, it would indeed be a grand finale to state the name of such a possible reader of the manuscript. What we know of St Augustine's Abbey in the mid-tenth century and later, though, is based almost entirely on its manuscripts, for very little evidence survives about people and events in this period.[60] Nevertheless, what is certain from this brief overview is that the Vercelli Book is not the anomaly it might seem to be. It can be seen as representing a spiritual and pastoral impulse emerging from a major monastery in the early years of the Reform movement, possibly under the influence of a leading figure of that movement, such as Dunstan himself, provocative as that might seem.[61] It is typical of later collections

---

[58] 'Eschatology in the Anonymous Old English Homilies', especially pp. 145–65. Gatch focuses on the ascetic, the penitential, and the spiritual or literal pilgrimage of the penitent. See also Éamonn Ó Carragáin, 'How Did the Vercelli Collector Interpret *The Dream of the Rood*?', in *Studies in Language and Literature in Honour of Paul Christophersen*, ed. by Philip Tilling, New University of Ulster, Department of English, Occasional Papers in Linguistics and Language Learning, 8 (Coleraine, 1981), pp. 63–104.

[59] If the manuscript were made for such a distinguished user, its function could be private or public. I am suggesting, in this inevitably over-simplistic interpretation, indirect public use — the manuscript's texts being read, absorbed, and subsequently performed. A priest could, of course, also have used the manuscript, but within the context of St Augustine's monastic abbey in the tenth century, I am not sure how, precisely. On preaching in the eighth and ninth centuries, see John Blair, *The Church in Anglo-Saxon Society* (Oxford, 2005), pp. 160–66. See also Sarah Foot, 'Parochial Ministry in Early Anglo-Saxon England: The Role of Monastic Communities', in *The Ministry: Clerical and Lay*, ed. by W. J. Sheils and Diana Wood, Studies in Church History, 26 (Oxford, 1989), pp. 43–54.

[60] See, for example, Nicholas Brooks, *The Early History of the Church of Canterbury: Christ Church from 597 to 1066*, Studies in the Early History of Britain (Leicester, 1984), esp. ch. 10; and *St Augustine's Abbey, Canterbury*, ed. by Richard Gem (London, 1997).

[61] It has often been pointed out, for example, that the Vercelli Book is conservative in its choice of texts and sources. Interestingly, just the same claim of conservatism has been proposed of Archbishop Dunstan himself, who is known to have been a regular visitor at St Augustine's. See Alan Thacker, 'Cults at Canterbury: Relics and Reform under Dunstan and his Successors', in *St*

made for personal but public use by those most responsible for disseminating religious teachings — senior ecclesiastics, monastic and regular. By looking forward to the company in which I have placed it, we can glimpse the role the Vercelli Book might have played in tenth-century Canterbury. And although this reading of the manuscript's form and function arrives at conclusions far removed from his own, I hope that Éamonn will enjoy reading and discussing the evidence on which it is founded.

Dunstan: His Life, Time and Cult, ed. by Ramsey, Sparks, and Tatton-Brown, pp. 221–45 (pp. 238–41).

THE DREAM OF THE ROOD AS EKPHRASIS

Paul E. Szarmach

To its everlasting credit Formalism (a.k.a. 'close reading') has rescued *The Dream of the Rood* from the junkheap of literary history. Over the last generation or so many scholars and critics have demonstrated the coherence, structure, thematic resonance, and unity of the poem, among many aesthetic attributes, while others, not the least of whom is the honoree, have shown how the poem is, in a sense, the interdisciplinary short poem par excellence in its meaningful relation to liturgy, archaeology, and forms of material and visual expression.[1] This paper seeks to extend the significance of the poem by considering it as an example of ekphrasis, that is, the verbal representation of the visual. Early medieval writers would not have understood the term, had they known it, in quite the way classical writers and rhetoricians would have done, and indeed as scholars and critics now do, but the verbal representation of the visual existed in the medieval,

I acknowledge with gratitude and thanks the generosity of Dr Zofia Kolbuszewska (Catholic University, Lublin), who shared her working bibliography on ekphrasis with me. I am grateful to Katherine O'Brien O'Keeffe, Elizabeth C. Teviotdale, and Jane Roberts for comments and contributions to my argument. All translations in this paper are mine, unless otherwise stated.

[1] Michael Swanton, in his rev. edn of *The Dream of the Rood* (Exeter, 1987), compiles a bibliography on the poem and the Ruthwell Cross through approximately 1987. Swanton's estimable edition provides the text of the poem for this paper. For scholarship after 1987 *Anglo-Saxon England* and the *Old English Newsletter* [*OEN*] offer annual bibliographies, the latter producing a bibliography in summer issues and a review of that bibliography in the subsequent winter issue. *OEN* is now online at <http://www.oenewsletter.org/OEN/>. Éamonn Ó Carragáin, *Ritual and the Rood: Liturgical Images and the Old English Poems of the 'Dream of the Rood' Tradition* (London, 2005) is the crowning achievement of a generation of work and well more than a score of Prof. Ó Carragáin's publications exemplifying interdisciplinary study.

precise term or no.[2] The emphasis here will be more on the 'how' of seeing and what 'seeing' quite means rather than on the content of the vision. To achieve some procedural clarity I will use 'viewing' to refer to looking at art and 'reading' to refer univocally to intellectual engagement with words on the page. Anglo-Saxon and early medieval theorizing about art will provide much of the context of understanding. Similar ekphrastic works will furthermore provide points of comparison. *The Dream of the Rood*, then, may thus be able to join Gawain's Pentangle Shield and Chaucer's walk through the Temple of Glass as vernacular intersections of the verbal and visual reflecting their respective cultural concerns. Anglo-Saxon art criticism provides the entry point for discussion.

In his homily *Dominica in media quadragesima* (I.12), Ælfric of Eynsham seeks to explain how to read the miracle of the five loaves and twelve fishes fed to the five thousand (John 6. 1–14):

> Ðis wundor is swiðe micel ⁊ deop on getacnungum; oft gehwa gesihð fægere stafas awritene. þonne herað he ðone writere ⁊ þa stafas ⁊ nat hwæt hi mænað; Se ðe cann þæra stafa gescead. he herað heora fægernysse. ⁊ ræt þa stafas. ⁊ understent hwæt hi gemænað; on oðre wisan we scawiað metinge. ⁊ on oðre wisan stafas. ne gæð na mare to metinge buton þ[æt] ðu hit geseo. ⁊ herige; Nis na genoh þ[æt] ðu stafas scawie. buton þu hi eac ræde. ⁊ þ[æt] andgit understande; swa is eac on ðam wundre þe god worhte mid þam fif hlafum. Ne bið na genoh þ[æt] we ðæs tacnes wundrian. oððe þurh þ[æt] god herian buton we eac þ[æt] gastlice understandon.[3]

> [This is a very great miracle and deep in its significations. Often someone sees beautifully written letters. He then praises the writer and the letters, and does not know what they mean. The one who understands the letters, he praises their beauty and reads the letters and understands what they mean. In one way we view a painting, in another the letters. Nothing more pertains to a painting except that you see it and praise it. It is not enough that you view the letters unless you read them and understand the signification. So is it

---

[2] Ruth Webb, '*Ekphrasis* Ancient and Modern: The Invention of a Genre', *Word and Image*, 15 (1999), 7–18, traces the development of the term. *Word and Image*, 15, no. 2 (1999) is a special, general issue on *Ekphrasis* edited by Mario Klarer. In its overall run the journal shows a particular interest in studies of the genre.

[3] *Ælfric's Catholic Homilies, The First Series: Text*, ed. by Peter Clemoes, EETS, SS, 17 (Oxford, 1997), p. 277. For discussion of the homily and its sources, see *Ælfric's Catholic Homilies: Introduction, Commentary and Glossary*, ed. by Malcolm Godden, EETS, 18 (Oxford, 2000), pp. 94–101. See also the entry by Malcolm Godden on *CH* I.12 in *Fontes Anglo-Saxonici: World Wide Web Register*, <http://fontes.english.ox.ac.uk/>, accessed January 2006. Benjamin Thorpe's edition and translation, *The Homilies of the Anglo-Saxon Church*, 2 vols (London, 1844–46) is of importance for the history of the subject, and indeed often serves as the hidden pony for Anglo-Saxonists; see Thorpe's first volume, pp. 180–93.

in the miracle that God wrought with those five loaves. It is not enough that we wonder over the sign or through it praise God unless we also understand it spiritually.]

Ælfric's meta-exegesis offers its complications. The comparison that Ælfric makes to reading miracles is double, that is, a contrast between looking at a painting and seeing beautiful letters. The double comparison has to be worked out first and then it has to be applied to the biblical problem at hand. Behind the double comparison and its application is a theory of literacy in the visual and in the verbal with an emphasis on meaning, but lurking in the comparison is some sense of beauty, of some 'fægernysse' in the letter-forms. Ælfric does not explain where the beauty comes from; neither, strictly speaking, does he offer a moral or intellectual critique of the observer attracted by it. Beauty is neither good nor bad; it is a simple given in the analogy presented. Ælfric's intellectual contrast is between two ways of looking: what you see is what you get; what you read is what takes you to another level of understanding. Ælfric clearly devalues the apparent commonsensical — or perhaps ultimately intuitive — reading of the letters as an art object because it is simple looking. Reading of the letters for their meaning is the significant act beyond the surface. Ælfric is no formalist, failing to see any value in abstract patterning (despite what contemporary Anglo-Saxonists praise in gold buckles and sword hilts and find in the procession of styles).[4]

Malcolm Godden documents and describes the complications of Ælfric's use of sources for this homily, which are some five in number with the possibility of 'show-through' as Bede, Alcuin, Haymo of Auxerre, and Smaragdus are in some relation with their ultimate source, Augustine's *Tractate* 24 on the Gospel of St John.[5] The

---

[4] See my 'Ælfric as Exegete: Approaches and Examples in the Study of the *Sermones Catholici*', in *Hermeneutics and Medieval Culture*, ed. by Patrick Gallacher and Helen Damico (Albany, 1989), pp. 237–47 (pp. 238–40 where I discuss this passage in connection with biblical exegesis).

[5] *Ælfric's Catholic Homilies*, ed. by Godden, pp. 94–101; Augustine, *In Iohannis Evangelium tractatus CXXIV*, ed. by Radbod Willems, CCSL, 36 (Turnhout, 1954), pp. 244–45. Here I cite the trans. by John W. Rettig, *St Augustine: Tractates on the Gospel of John*, 4 vols pub. to date (Washington DC, 1988–95), II, 232–33: 'But just as if we were to look at beautiful letters somewhere, it would not be enough for us to praise the writer's hand because he made the letters uniform, even, and elegant if we were not able to read what he had made known to us through them, so he who only looks at this deed is delighted by the deed's beauty so that he admires the artist; but who understands also reads, so to speak. For a picture is seen in one way, letters are seen in another way. When you have seen a picture, to have seen it, to have praised it, is all that is. When you have seen the letters, this is not all that is because you are put in mind also to read them. For you say, when you have seen letters, if perchance you do not know how to read them, "What do we think it is which was written here?" You ask what it is although you already see something.'

OE passage above is, as Godden styles it, 'a recasting' of Augustine, *Tractate* 24.2.5–25. Augustine's art criticism comes forward with more context and nuance, for he does observe that the miracles have 'linguam suam' ('their own discourse') and he word plays off Christ as the Word of God whose (miraculous) deed speaks as if a word. At this point Ælfric begins to follow Augustine when he cites the deep and profound nature of the miracle. Augustine works more binary pairs, however, contrasting a reading of the surface vs. a reading of the depth, a reading of the interior vs. a reading of the exterior. These contrastives are vintage Augustine as they suggest a way of thinking that will become a contrast between viewing a picture and reading letters. Augustine then amplifies the difference by a brief tableau in direct discourse where a viewer who does not know letters asks what he might be seeing. Implied in the vignette is some form of apparent curiosity, perhaps the undefined impulse to art. Ælfric, having already made the Augustinian point that a picture is viewed in one way and letters in another, avoids the tableau and proceeds directly to Augustine's major conclusion: the viewer sees and praises; the reader sees, praises, reads, and understands. Missing in Ælfric is Augustine's reference to sign theory, for Augustine says: 'Nonne similiter apices uidetis? Sed non similiter signa cognoscitis?' ('Do you not see the letter forms in a similar way? But do you not perceive signs in a similar way?').[6] Ælfric condenses and simplifies the Augustinian argument. Yet Peter Clemoes observes that Ælfric understands that written language is a combination of physical presence and meaning, distinguishable yet complementary.[7] In that inference one could see a latent sign theory — perhaps.

The Augustinian passage from the Ælfrician homily has become a key text in the study of Anglo-Saxon literacy. Seth Lerer incorporates Augustine's views in his extensive discussion of Asser and Alfred and their 'story of texts and their uses'.[8] Lerer links the Augustinian passage to Alfred's own encounter with beautiful letters and his attraction to them.[9] While Lerer looks beyond the surface of

---

[6] *In Iohannis Evangelium tractatus*, ed. by Willems, p. 245, with trans. as Rettig, with minor adjustments.

[7] Peter Clemoes, 'Language in Context: *Her* in the 890 *Anglo-Saxon Chronicle*', *Leeds Studies in English*, 16 (1985), 27–36 (p. 30).

[8] Seth Lerer, *Literacy and Power in Anglo-Saxon Literature* (Lincoln, 1991), pp. 61–96 for the whole discussion, p. 62 for the specific citation.

[9] Lerer, *Literacy and Power*, pp. 64–66. The passage for discussion is *Asser's Life of King Alfred*, ed. by William Henry Stevenson (Oxford, 1959), ch. 23, p. 20. For a translation, see Simon Keynes and Michael Lapidge, *Alfred the Great: Asser's Life of King Alfred and Other Contemporary Sources* (Harmondsworth, 1983), p. 75.

this anecdote to uncover Asser's doubts about Alfred's future success with texts, my own view is that the Augustinian passage might more positively function as a de facto script for Alfred's reaction to the beautiful letters. As Asser relates, Alfred acts out 'in real life' what Augustine describes in *Tractates* 24.2 with his confected tableau containing the unlettered questioner. Asser will eventually relate that Alfred learns to read, leaving his untutored state to become a translator of Latin texts (in the traditional view). With respect to Augustine's analysis (and Ælfric's), Alfred will see, praise, read, and understand. His intellectual life will be true to the art of reading.

However brief and therefore incomplete this Augustinian account of viewing and reading might be in accounting for the aesthetic response as such, it does establish the parallel between images and words and the superiority of reading over viewing.[10] The Augustinian account appears more theoretical than the above analysis would seem to indicate when placed next to Gregory the Great's pragmatism. It is Gregory who is at the beginning of the tradition that pictures function as do books and that they are accordingly valuable in teaching the illiterate. As Celia M. Chazelle argues, 'Gregory formulated arguments concerning the function of pictures in churches which, in the final analysis, were unprecedented in either western or eastern Christendom'.[11] It is traditional to maintain that Gregory is an Augustinian in very many ways, but his *Weltanschauung* tends towards practical administration of the Church with special reference to good leadership that a bishop must provide (compare his *Regula pastoralis*). Gregory's two letters to the maverick Bishop Serenus of Marseilles are the foundational texts (letters of July 599 and October 600). Serenus had apparently gone ahead to destroy sacred art in his diocese. Gregory's first letter admonishing Serenus on the matter apparently went unheeded — Serenus, in an evident ploy, claiming that it was a forgery! — and so Gregory had to write Serenus again from his papal chair. In the interim Serenus managed to split his diocese over his controversial actions. Gregory chides him in the first letter:

> Praeterea indico dudum ad nos peruenisse quod fraternitas uestra quosdam imaginem adoratores aspiciens eadem ecclesiis imagines confregit atque proiecit. Et quidem zelum uos, ne quid manufactum adorari possit, habuisse laudauimus, sed frangere easdem

---

[10] No doubt Otto Pächt, who gave the aphorism 'Am Anfang was das Auge', would not agree. See *Kunsthistoriker in eigener Sache*, ed. by Martina Sitt (Berlin, 1990), pp. 24–61, for a sketch of Pächt's life and works. My thanks to Elizabeth Teviotdale for this reference.

[11] Celia M. Chazelle, 'Pictures, Books, and the Illiterate: Pope Gregory I's Letters to Serenus of Marseilles', *Word and Image*, 6 (1990), 138–53 (p. 138). My debt to this essay is manifest.

imagines non debuisse iudicamus. Idcirco enim pictura in ecclesiis adhibetur, ut hi qui litteras nesciunt saltem in parietibus uidendo legant, quae legere in codicibus non ualent. Tua ergo fraternitas et illa seruare et ab eorum adoratu populum prohibere debuit, quatenus et litterarum nescii haberent, unde scientiam historiae colligerent, et populus in picturae adoratione minime peccaret.[12]

[Meanwhile I note that some time ago it reached us that your fraternity, seeing certain people adoring images, broke the images and threw them from the churches. And certainly we praise you for your zeal lest something manufactured be adored, but we judge that you should not have destroyed those images. For a picture is displayed in churches on this account, in order that those who do not know letters may at least read by seeing on the walls what they are unable to read in books. Therefore your fraternity should preserve those things and prohibit the people from adoring them, so that persons ignorant of letters may have something whereby they may gather knowledge of the story and the people may by no means sin through adoration of a picture.][13]

An excellent administrator's letter because it cloaks blame with enough praise to be palatable to the addressee, Gregory's missive takes a kind of middle-of-the-road position on images. It is right not to 'adore' something made by hand, but it is not right to destroy images since they have an educative function. Those who cannot read in books can 'read by seeing on the walls'. The word 'legere' begins to stretch its semantic field from its clear literal meaning to some kind of analogical cognitive activity, and the object of 'legere' can be both words and images. Serenus's disregard of the first letter gives Gregory a second chance to get to Serenus. Gregory more or less takes the gloves off, but amid the pummelling amplifies his remarks on the importance of images:

Aliud est enim picturam adorare, aliud per picturae historiam quid sit adorandum addiscere. Nam quod legentibus scriptura, hoc idiotis praestat pictura cernentibus, quia in ipsa ignorantes uident quod qui debeant, in ipsa legunt qui litteras nesciunt; quae praecipue gentibus pro lectione pictura est [. . .].[14]

[For it is one thing to adore a picture, another through a picture's story to learn what must be adored. For what writing offers to those who read it, a picture offers to the ignorant who look at it, since in it the ignorant see what they ought to follow, whence especially for gentiles a picture stands in place of reading [. . .].][15]

---

[12] Gregory the Great, *Registrum epistularum, Ep.* 9 (209), ed. by Dag Norberg, CCSL, 140A (Turnhout, 1982), p. 768.

[13] Trans. by Chazelle, 'Pictures, Books, and the Illiterate', p. 139.

[14] Gregory the Great, *Registrum epistularum, Ep.* 11 (10) ed. by Norberg, pp. 873–75.

[15] Trans. by Chazelle, 'Pictures, Books, and the Illiterate', p. 139.

and further:

> Frangi ergo non debuit quod non ad adorandum in ecclesiis sed ad instruendas solum-
> modo mentes fuit nescientium collocatum. Et [. . .] in locis uenerabilibus sanctorum
> depingi historias non sine ratione uetustas admisit.[16]

> [Thus that should not be broken which has been set in churches not for adoration but
> only to instruct the minds of the ignorant. And [. . .] the ancients reasonably permitted
> that stories of holy persons be depicted in venerable places.][17]

'Aliud [. . .] aliud' has the cast of an aphorism or a maxim that neatly addresses the
issue of idolatry, an issue always lurking in the discussion of holy images, and also
recalls Ælfric's 'on oðre wisan [. . .] on oðre wisan' above. The Gregorian stress
that a picture can be educative for those who do not know letters has almost a
Horatian ring to it, 'pro lectione pictura' (compare 'ut pictura poesis'). Here
Gregory injects the precedent of the past and what one might call 'best practices'
in the matter of images. Now, since the first letter did not capture Serenus's
benevolence, Gregory effectively tells Serenus what to say to his split congregation
so as to bring them back together again. Gregory-turned-Serenus repeats the earlier idea that it is not permitted to adore a hand-made thing. Serenus has to say
further that he was roused to a zealous reaction not because of the images but
because of the inappropriate adoration given them and that he allows images, but
not their adoration.[18] In these two letters the unity of the congregation and right
pastoral care in response to a crisis in a major church are behind Gregory's treatment of pictures on a church wall.

Chazelle makes several important observations in her close reading of these
two letters. Not all of these are germane to the topic of this paper, but it is still
useful to list them here so as to contextualize any latent principles or ideas about
(sacred) art.[19] These include the following: Gregory uses the 'adorare' to refer only
to God; he is interested not in portraits but with depictions of events or stories on
the wall; in the discussion of representations he focuses on 'sancti' who can be living

---

[16] Gregory the Great, *Registrum epistularum*, *Ep.* 11 (10), ed. by Norberg, p. 874.

[17] Trans. by Chazelle, 'Pictures, Books, and the Illiterate', p. 139.

[18] Ernst Kitzinger, 'The Cult of Images in the Age Before Iconoclasm', *Dumbarton Oaks
Papers*, 8 (1954), 83–150 (p. 85), renders the authoritative judgment: 'In the entire history of
European art it is difficult to name any one fact more momentous than the admission of the
graven image by the Christian Church'; Gregory gave 'a sanction which should be regarded as one
of the crucial events in the history of art'.

[19] Chazelle, 'Pictures, Books, and the Illiterate', in her section 'II' on the vocabulary, pp.
140–43, and subsequently, pp. 143–50, on larger issues.

or dead, Old Testament or New; Gregory says ambiguously that from pictures the illiterate 'scientiam historiae colligere[nt]' ('gather knowledge of the story'); Gregory's concept of the illiterate has its fuzzy features, which might allow for educated persons who could read and write. One may note here that there is no overt mention of the beauty of the art depicted or its attractiveness in any sense. One may ask, the knowledge transfer from art on the wall to the viewer occurs exactly how? The best explanation is that the viewer(s) come to the depiction with antecedent knowledge. The door to a (neo-)Platonic concept of interior or immanent knowledge might be there, but what the pragmatic Gregory seems to suggests is that the viewers have already heard about a particular depiction and that the wall-painting is, so to speak, a realization of the story that would amplify understanding of it and raise the viewer, ultimately, to the adoration of God. Chazelle argues cogently that the visual here thus cooperates with Christian preaching, which is the primary vehicle for knowledge transfer, often enhanced by 'story' for the audience that might need a narrative to attain knowledge of doctrine.[20] Without the verbal basis from preaching or teaching a viewer might take understanding in part from *tituli* or 'captions'. Thus does the mind of a sixth-century viewer before a picture on the wall correspond in part to a contemporary viewer looking at an abstract at a museum of modern art: how or why would a viewer before a particular Mondrian know that it was *Broadway Boogie Woogie* if there were no caption?

Gregory more directly proves himself Augustinian by adapting the parallel of words and images in his *Expositio in Canticis Canticorum*. Like Augustine, Gregory holds for the primacy of meaning, but he moves into a more analytical, less general treatment when he gets to some of the basic elements of the visual and the verbal:

> Sic est enim scriptura sacra in uerbis et sensibus, sicut pictura in coloribus et rebus: et nimis stultus est, qui sic picturae coloribus inheret, ut res, quae pictae sunt, ignoret. Nos enim, si uerba, quae exterius dicuntur, amplectimur et sensus ignoramus, quasi ignorantes res, quae depictae sunt, solos colores tenemus. Littera occidit, scriptum est, spiritus autem uiuificat. Sic enim littera cooperit spiritum, sicut palea tegit frumentum.[21]

> [For holy scripture is the same in terms of words and meanings as a picture is in terms of colours and things; and he is really too foolish who so concentrates on a picture's colours that he is unaware of the things that are depicted. For if we embrace the words that are spoken externally and pay no attention to their meanings, as if we disregard the things

---

[20] Chazelle, 'Pictures, Books, and the Illiterate', pp. 147–48.

[21] Gregory, *Expositio in Canticis Canticorum*, ed. by Patrick Verbraken, CCSL, 144 (Turnhout, 1963), p. 5.

that are depicted, we hold solely to the colours. The letter kills, as it has been written, yet the spirit gives life. For just as the letter covers the spirit, thus the chaff covers the grain.][22]

In this four-part comparison of colours and things (depicted), and words and meaning, formal or technical features of a picture do not take on any major significance; Gregory cannot imagine colour as a category even apparently if (say) a colour like blue could have a recurrent association, as it did later, with the Virgin Mary. Interestingly, one might, with a full Augustinian tooth, expect letters to be the equivalent to colours in this comparison, for any hierarchy of significance would seem to make words rather more directly important for meaning than colours for pictures. Perhaps colour was only the most obvious to Gregory's eye, or perhaps he valued colour more than other formal features, assuming that he recognized other features at all. The pursuit of the spiritual over the literal marks the passage as Augustinian.

Bede displays his Gregorianism when he considers the achievements of Benedict Biscop, founder of Wearmouth and Jarrow, in his homily celebrating the life and works of the monastic hero. Telling his audience that 'sumus eius filii', Bede relates with evident warmth and affection Benedict Biscop's generosity and how after trips he came back to Northumbria with holy books, relics of the saints and martyrs, architects, glassmakers, master singers, and a letter of papal privilege.[23] The list of good things that 'father' brought back ends with art for the church:

adportauit nunc pincturas sanctarum historiarum quae non ad ornamentum solummodo ecclesiae uerum et ad instructionem intuentium proponeretur aduexit uidelicet ut qui litterarum lectionem non possent opera domini et saluatoris nostri per ipsarum contuitum discerent imaginum.[24]

[he transported pictures of the holy histories which were put up, not only for the ornamentation of the church, but also for the instruction of those who looked at them, namely so that those who could not read might learn of the works of our Lord and Savior through gazing on images of these [works].][25]

---

[22] Trans. by Chazelle 'Pictures, Books, and the Illiterate', p. 147. I infer that Gregory's idea of 'colours' here is not particularly different from ours.

[23] Paul Meyvaert, 'Bede and the Church Paintings at Wearmouth-Jarrow', *Anglo-Saxon England*, 8 (1979), 63–77, considers Bede's various discussions of the artwork at Wearmouth-Jarrow as they appear in Bede's Homily on Benedict Biscop and in his *Historia abbatum*.

[24] Bede, *Homeliarum Evangelii libri II*, ed. by David Hurst, CCSL, 122 (Turnhout, 1955), p. 93.

[25] Trans. by Lawrence T. Martin and David Hurst, *Bede the Venerable: Homilies on the Gospels*, vol. I (Kalamazoo, 1991), p. 131.

As with Gregory, the stress is on pictures of 'holy stories', not portraits or other kinds of representation, which serve not only to adorn a church but also to instruct those looking at them. Bede considers a decorative possibility, which Gregory could not in his letters to Serenus, as well as an educative one, amplifying the latter point with a strong 'uidelicet' to indicate that those who are unable to read might discern the works of the Lord through viewing them. Perhaps 'ad ornamentum' implies some kind of aesthetic principle. Bede would seem to suggest that the literate and the illiterate can benefit from wall pictures. How this understanding comes to pass for either audience is taken for granted.

In *Historia abbatum*, 6, Bede gives more details of Benedict Biscop's generosity with 'ornamenta et munimenta', essentially amplifying the treatment found in the homily.[26] Relevant here on Bede's list from Benedict Biscop's fifth trip is the fifth set of 'spiritual merchandise' ('spriritalium mercium'):

> picturas imaginum sanctarum quas ad ornandam aecclesiam beati Petri apostoli, quam construxerat, detulit; imaginem uidelicet beatae Dei genetricis semperque uirginis Mariae, simul et duodecim apostolorum , quibus mediam eiusdem aecclesiae testudinem, ducto a pariete ad parietem tabulato praecingeret; imagines euangelicae historiae quibus australem aecclesiae parietem decoraret; imagines uisionum apocalipsis beati Iohannis, quibus septentrionalem aeque parietem ornaret, quatinus intrantes aecclesiam omnes etiam litterarum ignari, quaquauersum intenderent, uel semper amabilem Christi sanctorumque eius, quamuis in imagine, contemplarentur aspectum; uel dominicae incarnationis gratiam uigilantiore mente recolerent; uel extremi discrimen examinis, quasi coram oculis habentes, districtius se ipsi examinare meminissent.[27]

> [he brought with him pictures of sacred representation, to adorn the church of St Peter, which he had built; namely, a likeness of the Virgin Mary and of the twelve Apostles, with which he intended to adorn the central nave, on boarding placed from one wall to the other; also some figures from ecclesiastical [better: 'gospel'] history for the south wall, and others from the Revelation of St. John for the north wall; so that everyone who entered the church, even if they could not read, wherever they turned their eyes, might have before them the amiable countenance of Christ and his saints, though it were but in a picture, and with watchful minds might revolve on the benefits of our Lord's incarnation, and having before their eyes the perils of the last judgment, might examine their hearts the more strictly on that account.][28]

---

[26] *Historia abbatum*, 6, in *Venerabilis Baedae: opera historica*, ed. by Charles Plummer, 2 vols (Oxford, 1896), I, 368–70.

[27] *Historia abbatum*, 6, ed. by Plummer, I, 369–70.

[28] Trans. by J. Stevenson (1870) in *Bede's Ecclesiastical History of the English Nation* (London, 1970), p. 353.

This extensive listing continues the Bedan themes of the function of art. There are portraits and narrative panels, 'images' that adorn the church walls with scenes from the Gospels (Gregory's 'historia'). When the faithful enter the church, they reflect on the lovable face of Christ and his saints, they recall in their mind the gift of the Incarnation and the Last Judgement as if before their eyes, and they remember to examine themselves more strictly. The importance of memory is clear; the images join with what the faithful have otherwise heard or learned, and that is how the images teach by way of memory. Bede clearly points out that the images *are* images: Christ 'quamuis in imagine' ('though in image'); the Last Judgement, 'quasi coram oculis' ('as if before their eyes'). He does not confuse the image for any reality, transcendent or sublunary.

Bede relates that Benedict Biscop's sixth trip brings even more artistic treasures to Northumbria.[29] There are (again) pictures of the story of Christ ('dominicae historiae picturas'), but significantly there is a new kind of art work in typological images:

> [. . .] imagines quoque ad ornandum aecclesiamque beati Pauli apostoli de concordia ueteris et noui Testamenti summa ratione conpositas exibuit; uerba gratia, Isaac ligna, quibus immoraletur portantem, et Dominum crucem in qua pateretur aeque portantem, proxima super inuicem regione, pictura coniunxit. Item serpenti in heremo a Moyse exaltato, Filium hominis in cruce exaltatum conparauit.[30]

> [[. . .] and others to adorn St. Paul's church and the monastery, ably describing the connexion of the Old and New Testament; as, for instance, Isaac bearing the wood for his own sacrifice, and Christ carrying the cross on which he was about to suffer, were placed side by side. Again, the serpent raised up by Moses in the desert was illustrated by the Son of Man exalted on the cross.][31]

The appearance of typological panels showing the 'concordance' of Old and New Testaments raises the intellectual or educative level of any simple wall-hanging. If the viewer is to remember the meaning of typology by visual stimulus, the viewer must have some level of sophistication and training, whether monk or not. (The emphasis on the typology of the cross is certainly fortuitous for this paper.) The account of this successful trip ends on a note of artistic appreciation as well. Bede relates that Benedict Biscop brought along two silk *pallia* of 'incomparable work' ('incomparandi operis'), a comment that must pass for one of the few outright aesthetic judgements in Bede's description of artwork.

---

[29] *Historia abbatum*, 9, ed. by Plummer, I, 373.

[30] *Historia abbatum*, 9, ed. by Plummer, I, 373.

[31] Trans. by Stevenson, *Bede's Ecclesiastical History*, p. 355.

Bede would seem to have some awareness of the iconoclastic controversies and the issues concerning idolatry in an aside on Solomon's construction and decoration of the Temple. Describing how Solomon used carvings and sculpture of various flora and fauna and how Moses similarly made objects, Bede argues forcefully:

> Si enim licebat serpentem exaltari aeneum in ligno quam aspicientes filii Israhel uiuerent, cur non licet exaltationem domini saluatoris in cruce qua mortem uicit ad memoriam fidelibus depingendo reduci uel etiam alia eius miracula et sanationes quibus de eodem mortis auctore mirabiliter triumphauit cum horum aspectus multum saepe compunctionis soleat praestare contuentibus et eis quoque qui litteras ignorant quasi uiuam dominicae historiae pandere lectionem?[32]

> [Now if it was permissible to lift up a brazen serpent on a piece of wood so that the Israelites who beheld it might live, why should it not be allowable to recall to the memory of the faithful, by a painting, the exaltation of our Lord Saviour on the cross through which he wonderfully triumphed over the same author of death, and especially since their sight is wont also to produce a feeling of great compunction in the beholder, and since they open up, as it were a living reading of the Lord's story for those who cannot read?][33]

The Old Testament with its patriarchal precedents gives ample warrant to those living under the New Law who, by implication, have greater status, or so the tone of 'cur' seems to imply. The painting will appeal to the memory of the faithful, who will recall Christ's sacrifice and his miracles. To the recurrent stress on memory and recollection, Bede now adds another dimension in citing the affective impact of the paintings on the viewing faithful, whom compunction will accordingly seize.[34] Those who do not know letters, presumably also part of the audience, will experience as if a 'living reading' of the story of the Lord. Bede goes on to define the Greek 'pictura' as 'uiua scriptura' ('living writing'), which crosses the verbal-visual line. For Bede there would appear to be a special immediacy in a picture that makes it particularly effective in transmitting moral teaching and affective piety. What Bede is describing is essentially the experience of *The Dream of the Rood* where a living picture inspires the soul in tears to seek God. More generally, for the idea that art is the book of the illiterate, Duggan observes the

---

[32] Bede, *De templo* II, ed. by David Hurst, CCSL, 119A (Turnhout, 1969), pp. 212–13.

[33] Trans. by Meyvaert, 'Bede and the Church Paintings at Wearmouth-Jarrow', p. 69. As David Appleby aptly remarks, 'The symbol of the Cross was in some ways exceptional': 'Holy Relic and Holy Image: Saints' Relics in the Western Controversy over Images in the Eighth and Ninth Centuries', *Word and Image*, 8 (1992), 333–43 (p. 341).

[34] For a description of *compunctio cordis*, see Alcuin's *Liber de virtutibus et vitiis*, PL, 101, 620–21.

'central problem of memory, reading, and learning' is one that scholarship returns to again and again.[35]

This brief sketch of early medieval art criticism hardly makes a claim for comprehensiveness. Not included here is any pursuit of the Greek fathers, Paulinus of Nola, further Augustinian byways, or of course the remarkable thicket concerning the iconoclastic controversies and the *Libri Carolini*. Augustinian and early medieval sign theory, as applied to art, might have much to offer. Indeed, the *Libri Carolini* would seem to require a full-scale monograph of its own and a very subtle analysis to see if Anglo-Saxon art criticism and practice, ekphrasis included, owe anything to the iconoclastic controversies.[36] Otto Lehmann-Brockhaus and his five volumes are an open invitation to keep seeking early medieval art sources.[37] Two examples of vernacular ekphrasis may now complete the prolegomenon to *The Dream of the Rood*.

The narrative world of *Andreas*, a hagiographical romance in an epic style tangent here and there with *Beowulf*, is almost too busy as it relates how the apostle Andrew goes to rescue the apostle Matthew from Mermedonia, a city of cannibals.[38] Christ himself is in disguise as the Skipper who takes Andrew and his men on board for free and sails them through a storm at sea, appropriately described. The Captain asks Andrew to tell him more about Jesus [!], which leads into an account of Christ and the Jews. The disguise motif sets up possibilities for dramatic irony and a particular kind of comedy,[39] either of which suggests a self-conscious or even playful poet open to the possibilities of a narrative turned against itself.

---

[35] Lawrence G. Duggan, 'Was Art Really the "Book of the Illiterate"?', *Word and Image*, 5 (1989), 227–51 (p. 230), while offering a broad overview through the Middle Ages.

[36] The essays by Chazelle ('Pictures, Books, and the Illiterate'), Appleby ('Holy Relic and Holy Image'), and Duggan ('Was Art Really the "Book of the Illiterate"?') are important for establishing context. William J. Diebold, 'Verbal, Visual, and Cultural Literacy in Medieval Art: Word and Image in the Psalter of Charles the Bald', *Word and Image*, 8 (1992), 89–99, suggests how sophisticated visual literacy could be. For a comprehensive treatment, see now Herbert L. Kessler, *Seeing Medieval Art*, Rethinking the Middle Ages, 1 (Peterborough, 2004).

[37] Otto Lehmann-Brockhaus, *Lateinische Schriftquellen zur Kunst in England, Wales, und Schottland*, 5 vols (Munich, 1955–60).

[38] *Andreas and the Fates of the Apostles*, ed. by Kenneth R. Brooks (Oxford, 1961), remains the standard edition. It has to be said that throughout Brooks is uncomfortable with the literary features of the poem he has edited. All line references are to this edition. S. A. J. Bradley, *Anglo-Saxon Poetry* (London, 1982), pp. 110–53, offers a useful translation.

[39] See Edward B. Irving, Jr, 'A Reading of *Andreas*: The Poem as a Poem', *Anglo-Saxon England*, 12 (1983), 215–37, with special reference to parody and comedy at pp. 229, 233.

The disguise motif more importantly launches the theme of seeing and looking, which takes on major significance. What Andrew thinks he sees is not what is there. Christ's second encounter with the Jews, the occasion of ekphrasis, continues the theme. Having already been rebuffed once by the Jews, Christ returns to preach again with no immediate effect. The poet says the Jews did not receive Christ's holy teaching 'þeah he soðra swa feala | tacna gecyðde þær hie to segon' ('even though he had revealed so many true tokens where they were looking on' (Bradley's translation), lines 710a–11). The Jews were viewing the signs but were not understanding them. At this point Christ looks on the wall:

> Swylce he wrætlice   wundor agræfene,
> anlicnesse   engla sinra
> geseh, sigora frea,   on seles wage
> on twa healfe   torhte gefrætwed,
> wlitige geworhta.   (lines 712–16a)

[Thus, he, the Lord of Victories, saw *marvelous sculptures skilfully wrought*,[40] likenesses of his angels, on the wall of the hall on two sides, splendidly decorated, beautifully wrought.]

The carved images ('likenesses') adorn the wall of the Temple on two sides, recalling at least in a general way the use of pictures at Wearmouth-Jarrow as well as Gregory's own apparent expectations for the use of wall pictures.[41] The poet's eyes see their beautiful adornment and the audience's eyes are directed to this feature first. Christ now comments on the carved figures, explaining that they are Cherubim and Seraphim of the heavenly city who stand before the eternal Lord praising him. He then offers a piece of aesthetic criticism on artisanship:

> [. . .] Her amearcod is
> haligra hiw,   þurh handmægen
> awriten on wealle,   wuldres þegnas. (lines 724b–26)

[Here, the form of saints is depicted through the skill of hands — thegns of glory written on the wall.]

The hand strength makes the sculpture possible, but Christ's power is even greater, for he now suspends the laws of nature by calling for a miracle and a sign:

> 'Nu ic bebeode   beacen ætywan,
> wundor geweorðan   on wera gemange,

---

[40] The italicized words are as explained by Brooks in his edn, p. 86, n. to line 712.

[41] Penn Szittya, 'The Living Stone and the Patriarchs: Typological Imagery in Andreas Lines 706–810', *JEGP*, 73 (1972), 167–74, considers the image to be a fresco (p. 167).

> ðæt þeos onlicnes   eorðan sece
> wlitig of wage,   ond word sprece,
> secge soðcwidum [. . .].'   (lines 729–33a)

['Now I shall order a sign to be revealed, a miracle to come to pass among the people, that this likeness, beautiful as it is, will seek the earth from the wall, and speak words, talk in true words [. . .].']

Christ asks the likeness to seek the earth, which can be taken in two senses: come down from heaven to the earth, or come down from the wall to the ground. In either case (or both?) the likeness is beautiful and it will speak words, making it as if human. And so the 'wundor' — neuter singular — leaps from the wall and becomes a 'he' in reference:

> Ne dorste þa forhylman   hælendes bebod
> wundor fore weorodum,   ac of wealle ahleop,
> frod fyrngeweorc,   þæt he on foldan stod,
> stan fram stane.   Stefn æfter cwom
> hlud þurh heardne,   hleoðor dynede,
> wordum wemde;   wrætlic þuhte
> stiðhycgendum   stanes ongin. (lines 735–41)

[The venerable ancient work did not dare to disregard the Saviour's order with the result that he stood on the floor, stone from stone. Then a loud voice came through hard (stone), its voice resounded, spoke with words. The action of the stone seemed marvellous to the stubborn people.]

As a work of art ancient from days gone by, the stone figure once again merits the word 'wrætlic', but his ability to speak becomes more important to the narrative as the stone image proceeds to berate the Jewish elders. For their part the high priests, who 'soð ne oncneowan' ('did not recognize the truth'), declare that what they saw and heard was sorcery ('drycræftum', line 765). Again, they see with their own eyes, just as the illiterate might, but cannot read the signs that were given to them. In this passage there is the reverse of positive Gregorian transference when the Jews deny the God of their history and prove themselves a most unresponsive audience. The role of the beautiful or the well-made, as such, here seems secondary. It is a given of the narrative, but has no immediate function beyond the descriptive or ornamental, for there is no particular elaboration of the effects of beauty as in the Ælfric-Augustine passage above. At some level, perhaps, the beautiful stone attracts the eye, but the active role of the beautiful receives no acknowledgment. 'The living stone', as Penn Szittya so ably demonstrates, is one of three biblical images, the others being the Temple of Solomon and the Resurrection of the patriarchs, that make up the typological substratum of this passage.[42] The ekphrastic moment, one may further argue, creates the rhetorical moment that links all three images, for the living stone is a speaking stone as well. As an artistic object that speaks, the stone figure is, in Jean Hagstrum's terms, true ekphrasis.[43]

The second apposite example from Old English poetry is the celebrated, if not outright controversial, passage from *Beowulf* when Hrothgar 'reads' the runes on the hilt (lines 1687–98).[44] This ekphrastic moment is one of the 'twice-told tales' within the poem where an event gets a second telling that recapitulates and amplifies, sometimes with contrarious elements, the first. The hilt first appears when Beowulf is fighting for his life:

> Geseah ða on searwum   sigeeadig bil,
> ealdsweord eotenisc   ecgum þyhtig,
> wigena weorðmynd;   þæt [wæs] wæpna cyst, —
> buton hit wæs mare   ðonne ænig mon oðer
> to beadulace   ætberan meahte,
> god ond geatolic,   giganta geweorc.
> He gefeng þa fetelhilt [. . .].   (lines 1557–63a)

[Then he saw among the armor a victory-blessed blade, an old sword made by giants strong in its edges, the glory of warriors; it was the best of weapons except that it was bigger than any other man might carry it to battle, good and splendid, the work of giants. He grabbed the linked hilt [. . .].]

The poet stresses the sword as a killing machine, so to speak, and its pedigree as heroic, not aesthetic or artistic except for noting that the sword was 'hringmæl' ('patterned', line 1564b). It would be hard to squeeze any significant visual

---

[42] Szittya, 'Living Stone and the Patriarchs'.

[43] Jean H. Hagstrum, *The Sister Arts* (Chicago, 1958), p. 18 n.

[44] See Lerer, *Literacy and Power*, ch. 5: 'Hrothgar's Hilt and the Reader in *Beowulf*' (pp. 158–94), for a master reading in his project to investigate literacy and power. Allen J. Frantzen offers an extended reading of Hrothgar and the hilt in terms of narrative contexts: 'Writing the Unreadable Beowulf: "writen" and "forwritan", the Pen and the Sword', *Exemplaria*, 3 (1991), 327–57 (esp. pp. 342–55). See further Frantzen's *Desire for Origins: New Language, Old English, and Teaching the Tradition* (New Brunswick, 1990), pp. 184–90, and also Michael R. Near, 'Anticipating Alienation: *Beowulf* and the Intrusion of Literacy', *PMLA*, 108 (1993), 320–32, with special reference to 'Hrothgar's Sermon'. In an ensuing *PMLA* Forum, Near's article inspired a response by Frantzen and Gillian R. Overing, which was followed by Near's rejoinder: *PMLA*, 108 (1993), 1177–79. All my *Beowulf* citations are to *Beowulf and the Fight at Finnsburg*, ed. by F. Klaeber, 3rd edn with 1st and 2nd supplements (Boston, 1950); Klaeber's length marks and diacritics are not given in my citations.

meaning out of the passage above. In the recapitulation Beowulf tells his story to Hrothgar and adds some details. Beowulf says that he saw the sword 'on wage […] wlitig hangian' ('hanging on the wall, beautiful', line 1662). One might imagine that the sense of beauty here derives in major part from a sense of relief! Beowulf then gives the hilt to Hrothgar in his hand, which is surely the correct gesture in heroic courtesy. The poet intervenes in the narrative flow by praising the hilt in general terms as 'enta ærgeweorc' ('the old work of giants', line 1679a) and 'wundorsmiþa geweorc' ('the work of wondrous smiths', line 1681a) and by giving a brief précis of the strife with the Grendelkin. Hrothgar is now about to make a speech, which does not come to pass until after the poet takes lines 1687b–98a to describe the hilt in detail and Hrothgar's initial reaction to it. The poet says that Hrothgar 'hylt sceawode' (line 1687b). Bosworth-Toller gives five major meanings involving some idea of 'look' ranging from the simple act to various complex operations as in sense IV, 'inspect, examine, scrutinize'.[45] The *Dictionary of Old English Corpus* lists well over two hundred occurrences of 'sceawian' and its various forms.[46] Klaeber glosses the word as 'look at, view, examine, see, behold' in its nineteen occurrences in the poem.[47] Regarding what Hrothgar 'looked on', Klaeber observes that the ancient strife on the hilt is 'either a graphic illustration (which seems, on the whole, probable) or a runic inscription; both kinds are found together on the famous Franks Casket'.[48] Exactly what cognitive act did Hrothgar perform when the hilt was in his hand? In the Ælfric passage cited at the outset of this paper the two occurrences of the forms of *sceawian* suggest an association with the lowest level of perception, mere looking. Within *Beowulf* the word finds itself in contexts that suggest 'things out of the ordinary'. One 'looks at', for example, gold and treasure (lines 2285, 2744, 2748, 2793, 3075, 3084, and 3104), matters relating to the Grendelkin (for example Grendel's track, lines 132, 840, and 843; his dam's track, line 1391; his hand/claw, line 983; reconnoitring at the pond, line 1413), the dragon (line 2402), the sea-creature shot by an arrow (line 1440), Beowulf dead (line 3008). Perhaps treasure-gazing involves little

---

[45] *An Anglo-Saxon Dictionary*, ed. by Joseph Bosworth and T. Northcote Toller, 2 vols (Oxford, 1882–98), s.v. A sixth sense appears related to the form *gesceawian*.

[46] *Dictionary of Old English Corpus*, s.v. and in related forms.

[47] *Beowulf*, ed. by Klaeber, p. 391, s.v. *sceawian*.

[48] *Beowulf*, ed. by Klaeber, p. 189, n. to lines 1688–98. Frantzen, in 'Writing the Unreadable Beowulf', pp. 344–45, says: 'I propose that we regard the engraved sword hilt as a text, not as a set of pictures (as the usual interpretation of "runes" implies), and furthermore that we attend to the sense of secret mystery or magic that the "stæf" compounds generate.'

perception, but presumably tracking suggests some mental activity just as contemplating a dead Beowulf inspires some emotional reaction. The expression that may offer the closest idiom operating in *Beowulf* is 'hæl sceawedon' (line 204), when Beowulf is ready to set sail to Denmark and where Klaeber offers 'omens'.[49] The point is that Hrothgar does interpret the ancient strife depicted in 'runstafas' on the hilt. The cognitive activity is not *runstafas rædan* but *runstafas sceawian*, and that interpretation allows for an aesthetic dimension:

> Swa wæs on ðæm scennum   sciran goldes
> þurh runstafas   rihte gemearcod,
> geseted and gesæd,   hwam þæt sweord geworht,
> irena cyst   ærest wære,
> wreoþenhilt ond wyrmfah.   (lines 1694–98a)

[And so on the swordguard of bright gold it was properly marked through runestaves, set down, and told for whom that sword, best of irons, was first made, with twisted hilt and serpentine decoration.]

Runes are a third thing along with pictures and letters of the alphabet. Hrothgar does see, praise, read, and understand them, while the poet describes the hilt, especially its gold and its serpentine decoration. The description heightens the rhetorical effect of the passage, signalling its importance.[50] The runes note 'hwam þæt sweord geworht [...] wære' ('for whom/by whom the sword was fashioned'), thus serving a memorializing function.[51] That Hrothgar understands the meaning of what he is 'looking at' receives confirmation from what follows. The hilt prompts Hrothgar to meditate upon glory and Beowulf's achievements, which leads to a consideration of the negative example of Heremod and the celebrated Hrothgar's sermon. Through its design the hilt recalls ancient strife, 'showing it'. Perhaps, unlike Christian art, the runes do not amplify some narrative already known by the viewer but rather communicate the narrative directly (by magic?), but such a reading would need further substantiation. The hilt does become the medium or the occasion for moral teaching, which makes it parallel in formative effect to Christian art on one of Gregory's walls.

---

[49] For example, Bradley renders the expression neutral with '[...] watched for the favorable signs' (*Anglo-Saxon Poetry*, p. 417).

[50] In this effect the ekphrastic moment could be considered as ekphrasis in the manner of classical rhetoric.

[51] In *Beowulf*, ed. by Klaeber, n. to lines 1688–98, p. 191, a dative of agency is ruled out; Klaeber argues instead for a dative of benefit.

This sketch of early medieval art theory and two examples in Old English literature help place *The Dream of the Rood* in an ekphrastic context. *The Dream of the Rood* is the site of the intersection of several themes in early medieval art theory and represents the triumph over some inherent problems. Three of these major themes, traced above, are beauty, narrative, and meaning. Arguably, off these major themes comes a series of related themes and motifs realized in the poem. The most stunning feature of the poem is its immediate aesthetic impact.[52] The use of vision, which serves more to authorize the moral messages contained therein than to allow the suspension of realism (as earlier critics might have argued), invests the transformed Cross with a special beauty as the dreamer describes the gold and the gems that adorn it. The angels that behold the transformed Cross are likewise 'fægere þurh forðgesceaft' ('fair through creation', line 10), which one can also read in part as an epithet transferred from the Cross to the angels. Even though the dreamer is frightened, he can still consider what he views to be fair ('fægran', line 21). The emphasis on light and glory takes on a moral meaning when the dreamer advances the contrast: 'Syllic wæs se sigebeam, ond ic synnum fah [. . .]' ('Wonderful was that tree of victory, and I stained with sins', line 13). In this poem beauty indicates or reflects the moral or beatified state, which may very well be a rare linkage in the theory of early medieval art, and the lack of beauty is associated with sin. The poet has found a meaning or significance for beauty that neither Augustine nor Ælfric seems to wish to advance. The dreamer is furthermore a discerning viewer who through the gold can nevertheless perceive 'earmra ærgewin' ('the former strife of the wretched', line 19). The word used to describe his cognitive act is 'ongytan' (line 18), which generally conveys the sense of 'perceive, see, understand'. Bosworth-Toller (Sense VII, 'ongitan') offer as well 'recognize', as to recognize God's mercy. There is enough ambiguity in the use of 'ongytan' to keep from a confident estimate of its specific meaning here. Does the dreamer have a special way of looking or understanding within his mental faculties or, if 'recognize' means to recall something you somehow have known before, does he remember the story of the Crucifixion when he sees signs of the strife? Has he gone through the four stages that Augustine's proper sign-reader does to advance to understanding? In any case the dreamer does not 'read' (*rædan*) what he views, nor does he 'inspect' (*sceawian*) — assuming that these are separate cognitive

---

[52] Annemarie E. Mahler, '*Lignum Domini* and the Opening Vision of *The Dream of the Rood*: A Viable Hypothesis?', *Speculum*, 53 (1978), 441–59, speaks of 'the possibility of a [. . .] specific relationship between the poem and a particular object. Could the opening vision be an evocation of a reliquary cross, a *staurotheca*?'.

operations. The vision *qua* vision may empower the dreamer to perceive what he perceives, and in this way the transference of moral meaning takes place.

When the Cross begins to talk, the poem becomes more narrative than descriptive, thus fulfilling the Gregorian prescription for the function of art, 'scientiam historiae colligere'. The Cross tells its history from its perspective, which ranges from before biblical events, through them, and past them to moral history now and to Doomsday and the end of time. No doubt, any believing Christian would surely know the major points on this moral timeline, but many of the non-biblical specifics and even some of the devotional points could conceivably be new information grafted on to antecedent knowledge that the poem's audience might bring. In proper apocryphal mode the Cross 'fills in' the story of the Crucifixion, one of the defining moments in moral history. The conceit of a talking cross is doubly effective. The straightforward historical exposition makes the Cross almost human, which is arresting enough rhetorically, but the Cross is also an object of veneration raised to religious art. Its narration becomes in effect its own *titulus*,[53] describing what the dreamer is presumably perceiving as art (as if on the walls) and offering the more or less full *historia* that explains all that is seen. The visual and the verbal have a unique congruence in this poem, where the visual/material is embodied in words. The boundaries between the various kinds of 'seeing' or 'reading' or 'perceiving' become fluid as the poem becomes a record of mystical experience.

Just as the talking Cross has a double effect rhetorically, there is as well a double *titulus*. The 'Epilogue' (lines 122–56) functions as a second, morally directing *titulus*, outside of the vision and in the moral now, which explains the application of that vision to Christian life and conduct. For the dreamer the Cross is the familiar object of veneration, which can lead the dreamer to personal salvation. The effective 'caption' relates the saving power of the Cross and inspires the hope of the viewer in that saving power. The dreamer hopes that the Lord's rood will take him to eternal bliss. The dreamer describes his relation to the Cross: 'þe ic her on eorðan ær sceawode [. . .]' ('which I here on earth previously looked at', line 137). The use of *sceawian* in this ekphrastic context, as the discussion of

---

[53] See Elizabeth C. Teviotdale, 'Latin Verse Inscriptions in Anglo-Saxon Art', *Gesta*, 35 (1996), 99–110, who identifies some nineteen paintings and drawings in seven manuscripts, one carved stone, and one engraved portable altar which constitute the corpus of Latin inscriptions. In pp. 107–08, n. 4, she identifies these Old English *tituli*: a stone slab in Ipswich (E. Okasha, *Hand-List of Anglo-Saxon Non-Runic Inscriptions* (Cambridge, 1971), pp. 66–67); Oxford, Bodleian Library, MS Junius 11; the Franks Casket; and of course, the Ruthwell Cross.

Beowulf above suggests, has to be charged with more meaning than 'see' or 'behold'.[54] The connotation that the word must carry is 'the viewing of something outside of the ordinary'. For the poem's audience this caption-epilogue offers a devotional meaning to what the members of the audience must have seen and (heard) read. It is no prosaic afterword or homiletic afterthought, but rather an integral part of the viewing experience. The conventions of *ekphrasis*, as early medieval art practice and theory indicate, confirm the importance of the caption-epilogue as the means to ensure the successful transference of the meaning of this artistic, indeed mystical, experience.

Bede's comments on Old Testament/New Testament typology (as cited above) and the importance of compunction in the experience of viewing the Cross incorporate affective piety or, simply, emotion in the artistic experience. Other early medieval discussions of art, its effects, and its characteristics, certainly as adduced in this paper, do not particularly concern themselves with the emotional temper of the ekphrastic experience. In *The Dream of the Rood*, however, the dreamer is 'hreowcearig' ('sorrowful', line 25), all creation 'weop' ('wept', line 55), Christ and his *beornas* are respectively 'meðe' ('weary', lines 65, 69), *beornas* begin 'sorhleoð galan' ('to sing a song of sorrow', line 67), Christ and his Cross stood '[h]reotende' ('weeping', line 70), the dreamer experiences 'langung-hwila' ('times of longing', lines 126) — as if the general narration of the Crucifixion would need such specific reference and elaboration. The poet has thus gone beyond the art theory of his time, such as it was, to allow for human emotion. As John Burrow has reminded us, Emile Mâle demonstrates how Christ as the Suffering Servant and strong emotion are phenomena of the later Middle Ages, but *The Dream of the Rood* is an early exception to this general formulation.[55]

Ultimately, this paper suggests the triumph of art over criticism or, more sharply, ekphrasis and the experience of the verbal description of the visual over the discursive formulation of any particular ekphrastic moment. The comments made here and there in the early Middle Ages about art and its teaching function emphasize content over formal considerations, which is in line with the general anti-rhetorical position of the Church Fathers found, for example, in *De doctrina christiana*. How art teaches is something of a mystery except that it helps the

---

[54] As per Swanton in his rev. edn of *The Dream of the Rood*, p. 148, s.v.

[55] John Burrow, 'An Approach to *The Dream of the Rood*', *Neophilologus*, 43 (1959), 123–33 (pp. 123–24); repr. in *Old English Literature: Twenty-two Analytical Essays*, ed. by Martin Stevens and Jerome Mandel (Lincoln, 1968), pp. 253–67 (pp. 253–54). Jane Roberts reminds me that *Christ III* and several Vercelli Homilies manifest strong emotion.

viewer recall something already known. A given image needs its verbal explanation through *tituli* or perhaps by someone present and before the image to explain it. The attraction of the beautiful object may be a part in any illustrative example of the ekphrastic moment, but the function of beauty in general is underdescribed at best, as is any possible emotional reaction. In *The Dream of the Rood* the poet overcomes the problems inherent in any theories. The choice of the vision genre allows for the appearance of the speaking Cross of Christ, which teaches directly by narrating the Crucifixion in a detailed and nuanced account. The glorified Cross is an object of beauty, and that beauty takes on a moral meaning by contrast with the sin-stained dreamer. Beauty finds function in *The Dream of the Rood*. The Epilogue furthermore directs the audience to the meaning of the verbal-visual experience, as a proper *titulus* would. When the dreamer uses 'sceawian' to describe his cognition of the Lord's rood, his word choice may be pointing to the special way necessary to understand the extraordinary verbal-visual artefact. 'Reading' and 'seeing' do not convey, separately or together, the special act of understanding that the poet has described and explained and that in turn explains the full power of *The Dream of the Rood*.

THE DREAM OF THE ROOD AND GUTHLAC B AS A LITERARY CONTEXT FOR THE MONSTERS IN BEOWULF

Frederick M. Biggs

I have been arguing recently in a series of essays that many details in *Beowulf* may be seen as contributing to a single theme, a contrast in two models of succession, one reflecting an older Germanic system in which many members of a broadly defined kin-group may contend for the throne, the other espousing newer Christian ideals in which the candidates are restricted primarily to sons.[1] Breca, Unferth, Ecgtheow, Hondscioh, Æschere, the thief, Wiglaf, the female mourner, and, of course, Beowulf himself have all, among others, gotten tied up in the argument.[2] Yet I find whenever I try to explain this idea, I inevitably turn back to the monsters, confirming perhaps J. R. R. Tolkien's view that the poet has placed them at the centre of the work:[3] as images of fratricide and revenge, Grendel and his mother represent the likelihood that in the earlier system kin-violence will erupt at the death of a king; and a solitary hoarder of treasure, the dragon,

---

[1] 'The Naming of Beowulf and Ecgtheow's Feud', *Philological Quarterly*, 80 (2001), 95–112; 'Beowulf's Fight with the Nine Nicors', *Review of English Studies*, n.s., 53 (2002), 311–28; 'Hondscioh and Æschere in *Beowulf*', *Neophilologus*, 87 (2003), 635–52; 'Beowulf and Some Fictions of the Geatish Succession', *Anglo-Saxon England*, 32 (2003), 55–77; and 'The Politics of Succession in *Beowulf* and Anglo-Saxon England', *Speculum*, 80 (2005), 709–41.

[2] My current project is a re-examination of the historical, as opposed to the fictional, characters in the work.

[3] '*Beowulf*: The Monsters and the Critics', *Proceedings of the British Academy*, 22 (1936), 245–95. This essay has been reprinted many times, including in *Beowulf: A Verse Translation*, trans. by Seamus Heaney, ed. by Daniel Donoghue (New York, 2002), pp. 103–30.

calls attention to the greater possibility that a royal line may, with its own dire consequences, die out later. In this essay, following the lead of the scholar honoured in these pages,[4] I would like to suggest that monastic, meditative reading provides a possible source for the construction and reception of a work such as I propose *Beowulf* to be, even if the poem's interest is in politics rather than theology.

To turn, however, to *The Dream of the Rood* (the only possible choice once Éamonn has been invoked) is to nod first towards an at least partially secular tradition since many critics have sought to explain the speaking cross at its centre by referring to Anglo-Saxon *Riddles*.[5] While some may be wary of taking too seriously what is properly the domain of hobbits, these poems reveal a delight in challenging their audiences to sort through their clues to arrive at unexpected answers, although at times the focus shifts from simply discovering solutions (or distinguishing between proper and improper ones) to understanding some more essential meanings of the objects.[6] The conventional 'saga hwæt ic hatte' turns to reflection. It is not surprising, especially when remembering the manuscript context of the Exeter Book for these works, that a number of the shorter, enigmatic Old English poems, especially *Wulf and Eadwacer*, *The Husband's Message*, and *The Ruin*, have been aligned with this tradition.[7] The warning, then, is that a strategy of constructing poems that encourages their audiences to look beyond a

---

[4] See, for example, 'Cynewulf's Epilogue to *Elene* and the Tastes of the Vercelli Compiler: A Paradigm of Meditative Reading', in *Lexis and Texts in Early English: Studies Presented to Jane Roberts*, ed. by Christian J. Kay and Louise M. Sylvester, Costerus New Series, 133 (Amsterdam, 2001), pp. 187–201. Writing specifically on *Beowulf*, Éamonn has warned that 'it is dangerous to propose any single "theme" as the controlling principle of the poem', and so concentrates instead on its structure and the thematic concerns that are evident in its design; 'Structure and Thematic Development in *Beowulf*', *Proceedings of the Royal Irish Academy*, 66C (1967), 1–51 (p. 2). The following remarks are offered in the hope that they may contribute to this debate.

[5] See Margaret Schlauch, '*The Dream of the Rood* as Prosopopoeia', in *Essays and Studies in Honor of Carleton Brown* (New York, 1940), pp. 23–34; and, for further bibliography, *The Dream of the Rood*, ed. by Michael Swanton, new edn, Exeter Medieval Texts and Studies (Exeter, 1996), pp. 67, 79–92; quotations of the text will be from this edition, omitting long marks on vowels; translations are my own. Citing Peter Orton, Éamonn writes, 'the *Dream* reveals a mystery by means of a theological riddle': *Ritual and the Rood: Liturgical Images and the Old English Poems of the 'Dream of the Rood' Tradition* (London, 2005), p. 332.

[6] See Jonathan Wilcox's entry, 'Riddles, Old English', in *The Blackwell Encyclopaedia of Anglo-Saxon England*, ed. by Michael Lapidge and others (Oxford, 1999), pp. 393–94.

[7] See Anne L. Klink, *The Old English Elegies: A Critical Edition and Genre Study* (Montreal, 1992), pp. 25–26.

first, literal meaning may not be solely monastic but rather part of a wider literary culture.

In any case, there can be little doubt, as the scholarship of Éamonn and others has shown,[8] that *The Dream of the Rood* engages in a meditative reading to a particularly high degree. Although Éamonn, arguing that the poem is primarily devotional, has cautioned against considering it as taking part in the complex theological debate on Christ's nature outlined by Rosemary Woolf,[9] one of Woolf's ideas, relevant to the thesis of this essay, has won wider approval in later scholarship: the poet identifies the cross with Christ's human nature.[10] Woolf develops this idea by noting that 'The Cross not only experiences the extremities of pain but, having within itself the power to escape them, endures with a reluctance heroically subdued'.[11] Thomas D. Hill has offered a liturgical source for this insight in the Easter ritual of removing the cross from the altar on Good Friday and placing it, as described in the *Regularis concordia*, in a 'sepulchre' 'in imitation as it were of the burial of the Body of our Lord Jesus Christ'.[12] Moreover, James W. Earl has suggested that this identification explains Christ's silence in the poem as consonant with 'His ineffable transcendence' and contributes to our understanding of the speaking cross.[13] Even if the poet has not depicted the Rood as he has to make a precise theological point about the joining of God and man in Christ, by allowing the cross to embody Christ's humanity, he creates an occasion

---

[8] Indeed Éamonn has distinguished several different moments when the work can be seen as being read in this way; see 'How Did the Vercelli Collector Interpret *The Dream of the Rood*?', in *Studies in English Language and Early Literature in Honour of Paul Christophersen*, ed. by P. M. Tilling, Occasional Papers in Linguistics and Language Teaching, 8 (Coleraine, 1981), pp. 63–104; 'The Ruthwell Crucifixion Poem in its Iconographic and Liturgical Contexts', *Peritia*, 6–7 (1987–88), 1–71; and *Ritual and the Rood*. See also Susan Irvine, 'Adam or Christ? A Pronominal Pun in *The Dream of the Rood*', *Review of English Studies*, n.s., 48 (1997), 433–47.

[9] See 'How Did the Vercelli Collector', p. 98 and n. 70.

[10] 'Doctrinal Influences on *The Dream of the Rood*', *Medium Ævum*, 27 (1958), 137–53 (pp. 149–51); see also Michael J. Swanton, 'Ambiguity and Anticipation in "The Dream of the Rood"', *Neuphilologische Mitteilungen*, 70 (1969), 407–25; and *The Dream of the Rood*, ed. by Swanton, p. 69.

[11] 'Doctrinal Influences', p. 149.

[12] 'The Cross as Symbolic Body: An Anglo-Latin Liturgical Analogue to *The Dream of the Rood*', *Neophilologus*, 77 (1993), 297–301 (pp. 298–99).

[13] 'Trinitarian Language: Augustine, *The Dream of the Rood*, and Ælfric', forthcoming in *Source of Wisdom: Old English and Early Medieval Latin Studies in Honor of Thomas D. Hill*, ed. by Charles D. Wright, Frederick M. Biggs, and Thomas N. Hall.

for meditation that would presumably have been as rewarding for its original audience as it is for our own.

I would like to contribute to this discussion by noting that the structure of the Rood's speech reinforces Woolf's point by at times approximating the account of a human life, and specifically by patterning this life on Christ's; indeed by the end of the speech the abstract pattern takes precedence over even the details of Christ's triumph. The argument that comes closest to the points I would like to offer is developed by George S. Tate in support of his provocative claim that the rhetorical trope at the centre of this poem is chiasmus, which he finds specifically in the line, 'Rod wæs ic aræred. Ahof ic ricne Cyning' ('A Cross, I was set up. Raised I the great king', line 44).[14] A crossing pattern within a poem on the cross is a remarkable example of abstract thinking — Tate calls it 'a sort of rhetorical metaphor' — perhaps too good to be true.[15] In any case, Tate's argument leads him to note other specific correspondences between the Rood's 'life' and Christ's.[16] One detail, however, that he overlooks is that simply by beginning its speech by referring to its own origin, the Rood aligns its story with human biography:

> Þæt wæs geara iu,   (ic þæt gyta geman),
> þæt ic wæs aheawen   holtes on ende,
> astyred of stefne minum.   (lines 28–30a)

[That was long ago (I still remember it) that I was cut down at the end of the wood, removed from my root.]

Here, however, is a riddle: the cross is born at the moment when the tree from which it will be made is cut down. If the poet suggests that this is in some way

---

[14] 'Chiasmus as Metaphor: The "Figura Crucis" Tradition and "The Dream of the Rood"', *Neuphilologische Mitteilungen*, 79 (1978), 114–25. Tate acknowledges that the term 'chiasmus' 'does not appear in medieval rhetorical or grammatical handbooks', but argues that 'the late Latin transliteration of the Greek name tying the figure to X was merely a culmination of what was sensed all along' (p. 116).

[15] 'Chiasmus', p. 115. Although listing this article in his bibliography, Swanton does not mention Tate's claim in his note on line 44; *The Dream of the Rood*, ed. by Swanton, p. 119. Tate supports his idea further by discussing examples of acrostic arrangement in poems on the cross. See also Martin Irvine, 'Anglo-Saxon Literary Theory Exemplified in Old English Poems: Interpreting the Cross in *The Dream of the Rood* and *Elene*', *Style*, 20 (1986), 157–81; repr. in *Old English Shorter Poems: Basic Readings*, ed. Katherine O'Brien O'Keeffe (New York, 1994), pp. 31–63 (p. 55).

[16] 'Chiasmus', pp. 124–25.

similar to the saint, whose 'nativity' is celebrated on the day of his martyrdom,[17] the spiritual is near the surface right from the beginning of the speech.

As Tate and others note, the correspondences between the Rood and Christ are strongest in the depiction of the Crucifixion. First the cross is set up on a hill (line 33); then Christ ascends it (line 40). The Rood mentions only that it was pierced with nails and wounded ('Þurhdrifan hi me mid deorcan næglum; on me syndon þa dolg gesiene'; line 46: 'they pierced me with dark nails; in me the wounds are visible'), but notes that both are mocked ('Bysmeredon hie unc butu ætgædere'; line 48a: 'they mocked us both together'), and that it is covered with Christ's blood ('Eall ic wæs mid blode bestemed, | begoten of þæs guman sidan'; lines 48b–49a; 'I was covered completely with blood poured out from the man's side'). The cross and Christ appear as one: 'Crist wæs on rode' (line 56b; 'Christ was on the Rood'). Yet the Rood's account then separates them emphasizing Christ's deposition and burial (lines 57–69). It first describes the making of the sepulchre:

> Ongunnon him þa moldærn wyrcan
> beornas on banan gesyhðe;   curfon hie ðæt of beorhtan stane,
> gesetton hie ðæron sigora Wealdend.   (lines 65b–67a)

[Men then made a tomb for him in the sight of his slayers; they carved it from bright stone, and set therein the Lord of victories.]

It then stresses Christ's death by depicting a scene of mourning:

> Ongunnon him þa sorhleoð galan,
> earme on þa æfentide;   þa hie woldon eft siðian
> meðe fram þam mæran þeodne;   reste he ðær mæte weorode. (lines 67b–69)

[The sorrowful ones sang, then, a lament for him in the evening, when they, exhausted, wished to travel again from the great lord; he rested there with a small host.]

Moreover, while the Rood and the two other crosses stand weeping, Christ's 'corpse, the fair dwelling of the spirit, grew cold' ('hræw colode, | fæger feorgbold'; lines 72b–73a). It is only in the final lines of the narrative that the pattern is completed, but here remarkably with no reference to Christ's resurrection:

> Þa us man fyllan ongan
> ealle to eorðan;   þæt wæs egeslic wyrd!
> Bedealf us man on deopan seaþe.   Hwæðre me þær Dryhtnes þegnas

---

[17] See Jean-Charles Picard's section 'Des origines ou 9e siècle', in the entry on 'Saints' in the *Dictionnaire de Spiritualité*, ed. by Marcel Viller and others, 16 vols in 22 and Tables générales (Paris, 1937–95), XIV, 203–12 (p. 205).

> freondas gefrunon, ...
> gyredon me   golde ond seolfre. (73b–77)

[Then we all were cut down to the earth; that was a terrible fate! We were buried in a deep pit. Nevertheless the Lord's thanes heard of me there ... they adorned me with gold and silver.]

Like Christ, the Rood is taken down and buried, but in a breathtaking leap of some three hundred years, only it is raised up and glorified at the time of its rediscovery by Constantine's mother, Helena.[18] The Rood's story of its life ends at line 77 with Christ, presumably, still in the grave.[19]

The poet's strategy, it appears to me, is to force his audience to make the next step, to fill in the point of crucifixion, the resurrection. He does so by moving beyond the literal story to its abstract meaning: the pattern of death and resurrection established by the cross is itself so powerful that Christ's resurrection is present even though not mentioned. Indeed, if, as John V. Fleming has argued, the poet uses 'the thematic intimacy between Christ and His Cross' 'to bridge the gap between Christ and the Dreamer',[20] it may also resonate with the dreamer's concern for his sins at the start of the poem (lines 13b–14a and 21b) and his hope for salvation at the end (lines 135b–44a). Moreover, this device also allows the poet to tie the two parts of the work dramatically together. In the final lines, the dreamer turns from his eschatological reflections back to the harrowing of hell:

> Si me Dryhten freond,
> se ðe her on eorþan   ær þrowode
> on þam gealgtreowe   for guman synnum.
> He us onlysde   ond us lif forgeaf,
> heofonlicne ham.   Hiht wæs geniwad
> mid bledum ond mid blisse   þam þe þær bryne þolodan.

---

[18] The story is of course told elsewhere in the Vercelli Book in *Elene*.

[19] The break in the poem at this point has been noted by many readers, and is marked rhetorically by the Rood's address to the dreamer, 'Nu ðu miht gehyran, hæleð min se leofa; [...]' (line 78; 'Now you may understand, my dear man [...]'). See *The Dream of the Rood*, 4th edn by Bruce Dickens and A. S. C. Ross (London, 1954), who claim that the end of the poem (from line 78) is 'definitely inferior' (p. 18). Woolf speculates that the end may be a later addition; 'Doctrinal', p. 153, n. 34. See also Janet Duthie Collins, '*The Dream of the Rood*: An Internal Analysis', *LACUS Forum*, 26 (2000), 331–42. The differences she notes, however, may be the result of different subjects and styles of the two parts rather than evidence for their having been composed by different poets.

[20] '"The Dream of the Rood" and Anglo-Saxon Monasticism', *Traditio*, 22 (1966), 43–72 (p. 53).

> Se Sunu wæs sigor fæst   on þam siðfate,
> mihtig ond spedig,   þa he mid manigeo com,
> gasta weorode,   on Godes rice,
> Anwealda ælmihtig,   englum to blisse
> ond eallum ðam halgum   þam þe on heofonum ær
> wunedon on wuldre,   þa heora Wealdend cwom,
> ælmihtig God,   þær his eðel wæs. (lines 144b–56)

[May the Lord, who previously suffered here on earth on the gallows-tree for the sins of men, be to me a friend. He freed us and gave us life, a heavenly home. Hope was renewed with glory and bliss for those who suffered there. The Son, the almighty sovereign, powerful, and successful, was victorious on that journey, when he came with a great host of souls into God's kingdom, a joy to the angels and to all the holy ones who previously dwelled in glory in heaven, when their ruler, almighty God, came to his homeland.]

Far from being inappropriate,[21] these lines not only recall the heroic depiction of Christ in the Rood's speech, but also complete its story of the crucifixion. Of course, in the same way that the finding and adorning of the cross by Helena can celebrate Christ's resurrection, the harrowing points to the Last Judgement.

At the centre of *The Dream of the Rood*, then, is this complicated literary construct, the cross, that modern readers (and presumably Anglo-Saxon ones as well) may have found at first unsettling, but through a gradual process of scholarly debate (a modern form of monastic, meditative reading) have come to appreciate. Some of our respect for the work, I would suggest, derives precisely from the aptness of the construct to the theme: the gallows-tree seems a perfect image of fallen human nature redeemed by Christ's sacrifice. This is a remarkable poem, and yet to suggest that this technique is not exclusive to it, I would like to recall briefly an argument I have made about the poet's use of the saint's servant and sister in *Guthlac B*.[22]

In contrast to its Latin source, Felix's *Vita sancti Guthlaci*,[23] where the saint's servant and sister are clearly called Beccel and Pega, the Old English poem leaves the two nameless, suggesting that they represent concepts rather than people.[24]

---

[21] *The Dream of the Rood*, ed. by Albert S. Cook (Oxford, 1905), p. xlii; and *Dream*, ed. by Dickins and Ross, p. 18. For other explanations, see J. A. Burrow, 'An Approach to *The Dream of the Rood*', *Neophilologus*, 43 (1959), 123–33 (p. 132); and Fleming, '"The Dream of the Rood"', p. 68.

[22] 'Unities in the Old English *Guthlac B*', *JEGP*, 89 (1990), 155–65.

[23] *Felix's Life of Saint Guthlac*, ed. and trans. by Bertram Colgrave (Cambridge, 1956).

[24] For an opposing view, see Phyllis R. Brown, 'Beccel and the Theme of Death in *Guthlac B*', *Mediaevalia*, 19 (1996 for 1993), 273–97. While her interpretation is possible, neither the passages she cites nor the poem as a whole convince me that the poet uses the servant as she suggests.

Indeed, the poet develops his source to identify the servant after Guthlac's death with the saint's lifeless body, and his sister with the hope of the final reunification of the body and soul at the end of time. To cite just one example of each point, after the saint has died, the servant travels to his sister, but having delivered his message, he turns from her without any further direction:

> 'Ic sceal sarigferð
> heanmod hweorfan hyge drusendne . . .' (lines 1378b–79)[25]

['I, sorrowful and abject, must turn with drooping heart . . .']

The poem breaks off here with the image of a grieving, aimless servant who is in the same position as Guthlac's body, abandoned after the departure of its soul. Yet the message he has delivered from Guthlac promises that the sister and saint will be reunited in heaven:

> '[. . .] ⁊ þe secgan het
> þæt git a mosten in þam ecan gefean
> mid þa sibgedryht somud eard niman,
> weorca wuldorlean, willum neotan
> blædes ⁊ blissa.' (lines 1370b–74a)

['[. . .] and commanded [me] to say to you that the two of you are permitted to dwell together in the homeland, in the eternal bliss, with the peaceful band, [and] enjoy at will the glorious rewards of deeds, glory, and joy.']

As James L. Rosier has noted, these words promise that saint and sister will be together, 'somud', just as body and soul were previously.[26] *Guthlac B*, then, not only tells the story of the saint's death, but reflects on both the meaning of death itself, the separation of body and soul, and its ultimate conquest by using two ciphers, the servant and sister. While a servant seems a fitting expression of the saint's forsaken body, the sister appears a more potent symbol of its final reunion with the soul since by her gender she recalls Eve, through whom, as the poet has explained at the start of the work (lines 812–78b), death — the separation of body and soul — entered the world.

With these examples in mind, it seems reasonable to consider whether Grendel, Grendel's mother, and the dragon function in a similar way in *Beowulf*. Certainly,

[25] *The Guthlac Poems of the Exeter Book*, ed. by Jane Roberts (Oxford, 1979).

[26] 'Death and Transfiguration: *Guthlac B*', in *Philological Essays: Studies in Old and Middle English Language and Literature, in Honour of Herbert Dean Meritt*, ed. by James L. Rosier (The Hague, 1970), pp. 82–92 (p. 88).

Christian elements have long been recognized in the work,[27] and indeed a substantial amount of recent criticism has considered an important theological point: the poet's belief in the salvation or damnation of his main character and others in the historically pagan world in which he sets the poem. Yet while informative, this discussion has remained, for me at least, inconclusive, suggesting that it probably is not an issue that the poet hoped to address in his work.[28] It is also revealing that largely missing from this debate is a consideration of the roles of the monsters in the work. Even Andy Orchard, who has argued that the ultimate damnation of the main character, caused by his falling into the sin of pride, can be seen in his becoming like the monsters he fights, discusses monstrosity in general rather than these particular ones.[29] Indeed any argument for an exclusively Christian interpretation of the monsters seems doomed by Oliver F. Emerson's perception of a sharp difference between Grendel and his mother, with their religious associations, and the dragon, which has no biblical pedigree.[30]

Instead I would like to propose that the poet links Grendel and Grendel's mother to the kin of Cain, not to establish their reality in the minds of his audience, but rather to make us realize that they are fictional, and as such contribute to the theme of kin-violence associated with his Germanic model of succession. Since Dorothy Whitelock argued that 'the strongest evidence of all for belief in monsters' by the poet and his contemporaries appears in the work itself where 'it was found necessary to fit them into a Christian universe',[31] a number of scholars have looked for sources to validate the claim that Grendel and his mother descend

---

[27] For an overview with bibliography, see Edward B. Irving, 'Christian and Pagan Elements', in *A Beowulf Handbook*, ed. by Robert E. Bjork and John D. Niles (Lincoln, 1996), pp. 175–92. See also Paul Cavill, 'Christianity and Theology in *Beowulf*', in *The Christian Tradition in Anglo-Saxon England*, ed. by Paul Cavill (Cambridge, 2004), pp. 15–39.

[28] Two papers by equally learned scholars, Fred C. Robinson ('The Tomb of Beowulf') and Thomas D. Hill ('The Christian Language and Theme of *Beowulf*'), that reach opposing conclusions can be found reprinted in *Beowulf: A Verse Translation*, ed. by Donoghue, pp. 181–97 and 197–211.

[29] *Pride and Prodigies: Studies in the Monsters of the Beowulf-manuscript* (Cambridge, 1995), pp. 169–71. See also Christine Rauer who, while uncovering much useful information about dragons in hagiography, does not finally connect these traditions to the poem: *Beowulf and the Dragon: Parallels and Analogues* (Cambridge, 2000).

[30] 'In the later case, no single phrase or descriptive epithet applied to the firedrake can be tortured into any connection with devils, or creatures of evil in the Christian sense': 'Legends of Cain, Especially in Old and Middle English', *PMLA*, 21 (1906), 831–929 (p. 882).

[31] *The Audience of Beowulf* (Oxford, 1951), p. 76.

from Cain, with the most recent detailed survey appearing in Orchard's *Pride and Prodigies*. Here Orchard discusses several traditions that might contribute to a belief in post-diluvian giants, including the Hiberno-Latin *Reference Bible*, the Middle Irish *Duan in Cóecait Cest*, the Middle Irish *Sex aetates mundi* as well as a number of biblical passages that mention giants after the Flood and patristic and Anglo-Saxon elisions of biblical and classical giants.[32] Yet while it is possible that the *Beowulf*-poet knew one or more of these or similar traditions,[33] it is more likely that he would have known the Bible itself.[34] Genesis 7. 22 states that God destroyed all living things except those on the Ark: 'et cuncta in quibus spiraculum vitae est in terra mortua sunt' ('and all things wherein there is the breath of life on the earth, died').[35] While the descendants of Cain may be the source of pre-diluvian giants according to the common interpretation of the opening verses of chapter 6 of Genesis known in Anglo-Saxon England,[36] all would have died in the Flood. Indeed, while Orchard does, in his *Critical Companion to Beowulf*, provide a reference to his earlier discussion of the 'post-diluvian survival of giants and monsters', he writes: 'presumably, the *Beowulf*-poet is applying strict logic to the biblical tale: if the Flood was sent to destroy monstrous creatures, then the only ones who could survive were those who inhabited watery depths'.[37] Yet rather than challenging the Bible by suggesting that some of God's enemies escaped

---

[32] *Pride and Prodigies*, pp. 67–84.

[33] Ruth Mellinkoff admits that we 'cannot explain the poet's belief in terms of influence from a specific tradition, let alone a specific text': 'Cain's Monstrous Progeny in *Beowulf*: Part II, Post-Diluvian Survival', *Anglo-Saxon England*, 9 (1981), 183–97 (p. 197).

[34] He mentions the story of the Flood in lines 1687–93.

[35] Quoted from the *Biblia Sacra iuxta vulgatam versionem*, editio minor, ed. by Robert Weber (Stuttgart, 1984), but adding punctuation to the text. The translation is from the *Holy Bible; translated from the Latin Vulgate [. . .] the Old Testament first published [. . .] at Douay [. . .] and The New Testament first published [. . .] at Rheims* (Dublin, 1867). This point is also made in the surrounding verses, 21 and 23.

[36] See Augustine, who associates the 'sons of God' and the 'daughters of men' (Genesis 6. 2) with the descendants of Seth and Cain, respectively; *De civitate Dei* 15.23, ed. by Bernhard Dombart and Alfons Kalb, CCSL, 48 (Turnhout, 1955), pp. 489–90. This connection also appears in Bede's *Libri quatuor in principium Genesis usque ad nativitatem Isaac et eiectionem Ismahelis adnotationum*, ed. by Charles W. Jones, CCSL, 118A (Turnhout, 1967), p. 99; and Alcuin's *Interrogationes*, 96, *PL*, 100, 526. See also Ruth Melinkoff, 'Cain's Monstrous Progeny in *Beowulf*: Part I, Noachic Tradition', *Anglo-Saxon England*, 8 (1979), 146–47; and Orchard, *Pride and Prodigies*, p. 76.

[37] *A Critical Companion to 'Beowulf'* (Cambridge, 2002), p. 139.

destruction, the poet, I would argue, has used the stories from Genesis to indicate to his audience that these monsters are not in fact real.[38]

This possibility, that the poet refers to the Bible not to support but rather to deny the reality of his monsters, may allow us to see a reason for the ambiguity in his first description of Grendel. Here he does not, as he will later (lines 1255b–76a), establish a relationship of kin between his monster and Cain:

> [. . .] wæs se grimma gæst   Grendel haten,
> mære mearcstapa,   se þe moras heold,
> fen ond fæsten;   fifelcynnes eard
> wonsæli wer   weardode hwile,
> siþðan him Scyppend   forscrifen hæfde
> in Caines cynne — þone cwealm gewræc
> ece Drihten,   þæs þe he Abel slog;
> ne gefeah he þære fæðe,   ac he hine feor forwræc
> Metod for þy mane   mancynne fram.
> Þanon untydras   ealle onwocon,
> eotenas on ylfe   ond orcneas,
> swylce gigantas,   þa wið Gode wunnon
> lange þrage;   he him ðæs lean forgeald. (lines 102–14)[39]

[[. . .] that grim spirit was named Grendel, the famous wanderer who dwelt in the moors, the fen and stronghold; for a long time the unhappy man lived in the land of monsters after the Lord had proscribed him among Cain's kin — the eternal Lord avenged that killing in that Cain slew Abel; he [Cain] did not rejoice in that act of violence, but he, the Ruler, drove him away from mankind because of that crime. From that all the evil progeny were born, giants and elves and monsters, such giants as fought against God for a long time; he repaid them the reward for that.]

Rather than having been born into Cain's family, Grendel is forced to live among them after having been banished by God because of some crime he has committed, making him like Cain rather than related to him. This distinction also encourages the audience to interpret the chronology more loosely. Although strictly speaking, if Grendel lived among Cain's kin, he should have died in the Flood, if he, at some

---

[38] I have argued that he makes much the same point by including two versions of the competition with Breca. Unferth's account, which does not mention sea beasts, provides the core of what happened: Breca won a swimming race, a fact Beowulf confirms in his account with his descriptions of how each returned to land. Yet Beowulf includes monsters in his version, not to add more facts, but rather to comment on the significance of the action. See 'Beowulf's Fight'.

[39] References are to *Beowulf and the Fight at Finnsburg*, ed. by F. Klaeber, 3rd edn with 1st and 2nd supplements (Boston, 1950).

later time, is merely like Cain, then his 'reward' may also be similar — God's ven-
geance through Beowulf.

In contrast, then, to Whitelock's argument that the poet's inclusion of material from Genesis reveals his unquestioning belief in the reality of the monsters
he describes, I would argue that it shows him using stories from the Bible for his
own purpose. The association of Cain as the slayer of his own brother, a point that
he repeats (lines 1255b–76a), is significant to him because it reflects the problem
that he confronts in the Danish court, the likelihood of kin-violence's eruption
at the moment of succession. This is among the problems looming in the future
for the Danes, if one accepts Frederick Klaeber's interpretation that, in lines
1013–19, 1162b–68a, 1180b–87, and 1228–31, 'the poet intimates with admirable subtlety' that following Hrothgar's death, his nephew Hrothulf probably
'usurped the throne'.[40] Grendel's mother enters her son's conflict with Hrothgar
by avenging his death (lines 1255b–58a and 1276b–78), and yet the poet uses her,
and specifically her gender, to broaden his theme: as a woman she is at the centre
of kin relationships, which, while holding out the promise of strengthening a
people, seem too often to lead to violence. Around her the poet develops not only
Wealhtheow's doomed attempts to protect her sons,[41] but also Hildeburh's sorrow over the deaths of her brother and son (lines 1071–75).[42] Indeed, Beowulf's
account of Freawaru's failed marriage (lines 2020–31), itself linked to the burning
of Heorot (lines 82b–85), allows this theme to echo later in the poem. While
these two monsters hardly suggest a great host of contenders vying for the throne
at a king's death,[43] simply by placing them in a kin relationship — a mother and

---

[40] *Beowulf*, ed. by Klaeber, p. xxxii. Kenneth Sisam contests this interpretation; *The Structure
of Beowulf* (Oxford, 1965), pp. 80–82. His view, however, has not been widely accepted; see, for
example, Fred C. Robinson, 'History, Religion, Culture: The Background Necessary for Teaching
Beowulf', in *Approaches to Teaching 'Beowulf'*, ed. by Jess B. Bessinger, Jr, and Robert F. Yeager
(New York, 1984), pp. 107–22; repr. with an afterword, in Robinson, *The Tomb of Beowulf and
Other Essays on Old English* (Oxford, 1993), pp. 36–51 (p. 38). See also Thomas D. Hill, 'The
Confession of Beowulf and the Structure of *Volsunga Saga*', in *The Vikings*, ed. by Robert T.
Farrell (London, 1982), pp. 165–79 (pp. 174–75).

[41] See John M. Hill, 'The Economy of Honour', in *The Cultural World in Beowulf*, Anthropological Horizons, 6 (Toronto, 1995), pp. 85–107; and Stephanie Hollis, '*Beowulf* and the
Succession', *Parergon*, n.s., 1 (1983), 39–54.

[42] Her husband is also killed (lines 1146–53).

[43] The poet's description of the evil progeny that descend from Cain (lines 111–14a) suggests
a larger, more threatening group.

a son[44] — the poet evokes the strong and yet often complicated bonds that can lead to violence, and thus they stand for the dangers in the Danish court.

In contrast, the dragon is solitary, and so complements the changed perspective on succession in the final part of the poem. Although primogeniture was never the norm even in late Anglo-Saxon England, Christianity, with its emphasis on legitimate marriage, could have been perceived even from an early date as restricting the pool of candidates eligible to succeed and as emphasizing the rights of a king's direct heir.[45] The poet, I would argue, supports this change and yet he explores weaknesses in this newer system as well, asking the audience to consider what might happen if there is no eligible son to take the throne. Restricting the possible successors too much may have its own dangers, which the dragon embodies. It finds its hoard after the death of the last of a people who had owned it (lines 2236b–41a), and this treasure is finally buried with Beowulf (lines 3163–68), an apt image for the Geats, who seem to face imminent destruction at the poem's end because Beowulf has no son. Beowulf needs Wiglaf to defeat the dragon, and yet passing the kingdom to him would be disastrous because his armour would mark him for Swedish revenge (lines 2611–25a); in any case, he disappears from the end of the poem.[46] The dragon's threat is its singleness, a counterpart for the solitary king unable provide a successor, and so it is appropriate that in its rage after the theft the dragon destroys Beowulf's own home, the throne of the Geats (lines 2324–27a).

While it remains to be seen if these particular suggestions about the monsters in *Beowulf* are accepted by modern readers, Éamonn's work on specifically religious poems, such as *The Dream of the Rood*, may remind us of the possible sophistication of its original audience. That audience, I believe, would have been as surprised at first as we are by Grendel, Grendel's mother, and the dragon, and yet as they puzzled over the work, the poet's choices may have become clearer. A cross, a servant, a sister, two of Cain's kin, and a dragon may all be starting points for reflection even if the directions some lead may be to political, not religious, truths.

---

[44] Hrothgar's assertion that Grendel's father is unknown (lines 1355b–57a) contributes to the theme.

[45] I discuss this point in more detail in 'Politics of Succession'.

[46] I have developed this point in 'Beowulf and Some Fictions'.

THE SOLITARY JOURNEY:
ALONENESS AND COMMUNITY IN *THE SEAFARER*

Hugh Magennis

In his classes on *The Seafarer* in the late 1960s, I remember that Éamonn Ó Carragáin taught us two things in particular about the poem: one concerned the integrity and coherence of its text, even though the edition we were using, in *Sweet's Anglo-Saxon Reader*, relegated the closing sixteen lines to the notes at the end of the book;[1] the other thing he stressed — influenced especially, as he was quick to acknowledge, by Dorothy Whitelock's landmark article on the subject — was the centrality of the idea of Christian exile to the meaning of the poem.[2] Much has changed in approaches to *The Seafarer* since those days, but these two perceptions about the poem still provide an important foundation for its interpretation. Éamonn's inspirational teaching of this poem and others was what stimulated my dedication to Old English literature in the first place, and I am delighted to contribute to this volume in his honour by revisiting one of the poetic masterpieces to which he introduced me.

As is now universally accepted, *The Seafarer* is a religious poem which urges the necessity of rejecting the vain pleasures of the world and working to attain eternal

---

[1] *Sweet's Anglo-Saxon Reader in Prose and Verse*, 15th edn, rev. by Dorothy Whitelock (Oxford, 1967), p. 277. This dismemberment of the poem is also reflected in one of the teaching resources widely used today, Kevin Crossley-Holland, *The Anglo-Saxon World: An Anthology* (Oxford, 1984); see p. 56.

[2] Dorothy Whitelock, 'The Interpretation of *The Seafarer*', in *The Early Cultures of North-West Europe: H. M. Chadwick Memorial Studies*, ed. by C. Fox and B. Dickins (Cambridge, 1950), pp. 259–72; repr. in *Essential Articles for the Study of Old English Poetry*, ed. by Jess B. Bessinger and Stanley J. Kahrl (Hamden, 1968), pp. 442–57; also in *Old English Literature: Twenty-two Analytical Essays*, ed. by Martin Stevens and Jerome Mandel (Lincoln, 1968), pp. 198–211.

happiness in heaven. It is one of a number of poems on related religious themes in the Exeter Book, comprising *The Wanderer*, *Resignation*, and *The Riming Poem* as well as *The Seafarer* (all commonly also placed in the larger group of Old English 'elegies'),[3] and it can be usefully contextualized by reference to these other poems, as the present essay (I hope) illustrates. I argue that *The Seafarer* is to be distinguished in key respects from the other poems mentioned here, but there are also markers in them of a common approach. Like the other poems, for example, in presenting its Christian message *The Seafarer* exploits images and ideas inherited from the world of secular Old English verse,[4] images and ideas to do with heroic striving and with the communal life associated with the hall and its cherished activities. In *The Seafarer* these ideas and images are transformed, remade, in a context of the renunciatory recognition, urgently expressed in the poem, that life in this world is a dead life and that our true home is elsewhere. The heroic ideals of fame and reputation, familiar from *Beowulf* and other Old English secular poems, are reinterpreted in *The Seafarer* in spiritual and eschatological terms to refer to the striving of the individual for *eternal* glory. The individual (each person) should work while on earth

> þæt hine ælda bearn   æfter hergen,
> ond his lof siþþan   lifge mid englum
> awa to ealdre,   ecan lifes blæd,
> dream mid dugeþum.   (lines 77–80a)

[that the children of men may afterwards praise him, and that his esteem may live afterwards among the angels, for ever and ever, the glory of eternal life, joy among the hosts.]

---

[3] As in the collection edited by Anne L. Klinck, *The Old English Elegies: A Critical Edition and Genre Study* (Montreal, 1992); Klinck's book, now widely regarded as definitive, also includes *Deor*, *Wulf and Eadwacer*, *The Wife's Lament*, *Riddle 60*, *The Husband's Message*, and *The Ruin*. In the present study, citations of and references to Old English poems other than *The Seafarer* follow The Anglo-Saxon Poetic Records [ASPR], ed. by George Phillip Krapp and Elliott Van Kirk Dobbie, 6 vols (New York, 1931–53); references to *The Seafarer* are to *The Seafarer*, ed. by Ida Gordon, rev. with a Bibliography by Mary Clayton (Exeter, 1996); translations of Old English poems are my own. For *The Wanderer*, *Resignation*, and *The Riming Poem*, see *The Exeter Book*, ASPR, 3, pp. 134–37, 215–18, and 166–68, respectively.

[4] See, for example, S. B. Greenfield, 'Attitudes and Values in *The Seafarer*', *JEGP*, 51 (1954), 15–20; Peter Orton, 'Form and Structure in *The Seafarer*', *Studia Neophilologica*, 63 (1991), 37–55; repr. in *Old English Literature: Critical Essays*, ed. by R. M. Liuzza (New Haven, 2002), pp. 353–80; Graham Holderness, 'From Exile to Pilgrim: Christian and Pagan Values in Anglo-Saxon Elegiac Verse', in *English Literature, Theology and the Curriculum*, ed. by Liam Gearon (London, 1999), pp. 63–84.

The rewards of Christian heroic striving are in heaven. And the only *community* that matters is not that of the earthly hall, as celebrated in secular tradition, but is the heavenly community with its transcendent hall joys: *dream mid dugeþum*.

Abstracted from the poem, the unworldly message of *The Seafarer* sounds stern indeed. In the poem, however, it is a message expressed with considerable human warmth and understanding and with a spiritual assurance that is eager and even joyful, rather than stern. The human warmth and understanding come across in the lyric tone with which worldly pleasures, which the poem clear-sightedly rejects, are acknowledged. Alluding to the joys of the hall, the speaker juxtaposes what he ironically refers to as the 'entertainment' (*gomen*) of the kind of desolate seascape he has experienced with attractive social images of laughter and drinking:

> Hwilum ylfete song
> dyde ic me to gomene,   ganetes hleoþor
> ond huilpan sweg   fore hleahtor wera,
> mæw singende   fore medodrince. (lines 19b–22)

[Sometimes I took the song of the swan for my entertainment, the sound of the gannet and the noise of the curlew instead of the laughter of men, the gull singing instead of the drink of mead.]

And later on he pauses tellingly over evocations of the very things that he insists do *not* preoccupy the person setting out on the solitary sea-journey:

> Ne biþ him to hearpan hyge   ne to hringþege —
> ne to wife wyn   ne to worulde hyht —
> ne ymbe owiht elles   nefne ymb yða gewealc. (lines 44–46)

[His thought is not on the harp or on the receiving of rings; nor is his pleasure in woman or his joy in worldly things; nor is his thought about anything else except the rolling of the waves.]

Now it is interesting that included among worldly things here are not only the music of the harp and the receiving of rings, social joys associated with the hall, experienced by men together, but also the more private pleasure experienced by a man with a woman. The phrase *to wife wyn*, in its emphasis on the personal feelings of the man himself, does not even present the pleasure as mutual or shared, whereas the joys of the hall are by definition shared. One of the major developing concerns of the poem, and one which I wish to explore in this essay, is to do with the opposition between individual and communal experience, and between physical and cultural experience. The passage quoted just above is one of the places in *The Seafarer* where the individual, physical dimension is foregrounded in the speaker's thoughts. It is also highlighted in the description of the personal discomfort

endured by the seafarer in the opening lines and (as discussed further, below) in
the chilling image of the coming of death later on (lines 94–96).

The joyful spiritual quality that I have mentioned is apparent at the end of the
poem, though it is foreshadowed in the speaker's description of the beauties of
spring, when the person eager in mind is compelled by the attraction of the sea:

> Bearwas blostmum nimað,   byrig fægriað,
> wongas wlitigað,   woruld onetteð;
> ealle þa gemoniað   modes fusne,
> sefan to siþe   þam þe swa þenceð
> on flodwegas   feor gewitan. (lines 48–52)

[The woods take on blossoms, settlements become fair, fields brighten, the world quick-
ens; all these things urge the one eager in mind, the heart to the journey, in one who
thinks to venture on the paths of the sea.]

The speaker himself passionately experiences this attraction, associating it with
the joys of the Lord, which are 'hotter' ('hatran') — more intense — for him than
the dead, transitory, life on land, a life that is renounced in the poem:

> For þon nu min hyge hweorfeð   ofer hreþerlocan,
> min modsefa   mid mereflode,
> ofer hwæles eþel   hweorfeð wide,
> eorþan sceatas,   cymeð eft to me
> gifre ond grædig;   gielleð anfloga,
> hweteð on hwælweg   hreþer unwearnum
> ofer holma gelagu,   for þon me hatran sind
> Dryhtnes dreamas   þonne þis deade lif
> læne on londe.   (lines 58–66a)

[And so my mind now journeys in my breast, my spirit with the sea-flood, journeys widely
over the whale's domain, the expanses of the earth, and comes back to me yearning and
eager; the lone-flyer cries out, urges the heart irresistibly onto the whale-road and over the
waters of the ocean, for the joys of the Lord are hotter to me than this dead life, transitory
on land.]

Despite the hardship of the life of striving that the poem portrays, *The Seafarer*
embraces renunciation gladly, with a sense of appreciation of the pleasures being
given up but also a conviction that the voyage being embarked upon brings joy of
an entirely different and more satisfying order. And the poem ends with a rhetorically heightened appeal, inviting the audience to share in heroic striving, which
is presented as an honour ('geweorþade') granted by the Lord:

> Uton we hycgan   hwær we ham agen,
> ond þonne geþencan   hu we þider cumen;
> ond we þonne eac tilien   þæt we to moten

in þa ecan   eadignesse
þær is lif gelong   in lufan Dryhtnes,
hyht in heofonum.   Þæs sy þam Halgan þonc
þæt he usic geweorþade,   wuldres Ealdor
ece Dryhten,   in ealle tid.

Amen. (lines 117–end)

[Let us think where we may have our home, and then let us reflect how we may come
there; and let us then also work that we may be permitted to enter into that eternal
blessedness, where is the source of life in the love of the Lord, joy in heaven. For this,
thanks be to the Holy One that he has honoured us, the Prince of glory, the eternal Lord,
for all time. Amen.]

Through renunciation *The Seafarer* moves to a triumphant vision of love and joy
in these rhapsodic closing lines, which take on their full meaning only in the
defining context of the poem as a whole. And even in these lines themselves the
sense of heavenly joy is associated with the responsibility of striving while on
earth: the insistent use of the subjunctive mood in the verbs *agen, cumen, tilien,*
and *moten* underscores this responsibility. Heaven is not where we have our home
but where we *may* have our home, if we work towards it.

Also insistent in these closing line is the use of the first person plural pronoun
(*we* six times; *usic* once), directly relating the speaker and his addressees to the possibility of heaven. The movement of *The Seafarer* overall is from a preoccupation
with the individual physical and mental experience of the speaker, endured alone,
to an image of spiritual community in heaven. The speaker begins with a concentration on his personal life of hardship, which is presented in passive terms: things
happen to the speaker rather than being willed by him (*þrowade*, 'I suffered', line
3; *gebiden hæbbe*, 'I have experienced', line 4; *bigeat*, 'occupied [me]', line 6; *slat*,
'tore [me]', line 11; *bidan sceolde*, 'I had to remain', line 30; etc.). In recounting his
experience, he uses the language of emotional distress — he has felt *bitre breost-
ceare* ('bitter sorrow of heart', line 4), and sorrows have lamented hotly around his
heart ('ceare seofedun | hat' ymb heortan', lines 10–11) — and he also uses the
language of individual sense perception, as when he mentions the intense cold
which he felt in his feet (lines 8–22) and the hunger which tore at him from
within (lines 11–12), and that he 'heard' (*gehyrde*) the sea resounding (lines
18–19) and the birds shrieking (lines 19–22).

Above all, the emphasis on individual experience is highlighted by the insistent
use of the first person singular pronoun, forms of which occur five times in the
first nine lines and are sprinkled throughout the first half of the poem, but do not
reappear after line 66. And the specifying adjective *sylf*, 'self', used along with the
pronoun, appears in line 1 and then again at the key transition point when,

despite his previous experience, the speaker expresses his resolution to venture on the high seas (line 35). The speaker does not portray himself in his seafaring as a member of a crew or group who have endured things together but as a separate entity, enduring alone. It is not '*we* heard the sea resounding' but '*I* heard the sea resounding'. The speaker knows the sea and has often been on it, but he says nothing about other people being with him. Indeed, the only other person alluded to in the first part of the poem is the representative figure with whom the speaker contrasts himself, the 'landsman', who has no idea about the sea. The only companions the speaker acknowledges are the birds, and their bleak calls are what he hears instead of the laughter of men. He may or may not have had other people with him on his voyages, but if he had, their presence was not significant, as the hardship of those voyages was essentially experienced alone.

The speaker does not portray himself as one of a group of people together, sharing experience on his voyages. Nor, however, does he portray himself as wanting to belong to such a group, at least on earth. There are lingering images of the joys of society, but the speaker does not envy the landsman, and he does not look to society for relief from the cares he feels, which are most intensely those of physical and mental suffering. The feeling of loneliness is not highlighted in the overwhelming way that it is in two other religious 'elegies' of the Exeter Book, *The Wanderer* and *Resignation*.[5] It is not even said that when the speaker embarks on

---

[5] In *The Wanderer* the theme of exile provides the whole motivation for the speaker throughout the first half of the poem. This speaker is overwhelmed by the thought of his solitariness and he dreams of the social joys he once knew:

Þinceð him on mode   þæt he his mondryhten
clyppe ond cysse,   ond on cneo lecge
honda ond heafod,   swa he hwilum ær
in geardagum   giefstolas breac.
Ðonne onwæcneð eft   wineleas guma,
gesihð him biforan   fealwe wegas,
baþian brimfuglas,   brædan feþra,
hreosan hrim ond snaw,   hagle gemenged. (lines 41–48)

[It seems to him in his mind that he embraces and kisses his lord, and on his knee lays hand and head, just as at times beforehand in former years he had enjoyed gifts from the throne. Then he awakens again, a friendless man, sees before him the grey waves, sea-birds bathing and spreading their feathers, frost and snow falling, mixed with hail.]

The imagined and remembered social scenes seem all the brighter in contrast with the bleak reality of the speaker's present situation. But *The Wanderer* goes on to generalize from and meditate upon individual experience, a development that leads to the salutary perception that the quest for community on earth is a fruitless one and to the homiletic message that longed-for security lies elsewhere.

his longed-for spring voyage he will actually be going alone. But, as with his previous voyages, the presence or absence of others is not significant. Aloneness in *The Seafarer* is not a personal misfortune but an existential fact.

After the key transition of lines 33–38, which look forward to the voyage in spring, use of the first person singular is continued for a time, but from this point on the speaker also generalizes from his own individual experience, using the indefinite third person singular. He observes that there is no man so fortunate in the world that he should not have anxiety about his *sæfor* ('sea-voyage', line 42), and in the third and final mention of the landsman it is stated that this figure does not know what some people — not just the speaker — suffer on the paths of exile:

> Þæt se beorn ne wat,
> sefteadig secg,   hwæt þa sume dreogað
> þe þa wræclastas   widost lecgað. (lines 55b–57)

[That person does not know, the man blessed with comfort, what those suffer who direct their exiled tracks over the widest distance.]

After line 66, application of the first person singular is discontinued altogether, to be replaced by the indefinite third person singular and by pronoun phrases conveying totality and inclusion. Now, reference is to people in general through the use of the phrases *eorla gehwam* ('each of men', line 72), *monna gehwylc* ('every person', lines 90 and 111), *se þe* ('he who', lines 106 and 107), and *mon* ('person, one', line 109), and the focus on the speaker's own story disappears. The indefinite third

---

The speaker in *Resignation* (considered here as one poem), who has lived a life of poverty and hardship, relates that in his wretchedness he is driven from his homeland ('ic afysed eom | earm of minum eþle', lines 88–89) and says that the lone-dweller, 'a friendless exile' ('wineleas wræcca'), cannot endure longer when the Lord is angry with him:

> Ne mæg þæs anhoga,
> leodwynna leas,   leng drohtian,
> wineleas wræcca,   (is him wrað meotud). (lines 89b–91)

[Nor can the lone-dweller, deprived of the joys of society, endure for longer, the friendless exile (the Lord is angry with him).]

To the speaker in *Resignation* the world is an unloving place, where he has experienced rebuff and where the lone-dweller (such as himself) finds his misery increased by other people, enduring wounding words (lines 94–96). The speaker of *Resignation* seems to look to an end of exile, when he will return home, though he also declares dejectedly that he cannot love anyone in his homeland either:

> ic for tæle ne mæg
> ænigne moncynnes   mode gelufian
> eorl on eþle.   (lines 106b–08a)

[Because of calumny I cannot love in my mind anyone of the human race in my homeland.]

person has the effect of presenting experience as both individual — something undergone by people 'singularly', one at a time — and also common to everyone.

The speaker of *The Seafarer* sees himself as essentially alone but is aware that his predicament is not unique, either as a seafarer or as a human being. The insight upon which the whole development of the poem is based is that each person living in the world is essentially a separate entity who lives life alone. From this perspective, every man *is* an island (to coin a phrase). The blandishments of earthly community are really distractions from the fact of aloneness, and must be rejected as wholly unfulfilling. The poem is about the journey — which *is* fulfilling — which through an act of will and self-determination every individual needs to make in the light of this perception of aloneness. *The Seafarer* urges its audience to share this perception and to act appropriately in consequence. It moves from passive experience to active striving (*þenceð*, 'intends, is minded to', line 51; *hweorfeð*, 'turns', lines 58, 60; *gewyrce*, 'accomplish, bring about', line 74; *stieran*, 'steer, control', line 109; etc.), and in doing so it moves from individual to communal. In its closing, inclusive, appeal to its audience it adopts the first person plural pronoun, thereby implicitly constructing a spiritual community in which speaker and audience participate. Despite its rejection of ideas of community, therefore, *The Seafarer* is itself in its urgent address an expression of community. The lived experience of the seafarer is solitary, but in communicating this experience and using it to teach others the speaker engages in a communal act. And the application of the indefinite third person singular, suggestive of generality, links not only the speaker but also the audience with an imagined larger constituency beyond the text.

Each person lives life alone and will face death alone. A stark passage, which occurs as the poem draws to its conclusion, depicts a human body when old age comes upon it and then when life leaves it:

> Yldo him on fareð,   onsyn blacað,
> gomelfeax gnornað,   wat his iuwine,
> æþelinga bearn   eorþan forgiefene.
> Ne mæg him þonne se flæschoma,   þonne him þæt feorg losað,
> ne swete forswelgan   ne sar gefelan,
> ne hond onhreran   ne mid hyge þencan. (lines 91–96)

[Old age overtakes him, his face grows pale, the grey-haired one laments, knows that his friends of former days, the sons of noblemen, have been given over to the earth. Then, when life fails him, his body will not be able to swallow up sweetness or feel pain or stir a hand or think with the mind.]

This passage presents the epitome of the poem's remarkable emphasis on the individual and the physical, which had been evident right from the opening lines — 'be me sylfum' ('about myself', line 1). All communal experience in this world fades away in the face of the overwhelming physical reality of death, which afflicts the individual. Social loss, as represented here in the deaths of old friends, *iuwine* (line 92) — the word is found only here — is overtaken by physical loss, as the body itself fails. These friends who have died had been the sons of noblemen: the reference to them suggests the intimacy of friendship combined with associations of the good life of noble companionship. In their absence the old person is left alone, as death approaches.

As I have pointed out elsewhere, while Old English poetry is concerned centrally with ideals of cultural life, *The Seafarer* in its contemplation of death in the present passage focuses unblinkingly on the physical rather than the cultural basis of human life in the world.[6] It presents death as the extinguishing of individually experienced pleasure and pain. Life is pared down to its essentials, which are identified not as communal enterprises and activities but the basic functions of eating, moving, and thinking. Particularly striking in the quoted passage is the phrase *swete forswelgan*, 'to swallow up sweetness', in which the ingesting of food or drink is alluded to (a rare occurrence indeed in Old English poetry), and in which it is the physical rather than cultural nature of partaking in food or drink that is specified. *Swete forswelgan* portrays an image of taking rather than sharing, an image focussing on and combining individual sensation (*swete*) and eager physical consumption (*for-swelgan*, in which the prefix suggests the entirety or voraciousness of the action).[7] In my previous discussion of the passage, I stressed that this is an image which '"embodies" individual experience, and indeed possession, of the world (as feeling pain "embodies" impotence in the world), as that which is desirable is eagerly absorbed into the body'.[8] Here I wish to relate this point to the *poem's* preoccupation with the individual and the physical in human life. As death approaches in this passage, the old person's sorrow about the loss of earthly community gives way to concentration on the facts of sensation and consciousness.

And in the context of impending death, even issues of gender drop out of consideration. The language of the poem generally is strongly male in its orientation. The images of seafaring, of heroic striving for glory and reputation (see especially lines 72–80), and of a communal life centred on the warrior society of the hall, with its drinking and fellowship, are images of male life. Even the mention of the

---

[6] Hugh Magennis, *Anglo-Saxon Appetites: Food and Drink and their Consumption in Old English and Related Literature* (Dublin, 1999), pp. 127–28.

[7] See *Dictionary of Old English*, ed. by Angus Cameron and others (Toronto, 1986–; CD Rom edition, A–F, Toronto, 2003), s.v. *forswelgan*.

[8] *Anglo-Saxon Appetites*, p. 128.

pleasure experienced with a woman (line 45) is from a male perspective. The message of the poem may be applicable to women as well as men, but the life it vividly portrays is male, and its language, inherited from Germanic tradition, relates to the world of male experience, constructing a male discourse very different, for example, from that of the Old English poems with female speakers.[9] The discourse of *The Seafarer* remains markedly male, even in its image of the heavenly hosts (*dugeþum*, line 80), but in the face of death itself there is neither male nor female, as the basic functions of eating, moving, and thinking fail.

Other Old English poems, particularly those expressing the popular early medieval 'soul and body' trope, present salutary images of the body in death.[10] Poems such as *Judgement Day I* and *Soul and Body*[11] show the physical reality of death, describing bodily decay and disintegration in gruesome detail. This theme is present, with a strongly personal dimension, in one of the 'elegies' mentioned above in relation to *The Seafarer, The Riming Poem*:

> Me þæt wyrd gewæf,   ond gewyrht forgeaf,
> þæt ic grofe græf,   ond þæt grimme græf
> flean flæsce ne mæg,   þonne flanhred dæg
> nydgrapum nimeþ,   þonne seo neaht becymeð
> seo me eðles ofonn   ond mec her eardes onconn.
> Þonne lichoma ligeð,   lima wyrm friteþ,
> ac him wenne gewigeð   ond þa wist geþygeð,
> oþþæt beoþ þa ban   * * * an. (lines 70–77)

[Fate wove that for me and condemned me to that deed, that I should dig a grave [for myself]; and my flesh cannot escape that grim grave, when the arrow-swift day seizes me in its inescapable grips, when the night comes and grudges me my homeland and mocks

---

[9] On the latter, see Patricia A. Belanoff, 'Women's Songs, Women's Language: *Wulf and Eadwacer* and *The Wife's Lament*', in *New Readings on Women in Old English Literature*, ed. by Helen Damico and Alexandra Hennessey Olsen (Bloomington, 1990), pp. 193–203; Belanoff, '*Ides . . . geomrode giddum*: The Old English Female Lament', in *Medieval Woman's Song: Cross-Cultural Approaches*, ed. by Anne L. Klinck and Ann Marie Rasmussen (Philadelphia, 2002), pp. 29–46, 214–18; Helen T. Bennett, 'Exile and the Semiosis of Gender in Old English Elegies', in *Class and Gender in Early English Literature: Intersections*, ed. by Britton J. Harwood and Gillian R. Overing (Bloomington, 1994), pp. 43–58.

[10] See Rudolph Willard, 'The Address of the Soul to the Body', *PMLA*, 50 (1935), 975–83; T. A. Shippey, *Poems of Wisdom and Learning in Old English* (Cambridge, 1976), pp. 29–36; Douglas Moffat, *The Old English Soul and Body* (Woodbridge, 1990); Magennis, *Anglo-Saxon Appetites*, pp. 120–22.

[11] See ASPR, 3, pp. 212–15 (*Judgement Day I*); *The Vercelli Book*, ASPR, 2, pp. 54–59, and ASPR, 3, pp. 174–79 (*Soul and Body I* and *II*).

my dwelling-place here. Then the body will lie; the worm will eat my limbs, but will experience joy and partake in the feast, until only bones remain.]

Though they describe the physical reality of death, *The Riming Poem* and these other poems are not interested in emphasizing the physical reality of life, as *The Seafarer* is. They incite fear of death by juxtaposing images of earthly vanity to lurid depictions of post-mortem decomposition. *The Seafarer* is not about inciting fear of death but about instilling understanding of what life essentially is, and of the necessity of living life accordingly. *The Seafarer* does have the 'soul and body' theme of the uselessness of wealth from the perspective of the grave (lines 97–102), but it focuses not on the bodily decomposition of death but the inertness of death and the separateness of the individual in death.

The universality of the experience of old age and death is indicated in the poem by the use of the pronoun phrase conveying totality *monna gehwylc* ('every person', lines 90, 111). *The Seafarer* had begun with the preoccupation of the *ic*, 'I', with the facts of sensation and consciousness, as experienced by him. In its contemplation of the coming of death, the *ic* of the speaker's individual personal experience in life has merged into and been replaced by the inclusive, but unspecific, third person singular form.

In the closing lines a final shift of pronoun occurs, the first person plural (*Uton we*, etc.) being adopted, as the poem addresses its audience directly in what is its peroration. It has been suggested[12] that *The Seafarer* ends with 'the language of prayer'; if so, the first person plural pronoun makes it the language of communal, 'synactic', rather than private prayer.[13] In this respect, the speaker of *The Seafarer* is unlike that of *The Dream of the Rood*, say, who prays, in the singular, 'Si me dryhten freond' ('May the Lord be my friend', line 144), etc., or that of *Resignation*, whose tone is personal throughout: 'helpe min se halga dryhten' ('Help me holy Lord', line 2). And there is no direct address of the divinity in *The Seafarer*, the elements of prayer being appended, doxology-like, to the poem's larger rhetorical pattern.

The first person plural is also a definitive form of address at the conclusion of homilies, and by its use at the end of *The Seafarer*, especially accompanied as it is by the exhortatory marker *Uton* (line 117), the poem implicitly announces itself

---

[12] Klinck, *Old English Elegies*, p. 232.

[13] See Sarah Larratt Keefer, '"Ic" and "We" in Eleventh-Century Liturgical Verse', in *Unlocking the Wordhord: Anglo-Saxon Studies in Memory of Edward B. Irving, Jr*, ed. by Mark C. Amodio and Katherine O'Brien O'Keeffe (Toronto, 2003), pp. 123–46 (see esp. pp. 124–25).

as a homiletic discourse. There are two main ways in which the first person plural is used in Old English homilies. In her discussion of what she calls the 'positional rhetoric' of the Old English homilies, Mary Swan rightly distinguishes between a 'singular' sense of 'we', in which the speaker signals his separateness from and superiority over the audience — a 'royal' 'we', so to speak — and an inclusive sense of 'we', through which a common identity between speaker and audience is constructed.[14] To refer to two of Swan's examples from Ælfric's *Catholic Homilies*, the former is illustrated in statements like 'We sædon eow hwene ær [. . .]' ('We told you a little while ago [. . .]');[15] the latter in statements like 'Ac we sceolon witan [. . .]' ('but we must know [. . .]').[16] Both uses can be seen as rhetorical manoeuvres, with the former essentially meaning 'I', but depersonalized and implicitly aligning the speaker with a higher, institutional, authority, and the latter, on one level, meaning 'you', but playing down the distance between speaker and audience. The dichotomy between the two uses of 'we' is not absolute, however; in particular, it is clear that even when a speaker is being 'inclusive' there is still, integral to the dynamics of the discourse, an underpinning of institutional authority, a sense of the speaker representing a community larger than himself. Inclusive 'we', underpinned by this institutional authority, is particularly effective at the conclusion of homilies.

The phrase *Uton we* encapsulates the complex positional dynamics of homiletic discourse, as deployed at the end of *The Seafarer*. It both identifies the speaker with the audience, being an inclusive, first-person-plural formulation, and it distinguishes him from them, since it assumes a role of communal leadership, expressing an imperative, in the form of an invitation. As explained above, the poem renounces the idea of earthly community, the only community that matters being in heaven, but in its concluding homiletic address *The Seafarer* constructs a new idea of community on earth, in which the speaker invites his audience to participate, which indeed can be seen as foreshadowing the blessed community of heaven.

The use of the first person plural at the end of *The Seafarer* is given particular prominence by the context of the strongly personal tone of the earlier part of the poem. *The Seafarer* ends like a homily, but homilies proper — certainly medieval

---

[14] Mary Swan, 'Performing Christian Identity in Old English Preaching', paper delivered at the International Medieval Congress, University of Leeds, 2003: forthcoming publication.

[15] *Ælfric's Catholic Homilies: The Second Series: Text*, ed. by Malcolm Godden, EETS, SS, 5 (Oxford, 1979), XV (pp. 150–60), line 191.

[16] *Ælfric's Catholic Homilies: The Second Series*, ed. by Godden, XV, line 280.

ones — do not normally have a strongly personal dimension, since the speaker of a homily (even indeed when using the first person *singular*) speaks not for himself but in an institutional role. It would be unusual for homilies proper to have a strongly personal dimension, but such a dimension is apparent not only in *The Seafarer* but in two other religious poems of the Exeter Book, *The Wanderer* and *The Riming Poem*. Structurally, *The Seafarer*, *The Wanderer*, and *The Riming Poem* all move, in one way or another, from an account of personal experience, evoked in lyrical terms, to a general homiletic message, directly expressed in the closing lines. By their exploitation of this structure of lyric first-person-singular 'story' into homiletic exhortation, as by other features of their composition,[17] these poems identify themselves, in my view, as belonging to a particular literary sub-genre. A fourth text sometimes associated with them is *Resignation*, but the latter does not have the development from personal to homiletic. *Resignation* presents the most sustained personal utterance of any of these religious elegies, and some of its imagery, notably the journey motif, recalls that of *The Seafarer*. *Resignation* lacks the specific characteristics of the other three poems, however, and, though we might regard it as a 'potential' homiletic discourse, it is really a personal prayer.

In *The Seafarer*, *The Wanderer*, and *The Riming Poem* the homiletic message is given direct expression in the use of the first person plural at the end of the texts. These poems also make exhortatory use of the indefinite third person singular, a feature also of prose homilies. The indefinite third person refers both to representatives of a 'class' — for example, the seafarer (*The Seafarer*) or the wise man (*The Wanderer*) or the *eadig*, 'blessed person' (*The Riming Poem*) — and also to people in general: 'Til biþ se þe his treowe gehealdeþ' ('Good is he who keeps his faith', *The Wanderer*, line 112); 'Eadig biþ se þe eaþmod leofaþ' ('Blessed is he who lives humbly', *The Seafarer*, line 107).

The first person plural is authoritative, but it is also, in a homiletic context, the most inclusive form of address. The first person plural can be *exclusive*, of course ('*We* are not like *them*'), but its normal use in homilies is in terms of the relationship between speaker and audience, rather than serving to distinguish speaker and audience from some other group.[18] By comparison, the second person plural ('*I*

---

[17] See Klinck, *Old English Elegies*, pp. 231–33.

[18] There is some use of the 'exclusive' first person in Wulfstan's *Sermo Lupi ad Anglos*, for example, in which the speaker distinguishes between 'us' and heathens and between 'us' and Gildas's Britons: see *Sermo Lupi ad Anglos*, 2nd edn by Dorothy Whitelock (London, 1952), lines 26–36, 184–211.

am not like *you* people') represents a more oppositional and admonitory rhetorical choice, and while it occurs widely in Old English homilies, it is not favoured in their perorations. It does not appear in our homiletic poems in the Exeter Book.

The Seafarer carries the personal dimension further than the other poems under consideration. The sense of inclusiveness with which it ends is constructed from a starting point which appreciates the separateness of each individual in the world. The poem's acceptance of separateness and its exploration of the implications of separateness are among the features which contribute to the distinctiveness of *The Seafarer*, even among the religious elegies of the Exeter Book, with which in other ways it has much in common.

There has been much discussion in this essay of ideas to do with the individual and the self, ideas of personal feeling and experience. It has been put about that such ideas were invented only in the early modern period, or in the twelfth century.[19] Surely the Anglo-Saxons should not have been having such thoughts, whether in *The Seafarer* or in other texts where individuals seem to appear? But they *were* having them, though it has to be said that there are not many texts from the period where such ideas are in evidence. It *is* unusual for literary works from Anglo-Saxon England to express a developed interest in individual experience, but some of them do — most strikingly, I would suggest, the poem under consideration here.

Peter Lucas has also discussed the topic of individual experience with reference to *The Seafarer*.[20] He writes of the individualistic theme of spiritual quest in the poem, relating this to the elements of personal development and movement. As Lucas points out, such elements have been associated with literature of the twelfth century and later,[21] but their presence in *The Seafarer* is unmistakable, as in the

---

[19] Harold Bloom goes as far as to credit Shakespeare with the invention of the human: see his book *Shakespeare and the Invention of the Human* (London, 1999); see also Walter Ullmann, *The Individual and Society in the Middle Ages* (Baltimore, 1966); Colin Morris, *The Discovery of the Individual 1050–1200* (London, 1972) and also his 'Individualism in Twelfth-Century Religion: Some Further Reflections', *Journal of Ecclesiastical History*, 31 (1980), 195–206; Caroline Walker Bynum, 'Did the Twelfth Century Discover the Individual?', *Journal of Ecclesiastical History*, 31 (1980), 1–17.

[20] Peter J. Lucas, 'The Language of the Loner: From Splendid Isolation to Individual in Early English Poetry?', in *Text and Gloss: Studies in Insular Learning and Literature Presented to Joseph Donovan Pheifer*, ed. by Helen Conrad O'Briain, Ann Marie D'Arcy, and John Scattergood (Dublin, 1999), pp. 102–18.

[21] Lucas, 'Language of the Loner', pp. 103–04; see R. Southern, *The Making of the Middle Ages* (London, 1953), pp. 209–44; Morris, *Discovery of the Individual*, pp. 121–38.

poem longing for God is translated into 'self-motivated action that results in seeking the Lord in heaven'.[22] Other Old English scholars too have traced an interest in the experience of the individual in the poetry, notably Peter Clemoes, in a wide-ranging study that includes discussion of *The Wanderer* (but not *The Seafarer*) and other poems demonstrating awareness of the self,[23] and Fiona and Richard Gameson, whose essay on *Wulf and Eadwacer* and *The Wife's Lament* pointedly includes in its title the phrase 'The Discovery of the Individual in Old English Verse', a reference to Colin Morris's influential book *The Discovery of the Individual 1050–1200*.[24] The Gamesons identify the speakers of *Wulf and Eadwacer* and *The Wife's Lament* as 'individuals who give utterance to very personal expressions of powerful emotions'.[25]

Debates about when the individual was discovered can easily become sterile, since participants in them may not agree about definitions of key terms (Caroline Walker Bynum prefers to speak not about the discovery of the individual but about the discovery of the self);[26] taken in their own terms there is usually truth in the conflicting claims that are made. But it is noticeable that Old English literature has largely been excluded from such discussions. As indicated above, I would not wish to overstate the extent of preoccupation with concerns to do with the individual in pre-Conquest England but I welcome the contribution of Lucas and other informed scholars in helping to problematize the apparently widely accepted reductive view of this aspect of literary history.

The Seafarer in particular presents an outlook very different from the characterization of early medieval thinking offered, for example, by Morris, who in *The Discovery of the Individual* contrasts the 'Dark Ages' with the late Roman world: 'Religion was no longer a matter for personal decision, and the old community of love and fellowship was replaced by a quite different ideal of conformity to the norms accepted by society.'[27] My own discussion of *The Seafarer* has stressed

[22] Lucas, 'Language of the Loner', p. 117.

[23] Peter Clemoes, *Interactions of Thought and Language in Old English Poetry*, Cambridge Studies in Anglo-Saxon England, 12 (Cambridge, 1995), pp. 363–408.

[24] Fiona Gameson and Richard Gameson, '*Wulf and Eadwacer*, *The Wife's Lament*, and the Discovery of the Individual in Old English Verse', in *Studies in English Language and Literature: 'Doubt Wisely': Papers in Honour of E. G. Stanley*, ed. by M. J. Toswell and E. M. Tyler (London, 1996), pp. 457–74; for Morris's book, see note 19 above.

[25] 'Discovery of the Individual', p. 467.

[26] 'Did the Twelfth Century Discover the Individual?', p. 4.

[27] *Discovery of the Individual*, p. 24.

different facets of the poem from those highlighted in Lucas's article but equally pertinent, I think, to the question of literary expression of individual experience. In my view *The Seafarer* is a highly unusual Old English poem. Though coming from an age in which identity *was* characteristically constructed in communal terms, this poem bases its homiletic message on a recognition of the essential separateness of individuals from each other, focussing in particular at a key moment in the text on the fact of death as a distillation of physical individual experience. This would be a powerful message in any age; in the Anglo-Saxon period it is remarkable.

STAÞOL: A FIRM FOUNDATION FOR IMAGERY

Eric Stanley

It is a good rule when compiling a dictionary entry for a modern European language, such as English, to assume that, when literal and metaphorical uses are found side by side, the literal is the original and should take precedence in lexicography of any metaphorical sense or senses developed from it. Thus *nose*, the more or less prominent part of the face above the mouth, appears in a well-conducted dictionary entry before its metaphorical uses as when a journalist is said to have a good nose for a political scandal, or when a bottle of wine is said to have a good nose. Similarly, an entry *hand* would, no doubt, lead off with the human and simian forepaw, and only later such metaphorical uses are accorded their place, as a good hand in a game of cards, or that one must not show one's hand too soon. Such metaphorical usage has not moved away so far from the original sense, the olfactory organ or the prehensile limb, that that sense is not recalled when the word is used in a wider sense. In Old English the original sense of *mund* may be presumed to be 'hand', but that literal sense, etymologically related remotely to Latin *manus*, is rare, and wider senses such as 'protection, guardianship' are more common, and the Scandinavianism 'bride-price' is rare.[1]

For Modern English there are exceptionally words that have lost all contact with their original concrete meaning, especially where dead metaphors are involved. An example is *aftermath*, the second element of which, used on its own, is known to me only from the dictionaries: Modern English *math* and its doublet

---

[1] For OE *mund*, see E. G. Stanley, 'Words for the *Dictionary of Old English*', in *The Dictionary of Old English: Retrospects and Prospects*, ed. by M. J. Toswell, *Old English Newsletter, Subsidia*, 26 (1998), pp. 33–56 (pp. 39–47).

mowth are deverbative nouns, 'mowing', formed from *to mow*.[2] We have no means of telling in a dead language such as Old English how alive an original literal sense remained in the minds of native speakers when they used *staþol*, which is the subject of this paper in honour of Éamonn Ó Carragáin.

All the dictionaries and glossaries to collections of texts seem to be sure that some such sense as 'a firm foundation' underlies all senses of *staþol*; the following are some representative examples. Just before the end of what survives of the Harley Glossary breaks off we have: 'Fundamentum . siue dictum quod fundus fit domui . uel fundamen . *staþol* . [. . .] Fundamen . *staþol*.'[3] Somner's great seventeenth-century dictionary moves from the concrete to the metaphorical: '*Staþol*. ut *Staþelfæst*. itidem. fundamentum, firmamentum, cardo, status. a foundation, a ground-work: the firmament: the state, chief point, or issue of a matter.'[4] Lye and Manning's dictionary, handsomely printed in folio: '*Staðel. Staðol. Staðul.* Fundamentum, basis, firma sedes.'[5] Joseph Bosworth takes over, under sense 1., Lye and Manning's spellings and Latin meanings which he translates 'A foundation, basis, firm seat'; under 2., he gives Somner's 'The firmament; *firmamentum*'; and under 3., he has the metaphorical senses, 'A situation, station, position, state; *status, situs, positio*'; and he abridges that with the modification, under 3., 'A place, site, situation, station, position, state'.[6] Grein's *Sprachschatz*, s.v. *staðol*, follows the

---

[2] For the etymology of *aftermath*, see the references in E. G. Stanley, 'Polysemy and Synonymy and How These Concepts Were Understood From the Eighteenth Century Onwards in Treatises, and Applied in Dictionaries of English', in *Dictionary: History and Historical Lexicography*, ed. by Julie Coleman and Anne McDermott, Lexicographica Series Maior, 123 (Tübingen, 2004), pp. 157–83 (pp. 167–68).

[3] *The Harley Latin–Old English Glossary edited from British Museum MS Harley 3376*, ed. by Robert T. Oliphant (The Hague, 1966), pp. 207–08, F 1013–15. In all quotations in this paper abbreviations, contractions, and suspensions, as well as other editorial details, including punctuation and capitalization, have not been strictly followed. All translations are mine, unless otherwise stated.

[4] *Dictionarium Saxonico–Latino–Anglicum* [. . .], ed. by G. Somner (Oxford, 1659), sig. Ll2.

[5] *Dictionarium Saxonico et Gothico–Latinum*, ed. by Edward Lye and Owen Manning, 2 vols (London, 1772), II, sig [Sss2^{ro}–Sss2^{vo}], with many good quotations.

[6] *A Dictionary of the Anglo-Saxon Language*, ed. by J. Bosworth (London, 1838), p. 350. Bosworth, at pp. clxxv–clxxvi, acknowledges his debt to Lye; *A Compendious Anglo-Saxon and English Dictionary*, ed. by Joseph Bosworth (London, 1855), p. 209, abridges the dictionary entry of 1838; *Vorda Vealhstôd Engla and Seaxna: Lexicon Anglosaxonicum*, ed. by Ludwig Ettmüller, Bibliothek der gesammten deutschen National-Literatur, 29 (Quedlinburg, 1851), p. 735, s.v. *staðol*, mainly follows Bosworth's entry of 1838; as does *Caedmon's des Angelsachsen biblische Dichtungen*, 2 vols (vol. I, Gütersloh, 1854; vol. II: 'Ein angelsächsisches Glossar', Elberfeld and

earlier dictionaries in significations for the word used in poetry, and the full list of references to occurrences, some with meanings for individual uses, remains of great value.[7] Heinrich Leo's dictionary adds nothing substantial to the brief semantic information given in earlier dictionaries, except that for *ece staþelas* at *Christ*, line 661, he adds the contextual sense 'Aufenthalt', given by him perhaps because in his inconvenient arrangement under etymologically related verbs, in this case under *standan*, any sense derived from 'to sit, seat' might be thought inappropriate, though other lexicographers had been content with senses based on Latin *sedes*.[8] This brief list takes the record of dictionaries to modern times, to Toller's excellent continuations of 'Bosworth-Toller', which for parts of the alphabet not yet covered by the Toronto *Dictionary of Old English* are still the safest lexicographic guide, and to Clark Hall's and Sweet's lexicographic epitomes, both completed before Bosworth-Toller and *Supplement* were.[9]

The number of words of which *staþol* is an element is relatively considerable:[10] nouns, *staþolæht, staþolfæstness, gestaþolfæstness, unstaþolfæstness, staþolwong, burhstaþol, eðelstaðol, frumstaðol, modstaðol, modstaþolness, modstaþolfæstness,*[11]

Iserlohn, 1850 – the wrapper, omitting Iserlohn, but adding London to Elberfeld, dated 1851), p. 265, s.v. *staþol*.

[7] *Sprachschatz der angelsächsischen Dichter*, 2 vols, ed. by C. W. M. Grein, Bibliothek der angelsächsischen Poesie, 4 (Cassel, 1864), II, 473–74; retained in the revised edition by J. J. Köhler (Heidelberg, 1912–14), pp. 629–30.

[8] *Angelsächsisches Glossar*, ed. by Heinrich Leo, 2 parts, part 2, 'Alphabetischer Index', ed. by Walter Biszegger, under the direction of Moritz Heyne, the column numbers of part 1 continued as page numbers in part 2 (Halle, 1872–77), col. 61 of the continuous numeration.

[9] *An Anglo-Saxon Dictionary*, ed. by Joseph Bosworth and T. Northcote Toller, issued in 4 parts, with continuous page-numbering (Oxford, 1882–98), p. 912; with additions in Toller's *An Anglo-Saxon Dictionary Supplement*, issued in 3 parts, with continuous page-numbering (Oxford, 1908–21), p. 710. *A Concise Anglo-Saxon Dictionary for the Use of Students*, ed. by John R. Clark Hall (London, 1894); several times revised and reprinted, most recently 4th edn with a supplement by Herbert D. Meritt (Cambridge, 1960), p. 319. *The Student's Dictionary of Anglo-Saxon*, ed. by Henry Sweet (Oxford, 1897), p. 160. *Dictionary of Old English*, ed. by Angus Cameron, Ashley C. Amos, and Antonette diP. Healey (Toronto, 1986–).

[10] Minor spelling variants, such as <þ> ~ <ð> and the suffix <-ol-> ~ <-ul-> ~ <-el->, have been ignored. I list in parentheses, after the verb, forms directly derived from verbs. In my search for words I have been greatly helped by *A Microfiche Concordance to Old English*, ed. by Richard L. Venezky and Antonette diPaolo Healey, Publications of the Dictionary of Old English, 1 (Toronto, 1980).

[11] In Toller's attractive rendering, s.vv., 'stability of mind'; *modstaþolness* and *modstaþolfæstness* may be compared with such uses as *mod staþelian* 'give strength to (his) mind' (*Guthlac B*, line 1110).

westenstaþol; adjectives, *staþol, staþolfæst, staþolfæstlic, understaþolfæst, unstaþolfæst*; adverb, *staþolfæstlice*; verbs, *staþolian* (*staþoliend, staþolung*), *gestaþolian* (*gestaþolung*), *edstaðelian* (*edstaþeligend, edstaþelung*), *geedstaðelian* (*geedstaþeliend, geedstaþelung*), *gestaþolfæstan, gestaþolfæstnian* (*staþolfæstnung*), and the unique *gegrundstaþolian* which sums much of the metaphorical senses of many of these words.[12]

Very selectively, I now use quotations from the *Microfiche Concordance* as well as from Toller to illustrate some of the range of meanings of some of these words. Under the simplex, *staþel* 'foundation' at Psalter Gloss E 18:2 *firmamentum* is glossed 'trvmnesse ł staðel ł fesnesse' where *trumnes* and *fæstnes* render literally the *firm*ness of the *firmament*.[13] The verbs mean, according to Bosworth-Toller, 'to establish' (as in *ham staðelian* 'to establish a home' at *Genesis A*, line 1556, and compare *Christ and Satan*, lines 25, 275, and 344, Metrical Psalm 106. 35), 'found, settle', and metaphorically 'to confirm, make steadfast, endow with steadfastness', and 'to fix' as at *Christ B*, line 864, *hyht staþelian* 'base (our) hope firmly on' calqued on *figere*, and similarly *hyge staþeliað* 'base (their) thinking firmly on' (*Guthlac A*, line 66, and compare Metrical Psalms 61. 11), and, of the soul, *fæstlice ferð staþelian* 'to strengthen (her) soul firmly' (*Juliana*, line 270, and compare line 364, as well as *Elene*, lines 427, 796).[14] Blickling Homily 10 has 'þone rihtan

---

[12] The only occurrence is in what looks like an incomplete line of Ælfrician alliterative prose, *Aelfric's Lives of Saints*, ed. by Walter W. Skeat, EETS, OS, 76 (London, 1881), p. 196; St Agatha, lines 19–20: 'hi ne magon afyllan min fæstræde geþanc . þe is gegrundstaþelod' ('they cannot subdue my steadfast mind, which is well grounded and confirmed'). I have not included in this list the late and erroneous *weallstaðel* (for *wealhstod*), and I am grateful to Jane Roberts for drawing my attention to the fact that I had omitted *modstaðol*; see Bosworth-Toller, p. 695, and Alistair Campbell's *Enlarged Addenda*, p. 65.

[13] *Eadwine's Canterbury Psalter*, ed. by Fred Harsley, EETS, OS, 92 (London, 1889), p. 27. In the reading 'trvmnesse ł staðel ł fesnesse' presumably *staðel* stands for *staðelnesse*. The reading in the Vitellius Psalter, 'staðol ł trumne ł rador', may represent a faulty transmission of the word *staþolnesse* preserved correctly in the closely related Tiberius Psalter. For details, see Phillip Pulsiano, *Old English Glossed Psalters Psalms 1–50*, Toronto Old English Series, 11 (Toronto, 2001), p. 218.

[14] *The Christ of Cynewulf*, ed. by Albert S. Cook, 2nd edn (Boston, 1909), p. 167, n. on lines 850–66. Similarly 'swa ic in minne fæder, hellwarena cyning, hyht staþelie' ('even as I (the devilish creature) firmly established (my) trust in my father, the king of those that dwell in hell', *Juliana* lines 436–37). *The Junius Manuscript*, ed. by George Philip Krapp, Anglo-Saxon Poetic Records, 1 (New York, 1931), pp. 48, 136, 144, and 146. *The Exeter Book*, ed. by George Philip Krapp and Elliott Van Kirk Dobbie, Anglo-Saxon Poetic Records, 3 (New York, 1936), pp. 51, 120, and 364. *The Paris Psalter and the Meters of Boethius*, ed. by George Philip Krapp, Anglo-Saxon Poetic

geleafan fæste staðelian on urum heortum' ('ground firmly the true faith in our hearts').[15] Under *gestaðelian*, 'to erect, place, strengthen, fortify, repair, restore' are added to the meanings. Under *gestaðolfæstnian*, 'to make firm' is added by Toller in his *Supplement*; it glosses *solidare* in the Durham Ritual.[16] Verbs (based on *staþol*) with such meanings occur in both prose and verse. Wulfstan, by using his form of parallelism, delineates the meaning of the verb clearly: 'Ac staðelige man & strangige & trimme hi georne' ('but let them be firmly set and strengthened and strongly constructed'); *hi* refers to *On þisum þrim stapelum* two paragraphs before, 'on these three pillars', metaphorical pillars — men of prayer, of husbandry, and of war — on which (in a Christian nation) every royal throne must rest, so that this use too is not about erecting firmly some material structure.[17] Frequently the verb is used of God's act of Creation, as in glosses of Gallican Psalm 103. 5: 'Qui fundasti terram super stabilitatem suam', rendered in the Doway Bible 'Which hast founded the earth vpon the stabilitie therof', and in the Stowe Psalter 'þu ðe staþelodest eorðan ofer staðolfæstnysse his'.[18]

The simplex, often in the plural, *staþelas* and variants, renders *fundamentum* 'foundation' used metaphorically especially in verse, and there is a single occurrence, indefinite in sense, in the laws.[19] Charter language, whether authentic or not, includes, applied to protection of rights, the phrase *strang & staþelfæst* translated by the editor 'firm and unshaken', and applied to a benefaction, *þæt hit sig staðelfast* (etc.) is translated 'that it be unimpaired', and of an agreement 'that it

---

Records, 5 (New York, 1932), pp. 89 and 15. *The Vercelli Book*, ed. by George Philip Krapp, Anglo-Saxon Poetic Records, 2 (New York, 1932), pp. 77, 88.

[15] *The Blickling Homilies*, ed. by Richard Morris, EETS, OS, 58 (London, 1874), p. 111, lines 3–4.

[16] *Rituale Ecclesiae Dunelmensis: The Durham Collectar*, ed. by U. Lindelöf, Surtees Society, 140 (London, 1927), pp. 22, lines 5 and 6. For the source, see *The Durham Collectar*, ed. by Alicia Corrêa, Henry Bradshaw Society, 107 (1992), p. 154, no. 146 (I Peter 5. 10).

[17] *Die 'Institutes of Polity, Civil and Ecclesiastical': Ein Werk Erzbishof Wulfstans von York*, ed. by Karl Jost, Swiss Studies in English, 47 (Bern, 1959), pp. 56–57.

[18] *The Second Tome of the Holie Bible Faithfully Translated into English, out of the Authentical Latin* (Doway, 1610), p. 189; *The Stowe Psalter*, ed. by Andrew C. Kimmens, Toronto Old English Series, 3 (Toronto, 1979), p. 196.

[19] The difficulty of translating *be ðam staþole ures rices*, perhaps 'concerning the security of our kingdom', is well discussed by Felix Liebermann, *Die Gesetze der Angelsachsen*, 3 vols (Halle, 1898–1916), I, 88–89 [*Ine Prol.*], III, 68/3, n. 14; he follows Toller's 'fixed condition, state, position' and believes, as does *Quadripartitus*, that a more neutral sense such as 'situation' is the sense here.

stand firm'.[20] Often the adjective refers to and may be calqued on 'the firmament', 'fram ðissere unstæððigan worulde to his (God's) staðelfæstan rice', thus Ælfric towards the end of the first Easter homily; there may well be paronomastic emphasis on the stem element of the two adjectives, brought out in Thorpe's translation, 'from this un*stead*y world to his *stead*fast kingdom'.[21] Another lemma underlying several of the Old English adjectival uses is *stabilis* (and substantival, *stabilitatis*, especially in the Psalter glosses), a long way from any concrete sense of a material structure. A uniquely metaphorical use of the simplex in an adverbial phrase comes in *The Seafarer*, lines 109–10:

> Stieran mo*n* sceal strongum mode,   ond þæt on staþelum healdan,
> ond gewis werum, wisum clæne.

There are as many translations as translators of these lines, though *on staþelum* 'within bounds, in control, in check' is not chief among the problems. Among the points of doubt are not only the emendation *mod* to *mon* (line 109a), the precise meaning of *stieran*, but also if *werum* is or is not one of the Anglianisms occasionally found in the Exeter Book, a form, therefore, of *wærum* 'pledges' as some of the most sensitive scholars have suggested or accepted. On the other hand, there appears to be a general consensus that *stieran* means 'to govern, control, restrain', though often 'to steer' is listed in glossaries, perhaps mainly to indicate how the verb has developed semantically, without regard that 'to steer', understood as 'to give direction to', would fit well in lines 109–10:[22] 'One must give direction to a headstrong mind, and keep it in check, and true to one's pledges, and unblemished in one's habits.'

There is a relatively small number of literal uses of *staþol*. Among quotations listed by Toller are the following for the sense 'the lower, firmer part, base of a

---

[20] *Anglo-Saxon Writs*, ed. by Florence E. Harmer (Manchester, 1952), pp. 344–45 (no. 77), 352 (no. 85), 363 (no. 98), 367–68 (no. 102), 370–71 (no. 105), 372 (no. 106), and 402–03 (no. 113).

[21] *Ælfric's Catholic Homilies The Second Series: Text*, ed. by Malcolm Godden, EETS, SS, 5 (London, 1979), p. 160 (XV, lines 330–31). *The Homilies of Ælfric*, ed. and trans. by Benjamin Thorpe, II part VIII, Ælfric Society, 10 (London, 1846), p. 283; his rendering 'steadfast' (common among translators of Old English) owes more to the closeness, superficial and ultimately etymological, of *steadfast* to *staðolfæst* than to Modern English idiomatic usage.

[22] The following use is comparable (and Sweet's translation): 'Swa deð ðæt mod, ðonne hit wacorlice stiereð ðære sawle' ('So does the mind, when it vigilantly steers the soul'); *King Alfred's West-Saxon Version of Gregory's Pastoral Care*, ed. and trans. by Henry Sweet, EETS, OS, 45 (London, 1871), p. 433, lines 3–4.

pillar, trunk of a tree': with metaphorical application, 'hit bið unnyt ðæt mon hwelces yfles bogas snæde buton mon wille ða wyrtruman forceorfan ðæs staðoles' ('it is useless that one prunes the branches of every evil unless one is willing to eradicate the roots of the trunk');[23] *Andreas* lines 1503–04a, the saint commands the pillar to send forth floods to drown the heathen multitude: 'Læt nu of þinum staþole streamas weallan, | ea inflede' ('Let now floods surge forth out of thy pedestal, a river in spate');[24] from the charm 'For Unfruitful Land', 'Genim þonne on niht [. . .] feower tyrf [. . .] and gemearca hu hy ær stodon. Nim þonne ele and hunig and beorman and ælces feos meolc [. . .] and ælces treowcynnes dæl [. . .] and ælcre namcuþre wyrte dæl [. . .] and do þonne haligwæter ðæron, and drype þonne þriwa on þone staðol þara turfa' ('Then take at night [. . .] four turves [. . .] and note how they had been standing. Then take oil and honey and yeast and the milk from all the cattle [. . .] and some of every kind of tree [. . .] and some of every herb of note [. . .] and then put holy water on that and cause it to drip thrice on the base of those turves');[25] Toller adds, as a closely related sense 'that on which a thing depends', the Cleopatra gloss *cardo = staðul*.[26] The simplex comes at least once in *Riddle 88* at line 22, and probably also slightly damaged at line 5, but the context is too damaged to be useful. The two standard collected editions of Old English verse more or less agree on . . . *d ic on staðol* though Assmann is slightly less firm on the last two letters; the transcript preserved in the British Library is reported by Tupper as reading *od* and *staðol*.[27] The text of lines 19b–22 runs thus:

> Ic on wuda stonde
> bordes on ende. Nis min broþor her,
> ac ic sceal broþorleas bordes on ende
> staþol weardian, stondan fæste.

[23] *King Alfred's [. . .] Pastoral Care*, ed. and trans. by Sweet, p. 222, lines 14–16.

[24] *Andreas and The Fates of the Apostles*, ed. by Kenneth R. Brooks (Oxford, 1961), p. 48, and see the note on p. 113, justifying the sense 'pedestal'.

[25] *The Anglo-Saxon Minor Poems*, ed. by Elliott Van Kirk Dobbie, Anglo-Saxon Poetic Records, 6 (New York, 1942), p. 116, Metrical Charms, 1, lines 3–10.

[26] *Anglo-Saxon and Old English Vocabularies*, ed. by Thomas Wright and rev. by Richard Paul Wülcker (London, 1884), col. 376, 17.

[27] *Die Handschrift von Exeter*, ed. by Richard Paul Wülker and Bruno Assmann, Bibliothek der angelsächsischen Poesie begründet von Christian W. M. Grein, 3.1 (Leipzig, 1898), p. 233 (*Riddle 88* in their numbering). *The Exeter Book*, ed. by Krapp and Dobbie, p. 86. *The Riddles of the Exeter Book*, ed. by Frederick Tupper (Boston, 1910), pp. 60–61. The British Library transcript Additional MS 9067, made by Robert Chambers in 1831 and 1832, is described by Krapp and Dobbie, p. xv.

[I (one of the pair of horns) stand at the edge of the table. My brother is not here, but I, at the edge of the table, must hold the place where we stood, (must) stand firm.]

Whether *staþol* means, as I think, 'the place to which we were rooted' is obviously a matter of interpretation not of philological fact, but I think that sense is more in keeping with the semantics of the word than (among the editions of the last century), 'station, place' (Tupper), 'Standort, Stätte' (Trautmann), 'my place' (Mackie), 'place, foundation' (Williamson), *staþol weardian* 'den Platz einnehmen' (Göbel), or, perhaps best, 'meinen Standplatz behüten' (Pinsker and Ziegler).[28]

The compounds in which *staþol* is an element are often interesting, though again only a small number of them is literally the base, the lower part, the foundation of a material structure: *The Riming Poem*, line 22a *staþolæhtum steald*, with both words unique in the language, appears to mean 'I owned possessions held by secure right', or, less jurally, the noun has been rendered 'firm possessions',[29] and, as we have seen, in charter terminology *staþelfæst* refers to inalienable ownership. The compound *staþolwong* occurs twice, once in *Riddle 34*, line 8, the solution of which is generally accepted as 'rake' (lines 6–9):[30]

> aa heo þa findeð   þa þe fæst ne biþ,
> læteð hio þa wlitigan   wyrtum fæste
> stille stondan   on staþolwonge,
> beorhte blican,   blowan ond growan.

[It (the rake) always seeks out that one (plant) that is not firmly established, but it lets those beautiful, firmly rooted ones stand undisturbed on (their) rootfast ground, (lets them) shine brightly, (lets them) blossom and grow.]

---

[28] *Die altenglischen Rätsel*, ed. by Moritz Trautmann, Alt- und mittelenglische Texte, 8 (Heidelberg, 1915), p. 187 (the Riddle is numbered 86 in this edition); *The Exeter Book, part II*, ed. by W. S. Mackie, EETS, OS, 194 (London, 1934), p. 229 (the Riddle is numbered 87 in this edition); *The Old English Riddles of the Exeter Book*, ed. by Craig Williamson (Chapel Hill, 1977), p. 449 (glossary, the Riddle is numbered 84 in this edition); *Studien zu den altenglischen Schriftwesenrätseln*, ed. by Helga Göbel, Epistemata, Würzburger wissenschaftliche Schriften, Literaturwissenschaft, 7 (Würzburg, 1980), p. 427; *Die altenglischen Rätsel des Exeterbuchs*, ed. by Hans Pinsker and Waltraud Ziegler (Heidelberg, 1985), p. 133 (the Riddle is numbered 84 in this edition).

[29] See *The Old English Riming Poem*, ed. by O. D. Macrae-Gibson (Cambridge, 1983), pp. 30–31, and glossary, p. 60. The rhyme would be improved if the reading were *steold*, and some editors emend accordingly.

[30] *The Exeter Book*, ed. by Krapp and Dobbie, p. 197.

This use is clearly related to *on þone staðol þara turfa* of the Metrical Charm 'For Unfruitful Land'; my rendering 'rootfast ground', unattractively repeats *root* but is meant to convey the sense for the piece of ground where these plants favoured by the rake have their firm base. The compound *staðolwangas* is found at *Genesis A*, line 1912, in a context in which some scholars have not joined up manuscript *teon wit* to form a compound noun (lines 1911b–13a):[31] 'forðon wit lædon sculon | teonwit of þisse stowe, and unc staðolwangas | rumor secan' ('for this reason the two of us (Abraham addressing Lot) must direct brawling away from this place, and (must) find for ourselves more spaciously established dwelling-places'). The application here is very different from the gardening use in the Riddle. Modern English too has figurative uses, such as 'to put down roots', combining botanical wording with settling in a new home.

Compound nouns with *staþol* as first element include *burhstaðol*, which occurs rendering *fundus* in one of the more *outré* cures for chronic and incurable diseases; it is of little independent interest. The word is glossed by de Vriend 'foundation of the wall of a fortified place', and rendered by Cockayne as 'borough wall foundations'.[32] The compound *eðelstaðol* occurs once only, and the *Dictionary of Old English* defines it as 'established home, settlement', suitable for its occurrence at *Genesis A*, line 94, *eðelstaðolas*. The most recent editor of the poem, however, in his glossary gives 'lower creation, a home beneath another', and explains that further, 'the world being created for mankind'.[33] There is nothing in the semantics of the compound itself to suggest that the world created for mankind is lower than that home with God from which Lucifer fell, that Man's terrestrial home is beneath that other home where God and the angels loyal to God continue to dwell after Lucifer's Fall. The word *eðelstaðolas* 'the newly established homeland', established for Man, is given in contrast to the *wuldres eðel* 'the glorious

---

[31] See F. E. Dietrich, 'Zu Cädmon', *Zeitschrift für deutsches Alterthum*, 10 (1856), 310–67 (pp. 328–29, *teonwit* understood as 'insulting reproach, spiteful quarrel'); compare *Genesis A: A New Edition*, ed. by A. N. Doane (Madison, 1978), p. 171 for the text, with *teonwit* in place, and, pp. 292–93, some account of the scholarly history of the passage, expressed with a measure of irony, and without mention of Dietrich. See *The Junius Manuscript*, ed. by Krapp, p. 184 on line 1912, misguidedly emended at p. 58.

[32] *The Old English Herbarium and Medicina de Quadrupedibus*, ed. by Hubert Jan de Vriend, EETS, OS, 286 (London, 1984), pp. 236–37 (texts and source, I. 7) and 352 (glossary); *Leechdoms, Wortcunning, and Starcraft of Early England*, vol. I, ed. by T. Oswald Cockayne, Rolls Series, 35 (London, 1864), pp. 238–39 (texts and translation, 3 and 2–1 lines from bottom).

[33] *Genesis A*, ed. by Doane, p. 346; and compare the notes on lines 86b–111 at pp. 231–32, in which the hexaemeral tradition is explained.

homeland' of the Fallen Angels;[34] but *eðel* is not the subject of this paper, *staðol* is, and that word means in connection with landholding: possession established in such a way that one has rights of ownership, which, as the charters show, may be royally protected.

The compound *frumstaþol* occurs once only in the language, *Riddle 60*, line 3; that Riddle is somewhat insecurely solved as 'reed-flute, reed, staff with runes cut in it'. In this paper I am concerned only with the sense of the compound, not with the wider problem of the relationship, if any, of *Riddle 60* to *The Husband's Message* that follows it immediately with much damage to lines 2–8 of its text, and then at line 13, as if the layout for opening a new poem, a space and a large initial for the first word, *Hwæt*.[35] As *Riddle 60* is usually understood, the beginning is about the origins of the reed, later turned into a writing instrument. Some aspects of the use in this poem of 'minum gewunade | frumstaþole fæst' have been paralleled in various of the Old English poems. By his word-order and the alliterative emphasis on *minum* the poet is stressing that it is 'my, the reed's, accustomed first home' in which the reed stands fast however turbulent the sea, *æt merefaroþe* — not 'at the seashore' but 'by the sea in motion'; compare *Exodus*, line 474, 'æflastum gewuna ece staðulas' ('the eternal foundations (of the bottom of the Red Sea) accustomed to contrary tidal movements').[36] It is important to recognize that etymologically and vestigially in sense *staþol* has its root in *standan*; though inconvenient in arrangement for a dictionary, Leo's allocation of the noun under

---

[34] It goes with the uses of *eðel* as a simplex or as the first element of several compounds in this poem. In prose, we find *fæderedel* calqued on *patria*.

[35] There is the further complication that this 'riddle' is actually the beginning of *The Husband's Message* which immediately follows it; see *The Exeter Book*, ed. by Krapp and Dobbie, p. 225 text, pp. 361–62 notes, and pp. lix–lx the possible connection with *The Husband's Message*, to which are to be added the more recent discussions of the problem: Ralph W. V. Elliott, 'The Runes in *The Husband's Message*', *JEGP*, 54 (1955), 1–8; Robert E. Kaske, 'A Poem of the Cross in the Exeter Book: "Riddle 60" and "The Husband's Message"', *Traditio*, 23 (1967), 41–71; *Old English Riddles of the Exeter Book,* ed. by Williamson, pp. 315–18 (note on the Riddle numbered 58 in this edition, and with several more references to discussions of the problem); *Studien zu den altenglischen Schriftwesenrätseln*, ed. by Göbel, pp. 306–68 (by far the fullest discussion of the poem and the problem of connecting it with *The Husband's Message*); *Die altenglischen Rätsel des Exeterbuchs,* ed. by Pinsker and Ziegler, pp. 283–84 (note on the Riddle numbered 58 in this edition).

[36] See *Exodus*, ed. by Peter J. Lucas, Methuen's Old English Library (London, 1977), pp. 134–35, see the translation of lines 471b–76 and the note on line 474a.

the verb was not altogether malapropos.[37] The subsequent history of the noun has its main direction towards Modern English *staddle* (well represented in *OED*). Another, more difficult side has been less well charted. OE *stælhran* 'decoy reindeer' is familiar from its place in the account of Ohthere's voyage.[38] OE *stæl* is certainly related to *staþol*, and is recorded early. There was a rare sound-change[39] by which /æþel/ > /æːl/, a feature in the development of the personal-name element Æðel- > Æl-, Al-.[40] An example of this change, attested early, involves *mæðel* > *mæl* 'speech' and *staðol* 'support, position' (with /æ/ retracted before /u>o/ in the next syllable) and *stæl* 'place'. OE *stæl* (probably also *steall*) appears to be related to Middle English *stal stonden* 'to stand one's place, to be of use', perhaps = 'act as decoy'.[41] The roving wild reindeer are caught when they associate with the standing decoy deer that are standing still. At *Riddle 60*, line 3, there is, of course, no hint that the place where the reed stood originally was in any way connected with the function of being a decoy, only that the reed's incipience leads to its eventual usefulness. I am inclined, therefore, to translate *Riddle 60*, lines 1–7a as below:

[37] See *Angelsächsisches Glossar*, ed. by Leo, col. 61.

[38] *The Old English Orosius*, ed. by Janet Bately, EETS, SS, 6 (London, 1980), p. 15, line 10, and see her note on pp. 189–90.

[39] See Alistair Campbell, *Old English Grammar* (Oxford, 1959; last corrected reprint 1983), p. 171 § 421.

[40] Most fully recorded in Domesday Book (admittedly two hundred years later than the *Orosius*): Æðel- > Al-, see, for example, Æðelfrið > Aelvert, Aelverus, Æðelmær > Ælmarius, -merus, Æðelric > Ælric, Æðelsige > Ælsi, Æðelweard > Æluuard, Æðelwig > Ælwius, Æðelwine > Ælwinus; see Olof von Feilitzen, *The Pre-Conquest Personal Names of Domesday Book*, Nomina Germanica, 3 (Uppsala, 1937), pp. 182–91. Such forms are to be found also in coin inscriptions analysed for the reign of Edward the Confessor, who died in 1066 (only a little earlier than Domesday Book), by Fran Colman, *Money Talks: Reconstructing Old English*, Trends in Linguistics Studies and Monographs, 56 (Berlin, 1992), pp. 5, 15, 24, 26, 59–60, 75–76, 78–79, 166, 191, 203, 225, 232, 256, 261, 267, 282–83, 286, 307, 313, 322–23, and 328.

[41] See *The Owl and the Nightingale*, ed. by E. G. Stanley (London, 1960), p. 153, note on lines 1631–32 (unchanged in later editions). It is likely that, in this poem, *stal stonden* involves a pun on the sense 'decoy'; see *Middle English Dictionary*, s.v. *stonden* 34c. (d); but *MED* has nothing s.v. *stāl(e*, n. (4) 'decoy'); not explicitly adopted in his translation by Neil Cartlidge in *The Owl and the Nightingale*, ed. by Cartlidge, Exeter Medieval Texts and Studies (Exeter, 2001), p. 39, though *stale* 'decoy' is mentioned in the notes pp. 91–92. The long entry on the Frankish loanword into French in *Französisches Etymologisches Wörterbuch*, XVII, fascicle 83, ed. by Walther von Wartburg (Basel, 1962), pp. 206–10, s.v. **stal*, is no help; presumably this hypothesized Frankish etymon is thought to be cognate with the Old English word.

> Ic wæs be sonde   sæwealle neah
> æt merefaroþe,   minum gewunade
> frumstaþole fæst.   Fea ænig wæs
> monna cynnes   þæt minne þær
> on anæde   eard beheolde,
> ac mec uhtna gehwam   yð sio brune
> lagufæðme beleolc.

[I was by the sand[42] close to the sea-cliff by the sea in motion, standing firmly fixed in my accustomed first home. There was hardly anyone of mankind who saw my native land there in the wilderness, yet first thing every morning the shining wave played around me in marine embrace.]

The word *staþol* occurs relatively frequently in the Riddles, both as a simplex and in compounds: the simplex four times; and, each once, *staþolwong*, *frumstaþol*; as well as the very doubtful **wynnstaþol*. The manuscript at *Riddle 92*, line 3, has *wym staþol*; the metre of the emended half-line **wynnstaþol* is deficient, and that has led to various further emendations. No one has suggested *wynsū staþol* (that is, *wynsum staþol*) 'pleasant home for (my) roots'; I suggest that as less invasive of the text than most of the emendations that have been proposed.[43] The end of the Riddle is so badly damaged that the various names of trees proposed as solutions are imaginative speculations, among which Wyatt's *boc* 'beech' and 'book' is the most appealing.[44] In the much-anthologized book-moth *Riddle 47*, line 5 *þæs strangan staþol* 'its strong foundation' is generally accepted to refer to the *þrymfæstne cwide* 'the glorious (written) utterance' (line 4b):[45] the moth eats its

---

[42] The <o> of *sonde* is on an erasure, and though *sund* is not recorded with the preposition *be*, it is possible that the text originally had **be sunde* 'by the sea'.

[43] The emendation **wynnstaþol*, generally accepted (though not by all), was first suggested and first introduced into an edition by Assmann, in *Die Handschrift von Exeter*, ed. by Wülker and Assmann, p. 236 (Riddle number 92 in this edition). The fullest discussion of the many problems is by Göbel, *Studien zu den altenglischen Schriftwesenrätseln*, pp. 469–71, from which I have taken many details, as also from her discussion of the book-moth *Riddle 47*, pp. 226–55.

[44] *Old English Riddles*, ed. by Alfred J. Wyatt (Boston, 1912), p. 122 (the Riddle is numbered 90 in this edition). On the history of the word 'beech' see *The Vocabulary of English Place-Names* (Á–BOX), ed. by David Parsons and Tania Styles with Carole Hough (Nottingham: Centre for English Name Studies, 1997), pp. 118–19. Beech-trees did grow in early medieval England as far north as the Midlands, so that, even if it could be proved that the Riddle was written in Northumbria, its author would have heard about them (if he had never seen one); see K.-E. Behre, 'Buche § 3. Archäologisches', in (Johannes Hoops, ed. of 1st edn), *Reallexikon der Germanischen Altertumskunde*, vol. IV.1–2, 2nd edn (Berlin, 1979), pp. 58–59.

[45] I am not entirely persuaded that *cwide* is punningly at the same time 'utterance' from *cweþan* and *cwidu* 'cud', as suggested by Fred C. Robinson, 'Artful Ambiguities in the Old English

way through both the mighty intellectual food and its strong physical foundation that bears the ink on it, the vellum or parchment.

Halfway through *The Dream of the Rood* the three crosses on Golgotha are referred to in the first person plural by Christ's Cross, the speaker (lines 70–72a):[46]

> Hwæðere we ðær reotende   [r]ode hwile
> stodon on staðole   syððan [storm] up gewat
> hilderinca.

[However, for a long time we, the crosses, stood weeping there at (our) post from the time that the soldiers' onslaught had started up.]

Swanton has a good history of the various emendations proposed to make line 70 alliterate and to supply a subject at line 71b giving an alliterating syllable. For line 70, manuscript *reotende* 'weeping' is satisfactory in sense, as would be either of the emendations *greotende* or *hreotende* with the same meaning. But *hreotende* would give irregular alliteration, such as one might wish to defend if it were in the transmitted text but would not wish to introduce by emendation, though the assumption that <h> is labile might make that the lesser intrusion in this manuscript.[47] On the whole, I am inclined to follow those earlier scholars who left *reotende* unemended, and emended *gode* to *rode* 'crosses', nominative plural. In Insular script <g> and <r> are more alike than in modern hands or print (though not as similar as Insular <r> and <s>); **rode hwile* might have seemed difficult to a scribe who found *gode hwile* more comfortable. I am also impressed that Sievers, as late as December 1929 when scholars had embraced *stefn*, adhered to *rode*.[48] I believe that no one — with the possible exception of John C. Pope — had as fine an ear for Germanic verse as Sievers: excessive faith in his ear may have misled him into

"Book-Moth" Riddle', reprinted in his *The Tomb of Beowulf and Other Essays on Old English* (Oxford, 1993), pp. 98–104 (pp. 100–01): the gender does not fit with the preceding adjectival ending, masculine accusative, a fact to which Robinson himself refers (his footnote 12), and further, the sense of the adjective, 'glorious, mighty, majestic, illustrious', goes well with the religious book through which the moth pursues its inward study, but it does not go well with the partly digested food of the ruminant, even though rumination provides much food for thought. The Old English word is not recorded in such a metaphorical sense; see *Dictionary of Old English* s.v. *cwudu*.

[46] See *The Dream of the Rood*, ed. by Michael Swanton, Old and Middle English Texts (Manchester, 1970), p. 94 the text, p. 125 notes on lines 70 and 71.

[47] Compare *Andreas*, ed. by Brooks, p. 94, n. on line 936 *hrædlice* alliterating on /r/.

[48] See Sievers's *schallanalytische Bearbeitung*, in *Das altenglische 'Traumgesicht vom Kreuz'*, ed. by Hans Bütow, Anglistische Forschungen, 78 (Heidelberg, 1935), p. 184.

Schallanalyse (in which I have no faith). Modern editors have found it necessary to explain who *we* and *us* are at lines 70, 73, and 75;[49] *rode* makes that explanation redundant. It appears that the most generally accepted emendation in line 71b to provide a subject for *gewat* is *stefn*; *storm* 'tumult, uproar, onslaught' favoured by some earlier scholars seems preferable. That too had the support of Sievers. My main reasons for quoting these lines is to indicate that *on staðole standan* may be good Old English for 'to stand at one's post', as did the crosses on Calvary. It is as close as I get to the Ruthwell Cross inscription, which I think of as I think of Éamonn Ó Carragáin.

As often in Old English lexicology, it would be possible to expatiate on almost every use of a word under discussion. Literal senses must underlie metaphorical usage: they are the foundation on which the metaphors stand, in which they are rooted. A more scientific account of *staþol* in verse and prose than mine would make more of statistics — to return to the Modern English example, the *mowing* is statistically insignificant in the *aftermath* — but in the minds of the Anglo-Saxon enigmatists such deep-seated meanings are exploited, and so the Riddles occupy a larger proportion of this paper than is their statistical due. Literary significance is ponderable, yet not accurately weighable in ways that are significant in statistics.

---

[49] For example, see *The Dream of the Rood*, ed. by Alan S. C. Ross and Bruce Dickins, Methuen's Old English Library, 2nd edn (London, 1945), p. 30.

INTOXICATION, FORNICATION, AND MULTIPLICATION: THE BURGEONING TEXT OF GENESIS A

Andy Orchard

The roots of English poetry are hard to discern, but it clear that biblical verse in Old English has an impressive history: it is only at the end of the seventh century that vernacular verse emerges into view, and, strikingly, both Bede's account of Cædmon and the much later testimony of William of Malmesbury concerning Cædmon's contemporary Aldhelm (who died in 709 or 710) make it clear that both these fathers of English poetry composed Old English biblical verse.[1] Moreover, if no extant biblical narrative poem can be securely assigned to either poet, successive linguistic studies in recent years by scholars such as Thomas Cable, Robert D. Fulk and Denis Cronan all seem to uphold the traditionally asserted relative antiquity of the surviving biblical poems *Genesis A*, *Exodus*, and *Daniel*, at least.[2] Such a background surely makes the assessment of the style and putative influence of these poems a matter of more than mediocre

---

[1] For Cædmon, see Bede, *Historia ecclesiastica gentis Anglorum*, 5.22 [24]; for Aldhelm, see William of Malmesbury, *Gesta pontificum*, 5, and further Paul G. Remley, 'Aldhelm as Old English Poet: *Exodus*, Asser, and the *Dicta Ælfredi*', in *Latin Learning and English Lore: Studies in Anglo-Saxon Literature for Michael Lapidge*, ed. by Katherine O'Brien O'Keeffe and Andy Orchard, 2 vols (Toronto, 2005), I, 90–108, esp. p. 91.

[2] T. Cable, 'Metrical Style as Evidence for the Date of *Beowulf*', in *The Dating of 'Beowulf'*, ed. by C. Chase (Toronto, 1981), pp. 77–82; R. D. Fulk, *A History of Old English Meter* (Philadelphia, 1992), pp. 391–92; Denis Cronan, 'Poetic Words, Conservatism, and the Dating of Old English Poetry', *Anglo-Saxon England*, 33 (2004), 23–50. For a contrary view, detailing the problems in using linguistic tests for dating, see Ashley Crandell Amos, *Linguistic Means of Determining the Dates of Old English Literary Texts*, Medieval Academy Books, 90 (Cambridge, MA, 1990).

moment, especially since they are preserved in a manuscript (Oxford, Bodleian Library, MS Junius 11) that may be up to three centuries younger than their dates of composition.[3]

This paper will focus on the first poem in the Junius manuscript that contains all three of these biblical poems, namely *Genesis A*, so-called to distinguish it from the seamlessly incorporated *Genesis B*, that (as Sievers marvellously demonstrated) derives from an Old Saxon source part of which still survives.[4] Most commentators seem to suppose that *Genesis A* is earlier than *Genesis B*, the Old Saxon original of which seems to date from the ninth century.[5] The recognition by Charles D. Wright that part of *Genesis A* derives from Aldhelm's verse *De uirginitate* (produced between 690 and 709)[6] pushes the earliest possible date of composition of that poem up to a century earlier than *Genesis B*, and while the further parallels between *Genesis A* and Prudentius that have been pointed out are consistent with such a date, Prudentius was such a popular author throughout the Anglo-Saxon period that his influence offers no secure grounds for dating.[7] Nothing, however, precludes the eighth-century date for *Genesis A* suggested by Cable, Cronan, and Fulk.[8]

[3] For the date of the so-called Junius manuscript, see now Leslie Lockett, 'An Integrated Re-Examination of the Dating of Oxford, Bodleian Library, Junius 11', *Anglo-Saxon England*, 31 (2002), 141–73; Lockett puts the manuscript in the period *c.* 960–*c.* 980, some three hundred years after the putative dates of composition of the biblical verses of Aldhelm and Cædmon, both of whose works presumably pre-date the surviving biblical poems by an indeterminate span.

[4] *Der Heliand und die angelsächsische Genesis*, ed. by Eduard Sievers (Halle, 1875); *Genesis A: A New Edition*, ed. by A. N. Doane (Madison, 1978); Alger Nicolaus Doane, '"Paraphrasis poetica": The Integration of Traditional Art and Traditional Learning in the Old English Poem *Genesis A*' (unpublished doctoral dissertation, University of Toronto, 1971); Nancy Mohr McKinley, 'Poetry vs Paraphrase: The Artistry of *Genesis A*' (unpublished doctoral dissertation, Harvard University, 1991); David Marsden Wells, 'A Critical Edition of the Old English *Genesis A* with a Translation' (unpublished doctoral dissertation, University of North Carolina at Chapel Hill, 1969).

[5] See further *The Saxon Genesis: An Edition of the West Saxon 'Genesis B' and the Old Saxon Vatican 'Genesis'*, ed. by A. N. Doane (Madison, 1991).

[6] Charles D. Wright, 'The Blood of Abel and the Branches of Sin: *Genesis A, Maxims I* and Aldhelm's *Carmen de uirginitate*', *Anglo-Saxon England*, 25 (1996), 7–19.

[7] See Andy Orchard, 'Conspicuous Heroism: Abraham, Prudentius, and the Old English Verse *Genesis*', in *Heroes and Heroines in Medieval English Literature: A Festschrift for Professor André Crépin*, ed. by Leo Carruthers (Cambridge, 1994), pp. 45–58; updated and reprinted in *The Poems of MS Junius 11*, ed. by R. M. Liuzza, Basic Readings in Anglo-Saxon England (New York, 2002), pp. 119–36.

[8] See note 2 above.

The style of *Genesis A* is seldom commented on, and still more seldom in positive terms. But we have come a long way since the normally sensitive W. P. Ker demonstrated an unusual tin ear in describing *Genesis A* as 'mere flat commonplace, interesting as giving the average literary taste and the commonplace poetical stock of a dull educated man'.[9] Slowly we have recognized its poet's use of Hebrew etymologies, as well as of what now seems the Germanic poet's stock-in-trade of repeated formulas, echo-words, and envelope-patterns, as highlighted by the work of such scholars as Paul Battles, Roberta Frank, Larry McKill, Fred Robinson, Colette Stévanovitch, and Michael Wilson.[10] In this context, it is interesting to compare two passages which are clearly connected within the text of the Vulgate itself, namely God's injunction to Adam and Eve to 'Increase and multiply' (*crescite et multiplicamini*, Genesis 1. 28), and the obviously parallel injunction by God to Noah and his sons immediately after the Flood to 'Increase and multiply' (*crescite et multiplicamini*, Genesis 9. 1), a commandment echoed by God shortly afterwards, again to Noah and his sons (*crescite et multiplicamini*, Genesis 9. 7).[11] It is instructive to compare these three passages, not only in the Vulgate, but also in their vernacular renderings in *Genesis A*, to assess the traditional techniques that the *Genesis A*-poet chose to use in transforming the Latin source.[12]

[9] W. P. Ker, *The Dark Ages* (London, 1955), p. 256.

[10] Fred C. Robinson, 'The Significance of Names in Old English Literature', *Anglia*, 86 (1968), 14–58; Roberta Frank, 'Some Uses of Paronomasia in Old English Scriptural Verse', *Speculum*, 47 (1972), 207–26; [Horst Richard] Paul Battles, 'The Art of the *scop*: Traditional Poetics in the Old English *Genesis A*' (unpublished doctoral dissertation, University of Illinois at Urbana-Champaign, 1998); Paul Battles, '*Genesis A* and the Anglo-Saxon "Migration Myth"', *Anglo-Saxon England*, 29 (2000), 43–66; *La Genèse, du manuscrit Junius XI de la Bodléienne*, ed. by Colette Stévanovitch, Publications de l'Association des médiévistes anglicistes de l'enseignement supérieur, hors série 1, 2 vols (Paris, 1992); Larry McKill, 'A Critical Study of the Old English *Genesis A*' (unpublished doctoral dissertation, State University of New York at Stony Brook, 1974); Michael J. Wilson, 'The Rhetoric of *Genesis A*' (unpublished doctoral dissertation, Kent State University, 2002).

[11] In fact, the phrase also appears in the Vulgate at Genesis 1. 22 and 8. 17, but the poet of *Genesis A* ignores both these occurrences. In discussing the first two of the passages from *Genesis A*, I build on the work of Paul Battles, 'The Art of the *scop*', pp. 221–29, who discusses the wider implications of such repetition in his Chapter 3: 'Traditional Rhetoric: The Echo-Word', pp. 168–240.

[12] In general, on the Latin sources for Old English biblical verse, see Paul G. Remley, *Old English Biblical Verse: Studies in 'Genesis', 'Exodus', and 'Daniel'*, Cambridge Studies in Anglo-Saxon England, 16 (Cambridge, 1996), esp. pp. 94–167.

The first passage represents God's blessing on Adam and Eve, with terms drawn directly from the Latin indicated by <u>underlining</u> (*GenA* 196–205):[13]

```
196    Temað nu and wexað,    tudre fyllað
197    eorðan ælgrene,    incre cynne,
198    sunum and dohtrum.    Inc sceal sealt wæter
199    wunian on gewealde    and eall worulde gesceaft.
200    Brucað blæddaga    and brimhlæste
201    and heofonfugla.    Inc is halig feoh
202    and wilde deor    on geweald geseald,
203    and lifigende,    ða ðe land tredað,
204    feorheaceno cynn,    ða ðe flod wecceð
205    geond hronrade.    Inc hyrað eall.
```

['Be fruitful now and grow, fill the all-green earth with progeny, the kindred of the two of you, sons and daughters. Salt water will have to abide your dominion, and all the world's creation. Enjoy fruit-days and sea-bounty and the birds of the sky. The hallowed cattle and wild beasts are granted to your dominion, and the living ones that tread the land, the life-increased kindreds that the flood stirs throughout the whale-riding: all will obey you.']

As implied by the rather infrequent underlining in the Old English, the Latin is rather starker (Genesis 1. 28):

<u>crescite et multiplicamini</u> et <u>replete terram</u> et subicite eam et <u>dominamini</u> piscibus maris et <u>uolatilibus caeli</u> et uniuersis <u>animantibus quae mouentur super terram</u>.

['Increase and multiply, and fill the earth, and subdue it, and rule over the fishes of the sea, and the fowls of the air, and all living creatures that move upon the earth.']

Among the more obvious additions to the source, the poet of *Genesis A* has introduced a series of emphatic dual forms heading successive b-lines (*incre* [. . .] *Inc* [. . .] *Inc* [. . .] *Inc*), 'filler' half-lines of a more or less formulaic nature, all in the a-lines (*sunum and dohtrum*, line 198a; *brucað blæddaga*, line 200a; *wilde deor*, line 202a; *geond hronrade*, line 205a),[14] while in the opening line the adverb *nu* ('now',

---

[13] Quotations from Old English poems follow The Anglo-Saxon Poetic Records, ed. by George Phillip Krapp and Elliott Van Kirk Dobbie, 6 vols (New York, 1931–53); the short titles are those used in the Toronto database: Antonette diPaolo Healey, John Price-Wilkin, and Takamichi Ariga, *Dictionary of Old English Corpus on the World-Wide Web*, Society for Early English and Norse Electronic Texts (Ann Arbor: University of Michigan Press, 1997; rev. 2000). Biblical quotations are from the Vulgate, with translations from Douay-Rheims.

[14] The formula *sunum and dohtrum* (and equivalents) occurs at *GenA* 924, 1133, 1139, 1153, 1221, 1229, 1245, 1606, 1640, 1729, and 1764; *Phoen* 406; *PPs105,1* 2; *Rid9* 12 (one notes in passing its overwhelming occurrence in *Genesis A* itself, and there in clusters); the formula *bruc-*

line 196) adds to the immediacy of the situation, and is the more interesting in that it is not required by the metre. More substantial additions include the unique (and likely new-coined) compounds *brimhlæste* ('sea-bounty', line 200b) and *feorheaceno* ('life-increased', line 204a), the latter seemingly a calque on the Latin *animantibus*, as well as the half-line 'ða ðe flod wecceð' ('that the flood stirs', line 204b), evidently added to match the preceding half-line 'ða ðe land tredað' ('that tread the land', line 203b). Other additions filling out other half-lines include the words *tudre* ('progeny', line 196b), *ælgrene* ('all-green', line 197a), and *geseald* ('granted', line 202b), the last again evidently for reasons of style, since it completes the self-rhyming half-line *on geweald geseald*. It is worth highlighting all these changes, since a large number of them recur in later parallel passages in *Genesis A*.

Like another before him, the poet seems to have looked on his work and seen that it was good: certainly, the next two times the theme is repeated in *Genesis A*, at the point where God blesses Noah and his sons (*GenA* 1512–17 and 1532–35a), there is considerable verbal repetition linking back to the original passage, here highlighted by the use of **bold** (underlining again indicates a direct debt to the Latin source, while the symbol '*' signals an emendation, with the manuscript reading given in the margin):

1512	**Tymað nu and tiedrað**, tires **brucað**,	
1513	mid gefean fryðo; **fyllað eorðan**,	
1514	**eall** geiceað. Eow **is** eðelstol	
1515	**and*** holmes hlæst **and heofonfuglas***	*Not in MS; MS* heofon fugla
1516	**and wildu deor on geweald geseald**,	
1517	**eorðe ælgrene and eacen feoh***.	*With* r *written above* h
	* * *	
1532	**Weaxað and** wridað, wilna **brucað**,	
1533	ara on **eorðan**; æðelum **fyllað**	
1534	eowre from**cynne** foldan sceatas,	
1535	**teamum and tudre**.	

['Be fruitful now and multiply, enjoy honour, peace with joy; fill the earth; increase all. There is granted to your dominion a home-seat and the ocean's bounty and the birds of

blæddaga- is found in *GenA* 1201 and *Phoen* 674; the formula *wild- deor(-)* is found in *Dan* 388, 511, and 576; *Dur* 7; *GenA* 1516; *GuthA* 276; *GuthB* 907; *Jul* 597; *Met27* 20; *PPs79,13* 2; *SoulI* 82; *SoulII* 77; the compound *wil(d)deor-* is found in *Beo* 1430; *Dan* 504, 571, 621, 623, 649; *GuthA* 741; *MSol* 82, 286, 306; *PPs67,27* 1; *PPs103,1* 2; the phrase *geond hronrade* is unique to *Genesis A*, but can be parallelled by phrases such as *on hron-/hranrade* in *Beo* 10; *And* 266, 634, and 821.

the sky and wild animals, the all-green earth and the increased cattle [. . .]. Grow and flourish, enjoy delights, honours on the earth, fill the corners of the land with your noble progeny, your fruit and multiplication.']

Again, the Latin source might be cited for comparison, with parallels with the earlier Latin passage highlighted by *italics*:

[9. 1] *crescite et multiplicamini* et *implete terram* [9. 2] et terror uester ac tremor sit super cuncta animalia terrae et super omnes uolucres *caeli* cum *uniuersis quae mouentur* in *terra* omnes *pisces maris* manui uestrae traditi sunt. [*UL* dedi . . . sub potestatem] [. . .] [9. 7] uos autem *crescite et multiplicamini* et ingredimini *super terram* et *implete* eam

[[9. 1] 'Increase, and multiply, and fill the earth. [9. 2] And let the fear and dread of you be upon all the beasts of the earth, and upon all the fowls of the air, and all that move upon the earth: all the fishes of the sea are delivered into your hand [. . .]' [9. 7] 'But increase you and multiply, and go upon the earth and fill it.']

The numerous parallels between the Old English versions (indicated in bold) are separated, we note, by some sixty-four manuscript pages, comprising nearly 1400 lines of the text, including the 618 lines of *Genesis B*, but ignoring another perhaps two hundred lines (three leaves) lost after line 205. It will be immediately obvious that (to put it bluntly) there are far more words in **bold** (echoed in the Old English) than there are underlined (drawn from the Latin). Strikingly, the Anglo-Saxon poet actually eschews the obvious parallelism: whereas all three Latin passages have very similar minor variations on the theme *crescite et multiplicamini et implete [replete] terram [eam]*, no two Old English renderings of this fixed pattern are entirely the same; 'Temað nu and wexað [. . .] fyllað | eorðan' (196–97a) becomes 'Tymað nu and tiedrað [. . .] fyllað eorðan' (1512a and 1513b) which in turn appears as 'Weaxað and wridað [. . .] eorðan [. . .] fyllað' (1532a–33). Again, whereas in the Latin it is the second of the three variations on this theme which is the longest, in the vernacular the iterations become progressively shorter, from ten lines to six to four (or from fifty-seven words to thirty-two to seventeen), with the degree of reliance on the Latin source likewise diminishing from fifteen words to eight to four; but there remains throughout far more emphasis on overlapping words shared with the other two Old English passages than on terms taken from the Latin (the figures are twenty-seven words, twenty-five words, and nine words respectively).

The poet emphasizes his control over the material still further by ensuring that the whole of the passage concerning Noah and his sons (and containing the double injunction) forms a tight envelope pattern, beginning with 'Tymað nu and tiedrað' (line 1512a), a phrase mostly sanctioned by the Vulgate, and ending with

'teamum and tudre' (line 1535a), a phrase which is not.[15] In the same way, the
poet of *Genesis A* scrupulously observes a distinction between the second-person
dual pronouns and pronominal forms that God uses to Adam and Eve in the first
passage, and which the poet added to the source (*incre* [...] *Inc* [...] *Inc* [...] *Inc*)
and the second-person plural forms used in the second and third passages (*Eow*
[...] *eowre*), which are sanctioned by similar second-person forms in the Vulgate
(*uester* [...] *uestrae* [...] *uos*). The particular connections between the first and
second passages are stark indeed: if the word *eorðe* appears forty-six times in *Genesis A*, it is only *ælgrene* here, just as the jingling phrase *on geweald geseald* is unique
in Old English poetry to these two passages (though it is also found, in rather
different contexts, in Vercelli IX.186 and Vercelli I.234). If we accept the suggestion that the phrase has a vague parallel either in the phrase *manui uestrae traditi
sunt* (as in the Vulgate) or *dedi manui uestrae sub potestatem* (as in the Vetus
Latina), then we have to suppose that (as perhaps also with the introduction of
dual forms) the poet of *Genesis A* had in mind the second biblical passage even as
he rendered the first. Likewise, we note that the order of dominated creatures is
different in the Bible but the same here: the order fish (*piscibus maris*), fowl (*uola-
tilibus caeli*), beasts (*animantibus* [...] *super terram*) of Genesis 1. 28 becomes
beasts (*animalia*), fowl (*uolucres caeli*), fish (*pisces maris*) in Genesis 9. 1–2; in
Genesis A the order of the first biblical passage is maintained in both lines 200–02
(*brimhlæste* [...] *heofonfugla* [...] *wilde deor*) and lines 1515–16 (*holmes hlæst*
[...] *heofonfuglas* [...] *wildu deor*), in almost identical words, highlighted by the
non-biblical element *(-)hlæst* ('bounty') that, as noted above, was added by the
poet, like so many of the key linking elements that connect the three passages.

But perhaps the most fascinating aspect of the obviously deliberate overlap between these passages is the extent to which it seems to have been recognized by the
scribe, and perhaps too by another early reader, as will be clear from Figures 19
and 20.

In Figure 19, the verbal sequence 'temað nu ⁊ [...] tudre fyllað · eorðan [...]
hlæste · ⁊ heofonfugla · [...] ⁊ wilde deor · on geweald geseald · feorheaceno' can
be matched in Figure 20 by the strikingly similar sequence 'Tymað nu ⁊ tiedrað
· [...] fyllað eorðan · [...] hlæst · ⁊ heofonfugla · [...] ⁊ wildu deor · on geweald
geseald · [...] eacen feo'r'h'.

[15] See further Colette Stévanovitch, 'Envelope Patterns in *Genesis A* and *B*', *Neophilologus*, 80
(1996), 465–78.

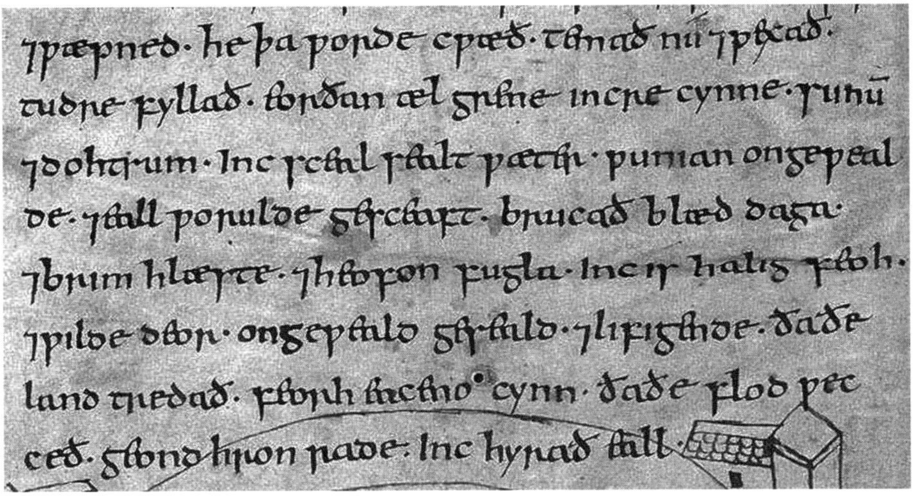

Figure 19. Oxford, Bodleian Library, MS Junius 11, p. 10, lines 7–14. From *Genesis A*, lines 195–205. By kind permission of the Bodleian Library, Oxford.

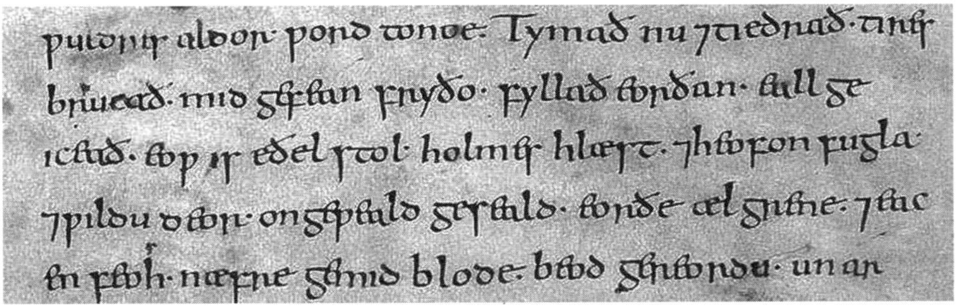

Figure 20. Oxford, Bodleian Library, MS Junius 11, p. 74, lines 10–14. From *Genesis A*, lines 1511–19. By kind permission of the Bodleian Library, Oxford.

Certainly, in Figure 20 the main scribe evidently wrote the ungrammatical form *heofonfugla* at 1515 (p. 74, line 12), most likely in echo of the earlier formulation (appropriate at 201 (p. 10, line 11), when it is a genitive following *brucað*), and someone (perhaps the main scribe: one cannot be clear) has erroneously added an *r* in line 1517 to the phrase *eacen feoh* (p. 74, line 14), again apparently as a deliberate echo of the unique compound *feorheaceno* in line 204 (p. 10, line 13). In other words, the scribe has apparently recognized the poet's repetition, despite the distance between the passages.

That the poet of *Genesis A* (and evidently the scribe of the Junius manuscript) could recognize and elaborate on verbal parallels present in the Vulgate text even over a considerable distance is perhaps not surprising, but it is clear from other passages that such recognition and highlighting of perceived thematic parallels represented a significant part of the poet's stock-in-trade. Consider for example, the massively expanded account of Noah's drunkenness, the first sin committed after the purging Flood, again with elements drawn directly from the Latin highlighted by underlining (*GenA* 1555–84a):

1555	Ða Noe ongan	niwan stefne
1556	mid hleomagum	ham staðelian
1557	and to eorðan him	ætes tilian;
1558	won and worhte,	wingeard sette,
1559	seow sæda fela,	sohte georne
1560	þa him wlitebeorhte	wæstmas brohte,
1561	geartorhte gife,	grene folde.
1562	Ða þæt geeode,	þæt se eadega wer
1563	on his wicum wearð	wine druncen,
1564	swæf symbelwerig,	and him selfa sceaf
1565	reaf of lice.	Swa gerysne ne wæs,
1566	læg þa limnacod.	He lyt ongeat
1567	þæt him on his inne*	swa earme gelamp,	MS innne
1568	þa him on hreðre	heafodswima
1569	on þæs halgan hofe	heortan clypte.
1570	Swiðe on slæpe	sefa nearwode
1571	þæt he ne mihte	on gemynd drepen
1572	hine handum self	mid hrægle wryon
1573	and sceome þeccan,	swa gesceapu wæron
1574	werum and wifum,	siððan wuldres þegn
1575	ussum fæder and meder	fyrene sweorde
1576	on laste beleac	lifes eðel.
1577	Þa com ærest	Cam in siðian,
1578	eafora Noes,	þæt his aldor læg,
1579	ferhðe* forstolen.	Þær he freondlice *MS* ferðe *with* h *above the line after* r
1580	on his agenum fæder	are ne wolde
1581	gesceawian,	ne þa sceonde huru
1582	hleomagum helan,	ac he hlihende
1583	broðrum sægde,	hu se beorn hine
1584	reste on recede.	

[Then Noah began for a second time to establish a home with his kinsman, and to till the earth for food; he toiled and worked, planted a vineyard, sowed a host of seeds, sought eagerly that the green earth might bring him bright-shining harvests, year-gleaming gifts. Then it came to pass that the blessed man became drunk with wine in his dwelling-places, slept feast-weary, and himself cast off the clothing from his body; as was not seemly, he lay then limb-naked. Little did he perceive that things had gone so wretchedly within his house, so that in his breast head-dizziness embraced his heart in his holy building. His mind was greatly constrained in sleep, so that, smitten in his consciousness, he was unable to cover himself with clothing with his hands and conceal his shameful parts, as was decreed [with a pun on *gesceapu* OE 'genitals'] for men and women, since the thegn of glory closed off the homeland of life behind our father and mother with a fiery sword. Then first there went in Ham, son of Noah, where his lord lay, deprived of his spirit. There he would not gaze in a friendly manner with favour on his own father, nor truly conceal the disgrace from his kinsmen, but laughing he told his brothers how that warrior rested in his hall.]

Compared with this lavish and full account, the Latin source seems bare indeed.

[9. 20] <u>coepitque Noe</u> uir agricola <u>exercere terram et plantauit uineam</u> [9. 21] bibensque <u>uinum inebriatus est</u> et <u>nudatus</u> in tabernaculo suo [9. 22] quod cum <u>uidisset Ham</u> pater Chanaan <u>uerenda</u> scilicet <u>patris</u> sui esse <u>nuda</u> nuntiauit duobus <u>fratribus</u> suis foras

[[9. 20] And Noe a husbandman began to till the ground, and planted a vineyard. [9. 21] And drinking of the wine was made drunk, and was uncovered in his tent. [9. 22] Which when Cham the father of Chanaan had seen, to wit, that his father's nakedness was uncovered, he told it to his two brethren without.]

The poet of *Genesis A* embellishes this passage significantly, and in the final line 'reste on recede' ('rested in his hall'), seems to gesture (as elsewhere in the poem) towards the accepted etymology of Noah's Hebrew name, which Jerome glosses as *quies* ('rest'), an etymology touted later in Anglo-Saxon England by (for example) Ælfric.[16] In this context, it is ironic that the passage begins with an uncharacteristic cluster of finite verbs denoting Noah's busy activity as he establishes his vineyard (*won* [...] *worhte* [...] *sette / seow* [...] *sohte* [...] *brohte*), in a section which not only goes well beyond the biblical source, but is highlighted by both rhyme and sound-play (for example in *staðelian / tilian*; *sohte* [...] *brohte*; *worhte* [...] *-beorhte* [...] *-torhte*; *sceaf / reaf*).

Apart from these adornments, the poet of *Genesis A* adds clear verbal parallels without warrant in the Latin source that extend both backwards, to his version of the expulsion of Adam and Eve from Paradise, and forwards, to his likewise embellished narrative of the taking of Sarah from Abraham by Abimelech. The debt to the poet's own earlier description of how Adam and Eve were expelled

---

[16] In general, see Matthias Thiel, *Grundlagen und Gestalt der Hebräischkenntnisse des frühen Mittelalters*, Biblioteca degli studi medievali, 4 (Spoleto, 1973), pp. 370–71; Ælfric alludes to this etymology in his *Letter to Sigeweard*. Compare the phrase *lagosiða rest* ('a rest from wandering on the waves', line 1486b) used by God to Noah earlier in the poem.

from Eden is signalled in the Noah-passage itself, with its reference to 'our father and mother' ('ussum fæder and meder', line 1575a), and indicated here in **bold**, with debts to the Latin source again highlighted by <u>underlining</u> (*GenA* 941–47):[17]

941	Hie þa wuldres weard <u>wædum gyrede</u>,	
942	scyppend usser; het heora **sceome þeccan**	cf. 1573
943	<u>frea frum**hrægle**;</u> het hie <u>from hweorfan</u>	cf. 1572
944	<u>neorxnawange</u> on **nearore lif**.	cf. 1570 and 1576
945	Him **on laste beleac** liðsa and <u>wynna</u>	cf. 1576
946	hihtfulne ham <u>halig engel</u>	
947	be frean hæse **fyrene sweorde**.	cf. 1575

[Then the guardian of glory, our creator, adorned them with clothes; the lord ordered them to cover their shameful parts with the first clothing, ordered them to turn from paradise to a more constrained life. A holy angel, according to the lord's command closed off the hopeful home of joys and delights with a fiery sword.]

[3. 21] fecit quoque Dominus Deus Adam et uxori eius tunicas pellicias et <u>induit eos</u> [3. 22] et ait ecce Adam factus est quasi unus ex nobis sciens bonum et malum nunc ergo ne forte mittat manum suam et sumat etiam de ligno uitae et comedat et uiuat in aeternum [3. 23] <u>emisit</u> eum <u>Dominus</u> Deus <u>de paradiso</u> uoluptatis ut operaretur terram de qua sumptus est [3. 24] eiecitque Adam et conlocauit ante paradisum <u>uoluptatis</u> <u>cherubin</u> et <u>flammeum gladium</u> atque uersatilem ad custodiendam uiam ligni uitae

[[3. 21] And the Lord God made for Adam and his wife garments of skins, and clothed them. [3. 22] And he said: 'Behold Adam is become as one of us, knowing good and evil: now therefore lest perhaps he put forth his hand and take also of the tree of life, and eat, and live for ever.' [3. 23] And the Lord God sent him out of the paradise of pleasure, to till the earth from which he was taken. [3. 24] And he cast out Adam: and placed before the paradise of pleasure a Cherubim, and a flaming sword, turning every way, to keep the way of the tree of life.]

One notes that *Genesis A* 1572–76 appears to draw heavily on lines 942–47, and that while the shared phraseology generally does not derive from the Latin sources of either passage (and is therefore not underlined), the shared phrase *fyrenum sweorde* ('fiery sword', lines 947 and 1575) clearly derives from the *flammeum gladium* ('fiery sword') that lies behind the earlier passage. As in the earlier passages expanding on the shared biblical injunction to 'increase and multiply' the poet seems keen here to point up the parallels between Noah on the one hand and Adam and Eve on the other.

---

[17] Compare Battles, 'The Art of the *scop*', pp. 227–28.

More surprisingly, perhaps, the account of Noah's drunkenness in *Genesis A* is also echoed in the poet's later description of the visit God makes to Abimelech, King of Gerar (*GenA* 2634b–2635 and 2641b–42):

2634	Com nihtes self,	
2635	þær se waldend **læg wine druncen**.	cf. 1563 and 1566
	* * *	
2641	Him **symbelwerig**	cf. 1564
2642	sinces[18] brytta þurh **slæp** oncwæð	cf. 1570

[He himself [= God] came at night where the ruler lay drunk with wine [...]. To him the giver of treasure (*or* 'giver of sins') weary with feasting, spoke through his sleep.]

The feasting, drinking, and subsequent sleeping, though certainly hinted at in the biblical text, is considerably embellished both in the Noah episode cited above and here with regard to Abimelech, most likely, as Paul Battles has suggested, to align this scene with the so-called 'sleeping after the feast' theme found elsewhere in *Beowulf* (no fewer than five times), as well as in *Andreas*.[19] What links all these accounts is ill-advised feasting (which, as Hugh Magennis has shown, in Anglo-Saxon England means drinking),[20] followed by ill-advised sleeping, disturbed by an evil consequence unforeseen to the feasting sleeper(s). Certainly, the poet of *Genesis A* heightens the feasting and sleeping references that are implicit in the biblical text, and adds entirely a reference to Noah's insouciance concerning the evil ahead (*He lyt ongeat*, line 1566b). More importantly, he repeats the theme with regard to Abimelech, where the biblical source specifies neither feasting nor sleeping at all. The possibility of direct literary borrowing between *Andreas* and *Beowulf* on the one hand and between *Beowulf* and *Genesis A* on the other have been the stuff of critical debate for many years,[21] and given the apparent antiquity

---

[18] The manuscript reads *synna* at this point. The phrase *sinces brytta* is also found in *GenA* 1857, and 2728; *synna bryttan* is also found in *El* 957.

[19] Battles, 'The Art of the *scop*', pp. 94–120; see too Brian McFadden, 'Sleeping after the Feast: Deathbeds, Marriage Beds, and the Power-Structure of Heorot', *Neophilologus*, 84 (2000), 629–46.

[20] Hugh Magennis, *Anglo-Saxon Appetites: Food and Drink and their Consumption in Old English and Related Literature* (Dublin, 1999).

[21] For the notion that *Andreas* borrows directly from *Beowulf*, see Anita Riedinger, 'The Poetic Formula in *Andreas, Beowulf* and the Tradition' (unpublished doctoral dissertation, New York University, 1985); Carole Hughes Funk, 'History of *Andreas* and *Beowulf*: Comparative Scholarship' (unpublished doctoral dissertation, University of Denver, 1997); Alison M. Powell, 'Verbal Parallels in *Andreas* and its Relationship to *Beowulf* and Cynewulf' (unpublished doctoral

of *Genesis A* it is perhaps worth considering whether the literary influence of *Genesis A* can be detected in any Old English poems that survive.

In attempting to assess which (if any) Old English poems are indebted to *Genesis A*, it is instructive to consider which poems share with it a significant overlap of rare or unusual diction. Denis Cronan has noted that no fewer than six poetic simplexes are uniquely shared by *Beowulf* and *Genesis A* and argues on the basis of other lexical links connecting *Genesis A*, *Beowulf*, *Exodus*, *Maxims I*, and *Widsith* that 'the most reasonable explanation of the conservative diction found in these poems is that these poems were composed in or around the eighth century'.[22] Intriguing further support for such a connection between the first two of these poems at least is offered by the alliterating doublet *weaxað and wridað* (*GenA* 1532, cited above), which in surviving Old English poetry is attested only in *Genesis A* (lines 1532, 1702, and 1902–03), *Charm for Unfruitful Land* (line 53), and *Beowulf* (line 1741); in all extant Old English, the doublet is only found elsewhere in Blickling Homily 16 and in *Alexander's Letter to Aristotle*, the close links of which to *Beowulf* have been recently reasserted.[23]

If we move beyond the level of the simplex, and consider compounds rarely or uniquely shared between *Genesis A* and no more than two other poems, a still more nuanced picture emerges. A list of such compounds is given in Appendix I below, rearranged to factor in the length of the poems involved and focussing only on surviving poems of over three hundred lines. The distribution is intriguing: if such compounds are found in a tiny proportion of verses overall (ranging from 0.12% to 2.29% for the poems cited), there is still an enormous step between the poem

---

dissertation, University of Cambridge, 2002). Anita Riedinger has also published a series of pertinent articles, including 'The Old English Formula in Context', *Speculum*, 60 (1985), 294–317; '*Andreas* and the Formula in Transition', in *Hermeneutics and Medieval Culture*, ed. by Patrick Gallacher and Helen Damico (Albany, 1989), pp. 183–91; and 'The Formulaic Relationship Between *Beowulf* and *Andreas*', in *Heroic Poetry in the Anglo-Saxon Period: Studies in Honor of Jess B. Bessinger, Jr*, ed. by H. Damico and J. Leyerle, Studies in Medieval Culture, 32 (Kalamazoo, 1993), pp. 283–312. See now Andy Orchard, *A Critical Companion to 'Beowulf'* (Cambridge, 2002), pp. 163–66. The putative connection between *Beowulf* and *Genesis A* is outlined in *Beowulf and the Fight at Finnsburg*, ed. by F. Klaeber, 3rd edn with 1st and 2nd supplements (Boston, 1950), pp. cx–cxiii.

[22] Cronan, 'Poetic Words', p. 48. The words in question are *dyhtig* 'strong' (*GenA* 1993; *Beo* 1287); *fær* 'ship, vessel' (*GenA* 1307, 1323, 1394, 1419, 1544; *Beo* 33); *freme* 'good, valiant' (*GenA* 2332; *Beo* 1932); *gombe* 'tribute' (*GenA* 1978; *Beo* 11); *heore* 'safe, pleasant, mild' (*GenA* 1468; *Beo* 1372); *secg* 'sword' (*GenA* 2001; *Beo* 684).

[23] Compare Orchard, *Critical Companion to 'Beowulf'*, pp. 25–39.

with the greatest overlap (*Judith*, with eight such compounds, representing one every forty-four lines or so), and the next largest degree of overlap (*Exodus*, with seven such compounds, representing one every eighty-four lines or so); in all other poems over three hundred lines such compounds appear fewer than once every hundred lines. This figure becomes still more striking when it is realized that fully half of these overlapping compounds occur in a single dense passage of only thirty-three lines of *Judith* (lines 6–38), representing a strike-rate for such rare or unique shared compounds of one every eight lines or so. The compound *ælfsciene* ('elf-bright', *Jud* 14a; *GenA* 1827a and 2731) is particularly interesting here, since in each case the referent, namely Judith and (twice) Sarah, is dangerously seductive from the point of view of characters in their respective poems, particularly in the case of the poor drunk war-lords (Holofernes and Abimelech) who seek unsuccessfully to sleep with them.[24]

The notion of some connection between *Judith* and *Genesis A*, particularly with regard to the Abimelech episode in the latter (lines 2621–2759), gathers support when the analysis moves beyond shared compounds and considers shared formulas; a list of twenty-six such parallel formulas is found in Appendix II below, and once again the distribution of such formulas is striking. No fewer than six of these parallels are found in a brief passage from *Judith* that runs from line 9 to line 32[25] and matches almost precisely the similar concentration of unique and rare shared compounds already noted: the thirty-three lines from *Jud* 6–38 contain three uniquely shared compounds and one uniquely shared formula with *Genesis A*, as well as one compound and five formulas that appear in no more than three other poems.[26] Likewise, six of the parallel formulas noted in Appendix II derive from the section of *Genesis A* dealing with the so-called war of the kings (*GenA* 1960–2095),[27] and no fewer than five of these parallels pertain to the

---

[24] On elves as dangerously seductive, see Alaric [Timothy Peter] Hall, 'The Meanings of *Elf*, and Elves, in Medieval England' (unpublished doctoral dissertation, University of Glasgow, 2005), pp. 71–76; for a different sense of *ælfscino*, see Heather Stuart, 'The Meaning of OE **ælfsciene*', *Parergon*, 2 (1972), 22–26.

[25] See Appendix II, nos [1]–[6].

[26] The phrase *gumena baldor* [1] is unique to *Genesis A* and *Judith*; *ofstum myclum* [2] is also found in *Elene* 44, 102, and 999; *folces ræsw-* [3] in *Andreas* 619 and 1086; *rof- rand- / rond-* [4] in *Elene* 50 and *Beowulf* 682, 1793, and 2538; *sinces brytta(-)* [5] in *Elene* 194, *Wanderer* 25, and *Beowulf* 607, 1170, 1922, and 2071 (for the manuscript form *synna brytta* in *GenA* 2642a, see note 18 above); *gumena aldor* [6] in *Dan* 548.

[27] See Appendix II, nos [4], [9], [12], [15], [17], and [23].

Abimelech episode.[28] The clear thematic connection between the biblical account of Abimelech's attempted seduction of Sarah in *Genesis A*, where, as we have seen, the Old English poet has added to his biblical source the traditional vernacular theme of 'sleeping after the feast', and the drunken post-prandial attempted seduction of Judith by Holofernes makes the notion of the direct influence of *Genesis A* on *Judith* an attractive possibility. With regard to the overlapping formulas linking the war of the kings in *Genesis A* and the account of the battle in *Judith* largely unwarranted by the source, it is worth highlighting the fact that two of the parallels noted are relatively extensive, and refer on the one hand to the beginning of the war of the kings in *Genesis A* and the beginning of the battle between the Assyrians and Jews in *Judith*, and on the other to the headlong flight of the foes that brings each respective encounter to an end.[29] It has been suggested in another article that in composing this section of his poem, describing a battle without warrant in his biblical source, the *Judith*-poet was led to borrow from another Old English poem known to him, namely Cynewulf's *Elene*,[30] and it may be that *Genesis A* has here been laid under similar contribution.

It is hoped that the evidence presented above will serve in some small part to support the notion that for later Anglo-Saxon authors, as for us, the antiquity and artistry of *Genesis A* were indeed a continuing revelation. Certainly, in the chain of textual associations that links Adam and Eve, and Noah, and Abimelech, as well as in the parallel textual connections between the war of the kings and Abimelech and the treatment of similar themes in *Judith*, it seems that the poet of *Genesis A* surely took to heart the biblical injunction to 'increase and multiply'.

---

[28] See Appendix II, nos [1]–[2], [5], [7], and [21].

[29] With regard to parallel [17], the beginning of the respective conflicts, one might note that the phrase *ecgum dihtig* in *GenA* 1993a is also found (as *ecgum dyhttig*) in *Beo* 1287a; the occurrence of the clearly similar phrase *ecgum þyhtig* in *Beo* 1558b makes one doubt whether the unique form *þyhtig* is indeed a genuine word at all, given the common scribal miscopying of *þ* or *ð* for *d* (and vice versa). With regard to parallel [23], the rout that signals the end of each conflict, one might note that the phrase *laðan cynnes*, found in *Jud* 310, is also found elsewhere in *Jud* 226 and *GenA* 2550 (see Appendix II, no. [16]), as well as in *Beo* 2008 and 2354.

[30] See Andy Orchard, 'Computing Cynewulf: The *Judith*-Connection', in *The Text in the Community: Essays on Medieval Works, Manuscripts, and Readers*, ed. by Jill Mann and Maura Nolan (Notre Dame, 2005), pp. 75–106.

Appendix I

Unique and Rare Shared Compound in Genesis A

[only poems over three hundred lines shown; * denotes an emended form]

Judith (349 lines; 8 compounds [2.29%])

ælfsciene 'elf-bright'	*GenA* 1827, 2731	*Jud* 14
aldorduguþ 'chief nobility'	*GenA* 2081	*Jud* 309
beddrest 'bed-couch'	*GenA* 2250, 2716	*Jud* 36
blachleor 'pale-cheeked'	*GenA* 1970	*Jud* 128
herbuende 'those living here'	*GenA* 1079	*Jud* 96; *MB* 29.60
ombihtscealc 'serving-man'	*GenA* 1870	*Jud* 38; *PPs* 133.1
torhtmod 'bright-minded'	*GenA* 1502	*Jud* 6, 93
þancolmod 'thoughtful-minded'	*GenA* 1705	*Jud* 172; *MB* 19.14

Exodus (590 lines; 7 compounds [1.19%])

deawigfeþere 'dewy-feathered'	*GenA* 1984	*Ex* 163
drenceflod 'drench-flood'	*GenA* 1398	*Ex* 364*
leodweard 'rule over a people'	*GenA* 1180, 1196	*Ex* 57
leodwer 'countryman'	*GenA* 1833	*Ex* 110
magoræswa 'leader of men'	*GenA* 1624	*Ex* 17*, 55*, 102
randwiga 'shield-warrior'	*GenA* 2829	*Ex* 126, 134; *Beo* 1298, 1793
tuddorteonde 'bearing fruit'	*GenA* 959	*Ex* 372

Guthlac B (510 lines; 6 compounds [1.17%])

feorhcwealm 'mortal pain'	*GenA* 1038, 1103	*GuthB* 915
foldwong 'ground-plain'	*GenA* 1951*	*GuthB* 1326; *ChristC* 974
gastgedal 'soul-parting'	*GenA* 1127	*GuthB* 862, 1138
sweglcyning 'heaven-king'	*GenA* 2659	*GuthB* 1082
wineþearfende 'needing a friend'	*GenA* 2482	*GuthB* 1347; *And* 300
yrfestol 'hereditary seat'	*GenA* 1629, 2177	*GuthB* 1319; *PPs* 68.36

Beowulf (3182 lines; 29 compounds [0.91%])

ærgestreon 'ancient treasure'	*GenA* 2148	*Beo* 1757, 2232; *ChristC* 996
agendfrea 'possessing lord'	*GenA* 2141, 2239	*Beo* 1883*
aldorgedal 'life-parting'	*GenA* 1071, 1959	*Beo* 805

bælfyr 'pyre-fire'	*GenA* 2857	*Beo* 3143; *Jln* 579
blondenfeax 'grey-haired'	*GenA* 2343, 2602	*Beo* 1594, 1791, 1873, 2962; *Brun* 45
burhloca 'city-enclosure'	*GenA* 2539	*Beo* 1928; *And* 940, 1038, 1065
feorhbana 'life-slayer'	*GenA* 1020, 2088	*Beo* 2465
folccyning 'people-king'	*GenA* 1974, 2074, 2754	*Beo* 2733, 2873
fyrdgestealla 'battle-companion'	*GenA* 1999	*Beo* 2873
gumcynn 'mankind'	*GenA* 1275	*Beo* 260, 944, 2765; *Ridd81* 17
guþcyning 'war-king'	*GenA* 2123	*Beo* 199, 1969, 2335, 2563, 2677, 3036
heafodmæg 'chief kinsman'	*GenA* 1200, 1605	*Beo* 588, 2151; *And* 942*
hordburh 'rich city'	*GenA* 2007	*Beo* 467
hronrad 'whale-riding'	*GenA* 205	*Beo* 10; *And* 266, 634, 821
leodburh 'people's city'	*GenA* 2503	*Beo* 2471
mereliþend(e) 'sea-traveller'	*GenA* 1407	*Beo* 255; *And* 353
randwiga 'shield-warrior'	*GenA* 2829	*Beo* 1298, 1793; *Ex* 126, 134
sawldreor 'life-blood'	*GenA* 1520	*Beo* 693
stanbeorh 'stone enclosure'	*GenA* 2214	*Beo* 2213
swyltdæg 'day of death'	*GenA* 1221	*Beo* 2798
wægliþend 'wave-traveller'	*GenA* 1395, 1432	*Beo* 3158; *Whale* 11
wælbedd 'bed of slaughter'	*GenA* 1011	*Beo* 964
wældreor 'slaughter-blood'	*GenA* 1016, 1098	*Beo* 1631
wæpnedmen 'virile man'	*GenA* 919	*Beo* 1284
wigsigor 'battle-victory'	*GenA* 2003	*Beo* 1554
wlitebeorht 'beauty-bright'	*GenA* 131, 188, 220, 1560, 1728, 1804	*Beo* 93; *MB* 25.4
wonhygd 'lack of mind'	*GenA* 1673	*Beo* 434
woruldcyning 'worldly king'	*GenA* 2337	*Beo* 1684, 3180*; *Az* 185
wuldortorht 'glory-bright'	*GenA* 119, 2770, 2875	*Beo* 1136; *And* 1457

Daniel (764 lines; 6 compounds [0.79%])

cynegod 'nobly good'	*GenA* 1590, 1736	*Dan* 196, 432; *Widsith* 56
folcgesiþ 'lordly companion'	*GenA* 2134	*Dan* 411; *MB* 1.70
herewosa 'battle-fighter'	*GenA* 85	*Dan* 628

reþemod 'angry-minded'   *GenA* 47, 1684,   *Dan* 33
                                         2494
þeownyd 'forced enslavement'   *GenA* 2030   *Dan* 293, 307; *El* 768
weorcþeow 'work-slave'   *GenA* 2262, 2721* *Dan* 74

Andreas (1722 lines; 13 compounds [0.75%])
æscberend 'spear-bearer'   *GenA* 2041   *And* 47, 1076, 1537
burhloca 'city-enclosure'   *GenA* 2539   *And* 940, 1038, 1065; *Beo*
                                                                 1928
goldburg 'gold-city'   *GenA* 2551   *And* 1655
heafodmæg 'chief kinsman'   *GenA* 1200, 1605   *And* 942*; *Beo* 588, 2151
hearmloca 'harm-enclosure'   *GenA* 91   *And* 95, 1029; *El* 695
hronrad 'whale-riding'   *GenA* 205   *And* 266, 634, 821; *Beo* 10
inflede 'flood-full'   *GenA* 232   *And* 1504
lifcearu 'life-care'   *GenA* 878   *And* 1428
mereliþend(e) 'sea-traveller'   *GenA* 1407   *And* 353; *Beo* 255
ræsbora 'battle-carrier'   *GenA* 1811   *And* 139, 385
wægþel 'wave-plank'   *GenA* 1358, 1446,   *And* 1711
                                         1496
wineþearfende 'needing a friend' *GenA* 2482   *And* 300; *GuthB* 1347
wuldortorht 'glory-bright'   *GenA* 119, 2770,   *And* 1457; *Beo* 1136
                                         2875

Christ A (426 lines; 2 compounds [0.47%])
magotudor 'child-offspring'   *GenA* 2766   *ChristB* 629
sibblufu 'kin-love'   *GenA* 24, 2516   *ChristB* 635; *Part* 8

Elene (1321 lines; 6 compounds [0.45%])
hearmloca 'harm-enclosure'   *GenA* 91   *El* 695; *And* 95, 1029
leodmæg 'people-kin'   *GenA* 2695   *El* 380
monrim 'number of men'   *GenA* 1763, 2749   *El* 650
stiþhydig 'stern-minded'   *GenA* 2897   *El* 121; *Jln* 654
þeownyd 'forced enslavement'   *GenA* 2030   *El* 768; *Dan* 293, 307
witebroga 'fearful punishment'   *GenA* 45   *El* 931; *Jln* 135, 196

Juliana (731 lines; 3 compounds [0.41%])
bælfyr 'pyre-fire'   *GenA* 2857   *Jln* 579; *Beo* 3143
stiþhydig 'stern-minded'   *GenA* 2897   *Jln* 654; *El* 121
witebroga 'fearful punishment'   *GenA* 45   *Jln* 135, 196; *El* 931

Metres of Boethius (**1750 lines; 7 compounds [0.4%]**)

beamsceadu 'shadow of a tree'	*GenA* 859	*MB* 8.28
folcgesiþ 'lordly companion'	*GenA* 2134	*MB* 1.70; *Dan* 411
gielpsceaþa 'boasting harmer'	*GenA* 96	*MB* 9.49
gumrinc 'man-guy'	*GenA* 1552	*MB* 26.53; *Ridd87* 4
herbuende 'here-dwellers'	*GenA* 1079	*MB* 29.60; *Jud* 96
þancolmod 'thoughtful-minded'	*GenA* 1705	*MB* 19.14; *Jud* 172
wlitebeorht 'beauty-bright'	*GenA* 131, 188, 220, 1560, 1728, 1804	*MB* 25.4; *Beo* 93

Christ C (**797 lines; 3 compounds [0.38%]**)

ærgestreon 'ancient treasure'	*GenA* 2148	*ChristC* 996; *Beo* 1757, 2232
folcdriht 'multitude of people'	*GenA* 1262	*ChristC* 1066
foldwong 'ground-plain'	*GenA* 1951*	*ChristC* 974; *GuthB* 1326

Battle of Maldon (**325 lines; 1 compound [0.31%]**)

heorþwerod 'hearth-retainers'	*GenA* 1605, 2039, 2076	*Maldon* 24; *Order* 91*

Christ A (**439 lines; 1 compound [0.23%]**)

monwise 'folk-custom'	*GenA* 1939	*ChristA* 77

Phoenix (**677 lines; 1 compound [0.15%]**)

blæddagas 'prosperous days'	*GenA* 200, 1201	*Phx* 674

Paris Psalter (**5040 lines; 7 compounds [0.14%]**)

elebeam 'olive-tree'	*GenA* 1473	*PPs* 51.7, 127.4
ferhþcofa 'spirit-enclosure'	*GenA* 2604	*PPs* 108.17
norþdæl 'north-part'	*GenA* 32	*PPs* 88.11
ombihtscealc 'serving-man'	*GenA* 1870	*PPs* 133.1; *Jud* 38
sæflod 'sea-flood'	*GenA* 1437	*PPs* 68.34
wingeard 'vinyard'	*GenA* 1558	*PPs* 77.47, 79.8, 79.14, 104.29, 106.36, 127.3
yrfestol 'hereditary seat'	*GenA* 1629, 2177	*PPs* 68.36; *GuthB* 1319

Guthlac A (**818 lines; 1 compound [0.12%]**)

hearmstæf 'harm-foundation'	*GenA* 939	*GuthA* 229

Appendix II

A Selection of Parallels between Genesis A *and* Judith

[punctuation and capitalization have been removed to facilitate comparison; emended forms are indicated by an asterisk]

[1] *Jud*   9   girwan up swæsendo   to ðam het se **gumena baldor**
    GenA 2694   ac ic me **gumena baldor**   guðbordes sweng

[2] *Jud*   10   ealle ða yldestan ðegnas   hie ðæt **ofstum miclum**
    Jud   70   ut of ðam inne   **ofstum miclum**
    GenA 2673   him þa Abraham   to **ofstum miclum**

[3] *Jud*   12   feran **folces ræswan**   þæt wæs þy feorðan dogor
    GenA 1669   swa þa foremeahtige   **folces ræswan**

[4] *Jud*   20   **rofe rond**wiggende   þeah ðæs se rica ne wende
    GenA 2049   rincas wæron* **rofe***   **randas** wægon*
            MS *waron*; *rofe* altered from *rore*; *wægon* altered from *wæron* (?)

[5] *Jud*   30   swiðmod **sinces brytta**   oðþæt hie on swiman lagon
    GenA 1857   his selfes sele   **sinces brytta**
    GenA 2642   **sinces* brytta**   þurh slæp oncwæð   MS *synna*
    GenA 2728   to Sarran   **sinces brytta**

[6] *Jud*   32   agrotene goda gehwylces   swa het se **gumena aldor**
    GenA 1863   ongæt hwæðere   **gumena aldor**

[7] *Jud*   67   wunode under wolcna hrofe   gefeol ða **wine** swa **druncen**
    Jud   106–07   þone sweoran him   þæt he on swiman **læg**
                druncen ond dolhwund   næs ða dead þa
    GenA 1563   on his wicum wearð   **wine druncen**
    GenA 2606   **wine druncen**   gewitan ne meahte
    GenA 2635   þær se waldend   læg **wine druncen**

[8] *Jud*   88–89   swyðe sorgum gedrefed   forgif me **swegles ealdor**
                sigor ond **soðne** geleafan   þæt ic myd þys sweorde mote
    Jud   124   **swegles ealdor**   þe hyre **sigores** onleah
    GenA 862   þa sona ongann   **swegles aldor**
    GenA 2542   þa ic sendan gefrægn   **swegles aldor**
    GenA 2807–09 sweotol is and gesene   þæt þe **soð** metod
                on gesiððe is   **swegles aldor**
                se ðe **sigor** seleð   snyttrum mihtum
    GenA 2879   swa him sægde   ær **swegles aldor**

[9] *Jud*   128   **blachleor ides**   hyra begea nest
    GenA 1970   **blachleor ides**   bifiende gan

[10] *Jud*   130   and hit ða swa heolfrig   hyre on **hond ageaf**
     GenA 2121   þurh **hand ageaf**   and þæs hereteames

[11] *Jud*   145   searoðoncol mægð   þa **heo on sið gewat**
     GenA 2267   to Sarran   ac **heo on sið gewat**

[12] *Jud*   178   **leoda ræswan**   on ðæs laðestan
     GenA 1656   **leoda ræswan**   leofum mannum
     GenA 2075   **leode ræswan**   him on laste stod

[13] *Jud*   201   **secgas ond gesiðas**   bæron sigeþufas*   MS *þufas*
     GenA 2067   **secgas and gesiððas**   **sigor** eft ahwearf

[14] *Jud*   184   **lengran lifes**   þæt he mid læððum us
     GenA 1841   **lengran lifes**   se us þas lade sceop

[15] *Jud*   206–07   wulf in walde   and se **wanna** hrefn
                         wælgifre **fugel**   wistan* begen   MS *westan*
     GenA 1983   wraðe **wæl**herigas   sang se **wanna fugel**

[16] *Jud*   226   landbuende   **laðum cynne**
     Jud   310   **laðan cynnes**   lythwon becom
     GenA 2550   **laðan cynnes**   lig eall fornam

[17] *Jud*   229–31   medowerige   mundum **brugdon**
                         scealcas **of sceaðum**   scirmæled swyrd
                         ecgum gecoste   slogon eornoste
     GenA 1991–93   hlud hildesweg   handum **brugdon**
                         hæleð **of scæðum**   hring**mæled sweord**
                         ecgum dihtig   þær wæs eaðfynde

[18] *Jud*   247   slegefæge hæleð   **slæpe** to**bredon**
     GenA 1588   Sem and Iafeð   ða of **slæpe** on**brægd**
     GenA 2666   sinces gesundne   þa **slæpe** to**brægd**

[19] *Jud*   267   **bælc forbiged**   beornas stodon
     GenA 54   **bælc forbigde**   þa he gebolgen wearð

[20] *Jud*   286–87   toweard getacnod   þæt **þære tide ys**
                         mid niðum **neah geðrungen**   þe we sculon nyde* losian
                                                              NOT IN MS
     GenA 2510–11   and his torn wrecan   **þære tide is**
                         neah geþrungen   gewit þu nergean þin

[21] *Jud*   300   **fægre** on fultum   **frea ælmihtig**
    GenA 852   þa com feran   **frea ælmihtig**
    GenA 904   **frea ælmihtig**   fagum wyrme
    GenA 1359   and eall þæt to fæsle   **frea ælmihtig**
    GenA 1427   **frea ælmihtig**   frecenra siða
    GenA 2760   þa com feran   **frea ælmihtig**
    GenA 2353   him þa **fægere**   **frea ælmihtig**

[22] *Jud*   302   **hæleð higerofe**   herpað worhton
    GenA 1709   **hæleð higerofe**   hatene wæron

[23] *Jud*   307–13   Þær on greot gefeoll
                   se hyhsta dæl   heafodgerimes
                   Assiria   **ealdorduguðe**,
                   laðan cynnes.   Lythwon becom
                   cwicera to cyððe.   Cirdon cynerofe,
                   wiggend on **wiðertrod**,   wælscel on innan,
                   reocende hræw.
    GenA 2080–85   Fleonde wæron*   NOT IN MS
                   Elamitarna   **aldorduguðe**
                   dome bedrorene,   oðþæt hie Domasco
                   unfeor wæron.   Gewat him Abraham ða
                   on þa **wig**rode   **wiðertrod** seon
                   laðra monna.

[24] *Jud*   323   cwicera cynna   þa seo cneoris eall
    GenA 1297   and **cynna gehwilc**   cucra wuhta
    GenA 1311   **cwic**lifigendra   **cynna gehwilces**

[25] *Jud*   338   gerenode **readum golde**   ond eal þæt se rinca baldor
    GenA 2406   reced ofer **readum golde**   ongan þa rodera waldend

[26] *Jud*   342   wuldor **weroda dryhtne**   þe hyre weorðmynde geaf
    GenA 1362   **weroda drihten**   þurh his word abead
    GenA 1411   gelædde þa wigend   **weroda drihten**

Understanding Hrothgar's Humiliation: *Beowulf* Lines 144–74 in Context

Jane Roberts

In his reading of 'Structure and Thematic Development in *Beowulf*', back in 1967, Éamonn Ó Carragáin demonstrated the importance of 'vital clues' supplied by the manuscript itself, its 'enigmatical sectional divisions', for reaching an understanding of the poem,[1] an approach that has over the intervening years become accepted normal practice not just for *Beowulf* but for other poems in the corpus of Anglo-Saxon poetry.[2] Recently, when thinking over the difficulties presented by the *gifstol* passage (lines 168–69), I found myself returning to his analysis, to see how he dealt with this crux. Ever a wise man, he passed it by, choosing rather to emphasize the larger issues in play. Taking 'Lines 1–188, Prelude — Fitt II' as the first unit for examination, he shows first how in the '*Exordium to the poem*' the poet sets out 'the heroic qualities which are to become one of the dominant themes: *þrym* (power, glory) and *ellen* (valour)'. Then, in fitt I, just as the building and glory of Heorot are balanced with its fate, 'so the origins of the Grendel tribe bring a prophecy of their end'. With fitt II 'violent action' comes to the fore, and 'humans and monsters are not merely contrasted, but clash'. Before the publication of Ó Carragáin's analysis of *Beowulf*, the manuscript divisions, if noted, were for the most part placed discreetly in the margins, as if an interruption

---

[1] 'Structure and Thematic Development in *Beowulf*', *Proceedings of the Royal Irish Academy*, 66C (1967), 1–51.

[2] For example, see Earl R. Anderson, 'Cynewulf's Elene: Manuscript Divisions and Structural Symmetry', *Modern Philology*, 72 (1974), 111–22, and, for a very recent contribution, Frederick M. Biggs, 'The Politics of Succession in *Beowulf* and Anglo-Saxon England', *Speculum,* 80 (2005), 709–41. The unity of fitt XXXI is central to Biggs's argument.

to the narrative; and indeed the absurd idea was widespread that they might reflect the completion of copying a folio.[3] Nowadays division markers tend to be more clearly presented, with the numbers given prominence and with space opened between fitts. This is the case in the recent edition of Mitchell and Robinson, who, although observing that divisions are sometimes lacking where 'modern readers would expect a narrative break', reach the conclusion that 'Some systematic correlation between fitt-divisions and narrative content may bespeak authorial origin of the segmentation'.[4] Recognition of the unity of the second fitt is accepted in this paper, and I shall explore the poet's use in it of a commenting device omnipresent in Old English poetry, extended reflection introduced by *swa*.

The second fitt presents the dilemma of a great leader of the Danes. Hrothgar's achievements are enviable. From fitt I we know that not only has he achieved 'heresped' ('success in war', line 64), but he has had built a 'medoærn micel' ('great mead-hall', line 69) in which he feasts his followers and shares out treasures generously and equitably.[5] Now he confronts an adversary that he and his men are unable to defeat, the grim and greedy Grendel who, for twelve long years, has slaughtered with impunity. Such is the enmity of that occupier of Hrothgar's hall (ironically, the poet uses the phrase 'healðegnes hete', line 142, signalling Hrothgar's loss of overall control of his hall) that anyone minded to escape must seek the greater security of staying far away from Heorot during the dark hours of night. In the manuscript there are two distinctive capital letters within the fitt: 'Swā' ('So', line 144) begins with a large round *s* and 'Hwīlum' ('Sometimes', line 175) with a large distinctive *h*, its final stroke curving to the left. These capitals suggest that there are three movements within fitt II, a blocking of text that disappears in the editions, and not improperly so. It is, after all, an editor's task to decide on what forms of punctuation will mediate between the manuscript and readers accustomed to modern norms. Thus, three editions that proved influential in the twentieth century vary considerably from one another in the paragraphs allotted fitt II. Klaeber has one indentation only, at line 164, whereas Wrenn makes five

[3] Henry Bradley, 'The Numbered Sections in Old English Poetical Manuscripts', *Proceedings of the British Academy*, 7 (1915–16), 165–87.

[4] *Beowulf: An Edition with Relevant Shorter Texts*, ed. by Bruce Mitchell and Fred C. Robinson (Oxford, 1998).

[5] Where no other source is indicated, *Beowulf* quotations in this paper are taken from *Beowulf and the Fight at Finnsburg*, ed. by F. Klaeber, 3rd edn with 1st and 2nd supplements (Boston, 1950).

paragraphs (lines 115–25, 126–43, 144–63, 164–69, and 170–88),[6] and Mitchell and Robinson settle for an undivided whole.[7]

The first movement of the second fitt (lines 115–43) describes the beginning of Grendel's attacks on Heorot, telling how, in the early dawn hours after the first onslaught, Hrothgar 'unblīðe sæt' ('sat, unhappy,' line 130), an image arrested by the nudging observation, 'wæs þæt gewin tō strang, | lāð ond longsum' ('the conflict was too hard, hateful and protracted', lines 133b–34a). At line 144 the poet pauses to make plain the uneasy state of Hrothgar's kingdom and, with 'Swā' (line 144) marking a change to commentary, explains (lines 144–74) that throughout the twelve years following the first attack Grendel posed a constant threat to Hrothgar. This is one of the poem's sometimes lengthy passages that draw attention to and expand on significant events in the narrative. So Grendel, 'wið rihte' ('wrongfully', line 144), held sway for twelve years, 'āna wið eallum' ('one against all', line 145), carrying on relentless persecution of the Danes, a creature from the marshes, aligned with images of darkness, death, and evil: essentially, 'Grendel wan | hwīle wið Hrōþgār' ('for a time Grendel waged war against Hrothgar', lines 151–52). A second 'Swā' (line 164) refocuses the explanation, drawing the elements together by contrasting the positions of Grendel and Hrothgar. In the editions the 'hē' of line 168 is generally identified with Grendel, but I shall argue for the alternative possible reading, that here the referent of 'hē' is Hrothgar.[8] In the absence of effective opposition, Grendel held Heorot during the darkness of night, and Hrothgar could not approach 'þone gifstōl':

> Swā fela fyrena   fēond mancynnes,
> atol āngengea,   oft gefremede,
> heardra hȳnða;   Heorot eardode,
> sincfāge sel   sweartum nihtum; —

[6] *Beowulf with the Finnesburg Fragment*, ed. by C. L. Wrenn (London, 1953; rev. edn 1958); *Beowulf with the Finnesburg Fragment*, ed. by C. L. Wrenn and W. F. Bolton, 3rd edn (London, 1973; repr. New York, 1982). Compare *Beowulf: A Student Edition*, ed. by George Jack (Oxford, 1944), where there is no new paragraph at line 164.

[7] *Beowulf*, ed. by Mitchell and Robinson. Editorial aims, including their decision 'to introduce no narrative breaks of our own' apart from a break between lines 2199 and 2200, are discussed further by Fred C. Robinson, 'Some Reflections on Mitchell and Robinson's Edition of *Beowulf*', *Medieval English Studies Newsletter*, 39 (1998), 27–29.

[8] Argued both by Stanley B. Greenfield, '"Gifstol" and Goldhoard in Beowulf', in *Old English Studies in Honour of John C. Pope*, ed. by Robert B. Burlin and Edward B. Irving, Jr (Toronto, 1974), pp. 107–17, and by David Clipsham, '*Beowulf* 168–169', *In Geardagum* (1974), 19–24. It has not been accepted into more recent editions.

nō hē þone gifstōl   grētan moste,
māþðum for Metode,   nē his myne wisse. —
Þæt wæs wrǣc micel   wine Scyldinga,
mōdes brecða.   Monig oft gesæt
rīce to rūne,   rǣd eahtodon.
hwæt swīðferhðum   sēlest wǣre
wið fǣrgryrum   tō gefremmanne. (lines 164–74)

[so that enemy of mankind, a terrible solitary wanderer,[9] often committed many wrongs, severe humiliations, occupying treasure-adorned Heorot during the dark nights; and he [Hrothgar] could not approach that noble seat, [his] treasure, because of the Creator, or know His purpose: for the ruler of the Scyldings it was a great agony, the impugning of his courage; many were seated often in counsel, deliberating what might be best for the stern-hearted to do against the terror of sudden attacks.][10]

In the final part of the second fitt (lines 175–88) as marked out by the large capital of 'Hwīlum' ('Sometimes', line 175), we learn that the best solution Hrothgar and his followers could devise was to make offerings at heathen shrines ('æt hærgtrafum', line 175) and pray to the devil. It is, as Paul Cavill points out, a bitterly ironical passage, for the poet distinguishes clearly 'between what his characters think they are doing, and what he knows they are doing' and he 'sympathises with their plight but does not identify with their world view'.[11] Overall, the central drive of fitt II establishes the humiliation of Hrothgar of the Scyldings.

Reading lines 144–74 as holding together is important to my argument.[12] The 'hē' of line 168 is the only subject pronoun in these lines, and its use may signal a

---

[9] Rather than the suggested interpretation 'attacker' of Alfred Bammesberger, 'Five *Beowulf* Notes', in *Words, Texts and Manuscripts: Studies in Anglo-Saxon Culture Presented to Helmut Gneuss on the Occasion of his Sixty-fifth Birthday*, ed. by Michael Korhammer, Karl Reichl, and Hans Sauer (Woodbridge, 1992), pp. 239–55 (p. 243 and n. 16), I accept the explanation to be found in the *Dictionary of Old English in Electronic Form A–F* (Toronto, 2003) for all five instances of this word.

[10] On checking through some of the many translations I realize I have arrived at a version that is close to John R. Clark Hall, *Beowulf and the Finnsburg Fragment* (London, 1911), p. 17: 'He (Hrothgar) could not visit that royal seat, that precious possession, because of the Creator, nor did he know His purpose'. Contrast the freer interpretation of Seamus Heaney, *Beowulf: A New Translation* (London, 1999), p. 8: 'He took over Heorot, | haunted the glittering hall after dark, | but the throne itself, the treasure-seat, | he was kept from approaching; he was the Lord's outcast.'

[11] 'Christianity and Theology in *Beowulf*', in *The Christian Tradition in Anglo-Saxon England*, ed. by Paul Cavill (Cambridge, 2004), pp. 15–39 (p. 27).

[12] Whether these lines are a grammatical unit it is impossible to say; see Bruce Mitchell, *Old English Syntax*, 2 vols (Oxford, 1985), §§ 1881, 3956, on the difficulty of demarcating the verse paragraph.

switch from Grendel. Up to this point Grendel, in his persecution of the Danes, has been presented as the active force. Overwhelmingly at the subject position in verb phrases that denote action or decision, Grendel 'rīxode' ('reigned', line 144), 'wan' ('fought', line 144), 'wan' ('waged war', line 151), 'henīðas wæg' ('pursued fierce enmity', line 152), 'sibbe [...] ne wolde [...] fēa þingian' ('did not wish for peace, to settle by payment', lines 154–56), 'ēhtende wæs' ('kept on persecuting', line 159), 'seomade ond syrede; [...] hēold' ('lurked and lay in wait; ruled over', line 161), 'gefremede' ('committed', line 165), 'eardode' ('lived in', line 166). By contrast, Hrothgar, powerless to act, 'torn geþolode' ('suffered troubles', line 147), and none of the senior men of the Danes dared hope for any redress at the murderer's hands ('nē [...] wēnan þorfte', line 157). The effect of the introductory negative adverb 'nō' (line 168) at the head of its clause, followed immediately by a pronoun subject, is adversative, setting up a sense of 'hē' as contrasted.[13] It may seem unusual that no negative particle *ne* stands before the finite verb 'moste', but the sequence is not uncommon in Old English poetry, where there is generally less piling up of negatives than in prose.[14] During the black of night Hrothgar could not go safely to the great seat where he was accustomed to give out treasure, and he could not go to the 'māþðum', an appositional word that intrigues me every bit as much as the other difficulties within the passage. In addition, the hapax legomenon *brecða*, explained as 'a broken condition, here used figuratively of grief' in the *Dictionary of Old English*,[15] is open to shading in translation, and the senses recorded both for *wræc* and *mod* allow for a range of interpretations.

Lines 168–69 have been subjected to an inordinate amount of scrutiny, a flavour of which may be quickly gained by consulting any good edition of the poem for its examination of the main difficulties endlessly mulled over by the critics or by plunging into more recent extended examinations.[16] To review them all in detail would be long, tedious, and ultimately non-productive. It is, however, necessary to look at ways in which the identification of 'hē' as Grendel is defended, and a representative selection follows. Klaeber (p. 134) pronounces magisterially, 'The pos-

---

[13] Arthur Gilchrist Brodeur, *The Art of 'Beowulf'* (Berkeley, 1959; repr. 1969), pp. 203–04, arguing that here *he* refers forward to 'wine Scyldinga' in line 170, discusses comparable switches.

[14] Mitchell, *Old English Syntax*, §§ 1609, 1615.

[15] The element occurs otherwise in *æbrecþ* and *eodorbrecþ*, each attested once only (see *Dictionary of Old English in Electronic Form A–F* (Toronto, 2003)).

[16] R. E. Kaske, 'The *Gifstol* Crux in *Beowulf*', in *Sources and Relations: Studies in Honour of J. E. Cross*, ed. by Marie Collins, Jocelyn Price, and Andrew Hamer, special issue, *Leeds Studies in English*, n.s., 16 (1985), 142–51 (pp. 143–44), provides an excellent overview of the range of interpretation to which the passage has been subjected.

sibility of identifying *hē* with the king is too remote to be seriously considered'. For Wrenn (p. 104) '**Hē** is almost certainly Grendel; for the idea is clearly of Grendel rather than Hrōþgār in view of what has gone before — nor would the king want to approach his throne in any case'. The tones of common sense lull the unwary reader into agreement: the phrase 'almost certainly' forestalls criticism, the sweeping assumption 'in view of what has gone before' gains acceptance, and the non sequitur of the clinching final statement goes unnoticed. More straightforwardly, Bammesberger observes 'Since in the two preceding clauses, Grendel functioned as subject it is to be assumed that *he* in l. 168 refers to Grendel';[17] and he adds that 'Since Hroðgar was in the habit of retiring from Heorot when night came, it stands to reason that Grendel, who was active at night only, could not participate in Hroðgar's munificence' — rather, Grendel despised treasure (with *formetode* from a verb **formetian* 'despise') and 'did not know its joy'.[18] It is irrelevant to this reading that Hrothgar and his people were accustomed to leaving the hall at nightfall because of Grendel (lines 644b–51). Nevertheless, Robinson finds **formetian* attractive, translating lines 168–70a: 'By no means did he [Grendel] have to show respect for the throne; he despised the precious thing, did not feel love for it.' But it is not essential to his argument that Grendel's disrespect for Hrothgar's throne is the issue here: 'By no means was he [Grendel] compelled by God to show respect for the throne, that precious thing, nor did he feel love for it. That was a great distress for the lord of the Scyldings, a heart-breaking thing.' More recently Scowcroft, declaring the identification of 'hē' as Hrothgar to be 'unconvincing', asks 'what would Hroðgar want with his gift-seat in the middle of the night?'[19] The short answer is access, and not just in the middle of the night but from dusk.

There is widespread discomfort too with 'māþðum', which is understood as equating with 'þone gifstōl' and often translated with a matching definite article which limits the word's possible range. Although the *gifstol* may be visualized as a great high seat ornamented with gold and jewels, akin to the chairs not coveted by Philosophy in Alfred's Boethius,[20] the mind need not conjure up the same

---

[17] Similarly, Marijane Osborne, 'The Great Feud: Scriptural History and Strife in *Beowulf*', *PMLA*, 93 (1978), 973–81 (p. 976), argues that 'the direct antecedent of the pronoun *he* is *feond mancynnes*' and that 'Grendel is thus once more identified with the Antagonist'; an interesting addition here is the observation that 'the Devil cannot approach an Altar'.

[18] Bammesberger, 'Five *Beowulf* Notes', p. 245.

[19] Mark R. Scowcraft, 'The Irish Analogues to *Beowulf*', *Speculum*, 74 (1999), 22–64 (p. 54 and n. 108).

[20] The seats 'mid golde [⁊] mid gimmū gerenodra' do not come directly from the Latin of Boethius, but are introduced when, circumnavigating *bibliotheca* (no Old English word is extant

image for *maþðum*. Even Greenfield who, in comparing Hrothgar's loss of *gifstol* with Beowulf's, makes it clear that for each 'the act of gold-giving, so central to his function as a good king' is 'frustrated', resorts to an appositional equivalence, '(that) treasure'; and this is the translation also of Kaske, who sees 'a pointed parallel and contrast between the treasure-adorned hall (with its gift-throne) which Grendel could possess, and the treasure of God's gift-throne which he could not'.[21] (Scowcraft's suggestion that Hrothgar would not have had reason to use the hall at night-time seems entirely to miss the point. Hrothgar's great hall no longer provided security from the terrors of darkness, for from dusk it lay silent, empty, and waiting for Grendel's arrival.) The difficulty presented by 'māþðum', which is not limited in reference by any qualifying article or possessive, is related to the potential range of reference for 'þone gifstōl', which I have trans-lated 'that noble seat'. The compound 'gift-seat' is, after all, a loan-translation, calqued on the Old English word, and 'seat of grace' over-theological for the context. The compound's elements look misleadingly familiar, with Klaeber's explanation 'GIFt-seat, throne' for both *Beowulf* occurrences seemingly straight-forward; but Klaeber includes a cross-reference to his entry for *eþelstol*, which he glosses 'native-seat, ancestral throne'. The resolved translation offered in his glossary 'throne' loses the element *stol*, and it is this element that allows the mind to consider a range of connotations. As simplex, *stol* is used for 'seat, stool', 'seat of authority', 'bishopric, see'; and as the base element in compounds it supports words with meanings as diverse as 'folding-stool', 'palace', 'privy', 'capital city', 'kingdom', 'see', 'sanctuary'.[22] Moreover, as 'māþðum' need not equate completely with 'þone gifstōl', it potentially affords a different perspective, one triggered in part by the description just given of Heorot as 'sincfāge sel' (line 167).[23] Should

---

for the idea of a room specially dedicated to books, for use as a library), Alfred writes of walls made with glass and thrones ornamented with gold and jewels. *King Alfred's Old English Version of Boethius*, ed. by Walter John Sedgefield (Oxford, 1899), p. 11, lines 26–28.

[21] Kaske, 'The *Gifstol* Crux in *Beowulf*', p. 147.

[22] These meanings, listed in *A Thesaurus of Old English*, ed. by Jane Roberts and Christian Kay with Lynne Grundy, 2 vols, King's College London Medieval Studies, 11 (London, 1995; 2nd impression, Amsterdam 2000), reflect the divisions made in standard dictionaries. *A Thesaurus of Old English*, ed. by Flora Edmonds, Christian Kay, Jane Roberts, and Irené Wotherspoon, is now available on-line at <http://libra.englang.arts.gla.ac.uk/oethesaurus/> (2005).

[23] It should be noted also that *maþ(þ)um* occurs relatively infrequently in the singular, most often of swords: *Beowulf*, lines 1528, 1902, 2055 and probably 1052, 3016; *Riddles* 55.13 (*The Exeter Book*, ed. by George Philip Krapp and Elliott Van Kirk Dobbie, Anglo-Saxon Poetic

this interpretation seem fanciful, compare the passage in which *gifstol* occurs in its other appearance in *Beowulf*:

Þā wæs Bīowulfe   brōga gecȳþed
snūde tō sōðe,   þæt his sylfes hām,
bolda sēlest   brynewylmum mealt,
gifstōl Gēata.   (lines 2324–27a)

[In truth then the horror of it was immediately evident to Beowulf, that his own home, the best of buildings, the noble seat of the Geats, was liquifying under waves of fire.]

The converging images in this three-fold variation are home, strength, and generosity; in contrast, the *gifstol* of Hrothgar, from which he had dealt out treasure, is inaccessible at night for twelve long years. Why, one wonders, did the Danes not set the hall ablaze to rid themselves of Grendel, for its eventual destruction amidst flames is foretold in the account of its construction (lines 67a–85). Hrothgar as the leader of the Danes had every reason to want to approach his *gifstol*, for his inability to do so at will exemplifies his diminished stature. He has lost control of great treasure, both his high-seat and his hall, for the 'hūsa sēlest' ('best of houses', line 146) was 'īdel' ('useless', line 145, an adjective resonating with notions of vainglory and loss of value).[24] Interestingly, Robinson identifies an 'opposition of artifice and nature' in the hall, 'a bastion of order and safety which throws light

Records, 3 (New York, 1936), p. 208). The 'mynelicne maþþum' and 'glædlicne maþþum' of *Widsith* lines 4 and 66 (*The Exeter Book*, pp. 149, 151) are left to the imagination, as is the '*gylden* maðm' of *Metres* 21.20 (*The Paris Psalter and the Meters of Boethius*, ed. by George Philip Krapp, Anglo-Saxon Poetic Records, 5 (New York, 1932), p. 185). Three instances of *maþ(þ)um* in the singular may be interpreted as 'a precious object, treasure': *The Gifts of Men*, line 60, *Maxims I*, line154 (*The Exeter Book*, pp. 139, 162), and *Andreas*, line 1113 (*The Vercelli Book*, ed. by George Philip Krapp, Anglo-Saxon Poetic Records, 2 (New York, 1932), p. 34). Typically the word is used of concrete treasures, in which use it lasts into Middle English only as a plural noun. Strikingly therefore, in Old English prose the singular refers to Mary (*Ælfric's Catholic Homilies: The First Series: Text*, ed. by Peter Clemoes, EETS, SS, 17 (Oxford, 1997), I, XXX (p. 430), line 43), to John the Baptist's head (*Ælfric's Catholic Homilies: The First Series*, ed. by Clemoes, I, XXXII (p. 456), line 159), to the Cross (*Ælfric's Catholic Homilies: The Second Series: Text*, ed. by Malcolm Godden, EETS, SS, 5 (Oxford, 1979), II, XVIII (p. 175), line 45; and *The Exaltation of the Holy Cross*, in *Ælfric's Lives of Saints*, ed. by Walter W. Skeat, EETS, OS, 76, 82, 94, and 114 (London, 1881–1900), II, XXVII (p. 144), line 5) and to the phoenix (*Early English Homilies from the Twelfth Century MS. Vesp. D. XIV*, ed. by Rubie D-N. Warner, EETS, OS, 152 (London, 1917), p. 147, line 21).

[24] See Kathryn Hume, 'The Concept of the Hall in Old English Poetry', *Anglo-Saxon England*, 3 (1974), 63–74 at p. 72 for discussion of the possibility that Heorot was 'automatically equated with Babel as built out of overweening pride'.

into the surrounding darkness' and what lies beyond, and he describes Beowulf as freeing 'the artifact of Heorot from Grendel's hold'.[25]

There are further difficulties within lines 168–69. Even if the identification of Hrothgar as the subject of these lines allows 'þone gifstōl' and 'māþðum' to be understood as the ceremonial seat and power base from which as ruler he shared out treasure in this world,[26] some readers of the poem are dismayed by the implications of 'for Metode, nē his myne wisse'. Worried by what they take to be an anachronistic viewpoint,[27] they forget that it is the poet's viewpoint and that he is at pains to make clear Hrothgar's helplessness in a pagan world. For a long time lines 168–69 were thought suspect. In Klaeber's words the passage is 'singularly awkward', and 'One might suspect an inept interpolation here',[28] a view still held in some later editions, for lines 168–69 were for Tolkien among three passages intruded or at least retouched.[29] But this great lord of the past is from a world as yet without the comforting teachings brought so memorably to Edwin's court by Paulinus. With 'Hwilum' ('Sometimes', line 175) the foreground narrative resumes momentarily, telling what action was taken by the Danes:

> Hwīlum hīe gehēton æt *h*ærgtrafum
> wīgweorþunga, wordum bædon,
> þæt him gāstbona gēoce gefremede
> wið þēodþrēaum. (lines 175–78a)

[Sometimes they pledged worship to idols in their heathen temples, asking with words (of prayer) that the slayer of souls should afford them help against the people's troubles.]

The poet has told us that Hrothgar, who knew not God's 'myne', was prevented by the Creator from approaching 'þone gifstōl'. If the leader cannot gain access to his centre of power, no more can his councillors help him to do so. Their only recourse, the poet hastens to add, is the customary 'hæþenra hyht' ('hope of the heathen', line 179). An *aglæca* ('awesome combatant', line 159) holds Heorot.

[25] Fred C. Robinson, *'Beowulf' and the Appositive Style* (Knoxville, 1985), p. 72.

[26] For a large array of alternative interpretations, see Betty S. Cox, *Cruces of Beowulf* (The Hague, 1971), pp. 56–72.

[27] Greenfield, '"Gifstol" and Goldhoard in Beowulf', p. 112, points out that '"ne his myne wisse" offers little difficulty', but see further Richard North, *Pagan Words and Christian Meanings* (Amsterdam, 1991), pp. 33–38.

[28] *Beowulf*, ed. by Klaeber, p. 135.

[29] J. R. R. Tolkien, *'Beowulf*: The Monsters and the Critics', *Proceedings of the British Academy*, 22 (1936), 245–95 (p. 282, n 34).

Clearly, help for Hrothgar's kingdom must come from outside, and it is time for
Grendel's adversary to appear. Fitt III opens first with a bridging statement about the
unrelenting misery of Healfeene's son ('maga Healfdenes', line 189) and his Danes
before announcing that 'Higelāces þegn' ('Hygelac's follower', line 194) has heard of
Grendel's deeds. The very way in which the despairing leader of the Danes and the
Geatish retainer are identified must prompt comparison between the two, even
before we learn that Hygelac's follower was 'moncynnes mægenes strengest | on þǣm
dæge þysses līfes' ('in might the strongest of mankind in that age of this life', lines
195–96). This hero from outside is a suitable opponent for not only Grendel but,
as it turns out, Grendel's mother too. Yet the audience does not hear Beowulf's
name until he announces it to Wulfgar when seeking to speak with Hrothgar:

> 'We synt Higelāces
> bēodgenēatas;   Bēowulf is mīn nama.
> Wille ic āsecgan   sunu Healfdenes,
> mǣrum þēodne   mīn ǣrende,
> aldre þīnum,   gif hē ūs geunnan wile,
> þæt wē hine swā gōdne   grētan mōton.' (lines 342–47)

[‘We are Hygelac’s companions at table; my name is Beowulf. I wish to explain my
mission to the famed lord Healfdene’s son, your prince, if he will grant (it) to us that we
may approach so great a man.’]

In this very formal speech Beowulf, it is often pointed out, introduces himself as
Hygelac's follower, but it is less often noted that he does not name Hrothgar. Again,
as at the beginning of fitt III, the two are implicitly compared in relation to
Hygelac on the one hand and Healfdene on the other. Like Grendel or the dragon
or Sigemund, Beowulf is an exceptional combatant, an *aglæca*.[30] Hrothgar, the
builder of Heorot, has done well, but he lacks the glamour of Hygelac and Healfdene.
Perhaps we should be less than surprised that, in later Scandinavian legends of the
Danes, his nephew Hrothulf achieves far greater glory. In slaying Grendel, Beowulf will outstrip his host; and the men returning from the mere once Grendel's
death is established are careful not to cast any slight upon 'glædne Hrōðgār, ac þæt
wæs gōd cyning' ('gracious Hrothgar, for that was a good king', line 863).[31]

---

[30] See Jane Roberts, 'Hrothgar's "admirable courage"', in *Unlocking the Wordhoard: Anglo-
Saxon Studies in Memory of Edward B. Irving, Jr*, ed. by Mark C. Amodio and Katherine O'Brien
O'Keeffe (Toronto, 2003), pp. 240–51, for discussion of the dangers presented to Hrothgar's
leadership by Beowulf's cleansing of Heorot.

[31] Compare Lauryn S. Mayer, *Worlds Made Flesh: Reading Medieval Manuscript Culture*
(New York, 2004), p. 99, on Beowulf's framing words of praise for Hrothgar in lines 270–79.

Such comparisons and contrasts create differences among the poem's central figures and events, with similes built on the adjective *(ge)lic* playing little part.[32] There are at most four direct similes in *Beowulf*, whereas *The Phoenix*, a poem approximately a fifth its length, has eight instances of *(ge)lic* in simile.[33] Three of the *Beowulf* similes flash by — a ship moves 'fugle gelīcost' (line 218), a horrible light shines 'ligge gelīcost' (line 727), Grendel's nails are a 'stȳle gelīcost' (line 985) — clunky in a poetry filled with metaphoric compounds. Careful explanation follows a fourth, the melting of the ancient sword blade in the mere, widening reference to remind the audience of the providential presence of the 'sōð Metod':

> þæt wæs wundra sum,
> þæt hit eal gemealt   īse gelīcost,
> ðonne forstes bend   Fæder onlǣteð,
> onwindeð wǣlrāpas,   sē geweald hafað
> sǣla ond mǣla;   þæt is sōð Metod. (lines 1607b–11)

[It was a marvel of marvels that it melted completely, like ice when the Father, who has power over times and seasons, releases frost's bond, loosening the water's chains: that is the true Lord.]

Any superstitious notions hovering about the powers of the blood of uncanny ogres are trumped. A fifth passage is sometimes numbered among the poem's meagre crop of similes:

> Līxte se lēoma,   lēoht inne stōd,
> efne swā of hefene   hādre scīneð
> rodores candel.   (lines 1570–72a)

[The flash blazed out — there was light in there — just as when the sun, heaven's candle, shines vividly.]

But here, with that simple device far more typical of writings in Old English, the commenting use of *swa*, the strange light in the underwater cave is juxtaposed with the light of heaven, and there is again a mediating suffusion of the mysterious.[34] Reflection can accommodate effective similitude, as in the elegiac representation of the depth of grief felt by Hrethel (lines 2443–52a) for his son Herebeald, whose death was an accident that happened when his brother Hæthcyn missed a

---

[32] *Beowulf*, ed. by Klaeber, p. lxiv, n. 5.

[33] *The Exeter Book*, ed. by Krapp and Dobbie, pp. 94–113, lines 230, 237, 302, 312, 387, 424, 585, and 601. Mitchell, *Old English Syntax*, § 1881, points out Campbell's recognition of lines 424–42 as one continuous paragraph.

[34] Mitchell, *Old English Syntax*, §3276, cites this passage in illustration of comparative clauses introduced by *efne / emne swa*.

mark he was shooting at, a slaying for which no blood money could be exacted ('feohlēas gefeoht', line 2441). In the generalizing comparison introduced by 'Swā', line 2444, the nameless only son hangs dead and there is no remedy; the setting is long past, and the sorrow for the unnamed father is endless. Yet, with a masterly switch in line 2461 to the past tense of 'þūhte him', the impression lingers that we have overheard the thoughts of Hrethel. Unfortunately Klaeber makes a new paragraph within line 2462 before 'Swā Wedra helm | æfter Herebealde heortan sorge | weallinde wæg' ('So the protector of the Weder-Geats felt surging heart sorrows for Herebeald', lines 2462b–64a); and he notes in his commentary that the 'pret. is fully justified. After a survey of the grounds and buildings the lonely father has retired'. Thus, his separation of these clauses cuts across the clever overlap between the nameless old man's sorrow and Hrethel's in the opening lines of fitt XXXV.

The reflective device (*efne*) *swa* (. . . *swa*),[35] omnipresent in Old English poetry and essential to what Greenfield has termed 'the authenticating voice' in *Beowulf*,[36] is a powerful tool, whether awaking in the audience quick realization of wider issues, as in lines 1570–72a, or effecting smooth introduction between contrasting narrative themes, as in lines 99–114.[37] In lines 144–74 the first 'Swā' introduces a devastating account of the destruction and fear Grendel had brought about, with the second 'Swā' of line 164 leading into the completion of this material. Lines 164–74 thus wrap up the movement begun at line 144. Here the scribe's choice of large capitals happily accords with reading lines 144–74 as a large unit within fitt II. Yet, the demarcation of syntactic units in Old English poetry is acknowledgedly a difficult editorial procedure, be it into paragraphs or indeed sentences.[38] The shorter the editor's paragraphs, the more likely they are to resemble the 'envelope' groups observed by Bartlett.[39] Her envelope patterns can,

---

[35] Mitchell, *Old English Syntax*, §§ 3290–94, describes such structures; see also §3330 for *swelce . . . swa*, and indeed § 2375 *swylc* (. . . *swylc*), also among the modes of reflection and comparison used by poets in Old English.

[36] Stanley B. Greenfield, 'The Authenticating Voice in *Beowulf*', *Anglo-Saxon England*, 5 (1976), 51–62.

[37] See Ó Carragáin, 'Structure and Thematic Development in *Beowulf*', p. 6, on this passage.

[38] Mitchell, *Old English Syntax*, §1881.

[39] Adeline Courtney Bartlett, *The Larger Rhetorical Patterns in Anglo-Saxon Poetry* (New York, 1935), p. 18, would set off lines 166–74 as having what she terms an 'Envelope frame', presumably, as is sometimes done in editions, splitting line 166. The fourth of Wrenn's five paragraphs in fitt II, lines 164–69, begins a little earlier.

however, be 'themselves parts of larger patterns',[40] and she identifies lines 129–93 'as suggestive of the Envelope pattern',[41] but without taking any account of the manuscript divisions. Fitt III, which opens with 'Swā' (line 189), smoothly redirects attention to the powerlessness of Hrothgar, word echoes serving to link the new fitt with what has gone before.[42] The scene is set for effective action, and straightaway Beowulf is introduced, as 'an excellent follower of Hygelac'. Klaeber indents for a new paragraph at line 193, but the abbreviation for 'þæt' in the manuscript is of normal size:

> Swā ðā mælceare   maga Healfdenes
> singāla sēað;   ne mihte snotor hæleð
> wēan onwendan;   wæs þæt gewin tō swȳð,
> lāþ ond longsum,   þē on ðā lēode becōm,
> nȳdwracu nīþgrim,   nihtbealwa mæst.
>   Þæt fram hām gefrægn   Higelāces þegn
> gōd mid Gēatum [...].   (lines 189–95a)

[So Healfdene's kinsman brooded incessantly over the sorrows of those times, and that wise man was unable to turn aside that trouble — the struggle which engulfed the people was very harsh, loathsome and protracted, cruel aggression, the most destructive terrors of the night. Hygelac's thane, an excellent man among the Geats, heard about it at home [...].]

At home, far away among the Geats, Beowulf has heard about the acts perpetrated by Grendel, and his immediate reaction is to commission the building of a ship in order to seek out Hrothgar 'þā him wæs manna þearf' ('when he was in need of men', line 201). The narrative proper has begun, in the foreground the adventurer who will give back to Hrothgar full possession of his *gifstol*.

---

[40] Bartlett, *Larger Rhetorical Patterns*, p. 19.

[41] Bartlett, *Larger Rhetorical Patterns*, p. 24, though a 'crude' example by comparison with others 'previously noted'.

[42] Florian Schleburg, *Altenglisch 'swa': Syntax und Semantik einer polyfunktionalen Partikel* (Heidelberg, 2002), §62 (pp. 71–73), comments on the use of *swa* as a sentence opener to introduce reflection on particular points, noting *Beowulf* line 144 among his examples; see further the index on his homepage at the University of Ravensburg (<http://www-englishlinguistics. uni-regensburg.de/Staff/Schleburg/home.htm>), where lines 164 and 189 are also cited as examples of this usage.

IMAGE AND ASCENDANCY IN ÚLFR'S *HÚSDRÁPA*

Richard North

O ld Icelandic poetry is related to the early medieval literature of the British Isles. Not only is the Icelandic language, often called 'Old Norse', cognate with that of the Anglo-Saxons; but from the early tenth century onwards the Norwegian culture of Ireland left her imprints, images, and people in a line from Cheshire to Cumbria and the Western Isles, from the Northern Isles as far as Iceland out in the Atlantic. One of these imprints is a poem of the late tenth century which is preserved in a prose treatise of the early thirteenth. The poem was composed about a new house in western Iceland for a patron and audience of mixed Norwegian-Irish descent. Indeed, *Húsdrápa* ('Eulogy of the House') imagines images in a house whose fate it has been lucky not to share. The house is long gone, but the poem survived, if less entirely than the great Cross of Ruthwell in 1642, by being broken up in pieces over a younger terrain. The ground in this case is *Skáldskaparmál* ('poetics'), part of the Prose *Edda* by the Icelandic mythographer Snorri Sturluson (1178/79–1241).[1] Snorri

---

[1] *Skáldskaparmál*, ed. by Anthony Faulkes, 2 vols (London, 1997). In the following quotations I treat Faulkes's verse-lines properly as half-lines by setting out each pair as one full line with caesura: this I call a 'line', though I still number by the half-line. I contract forms in Faulkes, with *vilk* for *vil ek* and so on. 'St.' is for 'stanza', 'Vs.' for 'verse'. *Snorra Edda* MS abbreviations R T U W: R: *Codex Regius, c.* 1325, copied from a now-lost exemplar of *c.* 1250–1300 (Copenhagen, Royal Library, GkS 2367 quarto); T: *Codex Trajectinus, c.* 1600, copied from a now-lost exemplar of *c.* 1250–1300 (Utrecht, Universiteitsbibliotheek, MS No. 1374); U: *Uppsala-Handskriften, c.* 1300 (Uppsala, University Library, DG 11); W: *Codex Wormianus, c.* 1340–50 (Copenhagen, Arnamagnaean Institute, AM [Arnamagnaean] 242 fol.). I am indebted to Jane Roberts and James Graham-Campbell for reading drafts of this paper, also to the latter for my references to Scandinavian art.

here refers to *Húsdrápa* twice by name; probably all thirteen verses he ascribes to Úlfr, its poet, belong to this poem. In the following essay I shall ponder what the lost images looked like and why they, the house, and the poem were commissioned. If this means attempting a new edition, so be it. In the process, however, we may see how those images of Old Norse myths which were carved and painted on wood for one purpose could be reinterpreted in poetry for another.

Let us start with the poet. According to *Laxdæla saga*, written in the mid-thirteenth century, Úlfr Uggason was hired by Óláfr Hǫskuldsson, a chieftain of Laxárdalr in western Iceland. One summer Óláfr, shortly after coming back with some timber from Norway, built a hall. In the spring, with the hall finished, he married his daughter, Þuríðr, there to a Norwegian named Geirmundr *gnýr* (or Geirmundr 'the clash') from Hordaland. Contextually this wedding has been dated *c.* 978 x *c.* 985, in the period of the Mammen style.[2] No expense was spared. According to the saga, Óláfr's house was

> meira ok betra en menn hefði fyrr sét. Váru þar markaðar ágætligar sǫgur á þilviðinum ok svá á ræfrinu; var þat svá vel smíðat, at þá þótti miklu skrautligra, er eigi váru tjǫldin uppi. (ch. 29)[3]

> [bigger and better than anyone had seen before. Carved on the wood of the wainscoting, and likewise on the ceiling, were noble stories; the workmanship was so good that the place seemed much showier when the tapestries were not hung.]

Earlier the craftsmen working for Óláfr are named as Án the White, his brother Án the Black, and Beinir the Strong (ch. 24). The work that endured, however, was that of a poet from southern Iceland. According to the fragment of *Laxdæla saga* that provides an older version than the complete but shortened text:[4]

> skal boð vera at áliðnum vetri í Hjarðarholti; þat boð var allfjǫlmennt, því at þá var algǫrt eldhúsit. Þar var at boði Úlfr Uggason ok hafði nýorta drápu um Óláf Hǫskuldsson ok

---

[2] *Laxdæla Saga*, ed. by Einar Ólafur Sveinsson, Íslenzk fornrit, 5 (Reykjavik, 1934), p. lix (an edition based on the complete but shortened text in Mǫðruvallabók (M)). Signe Horn Fuglesang, 'II. Decorative Arts', in *The Dictionary of Art*, ed. by Jane Turner, with Hugh Brigstocke (London, 1996), s.v. 'Viking Art', pp. 512–34, esp. 514–27 (p. 517) and 521–24 (pictorial narrative art). See also her 'Stylistic Groups in Late Viking Art', in *Anglo-Saxon and Viking Age Sculpture and its Context: Papers from the Collingwood Symposium on Insular Sculpture from 800 to 1066*, ed. by James Lang, British Archaeological Reports, British Series, 49 (Oxford, 1978), pp. 205–16, esp. pp. 205, 209.

[3] *Laxdæla Saga*, ed. by Einar Ólafur Sveinsson, p. 79. Translations are my own throughout.

[4] AM 162 E, fol. See *Laxdæla Saga*, ed. by Einar Ólafur Sveinsson, pp. lxxvii–lxxx.

um sǫgur allar, er skrifaðar váru á eldhúsinu, ok fœrði hann þar at boðinu. Þetta kvæði er kallat Húsdrápa ok er vel ort. Óláfr launaði vel kvæðit. (ch. 29)[5]

[the wedding party was to take place in Hjarðarholt when winter had passed; this party was attended by huge numbers of people because building on the great hall was now finished. Present at the wedding was Úlfr Uggason who had just composed a eulogy about Óláfr Hǫskuldsson and all the stories painted on the great hall, and he performed it there at the wedding. This poem is called 'Eulogy of the House' and it is a good piece of work. Óláfr paid well for the poem.]

So Úlfr finished his poem just in time. The marriage was not a success, for later Geirmundr ran off, but the wedding was: 'þótti Óláfr vaxit hafa' ('Óláfr was thought to have gone up in the world'; ch. 29). From this chapter it is already clear that Óláfr commissioned Úlfr to elevate him socially as the owner of the biggest, most splendid hall in Iceland.

Now for the poem. Unfortunately the author of *Laxdæla saga,* who knew *Húsdrápa*, gives no quotations. The thirteen verses surviving in *Skáldskaparmál* are probably a fraction of *Húsdrápa* as it was, for, as we have seen, the oldest surviving text of *Laxdæla* claims that Úlfr composed on 'all' the carvings of the hall, and the hall was massive. As to the order of events within *Húsdrápa*, Úlfr's verses have since been put in sequence so as to present three stories, all of them myths of Norse gods: one stanza tells of a duel between Heimdallr and Loki over Freyja's necklace, the *Brísingamen* (*Húsdrápa* '2'); five half-stanzas, two of which are sometimes joined, relate Þórr's fishing-trip with a giant which ends in a confrontation with the World Serpent (st. '3–6'); a further five half-stanzas tell of the procession of Freyr, Heimdallr, and Óðinn together with ravens and valkyries to Baldr's funeral pyre and then the launching of this ship (st. '7–11'); and a half-stanza survives in which the poet appears to sum up (part of) his work as something completed (st. '12').[6] This sequence of episodes could easily be changed. Baldr's death triggers the end of the world in Snorri's *Gylfaginning*, the mythography preceding *Skáldskaparmál*,[7] as it appears to do in his greatest source, the

---

[5] *Laxdæla Saga*, ed. by Einar Ólafur Sveinsson, p. 80. M has *ort kvæði* ('composed a poem') for *nýorta drápu*, and *þær* ('those [stories]') for *allar*.

[6] As in *Den norsk-islandske skjaldedigtning*, ed. by Finnur Jónsson, 4 vols (A I, II: diplomatic; B I, II: normalized) (Copenhagen, 1912–15) [henceforth *Skj*], A I, 136–38, esp. p. 136; B I, 128–30, esp. p. 128; and in *Den norsk-isländska skaldediktningen*, ed. by E. A. Kock (Lund, 1946–49) [henceforth *Ska*], I, 71–72, esp. p. 71.

[7] *Snorri Sturluson: Edda: Prologue and Gylfaginning*, ed. by Anthony Faulkes (Oxford, 1982), pp. 46–47 (ch. 49). On this sequencing of stanzas, see Margaret Clunies Ross, *Prolonged Echoes:*

Eddic poem *Vǫluspá*, as well as in *Lokasenna* (st. 28); but it also falls long before
the action in *Skírnismál* (st. 21–22) and *Vafþrúðnismál* (st. 54). Below I shall put
Úlfr's (half-)stanzas mostly in the time-honoured order. There is no way of telling
if Norse gods were all that was carved, then painted, on the walls and ceiling of
Óláfr's hall. But in their thematic groups the surviving verses of Úlfr's poem, when
interpreted, do help us imagine the style, colour, and function of the images which
his patron put there.

Dedication

The first verse of *Húsdrápa* is among fifteen half-stanzas Snorri quotes from late
tenth-century poets to illustrate the range of pre-Christian 'kennings', or peri-
phrases, for 'poetry'. Thirteenth is a half-stanza assigned to 'Úlfr Uggason', now
known as *Húsdrápa* '1':

> Hoddmildum ték Hildar   hugreifum Óleifi
> (hann vilk at gjǫf Grímnis)   geð-Njarðar lá (kveðja). (vs. 39)

[For the hoard-generous Óláfr who is brave in heart — him will I summon to the gift of
Grímnir — I draw a wave from Hildr's soul-Njǫrðr.]

So runs the text in RTW, three of the four main manuscripts of *Skáldskaparmál*.
Óðinn, or Grímnir as he is named here, stole poetry from the giants by drinking
it, as mead, in the mountain of the giants. To get the mead he seduced Gunnlǫð,
daughter of Suttungr, drinking one vat for each of the three nights he agreed to
spend with her. Afterwards he flew back in bird-shape to his citadel, with
Suttungr in hot pursuit, and spewed out the mead into vats that the Norse gods
had set out beneath him. Poetry was Óðinn's gift to mankind, but at the same
time Úlfr, in drawing a wave from Hildr's 'soul-Njǫrðr', presents Óðinn as war-
god. Through Hildr, the valkyrie who eponymizes 'battle' (*hildr*), Óðinn is the
sea-god (Njǫrðr) of the soul, who directs the slaughter in battle. This is a
straightforward kenning for poetry by the norms of the other surviving tenth-
century 'skaldic' or occasional poems.[8] There is a more baroque version of it in the
half-stanza in U:

Old Norse Myths in Medieval Northern Society, Studies in Northern Civilization, 7 (Odense,
1994), p. 260.

[8] Roberta Frank, *Old Norse Court Poetry: The Dróttkvætt Stanza*, Islandica, 42 (Ithaca, NY,
1978), pp. 42–49.

> Hjaldrgegnis telk Hildar   herreifum Óleifi
> (hann vilk at gjǫf Grímnis)   geðfjarðar lá (kveðja). (vs. 39)

[For Óláfr who is brave in war — him will I summon to the gift of Grímnir — I recount a wave of the fjord of the soul of Hildr's din-server.]

In this variant Úlfr refers to his poem as just one draught of the many which he pulls to order from the war-god's mead-vat. Probably because this version of the kenning is better developed, its verse is more often chosen as the first half-stanza of *Húsdrápa*.

The Duel of Heimdallr and Loki

At least two hall images underlie *Húsdrápa* '2', the only full stanza to survive as such from this poem. This stanza is quoted by Snorri at the end of his list of kennings for Norse gods in *Skáldskaparmál*. First he tells us that Heimdallr, among other sobriquets, has the names 'Loka dólg, mensœkir Freyju' ('Loki's foe, Freyja's necklace-seeker'), and a little later he is 'tilsœkir Singasteins ok Vágaskers', either 'striver for' or 'visitor to' what most scholars believe to be places, '*Singa*-stone' and 'Wave-Rock':

> þá deildi hann við Loka um Brísingamen. Hann heitir ok Vindlér. Úlfr Uggason kvað í Húsdrápu langa stund eptir þeiri frásǫgu; er þess þar getit at þeir váru í sela líkjum. (ch. 8)[9]

[that was when he struggled with Loki over the Brísing necklace. He is also called Wind-Shelter. Úlfr Uggason based a long passage on this tale when he composed Eulogy of the House; it is said there that they were in seal-shapes.]

Snorri seems to come back to this divine seal-duel in his kennings for Loki, whom he designates as 'son Fárbauta' ('son of Fárbauti' ('Fear-Beater')) and 'þrætudólg Heimdala[r] ok Skaða' ('wrestling-foe of Heimdallr and Skaði'). Snorri proceeds to illustrate Loki's wrestling with Heimdallr 'svá sem hér segir Úlfr Uggason' ('just as Úlfr Uggason says here'):

> Ráðgegninn bregðr ragna   rein– at singasteini
> frægr við firna slœgjan   Fárbauta mǫg –vári.
> Móðǫflugr ræðr mœðra   mǫgr hafnýra fǫgru
> (kynnik) áðr ok einnar   átta (mærðar þáttum). (vs. 64)

[Ready with a plan, the gods' land-warmer transforms for the blessing-jewel, renowned for facing the monstrously sly kinsman of Fárbauti. Mighty in spirit, the son of eight plus

---

[9] *Skáldskaparmál*, ed. by Faulkes, I, 19 (ch. 8).

one mothers — I proclaim [Óláfr] in strands of renown — is the first to get control over the dazzling sea-kidney.]

There are more semantic difficulties in this stanza than in the rest of the extant *Húsdrápa*.[10] Clearly there is a contest between Loki and Heimdallr, the one 'ready with a plan' and the other 'monstrously sly'; each gets a genealogy, with Loki as a giant's son in the first half-stanza, Heimdallr as divinely born in the second. But after that interpretations can vary. Finnur Jónsson was the first to read a tmesis in the first two long lines, reading an epithet for Heimdallr as the gods' watchman in *ragna rein-vári*.[11] Most have accepted this reading, which is in keeping with Heimdallr's known role as 'vǫrðr goða' ('gods' sentinel', *Lokasenna* 48); and the word 'rein', which can refer to a strip of land between fields, may be taken as Bifrǫst, Heimdallr's traditional 'road', the bridge between gods and giants.[12] On the other hand, the etymology of the once-attested 'vári' remains unclear. Finnur Jónsson related it to the adjective *varr* ('aware'),[13] but it has become customary to connect 'vári' with *verja* 'to defend', even if its long vowel fails to match with the short vowel and weak class of *verja*.[14] If Heimdallr is the gods' 'defender', the half-giant Loki could be seen as a dark allusion to Ragnarǫk, to the giants' assault on Ásgarðr at the end of the world.[15] A third reading of 'vári' as 'trusty one, the gods'

---

[10] *Skáldskaparmál*, ed. by Faulkes, I, 20 (ch. 16) and 168–69. Clive Tolley, 'Heimdallr and the Myth of the Brísingamen in *Húsdrápa*', *TijdSchrift voor Skandinavistiek*, 17 (1996), 83–98.

[11] Finnur Jónsson, 'Kenningers ledomstilling og tmesis', *Arkiv för nordisk filologi*, 49 (1933), 1–23 (p. 13).

[12] Johannes Fritzner, *Ordbog over det Gamle Norske Sprog*, 3 vols plus a Supplementary 4th vol. (Kristiania [Oslo], 1886–96 and 1972), III, s.v. 'Rein'. Finnur, 'Kenningers ledomstilling og tmesis', p. 13: '*ragna rein* "gudernes vej" [the gods' road]: Bivrost'; followed by Britt-Mari Näsström, *Forn-skandinavisk religion: En grundbok* (Lund, 2001), pp. 130–31: 'Den vise mäktige beskyddaren (= Heimdall) av gudarnas väg (= Bifrost)' ('The wise powerful protector of the gods' road').

[13] Finnur, 'Kenningers ledomstilling og tmesis', p. 13.

[14] Alexander Johannesson, *Altisländisches etymologisches Wörterbuch* (Bern, 1956), p. 149. Kurt Schier, 'Húsdrápa 2: Heimdall, Loki und die Meerniere', in *Festgabe für Otto Höfler zum 75. Geburtstag*, ed. by Helmut Birkhan and Otto Gschwantler (Vienna, 1976), pp. 577–88 (p. 578). Edith Marold, 'Kosmogonische Mythen in der *Húsdrápa* des Úlfr Uggason', in *International Scandinavian and Medieval Studies in Memory of Gerd Wolfgang Weber: ein runder Knäuel, so rollt' es uns leicht aus den Händen*, ed. by Michael Dallapiazza and others, Hesperides: Letterature e Culture Occidentali, 12 (Trieste, 2000), pp. 281–92 (p. 283, n. 4).

[15] Thomas Krömmelbein, *Skaldische Metaphorik: Studien zum Funktion der Kenningsprache in skaldischen Dichtungen des 9. und 10. Jahrhunderts*, Hochschul-Produktionen Germanistik-Linguistik-Literaturwissenschaft, 7 (Freiburg, 1983), pp. 222, 224–25.

confederate' is related to the feminine noun *vár* ('pledge').[16] This meaning too suits Heimdallr's role as the gods' watchman in the Last Days; according to Snorri in *Gylfaginning* (ch. 51) Heimdallr and Loki kill each other in Ragnarǫk.

In my turn, I suggest that *vári* is the *nomen agentis* of *værr* ('comfortable, snug', hence 'warm'). This is how Heimdallr's house is described in *Grímnismál* 13:

> Himinbiǫrg ero in átto,   enn þar Heimdall
>   qveða valda véom;
> þar vǫrðr goða   dreccr í væro ranni,
>   glaðr, inn góða miǫð.[17]

['Heaven-hills' are the eighth [god's abode], and it is there they say Heimdallr has power over deities; there in a warm house the gods' sentinel, gleaming, drinks the good mead.]

I link these forms on analogy with two other combinations: *skærr* ('white, pure') with *skári* ('young seagull', perhaps 'whitener', whose droppings whiten the rock); and *kærr* ('loving') and *kæra* ('to murmur, complain') with *Kári*, a name for the wind. This idea keeps Heimdallr's designation in *Húsdrápa* '2' related to his recovery of Freyja's necklace from Loki. In other words, the 'gods' land-warmer' recovers her Brísingamen in order to stop everything freezing to death in winter. The meaning of this otherwise unattested noun 'vári' is at least straightforwardly related to that of the neuter noun *vár* ('spring').[18] It can be identified with the word in 'Fárbauta mǫg vára', similarly positioned at the end of a line which Úlfr probably borrowed from *Haustlǫng*, a shield-poem nearly a century older than *Húsdrápa*.[19]

---

[16] Discussed in Schier, 'Húsdrápa 2', p. 578; favoured by Hans Kuhn, *Das Dróttkvætt* (Heidelberg, 1983), p. 296; rejected by Marold, 'Kosmogonische Mythen in der *Húsdrápa*', p. 283. 'Trusty one' is preferred to 'defender' in *Skáldskaparmál*, ed. by Faulkes, II, 421.

[17] *Edda: Die Lieder des Codex Regius nebst verwandten Denkmälern*, ed. by Gustav Neckel, rev. by Hans Kuhn, 2 vols., 5th edn (Heidelberg, 1983), I, 59–60.

[18] Johannesson (*Altisländisches etymologisches Wörterbuch*, p. 153) connects OIce *værr* ('freundlich, ruhig, angenehm') formally with *várar* ('feierliche versicherung') and *Vár* ('göttin des versprechen, treue').

[19] *The Haustlǫng of Þjóðólfr of Hvinir*, ed. by Richard North (Enfield Lock, 1997), pp. 4–5 (text 5/1–4) and 25–27 (note). Þjóðólfr's two long lines, whose meaning is disputed, are 'Fljótt bað foldar dróttinn Fárbauta mǫg vára | þekkiligr með þegnum þrymseilar hval deila', which I now translate as: 'Swiftly the handsome lord of the land [: Óðinn] bade Fárbauti's boy [: Loki] deal out the whale of the cracking rope of spring-times [: whale of the traces: plough-ox] among the thegns'. The scene is their serving up of Þjazi's meal. See also Tolley, 'Heimdallr and Brísingamen in *Húsdrápa*', pp. 93–94.

The next problem is the meaning of 'bregðr'. As Kurt Schier and others have noted, the simple verb *bregða*, which denotes sudden movement, may be transitive or intransitive, whereby Heimdallr either 'rushes (himself)', or 'jerks (something)' towards a place or object named *singasteinn*; with *við* as preposition, *bregða* may mean 'compete (with)'; in an adverbial phrase with *við*, as in *bregða einhverju við*, it may even mean 'to talk about something'.[20] Edith Marold prefers the transitive *bregða*, accepting no tmesis in the first half of *Húsdrápa* '2', but reading 'ragna . . . vári' as a kenning for Heimdallr, 'bregðr' as verb, and 'rein' as object: 'Der ratkluge, berühmte Wächter der Götter nimmt beim Singasteinn das Land vom überaus schlauen Sohn des Fárbauti weg.'[21] Mostly Marold follows Schier, who reads the Heimdallr-Loki contest as part of an otherwise forgotten creation myth in which Loki, having helped Heimdallr to raise the gods' rich earth from the sea, keeps some of this back in his mouth; they wrestle underwater until Heimdallr, the defender of the gods' rich earth takes this last piece of it from him.[22] The unique compound 'hafnýra' or 'sea-kidney' in the second half of Úlfr's stanza is accordingly explained as a kenning for 'earth'.[23] In general this reading works. The meanings of *bregðr* and *rein* are pliable enough to allow us to read this stanza with Schier as 'den Rest eines überaus weit verbreitetes dualistischen Schöpfungsmythos'.[24] But Schier throws the net out far from home: his parallels, inspired by Georges Dumézil, come from Eurasian mythology, Finnish, Russian, 'Ugric', and Turkish; Marold pushes it when she calls these 'osteuropäischen Erzählungen'. Consequently

---

[20] Fritzner, *Ordbog*, I, s.v. 'bregða'. Schier, 'Húsdrápa 2', pp. 579–81 (p. 580). *Skáldskaparmál*, ed. by Faulkes, II, 250. Marold, 'Kosmogonische Mythen in der *Húsdrápa*', p. 284.

[21] Marold, 'Kosmogonische Mythen in der *Húsdrápa*', pp. 283–85, esp. p. 284: 'the counsel-clever famed watchman of the gods takes the land away from the supremely sly son of Fárbauti at the *Singa*-stone'. Tmesis here was first rejected by E. A. Kock, in *Notationes Norrænæ*, 2 vols (Lund, 1923–41), § 240; in § 1952, however, Kock emends *rein at* to *reinar*, as in *ragna reinar vári*, a phrase which has much the same meaning as the kenning of Finnur Jónsson's which he opposed (as in *Ska*, I, 71, 2). Schier follows Kock with *reinar in 'Húsdrápa 2', p. 581.

[22] Kurt Schier, 'Die Erdschöpfung aus dem Urmeer und die Kosmogonie der Völuspá', in *Märchen, Mythos, Dichtung: Festschrift zum 90. Geburtstag Friedrich von der Leyens*, ed. by Hans Kuhn and Kurt Schier (Munich, 1963), pp. 303–34. See also his 'Húsdrápa 2', pp. 583–86; and 'Die Húsdrápa von Úlfr Uggason und die bildliche Überlieferung altnordischer Mythen', in *Minnjar og Menntir: Afmælisrit helgað Kristjáni Eldjárn, 6 desember 1976*, ed. by Guðni Kolbeinsson (Reykjavik, 1976), pp. 425–43, esp. pp. 427–33. Accepted, as an allusion to a myth of creation as male pseudo-creation, in Clunies Ross, *Prolonged Echoes*, pp. 173–74.

[23] Marold, 'Kosmogonische Mythen in der *Húsdrápa*', p. 284.

[24] Schier, 'Die Húsdrápa von Úlfr Uggason', p. 427.

Marold rules out the Brísingamen from *Húsdrápa* '2', relegating this necklace, in a footnote, to obscurity as one of Snorri's 'mythologischen Kombinationen': produced, presumably, whenever his Icelandic fails him.[25] Although Heimdallr cannot be called a creator god, Marold implies that Óðinn, who is one, might have been included in a part of the context now lost: Norse gods come in threes according to Dumézil.[26] If we keep Snorri in mind, however, it is worth noting that he makes no mention of Óðinn in Heimdallr's duel with Loki in *Húsdrápa*.

As we have seen, Snorri says that Heimdallr struggled with Loki for the Brísingamen. Loki's theft of this necklace is known from *Haustlǫng* (*c.* 900), in which the Norwegian skald Þjóðólfr of Hvinir calls Loki 'Brísings goða girðiþjófr' ('thief of the gods' Brísing-girdle'; st. 9) as he abducts the fertility goddess Iðunn to the land of the giants.[27] As we have *Húsdrápa*, Úlfr's stanza delivers one, if not two, kennings that can be interpreted as denotations for Freyja's necklace in line with one etymology of *brísa*, stem of the first element of *Brísingamen* ('necklace of the Brísingar') as 'to shine'.[28] There is 'hafnýra fǫgru' ('dazzling sea-kidney') in the dative after 'rædr' ('gets control over'). Birger Pering took this phrase to refer to the tradition of *vettenyrer*, kidney-shaped molucca beans washed up by the Gulf Stream on the shores of Norway, Iceland, and the Western Isles.[29] This interpretation of the unique *hafnýra* alludes to women's use of birth talismans that Freyja, as Gefjun or Gefn, might have given them from the sea; we may include this meaning as secondary.[30] The primary meaning, however, must reside in a kenning. The brightness and marine origin both suggest a golden treasure: more than two hundred skaldic kennings survive in which gold is indicated as the fire of the sea.[31] What is then

---

[25] Marold, 'Kosmogonische Mythen in der *Húsdrápa*', pp. 284–88, esp. p. 285 ('eastern European narratives') and n. 18 ('mythological combinations').

[26] Georges Dumézil, *Gods of the Ancient Northmen*, ed. by Einar Haugen (Berkeley, 1973). For a criticism of Dumézil's presentation of Norse mythology, see R. I. Page, 'Dumézil Revisited', *Saga-Book of the Viking Society*, 20 (1978–79), 49–69 (p. 68).

[27] *Haustlǫng*, ed. by North, pp. 6–7 and 40–41 (n. to 9/6–7).

[28] Birger Pering, *Heimdall* (Lund, 1941), p. 227. Tolley, 'Heimdallr and Brísingamen in *Húsdrápa*', p. 87.

[29] Pering, *Heimdall*, pp. 217–19. For an illustration (of 1700), see James Graham-Campbell, *The Viking Age Gold and Silver of Scotand (850–1150)* (Edinburgh, 1995), p. 180 (pl. 2).

[30] Audrey Meaney, 'Driftseeds and the Brísingamen', *Folklore*, 94 (1983), 33–39; Tolley, 'Heimdallr and Brísingamen in *Húsdrápa*', pp. 89–90; Näsström, *Fornskandinavisk religion*, p. 131.

[31] Rudolf Meissner, *Die Kenningar der Skalden: Ein Beitrag zur skaldischen Poetik* (Bonn, 1921), pp. 229–32 (§ 87. o: 'Die stärkste Gruppe der Goldkenningar').

unusual in 'hafnýra fǫgru' is the kidney-shape, which, if not to be explained purely as an allusion to *vettenyrer*, must be taken as representing something on the panels at Hjarðarholt. Perhaps this is a deformed circle representing a necklace.[32]

Úlfr's other kenning for Freyja's necklace, if he has one here, is to be seen in the phrase *at singasteini* in the first half of *Húsdrápa* '2'. Almost all commentators have decided to treat *singasteinn* as a place-name, although an airing of the older view of this as a kenning for the Brísingamen can still be found in erudite discussion.[33] The problem arises in the *singa*-element, for which no Old Icelandic cognate has been found. It might be possible to treat this as a now-lost adjective (**sinnigr* ?'ancient': Gothic *sinneigs*) with a thematic vowel for use in compounds.[34] This notion of 'Singasteinn' compares with 'Frecasteinn', a battle-site in the eleventh-century Helgi Lays.[35] No 'Singasteinn' is elsewhere recorded as a place-name, as one might expect, but the word seems comparable with 'Vágasker' ('Wave-Rock') in Snorri's typification of the Heimdallr-kenning 'tilsœkir Singasteins ok Vágaskers'. Yet it remains true that whereas 'Vágasker' is a place-name, the word 'singasteinn' may not be: when Snorri, in another case, tells us that Loki may be called 'þrætudólg Heimdala[r] ok Skaða' ('wrestling-foe of Heimdallr and Skaði'), he covers two separate stories with the same base-word.[36] Likewise, the base-word 'tilsœkir' may support two aspects of Heimdallr: 'visitor to Wave-Rock', as a stanza now missing from *Húsdrápa* might have told us; and 'striver for' an object, Úlfr's *singasteinn*.

As to the first element in this compound, Pering has seen *singa* as a miscopying of *signa*, a loanword from Latin *signum* ('sign, miracle'). Pering's idea is to define the *singasteinn* as an amulet in keeping with his reading of *hafnýra* as a birth-talisman,

---

[32] Schier, 'Húsdrápa 2', p. 583: 'Vielleicht wurde das Grundwort *nýra* "Niere" bestimmt durch die Art der Abbildung in der Schnitzerei von Hjarðarholt, so dass sich die Kenning unmittelbar aus der Ausschauung erklären liess.' Accepted in *Skáldskaparmál*, ed. by Faulkes, II, 299 (s.v. 'hafnýra').

[33] Krömmelbein, *Skaldische Metaphorik*, pp. 222–23.

[34] Discussed in Schier, 'Húsdrápa 2', p. 584. See Tolley, 'Heimdallr and Brísingamen in *Húsdrápa*', p. 82 ('The ready in counsel, famous guardian of the territory of the gods turns against the monstrously sly son of Fárbauti over the Gleaming Stone') and pp. 87–88.

[35] *Helgakviða Hundingsbana* I, 44, 53, *Helgakviða Hjörvarðssonar* 39, *Helgakviða Hundingsbana* II, 26.

[36] *Skáldskaparmál*, ed. by Faulkes, I, 19 (ch. 8). Margaret Clunies Ross, 'Why Skaði Laughed: Comic Seriousness in Old Norse Mythic Narrative', *Mál og Minne* (1989), 1–14. Richard North, 'Loki's Gender, or Why Skaði Laughed', in *Monsters and the Monstrous in Medieval Northwest Europe*, ed. by Karin E. Olsen and Luuk A. J. R. Houwen (Leuven, 2001), pp. 141–51.

but Schier rejects this interpretation on the grounds that *signum*, which is borrowed into thirteenth-century sagas in *signask* 'to bless oneself' and *prímsigning* (< *prima signatio*) does not appear in Icelandic texts as old as the late tenth century.[37] It is plausible, however, that the Christian Irish introduced Latin *signum* into Icelandic in the ninth century, particularly in the west where so many settlers, more in fact than given in *Laxdæla saga*, claimed Irish descent.[38] The Old Irish word *sén*, from *signum*, could mean 'the blessing of God': a verbal form such as *signid* ('he makes a sign') shows the word as used by Irish clergy such as the *papar* ('fathers') who lived in Iceland when the first settlers arrived; the cognate Scots Gaelic *seun* ('charm; an amulet to render a warrior invulnerable') gives a physical aspect to *signum* which fits with *steinn*.[39] The simplex can mean 'jewel': in 'breiða steina' ('broad jewels') it is used for gemstones in Freyja's necklace (*Þrymskviða* 16 and 19); the compound 'iarknasteinn' (*Vǫlundarkviða* 25) appears to mean 'gem' or 'pearl', as does the Old English cognate *eorcnanstan*.[40] As an unusual kenning, rather than a transparent descriptive term, the word *singasteinn* would refer to the sun as a 'jewel' whose rays bless creation. The thirteenth-century *Landnámabók* ('Book of Settlements') tells us that Þorkell *máni* ('moon'), law-speaker and astronomer, was a man

> er einn heiðinna manna hefir bezt verit siðaðr, at því er menn vitu dœmi til. Hann lét sik bera í sólargeisla í banasótt sinni ok fal sik á hendi þeim guði, er sólina hafði skapat; hafði hann ok lifat svá hreinliga sem þeir kristnir menn, er bezt eru siðaðir.[41]

---

[37] Pering, *Heimdall*, p. 219; Schier, 'Húsdrápa 2', p. 584.

[38] The Irish were there first, according to Ari's *Íslendingabók* (ch. 1), in *Íslendingabók–Landnámabók*, ed. by Jakob Benediktsson, Íslenzk fornrit, 1 (Reykjavik, 1986), p. 5. On the suppression of Irish ancestry in *Laxdæla saga*, in all but the heroes, see Preben Meulengracht Sørensen, 'Norge og Irland i *Laxdæla saga*', in *At Fortælle Historien: Studier i den gamle nordiske Litteratur. Telling History: Studies in Norse Literature*, Hesperides: Letterature e Culture Occidentali, 16 (Trieste, 2001), pp. 71–80, esp. pp. 74–75.

[39] Joseph Vendryes, *Lexique Étymologique de l'Irlandais Ancien: RS* (Dublin, 1974), s.v. 'sén': 'signe, présage, d'où bénédiction, bonheur [...] bénédiction de Dieu'; s.v. also 'sigen'. *Signum* was borrowed into Irish again as *sigen*, as in *sigen na crochi* ('sign of the cross'). *A Pronouncing and Etymological Dictionary of the Gaelic Language: Gaelic–English, English–Gaelic*, ed. by Malcolm Maclennan (Edinburgh, 1925), s.v. 'seun'. *Foclóir Gaeilge-Béarla*, ed. by Niall Ó Dónaill and rev. by Tómas de Bhaldraithe (Baile Átha Cliath [Dublin], 1977), s.v. 'séan'. Compare OIce *bjannak* ('blessing'), from Irish *beannacht*.

[40] *The Poetic Edda*, vol. II: *Mythological Poems*, ed., trans., and comm. by Ursula Dronke (Oxford, 1997), pp. 318–19.

[41] *Íslendingabók–Landnámabók*, ed. by Jakob Benediktsson, p. 46 (*Sturlubók*, ch. 9; also in *Hauksbók*, ch. 10).

[who was the most moral of any heathen men of whose case men had knowledge. In his final illness he had himself carried into the sun's rays and commended himself into the hands of the god who made the sun; he had also lived as cleanly as those Christian men who are the most moral.]

So the crux *singasteinn* in *Húsdrápa* '2', if metathesized from **signa-steinn*, may be read as 'blessing-jewel'. Óláfr Hǫskuldsson is said to have learned Irish from his mother Melkorka, his father's concubine, whose fabulous secret was that she was the daughter of Mýrkjartan, King of Ireland.[42]

In *Skáldskaparmál*, Snorri says that Heimdallr fights Loki in the shape of a seal. The change into seal's shape may be seen in *Húsdrápa* '2', if we take Úlfr's verb *bregðr* in the first half of the stanza to be an ellipse for *bregðr sér* 'transforms himself, changes shape'.[43] The idiom is used by Snorri three times in *Gylfaginning* to describe divine shape-shifting: in one, Loki 'changed into the shape of a woman' to hear about Baldr ('brá sér í konu líki', ch. 49); in another, 'into salmon-shape' to escape the gods ('brá hann sér í laxlíki', ch. 50); in a third, the gods 'changed Váli, Loki's son, into the shape of a wolf' ('brugðu Æsir Vála í vargs líki', ch. 50).[44] With 'kvað' for *kvazk* in stanza '3', there is already such an omission of *sér* in *Húsdrápa*.[45] In my interpretation, as the jewel hits the water, Heimdallr turns into a seal to save the Brísingamen from sinking out of reach. This would explain why Heimdallr is initially 'ráðgegninn' ('ready with a plan') and why, changing so fast, Heimdallr gets control ('rædr') over the necklace ('hafnýra fǫgru') before Loki ('áðr').[46] With these words

---

[42] *Laxdæla Saga*, ed. by Einar Ólafur Sveinsson, pp. 51 (end of ch. 20) and 57–59 (ch. 21).

[43] Fritzner, *Ordbog*, I, s.v. 'bregða': '5. forandre, omdanne noget (*e-u*) saa at det bliver af anden Beskaffenhed, andet Udseende end det havde før' ('5. change, alter something (*einhverju*) so that it becomes of another nature, another appearance from what it had before').

[44] *Gylfaginning*, ed. by Faulkes, pp. 45, 48, and 59. See also Gunnarr of Hlíðarendi, of everyone said 'at hann brygði sér hvárki við sár né við bana' ('that he changed his composure neither at wounds nor at his death'), in *Brennu-Njáls saga*, ed. by Einar Ólafur Sveinsson, Íslenzk fornrit, 12 (Reykjavik, 1954), p. 189 (ch. 77).

[45] *Skáldskaparmál*, ed. by Faulkes, I, 16–17 (ch. 4: vs. 54: RW (attributed to Bragi) and U; omitted in T). *Sér* for *sézk* is furthermore found in *Haustlǫng* 14; ed. by North, pp. 8, 58.

[46] Heimdallr's *ráð* is discussed in Tolley, 'Heimdallr and Brísingamen in *Húsdrápa*', p. 84, as comparable with the everlasting OE *ræd* (properly 'benefit') which Hama, a distant Anglo-Saxon analogue in *Beowulf*, lines 1197–1201, is shown to gain in taking the *Brosinga mene* away from Eormanric, its cunning Gothic owner. See also Richard North, *Heathen Gods in Old English Literature*, Cambridge Studies in Anglo-Saxon England, 22 (Cambridge, 1997), pp. 196–98. More sombrely, Krömmelbein (*Skaldische Metaphorik*, p. 224) connects *ráðgegninn* with Heimdallr's fine hearing in his role 'als ein endzeitlich programmierter Hüter' ('as a guardian programmed for the End Time').

Úlfr appears to capture the moment in the story at which both gods change into seals in pursuit of a necklace which he likens to the sun sinking in the western ocean.

Thus the story behind this stanza may be quite different from Schier's image of Heimdallr lifting earth from the sea. The myth as we have it in *Húsdrápa* is still a fragment; but *Sǫrla þáttr*, a story in the fourteenth-century *Flateyjarbók*, tells how Óðinn forced Loki to steal Freyja's necklace, then kept it from her until she arranged the war of the Hjaðningar, an endless sea-battle between two kings in which her magic constantly revives the dead.[47] The story of this battle is told in Bragi's *Ragnarsdrápa* (*c.* 850), as one of four extant representations of images on a shield.[48] The later *Sǫrla þáttr* is a composite story in that it appears to add Óðinn's necromancy to the simpler tale of Loki's theft of the necklace from Freyja (who got it by sleeping with the (many) dwarves who made it). There is no Heimdallr in *Sǫrla þáttr* to return the necklace to Freyja, but if *Sǫrla þáttr* contains a reflex of the story behind *Húsdrápa* '2', as most believe, it may be that he was replaced at some stage with Óðinn. Úlfr's verse can be read as praise for Heimdallr, who needs the necklace to end the winter and warm up life in Iceland with spring.

Elsewhere I have suggested that Heimdallr, having recovered the Brísingamen, is rewarded with the sexual favours of its owner.[49] *Lokasenna* is a poem probably of the early Christian period in the eleventh century, in which Loki, mocking the Norse gods one by one, deconstructs each of their divine mysteries by moralizing these as flaws of character. In *Lokasenna* 20, when Loki alleges the goddess Gefjun's prostitution with *sveinn inn hvíti* —

> Þegi þu, Gefion, þess mun ek nú geta,
>   er þik glapði at geði —
> sveinn inn hvíti, er þér sigli gaf
>   ok þú lagðir lær yfir.[50]

---

[47] *Flateyjarbók*, ed. by Guðbrandur Vigfússon and C. R. Unger, 3 vols (Christiania [Oslo], 1860–68), I, 275–83.

[48] *Skj*, B I, 1–4, esp. 3. For a recent text and discussion, see Karin Olsen, 'Bragi Boddason's *Ragnarsdrápa*: A Monstrous Poem', in *Monsters and the Monstrous*, ed. by Olsen and Houwen, pp. 123–39, esp. pp. 131–34.

[49] J. R[ichard] J. North, 'Words in Context: An Investigation Into the Meanings of Early English Words by Comparison of Vocabulary and Narrative Themes in Old English and Old Norse Poetry' (unpublished doctoral dissertation, Cambridge University, 1988), pp. 217–24; *Heathen Gods in Old English Literature*, pp. 221–26, esp. pp. 222–23 and n. 70. Accepted in *Poetic Edda*, II, ed., trans., and comm. by Dronke, pp. 360–61 (n. to *Lokasenna* 20) and in Tolley, 'Heimdallr and Brísingamen in *Húsdrápa*', pp. 85–86.

[50] *Poetic Edda*, II, ed., trans., and comm. by Dronke, pp. 337 (text) and 360–61 (note). My translation is adapted from that of Dronke.

['Hold your tongue, Gefjun, now will I tell of the one who seduced your senses — that blond boy who gave you a trinket and whom you laid your thigh over.']

— he seems to moralize the idea of Heimdallr restoring the Brísingamen to Freyja. Less satirically, Heimdallr is known as 'hvítastr ása' ('whitest of the gods') in *Þrymskviða* 15 and as 'hvíti Áss' ('the white god') in *Skáldskaparmál*.[51] Gefjun is identifiable with Freyja, one of whose names, 'Gefn', with a meaning such as 'giver', is formally related to Gefjun; in the same phrase in *Gylfaginning*, Freyja's name 'Mardǫll' suggests a connection between her and Heimdallr, in that the prefixes 'sea' (*marr*) and 'world' (*heimr*) go together as complements.[52]

The 'Heimdallr' name has been interpreted as 'world tree' (*heim-dallr*), an idea which sheds light on several of the curious things about him: his names Vindhlér ('wind-shelter') and Hallinskíði ('leant-board'); the name of his abode Himin-bjǫrg ('heaven-hill') and his position as the gods' watchman 'við himins enda' ('on the edge of heaven'); his ability to see over a hundred leagues; and the oddity which Úlfr reveals in *Húsdrápa* that Heimdallr is born of nine mothers (his roots).[53] Heimdallr's 'whiteness' seems related to the 'white loam' ('hvíta auri') which is poured on the bole of the World Tree in *Vǫluspá* 19.[54] In all, he is a mysterious god whose role, I suggest, as 'gods' land-warmer' in *Húsdrápa* '2' appears to be one of saving the sun, all life, and abundance from the giants. His procreation of renewal with Freyja, goddess of fertility, is entirely explicable in terms of the word *ráð* with which he is introduced on the first line. As 'ráðgegninn', it appears that Heimdallr is not only 'ready with a plan' to save the Brísingamen, but also 'ready with a family plan' for men and women. He is celebrated for this role in two other poems: as Rígr (Irish *rí*, 'king') in *Rígsþula*, a poem which can thus be associated with the Norse areas of Ireland; and in the first stanza of *Vǫluspá*, where the sibyl's voice asks silence from all humanity, the 'meiri ok minni mǫgo Heimdal[l]ar' ('greater and lesser sons of Heimdallr').[55] In *Rígsþula* we find Heimdallr going to bed between three sets of husband and wife for three nights in each

[51] *Edda*, ed. by Neckel and rev. by Kuhn, I, 113. *Skáldskaparmál*, ed. by Faulkes, I, 19 (ch. 8).

[52] *Gylfaginning*, ed. by Faulkes, p. 29 (ch. 35).

[53] Hugo Pipping, 'Eddastudier I', *Studier i nordisk filologi*, 16 (1925), 7–52, esp. pp. 8–19; 'Eddastudier II', *Studier i nordisk filologi*, 17 (1926), 120–30. On his nature, see Snorri's summary in *Gylfaginning*, ed. by Faulkes, pp. 25–26 (ch. 27). Pering interprets Heimdallr as a ram, in *Heimdall*, pp. 248–54, esp. p. 254: 'Er ist derjenige, "der zu Hause umhergeht"' ('he is the one "who walks around the house"').

[54] *Poetic Edda*, II, ed., trans., and comm. by Dronke, pp. 11–12, 127.

[55] *Poetic Edda*, II, ed., trans., and comm. by Dronke, pp. 7, 162–73, and 202–08, esp. p. 204.

case, begetting or helping to beget sons successively named 'Thrall', 'Churl', and 'Earl'. The poet introduces Heimdallr as 'ǫflgan ok aldinn ás kunnigan, ramman ok rǫskvan' ('a strong and aged sagacious god, robust and ripe-grown'; st. 1);[56] just as he is described as 'móðǫflugr' ('mighty in spirit') in *Húsdrápa* '2'. As the poet says of each set of parents in a refrain, 'Rígr kunni þeim ráð at segja' ('Rígr was able to offer them advice').[57] The saga tells us that *Húsdrápa* was performed not only in the spring, but at a wedding.[58]

Visually in *Húsdrápa* '2', if the word *þáttr* is taken literally, as 'strand', Úlfr may also be telling us that he found his Heimdallr-Loki tale on a tapestry. In skaldic verse the word *þáttr* appears to have been used figuratively to suggest 'strand (of destiny)' as early as the tenth century; the sense 'part (of a poem)', which has been regularly read into it here, appears to have no earlier example than *Húsdrápa*.[59] The fact that Úlfr's *þættir* is plural is a mild problem for the meaning 'part of a poem' which Finnur Jónsson chose for 'mærðar þáttum'.[60] 'Themes' might seem better, given Snorri's words for the handling of heroic and other stories by skalds: 'eptir þessum sǫgum hafa flest skáld ort ok tekit ýmsa þáttu'.[61] Even though a meaning such as this is probably primary, it seems that Úlfr plays on the meanings of *þættir* as he appears to do with *ráð* and other words in *Húsdrápa* '2'. In this case he would describe his poem as a tapestry, a 'text'. Fragments of tapestries have survived in the ninth-century Oseberg ship-find (a procession with men and women, wagons, and horses with riders), and in the Rolvsøy grave in Østfold (a group of people by a boat).[62]

---

[56] Translation from *Poetic Edda*, II, ed., trans., and comm. by Dronke, p. 162.

[57] *Rígsþula* 3/1–2, 5/1–2, 17/1–2, 33/1–2.

[58] Tolley, 'Heimdallr and Brísingamen in *Húsdrápa*', p. 93.

[59] John Lindow, 'Old Icelandic *þáttr*: Early Usage and Semantic History', *Scripta Islandica: Isländska sällskapets årsbok*, 29 (1978), 3–44, esp. pp. 22–24 and p. 24, n. 19: 'One might even imagine that the *þættir* are the stories behind the artwork in Ólafr pái's hall.' Lindow dates the poem to 985.

[60] *Skj*, B I, 128, 2: *kynni ek mærðar þáttum*: 'det gör jeg bekendt i et digterafsnit' ('I make this known in a section of the poem'). Krömmelbein adjusts to the plural, in *Skaldische Metaphorik*, p. 222: 'ich mache dies in den Abschnitten des Preisgedichtes bekannt'.

[61] *Skáldskaparmál*, ed. by Faulkes, I, 50: 'on these stories most poets have composed and taken various themes from them' (ch. 42).

[62] Signe Horn Fuglesang, 'Early Viking Art', in *Acta ad Archaeologiam et Artium Historiam Pertinentia*, Series altera, vol. I, ed. by Hjalmar Torp and J. Rasmus Brandt (Oslo, 1982), pp. 125–73, esp. pp. 170–71 and figs 40–41. David M. Wilson and Ole Klindt-Jensen, *Viking Art*, 2nd edn (London, 1980), pp. 82–83 and pl. XIXa.

We can see some of the images that underlie this stanza. Biographical terms such as 'ráðgegninn' and 'firna slœgr', or even the genealogies of Heimdallr and Loki, can hardly have been embroidered, carved, or painted. Eliminating these, however, we can focus on narrative actions which are centred on the two verbs 'bregðr' and 'rœðr'. If 'bregðr' means 'transforms', as I suggest, then there were at least two images of Heimdallr: one perhaps as a man, as he appears on the west face of the tenth-century Gosforth Cross in Cumbria;[63] another as the seal into which (Snorri says) he transforms when dealing with Loki. Loki as a seal is also necessary to the second image, as is a depiction of the Brísingamen with a kidney-shape ('hafnýra') and metallic boss or inset surface or outline ('fǫgru').[64] As Schier points out, individual images on surviving Scandinavian artefacts and monuments are often unintelligible if they are not related to a whole, one which provides the means of illuminating their meaning; conversely a picture may be interpreted solely through one of its details.[65] In this case, we can presume one human image with a definer, such as a horn, to give an idea of Heimdallr before his trans-formation; and another of two seals adjacent to a necklace, one of them right next to it. In all, these are two images. As large and splendid as such images doubtless were, however, the greater effect comes from the meanings we read into the lan-guage of *Húsdrápa* '2'.

Þórr, Hymir, and the World Serpent

Elsewhere in *Húsdrápa*, Úlfr deals with Þórr's fishing trip with the giant Hymir for the World Serpent. This is one of the most popular myths to survive from the

[63] Known by his horn, the 'Gjallarhorn', in a Doomsday scene: *The British Academy Corpus of Anglo-Saxon Stone Sculpture in England: General Introduction and Volume II*, ed. by Rosemary Cramp and R. N. Bailey (Oxford, 1988), pp. 100–09, esp. pp. 100–02 (ills 288–308).

[64] For metallic bosses on the Oseberg woodcarvings, see Wilson and Klindt-Jensen, *Viking Art*, pls XIV and XV(a) and (c). The word *fagr* means 'shining' (hence my 'dazzling'). For the sun: 'fagrhvél' ('shining-wheel'), in the *Þulur* (*Skáldskaparmál*, ed. by Faulkes, I, 133 (vs. 517/2). For Sigurðr's treasure: 'Grana fagrbyrðr' (his horse, 'Grani's shining burden'), in *Skáldskaparmál*, ed. by Faulkes, I, 60 (vs. 188). For a shield: 'fagr botn randar' ('rim's shining base'), in Bragi's *Ragnarsdrápa* (*Skáldskaparmál*, ed. by Faulkes, I, 51 (vs. 158)).

[65] Kurt Schier, 'Zur Problematik der Beziehung zwischen Bilddetail und Bildganzen', in *Medieval Iconography and Narrative: A Symposium: Proceedings of the Fourth International Symposium Organized by the Centre for the Study of Vernacular Literature in the Middle Ages*, ed. by Flemming G. Andersen and others (Odense, 1980), pp. 167–82, esp. pp. 168–69.

Viking Age in poetic and graphic form. Snorri writes an entertaining version in *Gylfaginning* and this story is also known in Bragi's *Ragnarsdrápa*, in works attributed to three other skalds of the ninth and tenth centuries, and in the Eddic, probably early fourteenth-century, poem *Hymiskviða*.[66] The same story is interpreted on an eighth-century Gotland memorial stone (Ardre VIII), on a tenth-century sandstone frieze in Gosforth, and on the Hørdum stone from Thy, Denmark, and less reliably (there is no Hymir) on the Altuna stone from Uppland, Sweden, both carvings of the eleventh century.[67] Snorri's synoptic version allows us to put the relevant part of *Húsdrápa* into a sequence. Snorri follows on from Þórr's failures to impress a giant named 'Útgarða-Loki' ('the Loki of the Outworld', a trickster). Þórr, having failed to lift more than a paw of the giant's cat from the ground, learns from his host the next day that this was the World Serpent (ch. 47); he returns to the Middle World but almost immediately sets out again, 'sem ungr drengr' ('as a young fellow'), on a mission to destroy him (ch. 48). He stays the night with a giant named Hymir whom next day he asks to accompany on a fishing trip. Hymir says he would be of little use to him 'er hann var lítill ok ungmenni eitt' ('seeing that he was a little youngster'). When he tells Þórr to get the bait, the god tears the head off his prize ox, carries this into the boat and rows off at full pressure, with Hymir in the bow rowing hard to keep up. Þórr twice makes Hymir row on when they reach the giant's favourite fishing grounds, and at the edge of the world Þórr throws out the ox-head on a hook and line; the World Serpent falls for this no less easily than Þórr was tricked earlier into taking

[66] *Gylfaginning*, ed. by Faulkes, pp. 44–45 (ch. 28). For Bragi's stanzas, see Olsen, 'Bragi Boddason's *Ragnarsdrápa*', pp. 127–31. The remaining skalds are Ǫlvir hnúfa (great-uncle of Egill Skalla-Grímsson), Gamli gnæfaðarskáld, and Eysteinn Valdason, respectively at *Skj*, B I, 6, 131, and 132. Discussed in Preben Meulengracht Sørensen, 'Thor's Fishing Expedition', in *At Fortælle Historien*, pp. 59–70, esp. pp. 62–67.

[67] Gabriel Gustafson and Fredrik Nordin, *Gotlands Bildsteine*, with drawings by Olof Sörling and photographs by Harald Faith-Ell, rev. by Sune Lindqvist, 2 vols (Stockholm, 1941), I, 18–24, esp. pp. 22–24 (§ 19) and ill. 311 (Ardre VIII). Peter Foote and David M. Wilson, *The Viking Achievement: The Society and Culture of Early Medieval Scandinavia* (London, 1970), pls 26.b–c. For Gosforth, see *British Academy Corpus*, ed. by Cramp and Bailey, pp. 108–09 (ill. 332). For discussion and reservations, see Signe Horn Fuglesang, 'Viking Art', in *Medieval Scandinavia: An Encyclopedia*, ed. by Phillip Pulsiano and Kirsten Wolf (New York, 1993), pp. 694–700, esp. p. 697: 'There has been, and still exists, a philological propensity to link haphazardly surviving pictures with equally fortuitously transmitted texts, disregarding elementary rules of methodological control.' See also John McKinnell, *Both One and Many: Essays on Change and Variety in Late Norse Heathendom*, with an Appendix by Maria Elena Ruggerini, Philologia, 1 (Rome, 1994), pp. 17–18 and figs 6 (Altuna), 7 (the Gosforth 'Fishing Stone'), and 13 (Hørdum).

him for a cat. When the Serpent sees Þórr he lashes back, forcing him to the edge of the boat; Þórr kicks against him, putting both feet through the boat on to the sea-floor. For a moment they eye one another, the Serpent blowing poison while Þórr gets his hammer. Then Hymir panics and cuts the line and the Serpent sinks back into the sea. Þórr throws the hammer after the monster, but perhaps in vain. Snorri's narrator (Hár), although he says that some think Þórr hits the Serpent and kills him, prefers to believe that the creature still lives encircling the earth.

Five fragments survive from Úlfr's treatment of a depiction of this myth on the walls of Hjarðarholt. If we follow the order of Snorri's narrative, supported by the version in *Hymiskviða*, the first verse would be *Húsdrápa* '4' (only in W: *Skj*, B I, 128, 4), which describes Þórr's stare at the Serpent:

> Innmáni skein ennis   ǫndótts vinar banda;
> áss skaut œgigeislum   orðsæll á men storðar.

[The inner forehead-moon of the powers' fierce friend shone; the renowned god shot terrifying rays at the necklace of the wood-realm [: World Serpent]]

Úlfr's kenning for Þórr's eye, 'innmáni', is reminiscent of 'ennitungl' ('forehead-moons'), Bragi's term in *Ragnarsdrápa* for the eight eyes of Gefjun's oxen.[68] The poet Egill appears to allude to the World Serpent in his *Arinbjarnarkviða* 5 (*c*. 960), describing his lucky escape from King Eiríkr in York; he says it was not safe to look at his enemy's 'tunglskin' ('lunar shine'): 'þás ormfránn ennimáni skein allvalds œgigeislum' ('when the all-powerful's serpent-glittering forehead-moon shone with terrifying rays').[69] In this way, Úlfr's imagery is traditional, but it is also possible in each case that he and Bragi emphasize the circle of the eye because this was an inlaid metallic image. In *Húsdrápa* '5', Úlfr describes the Serpent as a rope around the earth, Þórr as the enemy of monsters:

> En stirðþinull starði   storðar leggs fyrir borði
> fróns á fólka reyni   fránleitr ok blés eitri (vs. 316, also in vs. 210)

[But the taut rope of the wood-realm's leg, glittering-featured, stared from across the gunwale at earth-folk's adversary and blew poison.]

None of the stone carvings show the monster over the waterline. Since the word 'storð' appears in this verse as well as in *Húsdrápa* '4' above, it seems unlikely that

---

[68] Olsen, 'Bragi Boddason's *Ragnarsdrápa*', p. 124. Roberta Frank argues that 'the repeated image of a circle or shield rim' is Bragi's device to link the four (extant) episodes of *Ragnarsdrápa*, in *Old Norse Court Poetry*, pp. 108–110, esp. p. 109.

[69] *Egils saga Skalla-Grímssonar*, ed. by Sigurður Nordal, Íslenzk fornrit, 2 (Reykjavík, 1933), p. 259 (ch. 78).

they belonged to the same stanza. Marold would swell *Húsdrápa* here with two stanzas assigned to Bragi, on the strength of their burlesque.[70] If the first of these truly comes out of *Húsdrápa*, against its attribution to Bragi not long before the Jǫrmunrekkr-section of *Ragnarsdrápa* in *Skáldskaparmál*, then it is just possible that the second half of *Húsdrápa* '5' went as follows:

> þá er forns Litar flotna   á fangboða ǫngli
> hrøkkviáll of hrokkinn   hekk Vǫlsunga drekku. (vs. 153)[71]

[when the coiling eel of the Vǫlsungs' drink hung curled on the hook of the wrestling-challenger of the shipmates of old Litr.]

A stanza's second half often elaborates on the first: here the snake would blow poison when the giants' enemy hooked it up out of the sea. The kenning for Þórr in this verse might seem to refer to the story most fully known from *Skáld-skaparmál*, in which the giant Suttungr rows out to sea with two dwarves, killers of his uncle and aunt, threatening to leave them on a tidal rock unless they repay him with the mead of poetry.[72] The problem is that Þórr does not wrestle with giants.[73] With the name 'Litr', however, perhaps with the word *hrokkinn* also, the poet appears to allude to the story of Baldr's wild funeral, in which Þórr kicks the dwarf Litr into the pyre when the gods stop him from killing the giantess Hyrrokkin, the only creature who can dislodge Baldr's funeral ship.[74] Whether or not it was Úlfr, rather than Bragi, who composed the verse above, we can now proceed to *Húsdrápa* '3', which is attributed to Bragi in two manuscripts of *Snorra Edda* (RW) and to Úlfr in one (U; omitted in T):

> Þjokkvǫxnum kvað þykkja   þikling firinmikla
> hafra njóts at [W: hǫfgum]   hætting megindrætti. (vs. 54)

---

[70] Edith Marold, *Kenningkunst: Ein Beitrag zu einer Poetik der Skaldendichtung*, Quellen und Forschungen zur Sprach- und Kulturgeschichte der germanischen Völker, n.s., 80 (Berlin, 1983), pp. 109–10.

[71] *Skáldskaparmál*, ed. by Faulkes, I, 50 (ch. 42).

[72] *Skáldskaparmál*, ed. by Faulkes, I, 3 (*Gylfaginning*, ch. 57).

[73] How about *fangboði forns Litar flotna*, 'wrestling-challenger of the old Litr of sailors'? 'Litr', as a smaller person the crew kick around a ship, may be a woman; with *forn*, the old woman whom Þórr challenges to a wrestle is Elli, *kerling ein gǫmul*, in Snorri's tale of Útgarða-Loki. See *Gylfaginning*, ed. by Faulkes, p. 42: 'an old crone' (ch. 46). There is not much *gravitas* here.

[74] So Krömmelbein, *Skaldische Metaphorik*, pp. 81–83, who suggests that Þórr wrestles with Litr first. A god wrestling a dwarf?

[It is said the thick-grown stumpy-legs thought he was in monstrously big danger from the billy-goat-employer's [W: heavy] mighty haul.]

Hymir's fright, in Snorri's story, leads him to cut the line just as Þórr swings the hammer. With his verb *kvað*, Úlfr openly refers to such a story in his own time.[75] If he seems to remove himself from the images before him, it is really to acknowledge that the giant's thoughts are not depicted. His desire to supply these thoughts is an act of interpretation. It may show that here we are close to a group of narrative tableaux on a painted carved panel or on a tapestry. Úlfr's provision of a reason for what happens next, the cutting of the line, shows that the picture, as he sees it, may feature the World Serpent's head raised into a position from where it can frighten Hymir. Perhaps this is as high as the gunwale. The word *þikling* allows us to glimpse the modest size of Hymir's figure in relation to that of Þórr, who must stand close to the World Serpent if Úlfr's description of their face-off is based on an image.[76] With the word 'þjokkvǫxnum' we also appear to see the width of the giant's limbs offsetting his smaller size. In a stanza which is lost after this one Úlfr makes Hymir cut the fishing line. In spite of this, in *Húsdrápa* '6/5–8', Þórr succeeds in killing the Serpent:

> Víðgymnir laust Vimrar   vaðs af fránum naðri
> hlusta grunn við hrǫnnum.   Hlaut innan svá minnum. (vs. 56)

[The Wide-Wader of the ford of Vimur struck off into the waves the earhole's pediment from the glittering adder of the fishing line. He got it from Norway with images like this.]

In *Húsdrápa* '6/1–4', Þórr appears to pay Hymir for his sabotage:

> Fullǫflugr lét fellir   fjall-Gauts hnefa skjalla
> (ramt mein var [þat]) reyni   reyrar leggs við eyra. (vs. 55)

[The fully-endowed feller of the mountain-Gaut made his fist crack ([that] was a mighty injury) against the ear of the explorer of the reed's leg.]

This half-stanza appears to be the last one we still have in the section of *Húsdrápa* that deals with Þórr's fishing trip. In the foregoing two quotations I have chosen to reverse Snorri's order (one clear in the numbering of vs. 55 and 56). Until recently

---

[75] Russell Poole, but not Faulkes (edn, I, 137), reads *Þjokkvaxinn kvezk* [...] *þiklingr* in U, in *Viking Poems on War and Peace: A Study in Skaldic Narrative* (Toronto, 1991), pp. 52–53: 'The stoutly grown thick creature [giant] says he sees extremely great danger in Þórr's heavy and mighty catch.'

[76] Schier, 'Die Húsdrápa von Úlfr Uggason', p. 428: 'Man hat den Eindruck, in der anschaulichen Darstellung in diesen Strophen die Bildvorlage besonders deutlich zu erkennen.'

most commentators took the kenning for Þórr's opponent in vs. 55 ('reynir reyrar leggs') as a term for the Serpent, joining these lines to half-stanza vs. 56, which Snorri cites after a second attribution to Úlfr. Perhaps it is safe to assume that Snorri or one of his scribes followed the flow of his (complete) text of Úlfr's poem in their search for quotations. But these two verses are clearly separated in three of the four main manuscripts of *Skáldskaparmál* (RTW); and even where they are not (U), Faulkes points out that the initial capital *V* is placed out at the margin as well as a *v* (for *vísa*, 'verse').[77] Roberta Frank, moreover, identifies the words *reyni reyrar leggs* (in her words 'explorer [or rowan tree] of the hollow bone of the reed') as Úlfr's kenning for Hymir, not the Serpent.[78] In this case, we could follow Snorri's order of incident in *Gylfaginning* and place vs. 55 (Hymir) after vs. 56 (the Serpent).

In vs. 56 Þórr is presented as the victor against a giantess in the tale of his journey to the giant Geirrøðr. In vs. 55 he is presented no longer as a goat-driver (as he is on arrival at Hymir's house in *Hymiskviða* 7 and perhaps elsewhere in the house-carvings), but again in his role of giant-killer.[79] This suits what he does in context, slinging his hammer after the Serpent's retreating head, while it sinks back into the ocean, then knocking Hymir out of the boat with such force that he hits the sea-floor. It is all very quick; speed of action is also a feature of Heimdallr in *Húsdrápa* '2'.

'Ok segja menn', says Snorri of Þórr and the Serpent in his version, 'at hann lysti af honum hǫfuðit við grunninum' ('and people say he struck its head off into the deep'; ch. 48). This is probably how Úlfr saw it, although at least one scholar takes him to mean that the Serpent's head hits the waves still joined to its body.[80] Scholars disagree on whether the Serpent's death here, rather than in Ragnarǫk (as given in *Vǫluspá* 53), was Úlfr's innovation or an old variant to the Serpent's escape or indeed the only form of this myth prior to the Christianized eschatology of *Vǫluspá*.[81] Meulengracht Sørensen treats the Serpent's survival as the older mythic form, consistent with his idea that the story expresses Þórr's failure to

---

[77] *Skáldskaparmál*, ed. by Faulkes, I, 165–66.

[78] Frank, *Old Norse Court Poetry*, pp. 110–12, esp. p. 110.

[79] *Edda*, ed. by Neckel and rev. by Kuhn, I, 89.

[80] Krömmelbein, *Skaldische Metaphorik*, p. 225.

[81] On the possible debt of *Vǫluspá* to Revelation, see Richard North, 'End Time and the Date of *Vǫluspá*: Two Models of Conversion', in *Conversion and Colonization in Anglo-Saxon England*, ed. by C. E. Karkov and Nicholas Howe, Medieval and Renaissance Texts and Studies, 318 (Tempe, 2006), pp. 213–36.

disrupt 'a cosmic balance'.[82] But one cannot base this version on Bragi's ninth-century verses, as he does: not all of these have come down to us. Schier follows many others in comparing this myth with Indra's slaying of the dragon Vrtra, although he might cite the Greek myth of Apollo and Python nearer home.[83] In addition, it is unclear why Þórr's fishing trip is so widespread on Norse monuments if it really was a story of divine failure.[84] On balance, it seems better to define it as a tale of Þórr's triumph: a young triumph, if we agree with Meulengracht Sørensen that Þórr's guise here in *Gylfaginning* as 'ungr drengr' ('a young fellow') and Bragi's adverb 'snimma' ('in old times') in *Ragnarsdrápa* '14' both show that the story belongs to Þórr's early career.[85]

In other words, there is little in these verses of *Húsdrápa*, any more than in the Heimdallr-Loki stanza, to show Ragnarǫk weighing heavily on Úlfr's mind. Indeed the mood of his poem suggests otherwise. The kenning 'Víðgymnir Vimrar vaðs', which celebrates Þórr in another tale, seems to mean 'Wide-Wader [a giant's name] of the ford of Vimur': not only does he hold on while the Serpent's wake engulfs him and Hymir in their boat, but crossing the Vimur to get to Geirrøðr, Þórr and his human helper Þjalfi find themselves swamped in the urine of a giantess straddling the river. The latter tale is told in six stanzas (*Skáldskaparmál*, vs. 76–81) of the great *Þórsdrápa* which the skald Eilífr Goðrúnarson, probably a Norwegian, is thought to have composed for Earl Hákon of Norway (*c.* 975–*c.* 995) in the late 980s.[86] It also survives in an Eddic fragment and in Snorri's prose narrative after *Þórsdrápa*.[87] Þórr here survives the flood by lobbing a boulder at the giantess which stops her flow at its source. Úlfr's indelicate kenning puts Þórr's triumph in a light more suitable for a society wedding in Iceland.

[82] Meulengracht Sørensen, 'Thor's Fishing Expedition', pp. 66–67.

[83] Schier, 'Die Húsdrápa von Úlfr Uggason', pp. 434–35.

[84] Marold, 'Kosmogonische Mythen in der *Húsdrápa*', p. 290.

[85] Margaret Clunies Ross refrains from placing this story in mythic time, in *Prolonged Echoes*, p. 260.

[86] Ed. by Daphne L. Davidson, 'Earl Hákon and his Poets' (unpublished doctoral dissertation, Oxford University, 1983). Cited respectfully by Snorri in a sequence of nineteen stanzas, with two more probably part of it (vs. 44 and 53), in *Skáldskaparmál*, ed. by Faulkes, I, 15 (vs. 44), 16 (vs. 43), 25–30 (vs. 73–91), and 171–72 (note). *Skj*, B I, 139–44. Discussed as aetiology for Þórr's hammer, in Roberta Frank, 'Hand Tools and Power Tools in Eilífr's *Þórsdrápa*', in *Structure and Meaning in Old Norse Literature*, ed. by John Lindow, Lars Lönnroth, and Gerd W. Weber (Odense, 1986), pp. 94–107.

[87] *Skáldskaparmál*, ed. by Faulkes, I, 25 (ch. 18: vs. 72).

Baldr's Funeral

In *Gylfaginning* Snorri moves out from Þórr's fishing trip into the myth of Baldr.[88] This is the god whose young death at the instigation of Loki brings on Ragnarǫk, the end of Norse gods. First, in response to the anxiety of his mother Frigg, all things living and lifeless swear oaths to protect Baldr's life. Loki, however, thwarts their intention by making mistletoe, a plant too young to swear the oath, into the head of a spear which he hands to Hǫðr, blind brother of Baldr, to shoot at the god. Baldr falls dead. In their grief the gods try to get him back, and Hermóðr is sent riding down to the world below, meets Hel, and wins her promise to restore Baldr if all things living and lifeless agree to weep for Baldr's death. In all this Snorri paraphrases a lost Eddic poem which we could call *Baldrsmál*. He quotes what is possibly the final stanza of this poem at the moment an old crone in a cave, Loki in another form, thwarts the common purpose by refusing to weep for Baldr's death.[89] Into this myth of mortality Snorri weaves a paraphrase of what were probably the essentials of Úlfr's *þáttr* on Baldr in *Húsdrápa*. While Hermóðr sets off, the gods burn Baldr's remains on a funeral pyre. With the fire lit, a procession begins in which Snorri mentions chiefly gods and giants: first Óðinn, then Frigg, Óðinn's valkyries and ravens, Freyr 'í kerru' ('in a chariot') pulled by his golden boar, Heimdallr on his horse Gulltoppr, Freyja with her cats, and finally a host of frost-ogres and mountain-giants. In *Húsdrápa* '7', the protocol is different, as is the image of Freyr:

> Ríðr á borg til borgar   boðfróðr sonar Óðins
> Freyr ok fólkum stýrir   fyrst ok gulli byrstum. (vs. 63)

[Rides in first place, and on a boar with bristles of gold, the battle-wise Freyr to the stronghold of Óðinn's son and he guides the people.]

As yet the pyre is just *borg*, a fortification of logs, so it looks as if Úlfr treated Þórr's consecration towards the end of this *þáttr* separately from the scene with Hyrrokkin. With straightforward kennings and use of the present tense, Úlfr puts Freyr first, shows him riding on the boar without vehicle, and gives him a host (*folk*), something in keeping with Freyr's introductory epithet 'fólkvaldi goða' ('field-marshal of gods'; st. 3) at the head of *Skírnismál*.[90] The Oseberg tapestry procession might

---

[88] *Gylfaginning*, ed. by Faulkes, pp. 45–48 (ch. 49).

[89] Compare Snorri's quotation of *Skírnismál*'s final stanza at the end of his story of Freyr in *Gylfaginning*, ed. by Faulkes, p. 31 (ch. 37).

[90] *Poetic Edda*, II, ed., trans., and comm. by Dronke, p. 377.

be taken as support for the idea that the gods in the Hjarðarholt panels move from right to left.[91] Snorri, in his paraphrase of some of *Húsdrápa*, seems to bring Óðinn, Frigg, and their entourage forward to the head of the procession because he is keen to keep Óðinn as lord of the Æsir. If he leaves Úlfr's hierarchy otherwise unchanged, the god after Freyr is Heimdallr. In *Húsdrápa* '10':

> Kostigr ríðr at kesti   kynfróðs þeim er goð hlóðu
> hrafnfreistaðar hesti   Heimdallr at mǫg fallinn. (vs. 19)

[Heimdallr rides splendid on his horse to the pyre which the gods have loaded for the fallen son of the strangely wise tester of ravens.]

In this verse Baldr's funeral pyre is still not lit. Gulltoppr, Heimdallr's horse, was doubtless more elaborately described in the half-stanza which accompanied this one, given that Snorri names him as he does Freyr's boar earlier. In both cases it is the 'gold' of these mounts (Gullinbursti 'golden-bristle' and Gulltoppr 'gold-top') which is emphasized, as if a striking use was made of gold leaf on the original panel.

A couple of winged shapes in black paint are also to be glimpsed in Úlfr's kenning for Óðinn as the raven-god. With the adjective *kynfróðr* in particular, Úlfr describes Óðinn as 'strangely wise': from his practice of augury with Huginn and Muninn; wise also from the prophecy a sibyl gave him about Baldr's death (as in *Vǫluspá* 28–29);[92] possibly also 'kindred-fertile', by which he would connote Óðinn as the begetter on the princess Rindr of a new son to avenge Baldr, in a story to which the skald Kormákr Ǫgmundarson alludes with the proverb 'seið Yggr til Rindar' ('Yggr bewitched Rindr') in *Sigurðardrápa* (*c.* 960).[93] In any case, Úlfr has prepared us for Óðinn from Freyr's verse onwards. In the next passage from *Húsdrápa*, I join *Húsdrápa* '8' with '9', so as to make a complete stanza:[94]

> Ríðr at vilgi víðu   víðfrægr (en mér líða)
> Hropta-týr (of hvapta   hróðrmál) sonar báli. (vs. 8)
>
> Þar hykk sigrunni svinnum   sylgs valkyrjur fylgja
> heilags tafns ok hrafna.   Hlaut innan svá minnum. (vs. 14)

---

[91] Wilson and Klindt-Jensen, *Viking Art*, pp. 82–83 and pl. XIXa.

[92] *Poetic Edda*, II, ed., trans., and comm. by Dronke, pp. 14–15 and 136.

[93] *Skáldskaparmál*, ed. by Faulkes, I, 9 (v. 12) and 85 (vs. 308). *Skj*, B I, 69, 3.

[94] In defence of this join, it might be said that the initial consonant of the non-alliterating penultimate word in '2/4' seems to trigger the alliteration in '2/5–6': that is, '*mǫg*' leads on to '*Móðǫflugr ræðr mœðra mǫgr hafnýra fǫgru*'. This is also the effect of '*sonar*' in '8/4' with '*Þar hykk sigrunni svinnum sylgs valkyrjur fylgja*' in '9/1–2'.

[Rides to his son's exceedingly wide bonfire (while words of glory flow over my jaws) the God of Secrets widely renowned. There I think come valkyries and ravens following the wise-at-swallowing victory-tree to the holy sacrifice. He got it from Norway with images like this.]

By now the 'borg' is a 'bál', a 'pyre' that is lit. With 'Hropta-týr' Úlfr describes Óðinn as wise in the runic secrets which, as *hroptr rǫgna*, he has acquired from the dead ('the gods' master of things hidden'; *Hávamál* 142). Another aspect of Óðinn to which Úlfr alludes in this verse is the gift of the mead of poetry, a story implicit in the liquid image of poetry that rushes into and back out of the poet's mouth ('en mér líða [. . .] of hvapta'). The same image appears to underlie the kenning for Óðinn in vs. 14, *sigrunnr svinnr sylgs*, whereby the god's mighty ingestion of mead in Gunnlǫð's cave is hailed as a victory for wisdom of poetry.[95] Next, after Óðinn and his birds, Úlfr perhaps described Frigg, and then Freyja with her cats, before indicating the arrival of more giants.

Presumably his sequel to this was the death of Nanna, which seals Baldr's funeral at the launch. Snorri tells us that the gods have moved Baldr's body to Hringhorni, his ship near the shore. This vessel is the largest on earth. No one can launch it until they send for a *gýgr* ('ogress') named Hyrrokkin (perhaps 'Sooty-from-fire'), who arrives in troll style on the back of a wolf with a snake for reins. The four warriors from Valhǫll whom Óðinn appoints to hold her wild mount do so by cutting it down. Hyrrokkinn responds by shoving the ship out awkwardly stern first.[96] Fire flashes from the slipway and the earth shakes. In anger Þórr reaches for his hammer but the gods restrain him. To quote *Húsdrápa* '11' from Úlfr again in *Skáldskaparmál*:

> Fullǫflug lét fjalla   fram haf-Sleipni þramma
> Hildr, en Hropts of gildar   hjálmelda mar feldu. (vs. 242)

[The fully-endowed mountain-Hildr made the ocean-Sleipnir [: sea-horse: ship] trundle forwards while the empowerers of Hroptr's helmet-fires [: Óðinn's warriors] felled her steed.]

As no other narrative on Baldr's funeral survives, it is tempting to regard the lost half of this stanza, probably the first half, as Snorri's source for his description of

---

[95] The word *sylgs* is more often taken with *heilags tafns*, so as to make 'blood of the holy sacrifice': *Skj*, B I, 129, 8 ('blod'); E. O. G. Turville-Petre, *Scaldic Poetry* (Oxford, 1976), pp. 67–70, esp. p. 69; Clunies Ross, *Prolonged Echoes*, p. 270 ('"the drink of the holy carrion"', as the funeral feast); *Skáldskaparmál*, ed. by Faulkes, II, 409 ('sylgr').

[96] Þórr is held to be angry because Hyrrokkin produced 'the sort of cosmic disturbance that normally characterized his own actions', in Clunies Ross, *Prolonged Echoes*, p. 79.

the wolf and snake-reins. Striking is the resemblance between the first half-line of the above verse, 'fullǫflug lét fjalla', and the first half-line of *Húsdrápa* '6' (vs. 55), 'fullǫflugr lét fellir': almost as if Úlfr intended to use Hyrrokkin to recall Þórr's dispatch of Hymir, or vice versa. Then, who knows? Þórr may kill her: in a tenth-century fragment of an apostrophe of Þórr which Snorri attributes to Þorbjǫrn dísarskáld, Hyrrokkin is listed among the god's victims.[97]

After this, in *Gylfaginning*, and probably in a lost stanza of *Húsdrápa*, Baldr is laid on the pyre, 'ok er þat sá kona hans Nanna Nepsdóttir þá sprakk hon af harmi ok dó' ('and when his wife, Nanna daughter of Nepr, saw this, her heart burst with grief and she died').[98] Nanna is put on the same pyre, which Þórr consecrates with his hammer. When the dwarf named Litr runs innocently by, Þórr kicks him into the flames to join them.[99] At this unseemly moment, I suggest Úlfr focussed on the death of Nanna. Probably in *Húsdrápa* as in *Gylfaginning*, any comedy in Þórr's funeral brawl was offset by her great marital ideal. For the sake of a contemporary bride and groom, this may be the construction Úlfr wished to place on his patron's procession of images in Hjarðarholt.

Óláfr's Decorated Hall

Indicative of Úlfr's style is the phrase 'Þar hykk' ('There I think'). These words reveal a view more individual than any to be found in the other skaldic artistic commentaries preserved by Snorri. In his *Ragnarsdrápa*, Bragi pictures the World Serpent on his shield with the words 'þat erum sýnt' ('That is visible to me'); with the words 'sék far' ('I see the journey') Þjóðólfr conveys the opening image of the wayfaring Óðinn, Loki, and Hœnir on the shield which gave rise to *Haustlǫng*.[100] To the earlier poets the stories of gods and heroes are all history, for they happened long ago. The stories that went into and came out of disparate images on public slabs, shields, and panels were a renewable common property. Describing Jǫrmunrekkr, Bragi says 'Þat segik fall á fǫgrum flotna randar botni' ('I show this

---

[97] *Skáldskaparmál*, ed. by Faulkes, I, 17 (ch. 4): *Hyrrokkin dó fyrri* ('Hyrrokkin died earlier'). *Skj*, B I, 35; *Ska*, I, 74, 2.

[98] *Gylfaginning*, ed. by Faulkes, p. 46 (ch. 49).

[99] To become Baldr's servant in the next world, in the view of Näsström, *Fornskandinavisk religion*, p. 103.

[100] Olsen, 'Bragi Boddason's *Ragnarsdrápa*', pp. 127–28; *Haustlǫng*, ed. by North, pp. 2 and 14–15 (st. 1).

fall of men on the shining surface of the shield'), and 'þats á Leifa landa laufi fátt' ('that is painted on the leaf of Leifi's lands [: shield of the ship]');[101] Þjóðólfr confirms that he is not lying, the story of Þjazi is really there, with 'Þats of fátt á fjall Finns ilja brú minni' ('A memorial of that is painted on my bridge of the foot-soles of the Lapp of the fells [: shield]'; st. 13) and likewise with Þórr and Hrung-nir in 'Gǫrla lítk á Geitis garði þær of ferðir' ('I behold these expeditions clearly on the fortress of Geitr [: shield]'; st. 20).[102] Two or three generations later, appar-ently in *c.* 960, Kormákr invoked public knowledge of mythology in a poem which he composed in honour of Earl Sigurðr of Hlaðir and his son Hákon.[103] Kormákr punctuates his eulogy with asides which seem to have nothing to do with his subject, such as 'sitr Þórr í reiðum' ('Þórr sits in his chariot'; st. '5').[104] Taken together, however, they show that he was probably comparing Sigurðr with Óðinn and Hákon with Þórr.[105] Kormákr's asides have long been regarded as references to images on panels in Earl Sigurðr's hall in Trøndelag.[106] Snorri says of this type of aside, which he calls *hjástælt* ('abutted'), that 'skal orðtak vera forn minni' ('the expression must be old proverbial statements').[107] In *Húsdrápa*, a generation later, Úlfr in his turn delivers the stories presented in the *minni* of Hjarðarholt ('[memorial] images', st. '6' and '9'). His word 'hróðrmál' ('words of glory') is an expression for this activity in the verse above. Even in its poor fragmentary state, *Húsdrápa* is about praising Óláfr, and it is odd, but understandable, that this purpose is rarely emphasized in discussions of this poem.

In narrative action the present tense is more widespread in *Húsdrápa* than in the three earlier commentary poems. Úlfr's use of this tense probably shows that

---

[101] *Skáldskaparmál*, ed. by Faulkes, I, 51 (vs. 158); Olsen, 'Bragi Boddason's *Ragnarsdrápa*', p. 136 ('b').

[102] *Haustlǫng*, ed. by North, pp. 8, 10.

[103] On the date and conception of *Sigurðardrápa*, see Bjarne Fidjestøl, *Det Norrøne Fyrste-diktet* (Øvre-Ervik, 1982), pp. 92–93, and Poole, *Viking Poems on War and Peace*, pp. 50–51.

[104] Five others survive. *Skj*, B I, 69–70.

[105] Richard North, '*goð geyja*: The Limits of Humour in Old Norse-Icelandic Paganism', in *Quaestio: Selected Proceedings of the Cambridge Colloquium in Anglo-Saxon, Norse and Celtic*, vol. I (Cambridge, 2000), pp. 1–22, esp. pp. 11–14.

[106] Helmut de Boor, 'Die religiöse Sprache der Vǫluspá und verwandter Denkmäler', in *Deutsche Islandforschung 1930*, vol. I: *Kultur* (Breslau, 1930), pp. 68–142, esp. p. 84; repr. in his *Kleine Schriften*, 2 vols (Berlin, 1964), I, 209–83, esp. p. 229. Schier, 'Die Húsdrápa von Úlfr Uggason', pp. 439–40.

[107] *Snorri Sturluson: Edda: Háttatal*, ed. by Anthony Faulkes (Oxford, 1991), p. 10.

he is more interested than Bragi, Þjóðólfr, and Kormákr in mediating something of the outward form of the paintings before him. This does not mean that his past tense reveals the absence of underlying images, as was once proposed in the case of his verses on the World Serpent and Hyrrokkin.[108] What can be said of Úlfr's present tense is that it reveals an aesthetic approach. The comic impresario Þjóðólfr, thought to be less interested in the artistry of his shield, stints on the present tense: Þjazi, with his eagle-wings on fire, 'sviðnar' ('singes'; *Haustlǫng* 13);[109] and Loki, as he clings to a pole hanging from the airborne Þjazi, is called 'farmr Sigynjar arma sás ǫll regin eygja [. . .] í bǫndum' ('the cargo of Sigyn's arms, whom all the divine powers glare at in his bonds'; st. 7). The latter image of Loki is on an eighth-century picture on a stone in Gotland and also in a Last Days combination on the tenth-century Gosforth Cross.[110] But if it was also on Þjóðólfr's shield in Hordaland in *c*. 900, Þjóðólfr does not develop it into a story. There is a similar reserve in Kormákr, with only one present tense in the surviving *minni*: Þórr in the chariot 'Þórr sitr í reiðum', a painted relief or idol of Þórr which he juxtaposes with his patron's son. By contrast, the use of the present tense in *Húsdrápa* is sustained, delivering neither a narrative culmination nor an aside but a visual foreground.

This stylistic feature amounts to a poet's attempt at explication rather than description. As an observer of the Hjarðarholt carvings for the winter it took him to work on *Húsdrápa*, Úlfr would doubtless have been 'forced to extrapolate meaning' from 'selected, and suggestive, juxtapositionings' of motifs on the panels, just like the admirers of the bold heathen-Christian combinations in Gosforth in the first half of the tenth century.[111] His occasional, but sustained, uses of the

---

[108] Axel Åkerblom, 'Bruket av historiskt presens i den tidigare isländske skaldediktningen (till omkr. 1100)', *Arkiv för nordisk filologi*, 33, n.f., 29 (1917), 293–31, esp. pp. 296–98. Poole, *Viking Poems on War and Peace*, pp. 24–56, esp. pp. 51–54.

[109] Emended to *sviðna* by Åkerblom, in order to exclude the present historic from this graphic poem, in his 'Bruket av historiskt presens', p. 296. On Þjóðólfr's being more detached from shield-images than Bragi, see Hallvard Lie, 'Billedbeskrivende dikt', in *Kulturhistorisk leksikon for nordisk middelalder fra vikingetid til reformationstid* (Copenhagen, 1956–78), I, 543–44, esp. p. 544: 'synes ikke å ha vært ledet av en så klar kunstnerisk idé under sin formgivning'.

[110] Gustafson and Nordin, *Gotlands Bildsteine*, rev. by Lindqvist, I, 22–24 (§ 11). *British Academy Corpus*, ed. by Cramp and Bailey, pp. 102–03 (ills. 289, 291).

[111] Richard N. Bailey, 'Scandinavian Myth on Viking-period Stone Sculpture in England', in *Old Norse Myths, Literature and Society: The 11th International Saga Conference, 2–7 July 2000*, ed. by Geraldine Barnes and Margaret Clunies Ross (Sidney, 2000), pp. 15–23, esp. p. 21.

present tense illuminate a sequence of images beneath both what survives of the Heimdallr-Loki conflict in *Húsdrápa* '2' and Baldr's funeral procession in stanzas '7–10'. If we unite the images with what survives of their context, Úlfr's present tense gives focus to a golden disk or kidney shape, seals, the sea, a golden boar and horse, black ravens, and a conflagration over a ship. Other verses allow us to add a serpent and a wolf with rider and snakes. In the tenth-century Mammen style it appears that some of these images could have been bordered, or even drawn, with semi-naturalistic or ribbon-shaped quadrupeds and birds looped asymmetrically together, their heads emphasizing eyes and snouts in abrupt outlines.[112] The Möðrufell panel fragments, probably from the early eleventh century, have only leafless scrolls and tendrils, such as may have accompanied the figures in Hjarðarholt, whereas the three intertwined animals on a bone mount in Árnes (Romsdal og Møre) could show us something of Heimdallr and Loki; the lion-rider holding snakes on a memorial stone in Hunnestad (Skåne) might give an impression of Hyrrokkin; the lion and bird juxtaposed in flight on the now-destroyed Cammin Casket might help us to visualize Óðinn with his valkyries and ravens.[113] The colours are perhaps better imagined on the basis of the patron's nickname, Óláfr *pái* ('peacock'). This was a name bestowed on him either by his father at the age of twelve, according to *Laxdœla saga*, or by people in his adulthood, or, as seems most likely, by posterity in the eleventh century after his death.[114] Implicit in his peacock name is Óláfr's love of display. In his case this was perhaps visualized in the form of colours on ovals, eyes, and filaments painted on carvings all over his new house.

The memorial images that inspired *Húsdrápa* have long been taken as a key to the words 'hlaut innan svá minnum' (st. '6' and '9'). The meaning of this refrain is obscure, however. The verb *hljóta*, which primarily means 'to receive by lot',

---

[112] Signe Horn Fuglesang, 'The Axehead from Mammen and the Mammen Style', in *Mammen: Grav, Kunst og Samfund i Vikingetid*, ed. by Mette Iversen, with Ulf Näsman and Jens Vellev, Jysk Arkæologisk Selskabs Skrifter, 28 (Århus, 1991), pp. 83–107, esp. pp. 85, 97–102.

[113] Illustrated in Fuglesang, 'Axehead from Mammen', pp. 86–95 ('Mammen style: a handlist'), esp. pp. 87 (5c: Hunnestad lion-rider), 89 (13: Möðrufell panels), 90 (15: Cammin Casket), and 91 (17: Árnes bone mount).

[114] *Laxdœla saga*, ed. by Einar Ólafur Sveinsson, 39 (ch. 16). *Íslendingabók–Landnámabók*, ed. by Jakob Benediktsson, p. 143 (*Sturlubók*, ch. 105). The peacock skeleton and feathers found in the Gokstad ship-burial show that this creature was known to some in SE Norway in the middle of the ninth century. See Torleif Sjøvold, *Osebergfunnet og de andre vikingskipsfunn* (Oslo, 1957), pp. 54, 60.

could be used impersonally with a meaning such as 'to turn out', so as to render 'my memory of the interior has turned out thus'.[115] But this refrain could be elliptical, a *klofastef* ('split refrain') with its missing words to be found in the last line of a stanza now lost.[116] The strains imposed by treating the words 'hlaut innan svá minnum' as an entire phrase do not arise if we treat them as a *klofastef*. Accordingly, most scholars take the verb 'hlaut' as an auxiliary for the passive which is missing its subject and complement, as in '[The hall] was thus [adorned] within with [old] memorials'.[117] In my turn, I propose to look for another subject. The title of this work and its surviving mythological character have led commentators to make the 'house' the subject of the refrain as if this were all on which Úlfr composed. Yet in the story in *Laxdœla saga*, as we have seen, he is said first to have made the poem on Óláfr and second on the stories in the pictures (ch. 29), a priority which is also clear in the first extant verse of *Húsdrápa*. In this way it is more likely that Óláfr is the missing subject of 'hlaut innan svá minnum'. With a personal subject the verb 'hlaut' will mean that Óláfr either 'got' something or 'got to do' or 'had to do' something (if we assume an infinitive is the missing complement). Neither usage presents any difficulty in the verse of this period: Einarr *skálaglamm* ('cup-tinkle') Helgason, the Pindar of the Norse tenth century, follows both idioms when in one verse, speaking of his patron Earl Hákon of Norway, he says 'hans mæti knák hljóta' ('I did get precious things from him'; *Vellekla* 33) and in another, he says 'hljóta munk at ausa' ('I shall have to bail [the ship of poetry]'; st. 3).[118] The first construction seems to work better in the *Húsdrápa* refrain. Indeed the title itself can give us the missing object of 'hlaut': '[Óláfr] got [the house] with images like this within.' The advantage of this

---

[115] Krömmelbein, *Skaldische Metaphorik*, p. 225: 'So ist (mir) die Erinnerung (des Innern)'. Likewise *Snorri Sturluson: Edda*, trans. by Anthony Faulkes (London, 1987), pp. 68 and 74: 'within have appeared these motifs'.

[116] *Skáldskaparmál*, ed. by Faulkes, II, 313: 'hljóta'. Snorri defines the *klofastef* in *Háttatal*, ed. by Faulkes, p. 30 (vs. 70).

[117] *Lexikon Poeticum Antiquæ Linguæ Septentrionalis*, ed. by Sveinbjörn Egilsson, rev. by Finnur Jónsson (Copenhagen, 1931), s.v. 'hljóta': '[Hallen] blev således indvendig [prydet] med [gamle] minder'. So Turville-Petre, *Scaldic Poetry*, p. 69: 'Thus was the hall adorned with pictures?'; Frank, *Old Norse Court Poetry*, p. 112: '[the hall] was thus adorned within with memorials'; Poole, *Viking Poems on War and Peace*, p. 55: 'Inside thus, with old stories, was [the hall decorated]'; *Skáldskaparmál*, ed. by Faulkes, I, 159 (vs. 14); Marold, 'Kosmogonische Mythen in der *Húsdrápa*', p. 289: 'Es (das Haus) erhielt auf der Innenseite auch die (alten) Sagen(darstellungen)'.

[118] *Skáldskaparmál*, ed. by Faulkes, I, 62 (vs. 197) and 10 (vs. 18). *Skj*, B I, 117 and 123.

reading is that it includes not one but both subjects of Úlfr's eulogy around the verb. If it is thought that the adverb 'innan' is now redundant, we can take it in its primary sense, 'from within' rather than 'within'. This allows us to see Óláfr's new house coming from Norway. This idiom can be seen in two ways: not only in the conventional *fara út* ('go out (west), to Iceland') and *koma útan* ('go (east) from Iceland'), the obverse of treating *inn* and *innan* as terms for Norway; but also in Snorri's words when he says, for example, that when the Norwegians turned to St Óláfr on one occasion, 'fóru þá margir menn innan ór Þrándheimi' ('many men then came out of Trøndelag from the east').[119] The *innan* of *Húsdrápa*'s refrain, if the context supports a Norwegian link, especially one with Trondheim, may be understood as 'west', that is to say, 'from Norway'. The refrain might then be read as 'He [Óláfr] got it [the house] from Norway with images like this'. In both *Ragnarsdrápa* and *Haustlǫng* the poet appears to end by hailing both his patron and the shield on which he based his work.[120] At the end of *Húsdrápa*, therefore, it seems likely that Úlfr completed his refrain with Óláfr's name and a term for the house.

Conclusion of the Poem

The concluding lines of Úlfr's poem are now lost, although the first half of this stanza may be *Húsdrápa* '12', a verse cited late in *Skáldskaparmál*:

> Þar kømr á, en æri   endr bark mærð af hendi
> (ofrak svá) til sævar,   sverðregns (lofi þegna). (vs. 303)

> [There comes a river to the sea, while once again I have delivered renown (thus I lift up the praise of thegns) for the herald of sword-rain.]

In this verse Úlfr describes his poem as a tide of water. Having begun with the 'wave of the fjord' ('-fjarðar lá', U) of Óðinn in stanza '1' or just his 'wave' ('lá', RTW), somewhere in the middle (*Húsdrápa* '8') he conceives of poetry moving to and fro 'over my jaws', as if the teeth were rocks under the tide ('mér líða of hvapta'); finally he describes his poem flowing into the open sea in a shower of

---

[119] Kirsten Hastrup, *Culture and History in Medieval Iceland: An Anthropological Analysis of Structure and Change* (Oxford, 1985), pp. 52–54. *Snorri Sturluson: Heimskringla II*, ed. by Bjarni Aðalbjarnarson, 2nd edn, Íslenzk fornrit, 27 (Reykjavik, 1979), p. 72 (*Óláfs saga Helga*, ch. 56).

[120] *Skáldskaparmál*, ed. by Faulkes, I, 51 (vs. 158): 'Ræs gáfumk reiðar mána Ragnarr ok fjǫlð sagna' ('He gave me the moon of King Rær's chariot, did Ragnarr, along with a heap of stories'). *Haustlǫng*, ed. by North, p. 10 (st. 20; compare st. 13): 'Baugs þák bifum fáða bifkleif at Þórleifi' ('I have received the coloured cliff of the shield-rim, painted with tales, from Þórleifr').

(sword-)rain.[121] With these expressions, his verse echoes the sonorous conceits of Einarr skálaglamm. Einarr composed the *Vellekla* ('Gold-dearth') for Earl Hákon of Norway probably *c.* 990, not too long after the Earl's victory against the Danes in the battle of Hjǫrungavágr in *c.* 985.[122] 'The wholeness of Einarr's vision', Frank remarks, 'takes the form of a hydrocycle.'[123] In what can be deduced as the *Vellekla* proem, poetry is first the tide breaking on the shores of the fjords inside Norway ('Kvasir's blood'; the 'surf of the yeast of the fellows of the fjord's limb [: giants]', st. 1); then water on a tidal reef ('liquid of the rock of the guarding dwarves [: Suttungr's threatened victims]', st. 2); then the high seas as they swamp the ship's sides ('the flooding of War-God's wine-boat', st. 3); then the explosion of sea-spray around headlands ('Rǫgnir's [: Óðinn's] wave surges', 'the wave of Óðrørir's sea resounds against the flat rock of chants [: tongue]', st. 5); finally, the mountain force swelling with rain ('the wave of the mountain-Saxons' Boðn [: one of Suttungr's vats]' as it 'starts to swell', st. 6).[124] It is reasonable to suppose that Snorri would have quoted Úlfr's poetry kennings more fully if Úlfr had composed any that matched those of Einarr in *Vellekla*. But the 'hydrocycle' that we do see in Úlfr's kennings suggests that he was aware of Einarr's innovation and wished to emulate it in *Húsdrápa*.

The problem is that *Vellekla* has been dated at *c.* 990, *Húsdrápa* as early as *c.* 978.[125] At first the plausibility of the earlier date for *Húsdrápa* seems strengthened by a story about Úlfr Uggason which places him in the early 980s. In *Njáls saga* it is said that Úlfr lost an inheritance claim brought against him by Ásgrímr Elliða-Grímsson. When the plaintiff (fifth cousin of Járngerðr, Úlfr's wife) faces the prospect of losing his suit for the property now held by Úlfr, Gunnarr of Hlíðarendi

---

[121] Noted by Carol J. Clover, 'Skaldic Sensibility', *Arkiv för nordisk filologi*, 93 (1978), 63–81, esp. pp. 70–71.

[122] Foote and Wilson, *Viking Achievement*, pp. 358–40, esp. p. 136.

[123] Frank, *Old Norse Court Poetry*, pp. 60–62, esp. p. 60. See also Foote and Wilson, *Viking Achievement*, pp. 365–66; and Davidson, 'Earl Hákon and his Poets', pp. 186–89.

[124] Davidson, 'Earl Hákon and his Poets', pp. 160–61: *Kvasis dreyra* and *fyrða fjarðleggjar brim dreggjar* (*Vellekla* 1); *bergs geymilá dverga* (st. 2); *Her-Týs austr vín-Gnóðar* (st. 3); *eisar vágr Rǫgnis* and *þýt Óðrøris alda hafs við fles galdra* (st. 5); *Boðnar bára berg-Saxa tér vaxa* (st. 6). On reconstructing parts of *Vellekla*, see Fidjestøl, *Det Norrøne Fyrstediktet*, pp. 96–101.

[125] *Laxdæla Saga*, ed. by Einar Ólafur Sveinsson, pp. lviii–lix (*c.* 978); so Meulengracht Sørensen, 'Thor's Fishing Expedition', p. 61. Schier, 'Die Húsdrápa von Úlfr Uggason', p. 426 (*c.* 980). Frank, *Old Norse Court Poetry*, pp. 104–05 (*c.* 985).

saves the day by challenging the poet to a duel.[126] Úlfr backs down, humbled like the parvenu they seem to think he is. As the author of *Njáls saga* says, 'Úlfr hlaut at greiða fé allt' ('Úlfr had to pay up the whole amount'; ch. 60), perhaps alluding ironically to the refrain of *Húsdrápa*.[127] This case would have gone to court before Gunnarr's death in *c.* 990.[128] However, there are problems with a date for *Húsdrápa* in the 980s or before. It is not clear that Kjartan Óláfsson was born as early as 970, as Einar Ólafur Sveinsson supposes, or why his marriage (ch. 44), shortly after the conversion in *c.* 1000, should take place as many as fifteen to twenty-two years after that of his sister to the Norwegian (ch. 29).[129] Although Einar Ólafur Sveinsson dates Þuríðr's marriage to 978 on the basis of the ages of her sons by her second marriage, he has misgivings about the earlier chronology of *Laxdæla saga*.[130] Úlfr is known to have been active up to the years *c.* 996–98, during Þangbrandr's ill-fated mission to Iceland, when he is said to have composed a stanza in an oral correspondence with an anti-Christian zealot named Þorvaldr veili. Þorvaldr, portraying Úlfr as a protégé of Óðinn, asks him to join forces to kill the Christians; Úlfr, deriding Þorvaldr both as an amateur poet and as Þórr when this god is mocked by Óðinn on the wrong side of a fjord, cautiously declines.[131] In these ways it is quite possible that the Hjarðarholt panels were finished, Þuríðr first married, and *Húsdrápa* composed, as late as *c.* 995: later, at any rate, than the circulation of *Vellekla* in which Úlfr could have made an attempt to imitate Einarr skálaglamm.

If we leave the poets and turn to their respective masters in *Laxdæla saga* (ch. 29), we see that Óláfr gets the wood for his house from Earl Hákon. After years of marriage, Óláfr tells his wife one day that he wants to go to Norway. Buying a ship from nearby he sails to Hordaland, where by chance a local landowner who

---

[126] *Íslendingabók–Landnámabók*, ed. by Jakob Benediktsson, Genealogical Tables III.a and XXXV. Teitr Ketilbjarnarson, Ásgrímr's maternal grandfather, was the grandson of Þórðr skeggi, whose brother Ørlygi gamli was the grandfather of Þorgerðr Valþjófsdóttir, Járngerðr's paternal grandmother.

[127] *Brennu-Njáls saga*, ed. by Einar Ólafur Sveinsson, p. 152.

[128] *Brennu-Njáls saga*, ed. by Einar Ólafur Sveinsson, p. lxi.

[129] *Laxdæla Saga*, ed. by Einar Ólafur Sveinsson, pp. l–li.

[130] *Laxdæla Saga*, ed. by Einar Ólafur Sveinsson, p. lix: 'ekki er þess að dyljast, að mörg fyrri ártölin eru lítið annað en sennilegar ágizkunir' ('it cannot be denied that many of the earlier dates are little but likely guesses').

[131] For textual elucidation, see *Brennu-Njáls saga*, ed. by Einar Ólafur Sveinsson, pp. 262–63 (ch. 102). For interpretation, see North, '*goð geyja*: The Limits of Humour', pp. 20–21.

has heard of him, Geirmundr gnýr, comes down and invites him to stay. Geir-mundr is a retired viking and a retainer of Earl Hákon. As winter draws to an end, Óláfr reveals that he wants to get some timber. Geirmundr says that Hákon has the best forests, one of which will surely be placed at his disposal ('þér mun sú innan handar') if he visits the Earl and asks him. Geirmundr is right: in the spring, when Óláfr frames the question after another winter's stay, the Earl instantly grants him the royal timber, 'því at vér hyggjum, at oss sœki eigi heim hversdagliga slíkir menn af Íslandi' ('because in our opinion such men from Iceland don't visit us every day'; ch. 29). Hákon is here referring to Óláfr's lineage, widely touted as royal since Óláfr came back from Ireland; also to his wealth, increased as it is by the gifts of the Earl's predecessors, Queen Gunnhildr and her son Haraldr *gráfeldr* ('grey-cloak') Eiríksson (chs 21–22). From other sources the Earl is known to have had these rivals killed in Denmark before taking over their power in Norway in *c.* 975. Indeed Óláfr's allegedly warm friendship with Gunnhildr and her son might be read in the saga as his reason for approaching Earl Hákon by such roundabout means. Once they meet, however, Óláfr works his charm and Hákon presents him with an inlaid axe, an important treasure, before they part 'með inum mesta kærleik' ('with the greatest affection'). When Óláfr makes ready to sail, he finds that Geirmundr has secretly sold up his lands in the meantime and moved all his goods aboard Óláfr's ship; but Geirmundr is so rich that Óláfr takes him to Iceland anyway and invites him to stay. That summer work begins on the new hall with the carving of noble stories on panels, while the surly Geirmundr drifts about until he falls in love. Óláfr rejects the offer of marriage with Þuríðr that follows, but then 'berr Geirmundr fé undir Þorgerði, til þess er hann næði ráðinu' ('Geirmundr proffered money secretly to Þorgerðr until he secured the marriage'). Óláfr lets it go ahead, still voicing doubts to Þorgerðr, whom he mocks three years later for her (and her father's legendary) greed when Geirmundr runs off (ch. 30). But all the same Óláfr gives him a merchant ship. The wind drops and after two weeks' lying off at anchor, Geirmundr is tricked when Þuríðr switches Fótbítr ('Footbiter'), his beloved sword, with Gróa, their unfortunate daughter. Geirmundr curses her family with loss of its best man, sails off, and drowns with all hands off Stad in Norway.

The last part is made up, for the author could not know how Geirmundr's ship was lost if there were no survivors. The Norwegian's name also seems fictitious, for Geirmundr is too much like Guðmundr (Sǫlmundarson), the name of Þuríðr's second husband (ch. 31); nor is he introduced with a father or connections. Geir-mundr might be in the narrative so that his sword Fótbítr may be used later to kill Kjartan Óláfsson (ch. 49), in keeping with his curse, but this plot needs none of the other details: his generosity towards Óláfr when he comes to Hordaland, the secrecy with which he leaves, the lack of his own ship, his reason for staying with Óláfr, or why he returns to Norway. Nor is it clear why Óláfr mocks Þorgerðr for taking Geirmundr's money for their daughter, when he has taken money for the Norwegian's passage to Iceland. In short, the story looks worked on to protect Óláfr's reputation. The author blames Þorgerðr for her daughter's marriage, but if we focus on the plot of this story, rather than on the innocent motives attributed to Óláfr, it is he who chooses to bring home a retainer of Earl Hákon, invites him to stay, and sanctions a match between him and their daughter. In outline it appears that Óláfr could have brought the Norwegian to Hjarðarholt as a trophy son-in-law, together with Earl Hákon's timber, as part of the same project. It is tempting to believe that if 'Geirmundr' existed, he and the house were both put on show as evidence of a friendship between Óláfr and Earl Hákon of Norway.

In *Húsdrápa* the words 'frægr' for Heimdallr (st. '2'), 'orðsæll' for Þórr (st. '4'), and 'víðfrægr' for Óðinn (st. '6') indicate Óláfr's aim to be equally 'renowned' as a *goði* ('divine representative chieftain') to his people. In the saga records the audience he hopes to impress is made up of rich neighbours and other guests from all over Iceland, who contribute the 'lof þegna' ('praise of thegns') which Úlfr lifts up in the closing verse of *Húsdrápa*. Some years after the wedding, however, Óláfr is seen in *Laxdæla saga* showing off his house to the aged seer Gestr inn spaki. This occurs after Gestr's reading of the four dreams of his kinswoman Guðrún Ósvífrsdóttir (ch. 33). Gestr has come to stay with her family, for Ósvífr Helgason, Guðrún's father, is his first cousin once removed. Perhaps he agrees to see the house at Hjarðarholt because he has twice declined an offer from Óláfr to stay there. His praise when he sees the panels is material rather than aesthetic: 'kvað eigi þar fé til sparat bœjar þess' ('he said that no money had been spared on that farmstead'). He goes to the river with Óláfr escorting him personally, then lets slip a premonition of Kjartan's early death. This story shows Óláfr using his beautiful panels to compete with Ósvífr, an aim which can also be inferred from their original construction, even from the composition of *Húsdrápa* itself. Ósvífr's high-born kindred is given in ch. 33, from which it can be deduced that Óláfr is his third cousin once removed.[132] Although he is introduced after the famous wedding in ch. 29, he must have been on its guest list, though not mentioned

---

[132] *Laxdæla Saga*, ed. by Einar Ólafur Sveinsson, Genealogical Tables I, II.a, III.a, and IV. Ósvífr's great-grandfather Bjǫrn the Easterner was the brother of Unnr the Deep-Minded (or Deeply-Wealthy), whose grand-daughter Þorgerðr Þórsteinsdóttir was Óláfr's paternal grandmother.

there. Also omitted is the fact that Ósvífr had a brother, none other than the skald Einarr skálaglamm Helgason. Einarr is mentioned neither here nor elsewhere in *Laxdœla saga*. This is an odd omission, for the author probably knew *Egils saga*, in which Einarr is given as a friend of Egill Skalla-Grímsson, Óláfr's father-in-law.[133] The family relationships make it certain that Ósvífr was renowned locally as a brother of the retainer and leading skald of Earl Hákon. Traces of an imitation of Einarr's 'hydrocycle' in *Húsdrápa* make it reasonable to suppose that Úlfr was hired to put Óláfr, rather than Ósvífr or his brother, on the map as Hákon's man in Iceland.

If this was the glorious image of himself that Óláfr wished to broadcast in *Húsdrápa*, the cheerful style of Úlfr's mythology so close to the millennial conversion of Iceland becomes easier to explain. His context militates against the grim portents of Ragnarǫk. Rather this poem is a rampant celebration of Norse gods sometimes at war, sometimes in marital aspect, such as we find in *Þórsdrápa* and other eulogies composed for Earl Hákon of Norway. In Óláfr, the pagan revivalism of Hákon's decadent years seems thus to have crossed to western Iceland to flourish in flagrant disregard of the Christianity which was even then, in or before *c.* 995, working on the imagination of the poet of *Vǫluspá*. In contrast with the sublime ambitions of this poet, Úlfr's job was to stoke the jealousies of a province. The sequence of his stories, as we have seen, is unknown, as is the form of the tapestries and painted carvings on which he based his *Húsdrápa*. The house cannot be reassembled, as some hope the poem can be, or indeed as the best scholars know that most of the cross at Ruthwell has been. But if Úlfr's aim was to commemorate a patron, as the saga says, then *Húsdrápa* shows that the house does survive after all, as a witness to the ascendancy of one cousin over another.

---

[133] *Laxdœla Saga*, ed. by Einar Ólafur Sveinsson, p. xxvii. *Egils saga*, ed. by Sigurður Nordal, pp. 268–73 (ch. 78).

III. Reading Stones

CONVERTING THE ANGLO-SAXON LANDSCAPE: CROSSES AND THEIR AUDIENCES

Carol Neuman de Vegvar

In his 1904 essay 'The Cross in the Life and Literature of the Anglo-Saxons', William Stevens included what he considered a comprehensive list of the historically attested purposes of the cross-slabs and sculptural crosses that punctuated the Anglo-Saxon landscape.[1] Looking to text evidence of the period, Stevens saw these crosses serving as memorials or mortuary markers both for clergy and for secular magnates, as markers of sites of historic events such as battles or saints' miracles, as boundary markers for sanctified ground and sanctuary, and as standards of the presence of the faith, sometimes marking a site where, absent a church, services were offered for the cure of souls in remote places. These functions, however, represent the crosses as viewed and documented from the vantage points of the Church and, to an extent, their converts among the political elite. But what can such crosses reveal of the process of conversion of the rural laity, who are rarely mentioned in surviving texts and whose identification in the archaeological and artefactual record does little to reveal changing beliefs? Can the crosses show the modern viewer anything useful about the process of conversion of a landscape inhabited by barely visible people?

In the century that has elapsed since Stevens's essay was first published, much has been done to broaden his perspective, but the study of the crosses is not yet truly representative of a comprehensive cross-section of the Anglo-Saxon population, the initial audience of the crosses. Recent scholarship has compounded Stevens's focus on the elite and the learned by concentrating on the few crosses

[1] William O. Stevens, *The Cross in the Life and Literature of the Anglo-Saxons*, Yale Studies in English, 22 (New Haven, 1904), repr. in *The Anglo-Saxon Cross* (Hamden, 1977), pp. 58–65.

that have complex imagery, discerning elaborate iconographic constructs derived from texts that would have been accessible to an even tinier minority, the literate, not coincidentally the historical counterparts of the scholars currently producing such iconographic studies. We owe much to Éamonn Ó Carragáin, as well as to Carol Farr, Jane Hawkes, Fred Orton, and Catherine Karkov among others, who have done much to expand the definition of this elite to include the perspectives that gender differences and monastic or clerical versus lay status would bring to such complex monuments of Anglo-Saxon stone sculpture as the Ruthwell Cross.[2] But what of the rest of the viewing audience of such crosses, especially for the monuments placed outside ecclesiastical space, beyond the defined perimeters of churchyard or monastic enclosure?

Whether they were placed inside or outside the perimeters of ecclesiastical communities, actual knowledge of the intended functions of extant crosses is sparse, even for Northumbria where they are most numerous. Of the functions listed by Stevens, most are documented for particular instances, from which Stevens then educes a general practice that may or may not be justified. Bede's *Ecclesiastical History* (3.2) famously narrates that King Oswald raised a wooden cross before the battle of Heavenfield, which later becomes a site and vehicle of miracles associated with the sainted king, and Symeon of Durham notes that two crosses marked the tomb of Bishop Acca at Hexham and another the tomb of Bishop Æthelwald at Lindisfarne.[3] But neither author suggests that these

---

[2] Among others: Éamonn Ó Carragáin, 'The Necessary Distance: *Imitatio Romae* and the Ruthwell Cross', in *Northumbria's Golden Age*, ed. by Jane Hawkes and Susan Mills (Stroud, 1999), pp. 191–203 (p. 200), and 'Between Annunciation and Visitation: Spiritual Birth and the Cycles of the Sun on the Ruthwell Cross: A Response to Fred Orton', in *Theorizing Anglo-Saxon Stone Sculpture*, ed. by Catherine E. Karkov and Fred Orton (Morgantown, WV, 2003), pp. 131–87; Carol A. Farr, 'Worthy Women on the Ruthwell Cross: Woman as Sign in Early Anglo-Saxon Monasticism', in *The Insular Tradition*, ed. by Catherine E. Karkov, Michael Ryan, and Robert T. Farrell (Albany, 1997), pp. 45–61 (pp. 54–56); Jane Hawkes, 'Anglo-Saxon Sculpture: Questions of Context', in *Northumbria's Golden Age*, ed. by Hawkes and Mills, pp. 204–15; Fred Orton, 'Rethinking the Ruthwell and Bewcastle Monuments: Some Deprecation of Style; Some Consideration of Form and Ideology', in *Anglo-Saxon Styles*, ed. by Catherine E. Karkov and George Hardin Brown (Albany, 2003), pp. 31–67, and 'Rethinking the Ruthwell and Bewcastle Monuments: Some Strictures on Similarity, Some Questions of History', in *Theorizing Anglo-Saxon Stone Sculpture*, ed. by Karkov and Orton, pp. 65–92; Catherine E. Karkov, 'Naming and Renaming: The Inscription of Gender in Anglo-Saxon Stone Sculpture', in ibid., pp. 31–64.

[3] *Bede's Ecclesiastical History of the English People*, ed. and trans. by Bertram Colgrave and R. A. B. Mynors (Oxford, 1969), pp. 214–19; *Symeonis monachi opera omnia*, ed. by Thomas Arnold, Rolls Series, 2 vols (London, 1882–85), II, 33; Symeon of Durham, *A History of the*

installations reflected customary practice; one might even suggest that the need to observe and record these crosses at all suggests that their respective emplacements do not reflect predictable cultural norms. The remains of stone carving from the monastic communities at Jarrow, Monkwearmouth, Lindisfarne, Hartlepool, Wensley, and Whitby suggests that a cross-slab on or in the tomb was a more customary funerary monument at early Northumbrian monastic sites; and the restricted number of such slabs from monastic graveyards suggests that their use was limited and certainly not a requirement of deposition in monastic cemeteries, although a tradition of non-surviving wooden skeuomorphs, and perhaps also the carving of crosses in ephemeral wooden coffin lids, are certainly possible alternatives.[4]

For most of the extant monumental stone crosses and shaft fragments from Anglo-Saxon England, the problem of intended function is complicated both by their fragmentary state and the question of their original form, and by the lack of evidence in many cases as to original location. Since many of the so-called crossshafts lack an original apex, it is not certain how many of these originally terminated in a cross-head, and Fred Orton has rightly raised the question whether some of these may have taken a form or a variety of forms of monument other than crosses, including obelisks with their associations with Rome and *imperium*.[5] However, the substantial number of dissociated cross-heads among the catalogued fragments of stonecarving from early Anglo-Saxon England, along with the absence to date of any fragment that might be construed as an alternative type of terminal, such as the distinctive pyramidal apex of an obelisk, suggests that many

---

Church at Durham, vol. XII in *The Church Historians of England*, trans. by Joseph Stevenson (London, 1855; repr. Felinfach, 1993), p. 642; Rosemary Cramp, 'Early Northumbrian Sculpture at Hexham', in *Saint Wilfrid at Hexham*, ed. by D. P. Kirby (Newcastle upon Tyne, 1974), pp. 115–40 (p. 127, n. 38).

[4] Rosemary Cramp, *CASSS*, vol. I: *County Durham and Northumberland* (Oxford, 1984), Hartlepool nos 0–8, Jarrow nos 10–12, Lindisfarne nos 22–38, and Monkwearmouth nos 3–5; pt 1, pp. 97–101, 110–11, 124, 202–07, pt 2, pls 84–84, 94–96, 110, 199–201; James Lang, *CASSS*, vol. VI: *Northern Yorkshire* (Oxford, 2001), Wensley 8–9, pp. 224–27, ills. 883–86; Whitby 38–42, pp. 255–56, ills. 1037–1145.

[5] Fred Orton, 'Rethinking the Ruthwell Monument: Fragments and Critique; Tradition and History; Tongues and Sockets', *Art History*, 21 (1998), 65–106 (pp. 82–96); 'Northumbrian Sculpture (The Ruthwell and Bewcastle Monuments): Questions of Difference', in *Northumbria's Golden Age*, ed. by Hawkes and Mills, pp. 216–26 (pp. 219–20 and 225, nn. 1, 2, and 5); 'Rethinking the Ruthwell and Bewcastle Monuments', pp. 73–75, n. 26.

of the extant shafts were originally parts of standing crosses.[6] Where these crosses stood is less clear. Many English examples have been moved from their original locations, and their recorded history frequently indicates or implies more than one move. Further, the pre-Conquest history of the sites of these crosses is often obscure, so that it is uncertain if they have been moved locally or a considerable distance to their eventual find locations in churchyards or in the walls of later churches. Although weathering in some cases suggests that they spent a considerable portion of their history outdoors and exposed to wind and rain, this obviously cannot indicate when or where such exposure took place.

The process of the compilation of the *Corpus of Anglo-Saxon Stone Sculpture* to date has made evident what a small portion of the extant English shafts are carved with figural motifs which may by their iconographic content or by their very level of complexity give a sense of the audience for which they were intended. A significant number of shafts are carved primarily or entirely with ornamental motifs, of which one of the more frequent types are plant motifs that scholars have traditionally clustered under the heading of vine-scroll, regardless of degree of abstraction. Rosemary Cramp's invaluable *Grammar of Anglo-Saxon Ornament*, first published in 1984 as the 'General Introduction' to the first volume of the *Corpus*, confirms for the immediate context of Anglo-Saxon art a long-standing association of this motif from late antiquity onwards with the concept of Christ as the True Vine, as articulated at length in John 15.[7] Although Cramp is not the first to note this association, its statement in the *Grammar* gives it a kind of canonical status. Similarly, since W. G. Collingwood's 1927 *Northumbrian*

---

[6] Extant early obelisks in England that retain their pointed apices are from Roman sites; to date, to the best of my knowledge, no obelisk apex, either attached to a shaft or as an autonomous find, has been found on sites otherwise identified with Anglo-Saxon stone sculpture. See also C. R. Dodwell, *Anglo-Saxon Art: A New Perspective* (Manchester, 1982), pp. 113–15, on the use of the term 'pyramid' for a cross-shaft; Ó Carragáin, 'Between Annunciation and Visitation', pp. 181–86, on the possible transformation of tapered obelisks seen in Rome into Anglo-Saxon triumphal crosses; and also Richard N. Bailey, 'Innocent from the Great Offence', in *Theorizing Anglo-Saxon Stone Sculpture*, ed. by Karkov and Orton, pp. 93–103 (pp. 98–101), questioning Orton's identification of the Bewcastle shaft as an obelisk rather than a cross on the basis of the proportions of the shaft.

[7] Rosemary Cramp, *Grammar of Anglo-Saxon Ornament: A General Introduction to the Corpus of Anglo-Saxon Stone Sculpture* (Oxford, 1984), p. xxiv. See also Jane Hawkes, 'The Plant-Life of Early Christian Anglo-Saxon Art', in *From Earth to Art: The Many Aspects of the Plant-World in Anglo-Saxon England*, ed. by Carol Biggam (Amsterdam, 2002), pp. 257–80 (pp. 275–83), for a comprehensive overview of Christian vine symbolism.

Crosses of the Pre-Norman Age, the inhabited vine-scroll has been generically identified as the Tree of Life.[8] Most recent discussion of Anglo-Saxon vine-scroll has consequently taken meaning as a given and focussed instead on stylistic influences from the Mediterranean world, the range of possible models and media that may have served as conduits of the motif from south to north, and the internal stylistic affiliations of subgroups of these crosses, sometimes also seen as determinants of chronological sequencing.[9] In some contexts the assertion of a standard meaning for the vine-scroll motif may be accepted without demur, as for the shafts found in and near the abbey site at Hexham, a hub of ecclesiastical learning in the eighth-century period of the crosses where such references would be part of the common symbolic language of the ecclesiastical community.[10] However, that crosses elsewhere may have been 'influenced' by the Hexham shafts, whether by the sharing of models or of actual carvers, or more broadly of vine-scroll types or of compositional affiliations, may have little bearing on their meaning for a local audience, where both religious education and religious priorities may have been quite different.[11] Shafts ornamented primarily or entirely with vine-scroll motifs are found primarily in the Anglo-Saxon kingdom of Northumbria and its northern neighbours (Table 1). Many of these vegetal shafts, as at Lowther (Cumbria; Fig. 21), Edlingham (Northumberland; Fig. 22), and Patrington on Holderness (East Yorkshire), are often not associated archaeologically or via texts with early monastic communities or other early medieval ecclesiastical settings. Some of these crosses are associated with later churches, and the tendency for later churches to

[8] W. G. Collingwood, *Northumbrian Crosses of the Pre-Norman Age* (London, 1927), p. 39. The Tree of Life as metaphor is based on Ephesians 3. 17–19 (Hawkes, 'Plant-Life', pp. 276–78). See also Sally M. Foster, 'A Gazetteer of the Anglo-Saxon Sculpture in Historic Somerset', *Somerset Archaeology and Natural History*, 131 (1987), 49–80 (p. 60), on tree vines on stepped bases in West Camel, Kelston, Gloucester, and East Stour as possibly symbolic of Calvary.

[9] Johannes Brøndsted, *Early English Ornament* (London, 1924), pp. 16–93; Ernst Kitzinger, 'Anglo-Saxon Vine-Scroll Ornament', *Antiquity*, 10 (1936), 61–71; Cramp, 'Early Northumbrian Sculpture', pp. 133–37.

[10] Cramp, *CASSS*, vol. I, Hexham 1–4, pt 1, 174–78; pt 2, pls 167–76. The association of the vine-scroll motif with Christ as the living Vine is particularly evident on Hexham 2, which has vine-scroll motifs on three sides and a Crucifixion with two flanking figures on the fourth. Christ here wears a long *colobium*, a type associated in early Christian art with his triumph over death.

[11] Cramp, *CASSS*, vol. I, pp. 176–77; on proximity of vine types and compositional elements between Hexham 1 and Lowther and Stamfordham, and between Hexham 2 and Lancaster and Stamfordham.

conserve the siting of previous ones may suggest that the crosses have ancient associations with ecclesiastical sites. However, the embedding of many of these crosses in the actual fabric of later churches, as at Simonburn (Northumberland), Kendall (Cumbria), and Stamfordham (Northumberland), suggests that in such cases the cross was not considered an important visible legacy of the history of the site or a physical focus of the cult of sainted founders. For such crosses the find site is at the very least a secondary location, and any number of relocations prior to reuse as building material may be conjectured. Others have been found in clearly rural settings, such as the Edlingham shaft, found in 1901 by a spring in a glebe field five hundred yards from the later Church of St John the Baptist. There is at least the possibility that some of these crosses were originally raised in remote rural locations far from the nearest ecclesiastical community. Already in 1966, Rosalind Hill pointed out that a significant number of Northumbrian and later Anglo-Scandinavian carved crosses in general are not in pre-existing ecclesiastical centres but near Roman sites or along Roman roads, on hills overlooking or near good harbours, or at probable meeting places of local crofters, sites where churches were often later raised.[12] What would such an object mean to a less literate lay community, the primary population of these areas, who as a group would have been less sensitized to the nuances of the imported visual language of the church? What concerns would such an audience have brought to bear in reading these objects on their own terms?

What we know of the Anglo-Saxon landscape reveals that such an audience would have been rural and

Figure 21. Shaft from Lowther, Cumbria (Lowther 1a–bC), London, British Museum. Photo: © British Museum, by permission.

---

[12] Rosalind Hill, 'Christianity and Geography in Early Northumbria', in *Studies in Church History*, vol. III, ed. by G. J. Cuming (Leiden, 1966), pp. 133–39 (pp. 136–38).

Figure 22. Shaft from Edlingham (Edlingham 1D). Church of St John the Baptist, Edlingham, Northumberland. Photo: © Department of Archaeology, Durham University; photographer T. Middlemass, by permission.

predominantly agricultural. The argument is frequently voiced in early studies of the conversion of the Anglo-Saxons, by Stevens among others, that crosses were raised on lay estates as outdoor alternatives to churches.[13] In Bede's *Life of St Cuthbert* (9), both Cuthbert and his mentor Boisil are described as circuit-riding missionary priests carrying the faith to remote parts of the countryside, and no doubt this activity was the primary form of contact with the Church for most of the rural laity.[14] However, the association of this practice with the raising of

[13] John Godfrey, *The Church in Anglo-Saxon England* (Cambridge, 1962), p. 318; Henry Mayr-Harting, *The Coming of Christianity to Anglo-Saxon England*, 3rd edn (University Park, 1991), pp. 247–48; Hill, 'Christianity and Geography'.

[14] Bede's *Life of St Cuthbert*, 9, in *Two Lives of Saint Cuthbert*, ed. and trans. by Bertram Colgrave (Cambridge, 1940), pp. 184–87.

crosses rests on the misreading of a single text, Huneberc of Heidenheim's *Hodoeporicon of St Willibald*, which mentions a cross set up on a lay estate by a devout landholder as a focus for daily piety for the lay residents.[15] That such crosses were sometimes used as teaching stations is entirely possible; that they were consistently set up by the clergy as preaching stations and site markers for the outdoor celebration of the liturgy and identified as such by the rural population seems less provable. References in the correspondences of Boniface to Aldebert, a false prophet working in Francia who set up crosses and oratories in the fields as a way of drawing the people away from the public churches and was ultimately condemned by the Roman Synod of 745, suggest that remote liturgical sites outside the direct control of the clergy could be a danger to orthodoxy.[16]

The expectations that such an audience had of the Church and its symbols may have been rather different from what the clergy who came into contact with such people thought that they were bringing to them. In an environment where conversion was not a momentary event but a process that varied in speed, depth, and degree of permanence among social groups, belief structures and practices among the non-elite and non-literate rural laity are particularly difficult to pin down. Nonetheless, Bede's famous description in his prose *vita* of St Cuthbert of the rural communities as quick to resort to amulets and incantations in times of plague suggests a primarily pragmatic purposefulness in the deployment of the supernatural.[17] Similarly, Karen Jolly's work on both the Anglo-Saxon *Æcerbot* or

---

[15] Huneberc of Heidenheim, *Hodoeporicon of St Willibald*, ch. 1, in *Vita Willibaldi episcopi Eichstetensis et vita Wynnebaldi abbatis Heidenheimensis auctore sanctimoniale Heidenheimensis*, ed. by O. Holder-Egger, MGH, Scriptores, 15.1 (1887), pp. 80–117; trans. in *Soldiers of Christ; Saints and Saints' Lives from Late Antiquity and the Early Middle Ages*, ed. by Thomas F. X. Noble and Thomas Head (University Park, 1995), p. 146.

[16] *Die Briefe des heiligen Bonifatius*, ed. by Michael Tangl (Leipzig, 1912; repr. New York, 1965), letters 57 and 58; *The Letters of Saint Boniface*, trans. by Ephraim Emerton (New York, 2000), XLV, p. 74, and XLVI, p. 79; Alan Thacker, 'Monks, Preaching and Pastoral Care in Early Anglo-Saxon England', in *Pastoral Care Before the Parish*, ed. by John Blair and Richard Sharpe (Leicester, 1992), pp. 137–70 (p. 169). Dodwell, *Anglo-Saxon Art*, pp. 111–12, saw rural crosses as 'set up to displace former centers of heathen worship'; he argued that Boniface's objections to Aldebert's crosses were directed to the heretic's dedication of the crosses to himself and not to the crosses per se. But the Boniface texts specify that Aldebert's self-dedications were of his churches and oratories, not his crosses, and that the crosses were objectionable because they aided the heretic in seducing people away from the mainstream churches.

[17] Bede, *Life of St Cuthbert*, 9, in *Two Lives of Saint Cuthbert*, ed. and trans. by Colgrave, pp. 184–85.

field-blessing ritual and the healing rituals in *Bald's Leechbook* and the *Lacnunga*, which include material components that would have required the cooperation and often the active participation of the clergy, suggests that the lay agrarian population expected Christian religious activities to produce practical results by countering the hostile spells of witchcraft or the work of malign spirits.[18] Between pagan recidivism and Christian field and healing rituals the purpose was the same: the preservation of the lives and health of the people and the productivity of their fields and livestock by the application of ritual practice involving the supernatural.[19] In this context crosses covered with vegetal motifs may have taken on an entirely different level of meaning than they would have supported in, say, the heart of the ecclesiastical community at Hexham. These crosses may have been seen as weather crosses, deflecting harmful storms and providing spiritual insurance of a good harvest, or as sites of Christian Rogationtide rituals for the same purpose.

For farmers across early medieval Europe, as in modern agricultural communities, one major concern was the potential for storm damage to standing crops in the field. However, in the predominantly local agrarian economy of the early Middle Ages, where the success of crops was essential for the feeding of the regional population, bad weather could have far more substantial impact than in a modern economy with more mobile food supplies. Major storms and prolonged adverse weather conditions had sufficient impact to be considered worthy of inclusion in the historical record: in Ireland, the rainy summer of 759, the snowy winter and subsequent drought of 764, the thunderstorm of 2 August 783, the April blizzard of 855, and the windstorm on the feast of St Martin in 892 were all noted in the annals.[20] While some early medieval writers, such as Isidore of Seville, borrowed from classical authors such as Pliny to explain lightning, thunder, and hail as naturally occurring phenomena, for most early medieval observers storms were deliberately summoned and inflicted by the malice of demons or human evildoers

---

[18] Karen Louise Jolly, *Popular Religion in Late Saxon England: Elf Charms in Context* (Chapel Hill, 1996), pp. 169–74; and 'Father God and Mother Earth: Nature Mysticism in the Anglo-Saxon World', in *The Medieval World of Nature: A Book of Essays*, ed. by Joyce E. Salisbury (New York, 1993), pp. 221–52. *Æcerbot* ritual: London, British Library, Cotton MS Caligula A. VII; trans. by Bill Griffiths, *Aspects of Anglo-Saxon Magic* (Hockwold-cum-Wilton, 1996), pp. 173–78.

[19] Richard Kieckhefer, 'The Specific Rationality of Medieval Magic', *American Historical Review*, 99 (1994), 813–36.

[20] Nancy Edwards, *The Archaeology of Early Medieval Ireland* (London, 1990), p. 50.

with supernatural powers.[21] The Church initially accepted the existence of such malefactors, coining the term *tempestarii* or *emissores tempestatum* for those who would either foretell the weather or manipulate it for their own ends; the term *tempestarii* appears in documents from the eighth century onwards.[22] The Trullan Council of 692 and Carolingian church edicts from the *Admonitio generalis* of 789 to the Council of Paris in 829 condemn weather witches forcefully and repeatedly.[23] Penitentials both on the Continent and in the British Isles prescribe consistent penalties for these practices: the *Pseudo-Bedan* or *Albers Penitential*, possibly written in eighth-century Northumbria, assigns a seven-year penance, parallelling the slightly earlier *Burgundian Penitential* and the so-called *Roman Penitential* of Halitgar of Cambrai (*c.* 830).[24] Such ecclesiastical wrath was not limited to those deploying magic to summon storms; in 1310 the Council of Trier felt it necessary to condemn the use of sorcery to deflect hail and tempests.[25]

Even while it condemned the practice of weather magic, the Church made sporadic parallel attempts, beginning with the canons of the Council of Braga in 563, to condemn belief in its efficacy.[26] By the ninth century this condemnation of popular belief in storm magic began to take on noticeable momentum; Agobard of Lyons's early ninth-century treatise against such superstition was echoed in the Vienna Penitential, the Penitential of Silos, and the eleventh-century *Corrector*

---

[21] Monica Blöcker, 'Wetterzauber; Zu einem Glaubenskomplex des frühen Mittelalters', *Francia*, 9 (1981), 117–31; Adolph Franz, *Die Kirchlichen Benediktionen im Mittelalter*, 2 vols (Freiburg im Breisgau, 1901; repr. Graz, 1960), II, 19–28.

[22] J. F. Niermyer, '*tempestarius*', in *Mediae Latinitatis lexicon minus* (Leiden, 1997), p. 1016; Henry Charles Lea, *Materials Toward a History of Witchcraft*, 3 vols, arr. and ed. by Arthur C. Howland (Philadelphia, 1939; repr. New York, 1957), vol. I: for Carolingian imperial capitularies as well as the *Capitularies* of Herard, Archbishop of Tours (858), pp. 138–39; for *emissores tempestatum*, p. 186.

[23] For the Trullan Council, see John T. McNeill and Helena M. Gamer, *Medieval Handbooks of Penance: A Translation of the Principal Libri poenitentiales* (New York, 1938; repr. 1990), p. 227, n. 60. For the *Admonitio generalis* and Council of Paris, see Edward Peters, 'The Medieval Church and State on Superstition, Magic and Witchcraft: From Augustine to the Sixteenth Century', in *Witchcraft and Magic in Europe: The Middle Ages*, ed. by Bengt Ankarloo and Stuart Clark (Philadelphia, 2001), pp. 173–245 (pp. 198–200).

[24] McNeill and Gamer, *Medieval Handbooks*: Pseudo-Bedan or Albers Penitential, 1.4.14, p. 227; Burgundian Penitential, 20, p. 275; for Halitgar, 33, p. 305.

[25] Lea, *Materials*, p. 141.

[26] Franz, *Kirchlichen*, pp. 28–29; Lea, *Materials*, p. 143.

of Burchard of Worms.[27] Nonetheless, belief in the power of demons to control weather continued to be accepted by some leading ecclesiastical thinkers, including Thomas of Cantimpré, Thomas Aquinas, and Bonaventure.[28]

The holy was considered a sovereign defense against demonically inspired weather. Adolph Franz's classic 1960 catalogue of western formal ecclesiastical invocations for fruitful harvests traces both liturgical prayers and collects for the prevention of drought as well as storms, starting with the sixth-century Leonine Sacramentary, as well as the development of the processional liturgies of Rogation Days.[29] Saints or their relics were also believed to provide protection against storms, as well as to provide needed rain and to cause crops to grow with preternatural swiftness. Weather miracles are a common feature of the *Dialogues* of Gregory the Great.[30] Such thinking was also part of belief structures in both the Insular context and its Continental offshoots. Adomnán's seventh-century *Life of St Columba* includes both an incident where the saint causes a crop of barley to sprout and ripen in a month and a half, and a posthumous miracle where a drought is ended after the tunic in which the saint died is shaken over the fields and books he wrote are read on a site the saint frequented in his lifetime.[31] Similarly, St Leoba stills a tempest with cross-sign and holding her hands towards

---

[27] For Agobard of Lyon, *Liber contra insulsam vulgi opinionem de grandine et tonitruis*, see Franz, *Kirchlichen*, pp. 29–30; trans. by Paul Edward Dutton in *Carolingian Civilization: A Reader*, ed. by Dutton (Peterborough, Ont., 1993), pp. 189–91. For the Penitential of Silos, see McNeill and Gamer, *Medieval Handbook*, p. 289. For the *Corrector* of Burchard of Worms 68 and 194, see McNeill and Gamer, *Medieval Handbook*, pp. 331, 341. For *Poenitentiale Vindobonense*, 99, see F. W. H. Wasserschleben, *Die Bussordnungen der abendländische Kirche* (Graz, 1958), p. 422; trans. in Alan Charles Kors and Edward Peters, *Witchcraft in Europe, 400–1700; A Documentary History*, 2nd edn (Philadelphia, 2001), p. 64. For condemnation in Carolingian *capitularia* of practices against hail such as the baptism of bells or the hanging of plaques inscribed with magical signs or words on poles (*perticas*) or trees, see *Duplex legationis edictum*, 34 (published in 789), in Alfred Boretius, *Capitularia Regum Francorum*, vol. I, MGH Legum sectio, 2 (1833), p. 64 and n. 19.

[28] Lea, *Materials*, p. 143. On the range of medieval ecclesiastical opinion on the subject, see Franz, *Kirchlichen*, pp. 31–37.

[29] Franz, *Kirchlichen*, pp. 1–19, 45–123.

[30] St Gregory the Great, *Dialogues*, 1.4, 3.10–13, 15, 19, 36, trans. by Odo John Zimmerman (New York, 1959), pp. 24, 125, 127–28, 139, 141, 150, 177.

[31] *Adomnán's Life of St Columba*, 2.3, 2.44, ed. and trans. by A. O. Anderson and M. O. Anderson (Oxford, 1991), pp. 96–99, 172–73. The shaken cloak of a deceased saint (Eutychius) also produces rain in Gregory, *Dialogues* 3.15, trans. by Zimmerman, p. 141.

the sky, and the relics of St Sadalberga of Laon and bells blessed in her name could drive out thunder.[32] Such agricultural miracles feature particularly frequently in Irish saints' lives, where they continue into the later medieval period.[33] Bell ringing as well as less Church-associated noisemaking as a protection against storms, first documented in the preserved canon headings for the Synod of Estinnes in 744, the so-called *Indiculus superstitionum et paganiarum*, was still a focus of concern for Reformation-period Church disciplinarians in Germany.[34]

Of all Christian physical signs the cross was the most frequently deployed with affective intent, including the evocation of divine authority to control the weather. The Continental practice of raising weather crosses had the Church's endorsement. The practice may be described as early as a homily once attributed to St John Chrysostom, which enthusiastically describes crosses placed, among other locations, on mountains, in valleys, and on hills.[35] Another early source is the sixth-century *vita* of Caesarius of Arles (ch. 27), where the saint's misplaced staff is appropriated by a landowner and made into a cross for this purpose.[36]

---

[32] Rudolf, *Vitae Leobae abbatissae Biscofesheimensis*, 14, ed. by Georg Waitz, in MGH Scriptores, 15.1, pp. 118–31; trans. in *Soldiers of Christ*, ed. by Noble and Head, p. 270; Valerie I. J. Flint, *The Rise of Magic in Early Medieval Europe* (Princeton, 1991), p. 188. *Vita* of Sadalberga: *AA SS Septembris* VI (Brussels, 1970), p. 517.

[33] McNeill and Gamer, *Medieval Handbooks*, p. 41, n. 63; Charles Plummer, *Vitae sanctorum Hiberniae*, 2 vols (Dublin, 1997), I, pp. cxxxviii–cxxxix, clxxx, n. 3.

[34] For the *Indiculus* (Vatican City, Biblioteca Apostolica Vaticana, MS Palatinus lat. 577, fol. 7^{r-v}), see Alain Dierkens, 'Superstitions, christianisme et paganisme à la fin de l'époque mérovingienne: A propos de l'*Indiculus superstitionum* et paganiarum', in *Magie, Sorcellerie, Parapsychologie*, ed. by Hervé Hasquin (Brussels, 1982), pp. 9–26. For Reformation-era practices, see Flint, *Rise of Magic*, p. 189, n. 53; Gerhard Hirschmann, 'The Second Nürnberg Church Visitation', in *The Social History of the Reformation*, ed. by Lawrence P. Buck and Jonathan W. Zophy (Columbus, 1972), pp. 355–80 (p. 371); Max Siller, 'Zauberspruch und Hexenprozess: Die Rolle des Zauberspruchs in der Zauber- und Hexenprozessen Tirols', in *Tradition und Entwicklung: Festschrift Eugen Thurnher zum 60. Geburtstag*, ed. by Werner M. Bauer, Achim Masser, and Guntram A. Plangg, Innsbrucker Beiträge zur Kulturwissenschaft, Germanistische Reihe, 14 (Innsbruck, 1982), pp. 127–54 (p. 128–31). On folk practices against inclement weather, see Franz, *Kirchlichen*, pp. 37–44.

[35] *Contra Judæos et Gentiles: Quod Christus sit Deus*, IX, *PG*, 48, 813–36 (pp. 824–26); Eunice Dauterman Maguire, Henry P. Maguire, and Maggie J. Duncan-Flowers, *Art and Holy Powers in the Early Christian Church*, Illinois Byzantine Studies, 2 (Urbana, 1989), pp. 18–19.

[36] *Vita Caesarii episcopi Arelatensis*, ed. by Bruno Krusch, MGH Scriptores Rerum Merovingicarum, 15 (1910), pp. 433–501; *Caesarius of Arles: Life, Testament, Letters*, trans. William E. Klingshirn (Liverpool, 1994), pp. 56–57: 'Nor shall I be silent about the following very well-

Although this passage may describe an isolated event, other sources suggest a widespread practice of considerable duration. A tenth-century formulary from Schäftlarn (Munich, Bayerische Staatsbibliothek, Clm 17027, fols 124ʳ–127ʳ) evokes the power of the cross against floods and the 'murmurings of enchanters'.[37] More specific blessings for field crosses are preserved from Germany beginning with a twelfth-century manuscript, possibly from Prüm (Munich, Bayerische Staatsbibliothek, Clm 100, fols 69–73) and continue into thirteenth- and fourteenth-century German liturgical sources; in medieval France they are sometimes included in the liturgy for the Feast of the Discovery of the True Cross.[38]

Continental evidence for the widespread use of weather crosses to protect crops from storms suggests a possible alternative function for remotely situated Anglo-Saxon crosses, particularly those with vegetal motifs. There is no direct reference to the use of weather crosses in early medieval England. One later source may refer to the use of stone weather crosses in the Insular world, Martin's 1716 *Description of the Western Islands of Scotland*, which describes the use of a weather cross on North Uist in the Hebrides:

> There is a Stone in the form of a Cross in the Row, opposite to St. Mary's Church, about 5 foot high: the Natives call it the Water-Cross, for the ancient Inhabitants had a Custom of erecting this sort of Cross to procure Rain, and when they had got enough, they laid it flat on the ground, but this Custom is now disused.[39]

Disused, no doubt, because a sufficiency of rain in the Hebrides is rarely a problem; such a story may well have been invented by local residents having a joke at the expense of an earnest but gullible antiquarian standing in the rain to look at a bit of old stonecarving. However, more circumstantial evidence from the early

known event, which is said to have occurred once in the Alpilles. Constant bad weather kept destroying the property of a certain very noble man. The rain was most destructive, and powerful hailstorms devoured all the produce of the area. Every year, therefore, there was no hope of assistance for the place. It then happened that Caesarius's staff was left there by accident. From this staff the owner ordered a cross to be made. Fortified by his faith, he then put it up in a prominent place, so that the staff of the disciple and the cross of the master might counteract the incoming hailstones. In honour of his servant, God deigned to work so great a miracle there that after he had driven away the bad weather he made the place very fertile.'

[37] Flint, *Rise of Magic*, pp. 188–89; Franz, *Kirchlichen*, pp. 74–77.

[38] Franz, *Kirchlichen*, pp. 83–88; and see also pp. 12–14, 86–104 on later German and French sources.

[39] Martin Martin, *A Description of the Western Islands of Scotland*, 2nd edn (London, 1716; repr. Edinburgh, 1970), p. 59.

medieval period may permit the reinterpretation of some of the more rural vegetal crosses as understood by the laity at least in part as weather crosses. In an analogous ritual, the Anglo-Saxon *Æcerbot* ritual includes the burial of wooden crosses in the fields to enhance the growth of crops on unproductive land that may have been harmed by sorcery or witchcraft.[40] Church opposition to unsanctified weather sorcery, particularly the summoning of storms, is as strong in the Insular context as on the Continent, while the role of saints in manipulating the weather also parallels the Continental examples. In a context where weather played so powerful a role both in the realities of the lives of the agricultural community and in the ideational constructs of the Church, stone crosses carved with exclusively vegetal motifs may well have been seen by their local lay audiences as weather crosses. Just as Karen Jolly has suggested that the clergy must have been collaborative in the *Æcerbot* ritual, so a stone cross raised as a preaching station would have been more effective at reaching the laity if it offered a Christian alternative to non-Christian weather rituals; carving such a cross with vegetal motif would broadcast to local farmers the effectiveness of the new faith in a language they could clearly understand.

An alternative reading of the Anglo-Saxon vegetal crosses centred on the same protective relationship between Church and countryside is the possibility that these crosses may have served as stopping points and ritual stations for Rogationtide processions. Rogation processions were known from the fifth century onwards in Francia. According to Alcimus Avitus, sainted Bishop of Vienne, the formalization of penitential processions on the three days preceding the Feast of the Ascension for the protection of both the community and the land from natural calamities was instituted in 469 by his predecessor in the see of Vienne, St Mamertus, in the mid-fifth century; they were adopted at Clermont under Sidonius Apollinaris and quickly became popular across Francia.[41] In the early sixth century, Caesarius of Arles speaks of the widespread practice as involving a six-

---

[40] Jolly, 'Father God and Mother Earth', pp. 221–23.

[41] Prosper Guéranger, *The Liturgical Year*, 15 vols, *Paschal Time*, Bk 3, trans. by Laurence Shepherd, 3rd edn (Westminster, MD, 1949), pp. 130–32; K. A. Heinrich Kellner, *Heortology: A History of the Christian Festivals from their Origin to the Present Day* (London, 1908), pp. 191–92; Avitus, *Homilia de Rogationibus*, PL, 59, 289–94. See also Gregory of Tours, *Historia Francorum*, in *Gregorii Turonensis opera*, ed. by Wilhelm Arndt and Bruno Krusch, MGH Scriptores Rerum Merovingicarum (1885): Mamertus and Avitus at Vienne: 2.34, pp. 97–98; St Gall at Clermont-Ferrand, 4.5, p. 145; at Paris in 580, 9.6, p. 362; at Lyons in 588, 9.21, p. 379; at Tours and Nantes in 591, 10.30, p. 442.

hour procession of clergy and laity moving from place to place while singing canticles of supplication.[42] Canons of the first Council of Orléans in 511 and the Council of Tours in 567 both instituted fasting, and the former also mandated work release time for servants to permit them to participate.[43] Rogationtide processions reached England at least by the eighth century, deriving from the original fifth-century Frankish practice.[44] Abbot Cuthbert's letter to Cuthwin narrates Bede's last hours, in the year 739, spent with a single companion while the rest of the community was out on procession as was customary for the season.[45] In 747, the Synod of Clovesho laid out the requirements of Rogationtide for the Anglo-Saxon church, with three days of public processions bearing the cross and relics.

> Sexto decimo condixerunt capitulo: Ut Lætaniæ, id est, rogationes, a clero omnique populo his diebus cum magna reverentia agantur, id est, die septimo kalendarum Maiarum, juxta ritum Romanae Ecclesiae, quae et Laetania major apud eam vocantur. Et item quoque secundum morem priorum nostrorum, tres dies ante Ascensionem Domini in coelos cum jejunio usque ad horam nonam et Missarum celebratione venerantur: non admixtis vanitatibus, ut mos est plurimis, vel negligentibus, vel imperitis, id est, in ludis et equorum cursibus, et epulis majoribus; sed magis, cum timore et tremore, signo passionis Christi nostraeque aeternae redemptionis, et reliquiis sanctorum Ejus coram portatis, omnis populus genu flectendo Divinam pro delictis humiliter exorat indulgentiam.[46]

> [They agreed on the sixteenth capitulary: That the litanies, that is, Rogations, ought to be attended to by the clergy and the people on these days with great reverence, that is, on the seventh day of the *kalens* of May, according to the usage of the Roman church, where it is called the Laetania major. And also according to our pre-existing custom, the three days before the Ascension of the Lord to heaven should be venerated with fasting until the ninth hour and with the celebration of Masses. and without additional frivolities as is the custom among many, whether out of neglect or ignorance, that is in games and horse races and great feasts, but rather with fear and trembling, with the sign of the passion of Christ and of our eternal redemption, and the relics of his saints carried openly, the whole population should on bended knee humbly exhort Divine forgiveness for their sins.]

While the attempted correction of the laity about the penitential nature of Rogationtide and its possible replacement of or identification with pre-Christian

---

[42] Guéranger, *Liturgical Year*, p. 131.

[43] Orléans: canon 27; Tours: canon 17. Guéranger, *Liturgical Year*, p. 131.

[44] Franz, *Kirchlichen*, pp. 7–9.

[45] Godfrey, *Church*, p. 213; *Venerabilis Baedae: opera historica*, ed. by Charles Plummer, 2 vols (Oxford, 1896), I, pp. lxxvi, clxii.

[46] *Councils and Ecclesiastical Documents Relating to Great Britain and Ireland*, ed. by Arthur West Haddan and William Stubbs, 3 vols (Oxford, 1871; repr. 1964), III, 368.

vernal celebrations is certainly of interest, what is of consequence here for the stone crosses is the juxtaposition of calendar events by the clergy themselves. The synodiasts of Clovesho here consider together as interrelated practices the imported Frankish tradition of cross-bearing Rogation processions, which was only later introduced in Rome under Leo III (795–816), and the *letania maior*, a separate penitential procession of the Roman church that halted at an oratory dedicated to the cross.

The *letania maior* was a specifically Roman rite, a Christian replacement of the *ambarvalia*, a processional rite invoking the gods' blessing on field, orchard, and vineyard. The *ambarvalia* passed along the Via Flaminia to the Milvian Bridge where sacrifices were offered to the god Robigus, associated with *robigo*, or blight; in the early Roman calendars the festival is called the Robigalia.[47] Unlike the Rogation processions, which are tied to the feast of the Ascension and the variable calendar of the Easter cycle, the *letania maior* inherited a fixed date from the Robigalia, the twenty-fifth of April, and by the twelfth century was subsumed into the feast of St Mark, celebrated on the same calendar day.[48] The earliest evidence for the Roman *letania maior* is found in the *Registrum* of St Gregory, which contains a formula of announcement of a *letania maior* in 598; the stress here, as in the establishment of Rogation processions in Francia, is on penitence for sins that otherwise may elicit the wrath of God in the form of various and continual calamities.[49] The announcement specifies that the procession is to start from the *titulus*

---

[47] Kellner, *Heortology*, pp. 189–91; Edgar de Bruyne, 'L'Origine des processions de la chandeleur et des Rogations à propos d'un sermon inédit', *Revue Bénédictine*, 34 (1922), 14–26. The anonymous author of this sermon (Paris, Bibliothèque nationale de France, fonds latin, 18296, fol. 81) saw the *ambarvalia* as the origin of the Gallic rogations as well, but the *ambarvalia* as a rite are specific to the city of Rome.

[48] Ildefonso Schuster, *The Sacramentary (Liber Sacramentorum); Historical and Liturgical Notes on the Roman Missal*, 5 vols (London, 1924–30), II, 355–56.

[49] Walter Howard Frere, *Studies in Early Roman Liturgy*, vol. I: *The Kalendar*, Alcuin Club Collections, 28 (Oxford, 1930), pp. 98–99; *Grégoire le Grand, Registre des Lettres*, ed. by Pierre Minard, 2 vols (Paris, 1991), I, Appendice IV, pp. 457–58. Johannes Beleth, professor of theology at Paris (d. 1165) argued in his *Rationale divinorum officiorum* (ch. 123) that Pope Liberius (352–66) had substituted the *letania maior* for the *ambarvalia* (Mario Righetti, *Manuele di storia liturgica*, vol. II: *L'anno liturgico; Il Brevario* (Milan, 1955), p. 228). J. P. Kirsch 'Origine e carattere primitivo delle stazioni liturgiche di Roma', *Rendiconti della pontificia accademia romana de archeologia*, 3 (1925), 123–41, and A. G. Martimort, *L'Église en prière: Introduction à la Liturgie*, 3rd edn (Paris, 1965), p. 744, among others, accepted a direct derivation from the *ambarvalia*, but Righetti and also John F. Baldwin, *The Urban Character of Christian Worship: The Origins,*

of San Lorenzo in Lucina and travel to St Peter's. The Gregorian Sacramentary provides a more complete itinerary: after collect at San Lorenzo in Lucina, the procession set out along the Via Flaminia, stopping at the cemetery of St Valentinus and then crossing the Milvian Bridge before turning southward towards its destination at St Peter's. Between the bridge and its final destination, the procession stopped at a site the Sacramentary describes as 'ad crucem'.[50] The site was marked possibly as early as the sixth century by an oratory, the now-lost Capella di S. Croce on Monte Mario, which commemorated the vision of Constantine and may have held a relic of the True Cross. The oratory is identified as a stopping point for the *letania maior* in the time of Leo III (795–816).[51] It stood on the west

Development, and Meaning of Stational Liturgy, Orientalia Christiana Analecta, 228 (Rome, 1987), pp. 122, 164, 236, noted that the strongly penitential aspect of the Christian procession and the relatively late dates of the earliest extant liturgical sources suggest a less substantive continuum from pagan precedent.

[50] Jean Deshusses, *Le Sacramentaire Grégorien: ses principales formes d'après les plus anciens manuscrits* (Fribourg, 1971), pp. 211–12, 637. For overviews of the sources, see Baldovin, *Urban Character*, pp. 122, 126, 128–41, 159, 236, 239, and 260; and Joseph Dyer, 'Roman Processions of the Major Litany (*litaniae maiorae*) from the Sixth to the Twelfth Centuries', in *Roma Felix: Formation and Reflections of Medieval Rome*, ed. by Éamonn Ó Carragáin and Carol Neuman de Vegvar (Aldershot, forthcoming). The frequently cited address by Gregory to the people of Rome in response to the flood and ensuing plague of 589–90 (in Gregory of Tours, *Historia*, 10.1; pp. 407–09) lays out a *letania septiformis*, in which different components of the clergy and people converged from seven different churches for a service at Sta Maria Maggiore. This seems not to have been the normal pattern of the *letania* but rather to have been a response to the calamities of that particular year by renewing and enlarging upon tradition. The announcement of 598 and the Gregorian Sacramentary seem to reflect more normal practice, including the more usual early medieval processional route. By the twelfth century the route had changed to a more intra-urban focus, starting with processions from the church of S. Marco in Pallacinis and the Lateran, converging to Sta. Maria Nova in the Forum and continuing from there to the Vatican via St Mark's and the Mausoleum of Hadrian: Schuster, *Sacramentary*, pp. 356–57; Sible de Blaauw, 'Contrasts in Processional Liturgy: A Typology of Outdoor Processions in Twelfth-Century Rome', in *Art, Cérémonial et Liturgie au Moyen Âge*, ed. by Nicolas Bock and others (Viella, 2002), pp. 357–96 (p. 384). The date at which the route was shortened is debated in Bernhard Schimmelpfennig, 'Die Bedeutung Roms im päpstlichen Zeremoniell', in *Rom im Hohen Mittelalter: Studien zu den Romvorstellungen und zur Rompolitik vom 10. bis zum 12. Jahrhundert*, ed. by Bernhard Schimmelpfennig and Ludwig Schmugge (Sigmaringen, 1992), pp. 47–61 (p. 53).

[51] Frere, *Studies in Early Roman Liturgy*, p. 20, n. d; Augustus J. C. Hare, *Walks in Rome, Including Tivoli, Frascati and Albano*, 18th edn (London, 1909), p. 640; Ferrucchio Lombardi, *Roma: Le chiese scomparse; La memoria storica della città* (Rome, 1996), p. 435. In ruins by the late medieval period, the oratory was rebuilt by Bishop Pontius of Orvieto in 1350 and was restored

slope of Monte Mario near the surviving sixteenth-century church of S. Maria del Rosario. An eighteenth-century engraving by Giovanni Vasi (1710–82) shows S. Maria del Rosario in the foreground and the Capella di S. Croce in the distance (Fig. 23).[52] The identification of this chapel oratory as the 'ad crucem' of the *letania maior* extends its already unusually long processional route with a side trip up Monte Mario, although the extension would fit well with both the origins of the ceremony as a vernal field blessing and its later penitential function.[53]

   To Anglo-Saxon pilgrims the experience of the *letania maior* must have been an overwhelming and memorable spectacle, involving not only the clergy but also a substantial part of the lay population of Rome.[54] Crosses borne by the participant clergy and the halt of the entire procession at a chapel dedicated to the cross would have firmly associated the cult of the cross with this Roman penitential spring procession, with its ancient associations of field blessings.[55] The Anglo-Saxon clergy at Clovesho, who in their passion for *imitatio Romae* associated their knowledge of the *letania maior* with Frankish Rogation practices, also included the visible presence of the cross in their mandate for Rogation processions at home.[56] Stone crosses set up in the Anglo-Saxon countryside could extend and make permanent this association of the cross with Rogationtide; they could not only mark out predetermined stopping points for Rogation prayers but also served to remind the lay population, given to more secular and unrestrained vernal celebrations, of the Christian and penitential nature of Rogations. Further, they could mark out and sacralize the landscape as the site of Christian practice well

and richly furnished by the Mellini as a family chapel from the fifteenth century onwards; it was destroyed during the 1877–81 fortification of Monte Mario. I thank Professor Joseph Dyer (personal communication) for references to Hare and Lombardi.

   [52] Lombardi, *Roma*, p. 435.

   [53] Those readers who have had the pleasure of seeing early medieval Rome through the eyes and in the good company of Éamonn Ó Carragáin and who thereby count themselves among the happy veterans of 'Éamonn's Column' will not quibble at a few extra miles.

   [54] De Blaauw, 'Contrasts', pp. 373–75.

   [55] De Blaauw, 'Contrasts', pp. 377–80, describes an elaborate system of processional and stational crosses in use in the twelfth-century *letania*. Although the system of the eighth century is unknown, the prevalence of crosses in processions elsewhere in this period would suggest that they were also in use in Rome.

   [56] For pilgrimage to Rome, *imitatio Romae*, and creative approaches to liturgy in Anglo-Saxon England, see Éamonn Ó Carragáin, *The City of Rome and the World of Bede* (Jarrow Lecture, 1994).

Figure 23. Guiselle Vasi (1710–82): engraving of S. Maria del Rosario with Capella di S. Croce in the distance on Monte Mario; from his *Delle Magnificenze di Roma Antica e Moderna* (Rome, 1747–61), VII, 39. Photo: The Institute of Fine Arts, New York University, by permission.

beyond the spatial perimeters of ecclesiastical communities and the temporal limits of Rogationtide, bringing the land as well as its inhabitants permanently under the mantle and protection of the faith.

The two possible readings of the Anglo-Saxon vegetal crosses presented here, as weather crosses and as Rogationtide processional markers, may well have co-existed, side by side and in combination with more scripturally oriented readings. The relief sculpture of stone crosses was a specialty craft reserved to workshops affiliated with the Church; so the vegetal crosses could only be brought into being by the will of the clergy, for whom the vine-scroll no doubt primarily signified Christ as the True Vine or the Cross as the Tree of Life. But the polyvalent message of a vegetal cross in a rural landscape could also bridge the gap between church and laity, and pave the path to deeper and more widespread conversion. The placement of crosses in the Anglo-Saxon landscape, as on the Continent, may not only signal the actions and ideals of ecclesiastical and secular elites, but also have helped to christianize both the rural environment in which a majority of the population carried on their pursuit of agricultural subsistence and the practices by which they sought to insure a bountiful harvest. The not infrequent choice of vegetal motifs among Anglo-Saxon crosses may have permitted their occasional pragmatic interpretation as weather crosses or as places of Rogationtide prayer and blessing, suggesting that while the nominal religious identity of the rural population had been shifted to a new faith, their expectations that religious objects serve useful functions could be met halfway by a Church willing to save their crops along with their souls.

Table 1. Nonfigural crosses/shafts decorated primarily with vegetal motifs.
This list includes material published to date in *CASSS*, vols 1–VII.[1] Dates and provenance information follow *CASSS* data.

Title	CASSS Reference	Date	Provenance
Colyton 1 Devon	VII, 80–82, ills. 3–9	early 10c	fragments found embedded in tower/belfry, St Andrew now south aisle of nave
Croft on Tees 1 N. Yorkshire	VI, 89–92, ills. 147–52	late 8c–early 9c	first recorded 1886 as side of 14c aumbry in Milbanke Chapel, St Peter's now sill of chantry north window
Dacre 1 Cumberland	II, 90–91, ills. 235–39	early 9c	found c. 1900 in excavation near St Andrew's Church, at Dacre Castle by 1910 and in church by 1923 now inside chancel, south side
Digby 1 Lincolnshire	V, 325–26, ills. 462–65	mid-12c	purchased from antique dealer c. 1920, Lincolnshire now Lincoln, City and County Museum
East Stour 1 Dorset	VII, 101–02, ills. 57–64	9c	discovered in demolition of chimney-breast, 1939, possibly 'derived from' parish church of Christ Church now London, British Museum (1969/4-1).
Edlingham 1 Northumberland	I, 170–71, ills. 867–70	mid-8c	found 1901 by a spring in a glebe field 500 yards from Church of St John the Baptist now inside church
Escomb 1 Durham	I, 77, ills. 250–55	2nd ¼ 8c	probably found in fabric in 1879 restoration of St John the Evangelist now inside church porch
Falstone 1 Northumberland	I, 171–72, ills. 875–84	2nd ½ 9c	found in churchyard of St Peter and adjacent farm now Newcastle upon Tyne, Museum of Antiquities
Hauxwell 1 North Yorkshire	VI, 120–22, ills. 311–14, 316	late 8c–early 9c	St Oswald, in churchyard, on site since 1823, with associated socketed base
Heversham 1 Cumbria	II, 113–14, ills. 351–54	late 8c ?	inside porch of St Peter, Heversham, at least since 1893

Title	*CASSS* Reference	Date	Provenance
Hexham 1 Northumberland	I, 174–76, ills. 898–909	2nd ¼ 8c	fragments found at Hexham: at east end of St Andrew in foundations of warehouse near St Mary; and as cottage lintel at Dilston / now St Andrew, south transept
Hexham 3 Northumberland	I, 177–78, ills. 922–27	mid-8c	found 1854 as step in chemist's shop, Market Place by St Mary's, Hexham / now Monks' Dormitory, Durham Cathedral (catalogue no. IV)
Hexham 4 Northumberland	I, 178, ills. 933–36	mid-8c–1st ¼ 9c	found 1890 in demolition of old house, Market Street, Hexham / now Monks' Dormitory, Durham Cathedral (catalogue no. V)
Kendall 1 Cumbria	II, 120, ills. 380–83	late 8c–early 9c	probably found in restoration of Church of Holy Trinity in 1850 / now on south aisle windowsill
Lowther 1 Cumbria	II, 127–28, ills. 427–31, 436–43	late 8c–9c	reputedly from churchyard, St Michael, Lowther, later Lowther Castle / now London, British Museum (1967/4-4,1)
Lowther 2 Cumbria	II, 128–29, ills. 432–35	2nd ½ 8c	as for Lowther 1 / now Glasgow, Burrell Collection
Northallerton 1 North Yorkshire	VI, 180–81, ills. 662–64	8c	formerly on wooden stand beneath north window of All Saints; possibly at one time built into west façade / now on display, Jarrow, Bede's World Museum
Nunnykirk 1 Northumberland	I, 214–15, ills. 1192–96	early 9c	found c. 1850–60 in demolition of old cottage near Nunnykirk / now Newcastle upon Tyne, Museum of Antiquities, site possibly Bede's Uetadun
Patrington on Holderness East Yorkshire	III, 198–99, ills. 749–50	8c	found in a wall near church of St Patrick; presumed destroyed in air-raid on Hull Museum, World War II
St Leonard's Place 2 York	III, 108–09, ills. 365–68	9c	excavations near site of St Peter's Hospital, York / now Yorkshire Museum, York
Simonburn 1 Northumberland	I, 223, ills. 1233–35, 1240	last ¼ 8c–1st ¼ 9c	found in collapse of chancel arch, St Mungo, 1877 / now inside church porch

Title	CASSS Reference	Date	Provenance
Stamfordham 1 Northumberland	I, 225, ills. 1242–45	2nd ½ 8c	found in 1849 when old church was pulled down now Monk's Dormitory, Durham (catalogue no. XII)
Wensley 1/2 North Yorkshire	VI, 221–22, ills. 858–66	late 8c–9c	taken from interior east wall of Early English chancel in 1904 now fixed to sill of north sanctuary window, against splays
Wycliffe 3 North Yorkshire	VI, 270–71; ills. 1108–11	late 8c	St Mary, in alcove against north door of nave; previously in coach house and church porch; taken out of fabric at 1850 restoration.

[1] *CASSS*: Rosemary Cramp, vol. I: *County Durham and Northumberland* (Oxford, 1984); Richard N. Bailey and Rosemary Cramp, vol. II: *Cumberland, Westmorland and Lancashire North-of-the-Sands* (Oxford, 1988); James Lang, vol. III: *York and Eastern Yorkshire* (Oxford, 1991); Dominic Tweddle, Martin Biddle, and Birthe Kjølbye-Biddle, vol. IV: *South-East England* (Oxford, 1995); Paul Everson and David Stocker, vol. V: *Lincolnshire* (Oxford, 1999); James Lang, vol. VI: *Northern Yorkshire* (Oxford, 2001); Rosemary Cramp, vol. VII: *South-West England* (Oxford, 2006).

GREGORY THE GREAT AND ANGELIC MEDIATION: THE ANGLO-SAXON CROSSES OF THE DERBYSHIRE PEAKS

Jane Hawkes

The figural carvings decorating the remains of the Anglo-Saxon stone crosses of the Derbyshire Peak District have attracted considerable interest since they first came to public attention in the mid-eighteenth century during the burgeoning of antiquarian interest in such monuments.[1] It was an interest that ensured the survival of what were, at the time, damaged shafts and fragments that had been abandoned in the churchyards of Bradbourne, Bakewell, and Eyam and used as building fabric in the churches and adjoining walls (Figs 24–29).[2] Today they stand as one of the most celebrated group of pre-Scandinavian monuments of Anglo-Saxon Mercia, generally recognized as the products of a common sculptural centre flourishing in the region in the late eighth and early ninth centuries.

I am grateful to Richard Bailey, Katie Cubbit, Carol Farr, Kellie Meyer, Jennifer O'Reilly, and Tom Pickles for their advice and consideration of a number of points raised in this paper, as well as to Rosemary Cramp, Derek Craig, and Ken Jukes of the *CASSS* for their support with the research.

[1] For a full bibliography and conditions of the antiquarian history of this group of monuments, see the forthcoming volume of the *CASSS* on Derbyshire and Staffordshire by Jane Hawkes and Philip Sidebottom.

[2] A fragment of the cross-head, along with the shaft that incorporates the lower part of the cross-head, survives at Bakewell; at Bradbourne are the remains of the shaft and two pieces of a cross-head; at Eyam are the truncated remains of the shaft and cross-head. See T. E. Routh, 'Corpus of the pre-Conquest Carved Stones of Derbyshire', *DAJ*, 58 (1937), 1–46 (pp. 5–7, 18–20, 27–28), and John Moreland, 'George Forrest Browne, Early Medieval Sculpture and Nineteenth-Century Reformation Historiography', *JBAA*, 156 (2003), 150–66 (p. 154).

Figure 24 (above). Bakewell, Derbyshire: remains of cross-shaft and lower portion of cross-head: (a) west face, (b) east face, (c) south face, (d) north face. Photo: *Corpus of Anglo-Saxon Stone Sculpture*, Ken Jukes.

Figure 25 (below). Bakewell, Derbyshire: fragment of cross-head. Figure with book. Photo: Jane Hawkes.

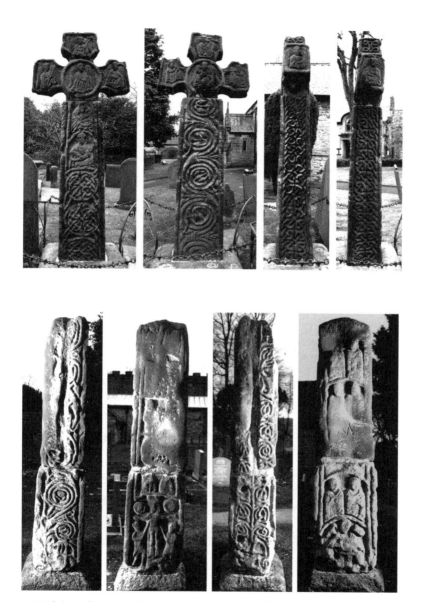

Figure 26 (above). Eyam, Derbyshire: remains of cross-shaft and cross-head: (a) west face, (b) east face, (c) south face, (d) north face. Photo: Jane Hawkes.
Figure 27 (below). Bradbourne, Derbyshire: remains of cross-shaft: (a) west face, (b) south face, (c) east face, (d) north face. Photo: Jane Hawkes.

Figure 28 (above). Bradbourne, Derbyshire: fragment of cross-head: (a) angel with trumpet, (b) angel with rod. Photo: Jane Hawkes.
Figure 29 (below). Bradbourne, Derbyshire: fragment of cross-head. Head of figure with foliate rod. Photo: Jane Hawkes.

Indeed, much of the scholarly discussion of this group of sculptures has been devoted to highlighting these issues of production through focussing on the many stylistic and formal features that they share.[3] The interlace and plant-scroll patterns filling the shaft at Eyam have been noted as being closely parallelled at Bakewell (Figs 24b–d, 26a–d), while the remains of an archer preserved at the base of the Bakewell shaft, shooting an arrow through the plant-scroll above him, is an arrangement and association of motifs found elsewhere at Bradbourne (Figs 24b, 27a, c),[4] where a further point of comparison is the common use of a Crucifixion scene (Figs 24a, 27b). Bakewell also shares with Eyam the setting of a single male figure in the end of one cross-arm (Figs 24c, 26d) and a quatrilobe interlace knot in the spandrels of the cross-arms, an unusual detail repeated on the cross-arm preserved at Bradbourne. Again, this latter fragment shares with the Eyam cross-head depictions of angels with staffs and trumpets (Figs 26a–b, 28, 29), while the figural style that has been used, not just for the angels in these cross-heads, but also for the figures on the cross-arm fragment at Bakewell and the shafts of the crosses, is common to all three monuments. Overall, it is an extensive catalogue of motifs that clearly demonstrates the likelihood of a shared centre, and therefore date of production.

However, in focussing on such details not only have these discussions, like most studies of Anglo-Saxon sculpture, provided insight to the techniques and methods of production of this distinctive type of public art through identifying their common features, they have also served to distinguish the differences between them.[5] In doing this they have laid the groundwork for further work on the material — most notably, that which has been devoted to exploring the motives of those responsible for the design of the monuments and their individual iconographic programmes. Here, the work of Éamonn Ó Carragáin has been fundamental. His seminal 1978 paper on the liturgy of the early Church and the carved decoration of the crosses at Ruthwell (Dumfries.) and Bewcastle (Cu.)[6] opened

---

[3] See, for example, Rosemary Cramp, 'Schools of Mercian Sculpture', in *Mercian Studies*, ed. by Ann Dornier (Leicester, 1977), pp. 191–233.

[4] See related fragments at Wirksworth (Philip C. Sidebottom, 'Stone Crosses of the Peak and the "Sons of Eadwulf"', *DAJ*, 119 (1999), 206–19), and remains of a shaft from Sheffield with an archer set in the plant-scroll (William G. Collingwood, *Northumbrian Crosses of the Pre-Norman Age* (London, 1927), fig. 53).

[5] See Richard N. Bailey, 'Innocent from the Great Offence', in *Theorizing Anglo-Saxon Stone Sculpture*, ed. by Catherine Karkov and Fred Orton (Morgantown, WV, 2003), pp. 93–103.

[6] Éamonn Ó Carragáin, 'Liturgical Innovations Associated with Pope Sergius and the Iconography of the Ruthwell and Bewcastle Crosses', in *Bede and Anglo-Saxon England: Papers in Honor*

up the manner in which these sculptures could be examined, iconographically. His approach situated the monuments within a specific cultural and intellectual context, and in so doing focussed on the figural rather than non-figural decoration, while at the same time calling attention to the possibility that the non-figural could be more than simply 'decorative' by emphasizing symbolic significances rather than issues of form and style.[7] More broadly speaking, Ó Carragáin's work has facilitated an approach that builds on the iconological methodology developed in art historical circles during the 1940s and 1950s, most notably in the work of Panofsky. His studies have enabled the application of this approach to art objects that are less explicitly related to specific documentation than are the works of the fourteenth- and fifteenth-century artists through which the iconological methodology was most famously articulated.[8] Some three decades later it is perhaps not inappropriate to examine the Derbyshire sculptures in the light of Ó Carragáin's work by considering the liturgical and exegetical literature circulating in the Anglo-Saxon world of the eighth and early ninth centuries.[9]

Angelic Settings

Although the vagaries of survival mean that much of the detail of the figural sculptures originally decorating the Peak District sculptures has been lost, their extant iconographic programmes are distinct in their selection and arrangement. The

of the 1300th Anniversary of the Birth of Bede, Given at Cornell University in 1973 and 1974, ed. by Robert T. Farrell, British Archaeological Reports, 46 (Oxford, 1978), pp. 131–47.

[7] For full discussion, see Éamonn Ó Carragáin, *Ritual and the Rood: Liturgical Images and the Old English Poems of the 'Dream of the Rood' Tradition* (London, 2005).

[8] Erwin Panofsky, *Iconography and Iconology: An Introduction to the Study of Renaissance Art* (New York, 1955). Despite the common association of this methodology with such works, it was applied earlier in Anglo-Saxon sculptural studies: Franz Saxl, 'The Ruthwell Cross', *JWCI*, 6 (1943), 1–19; Meyer Schapiro, 'The Religious Meaning of the Ruthwell Cross', *Art B.*, 26 (1944), 232–45, and 'The Archer in the Bowman and the Bird on the Ruthwell Cross and Other Works: The Interpretation of Secular Themes in Early Medieval Religious Art', *Art B.*, 45 (1963), 351–55; a response to Ernst Kantorowicz, 'The Archer in the Ruthwell Cross', *Art B.*, 42 (1960), 57–59. For a summary, see Kellie Meyer, 'Bird, Beast or Fish? Problems of Identification and Interpretation of the Iconography Carved on the Tarbat Cross-Slabs', in *Able Minds and Practised Hands: Scotland's Early Medieval Sculpture in the 21st Century*, ed. by Sally Foster and Morag Cross (London, 2005), pp. 243–57.

[9] See Richard N. Bailey, *The Meaning of Mercian Sculpture*, Vaughan Papers, 34 (Leicester, 1990), for initial iconographic discussion of the monuments at Bakewell and Eyam.

cross at Eyam, which displays the best preserved of the carvings, depicts figural images on only one, broad face of the shaft (Fig. 26a), while all four faces of the cross-head are filled with figural work (Fig. 26a–b). At Bakewell, the figural predominates on, but is not limited to, the broad (west) face of the shaft, as figural motifs are incorporated into the plant-scroll on the east face (Fig. 24a–b). This is also the case at Bradbourne, but here the plant-scrolls fill both narrow faces of the shaft, and the two broad faces are filled with the worn remains of figural panels (Fig. 27), while the cross-head seems, as at Eyam, to have been given over to figural motifs (Figs 26, 28, 29).

Not only does the arrangement of the carved ornament vary across these three monuments, however, the selection of figural motifs also varies. The Bakewell and Bradbourne shafts display numerous panels that are predominantly iconic portrait-type images, but which also include the Crucifixion amongst them: at the base of Bradbourne and at the top of Bakewell (Figs 24a, 27b). The shaft at Eyam, however, includes no such image, featuring only two panels of iconic portraits (Fig. 26a). Furthermore, while the cross-heads at Eyam and Bradbourne seem to have been filled with angels (Figs 26a–b, 28, 29), that at Bakewell included at least two non-angelic figures, one of whom carried a book (Figs 24c, 25). Clearly, the iconographic focus of these monuments, while having so much in common, used distinct means to convey their symbolic significance(s).

What is of note here is the manner in which the cross-heads of at least two of the monuments were filled with angelic figures. Elsewhere in the extant corpus of pre-Scandinavian sculpture this type of figure tends to be displayed on the shaft of the monument where angels feature as part of group images.[10] Even where they were depicted in cross-heads they form part of group schemes.[11] Only on the crosses of the Peak District are the angels crowded into the cross-heads as

---

[10] See Otley (Yorkshire), Halton (Lancashire), the Cross of St Oran, Iona, and the Kildalton Cross, Islay, in Collingwood, *Northumbrian Crosses*, fig. 52 (Otley) and fig. 92b (Halton); Jane Hawkes, 'Columban Virgins: Iconic Images of the Virgin and Child in Insular Sculpture', in *Studies in the Cult of Saint Columba*, ed. by Cormac Bourke (Dublin, 1997), pp. 107–35, figs 4–5 (Iona and Kildalton). For discussion, see Tom Pickles, 'The Church in Anglo-Saxon Yorkshire: Minsters in the Danelaw, *c.* 600–1200' (unpublished doctoral dissertaion, Oxford, 2006). I am grateful to him for the opportunity to discuss these issues. See also Ian Wood, 'Anglo-Saxon Otley: An Archiepiscopal Estate and its Crosses in a Northumbrian Context', *Northern History*, 23 (1987), 20–38.

[11] See Dewsbury, Yorkshire (Pickles, 'Church in Anglo-Saxon Yorkshire', and Collingwood, *Northumbrian Crosses*, fig. 73b), and St Martin's Cross, Iona (Hawkes, 'Columban Virgins', fig. 3, and discussion in Jane Hawkes, 'Figuring Salvation: An Excursus into the Iconography of the Iona Crosses', in *Able Minds*, ed. by Foster and Cross, pp. 259–75).

individual figures, while being absent from the panels of iconic portraits that fill the shafts.[12] This distinctive setting and focus on the angelic suggests that, despite the deplorable condition of much of the figural carving set in the shafts of these monuments (making clear identification of much of the subject matter impossible), they can, nevertheless, provide some insight into the potential iconographic function of the crosses.

Angelic Significances

As has been discussed elsewhere, interest in angels, their various roles, functions, and relationship with humanity, was widespread in the literature of early Christian Britain and Ireland where they make frequent appearances, not just as protagonists (messengers and psychopomps) in hagiographic and visionary texts,[13] but also as subjects accorded substantial consideration in liturgical and exegetical contexts.[14] In Anglo-Saxon England of the seventh, eighth, and ninth centuries much

---

[12] Although worn, the remains of the figures on the shafts at Bakewell and Bradbourne are sufficient to indicate they were not winged.

[13] See Adamnán's *Life of Columba*, iii.23, in *Life of St Columba, Founder of Hy*, ed. by William Reeves (Edinburgh, 1874), pp. 210, 225–29; the anonymous *Life of Cuthbert* [hereafter *VCA*], and that by Bede [hereafter *VCP*], in *Two Lives of Saint Cuthbert*, ed. and trans. by Bertram Colgrave (Cambridge, 1940): *VCA*, 1.4, pp. 66–69; 2.2, pp. 76–79; 2.7, pp. 72–73; 2.11, pp. 128–29; *VCP*, 2, p. 47; 7, pp. 53–54; Bede's *Ecclesiastical History* [hereafter *HE*], in *Bede's Ecclesiastical History of the English People*, ed. and trans. by Bertram Colgrave and R. A. B. Mynors (Oxford, 1969), 3.8, pp. 238–39; 4.3, pp. 344–45; 4.11, pp. 366–67; 4.23, pp. 412–13; 5.12, pp. 488–89; 5.19, pp. 526–27; and Æthelwulf's *De abbatibus*, ed. by Alistair Campbell (Oxford, 1967), lines 85–86, pp. 24–25.

[14] The primary exegetical works on the subject were those by Gregory the Great: his *Moralia in Job* [hereafter *Moralia*], ed. by M. Adriaen, 3 vols, CCSL 143–143B (Turnholt, 1979–85); his Homilies on Ezekiel [hereafter *H.Ez.*] and Luke (in *Homiliae in Hiezechielem prophetam*, ed. by M. Adriaen, CCSL, 142 (Turnholt, 1971) and *Homiliae in Evangelia*, ed. by R. Étaix, CCSL, 141 (Turnholt, 1999)), which featured as part of the Christmas office in the West by the ninth century (U. Nilgen, 'The Epiphany and the Eucharist: on the Interpretation of Eucharistic Motifs in Medieval Epiphany Scenes', *Art B.*, 49 (1967), 311–16); his *Dialogues* (hereafter *Dialog.*; *Grégoire le Grand: Dialogues*, ed. by A. de Vogüé and P. Antin (Paris, 1980)); and his *Pastoral Care* (hereafter *Past. Care*; *PL*, 77, 13–128). These formed the basis of subsequent Anglo-Saxon discussions of angels, most notably those of Bede: in his *HE* and Commentaries on the Tabernacle and the Temple (hereafter *De tab.* and *De temp.*; in Bede, *De tabernaculo, De templo, In Ezram et Neemiam*, ed. by David Hurst, CCSL, 119A (Turnholt, 1969)). But see also the early eighth-century anonymous Whitby *Life of Gregory* (hereafter *V. Greg.*; in *The Earliest Life of Gregory the Great*, ed. by Bertram Colgrave (Cambridge, 1968)). For the circulation of these texts

of this focus concerned the manner in which angels functioned as figures of contemplation in fellowship with humanity, a fellowship founded on the sharing of free will: for, 'the angelic nature [...] received free will at its creation, whether it wished to persevere in humility and remain within the presence of Almighty God, or yield to pride and fall from blessedness'.[15] Thus, while angels were regarded as heavenly creatures, they were also considered to be, like men, the 'fellow-servants' of God. This was deemed to be a truth revealed to John in his vision of the second incarnation (Revelation 19. 10), and was regarded as obliging humanity to 'be worthy of their [the angels'] respect and fellowship'.[16]

At one level, awareness of this fellowship is reflected liturgically, in the understanding that angels were the colleagues of men in prayer. Bede's comments on angels and the divine services make this clear,[17] as does his belief that angels were present at the canonical hours.[18] As Gregory had put it:

and their influences in Anglo-Saxon England, see Michael Lapidge, 'Surviving Booklists from Anglo-Saxon England', in *Learning and Literature in Anglo-Saxon England: Studies Presented to Peter Clemoes on the Occasion of his Sixty-fifth Birthday*, ed. by Michael Lapidge and Helmut Gneuss (Cambridge, 1985), pp. 33–90; Lapidge, *Anglo-Latin Literature 600–899* (London, 1996); Helmut Gneuss, *Handlist of Anglo-Saxon Manuscripts: A List of Manuscripts and Manuscript Fragments Written or Owned in England up to 1100* (Tempe, 2001); and general discussions in Paul Meyvaert, *Bede and Gregory the Great* (Jarrow Lecture, 1964); Alan Thacker, 'Bede's Ideal of Reform', in *Ideal and Reality in Frankish and Anglo-Saxon Society: Studies Presented to J. M. Wallace-Hadrill*, ed. by Patrick Wormald, Donald Bullough, and Roger Collins (Oxford, 1983), pp. 130–53 (pp. 130–35); Thacker, 'Monks, Preaching and Pastoral Care in Early Anglo-Saxon England', in *Pastoral Care Before the Parish*, ed. by John Blair and Richard Sharpe (Leicester, 1992), pp. 137–70 (pp. 152–60); Thacker, 'Memorializing Gregory the Great: The Origin and Transmission of a Papal Cult in the Seventh and Eighth Centuries', *Early Medieval Europe*, 7 (1998), 59–84; Henry Mayr-Harting, *Perceptions of Angels in History* (Oxford, 1998); and Hawkes, 'Figuring Salvation'. For a summary of liturgical contexts, see Richard N. Bailey, *Anglo-Saxon Sculptures at Deerhurst* (Deerhurst, 2005), pp. 11–14.

[15] Gregory, *H.Ez.*, I.vii.18, p. 94; trans. by Theodosia Gray, *The Homilies of Saint Gregory the Great on the Book of the Prophet Ezekiel* (Etna, CA, 1990), p. 74; see also Hawkes, 'Figuring Salvation'.

[16] *Hom. VIII*, ed. by Étaix, p. 56; see also Bede, *De temp.*, I.14.3, p. 185; *VCA*, 1.4, pp. 66–69; 2.2, pp. 76–79; 4.11, pp. 128–29; *VCP*, 2, p. 47; 7, pp. 53–54; and discussion in Mayr-Harting, *Perceptions of Angels in History*, p. 11.

[17] *Homeliarum Evangelii*, 2.10 'Post Pascha' (Luc. 24. 1–9), ed. by David Hurst, CCSL, 122 (Turnhout, 1955), pp. 246–52 (pp. 248–49).

[18] Recorded by Alcuin, 'Letter to the Brethren of the Church of St Peter', in *Councils and Ecclesiastical Documents Relating to Great Britain and Ireland*, vol. III, ed. by Arthur W. Haddan and William Stubbs (Oxford, 1871), pp. 470–71; see also Wood, 'Anglo-Saxon Otley', p. 31.

Quis enim fidelium habere dubium possit ipsa immolationis hora ad sacerdotis vocem caelos aperiri, in illo Iesu Christi mysterio angelorum chorus adesse, summis ima sociari, terram caelestibus iungi, unum quid ex visibilibus atque invisibilibus fieri.

[Which of the faithful can have any doubt that at the moment of the immolation, at the voice of the priest, the heavens are opened; that in that mystery of Jesus Christ, the choirs of angels are present, the lowest are bound to the highest, the earthly are joined with the heavenly, and out of the visible and the invisible a union is created.][19]

Indeed, it is no coincidence that almost every prayer in the Common of the Mass is an angelic prayer, the *Gloria* being composed around angelic praise at the Nativity, the *Sanctus* echoing the seraphic praise of the heavenly vision of Isaiah, and the *Agnus Dei* recalling the angelic adulation of the Lamb of the Apocalypse; all were prayers that had been established in the Mass by the eighth century. More generally, the whole mode of antiphonal singing was deemed to have derived from angelic worship in heaven,[20] and regardless of John the Deacon's infamous reservations concerning the quality of such choral practices north of the Alps in the ninth century — considering them to be 'unmodulated sounds like unto farm carts clumsily creaking up a rutted hill'[21] — it is clear that such liturgical practices were current in Anglo-Saxon England from the seventh century onwards.[22]

So intimate was the link between the angelic and the human reflected in such liturgical considerations that discussion of angels, particularly in the works of Gregory, tend to move seamlessly between the heavenly and human conditions. Thus, when discussing the disposition of angels in relation to the heavens in his Homilies on Ezekiel, Gregory considers them to be essentially 'stretched upward':

Facies et pennae extentae desuper describuntur, quia omnis intentio omnisque contemplatio Sanctorum super se tendit, ut illud possit adipisci quod in caelestibus appetit. Siue enim bono operi, siue vero invigilet contemplationi, tunc veraciter hoc quod agit bonum est, quando ei complacre concupiscit a quo est.

[19] *Dialog.* 4.60, p. 202; trans. by Odo J. Zimmermann, *Saint Gregory the Great: Dialogues* (New York, 1959), pp. 273–74; see Mayr-Harting, *Perceptions of Angels in History*, p. 25.

[20] Mayr-Harting, *Perceptions of Angels in History*, p. 14.

[21] *Vita Gregorii Magni*, 2.7 (hereafter *V. Greg. Mag.*; *PL*, 75, 59–242 (col. 91)); Meyvaert, *Bede and Gregory*, p. 8.

[22] See Bede, *Vita beatorum abbatum*, i.6, in *Venerabilis Baedae: opera historica*, ed. by Charles Plummer, 2 vols (Oxford, 1896), II, 369; *HE*, 4.18, 5.20, pp. 388–91; 530–31; *Alcuin: The Bishops, Kings and Saints of York*, ed. by Peter Godman (Oxford, 1982), pp. 98–100; and Éamonn Ó Carragáin, *The City of Rome and the World of Bede* (Jarrow Lecture, 1994).

[because the whole attention, the entire contemplation of the holy creatures, is directed above themselves in order that it may attain that which it seeks in the heavens. For whether he be watchful in good works, or in true contemplation, then truly that which he does is good when he desires to please him from whom he came.][23]

Here, the heavenly and angelic is indistinguishable from the human, but more significantly, the unity between the two is deemed by Gregory to lie in the shared activity of contemplating the divine. For, it is 'through the grace of contemplation' that angels and men 'yearn to taste eternal blessedness'.[24] It was a process that involved awakening 'the perception of the mind by understanding which is moved from within'.[25] It was thus that contemplation, by men and angels, enabled 'the spirit [...] to fix its eyes of faith on the single light of the Creator, because the God who created all things brings to life'. While angels, 'in gazing always on the Unchangeable are changed into immutability', humanity could

[Ponamus] ante oculos mentis quae illa natura sit quae tenet omnia, implet omnia, circumplectitur omnia, superexcedit omnia, sustinet omnia [...]. Huius naturae potentiam cum strictus in ea cogitat animus [...] quia eius intellectum concipit, qui et angelorum sensum sua incomprehensibilitate transcendit.

[place before the eyes of our minds that nature which holds all things, fills all things, encompasses all things, surpasses all things, sustains all things [...]. For when the spirit, intent on these things, ponders the power of this nature [...] the spirit receives an understanding thereof, which in its incomprehensibility transcends even the perceptions of the angels.][26]

However, while the shared act of contemplation demonstrated the link between angels and humans, and facilitated their necessary understanding of the transcendent, it was also a process regarded as crucial in integrating the inner life with the active. More specifically, it was deemed to be a critical element in the pastoral life of the priesthood.[27] In his *Moralia* Gregory makes it clear that 'by contemplation we rise to the love of God; by preaching we return to the service

---

[23] *H.Ez.*, I.iv.4, p. 49, trans. by Gray, *Homilies*, p. 42.

[24] *H.Ez.*, I.iv.4, p. 50, trans. by Gray, *Homilies*, p. 43.

[25] *H.Ez.*, I.viii.12, p. 107, trans. by Gray, *Homilies*, p. 83.

[26] *H.Ez.*, I.viii.15–16, pp. 108–09, trans. by Gray, *Homilies*, p. 84.

[27] See discussions in Robert A. Markus, *Gregory the Great and his World* (Cambridge, 1997), pp. 21–47; Thacker, 'Bede's Ideal', pp. 131–49; Thacker, 'Monks', pp. 152–53; Jennifer O'Reilly, 'Introduction', to *Bede: On the Temple*, trans. by Seán Connolly (Liverpool, 1995), pp. xvii–lv (pp. xxvi–xli).

of our neighbour'.[28] But, in order to avoid 'prioritizing' the contemplative over the active in the pastoral ministry, he also made it clear that

> Mira enim divinitatis pietate agitur, cum is qui perfecto corde ad contemplationem tenditur, humanis ministeriis occupatur; ut et multis infirmioribus eius mens perfecta proficiat et quo se ipse imperfectum respicit, inde ad humilitatis culmen perfectior assurgat.

> [It is by a wonderful divine benevolence that he who seeks contemplation with a perfect heart is occupied in serving others; so that his perfected mind may profit others weaker than him, and that he himself may rise to the summit of perfection in humility from the very imperfection he perceives in himself.][29]

For Bede, steeped in these ideals, the two were inextricably linked; as Thacker has pointed out, 'it seems never to have occurred to Bede to question the involvement of [the contemplative] in missionary and pastoral activity'.[30] Thus, just as the purpose of 'holy teachers' lay in 'being raised to supernal things they were also just as firm in their capacity of lifting others up to the love of supernal things by their teaching'.[31]

Thus angels were regarded as creatures that could be identified with both the heavenly and the human. With humanity they shared free will and contemplation of the Divine, and for humanity, while such contemplation was necessary if spiritual understanding was to be achieved, it was also a crucial aspect of the pastoral role of those serving the Church. In fact, contemplation was what made the Church of the Christian community 'as like to the angels'.[32]

Against the background of this complex of ideas it is not impossible that the apparent focus on the angelic, evidenced by the concentration of these figures in the cross-heads of the Derbyshire monuments, implies some reference to the ideas surrounding angels, to their fellowship with humanity, their role as figures of contemplation (the aim of which was to achieve understanding of the nature of the divine), and the importance of contemplation in the pastoral life of the Church.

---

[28] *Moralia*, VI.xxxvii.56, p. 326; see also *Moralia*, XXXI.xxv.49; *H.Ez.*, I.iii.9; and the discussion in Markus, *Gregory*, p. 23.

[29] *Moralia*, V.iv.5, p. 222; see also *H.Ez.*, II.ii.11; *H.Ez.*, II.vi.5; and stronger admonition in *Past. Care*, 1.5; with discussion in Markus, *Gregory*, pp. 24–25.

[30] Thacker, 'Monks', p. 153.

[31] *De tab.*, 2.9, p. 74; trans. by Arthur G. Holder, *Bede: On the Tabernacle* (Liverpool, 1994), p. 83; see also *De tab.*, 2.13, p. 86.

[32] *H.Ez.*, I.viii.6, p. 105; trans. by Gray, *Homilies*, p. 81.

Angelic Sculptures

As far as the cross at Eyam is concerned (Fig. 26), the figural panels associated with the angelic scheme depict the remains of the Virgin and Child at the truncated top of the shaft and, below, a prophet with an unfurled scroll.[33] Of these, the Virgin and Child panel functions, as do all such images, to signify the humanity of the Christ Child at the incarnation while the hierarchic attitude of the mother and child, and the manner in which the Child raises one hand in blessing, serve as signifiers of his inherent majesty and divinity. In early Christian images this aspect of Christ's nature is usually emphasized by the inclusion of attendant angels (with staffs).[34] Thus, while angels are not included within the same panel as the Virgin and Child at Eyam, the way they are crowded (holding floriated rods) into the cross-head above means that they can be regarded as indicators of the divinity of the godhead at the first incarnation. In this context the prophet set below the Virgin and Child serves, in keeping with such depictions in early Christian art, to under-line the manner in which this incarnation was regarded as fulfilling God's plan for salvation foretold in the Old Testament.[35] Overall, therefore, the iconographic programme reveals the salvation of humanity as foretold by the prophets, con-firmed in the incarnation of the Christ Child, and celebrated by the angelic host, signifiers of his divinity. Being concentrated in the cross-head, however, the angels also serve as reminders of the most appropriate manner in which such issues are to be regarded; they remind the viewer of the shared obligation of contemplation, leading the mind upwards in understanding of the divine. The angels blowing trumpets on the other side of the cross-head further complement these themes by providing clear references to the judgement of the Second Coming,[36] while their

[33] The scroll (signifying the words of his prophecy concerning the future coming of the Messiah) is represented by the unusual curved feature held across the body of the prophet, which twists to a point at one end.

[34] See the sixth-century icon at Mt Sinai (Gertrude Schiller, *Ikonographie der Christlichen Kunst*, vol. IV.2 (Gutersloh, 1980), pl. 414), the seventh-century icon at Sta Maria in Trastevere, Rome (*Europe in the Dark Ages*, ed. by Jean Hubert, Jean Porcher, and Wolfgang F. Volbach (New York, 1969), fig. 128), and the mid-eighth-century Iona carvings (Hawkes, 'Columban Virgins', figs 3–5).

[35] Gertrude Schiller, *Iconography of Christian Art*, vol. I, trans. by Janet Seligman (London, 1971), pp. 13–15.

[36] It is possible that the cross-head was reset the wrong way round on the truncated top of the shaft in the later eighteenth century — that originally, the angels with the trumpets were intended to be viewed in conjunction with the Virgin and Child and prophet. If so, these angels would still

association with the plant-scroll below links the Church and its sacraments with the process of incarnation, salvation, judgement, and resurrection (Fig. 26b).[37]

Here, it is also worth noting that the manner in which the figural decoration is organized across the monument emphasizes the single male figure set in the company of angels on the narrow end of the northern cross-arm (Fig. 26d). Whether he was intended to depict a specific individual (such as a prophet, apostle, or saint), if the angels are understood as figures of contemplation associating humanity with the heavenly, this figure serves dramatically to associate the human viewer standing below, being 'stretched upwards' in contemplation, with the angelic company of heaven. Overall, the iconographic scheme, through its focus on the angelic, emphasizes the act of contemplation, crucial at the level of each individual viewer, but also for the institution of the Church and those serving within it. The angels mediate understanding of the promise of salvation made possible by the incarnation (foretold by the prophets) and perpetually re-enacted in the regular celebration of the Eucharist in Christ's Church on Earth, and which will be fulfilled at the Second Coming.

At Bradbourne, although much of the figural decoration of the monument is damaged beyond identification, it is likely that the angelic figures of the cross-head fragments were originally associated with the Crucifixion and the archers set within the plant-scrolls on the shaft (Figs 27, 28, 29). In this context it is likely that, as Barbara Raw has argued, the archers can be regarded (through the exegetical tradition initially articulated by Augustine and Hilary of Poitiers), as symbolic of the preacher, his arrows being the word of God shot to arouse the love of humanity.[38] The references to sacrament and salvation expressed iconographically at Eyam are thus also articulated at Bradbourne, albeit through the invocation of a different set of signifiers.

---

present an iconographically coherent programme, serving as reminders of the second incarnation, a theme often invoked in discussions of the first incarnation.

[37] See E. S. Greenhill, 'The Child in the Tree', *Traditio*, 10 (1954), 323–71; Jennifer O'Reilly, *Studies in the Iconography of the Virtues and Vices in the Middle Ages* (New York, 1988), pp. 344–48; O'Reilly, 'The Trees of Eden in Medieval Iconography', in *A Walk in the Garden: Biblical, Iconographical and Literary Images of Eden*, ed. by Paul Morris and David Sawyer (Sheffield, 1992), pp. 167–204; Jane Hawkes, 'The Plant-Life of Early Christian Anglo-Saxon Art', in *From Earth to Art: The Many Aspects of the Plant-World in Anglo-Saxon England*, ed. by Carol Biggam (Amsterdam, 2002), pp. 257–80; and Hawkes, *The Sandbach Crosses: Sign and Significance in Anglo-Saxon Sculpture* (Dublin, 2002), pp. 90–93.

[38] Barbara Raw, 'The Archer, the Eagle and the Lamb', *JWCI*, 30 (1967), 391–94. This aspect will be discussed further in the forthcoming Corpus volume (see note 1 above).

Two other figural panels, however, also survive on the shaft in sufficient detail for their function within the iconographic programme to be considered (Fig. 30). These are the panels preserved at the base of the current north face of the shaft, directly opposite the Crucifixion on the south face (Fig. 27b, d). The uppermost of these portrays two clerical figures wearing *pallia* and grasping books; that below depicts a central clerical figure holding before him a book over T-shaped stand. Perched on his right shoulder is a bird while over his left is a rectangular object; below, he is flanked by two diminutive profile figures facing each other, both apparently with books before them. These distinctive features and their overall arrangement indicate that this lowermost image can be identified as Gregory the Great in his role as Scribe. Portraits of Gregory as Pope survive from an early date,[39] but during the ninth century an iconographic scheme emerged that depicted him writing and in the company of fellow scribes (who vary in number between one and three).[40] It is in this iconographic context that Gregory is associated with the bird,[41] and sometimes with an open manuscript in the upper confines of the surrounding frame — a detail that suggests the identity of the rectangular object set over the left shoulder of the Bradbourne figure.[42]

---

[39] *V. Greg. Mag.*, 4.83, cols 229–30; see the discussion in Meyvaert, *Bede and Gregory*. For early extant examples of Gregory as Pope, see the historiated initial in the mid-eighth-century copy of Bede's *Ecclesiastical History* (St Petersburg, Russian National Library, Cod. Q. v. I. 18, fol. 26ᵛ in Jonathan J. G. Alexander, *Insular Manuscripts, 6th to the 9th Century*, Survey of Manuscripts Illuminated in the British Isles, 1 (London, 1978), fig. 84); the miniature in the eighth-century collection of Gregory's Homilies (Vercelli, Archiv. Capitolare, MS CXLVIII, fol. 9ʳ, in the Princeton Index, 32/V582/AvCrs/5,9A); the miniature in the ninth-century gospel book of S. Gereon (Stuttgart, Württembergische Landesbibliothek, fol. 3ᵛ, in the Princeton Index, 32/S93/LLa/6,3B); and the ivory diptych panel dated variously to the sixth and ninth centuries at Monza (Wolfgang Braunfels, *Die Welt der Karolinger und ihre Kunst* (Munich, 1968), fig. 213).

[40] See, for example, the ninth-century ivory preserved at Vienna (A. Goldschmidt, *Die Elfenbeinskulpturen aus der zeit der Karolingischen und Sächsischen Kaiser: VIII–XI Jahrhundert* (Berlin, repr. 1969), Taf. LIV.122), and the miniature in a tenth-century missal (Halberstadt, Domgymnasium, MS 153, fol. 13ʳ, in the Princeton Index, 32/H129/LD/4,13A).

[41] John the Deacon's later ninth-century version of Gregory's *Life* explains that all images of Gregory portray him with the dove, but his account of the portrait then hanging in Gregory's monastery of St Andrew makes no mention of the motif (*V. Greg. Mag.*, 4.83, cols 229–30). Certainly extant manuscript images of the full-length standing figure of Gregory as Pope, produced between the eighth and eleventh centuries, do not include it (see above, note 39, and the discussion in *Earliest Life*, ed. by Colgrave, n. 110, and Meyvaert, *Bede and Gregory*, n. 17).

[42] See the miniature in the tenth-century copy of Gregory's Homilies on Ezekiel, Einseiedeln, Stiftsbibliothek, MS 156, p. 11 (Princeton Index, 32/Ei67/LSts/11,2).

Figure 30. Bradbourne, Derbyshire: detail of north face of cross-shaft. Clerical figures and Gregory as Scribe. Photo: Jane Hawkes.

While the scribal image of Gregory is commonly associated with Carolingian developments, being most famously depicted in the ninth-century ivory preserved at Vienna,[43] the association of his scribal activities with the dove of the Holy Spirit inspiring his work (on Ezekiel) has an earlier, eighth-century Anglo-Saxon literary source, being preserved in the Whitby *Life of Gregory*.[44] Here it is explained that

> Unde de ordinibus illorum, scilicet agminum tali tractavit ingenio, quali nequaquam sanctorum aliquis vel ante vel post eum invenimus fecisse alterum [...]. Hic vero eos non solum in suis distinxit agminibus, omnia ex sanctis confirmando scripturis, verum etiam ad nostrę consortia vitę, mundo corde quo beati tantum Deum videbunt, dirivavit. Iste igitur ille de quo ait Salvator, 'Omnis scriba doctus in regno cę lorum similes est homini patrifamilias, qui profert de thesauro suo nova et vetera.'

> [Gregory dealt with the orders of the angelic ranks with such skill as we have never been able to find in any other saint before or since [...]. Not only did Gregory divide them into orders, basing everything on the Holy Scriptures, but also, with that pure heart whereby the blessed alone shall see God, he even brought them into fellowship with this life of ours. It is he therefore of whom the Saviour says, 'Every scribe which is instructed unto the Kingdom of Heaven is like unto a man that is an householder which bringeth forth out of his treasure things new and old.']⁴⁵[45]

So laudable were his scribal skills, 'it is said that a certain member of Gregory's household [. . .] saw a white dove resting upon the man of God while he was engaged in writing these homilies on Ezekiel' — just as the dove of the Holy Spirit descended on Christ at his baptism.[46] The existence, preservation, and transmission of this event in an Anglo-Saxon context may go some way to explaining the depiction of Gregory preserved at Bradbourne, particularly as copies of the Whitby life seem to have been circulating in Mercia from the eighth century,[47] while the iconographic scheme itself is constructed within the long-established aulic tradition of the hieratic central figure surrounded by diminutive subsidiary figures, an iconographic tradition that was used elsewhere in Anglo-Saxon England, and indeed in Mercian art in the eighth century, to create scenes such as David Dictating the Psalms.[48]

[43] See above, note 40.

[44] I am grateful to Jennifer O'Reilly for her advice on this subject.

[45] *V. Greg. 25*, pp. 118–21.

[46] *V. Greg. 25*, pp. 120–23.

[47] See the discussion in *Earliest Life*, ed. by Colgrave, n. 99, n. 120; and Thacker, 'Memorializing Gregory'.

[48] Alexander, *Insular Manuscripts*, fig. 146; *The Vespasian Psalter: British Museum, Cotton Vespasian A.I*, ed. by David Wright (Copenhagen, 1967), pp. 71–72.

More significant, perhaps, in elucidating the potential iconographic significance of the overall programme once depicted at Bradbourne is the literary context of Gregory's scribal activities. In the Whitby life these are inserted into an account of his homiletic elucidation of Ezekiel's vision. This summarizes, not the entire collection of homilies, but rather the eighth homily of the first book: the homily most concerned with angelic nature, with the fellowship of angels and humanity, with the nature of contemplation and its function in the Christian life.[49] This is not to imply that the iconographic programme at Bradbourne is a visual commentary inspired by the *Life of Gregory*. It does, however, suggest that relevant to those responsible for this monument were the ideas propounded by Gregory concerning angels, their importance as figures of contemplation, and the role of contemplation in the pastoral life. The inclusion of Gregory as Scribe and the pairing of clerical figures in the panel implies that the importance he placed on the act of contemplation within the active pastoral life of the Church was intentionally being made explicit in the iconographic programme of the cross at Bradbourne.

Conclusions

Set in the heads of the Peak District crosses, the angelic figures can thus be understood to have acted as mnemonics inviting the viewer to consider the link between men and angels and their shared obligation of rightful contemplation of the godhead, such contemplation being a necessary precondition of proper understanding and the exercise of right action — particularly for the priesthood of the Church. The iconographic expression of these ideas indicates that, like their more well-known Northumbrian counterparts, these figural monuments were the products of a culturally and theologically sophisticated ecclesiastical milieu that wished to present themes expressly concerned with the Church and its pastoral role in the Christian community, themes that were perhaps intellectually esoteric, but which were nevertheless being given public expression in the form of sculptural stone monuments. By concentrating the setting of the visually arresting angels in the cross-heads of these monuments, the designers seem to have been concerned, on the one hand, to encourage the active participation of each viewer in that most central of processes (contemplation of the divine), while at the same time, to define their ecclesiastical role as one that integrated the contemplative with the active and the pastoral.

---

[49] See above, notes 25, 26, and 32.

The Winwick Cross and a Suspended Sentence

Richard N. Bailey

S t Oswald's church at Winwick on the Lancashire/Cheshire border is notable for three reasons: a chancel and vestry designed by Pugin; a sixteenth-century Latin verse inscription on the west wall in praise of St Oswald; and the transom of the largest cross to survive from Anglo-Saxon England. This paper is concerned with the cross, though St Oswald does put in a fleeting appearance. The apparent links of the sculpture to the Celtic west, together with a discussion which appeals to patristic and apocryphal texts — and invokes material from Rome and Italy — make this a particularly appropriate subject to offer Éamonn Ó Carragáin.

Location and Discovery

St Oswald's church is first mentioned in Domesday Book, by which time it was well endowed with a holding assessed at two carucates.[1] In the post-Conquest

---

[1] A full bibliography will be published in my forthcoming Cheshire and Lancashire volume of the *CASSS*. *The Transactions of the Historic Society of Lancashire and Cheshire*, 2 (1850), 115 record the gift of a (now lost) lithographed plate of the cross to the Society but the earliest surviving description is that of J. Robson, 'Historical and Antiquarian Notes on Warrington and its Neighbourhood', *Transactions of the Historic Society of Lancashire and Cheshire*, 4 (1852), 202–08 (p. 206). More substantial accounts with illustrations can be found in J. Romilly Allen, 'Description of Winwick Cross', *JBAA*, 1st series, 37 (1881), 91–93; G. Forrest Browne, 'Pre-Norman Sculptured Stones in Lancashire', *Transactions of the Lancashire and Cheshire Antiquarian Society*, 5 (1887), 1–18 (pp. 14–18); J. Romilly Allen, 'The Early Christian Monuments of Lancashire and Cheshire', *Transactions of the Historic Society of Lancashire and Cheshire*, 45 (1894), 1–32 (pp. 9, 23); J. Romilly Allen, 'The Early Christian Monuments of Cheshire and Lancashire', *Journal of the Architectural, Archaeological and Historic Society for Chester and North Wales*, 5 (1895), 133–74 (pp. 156–59); Henry Taylor, 'The Ancient Crosses of Lancashire: Hundred of West Derby',

medieval period the living was enormously wealthy and the parish comprised some eleven townships including the adjacent royal estate centre of Newton. All this would suggest that Winwick had been a minster church in the Anglo-Saxon period.[2] There is some doubt, however, as to the antiquity of that parochial status because Alan Thacker has persuasively argued that the territory which became the parish of Winwick had originally belonged to the church of Walton-on-the-Hill, whose rector still had a considerable holding in the area in the early thirteenth century.[3] Winwick's post-Conquest grandeur may thus be a consequence of reorganization begun by Æthelflæd and developed through the tenth century.[4]

The fragmentary cross-head is now set, upside down, on a windowsill on the north side of the nave (see Figs 31–37 below). The earliest published notices of its existence date to 1850 and 1852 by which time it had been placed outside the church against the east wall of the chancel — as part of the restoration of the church and its surroundings instigated during the incumbency of the energetic John Hornby, who also commissioned Pugin's work at the site.[5] The precise date of its discovery or recognition is uncertain: Henry Taylor, in his magisterial survey of Lancashire's crosses and holy wells attributes it to 1843 whilst a visiting party in 1909 was assured that it had been dug up in 1830.[6] Whatever the truth, the stone had obviously been available in the vicinity in the eighteenth century because part

---

Transactions of the Lancashire and Cheshire Antiquarian Society, 19 (1901), 136–238 (repr. with some alterations in Henry Taylor, *The Ancient Crosses and Holy Wells of Lancashire* (Manchester, 1906), pp. 204–10); J. Romilly Allen, 'Pre-Norman Cross-head at Winwick, Lancashire', *Reliquary and Illustrated Archaeologist*, 2nd series, 12 (1906), 134–35; William Farrer and J. Brownbill, *The Victoria History of the County of Lancaster*, vol. I (London, 1906), pp. 262–63.

[2] For the concept of Minster churches, see John Blair, *The Church in Anglo-Saxon Society* (Oxford, 2005), pp. 3–5, 80–83.

[3] D. J. Freke and Alan Thacker, 'Excavations at the Inhumation Cemetery at Southwell Farm, Winwick, Cheshire', *Journal of the Chester Archaeological Society*, 2nd series, 70 (1987), 31–38 (pp. 34–36).

[4] Blair, *Church in Anglo-Saxon Society*, pp. 309–10. Blair (p. 342) also suggests that the Oswald dedication is a reflex of an Æthelwoldian cult. For another view, see Eric Cambridge, 'Archaeology and the Cult of St Oswald in pre-Conquest Northumbria', in *Oswald, Northumbrian King to European Saint*, ed. by Clare Stancliffe and Eric Cambridge (Stamford, 1995), pp. 128–63 (p. 157).

[5] For the 1850 record see note 1 above. For 1852, see Robson, 'Historical and Antiquarian Notes'. For the role of the Revd Hornby, see William Beamont, *Winwick, its History and Antiquities* (Warrington, 1875), p. 61.

[6] Taylor, *Ancient Crosses and Holy Wells*, p. 205; 'Proceedings: Visit to Newton le Willows and Winwick', *Transactions of the Lancashire and Cheshire Antiquarian Society*, 27 (1909), 160–70 (p. 169).

of one main face carries a memorial inscription, neatly carved into a surface which has been cut back to remove the original pre-Norman ornament, reading:

Roger Lowe
Houghton
1721.
Thomas & Alice
Holcroft
1793.

We cannot know how much of the cross was available to the eighteenth-century mason but it was presumably at this date that the bosses on the inscribed face were hacked away and any substantial remaining traces of the ring on the head were removed.

At some date after 1911 the stone was taken into the church and placed on the windowsill in the north aisle. In that position it is now difficult satisfactorily to examine in detail the decoration on the ends of the arms, whilst the ornament on the reverse is totally inaccessible. Fortunately late nineteenth-century scholars commissioned or produced a series of photographs, rubbings, and drawings when the stone was set outside and thus easier to study (see Figs 31, 36, 37).[7] These records can be supplemented by a series of colour slides taken by Dr Ross Trench-Jellicoe when the stone was briefly on exhibition in Liverpool in 1990 and which he has generously allowed me to reproduced here (see Figs 32–35). The following description, adopting the format of the *Corpus of Anglo-Saxon Stone Sculpture*, is based upon a combination of these sources together with an examination of the carving in its present position.[8] Since this paper concentrates on the two figural panels, the rest of the decoration is only described in summary form.

Description

Transom of a ring-headed cross, of type 11A. Breadth: 150 cm. Height: 48 cm. Depth: 28 cm.

---

[7] Excellent photographs, though not of face C, appear in Taylor, 'Ancient Crosses'; Taylor, *Ancient Crosses and Holy Wells*; and the Romilly Allen Collection, London, British Library, Additional MS 37551 (no. XIII). The latter collection also has full-scale rubbings. Rubbings at a reduced scale appear in Browne, 'Pre-Norman Sculptured Stones'. Drawings, some with heavy restoration, can be found in Allen, 'Early Christian Monuments' (1894), p. 7, and Allen, 'Early Christian Monuments' (1895), facing p. 157. There is a further full set of early drawings, prepared by G. Rothwell, in the church.

[8] It should be noted that Allen's drawing, reproduced here, shows Face A upside down.

A (broad). The decoration is divided into three areas bordered by mouldings. At the centre is a flat boss carrying four inter-linked triquetra forming a cruciform shape. The upper half of this central section is filled by blocks of key pattern, the lower half by knotwork using Stafford knots. The two arms carry L-shaped blocks of key pattern and interlinked Stafford knots; the organization of the ornament is repeated from one arm to the other and is not set out as a mirror-image.

B (narrow). The figural scene on this face is bordered by an arris moulding; this is very broad at the bottom where it carries a long narrow slot which may represent later damage or originally have formed the setting for a metallic addition.[9] In the centre of the panel is a naked figure, with large head and hollow ears, who is suspended upside down from a strand emerging from the upper border; the feet are set in profile, the rest of the body is seen en face. His arms curve down alongside his head, one ending in a hand, the other apparently terminating as a stub. He is flanked by two figures, seen in profile, who also appear to be naked. They have pigtails, marked ears, long noses, round eyes, and open mouths — the left figure is depicted as though smiling, the other has a down-turned mouth. With one hand they each grasp the suspended figure's legs whilst one of their feet apparently passes behind or onto the victim's head. With their other hand they grasp a thin curved moulding which runs across their bodies to meet the lateral frame, disappearing behind (or into) the suspended man. A bulbous protrusion emerges from the lower part of their stomachs; this does not appear to be connected to the curved moulding.

C (broad). To the right the ornament has been removed for an eighteenth-century inscription. At the centre is a boss, which has been cut flat, surrounded by pelta-spiral ornament. In the left arm there was another boss, similarly now cut flat, surrounded by three quadrupeds, two with long interlacing tails.

D (narrow). The end of the arm is occupied by a framed figural scene. At the centre is a forward-facing human figure, with a flat head, hollowed ears, and fringed beard; the eyes, nose, and mouth are lightly modelled. He is dressed in a full long-sleeved garment (alb); over this are faint traces of a pointed chasuble. There are traces of decorative strips representing embroidery around the edges and neckline of the chasuble and there is a central bar of ornament up the front of the vestment; further decoration can be seen on the lower hem of the alb. The figure, whose booted feet face to his left, grasps the handles of two rectangular-shaped objects

---

[9] Slots and other traces of metalwork attachments are examined in Richard N. Bailey, *England's Earliest Sculptors*, Publications of the Dictionary of Old English, 5 (Toronto, 1996), pp. 7–11; Bailey, 'What Mean these Stones?', in *Textual and Material Culture in Anglo-Saxon England*, ed. by Donald Scragg (Cambridge, 2003), pp. 212–39 (pp. 227–39).

which narrow from base to top; below each of these is a triquetra. To the right of his head is a long-stemmed cross (probably of type B6) and there is a similar cross alongside his right arm. In the upper left corner is a church or reliquary with an off-centre door, inward-turning gable finials, and a central feature on the roof.

E (underside). The underside of each arm end is decorated with a single framed panel of key pattern. Between these panels and the curve of the cross's armpit is the stump of a ring.

Dating and the Broad Faces (Figs 31–33)

This is the largest pre-Norman cross to survive from England. Only a fragmentary cross-head from Lastingham in Yorkshire approaches these dimensions, and it is some 10 cm shorter.[10] Clearly this is an ambitious monument, in scale approaching the massive size of such crosses as those from Monasterboice (Co. Louth), Ray (Co. Donegal), and Iona.[11] The date of the carving is firmly indicated by the survival of the stub of the ring which once connected the arms of the cross.[12] All the evidence we have shows that the ring-headed form was not exploited in pre-Viking period Northumbria. The shape is one which belongs, in northern England, to the tenth and eleventh centuries, and its distribution points to an introduction from the west, either from Ireland or from western Scotland where the type existed at an earlier date.[13]

Some of the ornament on its main faces is not unexpected in Viking-Age Northumbria. Thus the organization of three free-style animals set around a boss

[10] James T. Lang, CASSS, vol. III: York and Eastern Yorkshire (Oxford, 1991), ills. 574–77.

[11] Iona, St Oran's Cross: 199 cm; Iona, St John's composite cross: 217 cm; Ray, Co. Donegal: 226 cm; Monasterboice, Muirdach's Cross: 212 cm. See the comparative drawings in Ian Fisher, Early Medieval Sculpture in the West Highlands and Islands, Royal Commission on the Ancient and Historical Monuments of Scotland and the Society of Antiquaries of Scotland, Monograph Series, 1 (Edinburgh, 2001), pp. 170–01.

[12] The remains of this ring may have been more apparent at an earlier date, for it is described in 1852 in terms of a 'wheel' by Robson, 'Historical and Antiquarian Notes', p. 206.

[13] W. G. Collingwood, 'The Dispersion of the Wheel Cross', Yorkshire Archaeological Journal, 28 (1926), 322–31; Richard N. Bailey, 'The Chronology of Viking-age Sculpture in Northumbria', in Anglo-Saxon and Viking-age Sculpture and its Context: Papers from the Collingwood Symposium on Insular Sculpture from 800 to 1066, ed. by James T. Lang, British Archaeological Reports, British Series, 49 (Oxford, 1978), pp. 173–203 (pp. 178–79); Bailey, Viking-Age Sculpture (London, 1980), pp. 70–71.

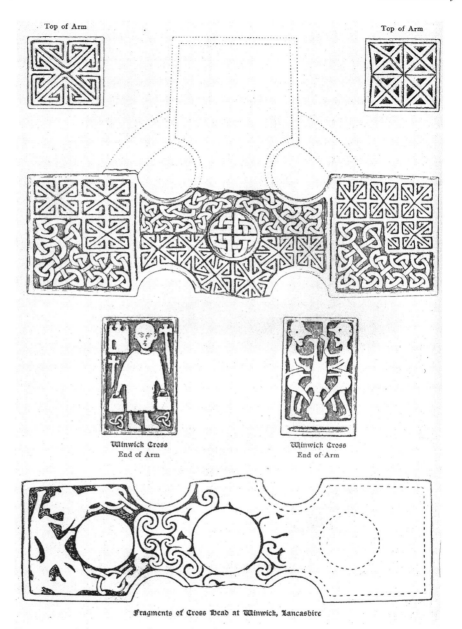

Figure 31. The Winwick cross-head. Face A, carrying the central decorated boss, is shown reversed. After J. Romilly Allen, *Journal of the Architectural [. . .] Society for Chester*, 5 (1895), 156.

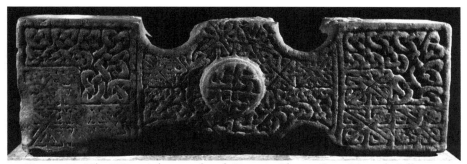

Figure 32. The Winwick cross-head, Face A. Photo: Ross Trench-Jellicoe.

Figure 33. The Winwick cross-head, Face C. Photo: Ross Trench-Jellicoe.

is repeated in the Tees valley at Winston in County Durham and Forcett in Yorkshire.[14] Similarly the run of Stafford knots also reflects a local taste, for this is a form of knotwork which had a restricted popularity to the west of the Pennines in tenth- and eleventh-century England.[15]

But, alongside these regional forms, there are important elements in the shape of the head and its decoration which seem to reflect tastes transplanted from Ireland or Scotland. The cross-head, which combines a block-ended arm, taller than it is wide, with small circular armpits and a narrow connecting ring set close

[14] Winston: Rosemary J. Cramp, *CASSS*, vol. I: *County Durham and Northumberland* (Oxford, 1984), ill. 774. Forcett: James T. Lang. *CASSS*, vol. VI: *Northern Yorkshire* (Oxford, 2001), ill. 250.

[15] Richard N. Bailey and Rosemary J. Cramp, *CASSS*, vol. II: *Cumberland, Westmorland and Lancashire North-of-the-Sands* (Oxford, 1988), pp. 34–40; Marilyn M. Brown and D. B. Gallagher, 'An Anglo-Viking Cross-shaft from Thornton le Moors, Cheshire', *Journal of the Chester Archaeological Society*, 66 (1983), 23–30.

to the armpit, is a type which is familiar on slabs in Scotland and, in free-armed form, in both Ireland and (once) in western Scotland.[16] It is not, however, a shape which can be readily parallelled in England.[17] Similarly, decoration built up from blocks of key pattern is not widely used in pre-Norman Northumbria, and certainly never on a cross-head, but it is very popular on sculptures in Ireland and Scotland.[18] The same can be said about the extremely competent version of spiral ornament at Winwick; this cannot be parallelled elsewhere among Northumbrian or northern Mercian carvings, but it is a persistent element in the decorative repertoire of carvings in Scotland and Ireland.[19]

The evidence of the two main faces of the cross is thus pointing to the Celtic world as a source for much of its inspiration. That conclusion forms a useful background to our main concern: the figural panels on the ends of the arms and their relationship to each other.

The Panel on Face D (Fig. 34)

When Ellacombe produced the first published sketch of this panel in 1872 he captioned it: 'campanarius antiquissimus in camisia vestitutus'.[20] In favourable lighting there is, however, no doubt that Ellacombe's *camisia* is in fact an alb overlaid by

---

[16] For Scotland, see J. Romilly Allen and Joseph Anderson, *The Early Christian Monuments of Scotland* (Edinburgh, 1903), figs 210, 227, 231, 309, 322, 393, and 397. For main discussion of the form, see I. Henderson, 'The Shape and Decoration of the Cross on Pictish Cross-slabs', in *The Age of Migrating Ideas: Early Medieval Art in Northern Britain and Ireland, Proceedings of the Second International Conference on Insular Art held in the National Museums of Scotland in Edinburgh, 36 January 1991*, ed. by R. Michael Spearman and John Higgitt (Edinburgh, 1993), pp. 209–18. For Ireland, see Peter Harbison, *The High Crosses of Ireland: An Iconographical and Photographic Survey*, 3 vols (Bonn, 1992), II, figs 38, 101, 109, 221, 405, 427, and 446.

[17] Though ringed versions of Type 11 heads are recorded in the tables of the volumes of the *CASSS*, none closely resembles the proportions or the combination and placing of the various elements of Winwick.

[18] Northumbrian sculptural key patterns tend to occur in single panels, not in adjacent blocks as at Winwick. For some Irish and Scottish examples on cross-heads, see Harbison, *High Crosses*, II, figs 105, 152, 365, and 446; Allen and Anderson, *Early Christian Monuments*, figs 32, 51, 151, 227, 231, 235, 305, 306, 309, 314, and 322.

[19] Spirals on cross-heads: Harbison, *High Crosses*, II, figs 15, 155, 398, and 516; Allen and Anderson, *Early Christian Monuments*, figs 66, 139, 235, and 393.

[20] H. T. Ellacombe, *The Church Bells of Devon* (Exeter, 1872), p. 526.

Figure 34. The Winwick cross-head, Face D. Photo: Ross Trench-Jellicoe.

a chasuble. This figure is therefore a priest who is shown wearing full Mass vestments, which carry elaborate detail carved in low (and now almost totally obliterated) relief. Below the alb his feet are set in high-ankled shoes of the same type as are worn by an angel on a carving from Slaidburn in West Yorkshire and by clerics and saints on various Pictish sculptures.[21] Similar priestly figures are found on Viking-Age carvings elsewhere in Northumbria at Brompton in Yorkshire and, closer to hand and with an equally elaborate chasuble, at Neston in Cheshire.[22] Both of these latter figures carry maniples whilst the Neston man also holds a chalice aloft. They are not, however, accompanied by the plethora of supporting images which are found in the Winwick carving. These warrant closer examination.

In the upper left corner of the panel is a tower-like structure, with two finials flanking a taller form which may be cruciform in shape.[23] There is a narrow arched door in the lower left. It is possible that this feature was intended to represent a reliquary of some kind: forms in metalwork with end finials and/or suspension loops are known and some of these have raised ornament at the centre of the ridge.[24] But the presence of a seeming door and the tall vertical shape suggest that this is a towered church, and it may not be entirely coincidental that coinage from Chester of *c.* 920 has remarkably similar forms among its decorative novelties.[25]

[21] Slaidburn: Bailey, *Viking-Age Sculpture*, fig. 68. St Vigean's Angus: George Henderson and Isabel Henderson, *The Art of the Picts* (London, 2004), pls 204, 221. In general, see I. Henderson, 'Primus inter Pares', in *The St Andrews Sarcophagus*, ed. by Sally M. Foster (Dublin, 1998), pp. 97–167 (pp. 157–58).

[22] Brompton: Lang. *CASSS*, VI, ill. 40. Neston: R. H. White, 'Viking-period Sculpture at Neston Cheshire', *Journal of the Chester Archaeological Society*, 69 (1986), pp. 45–58, fig. 1. A different kind of priestly representation, with book satchel or rational, is found on a series of Yorkshire sculptures: Lang, *CASSS*, III, ills. 254, 728, and 833.

[23] Allen's drawing shows the central element as a trefoil or cruciform shape. This is also how he restores it in his rubbing preserved in BL Additional MS 37551 (84), though the rubbing itself is not very clear.

[24] In general on reliquaries, see Martin Blindheim, 'A House-shaped Irish-Scots Reliquary in Bologna, and its Place among the Other Reliquaries', *Acta Archaeologica*, 55 (1984), 1–53; Susan Youngs, *The 'Work of Angels': Masterpieces of Celtic Metalwork, 6th–9th Centuries AD* (London, 1989), pp. 129–30. The Mortain reliquary has finials and a central cross but these are later additions: see Leslie Webster and Janet Backhouse, *The Making of England: Anglo-Saxon Art and Culture AD 600–90* (London, 1991), pp. 175–76.

[25] M. Dolley, 'Appendix II: The Numismatic Evidence', in H. M. Taylor, 'The Origin, Purpose, and Date of Pilaster Strips in Anglo-Saxon Architecture', *North Staffordshire Journal of Field Studies*, 10 (1970), 21–47 (pp. 42–43 and fig. 9). Note also the depiction of a mausoleum

The priest is carrying a pair of bells or buckets. Bishop Forrest Browne favoured the bucket interpretation;[26] in his support we could cite the numerous buckets carried by the diminutive figures on the ninth-century *Drogo Sacramentary* ivory cover, to argue that this type of object was used liturgically and could thus be an appropriate attribute of a priest.[27] As supplementary evidence we could call on the eighth-century bronze bucket from Hexham, to demonstrate that these containers were perfectly familiar in Northumbrian contexts.[28] Close examination of the carving, together with the evidence supplied by the photographs produced for Henry Taylor in the late nineteenth century (which were taken in very favourable light) convince me, however, that both of these objects are actually hand-bells.[29] These are of course a familiar survival, often in reliquary form, from the Celtic world. The majority of examples come from Ireland where they were central to the ecclesiastical tradition. In his definitive study, Cormac Bourke was able to distinguish two types.[30] The form represented here at Winwick, which tapers from mouth to crown and has its handle fixed part-way in along the top, has all the characteristics of his Class 2, whose distribution is markedly to the north and east of Ireland. Whilst we can assume that the Anglo-Saxon church was familiar with such objects — acolytes carrying a pair of bells are shown accompanying the funeral of Edward the Confessor on the Bayeux Tapestry[31] — it is

---

at Heysham, Lancs, with three crosses topping its roof: Jane Hawkes, 'Sacraments in Stone: The Mystery of Christ in Anglo-Saxon Sculpture', in *The Cross Goes North*, ed. by Martin Carver (York, 2003), pp. 351–70 (pl. 22.2).

[26] Browne, 'Pre-Norman Sculptured Stones', p. 17.

[27] J. Hubert, J. Porcher, and W. F. Volbach, *Carolingian Art* (London, 1970), pls 214–15.

[28] Richard N. Bailey, 'The Anglo-Saxon Metalwork from Hexham', in *Saint Wilfrid at Hexham*, ed. by D. P. Kirby (Newcastle upon Tyne, 1974), pp. 141–67 (pp. 141–50). See also the bucket from Skei Norway: Henderson and Henderson, *Art of the Picts*, pl. 176. Liturgical buckets are mentioned in lists of church possessions: Caecilia Davis-Weyer, *Early Medieval Art 300–1150: Sources and Documents* (Englewood Cliffs, 1971), pp. 95–96; A. J. Robertson, *Anglo-Saxon Charters* (Cambridge, 1939), p. 72; *Liber Eliensis*, ed. by E. O. Blake (London, 1962), p. 194.

[29] Taylor, *Ancient Crosses and Holy Wells*, pls between pp. 204 and 205.

[30] Cormac Bourke, 'Early Irish Hand Bells', *Journal of the Royal Society of Antiquaries of Ireland*, 110 (1980), 52–66. See also Cormac Bourke, 'The Hand Bells of the Early Scottish Church', *Proceedings of the Society of Antiquaries of Scotland*, 113 (1983), 464–68, and Cormac Bourke, 'Insignia Columbae II', in *Studies in the Cult of Saint Columba*, ed. by Cormac Bourke (Dublin, 1997), pp. 162–83.

[31] D. M. Wilson, *The Bayeux Tapestry* (London, 1985), pl. 29.

nevertheless significant that, in terms both of survival of and documentary emphasis on this type of object, the Winwick bells are once more leading us towards Celtic areas.

This comment becomes even more significant when we assemble the evidence for representations of figures with bells elsewhere in Insular sculpture before *c.* 1200. There are only five such examples; on all, the figure also carries a crosier, and they all come from Ireland. To these can be added the priest depicted on the Shrine of the Stowe Missal.[32] It is clear that, on these Irish examples, the bell is being used as an ecclesiastical marker; this must also be at least part of the function here at Winwick.

The presence of *two* bells is slightly unexpected since these objects are usually made, conferred, bequeathed, and indeed rung singly. But the Bayeux Tapestry suggests that such pairing might have funeral associations. More significantly perhaps, Cormac Bourke has drawn my attention to a passage in the *Life of Maedhog* in which the saint leaves two bells to Drumlane church to be used for excommunication.[33] The Winwick bells are thus not only symbols of a priest, but probably also indicative of his authority.

The other elements set around the priest are equally symbolic of sanctity and power. The two crosses clearly fulfil this function but so also do the triquetra at the base of the panel. This form of ornament is, of course, frequently employed in Insular ornament, often in the arms of crosses or to fill triangular spaces. In such contexts it is difficult to know how far to invest the motif with symbolic meaning. Despite this it has often been claimed that the triquetra is a Trinitarian symbol.[34] Sadly, there are no accompanying inscriptions in early medieval art which would help confirm this identity, such as occur with the triangles and interlinked circles of a later medieval period.[35] It is therefore helpful to draw on evidence which is well

---

[32] Carndonagh, Old Kilcullen, White Island, Killadeas, Glendalough, Shrine of Stowe Missal: Harbison, *High Crosses*, fig. 87; Françoise Henry, *Irish Art in the Early Christian Period to A.D. 800* (London, 1965), pl. 73; Henry, *Irish Art During the Viking Invasions, 800–1020 A.D.* (London, 1967), pls 9, 14; Henry, *Irish Art in the Romanesque Period 1020–1170 A.D.* (London, 1970), p. 183, pl. 30.

[33] *Bethada Náem nÉrenn: Lives of Irish Saints*, ed. and trans. by Charles Plummer, 2 vols (Oxford, 1922), I, 270; II, 262.

[34] Martin Blindheim, *Graffitti in Norwegian Stave Churches c. 1150–1350* (Oslo, 1985), p. 52; Hallvard Trætteberg, 'Triquetra', in *Kulturhistoriskt leksikon for nordisk middelalder fra vikingetid til reformationstid* (Copenhagen, 1956–78), XVIII, cols 634–36.

[35] E. M. Magerøy, 'En komplett treenighet fra Island', *ICO: den Iconographiske Post*, 2–3 (1975), 25–35.

distanced from the Insular art world: the sculpture of eighth- and ninth-century Italy. Here triquetra frequently occur on ciboria and on closure and altar slabs where they are associated with crosses, grape clusters, and other symbols of the Church and the Eucharist.[36] On these carvings it is difficult to resist the conclusion that they are charged with Christian symbolism. Similarly in Britain we find triquetra, at a variety of dates, placed in highlighted positions on sculptures: alongside a cross on the slab from Killaghtee (Donegal), above clerics at St Vigeans (Forfarshire), on top of a disc-headed cross from Iona, above the cross at St Madoes (Perthshire), surrounded by a series of symbols at Meigle (Perthshire), accompanying an angel at Slaidburn (Yorkshire), and on the end of a hogback from Plumbland (Cumbria).[37] Given such emphasis, they must here also be invested with symbolic significance. Admittedly, St Augustine may only have lent his written authority to the use of the triangle as an appropriate symbol for the Trinity, but his continual recourse to the value of the numeral three in his struggles to explain the essential unity of the threefold godhead do offer further support to the argument that the triquetra provides a very appropriate symbolic expression of the Trinity.[38]

In summary then, this panel is a visual statement of the power and authority of the priest and the Church, based upon the Trinity and the cross, using a symbolism which would be readily understood in late Anglo-Saxon England even though its representation owes much to Irish antecedents.

The Panel on Face B (Fig. 35)

It is with the scene on this second panel that major interpretative challenges arise — and which now involves me in a confession of error. When I published this

[36] Mario Rotilo, *CSA, 5: La Diocesi di Benvento* (1966), no. 42; Pani Ermini, *CSA, 7 (1): La Diocesi di Roma, La IV Regione Ecclesiastica* (1974), no. 32; Trinci Cecchelli, *CSA, 7 (4): La Diocesi di Roma, La I Regione Ecclesiastica* (1974), no. 232; Melucco Vaccaro and L. Paroli, eds, *CSA, 7 (7): La Diocesi di Roma, Museo dell'Alto Medioevo* (1995), no. 30; Joselita Serra, *CSA, 8: La Diocesi dell' Alto Lazio* (1974), nos 173, 183, 274, 350; Anna Maria Ramieri, *CSA, 11: La Diocesi di Ferentino* (1983), nos 12, 14, 44. Gioia Bertelli, *CSA, 15: La Diocesi della Puglia Centr–Settentrionale* (2002), no. 310; Donatella Scortecci, *CSA, 16: La Diocesi di Orvieto, Spoleto* (2003), no. 84.

[37] Killaghtee slab: Henry, *Irish Art to A.D. 800*, pl. IV. St Vigeans: Henderson and Henderson, *Art of the Picts*, pl. 220. Meigle and St Madoes: Allen and Anderson, *Early Christian Monuments*, figs 310 and 342. Iona: Fisher, *Early Medieval Sculpture*, fig. 17. Slaidburn: Bailey, *Viking-Age Sculpture*, fig. 68. Plumbland: Bailey and Cramp, *CASSS*, II, ill. 535.

[38] For St Augustine's comments on the symbolism of the triangle, see *PL*, 33, 455.

Figure 35. The Winwick cross-head, Face B. Photo: Ross Trench-Jellicoe.

panel in 1980 I boldly identified it as the death of Isaiah, sawn in half at the hands of Manesse.[39] I did this on the basis of illustrations in a paper by Richard Bernheimer which assembled several examples of the iconography of this episode.[40] At the time I was unaware of the fact that Romilly Allen had eventually reached an identical conclusion about the meaning of the panel.[41]

Though the Isaiah story emerges from non-canonical sources it was clearly known to the early Christian world where it was used as the explanation for one of the fates suffered by the faithful in the past as listed in Hebrews 11. 37: 'they were stoned, they were sawn asunder, were tempted, were slain with the sword'.[42] Isaiah's distinctive form of execution was invoked by, among others, Augustine, Ambrose, and Jerome in works which were circulating and being exploited in both Anglo-Saxon England and contemporary Ireland.[43] Bede's commentaries on Mark and Luke reproduce a passage from St Augustine referring to this episode, and borrowings elsewhere in his writings show that he was familiar with other texts which record the story.[44] The same patristic texts are quoted by other writers, like Aldhelm and Ælfric, even if they do not directly refer to the execution, whilst Helmut Gneuss's invaluable listing of surviving manuscripts further confirms that these and other sources of the narrative were well known in Anglo-Saxon England.[45]

---

[39] Bailey, *Viking-Age Sculpture*, pp. 159–61; Bailey, *England's Earliest Sculptors*, pp. 80–81; Bailey, 'What Mean these Stones?', pp. 221–22.

[40] Richard Bernheimer, 'The Martyrdom of Isaiah', *Art B.*, 34 (1952), 19–34.

[41] Allen, 'Pre-Norman Cross-head', pp. 134–35.

[42] *Ascensio Isaiae: Textus*, ed. by P. Bettiola, *CCSA*, 7 (1995). A translation with introduction is that by M. A. Knibb, 'Martyrdom and Ascension of Isaiah', in *The Old Testament Pseudoepigraphia*, ed. by J. H. Charlesworth, 2 vols (New York, 1985), I, 143–64.

[43] Augustine, *De consensu evangelistarum*, ed. by Franciscus Weihrich, CSEL, 43 (Vienna, 1904), p. 340. Ambrose, *Expositio evangelii secundum Lucam*, ed. by M. Adriaen, CCSL, 14 (Turnhout, 1957), pp. 340, 380. Jerome, *In Esaiam*, ed. by M. Adriaen, CCSL, 73A (Turnhout, 1963), pp. 640–41. Jerome, *Opera exegetica*, ed. by D. Hurst and M. Adriaen, CCSL, 77 (Turnhout, 1969), p. 247.

[44] Bede quotes Augustine's *De Consensu* in his commentaries on Mark and Luke: Bede, *In Lucae evengelium expositio* opera, ed. by David Hurst, CCSL, 120 (Turnhout, 1983), pp. 405, 633. His familiarity with the Ambrose and Jerome texts listed in note 43 is well evidenced: see the indices of his works in CCSL, 118–23 (Turnhout, 1955–2001). Surviving texts from Anglo-Saxon England of his commentaries on Mark and Luke are listed in Helmut Gneuss, *Handlist of Anglo-Saxon Manuscripts: A List of Manuscripts and Manuscript Fragments Written or Owned in England up to 1100* (Tempe, 2001), p. 156.

[45] For surviving manuscripts written or used in England containing the texts listed in note 43, see Gneuss, *Handlist*, pp. 152 (Ambrose), 154, 155 (Augustine), 169 (Jerome). For familiarity

Knowledge of the episode would be further reinforced by familiarity with *De ortu et obitu patrum*, attributed to Isidore, and its (Insular) pseudo-Isidore version whose texts have survived in some numbers from Anglo-Saxon England; use of these sources is again well evidenced in Anglo-Saxon works.[46] I was thus fairly convinced of the validity of this identification even though the particular form of inverted dismemberment was not otherwise documented before the fourteenth century; there was, after all, a good deal of variety attested by pre-tenth-century examples in Western Europe.[47] This view was further reinforced when Richard Hall published two small bow saws from York and Dublin which showed that the form of tool seemingly shown in the carving was known in tenth-century Britain.[48]

Despite all this assemblage of textual support I must now withdraw this proposal. For it was based upon a false premise: the accuracy of Allen's drawing of the scene (Fig. 36).[49] This shows the outer figures each grasping the leg of the inverted man whilst their other hands hold a thin curving linear object which passes into, or behind, the lower body of the central figure. Allen showed the return of this curved element as a straight line below, thus suggesting the blade of a bow-saw. Given that Allen's drawing had been produced in the late nineteenth century when the

with these texts elsewhere in Anglo-Saxon England, see J. D. A. Ogilvy, *Books Known to the English 597–1066* (Cambridge, MA, 1967); *Sources of Anglo-Saxon Literary Culture: A Trial Version*, ed. by F. M. Biggs, T. D. Hill, and Paul E. Szarmach (Binghamton, 1990).

[46] *PL*, 83, 129–59 (col. 142); *Liber de ortu et obitu patriarcharum*, ed. by J. Carracedo Fraga, CCSL, 108E (Turnhout, 1996), p. 19. For surviving manuscripts from Anglo-Saxon England, see Gneuss, *Handlist*, p. 263. For use of these texts by Bede, Aldhelm, and the Old English Martyrologist, see CCSL, 121 (Turnhout, 1983), pp. 10, 107; *Aldhelm: The Prose Works*, trans. by Michael Lapidge and Michael Herren (Cambridge, 1979), p. 176; James E. Cross, 'On the Library of the Old English Martyrologist', in *Learning and Literature in Anglo-Saxon England: Studies Presented to Peter Clemoes on the Occasion of his Sixty-fifth Birthday*, ed. by Michael Lapidge and Helmut Gneuss (Cambridge, 1985), pp. 227–49 (p. 243).

[47] Pre-1200 representations in Western Europe have Isaiah set in a variety of positions: upright, lying on table, kneeling, bound to a column. The scene is very popular in English psalters after the Conquest: see C. M. Kauffmann, *Romanesque Manuscripts, 1066–1190*, Survey of Manuscripts Illuminated in the British Isles, 3 (London, 1975), nos 70, 103; Nigel J. Morgan, *Early Gothic Manuscripts*, Survey of Manuscripts Illuminated in the British Isles, 4.1 (London, 1982), nos 24, 32, 63, and 75.

[48] Richard Hall, 'Bow Saw', in *Craft, Industry and Everyday Life: Bone, Antler, Ivory and Horn from Anglo-Scandinavian and Medieval York*, ed. by A. MacGregor, A. J. Mainman, and N. S. H. Rogers (York, 1999), pp. 1945–48 (p. 1948).

[49] Allen, 'Description of Winwick Cross'; and also his *Early Christian Symbolism in Great Britain and Ireland* (London, 1887), p. 329.

Figure 36. The Winwick cross-head, Face B. After J. Romilly Allen, *Early Christian Symbolism in Great Britain and Ireland* (London, 1887), p. 329.

panel was more readily accessible, I accepted his interpretation of the forms. But I was wrong so to do. Had I paid more attention to the rubbing produced at about the same date by Forrest Browne, I would have seen that, whilst he also recorded a saw-like form, he had clearly signalled that the 'blade' was a restoration on the basis of the protrusions from the lower bodies of the flanking figures.[50] Interestingly, Allen's own rubbing of the panel in London, British Library, Additional MS 37551 (85) shows that he also initially saw these protrusions as having no link between them or any connection to the curving linear feature(s). The late nineteenth-century drawing now kept in Winwick church more accurately shows what can now be discerned on the cross itself — that there never was a blade (Fig. 37).[51] The figures are thus either binding the central victim or poking at him with narrow instruments; the protrusions may represent deformities on the flanking figures or, less likely, be (marginally misplaced) genitalia. In summary, Anglo-Saxon England certainly knew the story of Isaiah's martyrdom, but this is not a representation of it.

What then is portrayed here? A long-standing local tradition recognized in this panel the dismemberment of the Northumbrian King Oswald after the battle of Maserfelth in A.D. 642 — an act which was to scatter a multiplying set of his bodily relics across Britain and Europe.[52] This interpretation depended in part upon the identification of the local place name 'Makerfield' with Bede's *maserfelth* — an identity which is philologically impossible and which has recently been effectively discredited.[53] It also, however, depended upon the church's dedication and the proximity of a St Oswald's well.[54] We cannot be certain about the antiquity of the well, though the saint is regularly associated with water sources.[55] Nor can we be sure about the period in which the church received its present name, though it was clearly

[50] Browne, 'Pre-Norman Sculptured Stones', pl. V.

[51] This drawing is not dated but is clearly late nineteenth century.

[52] Browne, 'Pre-Norman Sculptured Stones', pp. 16–17, is the first to identify Oswald scenes on the cross though earlier writers had seen the cross as associated with the saint: Beamont, *Winwick*, pp. 8, 61. For the dismemberment and the cult, see the essays in *Oswald*, ed. by Stancliffe and Cambridge, and Peter Clemoes, 'The Cult of St Oswald on the Continent', in *Bede and his World: The Jarrow Lectures 1958–1978*, ed. by Michael Lapidge (Aldershot, 1994), pp. 589–610.

[53] Clare Stancliffe, 'Where Was Oswald Killed?', in *Oswald*, ed. by Stancliffe and Cambridge, pp. 84–96.

[54] Taylor, *Ancient Crosses and Holy Wells*, pp. 210–11.

[55] For the association of the Oswald cult with wells, see the index in *Oswald*, ed. by Stancliffe and Cambridge, p. 291, and Blair, *Church in Anglo-Saxon Society*, pp. 226, 475–77.

Figure 37. The Winwick cross-head, Face B. After drawing in St Oswald's church. Reproduced by permission of the rector and churchwardens.

dedicated to St Oswald by the date of the Domesday Book compilation.[56] Despite these uncertainties a depiction of Oswald's dismemberment would still remain a possibility.[57] But that explanation can be firmly rejected on two grounds: first, there is no saw, and thus no dismemberment; secondly, the nakedness of all the participants would pose major problems for any identification with an Oswald depiction.

With Isaiah and Oswald thus removed from the scene, we can perhaps take a more positive approach to interpretation, and narrow down the possibilities, by drawing on the evidence of analogous figural compositions on other Insular sculptures. Significantly, in the light of what has gone before, these come from Ireland and Scotland. One is from St Vigeans (Forfarshire) whilst the other six are from Ireland: Arboe (Co. Tyrone), Castledermot (Co. Kildare), Kells (Co. Meath; two scenes), Monasterboice (Co. Louth), and Ullard (Co. Kilkenny).[58] All show figures flanking or alongside a naked and reversed third person, often grasping his legs; they have recently been conveniently listed and illustrated by Peter Harbison whose commentaries and tables summarize the interpretations offered for them.[59] Among these scenes, Arboe offers a very close parallel to Winwick in the manner in which the naked victim's arms curve downwards around his head whilst Ullard provides an analogy for the seemingly distorted — almost animal-like — faces of the flanking figures. In Ireland and Scotland the scenes are interpreted, with varying degrees of confidence, as the Judgement of Solomon, the Massacre of the Innocents, the Fall of Simon Magus, and Saints Paul and Anthony overcoming the Devil.[60] Whilst offering parallels for the basic composition of the Winwick scene, however, they do not offer any real clue as to its meaning. We can probably reject the possibility that it shows the Judgement of Solomon; the early ninth-century Stuttgart Psalter (Stuttgart Württembergische Landesbibliothek, biblia fol. 23, fol. 83ᵛ) admittedly shows that the threatened child can be of adult pro-

---

[56] For the date of this dedication, see note 4 above.

[57] St George, in Byzantine art, was occasionally portrayed in the sawn position of Isaiah; see Leslie Ross, *Text, Image and Message: Saints in Medieval Manuscript Illustrations* (Westport, 1994), p. 152. Had the Winwick figure been shown as sawn, then a similar transfer of iconographies might have been envisaged.

[58] St Vigeans: Henderson and Henderson, *Art of Picts*, pl. 221 (Ross Trench-Jellicoe is preparing a study of this sculpture). For Arboe, Castledermot, Kells, Monasterboice, and Ullard, see Harbison, *High Crosses*, II, fig. 642; III, figs 978, 749, 751, 955, and 956.

[59] Harbison, *High Crosses*, I, 222–23, 246–47, 306–07, and tables 1–4.

[60] The iconography of the Massacre and Judgement scenes can be very similar: see L. Brubaker, *Vision and Meaning in Ninth-Century Byzantium* (Cambridge, 1999), figs 18 and 25. Harbison, *High Crosses*, I, 289 and 307, rejects earlier claims for Simon Magus on Irish sculptures.

portions in such scenes but the Irish evidence confirms that the flanking figures would be expected to be both clothed and probably holding swords.[61] Similarly, clothed and (usually) armed figures would be expected for the Massacre.[62] Saints Paul and Anthony, if correctly identified in Ireland, are also shown both clothed and equipped with pastoral crosiers and thus again are unlikely to figure at Winwick.[63] As for the failed flight of Simon Magus, there is no doubt that the story was well known in Anglo-Saxon England.[64] But once more it is difficult to account for the nakedness of all the participants if this were the subject of the Winwick panel.

There are thus sculptural analogies from the Celtic world for the basic composition of two figures flanking a third who is shown reversed. And these carvings show, by their context, that this figural scheme was capable of a variety of realizations and meanings. But none of them has the distinctive characteristics of the Winwick scene, in which all of the participants are naked and — a crucial difference — the central figure appears to be suspended by one of his feet.

The combination of a suspended naked victim, flanked by repulsive and equally naked figures who appear to be binding or prodding the man between them, does however fit with both depictions and literary descriptions of a soul in hell which survive to us from the late Anglo-Saxon period. This, I suggest, is the meaning of the Winwick scene; its iconography draws upon a complex of interrelated 'attack and suffering' scenes, which are exemplified on early medieval sculpture from Ireland and Scotland, but invests the type with a new meaning.

The early medieval conception of hell depended upon a series of sources. Among these, the most significant within the Insular world was the *Visio Sancti Pauli*, a text which existed in a variety of forms and whose shorter redactions show significant connections with England and Ireland in their manuscript tradition.[65]

---

[61] Stuttgart Psalter: Harbison, *High Crosses*, III, fig. 752. Harbison identifies the Judgement of Solomon at Castledermot and Kells. A scene on a sculpture at Bakewell (Derbys.) with reversed and flanking figures may represent the Massacre; here one of the flanking clothed figures holds a sword: G. Forrest Browne, 'On the Pre-Norman Sculptured Stones of Derbyshire', *Journal of the Derbyshire Antiquarian and Natural History Society*, 8 (1886), 164–86.

[62] Harbison, *High Crosses*, I, 246–47.

[63] Harbison, *High Crosses*, I, 306–07.

[64] *Sources: Trial Version*, ed. by Biggs, Hill, and Szarmach, pp. 59–60.

[65] *Visio Sancti Pauli: The History of the Apocalypse in Latin together with Nine Texts*, ed. by T. Silverstein (London, 1935). For the Insular interest, see Charles D. Wright, 'The Insular Vision of Hell', in Wright, *The Irish Tradition in Old English Literature* (Cambridge, 1993), pp. 106–74. For Anglo-Saxon familiarity with *Visio* texts, see the summaries in *Visio*, ed. by Silverstein, p. 6; Antonette diPaolo Healey, *The Old English Vision of St Paul* (Cambridge, MA, 1978), pp. 41–57; and *Sources: Trial Version*, ed. by Biggs, Hill, and Szarmach, pp. 66–67.

In these texts, and in the Insular Latin and vernacular literature dependent on them — as well as in Anglo-Saxon art — all of Winwick's elements are present. The vulnerable nakedness of the soul is stressed in the *Visio Pauli* and *Christ and Satan*;[66] it is depicted on the early ninth-century Rothbury Cross and is frequently shown in late Saxon manuscripts and ivories.[67] Commonplace also in art is the fact that the devils are both wingless and naked, and several commentators have noted that there is a strong English tradition of portraying them as hideously threatening, with distorted features and with genitalia on display.[68] The souls are both bound and tortured in *Christ III* and are depicted as such in manuscripts — the devils using a variety of long thin objects (spears, flails, forks, and hooked instruments) which may be what is being held by the flanking figures at Winwick.[69] The reversed suspension of the souls is a theme which is present both in redactions of the *Visio Pauli* and in other apocryphal Latin texts.[70] One version

[66] *Visio*, ed. by Silverstein, p. 28 and throughout; *Christ and Satan: A Critical Edition*, ed. by Robert Emmett Finnegan (Waterloo, Ont., 1977), line 134.

[67] Rothbury: Cramp, *CASSS*, I, ill. 1224. Late Saxon manuscripts: Louis Jordan, 'Demonic Elements in Anglo-Saxon Iconography', *Sources of Anglo-Saxon Culture*, ed. by Paul E. Szarmach, Studies in Medieval Culture, 20 (Kalamazoo, 1986), pp. 282–317 (figs 17 and 21); W. Noel, *The Harley Psalter* (Cambridge, 1995), pl. 57; *The Utrecht Psalter in Medieval Art: Picturing the Psalms of David*, ed. by Koert van der Horst, William Noel, and Wilhelmina C. Wüstefeld (Utrecht, 1996), fig. 30a; John Beckwith, *Ivory Carvings in Early Medieval England, 700–1200* (London, 1974), pl. 23. Naked sinners figure on the Monasterboice cross: Harbison, *High Crosses*, III, fig. 940.

[68] For wingless devils, see Elżbieta Temple, *Anglo-Saxon Manuscripts 900–1066*, Survey of Manuscripts Illuminated in the British Isles, 2 (London, 1976), pls 200, 265; Noel, *Harley Psalter*, pls 44, 57. A naked wingless devil is depicted on the Monasterboice cross: Harbison, *High Crosses*, III, fig. 940. On the repulsiveness of devils in English art, see Jordan, 'Demonic Elements', pp. 303–06; Dimitri Tselos, 'English Manuscript Illumination and the Utrecht Psalter', *Art B.*, 41 (1959), 137–49 (p. 139). Genitalia can be seen on wingless devils in the Harley Psalter: see *The Utrecht Psalter*, ed. by van der Horst, Noel, and Wüstefeld, fig. 7 on p. 127, and note the comments there of William Noel on p. 126: 'Anglo-Saxon artists had a fascination with demonology and the Harley artist chose to emphasize their demonic nature, depriving them of their wings and making their genitalia more conspicuous.'

[69] *The Christ of Cynewulf*, ed. by Albert S. Cook (Boston, 1900), lines 1620–23. Devils with various instruments of torture (slender spears, flails, hooks) are depicted in the Caedmon manuscript and in the Harley copies of the Utrecht Psalter: see Jordan, 'Demonic Elements', pls 12 and 14. See also the instruments in the Utrecht Psalter and the Eadwine Psalter, C. R. Dodwell, *The Pictorial Arts of the West 800–1200* (New Haven, 1993), pls 50, 342.

[70] *Visio*, ed. by Silverstein, pp. 31, 42. For a general survey of hanging, including hanging by feet, in hell, see M. Himmelfarb, *Tours of Hell: An Apocalyptic Form in Jewish and Christian Literature* (Philadelphia, 1983), pp. 84–92.

of it, in which they are suspended from trees, was much exploited in Anglo-Saxon and Irish vernacular literature, and is a theme which has been fully explored by Charles Wright.[71] But a treeless and reversed suspension is also found, among the catalogues of suffering, in other pre-Conquest texts dependent on the *Visio Pauli*. It occurs, for example, in the Carolingian-period Latin homiliary preserved in Cambridge, Pembroke College, MS 125, an eleventh-century manuscript from Bury St Edmunds.[72] Here the *Omelia in Ascensione Domini* includes a list of hell's tortures beginning 'Et iterum: Viderunt animas peccatorum in poenis miserabiliter a daemonibus alligatas [...] Alii enim pendunt ibi ex pedibus, alii ex manibus' ('And afterwards they saw the souls of sinful men in torment miserably bound by devils [...] some hung there by the feet and others by the hands').[73] The same sequence is repeated in an anonymous Old English homily, dependent on a Pembroke-type antecedent, but here the reversed suspension is given the validation of *halige gewritu*: 'And eft hi gesawon synfulra manna sawla on witum earmlice fram deoflum gewriðene [...] Sume þær hangiað be þæm fotum, þæs þe halige gewritu onwrigen habbað, and sume þær hangiað be þam handum' ('And afterwards they saw the souls of sinful men in torment miserably bound by devils [...] some hung there by the feet, as holy writings have revealed to us, and some hung there by the hands').[74] If, moreover, one or both of the hands of the victim are represented at Winwick as being amputated then this is yet another of the punishments awaiting the damned in hell.[75]

I know of no other depiction of suspended souls in Insular pre-Norman art, though the theme is one which does appear in two early twelfth-century psalters.[76] In those later works, however, there are numerous souls who are suffering in this way. Here at Winwick the stress is on the drama of individual damnation just as it is on the *c.* 1070 Gunhild Cross where two devils flank a naked, but upright, soul.[77]

---

[71] *Visio*, 42, ed. by Silverstein, pp. 69–72. Wright, 'Insular Vision', pp. 113–21.

[72] *Cambridge Pembroke College MS 25*, ed. by James E. Cross (London, 1987).

[73] *Pembroke MS 25*, ed. by Cross, p. 192 (my translation).

[74] *Pembroke MS 25*, ed. by Cross, p. 193 (my translation).

[75] See *Visio*, ed. by Silverstein, p. 28, and S. Semple, 'Illustrations of Damnation in Late Anglo-Saxon Manuscripts', *Anglo-Saxon England*, 32 (2003), 231–45.

[76] Munich, Bayerische Staatsbibliothek, Clm 835 and Cambridge, Trinity College, MS B. 11. 4; see Morgan, *Survey of Manuscripts*, nos 23 and 51.

[77] Beckwith, *Ivory Carvings*, pp. 44–47. A similar focussing on an individual soul can be found in the Harley Psalter: see Semple, 'Illustrations', pl. VIII.

If all this can be accepted, then we must consider the relationship between the two figural panels, whilst recognizing that we now only have a very small part of the total original carving. I suggest that the link is relatively straightforward. On one end is the power of the priesthood and Church, founded on the Trinity, which can save the sinner through the sacraments of baptism, Eucharist, and confession; on the other an admonitory example of what failure to turn to that salvation will involve.[78] As a commentary on these scenes I turn to Archbishop Wulfstan and the *Institutes of Polity*:

> Mycel is and mære, þæt sacerd ah to donne folce to þearfe, gif he his drihtne gecwemð mid rihte. Mycel is seo halsung and mære seo halgung, þe deofla afyrsað and on fleame gebringað, swa oft swa man fullað oþðon husel halgað [...] [but, if a priest has tried and fails to persuade the sinner] se þe woh drifð and geswican nele, he sceal habban þæs éce wite, þæt is, þæt hi þonne sceolan to helle faran mid sawle and mid lichoman and mit deofle wunian on hellewitum.[79]

> [What a priest has to do for the benefit of the people is great and wonderful, if he wish to propitiate his Lord aright. Great is the exorcism and wonderful the consecration which drives away devils and puts them to flight as often as baptism is performed or Eucharist consecrated [...] he who pursues evil and will not desist, he must endure eternal torment that is, they must then go to hell with soul and with body and dwell with the devil in hell torments.][80]

The Winwick Cross has always been an impressive piece of sculpture. It can now be seen in its tenth-century context, strongly influenced in its shape, abstract ornament, and iconographical organization by the Celtic west but expressing a Christian message which was well understood in Anglo-Saxon England. Given Éamonn Ó Carragáin's published interests in the orientation of crosses we might add one more speculation. The broad sides of most pre-Norman crosses were set to face east or west. The narrow sides would thus face north and south. Winwick's scene of hell would most appropriately look to the north, for it was in the north-west quarter that the Anglo-Saxons, thoughtfully reading Isaiah 14. 12–14 and patristic commentaries, knew it to be located.[81]

---

[78] Elements of this contrast may be paralleled on a cross-head from Crofton (Yorkshire) where a cross-carrying bishop is set off against a reversed ?devil; see W. G. Collingwood, 'Anglian and Anglo-Danish Sculpture in the West Riding', *Yorkshire Archaeological Journal*, 23 (1915), 129–229 (p. 161).

[79] *Die 'Institutes of Polity, Civil and Ecclesiastical': Ein Werk Erzbishof Wulfstans von York*, ed. by Karl Jost, Swiss Studies in English, 47 (Berne, 1959), pp. 104, 107–08.

[80] *Anglo-Saxon Prose*, trans. by Michael Swanton (Letchworth, 1978), pp. 132–33.

[81] T. D. Hill, 'Some Remarks on "The Site of Lucifer's Throne"', *Anglia*, 87 (1969), 303–11.

THE REPRESENTATION OF THE APOSTLES IN INSULAR ART, WITH SPECIAL REFERENCE TO THE NEW APOSTLES FRIEZE AT TARBAT, ROSS-SHIRE

George Henderson

The Western Church has traditionally celebrated 15 July as the feast of the division or dispersal of the apostles, when having cast lots among themselves, they set off in various different directions[1] to fulfil Christ's command, reported in Matthew 28, 'Going therefore teach ye all nations'. In the Acts of the Apostles 1, the world-wide mission of the apostles is again emphasized, *usque ad ultimum terrae*, with the eventual consequence of the conversion of the inhabitants of the British Isles to Christianity, and the depiction of the apostles by Insular artists — the subject of the brief survey attempted here.

The word 'apostle', meaning one who is sent, a messenger, of course implies this mission, this news-bearing function. Luke 6 tells how Jesus chose twelve out of the number of his disciples and called them apostles. The list of the twelve apostles varies slightly in other Gospels, but there are twelve when they are first ordained and commissioned by Christ on a mountain in Judea. With Judas Iscariot out of the picture, eleven apostles only are left when Christ repeats his commission on a mountain in Galilee, from which he then ascends into heaven. The number of apostles is made up again to twelve, as recorded in Acts 1. 26 by the selection of Matthias, 'And he was numbered with the eleven apostles'. Acts 9 reports the conversion of Saul of Tarsus into St Paul and his introduction to the apostles, and so important does he become in the Christian Church that he comes

---

[1] *Eusebius, the Ecclesiastical History and the Martyrs of Palestine*, 3.1, ed. by Hugh J. Lawlor and J. E. L. Oulton, 2 vols (London, 1927), I, 65; Socrates, *History of the Church in Seven Books*, 1.19 (London, 1853), p. 51.

to share the leadership of the apostles with St Peter, with the same feast day, 29 June, and is represented in art as one of the twelve, for example in the now destroyed fifth-century mosaic in the Church of St Agata in Suburra in Rome[2] where he ousted St Matthias from the company of twelve.

As soon as Christian art officially began, in the reign of Constantine I, images of Christ's twelve apostles were made. Appropriately, since in the Canon of the Mass it is the apostles' names that stand first in the list of those with whom Christians are in communion, figures of the apostles were placed on a silver screen colonnade, or on a ciborium, behind or over the altar of the Basilica dedicated to the Holy Saviour at the Lateran,[3] sitting six and six on either side of an enthroned Christ. This sitting imagery is derived from gospel texts. In Matthew 19, Christ says to the apostles, 'when the Son of Man shall sit on the seat of his majesty, you also shall sit on twelve seats judging the twelve tribes of Israel'. In the early fifth-century apse mosaic in the Church of S. Pudenziana in Rome[4] the apostles are seen grouped in a curve, originally six and six, at either side of Christ, against a city-scape of the Heavenly Jerusalem. As at St Agata, the apostles' heads are not nimbed. In a fifth-/sixth-century ivory panel in Dijon,[5] Christ, represented as

---

[2] John Osborne and Amanda Claridge, *Early Christian and Medieval Antiquities*, vol. II: *Other Mosaics, Paintings, Sarcophagi and Small Objects*, Paper Museum of Cassiano dal Pozzo, series A, part 2 (London, 1998), pp. 49–53, figs 163–66. Here Christ, who alone is nimbed, holds an open book, while six out of the twelve apostles hold scrolls. All the figures are identified by inscriptions.

[3] Caecilia Davis-Weyer, *Early Medieval Art 300–1150: Sources and Documents*, Medieval Academy Reprints for Teaching, 17 (Toronto, 1986), p. 11; Richard Krautheimer, *Rome: Profile of a City, 312–1308* (Princeton, 1980), p. 22.

[4] Osborne and Claridge, *Early Christian and Medieval Antiquities*, II, 74–75, fig. 176; Ernst Kitzinger, *Byzantine Art in the Making, Main Lines of Stylistic Development in Mediterranean Art 3rd–7th Century* (London, 1977), pp. 41–43.

[5] Wolfgang Fritz Volbach, *Die Elfenbeinarbeiten der Spätantike und des frühen Mittelalters* (Mainz, 1952), no. 148, pl. 49, p. 73. The sixth-century Antioch Chalice in the Metropolitan Museum, New York, provides another example of the apostles, seated, in company with Christ. Ten apostles sit like philosophers in high-backed chairs, in a setting of vine branches, holding scrolls in their left hands and stretching out their right hands in acclamation of two principal, presiding, figures, one on either side of the cup, one bearded with a lamb at his right hand and an eagle with spread wings at his feet, the other beardless, making an expository gesture with his right hand and holding a scroll in his left. In the exhibition catalogue *Age of Spirituality: Late Antique and Early Christian Art, Third to Seventh Century*, ed. by Kurt Weitzmann (New York, 1979), no. 542, p. 606, both these figures are identified as Christ, the bearded version being the resurrected Lord, ruler of heaven. The lamb is seen to refer to the Apocalpyse, but surely it cannot, as suggested, imply the Last Judgement, but rather points to the identity of the bearded figure as the Ancient

much larger than the apostles and again alone having a nimbus, presides over a council of the apostles seated in a ring. They might be composing the Apostles' Creed or formulating the canon of holy writ, because scrolls of the scriptures are stacked in the basket in the middle of the floor.

The most usual images of Christ and the apostles represent the actual commission — their being sent out to preach. A monumental version of that subject was placed in the 790s in the apse of the grand reception/dining hall, the Aula Leonina, in the Lateran Palace.[6] The composition of the mosaic is recorded by various antiquaries but survives itself only in what is essentially an eighteenth-century copy (Plate 8). Christ stands on the mount, out of which flow four streams, the four rivers of Paradise, symbolizing the four life-giving Gospels. The inscription below the mosaic identifies the scene as the commission in Matthew 28. 19, 'Going therefore teach ye all nations', and quite accurately only eleven apostles are shown, since when Christ spoke to his disciples after the Resurrection, Judas had not yet been replaced as an apostle by Matthias.

An elegant Anglo-Saxon version of this same subject is one of a select group of illustrations painted in a fragmentary gospel lectionary, of around 1000, now in the Getty Manuscripts Library, Los Angeles. Christ, cross-nimbed, sits on the mound, down which the four streams are tumbling. A nice touch of naturalism is the inverted reflection of Christ's right foot in the stream below him, emphasizing the solid reality of his risen body. The apostles stand listening to Christ's words, three on either side, the space on the page being limited.[7] That type of composition, Christ seated, some, if not all, of the apostles in attendance, had become a useful convention or stereotype. It is employed in the early ninth-century Psalter in Stuttgart to illustrate the phrase *in consilio sanctorum* in Psalm 88. 7, 'God who is glorified in the assembly of the saints'.[8] Christ is seated, enthroned, flanked on one side by St Peter who holds the keys as *clavicularius regni caelestis*,

---

of Days, of Revelation 5. The same problem raised by the apparent duplication of figures of Christ is seen in the Anglo-Saxon Easby Cross.

[6] Davis-Weyer, *Early Medieval Art*, pp. 88–92; Krautheimer, *Rome*, pp. 115–16.

[7] MS 9, fol. 2, formerly Damme, Belgium. Elżbieta Temple, *Anglo-Saxon Manuscripts 900–1066* (London, 1976), no. 53, pp. 72–73 and pl. 173. For detail, see George Henderson, 'The Idiosyncrasy of Late Anglo-Saxon Religious Imagery', in *England in the Eleventh Century*, Proceedings of the 1990 Harlaxton Symposium, ed. by Carola Hicks (Stamford, 1992), pp. 239–49, pl. 19.

[8] Stuttgart, Württembergische Landesbibliothek, Biblia fol. 23, fol. 103ᵛ, for which see J. Eschweiler and Florentine Mütherich, *Der Stuttgarter-Bilderpsalter*, vol. I: *Facsimile* (Stuttgart, 1965); vol. II: *Untersuchungen* (Stuttgart, 1966).

and on the other side by Saints Paul and John. At Psalm 18. 3, when the text says there is 'no speech or language where their voices are not heard', the artist of the Stuttgart Psalter interprets these words as the start of the mission of the apostles to the whole world, and represents the twelve engaged in earnest debate, standing in a row, centred on St Peter.[9] The apostles are differentiated by the style and colour of their hair, black, red, or grey. Some are bearded, others clean-shaven. Their mantles and robes also vary in colour (Plate 9). One thing that they have in common is their bare feet. In the High Middle Ages it is a diagnostic feature of the apostles that they are bare-footed, whereas Old Testament Prophets wear shoes.[10] This convention with regard to the apostles originates in the command of Christ recorded in Matthew 10. 10, that for their journey they should not take 'two coats, nor shoes (*calceamenta*), nor a staff'. In early Christian art this particular injunction is ignored, in favour of the version of the instructions in Mark 6. 8–9, 'that they should take nothing for the way, but a staff only [. . .] but to be shod with sandals' (*calceatos sandaliis*). That is how the apostles are consistently represented in the fifth and sixth centuries, for example in the Dijon ivory panel and in the mosaics at Ravenna, such as those on the vault of the Arian Baptistery.[11]

In due course these visual concerns made their impact on the Insular world. Seventh- and eighth-century Irish scholars took a keen interest in the physical appearance of the individual apostles, not only in what they had in common, their sandals that 'never wear out or get soiled', but also in their multicoloured tunics, their varied complexions, and the different styles and colour of their hair, lore compiled in lists and preserved in the eighth-century Irish Reference Bible and elsewhere, and evidently derived from imported descriptions of the conventions of Roman painting[12] — just those later reflected in the Stuttgart Psalter's Psalm

---

[9] The Stuttgart Psalter, fol. 22[v], illustrating the words 'in omnem terram exivit sonus eorum; et in fines orbis terrae verba eorum'.

[10] See for example the two central portals on the transepts of Chartres Cathedral. On the north front of the Prophets, Isaiah, Jeremiah, Elijah, etc. are shod, whereas on the south the twelve apostles have bare feet; Willibald Sauerländer, *Gothic Sculpture in France 1140–1270* (London, 1972), pls 82–83 and pp. 110–11.

[11] Kitzinger, *Byzantine Art in the Making*, fig. 104. However, Origen, the third-century scholar and teacher, took this and other injunctions in St Matthew's Gospel literally; see *A New Eusebius*, ed. by James Stevenson (London, 1968), p. 204.

[12] Dáibhí Ó Cróinín, 'Cummianus Longus and the Iconography of Christ and the Apostles in Early Irish Literature', in *Sages, Saints and Storytellers, Celtic Studies in Honour of Professor James Carney*, ed. by Donnchadh Ó Corráin, Liam Breatnach, and Kim McCone, Maynooth Monographs, 2 (Maynooth, 1989), pp. 268–79.

18 illustration. However, these traditional specifications are not strikingly apparent in the extant Irish representations of the apostles. On the base of the North Cross at Ahenny, Co. Tipperary (Fig. 38) the apostles, if so they be, wear shoes and stand sideways in a row, three facing right, three facing left, converging on a centrally placed figure holding a book.[13] The cowls attached to the mantles of these profile figures and their conspicuous hooked croziers emphasize more their ecclesiastical than their apostolic status. On the base of the west face of the Cross of the Scriptures at Clonmacnois, Co. Offaly, the same composition, weathered but more conventional in the appearance of the figures, seems very likely to represent Christ giving his commission to six of his apostles.[14] Unproblematic, too, are the twelve figures on the east face of the West Shaft at Old Kilcullen, Co. Kildare. They stand framed, in three blocks of four, upright, frontal, shoulder to shoulder, some at least holding books, and all with flat caps of rigid hair crowning solemn bearded faces. The uppermost rank of four are less hieratic than the others and seem to incline inwards, forming two conversing pairs.[15] The comparatively naturalistic length of these figures and the intention to differentiate in some measure among them, are not factors in the representation of the twelve apostles gathered below the Crucifixion scene on the base of the west face of the Moone Cross, Co. Kildare.[16] The highly schematized identical figures, resolutely frontal in three rows of four, depend wholly on there being twelve of them to make their identity plain (Fig. 39).

Four groups of three frontal figures, closely wrapped in mantles, surround the Crucifixion on the cross-head of the North Cross at Castledermot, Co. Kildare. The similar figures, in pairs, up the south side of the South Cross are again recognizable as apostles not from any individual trait or attribute but numerically and because they stand, appropriately, above the scene of Christ's miraculous multiplication of loaves and fishes, with its obvious sacramental significance.[17] In the context of heroic and typologically weighty scenes from the Old Testament, and a few narrative scenes from the New Testament, blocks of frontal figures, not invariably adding up to twelve, reasonably lay claim to being apostles on several other Irish

[13] Peter Harbison, *The High Crosses of Ireland: An Iconographical and Photographic Survey*, 3 vols (Bonn, 1992), I, 12–13, 291–94; II, fig. 16.

[14] Harbison, *High Crosses*, I, 51; II, figs 139, 144.

[15] Harbison, *High Crosses*, I, 60; II, fig. 532.

[16] Harbison, *High Crosses*, I, 155; II, figs 514–15.

[17] Harbison, *High Crosses*, I, 37, II, fig. 101; I, 39, II, fig. 108.

Figure 38. North Cross, Ahenny, Co. Tipperary. Photo by permission
of the Commissioners of Public Works in Ireland.

Figure 39. Apostles, detail of west face of the Moone Cross, Co. Kildare.
© The Department of Arts, Culture & the Gaeltacht, Heritage Services,
St Stephen's Green, Dublin 2, Ireland.

monuments. Where on certain panels only two figures stand flanking a seated figure, as on the east face of the Cross of the Scriptures at Clonmacnois and on the west face of Muiredach's Cross at Monasterboice, Co. Louth, the princes of the apostles, Saints Peter and Paul, can be identified, receiving respectively keys and a book.[18] On Muiredach's Cross both apostles wear heavy moustaches.

Christ's commission to the apostles after the Resurrection is immediately followed by the Ascension. In Irish sculpture the Ascension does not involve the representation of the apostles. The one possible Ascension, at the top of Muiredach's Cross, shows only Christ, frontal, with raised arms, supported on either side by angels.[19] However, the miniature in the fragmentary gospel book in Turin, of acknowledged Irish manufacture, is inscribed with the text of Acts 1. 11, the words addressed by the angels to the apostles after the Ascension.[20] Above the inscription is Christ, bust-length in a decorative mandorla attended by angels, and below the inscription, in a series of small rectangles, are bust-length figures of the apostles, St Paul being added to make the number up to twelve, in the rectangle second from the top left. Each apostle is captioned, starting with St James at the top left and ending with St John at the bottom right. All are frontal, youthful, and beardless. Their hair is flattened, pressed against the upper frame of their rectangular compartments, exactly as in the sculptured figures on the east face of the West Shaft at Old Kilcullen.

Another scene whose visualization involves the formal presence of all twelve apostles is that, already cited, based on Matthew 19, when the apostles accompany Christ in majesty at his Second Coming. Again the representation of apostles in this context on the Irish monuments, such as Arboe (Co. Tyrone), Armagh, and Drumcliff (Co. Sligo), is ambiguous, the apostles, if so they be, being reduced to heads merely and any features blurred by weathering.[21] The fullest Irish representation of the subject is in the miniature in St Gall, Stiftsbibliothek, cod. 51, where the twelve are represented craning their necks, looking up as at the Ascension, to

[18] Harbison, *High Crosses*, I, 49, II, fig. 132; I, 144, II, fig. 481.

[19] Harbison, *High Crosses*, I, 145, 290–91, and II, fig. 481. The pose of the ascending Christ is similar to that of the ascending Enoch on p. 61 of Oxford, Bodleian Library, MS Junius 11; Temple, *Anglo-Saxon Manuscripts*, pl. 189. However, human witnesses are included in the lower portion of that drawing.

[20] Turin, Biblioteca Nazionale, Cod. O. IV. 20, fol. 1a^v; J. J. G. Alexander, *Insular Manuscripts, 6th to the 9th Century*, Survey of Manuscripts Illuminated in the British Isles, 1 (London, 1978), p. 81 and pl. 279.

[21] Harbison, *High Crosses*, I, 16, 22, 71, and 296–97; II, figs 32, 47, and 219.

the figure of the blessing Christ in the upper zone, flanked by two angels blowing trumpets.[22] The apostles form two rows of bust-length, or waist-length, figures, wearing heavy mantles and each supporting a book with the one visible long-fingered hand. Their draperies are variously coloured and patterned, and they are all young and beardless, with high smooth wig-like hair ending in a single lobe on the receding cheek and cascading behind the opposite shoulder. The six apostles at the left of the miniature look diagonally upwards to the right; the six at the right look diagonally to the left. Although the visual forms employed in the images have some resemblance to that of the apostles on St Cuthbert's coffin,[23] there is no sense of interchange between the individual apostles.

The numerical emphasis apparent in Irish representations of the apostles features also in the inscription composed by Bede for display in the cathedral church of Lindsey above an altar dedicated to the apostles, described as Christ's 'four-times three cohort' (*quater ternae [. . .] cohortis*).[24] Bede records that Benedict Biscop brought from the Continent, for the beautification of St Peter's church at Wearmouth, Northumberland, a substantial frieze representing the twelve apostles, presumably individualized according to the traditions of Roman painting.[25] The specificity with which the *puerulus* at Selsey, in another of Bede's narratives, described the physical attributes of his heavenly visitors, Saints Peter and Paul, and the promptness with which the Repton-trained St Guthlac knew St Bartholomew, might suggest that the instruction of novices in seventh-century England involved familiarizing them with depictions of individual apostles.[26] The bust-length apostles incised on the boards of St Cuthbert's Coffin at Durham are captioned in the order in which they appear in the Canon of the Mass, but only Saints Peter and Paul are given the standard portrait likenesses and attributes, St Peter tonsured and holding his keys, St Paul bald with a ragged beard.[27] The others are all the same in appearance, youthful and beardless. Their faces are

---

[22] St Gall, Stiftsbibliothek, cod. 51, p. 267; Alexander, *Insular Manuscripts*, pl. 206.

[23] See note 27 below.

[24] Michael Lapidge, *Bede the Poet* (Jarrow Lecture, 1993), pp. 2–3.

[25] Bede, *Historia Abbatum*, ed. by Charles Plummer (Oxford, 1896), pp. 369–70; George Henderson, *Bede and the Visual Arts* (Jarrow Lecture, 1980), pp. 13–16.

[26] *Bede's Ecclesiastical History of the English People*, 4.14, ed. and trans. by Bertram Colgrave and R. A. B. Mynors (Oxford, 1969), pp. 378–79; *Felix's Life of Saint Guthlac*, ed. and trans. by Bertram Colgrave (Cambridge, 1956), pp. 96–97.

[27] Ernst Kitzinger, 'The Coffin Reliquary', in *The Relics of Saint Cuthbert*, ed. by C. F. Battiscombe (Oxford, 1956), pp. 265–73 and pls IV, V, and VIII.

represented in a three-quarters pose alternatively towards the right or the left, giving the impression of collegiate consultation as in the Stuttgart Psalter's 'Mission' illustration, and hinted at in the two upper pairs carved on the West Shaft at Old Kilcullen. As the apostles on St Cuthbert's Coffin turn towards right or left their locks of hair blow back onto the opposite shoulder, the receding cheek being kept clear of hair.

In the panel at the bottom of the broken shaft of the Rothbury Cross, Northumberland, the attention of the apostles is dramatically coordinated in the scene of Christ's Ascension.[28] Like Saints Peter and Paul receiving their authority from Christ on Muiredach's Cross, the apostles at Rothbury wear heavy moustaches. The Rothbury scene resembles the miniature of the Second Coming in St Gall cod. 51, since the apostles are closely clamped together, some, where there is room, holding books, and twisting their heads to look upwards at Christ seated in his mandorla. The Rothbury sculptor has carefully reflected the gospel text in that only eleven apostles are present at the Ascension, the same historical accuracy that we noted in the Commission to the Apostles Mosaic in the Aula Leonina.[29] In the twelve bust-length figures of the apostles on the shaft of the Easby Cross, North Yorkshire, grouped in Bede's way as a 'four-times three cohort', knowledge of an excellent early Christian model is reflected in the varied facial types and the slight differences in the tilt of the heads, giving unusual life and dignity to the images (Fig. 40). No other surviving Anglo-Saxon sculpture of the period attains to this level of naturalism.[30] The cross-shaft at Otley, West Yorkshire, also shows classical

---

[28] Rosemary Cramp, *CASSS*, vol. I: *County Durham and Northumberland* (Oxford, 1984), pt 1, p. 219, pt 2, pls 213, 1218.

[29] Cramp, *CASSS*, vol. I, notes the presence of eleven witnesses at the Ascension, but suggests that the four holding books are 'possibly the Evangelists'. Jane Hawkes, 'The Rothbury Cross: An Iconographic Bricolage', *Gesta*, 35 (1996), 73–90 (pp. 81–83), describes the presence of eleven figures as 'canonically accurate', yet likewise identifies the four with books as 'presumably' the Evangelists. It would not be 'canonically accurate' to place Saints Mark and Luke among the eleven apostles who witnessed the Ascension, nor is it the case that the apostles either regularly all hold books or are all empty handed, as stated by Hawkes, the important example of the mosaic at St Agata in Suburra, noted above, proving the contrary. In the Stuttgart Psalter Psalm 18 illustration, while the other apostles are empty handed, St Peter holds up a scroll. Only some of the apostles at Easby display books, not for want of room.

[30] For description, discussion, and illustrations, see James Lang, *CASSS*, vol. VI: *Northern Yorkshire* (Oxford, 2001), pp. 98–102, and also James Lang, 'The Apostles in Anglo-Saxon Sculpture in the Age of Alcuin', *Early Medieval Europe*, 8 (1999), 271–82 (p. 273). Lang maintains that 'the variety of postures given to the apostles' heads is Carolingian rather than Late Antique', but, for example, inclined heads occur in the St Matthew and St Bartholomew figures from St Agata

influence, but there the sense of a benign assembly is dissolved. Bust-length figures, individually framed, turn abruptly alternately to the left and the right. In the deep but confined space they are not nimbed, but they hold up books, as some of the Easby apostles do. The Otley scheme included bust-length angels, which parallels the archangel/apostle imagery of St Cuthbert's Coffin, and the individual portraits seem likely to have been identified, in captions painted on the blank panels below each bust. However, since only three such figures survive, their identity as apostles, as opposed to evangelists, remains uncertain.[31]

The Hedda Shrine at Peterborough displays six standing nimbed figures, under arches, along both the front and back. Two of those on the front are Christ, identified by his cross-nimbus, and the Virgin Mary, cowled, holding a leafy stem. The Virgin was included with the twelve apostles in the imported panel painting at Wearmouth. The ten other figures on the Hedda Shrine are doubtless apostles, since one of them is St Peter, on Christ's left, holding his keys. The remaining figures, though much more wooden and linear than those at Easby, are in their own way carefully differentiated by variations in the fall of their ample mantles and by varied treatment of head types and hair. On the back the first figure on the right is a beardless youth, while the third from the left has a spade beard and markedly

in Suburra, and are in fact ubiquitous in late antique art. They are strikingly apparent among the groups of apostles in the sixth-century mosaics of gospel scenes at Sant'Apollinare Nuovo, for which see, for example, L. Colonna, *Ravenna the City of Mosaic* (Ravenna, [n.d.]), pp. 43, 50–51. The open gesture of Christ's right hand (Lang refers correctly to a single spread palm, but oddly then refers to both hands in his discussion on p. 101) closely parallels the simple expository gesture of the Saviour seated on the world globe at St Agata. At Easby the bearded frontal apostle at the top of the first group of six is consistent in appearance with St Paul, and a Petrine type of head might have appeared in the now missing figure immediately below the seated Christ. Saints Peter and Paul will necessarily be among the twelve figures represented, but Lang introduces another problem by affirming that the two heads of a rather distinct character, heavy jowled, on either side of Christ are those of Saints Peter and Paul. Such duplication of two of the apostles also seen below seems unlikely. However, Christ himself, this time blessing, is repeated in the roundel at the head of the cross. Lang does not identify the bust-length figure in the roundel on the reverse of the cross-head. A third Christ on the same monument presents the same kind of problem as we noted in the second figure on the Antioch Chalice, and perhaps the same solution could be offered, since God the Father is certainly represented in earlier and later Anglo-Saxon art. The bold wreath-like framing roundel gives particular emphasis to the figure within.

[31] Rosemary Cramp, 'The Position of the Otley Crosses in English Sculpture of the Eighth to Ninth Centuries', in *Kolloquium uber spätantike und frümittelalterliche Skulptur*, ed. by V. Milojčić, 3 vols (Mainz, 1968–72), II, 55–63. Lang, 'Apostles in Anglo-Saxon Sculpture', p. 273, incorrectly states that the shaft at Otley has 'figure carving which is restricted exclusively to the Apostles'.

Figure 40. Apostles and Christ from shaft of Easby Cross, London, Victoria and Albert Museum. Photo: Victoria and Albert Picture Library.

upstanding spiky hair.[32] On another possible shrine, now in fragments, at Breedon-on-the-Hill, Leicestershire, a quite different principle of design is employed. The surviving panels represent the apostles as identical bewigged puppet-like figures in full skirts and mantles, each under his own arch but processing boldly, six towards the right, the other two extant figures to the left, journeying as if converging on a centrally placed Christ,[33] as on the base of the North Cross at Ahenny.

Turning now to Pictland, the least familiar province of the British Isles in respect of images of the apostles, their mission conceived as a journey is perhaps represented by the two cowled figures, carrying staves, who move down the right side of the fragmentary arch from Forteviot, Perthshire, turning their back on an altar cross and lamb perched on the apex of the arch.[34] More standard imagery, of the kinds we have met with already, are the tonsured key-bearing St Peter and the bearded St Paul, placed beneath the image of the Virgin and Christ-child at Brechin, Angus,[35] and the block-like figures in two frontal rows of six each, at Dunkeld, Perthshire — visualization of the apostles wholly in the spirit of the sculpture of the North and South Crosses at Castledermot, apostolic simply because numerically sufficient.[36]

The Pictish contribution to the imagery of the apostles was notably enriched by the discovery at Tarbat, Easter Ross, in 1995 of the fragment of a cross-slab (Fig. 41) carrying on its reverse a group of figures who in their collegiate solemnity, although not nimbed, could only be apostles.[37] The Tarbat sculpture is broken across diagonally, so that only one figure, that at the extreme right, survives full-length down to the heel of his left foot. Below the ankle the surface of his foot is

---

[32] Richard N. Bailey, *England's Earliest Sculptors*, Publications of the Dictionary of Old English, 5 (Toronto, 1996), pp. 9–10, 58–59. Bailey identifies these two figures as respectively St John and St Andrew.

[33] Rosemary Cramp, 'Schools of Mercian Sculpture', in *Mercian Studies*, ed. by Ann Dornier (Leicester, 1977), pp. 191–233 (pp. 220–21). See also David M. Wilson, *Anglo-Saxon Art from the Seventh Century to the Norman Conquest* (London, 1984), p. 82, pl. 90.

[34] George Henderson and Isabel Henderson, *The Art of the Picts* (London, 2004), pp. 144–45 and pl. 211. On the significance of the lamb and the cross, see Éamonn Ó Carragáin, *The City of Rome and the World of Bede* (Jarrow Lecture, 1994), pp. 29–30. See also Friedrich Wilhelm Deichmann, *Ravenna, Hauptstadt des spätantiken Abendlandes*, vol. I (Weisbaden, 1969), pls 161, 170.

[35] Henderson and Henderson, *Art of the Picts*, p. 148 and pl. 215.

[36] Henderson and Henderson, *Art of the Picts*, p. 147, and pl. 214.

[37] Notwithstanding which, the archaeologists who located and retrieved the sculpture published it as the 'Monk Stone', in *Tarbat Discovery Programme Bulletin*, 2 (York, 1996), p. 19. See also Henderson and Henderson, *Art of the Picts*, pls 206 and 213, and p. 146.

Figure 41. Fragment of cross-slab, Tarbat, Easter Ross.
© Tom and Sybil Gray Collection.

unfortunately broken away, but on his ankle is a neat circular pad, and a strap runs up vertically to the hem of his robe. This apostle did not wear a conventional sandal, but some kind of buskin.[38] His companions were also presumably shod. The tip-toe, dancing, pose of the Tarbat apostle is similar to that of the figures in a frieze at Castor, near Peterborough.[39] At Tarbat all the figures are heavily built and wear robes and mantles, their drapery being represented by shallow repeated diagonal scoring, giving a pleated look reminiscent of the drapery over the shoulder of the Evangelists in the Lindisfarne Gospels.[40] That the sculptor was copying a painted model is suggested by the markedly flat surface of the figures and the clear silhouette that they present against the background plane. The apostle at the right, who is at the outer edge of the original sculpture, holds a book out towards the left, breaking his outline. The elbows of the other two also project, but it is uncertain if they carry anything. The head of the right figure has no projecting or undulating hair and might be tonsured. He has a square collar to his tunic, clear of his short rounded beard. The burly figure next to him has a beard covering his chest and has thick hair with matted locks on both sides of his face but markedly sprawling on his right side (the viewer's left). The next apostle beyond him has a short beard, again clear of his square collar, and smooth rounded hair falling in two neat scrolls against his right cheek, with only one scroll on his collar at the other side. The greater quantity of hair on one side than on the other is reminiscent of the device used in the apostles on St Cuthbert's Coffin to emphasize the three-quarters pose of the heads, but has no such meaning here, since the Tarbat apostles' faces are fully frontal. The broken-off head and collar of another potential apostle was retrieved from a separate site at Tarbat in 1999.[41] Here the hair lies close to the brow and cheek and runs smoothly down on to the shoulder. The heavy eyebrows are linked above the flat nose and the eyes are large and oval. Though a fragment only, the surface of this head is better preserved than those in the Apostles Frieze, but perhaps not only for this reason it gives a more stylized and decorative impression than that given by the other heads.

---

[38] George Henderson, 'Insular Art: Influence and Inference', in *Under the Influence: The Concept of Influence in the Study of Illuminated Manuscripts*, ed. by Alixe Bovey (Turnhout, 2005), pp. 11–20, fig. 4.

[39] T. D. Kendrick, *Anglo-Saxon Art to A.D. 900* (London, 1938), pp. 177–78 and pl. LXIX.

[40] London, British Library, Cotton MS Nero D. IV, fols 25ᵛ, 93ᵛ, 137ᵛ, and 209ᵛ; Janet Backhouse, *The Lindisfarne Gospels* (Oxford, 1981), pls 23, 27, 30, and 33.

[41] Press report, *The Press & Journal* (N. Scotland), Wednesday, 1 September 1999, p. 3.

At the far left of the frieze of three apostles is what remains of a fourth head, with a much larger rounded silhouette, suggesting a nimbus, though irregular in surface and not apparently given any cruciform marking (Fig. 42). The surviving shoulder of this figure slopes down at a much lower level than the shoulders of the three other figures, making clear that this figure sits while the others stand. The natural conclusion is that the original composition was the familiar one of a seated Christ flanked on either side by three apostles, six in all. There is, however, an intriguing problem in respect of this reconstruction. The Apostles Frieze was evidently part of the back face of a cross-slab. There survives on the front the top left-hand section of the cross-head, consisting of a narrow ring with an incomplete square-ended panel of spiral work set diagonally across it (Fig. 43). A slim dragon-like animal crouches with folded-up legs on the upper corner of this panel, and above it another rectangular panel of spiral work, outside the cross-head proper, formed the top left corner of the cross-slab.[42] The corner of a similar diagonally set panel, evidently from the bottom right of the cross-head, survives attached to the well-known Tarbat commemorative inscription carved in relief letters on the narrow side of this same demolished cross-slab.[43] If the whole content of the top left portion of the front of the slab is simply repeated in reverse, the breadth of the monument, so reconstituted, is such that the composition on the back requires not three, but four, figures to the left of the seated figure.

There are currently two other reconstructions of the Tarbat cross-slab. One, unpublished, by Ian G. Scott, late of the Royal Commission, envisages a tall wide monument, the diagonal panels being slotted in between the upright and transverse arms of a grand Latin cross. The breadth of the monument is the corollary of the unexplained supposition that ten figures were represented in a row on the back of the monument, and it is significant that this even number of figures takes no cognizance of the seated pose of the figure fourth from the right. An even broader monument is envisaged in a second reconstruction, by Elizabeth Hooper of the University of York Archaeology Department, published in the *Tarbat Discovery Programme Bulletin* for 1996.[44] There the diagonal panels are placed like huge studs on the narrow ring linking the large vertical and horizontal stepped arms of the cross. On the back Hooper proposes thirteen figures, twelve standing apostles with Christ upright in their midst, six on either side. Again no note is

---

[42] Henderson and Henderson, *Art of the Picts*, p. 219 and pl. 317.

[43] J. Romilly Allen and Joseph Anderson, *The Early Christian Monuments of Scotland* (Edinburgh, 1903; repr Balgavies, 1993), II.3, figs 96 and 96A, opp. p. 83.

[44] See fig. 9 in the *Tarbat Discovery Programme Bulletin* referred to in note 37 above.

Figure 42. Detail of Apostle frieze from cross-slab, Tarbat, Easter Ross.
© Tom and Sybil Gray Collection.

Figure 43. Front of fragment of cross-slab, Tarbat, Easter Ross.
© Tom and Sybil Gray Collection.

taken of the seated figure, fourth from the right. Both these reconstructions, and the scale and format of the cross-head they envisage, founder on their neglect of this basic visual fact.

Having in mind the evidence of the apostle frieze as we have it, we might tentatively envisage the cross-head as consisting of a shallow moulded ring linking the arms of a cross disposed diagonally, that is, a saltire cross (Fig. 44). Adopting the horse-shoe form of the diagonal panels, reasonably proposed by Scott, since they do appear to taper, there results a second cross bound by the first, a conventional Greek cross with curved arms, incidentally the shape of St Cuthbert's pectoral cross now in Durham.[45] The diagonal bars of the main cross, which certainly existed on the monument however it is to be reconstructed, although difficult to parallel in stone sculpture of this period, are paralleled on pages in the Book of Kells. A saltire design is made of the fantastically extended legs of a lion on the last text page of St Mark's Gospel, and a strong saltire design is displayed in the carpet page before the opening of St John's Gospel.[46]

Whatever the aesthetic merits of this proposed reconstruction of the cross-head on the front of the Tarbat monument, it takes into account the surviving composition on the back, with its hint of a central focus to the original design. I have noted the problem of the number of the figures needed at Christ's right hand, four instead of three, making for unbalance. A possible solution to the problem of an unequal group of apostles and an off-centre Christ would be the presence of a standing figure of the Virgin. As noted above, the Virgin was included along with the twelve apostles in some unknown composition on the large-scale panel painting at St Peter's, Wearmouth. The Virgin stands at Christ's right hand on the front of the Hedda Shrine, reducing the number of the apostles there to two, and two, at the extremes of the composition. For a standing Virgin, placed next to a seated Christ, we could invoke the *Gloria in excelsis* design on fol. 89[v] of the Utrecht Psalter and its later derivative on fol. 75[r] of the Winchester, New Minster, prayer-book.[47] For the accoutrements and appearance of this

[45] Rupert Bruce-Mitford. 'The Pectoral Cross', in *Relics of Saint Cuthbert*, ed. by Battiscombe, pp. 323–24 and pl. XV.

[46] Dublin, Trinity College Library, MS 58, fols 187[v], 290[v]; Bernard Meehan, *The Book of Kells* (London, 1994), pls 31, 36.

[47] Utrecht, University Library, MS 32, and London, Brtish Library, Cotton MS Titus D. XXVII, for which see *The Utrecht Psalter in Medieval Art: Picturing the Psalms of David*, ed. by Koert van der Horst, William Noel, and Wilhelmina C. M. Wüstefeld (Utrecht, 1996), pp. 252–53 and figs 36d, 36a.

Figure 44. Reconstruction of cross head, cross-slab,
Tarbat, Easter Ross. © George Henderson.

postulated figure of the Virgin, it is tempting to invoke the frontal (though seated) figure of the woman riding above the hunting scene on the back of the Hilton of Cadboll cross-slab, 14 km south-west of Tarbat.[48] The appearance and stance of the Tarbat apostles clearly does not accord with a more exalted form of imagery, the Apocalyptic scenario of God the Father accompanied by Christ the Lamb, at His right side.

The Tarbat Apostles Frieze is framed by a broad band above and below, and is the lower of two zones of sculpture. The upper zone looks surprisingly different in subject matter, containing a menacingly prowling bear in its top right corner and two massive lions facing one another over the neatly truncated hinder part of a slim-legged animal, a calf or deer. It has been suggested elsewhere[49] that this scene represents an unusual and original typological image, drawn from Genesis and a text of the prophet Jeremiah, and that exegesis smooths away the apparent discrepancy between the human figures below, the animals above. We have seen in the Irish examples of sculptured groups of apostles that these are often fairly loosely aligned to scriptural subjects drawn from both the Old and the New Testament. On the base of the west face of the Cross of the Scriptures at Clonmacnois the Apostles Frieze is the upper of the two framed zones, not the lower as at Tarbat. Scenes from the passion are displayed on the shaft above the apostles, while Old Testament narrative scenes appear on the opposite, east, face of the shaft.[50] In Anglo-Saxon England, the cross-shaft or rather pillar at Masham, North Yorkshire,[51] juxtaposes Old Testament heroes, David and Samson, with figures of the apostles, in the same kind of generalized historical comparison. The Pictish example, if we read it aright, seems to emphasize contrast rather than consensus in the choice of images from the two Testaments.

The Tarbat frieze of apostles is iconographically and stylistically informative, indeed explicit. The stage of absorption and adaptation of Continental models is similar to that represented by the Hedda Shrine in the Anglo-Saxon Midlands, while the clarity of its outlines and its scored and serrated surface treatment argue its connection with panel and perhaps also manuscript painting. The marked attention which the sculptor gives to different facial types and to different arrangements of hair connects Tarbat to the kind of information which we have

---

[48] Henderson and Henderson, *Art of the Picts*, pp. 46, 128; pls 50, 187.

[49] Henderson and Henderson, *Art of the Picts*, p. 142.

[50] Harbison, *High Crosses*, II, figs 144, 139, and 132.

[51] Lang, *CASSS*, VI, 169–71.

seen valued and preserved in the Irish Reference Bible and doubtless also available for study in imported models, such as that reported at Wearmouth. The happy chance of the recovery of this fragment increases our awareness of the whole Insular Church's devotion to the apostles,[52] which provided inspiration for so many, interestingly diverse, visual representations of them. Contemplation of these images must in itself have engendered a sense of fellowship with the wider Christian world — that sense of shared faith and practice so many aspects of which have been marvellously illuminated by the dedicatee of this paper.

---

[52] Another noteworthy contribution of the Picts to the imagery of the apostles is of course the sculpted illustration of the text of the Catholic Epistle of St James 2. 2–3, for which see Henderson and Henderson, *Art of the Picts*, p. 157, pl. 230.

A Suggested Function for the Holy Well?

Niamh Whitfield

The veneration of natural springs, so-called holy wells (Plate 10), is a widespread tradition in Ireland, often associated with a votive tree (*bile*) (Plate 11). How far back in time the tradition originated is impossible to say. Among the pagan Celts in Europe sacred springs seem to have become foci for healing rituals in the pre-Roman period towards the end of the Iron Age,[1] and the Irish may have been influenced by this. On the other hand, Eamonn Kelly has recently suggested that the tradition of the sacred spring in Ireland may have been introduced from Roman Britain.[2] Whatever its ultimate origins, as Kelly pointed out its importance in Irish Christianity is demonstrated by the fact that virtually every other early Irish saint whose life has come down to us is credited with the miraculous production of at least one well. Their strong links with Irish Christianity were also commented on by Ann Hamlin, who remarked:

In addition to Éamonn Ó Carragáin himself, I would like to thank the following for invaluable help with sources: Edel Bhreathnach, Cormac Bourke, Thomas Owen Clancy, Carol Farr, Ian Fisher, Peter Harbison, Anthony Harvey, Jane Hawkes, Conleth Manning, Rachel Moss, Jenifer Ní Ghrádaigh, Donnchadh Ó Corráin, Raghnall Ó Floinn, Catherine Swift, and Susan Youngs. I am grateful also to Adrian Whitfield and Jane Roberts for their comments on the text, and to Jenifer Ní Ghrádaigh, and Charles Thomas for permission to use their work to illustrate this paper.

[1] Miranda Green, 'The Archaeology of Religion in Pagan Celtic Europe', in *Celtica Helsingiensia: Proceedings from a Symposium on Celtic Studies*, ed. by Anders Ahlqvist and others, Commentationes Humanarum Litterarum, 107 (Helsinki, 1996), pp. 27–28.

[2] Eamonn P. Kelly, 'Antiquities from Irish Holy Wells and their Wider Context', *Archaeology Ireland*, 16 (2002), 24–28.

There must be several thousand holy wells in Ireland, many of them at early church sites. There were pressing practical reasons for building a church close to a good water supply, and it is surely this source which has sometimes come to be regarded as a holy well.[3]

Any visitor to early Christian church sites in Ireland must indeed be struck by how often a church is found in association with one or more holy wells. According to the life by Tírechán, composed in the late seventh century, St Patrick himself felt that it was important to have a well close to a church, for after he had founded a church at Drummae (possibly by Lough Gara), he dug a well there.[4] What is more, a number of Irish holy wells have freestanding inscribed early medieval cross-slabs next to them,[5] as do some from Scotland.[6] Why should this be? Charles Doherty has recently proposed that the use of wells formed part of a general Christianization of the landscape by early churchmen in Ireland.[7] Here I would like to be more

---

[3] Kathleen Hughes and Ann Hamlin, *The Modern Traveller to the Early Irish Church* (London, 1977), pp. 108–09. For further accounts of holy wells, see Philip Dixon Hardy, *The Holy Wells of Ireland, Containing an Authentic Account of those Various Places of Pilgrimage and Penance which are still Annually Visited by Thousands of Roman Catholic Peasantry* (Dublin, 1836); William Gregory Wood-Martin, *Traces of Elder Faiths of Ireland: A Folklore Sketch. A Handbook of Irish Pre-Christian Traditions*, 2 vols (London, 1902), II, 46–115; W. S. Cordner, 'The Cult of the Holy Well', *Ulster Journal of Archaeology* (1946), 24–36; Patrick Logan, *The Holy Wells of Ireland* (Gerrards Cross, 1980); Janet Bord and Colin Bord, *Sacred Waters: Holy Wells and Water Lore in Britain and Ireland* (London, 1985); Arthur Gribben, *Holy Wells and Sacred Water Sources in Ireland and Britain: An Annotated Bibliography* (New York, 1992); Walter L. Brenneman and Mary G. Brenneman, *Crossing the Circle at the Holy Wells of Ireland* (Charlottesville, 1995); Susan Connolly and Anne-Marie Moroney, *Stone and Tree Sheltering Water: An Exploration of Sacred and Secular Wells in Co. Louth* (Drogheda, 1998); Anna Rackard and Liam O'Callaghan with Angela Bourke, *Fishstonewater: The Holy Wells of Ireland* (Cork, 2001); Elizabeth Healy, *In Search of Ireland's Holy Wells* (Dublin, 2001).

[4] Ed. and trans. by Ludwig Bieler with a contribution by Fergus Kelly, *The Patrician Texts in the Book of Armagh*, Scriptores Latini Hiberniae, 10 (Dublin, 1979), pp. 148–49, § 31. 1.

[5] For instance, Tobermalogga/Tobar na Molaige at Ballywiheen, Dingle, Co. Kerry, and a number of other holy wells in the same peninsula. See Judith Cuppage, *Archaeological Survey of the Dingle Peninsula: A Description of the Field Antiquities of the Barony of Corca Dhuibhne from the Mesolithic Period to the 17th Century A.D.* (Dublin, 1986), no. 828, pp. 276–77, fig. 156a, and p. 353, fig. 209. I am grateful to Ian Fisher for pointing this out to me.

[6] For an example, see Ian Fisher, *Early Medieval Sculpture in the West Highlands and Islands*, Royal Commission on the Ancient and Historical Monuments of Scotland and the Society of Antiquaries of Scotland, Monograph Series, 1 (Edinburgh, 2001), p. 150, no. 78.

[7] Charles Doherty, 'Kingship in Early Ireland', in *The Kingship and Landscape of Tara*, ed. by Edel Bhreathnach (Dublin, 2005), pp. 3–31 (pp. 6–11).

specific about how this was achieved, taking a cue from Ann Hamlin's comment and looking for 'pressing practical reasons' to explain the phenomenon. What follows is offered as a small tribute to Éamonn Ó Carragáin in gratitude for his friendship and in recognition of the profound effect his scholarship has had on our understanding of late antique and early medieval Christian ritual and art.

The testimony of Adomnán makes it clear that in the late seventh century, as now, water from certain sacred wells was used for cures. This is explicitly stated at the end of his account of a well with evil properties which St Columba blessed in Pictland.[8] However, I would suggest that some holy wells, particularly those in the vicinity of churches, may also have played an important role in the sacrament of baptism. Water, after all, is essential for this rite which all Christians must undergo in order to be admitted to the fellowship of the Church, cleansed of past sins, and reborn to new and eternal life. Without it there is no salvation.

At the time of its conversion to Christianity Ireland had no grand tradition of architecture comparable to that in the Romanized world. At least one Irish holy well used for baptism, that at St Doulagh's Church, Balgriffin, Co. Dublin, approached down two steps, lies within an octagonal structure, the form particularly associated with baptisteries during the early medieval period on the Continent (Fig. 45).[9] Could the holy well have been the Irish counterpart to the detached baptisteries attached to large Continental churches of this period or to church fonts? Alternatively, if baptism did not always actually take place in the wells themselves, could their water have been used during the sacrament?[10]

There is evidence from Britain to suggest that this was the case there, and that both wells themselves and water taken from wells were used during baptism. James Rattue has pointed out that eighty-three wells in England are recorded as having been used for baptisms at one time or another,[11] some perhaps as long ago as the early

---

[8] *Adomnán of Iona: Life of St Columba*, II.11, trans. by Richard Sharpe (Harmondsworth, 1995), pp. 162–63.

[9] Rachel Moss, 'St Doulagh's Church', *Irish Arts Review* (Summer 2003), 123–25 (p. 125). The date of this structure, which lacks any known parallels within Ireland, is uncertain. As Rachel Moss points out, it is possible that whoever was responsible for its construction was inspired following a trip to Europe.

[10] The same proposal was independently made by Mary Low, whose work the writer belatedly discovered when this paper had been completed; see Mary Low, *Celtic Christianity and Nature: Early Irish and Hebridean Tradition* (Edinburgh, 1996), pp. 62–64.

[11] James Rattue, *The Living Stream: Holy Wells in Historical Context* (Woodbridge, 1995), p. 66.

Figure 45. Octagonal baptistery over a holy well by St Doulagh's Church,
Balgriffin, Co. Dublin. Sketch of 1836 in the Society of Antiquaries of London
by Captain Edward Jones. Photo: Niamh Whitfield.

Anglo-Saxon period,[12] while John Blair has noted that until recent times parishioners
at Bisley, Surrey, were still baptized in St John the Baptist's well, not far from the parish church, and in the nineteenth century at Halton, Lancashire, the baptismal water
was brought to the church from St Wilfrid's well.[13] There is also evidence that in
Wales in the early centuries of the Christian era people were baptized in wells. Moreover, water from such wells is known to have been carried to the fonts of churches
for baptism in some parts of Wales as late as the end of the nineteenth century.[14]

In Ireland holy wells are also said to have been used for baptism in relatively
recent times, for example at St Mullins, Co. Carlow, where baptism by immersion

[12] Sarah Foot, '"By Water in the Spirit": The Administration of Baptism in Early Anglo-
Saxon England', in *Pastoral Care Before the Parish*, ed. by John Blair and Richard Sharpe
(Leicester, 1992), pp. 171–92 (p. 181).

[13] John Blair, *The Church in Anglo-Saxon Society* (Oxford, 2005), p. 463, n. 166.

[14] Francis Jones, *The Holy Wells of Wales* (Cardiff, 1992), p. 34.

is said to have been carried out until about 1800.[15] Victor de Waal, who most recently drew attention to this practice, remarked that 'the wells had been sacred to pagan deities [. . .] and it was natural that they should become the focus for adherence to the new faith'.[16] His view, like mine, is that the use of water from holy wells for baptism probably goes back to the beginnings of Christianity itself in Ireland.

The early lives of the Irish saints provide plenty of evidence to support this proposition. They demonstrate, moreover, that the hagiographers did not consider baptism in a spring (Latin: *fons*; Old/Middle Irish: *tipra* or, more recently, *tiprait*)[17] as anything out of the ordinary.

St Patrick's Association with Wells

According to Tírechán, St Patrick himself used wells for many baptisms, apparently at places where annual assemblies were held.[18] One of the best known incidents concerns the two daughters of King Loíguire, fair-haired Ethne and red-headed Fedelm, baptized at a well called Clébach[19] on the eastern slopes of Cruachu.[20] These two young women encounter Patrick and a group of bishops by the well where they had come to wash in the morning, as was their custom. Patrick engages them in theological debate. and they are converted and baptized. Afterwards they express a wish to see the face of Christ. and Patrick explains that to do this they must first receive the sacraments and taste death. Undaunted, they ask for the sacraments and die forthwith. Later they are buried near the well. Not surprisingly, their foster-father, the druid Caplit, comes and weeps. But he too is

---

[15] Victor de Waal, 'The So-called Omission of the Baptismal Formula in the Order of Baptism in the Stowe Missal', *Peritia*, 13 (1999), 255–58 (p. 258).

[16] De Waal, 'Omission of the Baptismal Formula', p. 258.

[17] *Tipra/tiprait* may be translated as 'well, spring, fountain or source'; see the *Dictionary of the Irish Language*, ed. by The Royal Irish Academy, compact edn (Dublin, 1983), 'T', 186.40. Henceforth *DIL*.

[18] Catherine Swift, 'The Social and Ecclesiastical Background to the Treatment of the Connachta in Tírechán's Collectanea' (unpublished doctoral dissertation, University of Oxford, 1994), pp. 143–45, 245, and 269.

[19] *Patrician Texts*, ed. and trans. by Bieler, pp. 142–45, § 26.

[20] Local belief identifies this well as Orgulla Well, near Tulsk, Co. Roscommon. See Logan, *Holy Wells of Ireland*, p. 50. Liam de Paor also recorded this belief; see de Paor, *Saint Patrick's World: The Christian Culture of Ireland's Apostolic Age* (Dublin, 1993), p. 163.

converted and baptized and has his head shorn in the Christian manner. Eventually even the latter's sceptical brother, Máel, is baptized at the well of Clébach.

Another incident described by Tírechán concerns the baptism of a 'worshipper of idols' called Erc at the well of Loígles:

> Sanctus quoque dixit: 'Si babtisma Domini accipies, quod mecum est?' Respondit: 'Accipiam', et uenierunt ad fontem Loigles in Scotica, nobiscum 'Vitulus Ciuitatum'. Cumque aperuisset librum atque babtizasset uirum Hercum, audiuit uiros post tergum suum se inridentes ad inuicem de rei illius consideratione, quia nescierunt quid fecerat; et babtitzauit tot milia hominum in die illa.

> [The holy man [Patrick] said 'Will you receive the baptism of my Lord which I bring with me?' He [Erc] answered 'I will receive it.' And they went to the well of Loígles[21] in Irish, in our language [Latin] 'calf of the cities'. And when he had opened the book and baptized the man named Erc, he heard men behind his back laughing at him, for they did not understand what he had done. And he baptized many thousand men on that day.][22]

In addition, Tírechán referred to two further wells where baptisms were performed, the second of which, interestingly, was considered sacred in pagan times, a point discussed in uncharacteristic detail by Tírechán:

> Et uenit in regiones Corcu Temne ad fontem Sini, in quo babtitzauit milia hominum multa <et> fundauit aeclessias tres. Et uenit ad fontem Findmaige qui dicitur Slan, quia indicatum illi quod honorabant magi fontem et immolauerunt dona ad illum in modum dii. Fons uero quadratus fuit et petra quadrata erat in ore fontis (et ueniebat aqua super petram .i. est per glutinationes) quasi +uestigium regale+, et dixerunt increduli quod quidam profeta mortuus fecit bibliothicam sibi in aqua sub petra, ut dealbaret ossa sua semper, quia timuit ignis exust<ion>em; qui[a] adorabant fontem in modum dii. Et indicate est Patricio causa adorationis [...] et Patricius ait illis: 'Eleuate petram; uideamus quid sub est, si ossa an non, quia dico uobis; sub ea ossa hominis non sunt; sed puto aliquid de auro et argento per glutinationem petrarum +minime de uestris reprobis immolationibus.'

> [And he [Patrick] came to the territory of Corcu Temne to the well of Sine where he baptized many thousands of men and founded three churches. And he came to the well of Findmag which is called Slán because he had been told that the druids honoured the well and offered gifts to it as to a god. The well is of square shape and the mouth of the well was covered with a square stone (and water [flowed] over the stone, that is through ducts closed with cement) like a regal trail (?), and the infidels said that some wise man had made for himself a shrine in the water under the stone to bleach his bones perpetually because he feared the burning by fire; and they worshipped the well as a god. And Patrick was told the reason for its worship [...] and Patrick said to them: 'Lift the stone; let us see

---

[21] This well was 'apparently on the Hill of Tara'; see de Paor, *Saint Patrick's World*, p. 156.

[22] *Patrician Texts*, ed. and trans. by Bieler, pp. 132–35, § 13. 3–4.

what is under it, whether bones or not, for I am telling you: under it there are not the bones of a man, but — so I believe — some gold and silver from your wicked sacrifices leaks through the cementing of the stones.']²³

He also carried out a baptism at the second well, Slán, on a man called Caeta or Cata.²⁴

Furthermore, in two other early lives of St Patrick, the *Vita Secunda* and *Vita Quarta* (both said by Francis John Byrne and Pádraig Francis to derive from a lost eighth-century original),²⁵ as well as in the *Bethu Phátraic* or *The Tripartite Life of Patrick*,²⁶ which dates to between the ninth and eleventh centuries, the story is told of the saint's own baptism in water from a spring that miraculously welled up from the ground. Having informed us that Patrick was born in Campus Taburne, the version in the *Vita Secunda* continues:

> Hic autem natus est super lapidem, qui adhuc honorifice habetur. [. . .] Ille autem baptizari portatus est ad alium sanctum a natiuitate caecum tabulata facie, cui acqua defuit. Fertur autem quod Gornias fuerit nomen sacerdotis Patricium baptizantis. Qui de manu infantis signum crucis in terra posuit et inde eruptit fons, et lauit faciem et aperti sunt oculi eius, et relegit baptismum qui numquam litteras didicit — tres uirtutes simul — et postea baptizatus est. Aedificata est autem ecclesia super fontem in quo baptizatus est. Ipse autem fons est iuxta altare, habens figuram crucis, ut periti aiunt.²⁷

---

²³ *Patrician Texts*, ed. and trans. by Bieler, pp. 152–53, § 39, 2–5. This account of the well of Slán has led to differing interpretations. Nicolas B. Aitchison argues that it reflects the Iron Age pagan practice of depositing votive offerings in watery places such as bogs, lakes, and rivers ('Votive Deposition in Iron Age Ireland: An Early Medieval Account', *Emania*, 15 (1996), 67–75). On the other hand, Eamonn Kelly, without referring specifically to this example, suggests that Irish holy wells should be regarded as shrines rather than natural water features and that the practice of placing votive offerings in them may have originated in the classical world ('Antiquities from Irish Holy Wells', pp. 24–28). The case for a Christian interpretation of the well of Slán is put by Catherine Swift, who argues that the description of this well recalls early liturgical ceremonies for altar dedications, which involve the cementing of relics into place with exorcised water and chrism ('Social and Ecclesiastical Background', p. 270, n. 7); see also Michel Andrieu, *Les Ordines Romani du Haut Moyen Âge*, Spicilegium Sacrum Lovaniense, 4 (Leuven, 1956), pp. 394–400.

²⁴ *Patrician Texts*, ed. and trans. by Bieler, pp. 153–54, § 39. 7.

²⁵ F. J. Byrne and Pádraig J. Francis, 'Two Lives of Saint Patrick: *Vita Secunda* and *Vita Quarta*', *Journal of the Royal Society of Antiquaries of Ireland*, 124 (1994), 5–117 (p. 5).

²⁶ *The Tripartite Life of Patrick*, ed. by Whitley Stokes, Rolls Series, 2 vols (London, 1887), I, 8–9.

²⁷ *Four Latin Lives of St Patrick: Colgan's Vita Secunda, Quarta, Tertia, and Quinta*, ed. by Ludwig Bieler, Scriptores Latini Hiberniae, 8 (Dublin, 1971), p. 52, § 2–3.

[Here then he was born upon a stone which is still held in honour [. . .]. He was brought there to be baptized to a certain holy man who was blind from birth with a 'table face', and who had no water at hand. It is said moreover that Gornias was the name of the priest who baptized Patrick. He made the sign of the cross with his hand over the child, placing him on the ground and from there a spring welled up and he washed his face in it and his eyes were opened, and he read the baptismal rite although he was illiterate (three miracles at the same time!) and afterwards Patrick was baptized. Moreover, a church was built over the spring in which he was baptized. This spring is next to the altar, having the shape of the cross, as the experts say.][28]

The *Tripartite Life of Patrick* records further instances of baptism with well water. This is implicit in the account of the baptism by Patrick of the men of the east of Meath at Tech Laisrenn. Interestingly, the account of the baptism is followed by the statement that 'his [Patrick's] well is in front of the church' and a further statement that the tomb of the female founder of the church, Bice, 'stands to the north of the well'.[29]

The locations of other baptismal wells are also described in the *Tripartite Life*. One example is the well at Naas, which is described as follows:

> Atá lathrach apupaill isindfaigthi indúne frisligid anair, ocus ata atipra fridun antuaith, dú robaithis damacc Dunlangi, Ailill ocus Illand, ocus dú robaithes dí ingin Ailella Mogain ocus Fedelm.

> [The site of [Patrick's] tent is in the green of the fort, to the east of the road, and to the north of the fort is his well wherein he baptized Dunling's two son, Ailill and Illam, and Ailill's two daughter's, Mogain and Fedelm.][30]

Another example is the well of Óen-adarc, 'one-horn', so called because of a steep little hillock near the well. There Patrick baptized a pregnant woman, Fedelm, and her son, both of whom he had just brought back from the dead.

> Et suscitata illa praedicauit turbis de poenis inferni et praemís coeli, et per lacrimas rogauit fratrem suum ut Deo per Patricium crederet [. . .]. Et in illo die .xii. milia babtizati sunt in fonte Oenadarce, et dicitur
>> Baithsithir in oenlaithiu
>> dá se míli már
>> im secht maccu Amalgada
>> ised ón ba slán.

---

[28] Byrne and Francis, 'Two Lives of Saint Patrick', p. 21, § 2–3.

[29] 'Fir oirthir Midi ros bathess Patraic oc toig Laisrend indess itá athiprae indorus inna cilli. Facaib dís dia muintir ann .i. Bice ocus Lugaid, ocus ata ferta Bice fri tiprait antúaid': *Tripartite Life*, ed. by Stokes, I, 76–79.

[30] *Tripartite Life*, ed. by Stokes, I, 184–85.

[And when she was brought to life she preached to multitudes of the pains of hell and the rewards of heaven and with tears besought her brother to believe in God through Patrick [...]. And in that day twelve thousand were baptized in the well of Oen-adarc, and it was said:

> In one day are baptized
> twice six great thousand
> together with Amalgaid's seven sons:
> that was well.][31]

The tradition that St Patrick baptized converts in well water is recorded also in *Acallam na Senórach* or *Tales of the Elders of Ireland*, which may date to the twelfth century. A famous colloquy between Patrick and the Fenian hero, Caílte, is described. In an exchange between Patrick and his priests and Caílte and his men, the following dialogue takes place:

'Athchuinghidh dob áil liumsa d'iarraid ortt, a Cháilti,' ar Pátraic. 'Dá rabh ocumsa do niurt nó do chumung sin do ghébthar,' ar Cáilte; 'ocus abair cidh edh hí.' 'Topar fíruisci d'fagbáil inar bfocus annso, assa fétfamáis tuatha Breagh 7 Midhi 7 Uisnigh do baistedh,' ar Pátraic. 'Atá ocumsa dhuitse sin, a uasail 7 a fíreoin!' ar Cáilte. Ocus táncatar rompu tar cladh na rátha a(mach), 7 ro gab-sum lámh Pátraic ina láimh, 7 [ní deachadur acht náoi sbáis ón dorus amach antan . . .] itchonncatar in lochtobar grinn glainidi ina fiadhnaise. 7 ba hadbal leo mét 7 reime in bhilair 7 ind fochluchta ro bhói fair.[32]

[There is something I would ask of you, Caílte', said Patrick. Caílte replied, 'If my strength and powers suffice, it will be granted. Tell me what you wish.' Patrick answered, 'Could you find us a well of pure water close by, so that we might baptize the peoples of Brega, Meath, and Usnagh?' 'I shall indeed find one for you, noble and righteous one', said Caílte. He took Patrick by the hand and together they went over the ramparts of the fortress. Just nine steps from the portal they saw a lovely crystal-clear spring and were amazed at the thick growth of watercress and brooklime surrounding it.][33]

The name of this well too, *Tráig Dá Ban*, is recorded, and it is, moreover, celebrated in a praise poem by Caílte.

[31] *Tripartite Life*, ed. by Stokes, I, 134–35.

[32] *Irische Texte mit Übersetzungen und Wörterbuch*, 4th series, pt 1, ed. by W. H. Stokes and E. Windisch (Leipzig, 1900), p. 3. I thank Edel Bhreathnach for drawing this passage to my attention.

[33] Ann Dooley and Harry Roe, *Tales of the Elders of Ireland: A New Translation of 'Acallam na Senórach'* (Oxford, 1999), p. 5.

Other Irish Saints Associated with Wells

Not only do lives of St Patrick refer to baptisms in wells, so too do other Irish saints' lives. St Brendan of Clonfert's baptism in well water was immediately followed by a miracle that provided a handsome fee for the ceremony:

> Iarsin ro lingestair tri muilt asin tioprait in ro baistedh, conidh iatt sin feich baistedha Brenainn.

> [Afterwards three wethers leapt forth from the fountain in which he was baptized, and they formed Brendan's baptism fee.][34]

And St Buite of Monasterboice was said to have been baptized in infancy in water from a miraculous spring, as was St Patrick. Conleth Manning, in this discussion of the account of his baptism in the Latin life, suggests that this well was located at Toberboice ('St Buite's well'), in the townland of Mell on the outskirts of Drogheda, Co. Louth.[35] Following the birth of the infant, Buite (Latin, *Boecius*), his parents were anxious to baptize him. Priests, however, were not to be found locally. Fortunately, some clerics sailed into a nearby harbour, and their leader ('ille qui primus et principalis inter illos fuit') explained that God had sent them to baptize a little boy ('paruulum'). However, he also explained that baptism had to be performed in pure water ('in simplici aqua'), so the nearby river would not do because it was mixed with sea water. He therefore commanded that the infant's hands be set upon the ground and when this was done

> confestim fons purissimus mellei saporis ex eodem loco ebulliuit; qui ob insoliti miraculi signum usque hodie Mellifons nominatur. Denique uir ille sanctus, paruulum aqua perfundens, totum baptismatis ordinem compleuit, eumque Boecium nominauit.[36]

> [immediately a very pure spring with the savour of honey bubbled up from the very place which, because of the sign of the unusual miracle, even today is called Mellifons. Then that holy man, sprinkling the little boy with water, completed the whole rite of baptism and named him Boecius.][37]

In Adomnán's *Life of St Columba*, composed at the end of the seventh century, the story of a comparable miracle is told:

---

[34] *Bethada Náem nÉrenn: Lives of Irish Saints. Edited from the Original MSS, with Introduction, Translations, Notes Glossary and Indexes*, by Charles Plummer, 2 vols (Oxford, 1997), p. 45, § 8, in both vols.

[35] Conleth Manning, 'St Buite, Mellifont and Toberboice', *Peritia*, 3 (1984), 324–25; Connolly and Moroney, *Stone and Tree Sheltering Water*, pp. 36–37.

[36] *Vitae Sanctorum Hiberniae,* ed. by Carolus [Charles] Plummer (Oxford, 1910), I, 87.

[37] Trans. by Adrian Whitfield.

Alio namque in tempore, cum sanctus in sua conversaretur perigrinatione, infans ei per parentes ad babtizandum offertur iter agenti. Et quia in vicinís aqua non inveniebatur locís, sanctus ad proximam declinans rupem flexís genibus paulisper oravit; et post orationem surgens ejusdem rupis frontem benedixit. De qua consequenter aqua abundanter ebulliens fluxit, in qua continuo infantulum babtizavit [. . .] ubi hodieque fonticulus sancti nomine Columbae pollens cernitur.[38]

[Once during [St Columba's] life of pilgrimage he was on a journey when a child was brought to him for baptism by his parents. But there was no water to be found on the spot. So the saint turned to the nearest rock, where he knelt and prayed for a while. When he stood up, he blessed the face of the rock, and at once water bubbled out from it in great quantity. Thereupon he baptized the child [. . .] and a little spring is still to be seen there which is powerful in the name of Columba.][39]

Yet another saint whose baptism required a miracle because of the lack of available running water is St Mochuda:

Ro lamnaigh an inghen, 7 beiridh mac fri taobh Maingi; 7 ni raibhe uiscce foran tulaigh sin; 7 maighis sruth assa taobh, 7 doberar Aidarnas chuca, 7 baistis asin sruth é.

[The woman [his mother] was delivered and bore a son beside the river Maine; and there was no water on that hill; and a stream broke forth from the side of it. And Aidanus [a priest], was fetched to them, and baptized the child [with water] out of the stream.][40]

The lives of the Welsh saints describe similar incidents. To quote Francis Jones,

In the Lives, wells associated with a saint's baptism were either already in existence and became hallowed by the baptism of the infant, or, on the other hand, suddenly flowed to provide water for the ceremony. When Cadoc was baptized a large fountain arose at the prayer of the priest, whereupon the enterprising babe leaped into it and 'dipped himself thrice in the water in the name of the Holy Trinity'.[41]

Discussion

Such references to miraculously created springs originated, as Jennifer O'Reilly has observed, in a miracle performed by Christ 'Who brings forth water from the

---

[38] *Adomnan's Life of Columba*, ed. and trans. by A. O. Anderson and M. O. Anderson (London, 1961), 11.10, pp. 346–49.

[39] This translation is by Sharpe, *Adomnán of Iona: Life of Columba*, II.10, pp. 162–63.

[40] *Bethada Náem nÉrenn*, ed. and trans. by Plummer, I, 291, § 5; II, 282, § 5.

[41] Jones, *Holy Wells of Wales*, p. 33.

rock' (Psalm 77. 16), which itself harks back to the Old Testament story in which Moses struck water from a rock during the journey through the desert.[42]

The inclusion of the name of the Holy Trinity in the baptismal rite derives from a passage at the end of Matthew's Gospel, quoting Christ's instructions to his disciples to go out to teach all nations and to baptize them in the name of the Father, Son, and Holy Ghost (Matthew 28. 19),[43] a command which explains the practice of applying the waters of baptism three times during the ceremony, once for each Person of the Trinity. Like other rituals of the Church, baptism only gradually assumed a fixed form, and in some places, for instance Spain, baptism by single immersion seems to have been practised. However, in the case of early medieval Ireland, there is evidence for the canonical three immersions. The sole surviving source to record an early Christian Irish liturgy of the rite of baptism is found in the Stowe Missal, a manuscript probably written in Tallaght in the late eighth or early ninth century.[44] There the infant or catechumen is anointed twice with chrism (sacred oil), and purified three times with water.[45] Moreover, Donnchadh Ó Corráin has drawn attention to an earlier Irish text which provides further evidence for triple emersion, *Apgitir Chrábaid* (the Primer of Piety), dated to *c.* A.D. 600,[46] attributed to Colmán mac Beognai, abbot of Lann Elo.[47] The passage about baptism starts by referring to 'the three waves that pass over a person in baptism' ('inna téora tonna tíagde tar duine i mbáthius'). It then lists the three renunciations made by the candidate (the world, the devil, and the lusts

---

[42] Jennifer O'Reilly, 'Reading the Scriptures in the *Life* of Columba', in *Studies in the Cult of Saint Columba,* ed. by Cormac Bourke (Dublin, 1997), pp. 80–106 (p. 87).

[43] I am grateful to Jennifer O'Reilly for pointing this out to me.

[44] George F. Warner, *The Stowe Missal. Ms D II 3 in the Library of the Royal Irish Academy, Dublin*, Henry Bradshaw Society, 32 (1915), pp. xxxii–xxxvi. The manuscript of the Stowe Missal was added to on many occasions and the liturgy for the rite of baptism was added after the basic text of the Mass was recorded, although how long afterwards is unclear. See Thomas O'Loughlin, *Celtic Theology: Humanity, World and God in Early Irish Writings* (London, 2000), p. 130.

[45] Jane Stevenson, 'Introduction', in Frederick Edward Warren, *The Liturgy and Ritual of the Celtic Church*, 2nd edn, ed. by Jane Stevenson (Woodbridge, 1987), pp. xi–cxxviiii (p. liv). Note that Warren transcribes, without translating, the original text of the Stowe Missal on pp. 207–20.

[46] Vernam E. Hull, 'The Date of Aipgitir Crábaid', *Zeitschrift für celtische Philologie*, 25 (1956), 88–90. The date, which was accepted by Rudolf Thurneysen and David Greene, was based on certain archaic forms in the text, for example archaic *tre* and intervocalic u in *anuis* (Donnchadh Ó Corráin, personal communication).

[47] Donnchadh Ó Corráin, personal communication. I am very grateful to Professor Ó Corráin for drawing this text to my attention and for his translation and comments on the passage.

of the body), and goes on to state that he if breaks these renunciations he must again 'pass through three pools — a pool of tears of repentance, a pool of blood in penitence, a pool of sweat in labour' ('maní tudig tre [t]relind a frithissi [. . .] .i. lind dér aithirge, lind fola i pennaind, lind n-aillse i llebair').[48]

Furthermore, as Éamonn Ó Carragáin himself has explained to me, the emphasis on pure running water in the Irish saints' lives has a sound basis in liturgy, because running water was essential for the rite of baptism, which was modelled on the baptism of Christ in the waters of the River Jordan (Matthew 3. 13–17; Mark 1. 9; Luke 3. 21).[49] Indeed, a reference to Christ's baptism in the Jordan is to be found in the Stowe Missal, in a prayer that reads: 'Exorcyzo té et per iesum christum [. . .] et ab ionne in iordane in té babtizatus est'[50] ('I exorcize thee [. . .] through Jesus Christ [. . .] who was baptized [. . .] by John in Jordan').[51] References to the purifying effects of water abound in this rite, and the sacrament itself is preceded by a recitation of Psalm 41/42, 'sicut cervus desiderat', which refers to the spiritual benefits of such water.[52] The Authorized Version of the passage reads: 'As the hart panteth after the water brooks, so panteth my soul as after thee, O God.' The same psalm is included at this point of the ceremony in the Gelasian Sacramentary,[53]

---

[48] Vernam E. Hull, 'Apgitir Chrábaid: The Alphabet of Piety', *Celtica*, 8 (1968), 44–89 (pp. 74–75, § 30). In the introduction Hull revises his earlier opinion about the early date of this text. However, Professor Ó Corráin (personal communication) argues that this is a mistake: 'The author is a monk writing a spiritual primer for his fellow-monks and for students. Among his sources are the works of John Cassian (Conferences and Institutes), a matter that places him firmly in the learned Latin tradition. What has been less noticed is the polished nature of the prose. This is [. . .] a mature example of a sophisticated and learned style, consciously based on the technique of Latin school rhetoric: one notes parallelism, gradatio, asyndeton in series of parallel clauses, alliteration, and word play. These characteristics recur in vernacular legal texts of the next century, e.g. *Bretha Nemed*.'

[49] I am grateful to Professor Ó Carragáin for discussing with me the baptism liturgy in the period in question. For a very lucid account of the liturgy of baptism, see his *Ritual and the Rood: Liturgical Images and the Old English Poems of the 'Dream of the Rood' Tradition* (London, 2005), pp. 123–26.

[50] Warner, *Stowe Missal*, p. 28.

[51] Translation by Edward Charles Whitaker, in *Documents of the Baptismal Liturgy*, 2nd edn (London, 1970), pp. 217–18, § 18 (where the relevant passage of the rite recorded in Latin in the Stowe Missal is translated into English).

[52] Whitaker, *Baptismal Liturgy*, p. 217, § 16; Ó Carragáin, *Ritual and the Rood*, p. 125.

[53] Whitaker, *Baptismal Liturgy*, p. 185 (where it is listed as Psalm 41, its number in the Vulgate). A sacramentary is a service book containing the prayers recited during Mass and other Christian rites. Several distinct rites were current in the West before *c.* 700, the two most influen-

dated to the eighth century but recording a rite which probably goes back at least to the sixth century.[54]

In outline, the sacrament of baptism consists of a symbolic near-death experience, followed by rebirth as a Christian, the anointing with chrism (in order to be endowed with the grace of the Holy Spirit), and the taking of communion; as explained by Éamonn Ó Carragáin: 'Like Christ [the neophytes] died symbolically entering into his death in the waters of the font; and from the font they rose to new life, fed by his body.'[55] The irreducible core of the rite, however, is the application of water, while the celebrant says 'Baptizo te, N., in nomine Patris et Filii et Spiritus Sancti'.[56]

In considering whether Irish holy wells were used for baptism in early medieval Ireland, it is important to bear in mind that there were four possible variants in the rite: submersion, immersion, affusion, and aspersion.[57] In submersion, or total immersion, the candidate goes briefly, but entirely, under the water. In immersion the head alone was dipped in water, with or without the candidate having to stand in it. In affusion (see Figs 46 and 47) water was poured over the head of the neophyte from a vessel, so that it streamed down the body. In aspersion water was sprinkled on the head, as in the modern ceremony.

Reviews of the archaeological evidence from across the Roman empire have concluded that submersion, or total immersion, was rare in late antiquity,[58] and this may also be true of early medieval Ireland. The evidence is inconclusive. It is hard to know if the passage from *Apgitir Chrábaid* cited above, with its references to the 'three waves that pass over a person in baptism' and the three pools ('trelind')

tial being the Roman, used in Rome and southern Italy, and the Gallican, used in much of western Europe. By A.D. 700 the Roman sacramentary reached Gaul where it was modified by Gallican usage, and the mixture of rites resulted in the Gelasian Sacramentary (spuriously attributed to the late fifth-century Pope Gelasius I). See Michelle P. Brown, *Illuminated Manuscripts: A Guide to Technical Terms* (London, 1994), p. 112. For a fuller, very clear discussion, see Stevenson, 'Introduction' to Warren, *Liturgy and Ritual*, pp. xi–xx. Note that the original text of the Order of Baptism from the Stowe Missal is transcribed (but not translated) there on pp. 213–25.

[54] Whitaker, *Baptismal Liturgy*, pp. 185–86, § 87.

[55] Ó Carragáin, *Ritual and the Rood*, pp. 125–26.

[56] For further discussion of baptism in the early Celtic church, see Stevenson, 'Introduction' to Warren, *Liturgy and Ritual*, pp. xxiii, liii, and liv.

[57] Foot, '"By Water in the Spirit"', pp. 178, 183; Charles Thomas, *Christianity in Roman Britain to AD 500* (London, 1981), pp. 204–27 (p. 204).

[58] Thomas, *Christianity in Roman Britain*, pp. 205–06.

Figure 46 (left). Detail from the tombstone of Innocens, Aquileia (fifth century). Baptism by affusion as water descends on the child from the Holy Ghost as a dove. Drawing after Charles Thomas, *Christianity in Roman Britain to AD 500* (London, 1981), fig. 39.

Figure 47 (right). Baptism of Christ on the broken cross at Kells, Co. Meath (late ninth to tenth century), showing baptism by affusion as water descends on Christ from a ladle-like object. Drawing after J. Romilly Allen, 'The Celtic Brooch and How it Was Worn', *Illustrated Archaeologist* (1894), 165.

through which the penitent must symbolically pass again, is to be taken literally. But perhaps it was not, given that depictions of the Baptism of Christ on ninth-to tenth-century Irish high crosses such as that at Killary, Co. Meath and the broken cross at Kells, Co. Meath (Fig. 47) clearly show baptism by affusion, water being poured over the head of the neophyte from a ladle-like object, similar to the decorated copper-alloy ladle from the Derrynaflan hoard.[59] Interestingly, similar objects which have been identified as baptismal skillets occur in Anglo-Saxon contexts (for example, one recently discovered at Shalfleet, Isle of Wight, dated to the seventh to eighth century),[60] while baptismal scenes on tenth-century Anglo-Saxon stone crosses in the Chapter House in Durham show baptism by affusion with the use of such skillets.[61] Submersion, of course, can only take place in water that is relatively deep, and many Irish holy wells are now, at least, shallow. So submersion in holy wells may have presented practical problems, though some which

[59] Peter Harbison, 'The Derrynaflan Ladle: Some Parallels Illustrated', *Journal of Irish Archaeology*, 3 (1985/86), 55–58, pls I and IV.

[60] Frank Basford, 'An Early Christian Baptismal Skillet from Shalfleet, Isle of Wight', *Current Archaeology*, 17 (May/June 2006), 567.

[61] Harbison, 'Derrynaflan Ladle' p. 58, pls V and VI.

now have steps down to them (for example, those at Aghagower, Co. Mayo,[62] Faughert Upper, Co. Louth,[63] and see above, Fig. 45), like many in Wales, may have been deep enough. It is also possible that wells were dug out to make them deeper in the early Middle Ages. Alternatively, streams, rivers, lakes, or even waterfalls may have served instead. Bede tells us that Paulinus, on occasion, baptized the Northumbrians in rivers;[64] Irish clerics may have done likewise. However, if the Irish more commonly administered baptism by immersion or affusion, as seems to have been the norm across the late antique world from east to west,[65] then holy wells would have been eminently suitable places for the rite.

In the case of affusion, and also aspersion and maybe even immersion of the head alone, a vessel of some sort may have been required, in addition to a ladle, if such were used for affusion, as the high crosses indicate. Perhaps, as Cormac Bourke has suggested, some of the surviving, highly ornate buckets with wooden bodies and ornamented metal coverings may have played a role in baptismal ceremonies,[66] for example those from Clonard (Co. Meath), Skei (Trøndelag, Norway), and Birka (Uppland, Sweden) (Fig. 48).[67] Both the Skei and Birka buckets are decorated with incised vine-scrolls, a motif associated with the Eucharist, perhaps referring to the taking of communion at the end of the rite. Bullaun stones, that is, stones with hollows which fill with water which, like holy wells, are revered and often occur on church sites,[68] would, of course, also have been suitable for aspersion.

[62] My own observation.

[63] Ian Fisher, personal communication.

[64] Bede, *Historia Ecclesiastica Gentis Anglorum*, 2.14.16.

[65] Thomas, *Christianity in Roman Britain*, p. 206.

[66] Cormac Bourke, personal communication.

[67] James Graham-Campbell, 'National and Regional Identities: "The Glittering Prizes"', in *Pattern and Purpose in Insular Art: Proceedings of the Fourth International Conference on Insular Art held at the National Museum & Galley, Cardiff 3–6 September 1998*, ed. by Mark Redknap and others (Oxford, 2001), pp. 27–38, figs 3.3 and 3.4 respectively.

[68] For a fuller discussion of bullaun stones in Ireland, see Peter Harbison, *Pilgrimage in Ireland: The Monuments and the People* (London, 1991), pp. 223–26. There is evidence for the use of water from similar stones in the later Anglo-Saxon period in England. Baptism using water from such a stone is described in the eleventh-century Anglo-Saxon life of St Rumwold, who was supposedly the son of a Christian daughter of Penda, the seventh-century King of Mercia, and an unidentified King of Northumbria. At the moment of his birth Rumwold cried aloud and demanded baptism. He then ordered the servants standing around to fetch a hollow stone lying a little distance away, in which the water of holy baptism was blessed by the two priests who performed the rite. See Foot, '"By Water in the Spirit"', pp. 171–72.

Figure 48. Vine-scrolls on bucket from Birka, grave 507. Drawing after H. Arbman, *Birka I. Die Gräber* (Tafeln) (Stockholm, 1940).

Baptismal fonts would have performed the same function, but there is little proof of their use in Ireland before the later Middle Ages. The odd stone container that remains, which may have served this purpose, is difficult to date.[69] There may have been wooden fonts but none survives. The same is true of Anglo-Saxon England. The very shaky evidence for freestanding stone fonts there from this period has recently been reviewed by Richard Bailey. He has identified one possible Anglo-Saxon purpose-built font made of stone, decorated with vine-scrolls and spirals and dated on stylistic grounds to *c.* A.D. 800, that at Deerhurst, Gloucestershire.[70] Nevertheless, as he remarks,

We are still left with the problem of how the numerous documentary instructions on the necessity for infant baptism were fulfilled within the period; were portable, perhaps

[69] A case in point is the large granite basin at St Maelruan's Church of Ireland Church at Tallagh, Co. Dublin, to which Cormac Bourke has kindly drawn my attention.

[70] Richard N. Bailey, *Anglo-Saxon Sculptures at Deerhurst* (Deerhurst, 2005), pp. 14–23, pls 6–8.

wooden, containers employed or did wells and rivers figure in what Richard Morris felicitously described as 'al fresco initiation'?[71]

John Blair has likewise pointed out that stone fonts dated to this early period in England are hard to find. He suggests that we cannot exclude the possibility that before *c.* 1050 small churches did not have fixed containers for baptismal water, and he speculates that monolithic fonts were probably an aspect of the 'Great Rebuilding' movement, only becoming common with permanently built local churches during the later eleventh century. He adds:

> While there is no means of proving that the priests had previously baptized the laity at outdoor holy wells, it seems not unlikely; this practice, and that of filling fonts from holy wells, are recorded later in remote parts of Britain and may be archaic survivals.[72]

The situation in Ireland may have been similar. The second decree of the Synod of Cashel, held in the year 1172 and summoned by Henry II in order to enact 'measures beneficial to the church and with the amelioration of the existing conditions of the church' was that 'infants be catechized before the doors of the church, and baptized in the holy font in baptisteries'.[73] This had already been prescribed by Gilla Espaig of Limerick,[74] which rather suggests that baptism in a church font was not yet standard practice. This is also indeed suggested by the remark made by Abbot Benedict, in his account of the life of Henry II, that before the Synod of Cashel the uncanonical custom in many parts of Ireland had been that when a child was born 'the father, or somebody else, immersed him three times in water, and that if he was a rich man, three times in milk'.[75] This

---

[71] Bailey, *Anglo-Saxon Sculptures at Deerhurst*, p. 17; see also Richard Morris, 'Baptismal Places: 600–800', in *People and Places in Northern Europe 500–1600*, ed. by Ian Woods and Niels Lund (Woodbridge, 1991), pp. 15–24 (p. 20).

[72] Blair, *Church in Anglo-Saxon Society*, pp. 461–62.

[73] 'Et de utilitate ecclesie et statu eius in meliorem formam perducendo ibidem concilium celebrarunt [. . .] quod infantes ante fores ecclesie catezizentur, et in sacro fonte in ipsis baptismalibus ecclesiis baptizentur': Giraldus Cambrensis, *Expugnatio Hibernica: The Conquest of Ireland*, ed. by A. B. Scott and F. X. Martin (Dublin, 1978), pp. 98–99. All the sources cited in this paragraph derive from an unpublished lecture by Donnchadh Ó Corráin, 'The Council of Cashel, or How the Irish Bishops Gave Up' (Nineteenth Irish Conference of Medievalists, 24 June 2005). I am very grateful to Professor Ó Corráin for giving me a copy of this lecture.

[74] James Ussher, *The Whole Works of the Most Reverend James Ussher*, 17 vols (Dublin, 1847–64), IV, 505.

[75] 'Cum puer nasceretur, pater ipsius vel quislibet alius eum ter mergeret in aqua, et si divitis fuerit filius, ter mergeret in lacte': *Gesta Regis Henrici Secundus Benedicti Abbatis: The Chronicle*

statement, however, should not necessarily be taken at face value, and the suggestion that milk rather than water was used for baptism may be just one of the many slurs on the Irish church made by the Normans in the twelfth century.[76]

Conclusions

The evidence from saints' lives suggests that in the early centuries of Christianity in Ireland baptism in springs or holy wells was common, an inference supported by folklore tradition, twelfth-century historical sources, and comparative evidence from Anglo-Saxon England. We may speculate, therefore, that in early medieval Ireland baptisms were sometimes, at least, performed using water from holy wells or in holy wells themselves. In an organized Christian community where running water was essential for the baptismal rite, it would have been convenient to build churches near springs. Could this be one reason why holy wells, fed by local springs, are often found in the vicinity of early Christian churches and burial places in Ireland? Given the general lack of evidence for self-standing baptisteries or even for fonts in early medieval Ireland, it looks more than likely that such holy wells were important centres at which baptismal ceremonies were performed.

of the Reigns of Henry II and Richard I A.D. 1169–1192 Commonly Under the name of Benedict of Peterborough, ed. by Williams Stubbs , 2 vols, Rolls Series [49] (London 1867), I, 28.

[76] Jane Hawkes, personal communication.

Sacred Cities?

Michael Ryan

To Éamonn in memory of many al fresco celebrations in Rome and Venice

One abiding characteristic of significant early Irish ecclesiastical sites is the presence not of a single great church but rather of a multiplicity of small churches — what might well be called a 'sacred city'. The reasons for this are unclear, and the topic has rarely been discussed. Liam de Paor referred to clusters of churches as a characteristic of pre-Norman Irish sites. Both Kathleen Hughes and Anne Hamlin considered the practice of building a number of churches, and concluded that it was never the custom to rebuild or enlarge existing ones.[1] They noted that, at some sites, a church reserved for the use of women is usually located at some distance from the focus of the ecclesiastical settlement. Surviving women's churches are known at Clonmacnoise and Lemanaghan, Co. Offaly.[2] Tomás Ó Carragáin speculates that one explanation for the clusters of individual churches may be the great increase in private Masses from the eighth century onwards, which prompted the proliferation of altars in Continental and

---

[1] On church clusters, see Laim de Paor's unpublished excavation report on Inis Cealtra (file Dúchas: The Heritage Service, Dublin), and also Frank Mitchell and Michael Ryan, *Reading the Irish Landscape* (Dublin, 1997), pp. 295–96; Michael Ryan, 'The Derrynaflan Hoard and Early Irish Art', *Speculum*, 72 (1997), 995–1017 (p. 1017); and Kathleen Hughes and Ann Hamlin, *Celtic Monasticism: The Modern Traveller to the Early Irish Church* (repr. New York, 1981), pp. 68–69. Michael Herity provides a useful overview in 'The Layout of Irish Early Christian Monasteries', in *Ireland and Europe: The Early Church*, ed. by Michael Richter and Prionsias Ní Chatháin (Munich, 1984), pp. 105–16.

[2] On women's churches, see Hughes and Hamlin, *Celtic Monasticism*; Peter Harbison, *Pilgrimage in Ireland: The Monuments and the People* (London, 1991), pp. 89–90; and Elizabeth FitzPatrick and Caimin O'Brien, *The Medieval Churches of Co. Offaly* (Dublin, 1998), pp. 40–49 (Clonmacnoise) and 12–15 (St Mella's Cell, Lemanaghan).

Anglo-Saxon churches (see below).[3] But we simply do not know how many clergy were in priestly orders in a typical Irish church community. Numbers may have been small, and private Masses could have been accommodated readily by successive use of single altars in churches of modest size.

The *Liber angeli* mentions two churches at Armagh, one reserved for bishops, priests, and anchorites, and the other for virgins, penitents, and those legitimately married.[4] Con Manning suggests that by the twelfth century annalists were using what amounted to a formula when describing raids on church foundations — they are often described as having been burned *cona tempaillaib* ('with their churches'). A cluster of churches was therefore normal on important sites.[5] Peter Harbison assumes that they were especially characteristic of pilgrimage centres.[6] Dissenting voices include J. Blair and R. Stalley,[7] who believe that the pattern of multiple churches is no more distinctive of Irish sites than of other early medieval ecclesiastical complexes; the subsequent growth of towns has obscured their similarities. Differences in preservation as a result (in Ireland) of frequent abandonment of sites except for burial purposes and (elsewhere) of continuous use and development into urban settlements may well account for the apparent but misleading distinctiveness of the Irish clusters. The Irish early medieval church in this, as in many other matters, was closer to mainstream practice than is often realized. It only became an anomaly when the native clergy continued to cling to the older tradition long after the practice of consolidating the liturgy under the roof of a single large structure with numerous altars became the norm in the Carolingian world.

We do not know how many churches once stood on great sites such as Armagh, Clonmacnoise, Kells, and Lismore. The failure of wooden churches to

---

[3] In the proceedings of the Bangor conference, *The Archaeology of the Early Celtic Church*, ed. by N. Edwards, forthcoming.

[4] Discussed in N. B. Aitchison, *Armagh and the Royal Centres in Early Medieval Ireland* (Woodbridge, 1994), p. 240.

[5] Conleth Manning, ' References to Church Buildings in the Annals', in *Seanchas: Studies in Early and Medieval Irish Archaeology, History and Literature in Honour of Francis John Byrne*, ed. by Alfred P. Smyth (Dublin, 2000), pp. 37–52, table p. 45 (wooden church at Clonmacnoise in 1167) and stone and wooden churches in a cluster at Armagh (at p. 50).

[6] Harbison, *Pilgrimage*, p. 124.

[7] J. Blair, 'Anglo-Saxon Minsters: A Topographical Review', in *Pastoral Care Before the Parish*, ed. by John Blair and Richard Sharpe (Leicester, 1992), pp. 226–66 (pp. 247–58, 264–65); R. Stalley, 'Ecclesiastical Architecture before 1169', in *A New History of Ireland I Prehistoric and Early Ireland*, ed. by D. Ó Cróinín (Oxford, 2005), pp. 714–43 (pp. 719–20).

survive and the poor prospects for excavation caused by generations of burial make even a guess at this almost pointless. That there were wooden and earthen churches is amply attested by the historical and archaeological records. In Kerry, both at Church Island and at Illaunloughan, stone churches were preceded by wooden and sod-built structures respectively.[8] The limited distribution of surviving stone churches obliges us to infer that timber remained an important material for church building up to the period of the Anglo-Norman invasion, if not later. We cannot know whether stone churches were matched in size by wooden examples — since both were in use side by side on several sites, there was probably a rough equivalence of scale. Many of the surviving earliest stone churches tend to be relatively small and some of them have come to be termed 'oratories', their function as churches (in the sense of buildings capable of serving the pastoral needs of a community) supposed to have been limited. We actually know very little of pastoral care in early medieval Ireland and of how the sacraments were made available to the laity, although Richard Sharpe[9] has outlined the convincing evidence for a significant network of churches which could have provided such services. Ó Carragáin (*fils*) has supported this with detailed archaeological evidence, showing that many of the surviving drystone churches of west Kerry could have provided a network of places of more than sufficient size to accommodate the pastoral care of the inhabitants. However, not all churches would have been congregational — the very small examples associated with eremitical sites being a case in point.[10] (I am grateful to Dr Ó Carragáin for permitting me to discuss his forthcoming paper which examines these issues in even greater detail.[11])

Larger Irish stone churches begin with the construction in the early tenth century of the Cathedral of Clonmacnoise under the patronage of an exceptionally

---

[8] See Jenny White Marshall and Claire Walsh, *Illaunloughan Island: An Early Medieval Monastery in County Kerry* (Bray, 2003), pp. 23–26 (sod-built structure) and 33–34 for a possible further sequence of earth and wooden chapel to church, and references to such a sequence elsewhere, as at Church Island and St Vogue's, Co. Wexford.

[9] Richard Sharpe, 'Churches and Communities in Early Medieval Ireland: Towards a Pastoral Model', in *Pastoral Care before the Parish*, ed. by Blair and Sharpe, pp. 82–109.

[10] Tomás Ó Carragáin, 'A Landscape Converted: Archaeology and Early Church Organisation on Iveragh and Dingle, Ireland', in *The Cross Goes North: Processes of Conversion in Northern Europe, AD 300–1300*, ed. by Martin Carver (York, 2003), pp. 127–52 (pp. 129–30).

[11] Tomás Ó Carragáin, 'Church Buildings and Pastoral Care in Early Medieval Ireland', in *The Parish in Medieval and Post-Medieval Ireland*, ed. by R. Gillespie, S. Duffy, and E. FitzPatrick (Dublin, forthcoming).

powerful king, Flann Sinna.[12] This was followed at the turn of the century by churches at Inis Cealtra and Clonfert — both of them also evidently the result of the patronage of powerful rulers — and others less well documented.[13] The emergence of stone architecture in the eighth century, and the fairly widespread use thereof in the ninth and tenth centuries, may have had a great deal to do with the ambitions of ecclesiastical foundations and their alliances with formidable kings whose authority transcended their traditional spheres of influence and who were capable of commanding much greater wealth than their predecessors.

Excavation evidence has demonstrated the existence of single altars in a couple of instances. At Caherlehillan a large posthole in a small church seems to have been the support for an altar. The late Liam de Paor excavated a large rectilinear earth and wattle structure at Inis Cealtra, interpreted as a church, where stains probably representing the site of an altar were identified. It seemed to him that the position of the altar was adjusted as the building was renewed during the course of its use.[14] Altars exist in a number of stone churches. A fine example is to be seen in the chancel of St Caimin's on Inis Cealtra, but relatively modern reconstruction may be suspected there and in many other cases. The norm therefore appears to have been that churches had single altars, there being no space for additional ones in the small unicameral structures which appear to have been standard, to judge by surviving stone examples.

When chancels were added to Irish pre-Romanesque churches, these too could have accommodated only a single altar. The addition of chancels, however, indicates an elaboration of liturgy and significantly increased separation of congregation and celebrant in the twelfth century. The addition of south doorways to some churches at this time also suggests a change in liturgy and a reordering of space, with perhaps an emphasis on procession within the church (Plate 12a). A procession would have been difficult to manage in a small church with a single western entrance, where it would have had to make its way through a (presumably) standing congregation. Complex liturgical processions could possibly have been staged in wooden churches such as that described by Cogitosus at Kildare in

---

[12] Manning, 'References to Church Buildings'.

[13] Useful surveys are Harold Leask, *Irish Churches and Monastic Buildings*, 3 vols (Dundalk, 1955–60), vol. I; Françoise Henry, *Irish Art during the Viking Invasions, 800–1020 A.D.* (London, 1967), and Henry, *Irish Art in the Romanesque Period 1020–1170 A.D.* (London, 1970).

[14] Unpublished preliminary report, National Monuments Service.

the seventh century, with its separate entrances for different classes within the congregation.[15]

We have perhaps neglected the importance of processions in the early Irish church. While the *Liber angeli* records one at Armagh, the classic exemplar of processions was the Roman liturgy, and Armagh modelled itself liturgically on Rome.[16] At Rome the numerous churches were stations of an imposing liturgical tradition. Processions to major basilicas and other churches formed an essential part of the seasonal liturgical cycle and would have seemed particularly impressive to pilgrims.[17] The Roman practice was extensively copied in major cities within Francia and perhaps also in Anglo-Saxon England.[18] A reflection of the Roman liturgy is also to be found in the great monastic and other churches which had a multiplicity of altars. These formed stations on complex intramural processions at important feasts. R. K. Morris has speculated that a stational liturgy on the Roman model was practised at York, which had a number of early medieval churches but also had an example of its compression within a single building. According to Alcuin, the church of Alma Sophia had thirty altars.[19] A stational liturgy using a cluster of churches was certainly possible in contemporary Ireland.

The western drystone churches such as Gallarus are sometimes in exceptionally austere island settings such as Skellig Michael (Plate 12b), Illauntannig, and elsewhere.[20] Others located on the mainland were clearly close to populated areas and

[15] See Carol Neuman de Vegvar, '*Romanitas* and Realpolitik in Cogitosus's Description of the Church of St Brigit, Kildare', in *The Cross Goes North*, ed. by Carver, pp. 153–70, for a fresh analysis of the Kildare church and its significance.

[16] Aitchison, *Armagh and the Royal Centres*, pp. 207–10.

[17] John Baldovin, *The Urban Character of Christian Worship: The Origins, Development, and Meaning of Stational Liturgy*, Orientalia Christiana Analecta, 228 (Rome, 1987); Éamonn Ó Carragáin, '*Traditio Evangeliorum* and *Sustentatio*: The Relevance of Liturgical Ceremonies to the Book of Kells', in *The Book of Kells: Proceedings of a Conference at Trinity College Dublin 6–9 September 1992*, ed. by Felicity O'Mahoney (Aldershot, 1994), pp. 398–436 (pp. 411–14).

[18] Éamonn Ó Carragáin, *The City of Rome and the World of Bede* (Jarrow Lecture, 1994), analyses the impact of the Roman liturgy in the Anglo-Saxon world and especially on the monasteries of Monkwearmouth and Jarrow and, in passing, on the Irish church also.

[19] R. K. Morris, 'Alcuin, York and the *alma sophia*', in *The Anglo-Saxon Church: Papers on History, Architecture and Archaeology in Honour of Dr H. M. Taylor*, ed. by L. A. S. Butler and R. K. Morris, Council for British Archaeology Research Report, 60 (London, 1986), pp. 80–89.

[20] Peter Harbison, *The Golden Age of Irish Art: The Medieval Achievement 600–1200* (London, 1999), p. 194; Tadg O'Keefe, 'Architectural Traditions of the Early Medieval Church in Munster', in *Early Medieval Munster*, ed. by Michael A. Monk and John Sheahan (Cork, 1998), pp. 112–24 (p. 114).

could therefore have formed part of the pattern of pastoral provision postulated by Sharpe. Recently it has been argued that these very small churches were entered by senior clergy who completed in seclusion the celebration of Mass after the Gospel had been read, the preliminaries having taken place al fresco while the elements were being prepared inside. This argument is based partly on details of the Stowe Missal liturgy, and also on an anecdote in Adomnán's *Vita Columbae* concerning a visit of four brother abbots to the saint on the island of Hinba, wherein Columba is said to have 'entered the church with them as usual on the Lord's day after the Gospel had been read'.[21] Lay people, it is argued, remained outside while the sacred mysteries were celebrated out of sight. There are many difficulties with this interpretation, not least of which is that where the church was in a monastic setting it must surely have been conceived as being of sufficient size to enable the entire community of monks to assemble within it for divine office.[22] Infrequency of communion — which seems to have been the common

[21] J. W. Hunwicke, 'Kerry and Stowe Revisited', *Proceedings of the Royal Irish Academy*, 102C (2002), 1–19, esp. pp. 2–4. The four abbots are named as Comgall moccu Aradi, Cainech moccu Dalen, Brendan moccu Altae, and Cormac Ua Liatha(fada)n. However, the occasion described by Adomnán was an exceptional one, where the saint was in the company of three great monastic founding-saints. We must also bear in mind the possibility of idiosyncratic local practices which were by no means standard in an age before wide liturgical uniformity. In a note on this episode, Richard Sharpe suggests that the opening of the Mass was celebrated in the open air — a practice which would be appropriate for the cathecumens in the case of a church of small size — with the priest entering 'the church building as he would the sanctuary'. However, Hinba may be atypical since, as Sharpe notes, on Iona all the monks entered the church. *Adomnán of Iona: Life of St Columba*, trans. by Richard Sharpe (Harmondsworth, 1995), p. 219. Furthermore, the episode could reflect practice current in the time of the *Vita*'s composition rather than in the age of Columba. Hence it may constitute evidence for liturgical fashions as they were developing in these islands at the end of the seventh century, when Roman influences were gradually making headway — especially in Northumbria where, thanks to John the Archcantor, there was a deliberate attempt to bring the celebration of the Mass into conformity with Roman traditions. In early Roman *ordines*, the Bishop of Rome remained in the sacristy of the stational church until preparations for the celebration were complete; he then entered giving the signal that the liturgy could proceed. Is Adomnán's anecdote about Columba and the visiting abbots a confused account of something based on this practice?

[22] John Ryan, *Irish Monasticism: Origins and Early Development* (London, 1931), pp. 287–88, discusses the presence of large churches as distinct from oratories and especially churches of wood and of wicker. He observes that the 'church in every monastery must have been large enough to hold the whole community' and speculates that the members of a parish community may have stood around in the open air while Mass was celebrated within the church (pp. 288–89). Manning, 'References to Church Buildings', pp. 46–47, lists the annalistic entries which document the

pattern — may have meant that only relatively small churches were needed, as congregations at any one time may not have been large. In some areas, especially in the west, populations may have been very small and this, too, must be factored in. Hunwicke bases much of his argument on the very small size of certain churches on Kerry sites (at Kilabounia and Illaunloughan, for example) along with the abovementioned anecdote in Adomnán's *Vita Columbae*.[23] The diminutive churches, like the remains of a tiny structure on the South Peak of Skellig Michael, may simply have served the needs of a hermit or small group of ascetics and may have had no wider pastoral function — something which is in any event inconceivable in the case of the Skellig hermitage.

The problem is that Hunwicke bases his argument on texts which have no particular reference to small churches or which are equivocal or contradictory. For example, the Stowe Missal, on which he grounds much of his argument, originated at Lorrha, a sizeable church foundation very far removed from the early Kerry sites. There is no compelling reason to believe that at the time of composition of Stowe, Lorrha could not have had a church capable of holding a substantial congregation.[24] Kildare is cited as a place where the open-air celebration is, as it were, brought indoors, but the exclusivity of those who assisted at the mysteries was retained by the internal partitions. The idea that Mass was frequently celebrated in the open air, with the small churches of the western type serving merely as sacristies or as a holy of holies where only the élite witnessed the sacred mysteries, is by no means convincing. The Irish church belonged to an essentially Latin tradition where, unlike the practice in the Byzantine rites, public, openly visible celebration of the Eucharist was central. The regular designation of smaller Irish churches as 'oratories' is more than a little tendentious, as Manning has recently

---

fact that some churches were very capacious, as demonstrated by the numbers recorded as having been burnt or otherwise slain within them, for example in the wooden churches of Trevet in A.D. 850 (260 people) and Drumraney in A.D. 948 (150), and in the stone churches of Ardbraccan in 1031 (200) and Lusk in 1089 (180).

[23] Hunwicke, 'Kerry and Stowe Revisited'.

[24] One minor piece of evidence which might suggest that the author had celebration within the church in mind is the reference in a tract on the Mass in the Stowe Missal to the 'dove over the altar'. Unless it refers to a spiritual dove or a free-flying bird on the wing, it is likely to imply the existence of one of those metal doves in which the reserved consecrated Eucharist was held in early medieval churches on the Continent. The text is in *The Stowe Missal*, ed. by George Warner (London, 1915), p. 37 and n. 2. Such an object was unlikely to be trusted to the vagaries of the Irish climate.

noted.[25] Nussbaum in 1965 proposed a variant of this where he envisaged open-air Masses taking place at cross-slabs.[26] This might meet the objections of those who insist that the celebration of the Eucharist was publicly visible as in the Roman *ordines*. There is no really convincing evidence for regular open-air Masses in any Irish text. Documentary evidence, such as it is, assumes that the Mass was celebrated in church.

On many western ecclesiastical sites altar-like features (variously called *leachta*, *altóir*, and *ulaí*) are found, which signify cuboid structures of drystone, occasionally surmounted by a cross or cross-inscribed stone (Plate 12b). There are especially well-known examples on Tory Island, Inishmurray (Plate 13a), Rathlin O'Beirne, Caher Island,[27] and Skellig Michael. Several examples act as plinths for vertically set cross-slabs which, according to Michael Herity's cogent argument, were made especially for their positions.[28] He has assembled a substantial body of evidence to suggest that they were exclusively stations on pilgrimage rounds, a purpose many of them serve to this day. Herity has dated most of the cross-slabs to the sixth to seventh centuries A.D., and thus the development of the pilgrimages to a very early period. This is disputed, as many authors have been sceptical about that very ancient dating. O'Sullivan's excavations at Inishmurray have shed some light on the age of two examples, and he suggests that they were put up towards the end of the first millennium.[29] The excavations at Illaunloughan show that a *leacht*-like feature acts as support for the wall of a stone church and its stones are keyed into it.[30] The early medieval dating of certain *leachta* is not therefore in doubt.[31] If the

---

[25] Manning, 'References to Church Buildings', pp. 37–38.

[26] Otto Nussbaum, *Der Standort des liturgen am Christlichen Altar vor dem Jahre 1000 eine archaeologische und liturgiegeschichtliche Untersuchung*, 2 vols (Bonn, 1965), I, 366–71.

[27] M. Herity, 'The Antiquity of *An Turas* in Ireland', in Herity, *Studies in the Layout, Buildings and Art in Stone of Early Irish Monasteries* (London 1995), pp. 91–125.

[28] Herity, 'Antiquity of *An Turas*', p. 120, where he speaks of the 'harmony between slab and *leacht*'.

[29] J. O'Sullivan and Tomás Ó Carragáin, *The Sacred Landscape of Inishmurray: Survey and Excavation 1997–2000*, Department of the Environment Heritage and Local Government Monograph (Dublin, forthcoming).

[30] White Marshall and Walsh, *Illaunloughan Island*, pp. 46–48. A similar arrangement occurs on the large oratory on Skellig Michael; p. 49, pl. 38.

[31] White Marshall and Walsh, *Illaunloughan Island*. They point to clear constructional evidence at Skellig Michael which demonstrates that one *leacht* predates a drystone church and another appears to be contemporary with early medieval paving.

leachta are a comparatively late phenomenon they could form part of an ordering of ecclesiastical sites from the eighth to ninth century onwards, when *memoriae* began to be erected over the graves of founding saints and the larger churches began to take seriously their symbolic role as sacred cities. The encouragement of domestic rather than foreign pilgrimage begins to feature at this time. Somewhat later, as de Paor noted, there was a massive reorganization at Inis Cealtra to accommodate increased pilgrimage.[32] As we have seen, it is during the tenth century that we begin to get evidence of the construction of substantial churches in stone and complexes of features, including high crosses, which must have made the sacred centres of these places extremely imposing to the contemporary audience. Herity's thesis that the pilgrimages associated with many of the ancient church sites today are themselves ancient and the cross-slabs, pillars, and altar-like features continue to serve the purposes for which they were erected, seems — despite some chronological adjustment — to be sound.

Examples of slabs on Inishmurray — at Tríonoíd Mór and Reilig Odhráin — are carved with five crosses and are reminiscent of altar stones, but they are vertical pillars and not therefore the recumbent slabs on which Mass was celebrated (Figs 49 and 50).[33] The crosses are not laid out as one would find them on altar stones, although they may have formed a pattern of Eucharistic import. There are examples of true altar stones in the principal enclosure where there were three churches (Fig. 51).[34] There are also *leachta* within the enclosure but none incorporates an altar stone (Plate 13b). The evidence of survey and excavation combine to suggest that the altar-like features were built as stations on pilgrimages and not for other forms of liturgical activity. In short, while early medieval in date, they are not primary features of early church sites, as far as we can tell. Tomás Ó Carragáin suggests that where the altars on Inishmurray occur in cemeteries, they may well have been the sites of Mass said *in coemeterio* or perhaps for the saying of private Masses where they occur within the main enclosure.[35] Multiplication of altars had complex origins. In certain instances the numerous altars clearly substituted for the multiplicity of churches in urban liturgies and enabled them to be

[32] Liam de Paor, unpublished report, National Monuments Service, Dublin.

[33] W. F. Wakeman, *A Survey of the Antiquarian Remains on the Island of Inishmurray (Inis Muireadhaig)* (Dublin, 1893), fig. 72, p. 110; fig. 84, p. 152.

[34] Wakeman, *Antiquarian Remains on the Island of Inishmurray*, fig. 47, p. 99; fig. 48, p. 101; fig. 49, p. 102.

[35] O'Sullivan and Ó Carragáin, *Sacred Landscape of Inishmurray*.

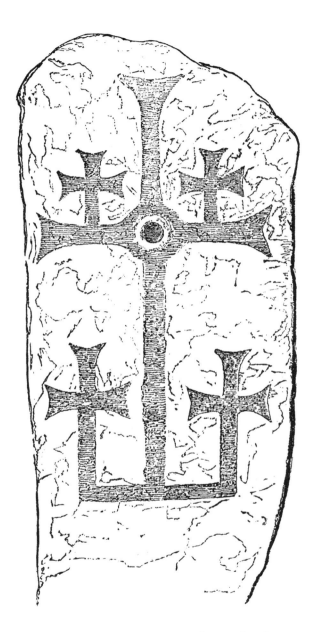

Figure 49. Pillar stone, Inishmurray, Co. Sligo. After drawing in W. F. Wakeman, *A Survey of the Antiquarian Remains on the Island of Inishmurray (Inis Muireadhaig)* (Dublin, 1893), p. 110, fig. 72.

Figure 50. Pillar stone, Inishmurray, Co. Sligo. After drawing in Wakeman,
Antiquarian Remains on the Island of Inishmurray, p. 152, fig. 84.

recapitulated under a single roof.[36] The tendency to increase the number of altars
was reinforced by the need to accommodate growing collections of relics — or the

---

[36] For example at the often studied church of Centula-St Riquier. See the summary by
Elizabeth C. Parker, 'Architecture as Liturgical Setting', in *The Liturgy of the Medieval Church*,
ed. by Thomas J. Heffernan and E. Ann Matter (Kalamazoo, 2001), pp. 273–326 (pp. 286–91).

Figure 51. Altar stone, Inishmurray, Co. Sligo. After drawing in Wakeman,
Antiquarian Remains on the Island of Inishmurray, p. 99, fig. 47.

concentration of relics previously held in separate buildings — and the saying of
commemorative and private Masses at side altars.[37] In Ireland, as we have seen,

[37] Walter Horn and Ernest Born, *The Plan of St Gall*, 3 vols (Berkeley, 1979), I, 208, 223.
White Marshall and Walsh, *Illaunloughan Island*, also speculate on the purpose of the numerous
open-air altar-like features and relate them to the development of liturgies around multiple altars
such as are mentioned in the *Regulis concordia* of Anglo-Saxon England and of the well-known
liturgical patterns at Centula-St Riquier (p. 53).

there seems to have been no provision whatever for more than one altar within pre-Norman churches, and this harks back to the earliest church traditions in the west where a single altar was the norm. Just as important in the development of Irish ecclesiastical architecture was the evident reluctance to build churches over the graves of saints or to translate their relics into churches. The general custom was to protect the grave with some form of small tomb shrine or to build *memoriae* (Plates 14, 15, and 16).[38] Thus there was a strong tendency in the early Irish church to continue to follow the early Christian model of building complexes of structures for religious purposes, and there was no need to expand individual churches to accommodate elaborate shrines and means of access to them for pilgrims. There was therefore little pressure to build large structures even if resources had been available for that purpose.

I argue elsewhere that the Irish church clusters represent also, at least partly, a conscious attempt in many cases to produce a simulacrum of Rome itself,[39] but perhaps it would be better to suggest that as they represented an ancient tradition, they presented a happy opportunity to replicate the Holy City when competition amongst pilgrimage destinations became intense. I would argue that the complex city liturgies such as we have in the early Roman *ordines* were aspired to in Ireland, particularly when the status of bishops began to rise to the levels more normal in international Church organization. There is no way of demonstrating this conclusively, but Irish writers of the period often refer to church sites as 'cities', and the term *ruam* is applied to a foundation with a cemetery because it resembled Rome where the martyrs and princes of the world were buried.[40] The term was in use from at least the eighth century. The creation of a setting for a stational liturgy (essen-

[38] Harbison, *Pilgrimage*, pp. 47–56. For a general discussion, see now Tomás Ó Carragáin, 'The Architectural Setting of the Cult of Relics in Early Medieval Ireland', *Journal of the Royal Society of Antiquaries of Ireland*, 133 (2003), 130–76.

[39] Michael Ryan, 'Eucharistic Vessels, Architecture and Liturgy in Early Medieval Ireland', in *De re metallica: The Uses of Metal in the Middle Ages*, edited by Robert O. Bork and others (Aldershot, 2005), pp. 125–46.

[40] *Dictionary of the Irish Language (compact edition)*, Royal Irish Academy (Dublin, 1983), p. 512. It is clear that the word had the meaning of 'cemetery', but the metaphorical use of the city's name in this way is very telling. See *Féilire Oengusso Céli Dé: The Martyrology of Oengus the Culdee*, ed. by Whitley Stokes (London, 1905), p. 25. See also John Hennig, 'Ireland's Contribution to the Martyrological Tradition of the Popes', in *Medieval Ireland, Saints and Martyrologies, Selected Studies*, ed. by Michael Richter, Variorum Reprints (Northampton, 1989), XI, who discusses the development of an early Irish form of the word *Roma*, i.e. *ru(fada)am*, which became a general term for a holy place and especially of one with a cemetery (pp. 10–11).

tially an urban liturgy) sits very comfortably with the occasional discouragement in Ireland of foreign pilgrimage[41] and the substitution of a simulation of that experience on native holy sites.[42] As we now know, Irish ecclesiastical sites were not haphazard accumulations of buildings.[43] Within their churches, the laity were admitted to the celebration of the Mass. We can safely conclude that open-air Eucharistic celebrations were the exception rather than the rule.

[41] Kathleen Hughes, *The Church in Early Irish Society* (London, 1966), p. 176, notes that St Máelruain forbade his followers to go abroad on pilgrimage because they would be 'deniers of Patrick in heaven and of the Faith in Ireland'. See also Ó Carragáin, '*Traditio Evangeliorum*'.

[42] There is nothing in the Irish record quite as explicit as the re-creation of Jerusalem by the Emperor Lalibela in Ethiopia, where the topography of the holy city and its surroundings were re-created in the Tigre mountains by a series of eleven churches, a stream named *Yordanes*, and the naming of surrounding hills after important sites in the life of Christ. See Roderick Grierson, 'Dreaming of Jerusalem', in *African Zion: The Sacred Art of Ethiopia*, ed. by Grierson (New Haven, 1993), pp. 5–17 (pp. 12–13). I am grateful to Professor Neumann de Vegvar for drawing my attention to this interesting parallel. Éamonn Ó Carragáin ('*Traditio Evangeliorum*', pp. 411–13) details one instance in the life of St Berach, where not only are his followers discouraged from going to Rome but crosses dedicated to Saints Peter and Paul are erected as suitable substitutes for the pilgrimage.

[43] Aitchison, *Armagh and the Royal Centres*, pp. 211–15; Stalley, 'Ecclesiastical Architecture before 1169'; Leo Swan, 'Monastic Proto-towns in Early Medieval Ireland: The Evidence of Aerial Photography, Plan Analysis and Survey', in *The Comparative History of Urban Origins in Non-Roman Europe: Ireland, Wales, Denmark, Germany, Poland and Russia from the Ninth to the Thirteenth Century*, ed. by H. B. Clarke and A. Simms, British Archaeological Reports, International Series, 255 (Oxford, 1985), pp. 77–102.

Nineteenth-century Travellers to Early Christian Sites in Co. Kerry

Elisabeth Okasha

É amonn Ó Carragáin has always been interested in inscribed and carved stones, of course in Anglo-Saxon monuments like the Ruthwell Cross, but also in Irish high crosses and cross-slabs. The Dingle peninsula in Co. Kerry, although without any carved high crosses, is rich in early Christian remains and monuments. Four sites in particular, Gallarus, Kilfountan, Kilmalkedar, and Reask, have produced stones that are both carved and inscribed. Some of these stones were among the first to be recorded from Ireland, having been described in the early nineteenth century. Travel to Dingle at this period was not easy, but nevertheless there were early travellers to these sites. Four prominent figures emerge: Henry Pelham, who visited the area in 1804; Lady Henrietta Chatterton, who undertook a tour in 1838; George Petrie, whose *Ecclesiastical Architecture* was published in 1845; and John Windele, who visited Kerry for a week in June 1838 and again in September 1848 and who kept a diary of his journeys. This paper examines the evidence of these early travellers to the Dingle peninsula sites and assesses the importance of their contribution to our understanding of the area, the sites, and the stones. It is offered to Éamonn in the certain knowledge that his interest in travel will be enhanced, not diminished, by his retirement from formal teaching.

Dingle, Co. Kerry

There are many early Christian remains and monuments in the Dingle peninsula. However, there are only four sites which contain stones that are both carved and also have a text inscribed in roman script. These sites, at Gallarus, Kilfountan, Kilmalkedar, and Reask, are all situated in quite close proximity to each other. Kilfountan is to the north of Dingle harbour, while the other three are all near Smerwick harbour. As is common with early Christian sites in south-west Ireland, these four are hardly mentioned in the early annals and little is known of their history.

At Gallarus (National Grid Reference [=NGR] 03933, 10486), the site is delineated by the partial remains of a large stone-walled enclosure. As well as the well-known boat-shaped oratory, there is a *leacht* (rectangular mound of stones) consisting of a low stone mound. The carved and inscribed stone now stands at one end of the *leacht*. There are no other carved or inscribed stones at the site.[1]

At Kilfountan (NGR 04255, 10330) the enclosure is defined by a stone-faced earthen bank and contains the remains of a dry-stone oratory and a rectangular building. As well as the stone under discussion here, a *bullaun* (holed) stone and a quern-stone were also found at the site. The carved and inscribed stone is loosely set into a mound of stone in the vicinity of the ruined oratory. As well as the roman inscription, this stone also contains an ogham text.[2]

By contrast, the early Christian and medieval site at Kilmalkedar (NGR 04027, 10617) covers a large area and contains a number of buildings and monuments. These include St Brendan's oratory and the remains of the twelfth-century church. There are several free-standing stones, including an ogham stone, the carved sun-dial stone, a plain stone cross, and some *bullaun* stones. There is also a large number of small cross-slabs and other grave-markers of uncertain date. The stone under discussion here is cemented into a modern base and is situated near the chancel arch in the ruins of the church. A second early stone, Kilmalkedar 2, is now lost.[3]

The site at Reask (NGR 03669, 10433) differs from the others under discussion in having been fully excavated in modern times.[4] These excavations revealed three broad phases of use. The first was a cemetery of fourth- to seventh-century

---

[1] For descriptions and illustrations of the site and stone, see Judith Cuppage, *Archaeological Survey of the Dingle Peninsula: A Description of the Field Antiquities of the Barony of Corca Dhuibhne from the Mesolithic Period to the 17th Century A.D.* (Dublin, 1986), pp. 286–89 and figs; and Elisabeth Okasha and Katherine Forsyth, *Early Christian Inscriptions of Munster: A Corpus of the Inscribed Stones* (Cork, 2001), pp. 147–50 and figs.

[2] For descriptions and illustrations of the site and stone, see Cuppage, *Archaeological Survey*, pp. 302–04 and figs; and Okasha and Forsyth, *Early Christian Inscriptions*, pp. 161–65 and figs.

[3] For descriptions and illustrations of the site and stones, see Cuppage, *Archaeological Survey*, pp. 308–23 and figs; and Okasha and Forsyth, *Early Christian Inscriptions*, pp. 165–71 and figs.

[4] T. Fanning, 'Excavation of an Early Christian Cemetery and Settlement at Reask, County Kerry', *Proceedings of the Royal Irish Academy*, 81C (1981), 67–172.

date and the third a *ceallúnach* (clandestine burial ground), used for clandestine burial until modern times. The main phase of development is loosely dated from the eighth to the twelfth centuries. It incorporated 'elements of worship, burial and a range of domestic activity and craftsmanship of a broadly "monastic" character'.[5] The two carved and inscribed stones date from this phase of the site and both now stand within the ecclesiastical site. There are also ten other cross-slabs, as well as some fragments.[6]

Early Travellers

Four of the people who travelled to the Dingle peninsula before 1850 left a written record of the stones they observed there. Listed chronologically, these early travellers were Henry Pelham (1749–1806), George Petrie (1790–1866), John Windele (1801–65), and Lady Henrietta Chatterton (1806–76). They form an interesting group. Although all of them lived for some time in Ireland, only two were Irish, Lady Chatterton being English by birth and Henry Pelham being American, although with an English father.

Henry Pelham was born in February 1749 in Boston, Massachusetts. Following in the footsteps of his father, Peter Pelham, he became a painter, specializing in historical subjects and miniatures. Some of his work was exhibited at the Royal Academy, London, in 1777 and 1778. Subsequently he came to Ireland and worked as an agent on Lord Lansdowne's estates in Co. Kerry. He married a daughter of William Butler of Castlecrine, Co. Clare, but they had no children. His greatest claim to fame is that he was the younger half-brother of the painter John Singleton Copley (1738–1815), whose widowed mother had married Peter Pelham in 1747. Copley's painting *A Boy with a Squirrel* (1765) is a portrait of Henry Pelham. This oil painting was apparently executed in America and then sent to London where it was exhibited. The painting is now in the Museum of Fine Arts, Boston, having been donated to the Museum in 1978 by the great-granddaughter of the artist. Henry Pelham died in an accident in 1806, drowning in the river at Kenmare.

Pelham described and drew the carving and text on the stone Kilmalkedar 1 as part of his contribution, entitled 'Ogham Inscriptions', which was published

---

[5] Cuppage, *Archaeological Survey*, p. 339.

[6] For descriptions and illustrations of the site and stones, see Cuppage, *Archaeological Survey*, pp. 336–45 and figs; Okasha and Forsyth, *Early Christian Inscriptions*, pp. 175–82 and figs.

in volume VI of Charles Vallencey's *Collectanea de rebus Hibernicis*. The 'Observations' given in this essay are apparently Vallencey's own. Charles Vallencey (1721–1812) was an English army officer, who was born in Windsor and died in Dublin. He was stationed for some time in Ireland and rose to the rank of General in 1803. As a military engineer he drew up plans for Mellows Bridge over the River Liffey and for the general defence of Dublin.[7] He was also interested in Irish history and antiquities. However, the entry on him in the *Dictionary of National Biography* is vituperative, in particular on the fact that he wrote about the Irish language when he had neither acquired the language nor read the literature. The comment given there on some of his books, including the *Collectanea*, reads: 'Their facts are never trustworthy and their theories are invariably extravagant.'[8] However there is no reason to suppose that Pelham's drawings or contribution to the *Collectanea* were included in this general condemnation.

George Petrie was born in Dublin in 1789. He was an antiquary, a painter, and a writer, and he worked for the Ordnance Survey between 1833 and 1846. Among his many interests were Irish architecture and antiquities, Irish music, and the decorative arts. He contributed articles on antiquarian subjects to academic journals, including many to the *Dublin Penny Journal*, which ran from 1832 to 1836. He also collected Irish tunes and played them on the violin. He was elected to the Royal Irish Academy in 1828 and to its council in 1829, and he worked hard to improve its library and museum. The University of Dublin honoured him with the degree of LL.D. in 1847. He died in Dublin in January 1866.

In 1833 Petrie won a gold medal from the Royal Irish Academy for a work entitled 'Essay on the Origin and Uses of the Round Towers of Ireland'. This, with many additions, was published as *Ecclesiastical Architecture* in 1845. In this he recorded visits to Kerry and included accounts and illustrations of the stones Gallarus and Kilmalkedar 1. Petrie continued to visit and examine inscribed stones and at his death left copious unpublished notes. These were edited by Margaret Stokes and published posthumously in two volumes, volume II containing the stones in Kerry.[9] Although Stokes included drawings of many of the stones,

---

[7] E. G. Quin, 'The Collectors of Irish Dialect Material', in *The English Language in Ireland*, ed. by Diarmaid Ó Muirithe (Dublin, 1977), pp. 115–26 (p. 115).

[8] N. Moore, 'Vallencey, Charles (1721–1812)', *Dictionary of National Biography*, 58 (1899), 82–83 (p. 83).

[9] George Petrie, *Christian Inscriptions in the Irish Language*, 2nd edn ed. by Margaret Stokes, 2 vols (Dublin, 1878), vol. II.

these were not often done from the stones themselves; instead she drew from the drawings, the lithographs, and the photographs of others.

John Dillon Windele was born in Cork in 1801, of a Catholic Kerry family. He was interested in Irish antiquities and the Irish language and was elected as an early member of the Kilkenny Archaeological Society, which later became the Royal Society of Antiquaries of Ireland. He worked in the Sheriff's Office in Cork city but was locally prominent as an antiquarian and historian, and was President of the Cork Cuvierian Society (which later became the Cork Historical and Archaeological Society) for the session 1847–48. Like Petrie, he contributed to the *Dublin Penny Journal* as well as to other academic journals. In his prime he was a great walker and apparently thought nothing of covering thirty to forty miles in a day on 'antiquarian rambles'.[10] He was particularly interested in ogham stones and saved many from destruction by moving them into his own house.[11] Some of these later went to the Royal Cork Institution and five from there subsequently came to University College Cork, where they remain.[12] He died in Cork in August 1865, and was survived by a son and three daughters.

Windele's diaries are preserved in the Royal Irish Academy in a large number of manuscript volumes of his papers. These papers contain a wealth of material but unfortunately they are mostly unpublished and largely unindexed. Some portions of the diaries relating to Windele's travels in Munster were transcribed in the *Journal of the Cork Historical and Archaeological Society*, but not the parts relating to Kerry. In his diaries Windele mentions carved and inscribed stones other than oghams that he had seen, for example at Gallarus and Kilmalkedar; he was in fact the first person to draw and record inscribed stones at Kilfountan and Reask. Some portions of his diary relating to journeys to Kerry in June 1838 and September 1848 are transcribed in the Appendix.

Lady Chatterton was born in London in November 1806 as Henrietta Georgina Marcia Lascelles Iremonger. In 1824 she married Sir William Abraham Chatterton of Castle Mahan, Co. Cork. They lived in Munster until the Famine when they moved back to England. Lady Chatterton was widowed in 1855 and in 1859 she married Edward Heneage Dering. He became a Catholic in 1865 and

[10] Anon., 'Three Memorable Cork Archæologists', *Journal of the Cork Historical and Archaeological Society*, 2nd series, 6 (1900), 32–47 (p. 38).

[11] E. I. Carlyle, 'Windele, John (1801–1865)', *Dictionary of National Biography*, 62 (1900), 166.

[12] P. Canon Power, *The Ogham Stones, University College Cork* (Cork, 1932), p. 10; Damian McManus, *The Ogam Stones at University College Cork* (Cork, 2004), p. 10.

in 1875, shortly before her death, Lady Chatterton also converted. She died in Malvern Wells in February 1876. Lady Chatterton wrote novels, stories, travel accounts, poems, and other short works. One of her early books was *Rambles in the South of Ireland during the year 1838*; this was published in 1839 and ran to two editions, both in that year. In this work Lady Chatterton described and illustrated the stone Kilmalkedar 1, first mentioned by Pelham, and also the Gallarus stone, which she was the first to record in print.

Although we have no evidence that any of these travellers actually met any of the others, it is of course possible that some of them did. Some of them were, at least, aware of the existence of some of the others. Windele, for example, refers to the work all the other three.[13] It also seems that Windele and Lady Chatterton either met or corresponded. On 16 June 1838, Windele noted that he had insuffi-cient time to visit all the places that he wanted to, including the church at Kinard. A later postscript at the bottom of the page, dated 22 November 1838, added: 'This Church was afterwards visited by Lady Chatterton who saw the Ogham Inscription there.'[14] However, Lady Chatterton's book was not published until 1839, indicating that the information came to Windele by some other means.

The Evidence Provided by Early Travellers, Site by Site

Gallarus

Three of the four early travellers visited Gallarus and described the stone there. The earliest were Windele and Chatterton, both of whom went to Gallarus in 1838. Chatterton's visit there was in March 1838 and Windele's was in June, probably 13 June 1838. They recorded the stone in what was presumably the same location, Windele saying that it was 'at the NE angle of the Cell in the little burying ground attached'.[15] Windele's drawing shows the stone erect. Chatterton described the stone simply as near the east end of the oratory, adding that it was not upright but 'in a slanting position',[16] although her drawing also shows it erect. The subsequent

---

[13] Dublin, Royal Irish Academy, John Windele manuscripts, Windele 12.C.11: on Pelham, p. 186; on Petrie, pp. 275–80; on Lady Chatterton, pp. 177, 281, and 393.

[14] Windele 12.C.11, p. 201.

[15] Windele 12.C.11, p. 199.

[16] Lady Chatterton, *Rambles in the South of Ireland during the year 1838*, 2nd edn, 2 vols (London, 1839), I, 137.

history of the stone indicates that many years later it did indeed fall down and was then re-erected on a patch of grass. By 1986 it was in its present position.[17]

The stone is a tall, slim pillar, with a cross and some other decorative elements incised on one face. Beneath the decoration is incised a text in two lines reading downwards. It reads COLUM [-] MEC. The first word is the personal name Colum, but the rest is not now interpretable. In 1838 apparently neither Windele nor Chatterton could read any of the text. Chatterton indeed admitted that, although she sketched the stone, it was 'very little to my edification'.[18] She interpreted the stone as a grave-stone. This may have been its original function although no grave has been found at the site.

Petrie visited Gallarus at some time before 1845 and drew the decoration and text on the stone. He also took the stone to be a grave-stone. He gave the stone as an example of an upright stone, which suggests that it was then still erect. His drawing in fact shows the stone on its side, but it was presumably printed like that to aid the reader, since the text on the stone then reads horizontally as print. He described the text as 'not perfectly legible in all its letters' which is certainly the case today. He interpreted part of the decoration as lettering, so that he read three further 'letters' at the beginning of each line.[19] His reading of the first line was LIE COLUM and of the second MEC [...] MEL and he translated the whole as 'the stone of Colum son of [...] Mel'.[20] Petrie was therefore the first person to make any sense of this text.

After Windele had read Petrie's account of the stone, he copied out parts of it, including a copy of Petrie's drawing, his reading of the text, and his translation.[21] Windele added his own comments to some of his quotations from Petrie. For example, he quoted Petrie as saying that the early Irish 'founders' of oratories lived nearby in circular stone houses, to which Windele added '(!) - assertion'. Again, Petrie said that when these early Christian founders died, their graves were marked by 'upright Pillar Stones', to which Windele added '(Where?)'.[22] However, Windele made no comment on Petrie's reading and translation of the text, which seems to imply that he accepted it.

---

[17] Okasha and Forsyth, *Early Christian Inscriptions*, p. 148.

[18] Chatterton, *Rambles in the South of Ireland*, I, 137.

[19] George Petrie, *The Ecclesiastical Architecture of Ireland, anterior to the Anglo-Norman Invasion* (Dublin, 1845), p. 134.

[20] Petrie, *Ecclesiastical Architecture*, p. 134.

[21] Windele 12.C.11, p. 278.

[22] Petrie, *Ecclesiastical Architecture*, pp. 133–34; Windele 12.C.11, p. 278.

Kilfountan

Windele was the first person to record this stone, which he examined on 4 September 1848 during his visit to Kerry that year. None of the other three early travellers described this stone, with the exception of Petrie who saw it after the publication of his work in 1845. Windele and his companions left Dingle on 4 September, en route to Kilmalkedar. They left the road to walk to Kilfountan, which Windele described as 'a cealluragh adjoining a boggy heath' and 'uninclosed'. The ruined oratory is described and the stone is said to be 'Near its S E angle but a few feet from it'.[23] It appears that Windele was describing the stone as being near the south-east angle of the oratory. When Petrie visited Kilfountan, some time between 1845 and his death in 1866, he said it was 'about ten feet from the north-east corner of the church'.[24] It may be that the stone had been moved between 1848 and the date of Petrie's visit. Alternatively, Windele might have meant that the stone was near the south-east angle of the *cealluragh*. Since, however, Windele did not observe the remains of the enclosure (which is defined by a stone-faced earthen bank), this seems less likely. When Stokes visited Kilfountan in 1868, she said simply that the stone was 'near the side of a road',[25] which may have been where Petrie saw it.

The back and sides of the Kilfountan stone are plain but the front (the west face) contains an elaborate cross design, which is not unlike that on Reask 1. Indeed Fanning, describing it as 'poorly executed', saw it as 'possibly a poor copy' of the Reask stone.[26] However the design can be defended as an unusual combination of several disparate elements.[27] Both the roman and ogham texts read upwards; the former is incised on the west face below the cross, while the latter is set on the south-east angle of the stone.

The ogham text reads EQODD-, but its meaning is unclear.[28] Despite his interest in ogham stones, Windele failed to read this text: 'The Oghams would appear to be Mere initials or forming part of some lost Stenographic inscription.'[29]

---

[23] Windele 12.C.11, p. 416.

[24] Petrie, *Christian Inscriptions*, p. 5.

[25] Petrie, *Christian Inscriptions*, p. 5.

[26] Fanning, 'Excavation [. . .] at Reask', p. 140.

[27] Okasha and Forsyth, *Early Christian Inscriptions*, p. 163.

[28] Okasha and Forsyth, *Early Christian Inscriptions*, p. 163.

[29] Windele 12.C.11, p. 417.

The roman text reads [F]INTEN, where the first letter is damaged. Windele read this as -INTEN which he interpreted as the name 'Intin or Fintan from whom the place has been called'.[30] Windele's drawing shows a line at right angles to the I of INTEN. This line is still visible and is now interpreted as part of a damaged F.[31]

Kilmalkedar

All four early travellers visited Kilmalkedar and described the stone numbered Kilmalkedar 1. There was a second early stone from the same site, Kilmalkedar 2, but it is now lost. It was an inscribed cross-slab which was first recorded in 1889.[32] It was not mentioned by any of the four early travellers to Kerry and may not have been found by then. It was still in existence in a broken state in 1965, but by 1986 was lost.[33] The text read DNE-, an abbreviated form of *Domine* ('O Lord'), the same text as occurs on Reask 1. A full description of Kilmalkedar 2 is given by Okasha and Forsyth.[34]

Kilmalkedar 1 is a pillar-stone which is broken at the top. The remains of a cross are incised on each broad face, while the texts are inscribed on the left side of the stone. Both texts are in half-uncial script and read vertically downwards. Text (a) is in large letters and reads DNI, with an abbreviation mark above the N, standing for *Domini* ('of the Lord'). This text was obviously incised first, followed by text (b). Text (b) is in smaller letters and is fitted in around text (a). It is a Latin alphabet with the letter A missing where the stone is broken. The letters from B to X are clearly legible although J, V, and W were not of course included. Following X the letters are less clear, but may well have been Y and Z, with the final 'letter' perhaps the manuscript abbreviation for *et* ('and').[35]

The first person to record this stone was Pelham in 1804. He described the stone as then standing in the churchyard 'about five yards from the church door'.[36]

---

[30] Windele 12.C.11, p. 417.

[31] Okasha and Forsyth, *Early Christian Inscriptions*, p. 163.

[32] J. Romilly Allen, *The Monumental History of the Early British Church* (London, 1889), p. 120.

[33] Cuppage, *Archaeological Survey*, p. 311.

[34] Okasha and Forsyth, *Early Christian Inscriptions*, pp. 169–71.

[35] Okasha and Forsyth, *Early Christian Inscriptions*, pp. 166–68.

[36] Henry Pelham, 'Ogham Inscriptions', in Charles Vallencey, *Collectanea de rebus Hibernicis*, 6 vols (Dublin, 1786–1804), VI, 182–91 (p. 183).

Pelham was meticulous: he 'carefully made several drawings of it, under different circumstances of light, which, on comparing with each other, I found perfectly to correspond; so that the drawing may be depended on'.[37] His drawing shows almost all of the text, although the blank part of the bottom of the stone was then apparently beneath the surface of the ground.

Chatterton and Windele both knew of Pelham's drawing since they both referred to it. It may well be that Pelham's description and drawing of the stone encouraged both of them to go to Kilmalkedar. Chatterton and Windele both drew the stone on their, separate, visits to Kilmalkedar, Chatterton in March 1838 and Windele on 13 June 1838. Their drawings of the stone, and descriptions of its location, agree with each other but not with Pelham's: both drawings show the stone with considerably more of it set into the ground than does Pelham's drawing. Windele described the stone as standing eight feet to the west of the door,[38] while Chatterton said it was 'near the entrance of the church'.[39] Windele noted the discrepancy in location with the earlier account but concluded that Pelham was simply 'wrong'.[40]

What in fact seems to have happened is that the stone was moved between 1804 and 1838. It was placed nearer to the church and more of it was dug in beneath the ground. This could have been because in its earlier position it was felt to be too vulnerable to the elements or to potential vandalism. However, by 1845, the stone had apparently been moved again. Petrie said that it was being 'used as a grave-stone in the church-yard', and his drawing shows the complete text as well as some of the blank part beneath.[41] Windele did not note anything about the stone or its location on his visit on 4 September 1848. However, he did admit that this visit was 'Merely one of reinspection and cursory'.[42] The subsequent history of the stone indicates that it was moved again several times.[43]

Pelham did not attempt to interpret the text. Vallancey, however, in whose work Pelham published his account, was less cautious: '*Observation. —* There are very evidently two kinds of characters on this stone. One the *Ogham*, on each side

---

[37] Pelham, 'Ogham Inscriptions', pp. 183–84.

[38] Windele 12.C.11, p. 84.

[39] Chatterton, *Rambles in the South of Ireland*, I, 156.

[40] Windele 12.C.11, p. 84.

[41] Petrie, *Ecclesiastical Architecture*, p. 134.

[42] Windele 12.C.11, p. 427.

[43] Okasha and Forsyth, *Early Christian Inscriptions*, pp. 165–66.

of a line; the other a running character, which appears to be a mixture of Phœnician, Pelasgian, and Egyptian.'[44] This 'observation' was quoted by both Chatterton and Windele in 1838, although both implied some sort of doubt as to its accuracy. Windele said Vallancey had 'pompously described' the stone, while Chatterton noted that the letters on the stone closely resembled those on a twelfth-century Irish reliquary.[45] Windele said that Lewis had followed Vallancey's description, although all that Lewis actually wrote was that 'Some of the tombstones are inscribed with Ogham and other ancient characters'.[46]

Windele interpreted the text as 'merely the Roman Irish alphabet which commenced on that part of the Stone, above the circle now broken off'.[47] This entry is not dated; it follows entries which must date from after 1839, since Lady Chatterton's work is quoted,[48] but immediately precedes the entry for 16 June 1838.[49] Windele's drawing and transliteration show the letters C to N, followed by DNI. However he failed to identify DNI correctly and thus transliterated the text as A to R with 'the rest effaced'.[50] This interpretation was, however, a considerable improvement on that offered by Vallancey. Windele's interpretation clearly pre-dates 1845 when Petrie published a correct interpretation of both texts, adding some mildly caustic remarks about Vallancey's scholarship.[51]

Reask

Windele was the first person to record the two carved and inscribed stones from Reask. None of the other three early travellers described these stones. Windele first visited Reask in June 1838, probably on 13 June, but failed to find all three stones he had been told about. He did, however, examine and sketch Reask 1.[52] This is a tall, thin sand-stone slab or pillar, plain on the back and sides but

---

[44] Pelham, 'Ogham Inscriptions', p. 184.

[45] Windele 12.C.11, p. 84; Chatterton, *Rambles in the South of Ireland*, I, 156n.

[46] Samuel Lewis, *A Topographical Dictionary of Ireland*, 2 vols (London, 1837), II, 178.

[47] Windele 12.C.11, p. 186.

[48] Windele 12.C.11, p. 177.

[49] Windele 12.C.11, p. 201.

[50] Windele 12.C.11, p. 186.

[51] Petrie, *Ecclesiastical Architecture*, pp. 134–35.

[52] Windele 12.C.11, p. 149.

containing an elaborate cross on the face. Windele described the whole stone as a 'cross'. He drew the inscription correctly, but did not attempt a reading. The text reads DNE, an abbreviation of *Domine* 'O Lord'.

On 4 September 1848 Windele returned to Reask which he then described as a 'Cealuragh or ancient and now neglected burial place'.[53] He made sketches of the stones that he had previously 'omitted', that is, Reask 2 and the carved but uninscribed cross-slab that is now preserved in the National Museum, Dublin.[54]

Reask 2 is a small, slender sand-stone pillar which contains two inscribed texts, one on the east face and one on the west face. In each case the text is set vertically beneath an incised linear cross. The text on the west face reads DNS, an abbreviated form of *Dominus* 'Lord'. Windele's drawing shows this text clearly. However he misinterpreted the half-uncial S as an I and read the text as DNI 'of the Lord', comparing it to the text on Kilmalkedar 1.

The text on the east face reads DNO, an abbreviated form of *Domino* 'to/from the Lord'. Windele's drawing shows the letters accurately, but he failed to offer a reading or interpretation, suggesting that he did not find the text easy to read. The form of D is certainly unusual and the text reads upwards, while that on the west face reads downwards. However, since Windele was accustomed to deciphering ogham texts, this orientation in itself would have been unlikely to have caused him difficulty.

Reask 1 has remained at Reask since June 1838 when Windele examined it. It is possible that it is in the same position now as it was then, and Fanning considered that it might even be in situ.[55] Reask 2 and the carved cross-slab now in the National Museum were subsequently moved to Adare Manor, Co. Limerick. According to the Countess of Dunraven, this removal took place 'about ten years ago', that is, around 1855.[56] Windele's evidence for the location of the stone at Reask in September 1848 is thus in accordance with this date. In 1971 Reask 2 was still at Adare, standing 'in a grove of trees in the manor grounds';[57] the other

---

[53] Windele 12.C.11, p. 435.

[54] Cuppage, *Archaeological Survey*, pp. 341–42, fig. 205 (e), Stone E.

[55] Fanning 'Excavation [...] at Reask', p. 152.

[56] C. W. Quin, Countess of Dunraven, *Memorials of Adare Manor. With historical notices of Adare by her son, the Earl of Dunraven* (Oxford, 1865), p. 153.

[57] Thomas Fanning, 'Two Cross-inscribed Stones from Reask, Co. Kerry, at Adare Manor', *North Munster Antiquarian Journal*, 14 (1971), 25–28 (p. 25).

stone was then kept inside the Manor itself.[58] However by 1975 Reask 2 was again at Reask.[59]

Conclusions

The accounts of early travellers to the inscribed stones of the Dingle peninsula are certainly of general interest to modern scholars working on early Christian stones. As far as the inscribed stones are concerned, it is fascinating to trace the way in which interpretations moved from the fanciful, for example Vallancey's description of Kilmalkedar 1 ('a running character, which appears to be a mixture of Phœnician, Pelasgian, and Egyptian') to Petrie's sober, and correct, account of the text as a Latin alphabet. However, the most helpful information given by the early travellers is their information on where the stones then were and what was the state of their texts. It is these personal observations that enable us to trace the early history of the stones.

The accounts of the early travellers are also of much interest in highlighting some aspects of social history of the early nineteenth century. Firstly, there was the problem of getting to Kerry and then of reaching the places mentioned. With no cars and no asphalted roads, travel was not easy. We have no information as to how Pelham travelled but, as an estate factor, he might well have been on horseback. Lady Chatterton and her party hired a coach and post-horses to reach Kerry and then hired or borrowed local transport, on different occasions carts, carriages, or horses. Petrie may well have done the same. Windele, perhaps indicative of his lower social standing, travelled to the area by 'Public Car',[60] and then hired transport locally, on one occasion at 12s. 6d. per day.[61]

Secondly, people did not apparently travel alone. Lady Chatterton was in a mixed group which presumably included her husband; she also had a maid with her.[62] Windele travelled with two or three male friends. On both journeys he was accompanied by Abraham Abell, another Cork antiquary. In 1838 they had with them Fr Mathew Horgan and William Willes, also Cork antiquaries, and in 1848

---

[58] Fanning, 'Two Cross-inscribed Stones from Reask', p. 27.

[59] Thomas Fanning, 'Excavations at Reask', *Journal of the Kerry Archaeological and Historical Society*, 8 (1975), 5–10 (p. 10).

[60] Windele 12.C.11, p. 85.

[61] Windele 12.C.11, p. 82.

[62] Chatterton, *Rambles in the South of Ireland*, I, 59, 70.

John Gallwey accompanied Windele and Abell. Windele subsequently noted that Abell died in 1851 and Gallwey, of the cholera, in 1849.[63] Horgan also died in 1849 and Willes in 1851. Both Windele and Lady Chatterton obtained local people to accompany and/or to guide them to the actual sites. On occasion, Windele and Lady Chatterton were both helped by the same person, for example by Fr Casey, described by Windele as the parish priest of Ferriter and Dunquin.[64]

Thirdly, even with the benefit of locally hired transport, difficulties remained. Accommodation was usually in local inns, where levels of comfort could differ quite widely. Sometimes the local mode of transport provided was deemed inappropriate for women. On one occasion, Lady Chatterton and her maid could not sit for fear of falling off and so had to lie on the 'primitive concern' provided; this 'consisted of a few flat boards nailed together, laid on two long poles'.[65] However on another occasion they were lent an 'open carriage and a fine pair of black horses'.[66] In any event, of necessity there was much walking, sometimes over rough terrain. On one occasion, the ascent of a hill overcame one member of Windele's party.[67] We can understand Lady Chatterton's comment that her journey in Ireland had been a 'tour in some of its wildest districts'.[68] Windele showed incredible stamina. For instance, on 4 September 1848, not only did he visit three of the four sites under discussion but also several others, making sketches of at least fourteen stones or architectural features. Again, on 6 September 1848, he listed eight places visited.[69] To those of us who have undertaken this type of field-work, this is nothing short of extraordinary.

Fourthly, in terms of social history, there are the comments made by Lady Chatterton, the aristocrat, and Windele, the city gentleman, on the inhabitants of Kerry. In June 1838, for example, Windele noted that Irish was 'the only language of the people', by which he presumably meant certain of the people, since those who helped and entertained him are clearly described as speaking English. On the same occasion, and presumably of the same class of people, he noted 'red

[63] Windele 12.C.11, p. 498.

[64] Chatterton, *Rambles in the South of Ireland*, I, 144; Windele 12.C.11, pp. 80, 149.

[65] Chatterton, *Rambles in the South of Ireland*, I, 59.

[66] Chatterton, *Rambles in the South of Ireland*, I, 99.

[67] Windele 12.C.11, p. 82.

[68] Chatterton, *Rambles in the South of Ireland*, I, un-numbered page, *advertisement*.

[69] Windele 12.C.11, p. 471.

Petticoats abundant'.[70] Lady Chatterton gave a detailed description of Fr Casey's house near Kilmalkedar, a description that clearly indicates how primitive she found it.[71] Windele can approve wholeheartedly of Pugin's new Catholic cathedral in Killarney and shortly afterwards be complaining of being stung by gnats as he sketched an ogham stone.[72]

Finally, it is worth noting that Windele never once makes any explicit mention of the Famine, nor even of conditions of extreme poverty, although in 1848 signs of these are unlikely to have been invisible in Co. Kerry. His reticence on this point is difficult to explain. Nevertheless, his diaries contain fascinating glimpses of life in the area in the middle of the nineteenth century. It is due to the interest of his comments and descriptions, as much as to the explicit information provided on the inscribed stones, that parts of Windele's diaries are transcribed in the Appendix.

---

[70] Windele 12.C.11, p. 82.

[71] Chatterton, *Rambles in the South of Ireland*, I, 144–48.

[72] Windele 12.C.11, pp. 379, 389.

Appendix

Portions of Windele's diaries describing journeys to Kerry in June 1838 and September 1848, as well as notes from books he had read about the area and its antiquities.

Transcribed with the kind permission of the Royal Irish Academy

Windele's notebook 12.C.11 contains diary entries, sketches of stones and of buildings, comments on books read, comments on lectures heard, and similar things. The entries are not necessarily chronological. All are written in ink except for the occasional pencil note: some of these notes have information later incorporated into the text, as on p. 84. On other occasions, as in the heading on p. 149, the pencil has later been inked over.

In the transcriptions, indentation and the starts of new lines are as in the original. Punctuation also follows the manuscript, except when a dot seems more reasonably to be interpreted as an ink blot than a full stop. Underlining is as in the manuscript and the spelling also follows that of the manuscript. However word-division has been added, since Windele tended to join several words together. Upper case letters are as far as possible as in the original, although on some occasions, particularly with the letters S and W, it is not clear whether an upper or lower case letter was intended. Small letters set high up in the line (as in 'Mr') are not indicated. On occasion there is more than one possible reading, and a few words are not legible: these are indicated by the use of square brackets. Italics are used throughout to indicate editorial additions and explanations.

Undated: notes taken from printed sources

Windele 12.C.11, p. 78:

After mention of various other places, this part starts with the words Lewis *and* beneath *from Vallancy in the margin. Then*:

At Kilmelchedor besides the <u>Ogham</u> there is another
Inscription in a running character of Various ancient
letters _

Above the word Ogham *in the first line, with an insertion sign, is*: on each side of this line, *written in small script. The final word is* Valcy, *presumably for Vallancy. After the word* character *in the second line is a mark of insertion and above is written in small script*:

a mixture of Phenician Pelasgian & and Egyptian Valcy [*the last presumably for* Vallancy]

Following the word letters *are three lines written in small script*:
It is a stone of the Green Mountain Kind it stands in the same Church yard at 5 yards
from the Church door & is inscribed with a variety of chacters – The flourished cross on the broad
side of the stone is later than the Inscription.
The rest of the page is about other places

Travels 11–16 June 1838
Windele 12.C.11, p. 82:
          11 June 1838
     Left Cork for Dingle accompanied by Abraham Abell
Wm Willis & the Revd Mathew Horgan PP of Blarney &
Whitechurch, passed thro Mallow, Kanturk - King Williams
Town a most interesting experiment, the Houses built in a
Bog - Castleisland and rested for the Evening at
the Hotel [*mark of insertion and* Tralee *above*] Where we saw J J O'Flaherty [*mark of insertion and* an old friend *above*] now Editor of
the Tralee Mercury and with whom we had a colloquy
on Round Towers.
     12th Tuesday - Visited the Town & Left it passing [*above the last three words in a hired Car*]
through Blennerville seeing the Ship Canal [canal *with a second* n *crossed out*] now in progress
Passed under Curraheen where a new Chapel has been built
Visited a [*mark of insertion and* round *above the line*] fort & entered its Chambers,
this at Derry Kay [*mark of insertion and above the line* Between the road & the Bay] ascended
by the Fionna Glaissa a Beautiful falling Stream - hired a
Guide at Camp or Coom & ascended Cahir Conree deeply envelloped
in Clouds concealing all prospect - Father Mat failed in the
ascent - Proceeded to Dingle stopping a moment at Ballinysteenig
looking at the Ogham - & dined at Mrs Jeffcotts at 10 °Clock PM
     13th Retained our Car at 12/6 per day & proceeded Westward
by Dingle Harbour to Kilmelchedor - The road bad -
Irish the only language of the people - red Petticoats
abundant - Kilmelchedor lies in a plain at foot of the mount-
Smerwick bay Gallerous etc in view -

Windele 12.C.11, p. 84:
1838
13 June
Drawings of Kilmalkedar 1, labelled west face *and* East face
Facing the West door of the church is a small
Common [brown *crossed out, next word written above*] green Stone 2 feet high and about one in
breadth, & 3 inches in thickness it stands 8 feet to the
West of the door and is the Stone so pompously
described by Vallancey (Vol 6 Collectanea) & followed in
Lewis's Topographical dictionary as Containing a quadruple
inscription in Phenician Egyptian Pelasgic & Ogham.
Vallancy Says it stands 5 yards from the Church, he is wrong

Windele 12.C.11, p. 149:
After the first line, which forms a heading, the text is written beside Windele's sketch of Reask 1
Riesk about a quarter of a Mile S E of Ballinrannig
Mr Casey informed
us that here were
3 stones (I forget
Whether he said
Inscribed) besides
a cross. We found
none but the
cross altho there
were some low
rude stones,
but uninscribed
Mr Casey was
unfortunately unable
to accompany us
as a guide being
called away from
us on a Sick call

Windele 12.C.11, p. 186:
The church appears to have been anciently Stone
roofed a portion of which roof still remains!

Facing its Western door is a Small Common green
Stone, 2 feet in height & about one in breadth & 3 inche[s]
in thickness. It stands 8 feet to the West of the door and is
the Stone so pompously described by Vallancy (6th Vol
Collectanea) who is followed by the Writer in Lewis's
Dictionary, as containing a <u>quadruple</u> inscription in
Phœnician Egyptian Pelasgic & Ogham! Vallancy says
also that it stands 5 yards from the Church! His
authority doubtless was Pelham the intended historian
of Kerry.

This Stone seems to me to be only a fragment
of a larger one Which was once sculptured with the
Druidic circle on which the Christians as usual imposed
the cross The fracture took place across the Circle. The
Inscription seems to have been merely [but *crossed out*] the Roman Irish
alphabet which commenced on that part of the Stone,
above the circle now broken off; thus.
*There follows a drawing, similar to that given on p. 187, of the letters C to N, followed
by* DNI, *and then the following*:
A B C D E F G H I K L M N [*last two letters above decoration*] P R the rest effaced

Windele 12.C.11, p. 187:
Two drawings of Kilmalkedar 1, one labelled in two lines Western face of the Stone
/ facing the door *and the other labelled* Eastern face

Windele 12.C.11, p. 199:
*Following labelled drawings of the inside of the doorway and the outside east window
of the oratory at Gallarus, the text resumes*:
This arch is formed by overlaying
and is very acute resembling the first Style of the Gothic to which
order however it does not belong, it is Pelasgic. The door is of the
same style of the
window [be *or* but] ancient
it proves the
antiquity of the
arch -
*To the right of the last five lines is a drawing of the Gallarus stone erect. To the right
of the drawing is the following text*:

Stone at the NE
angle of the Cell
in the little burying
ground attached -
It is 4f high, 9 inches
broad

Windele 12.C.11, p. 201:
16th June
1838
The first two lines are written alongside the two lines of the date
    With Ballintaggart ended our researches
    in this highly interesting district after the
ancient Cryptography Our three days labour had
well rewarded our toil & exertions and days of
toil but pleasant withal they were They certainly
were not spent in much indulgeance. as, always
breakfasting about seven OClock in the morning our
hours of dinner were 10 and 11 and on one occasion
12 °Clock at night! Pity however that our time
was limited as the Week we had expended was
quite insufficient for all the localities indicated to us
Witness -
    √ Skellig where there is more than one ogham
    √ Ballyreagh - 2 Miles NW from Dingle
    √Cahir caillaire, Parish of Dingle 3 miles from Town in a Glen
    Owen Masters house on the high road midway between
                Tralee & Dingle on the road
    X Kinnard church between Minard & Ballinystinig
    West Minard over Val Quins door an inscribed stone
    The old church near the Short Strand &
X This Church was afterwards visited by Lady Chatterton who saw the Ogham
Inscription
there - 22 Nov 1838

Undated, but after 1845
Windele 12.C.11, p. 278:
The page contains notes, not exact quotations, taken from Petrie, Ecclesiastical
Architecture, *pp. 133–34, with some comments.*

These were the first Stone edifices erected
for Christian uses in Ireland - 133 I am inclined
to believe they [were *crossed out*] may be more ancient than
the period assigned for the conversion of the Irish
generally by St Patk.
    Adjacent to them may be seen the remains
of the circular stone houses which were the
habitations of their founders (!) - assertion)133
    And their graves are marked by upright
Pillar Stones. (Where?) Sometimes bearing
inscriptions in the <u>Ogham</u> Character, as found
on Monuments presumed to be pagan
The above paragraph has ogham *in the margin between the first two lines and
between the third and fourth the following in three lines*:
he must mean
that at Bally
reagh
    (But if the cell be pagan and not christian, as
    Mr P <u>supposes</u>, the presumption that the ogham
    is pagan also will not be very erroneous)
and in other instances as at the Oratory of Gallerous
with an inscription in the Græco Roman or
Byzantine character of the 4th or 5th Century
    He then copies the Stone
There follows a copy of Petrie's drawing
lie colvm mec . . . mel The Stone of Colum son of Mel
*The transliteration attempts to copy the script on the stone, but the translation is in
Windele's usual writing*

Windele 12.C.11, p. 279:
It is this and the alphabet stone, which I suspect
Has christianised the cells of Gallerous.
Then there follows different material

Travels 1–8 September 1848
Windele 12.C.11, p. 415:
Following some other material:
    We returned to Dingle at 6 °Clock and
dined with Mr M Galway at Ballybeg and spent

a Very agreeable evening. A. was glorious and
kept up a running fire with old Mr Nelligan
the Apothecary until exhausted by speaking Latin
Sentences out of Lillys grammer, he dropped asleep
much to the shame of Jn° Gallwey. On his waking
he called out for his friend Nelligan and asked
his host were not we, that is, N, A & myself
an admirable triad. N. a <u>boy</u> of 90, himself (A)
a child of 70, and I an infant of 50.) Going
home he saw double, a tailor wending his way
before us he protested was the largest man ever
seen by him, being at least 10feet 7 in his eyes.

Windele 12.C.11, p. 416:
Just as we reached the hotel, the striking of the
Clock filled him with wonder as he declared
there were 7 clocks all chiming together.
     4th September
     The morning fine, left Dingle at Half past
7, Jno Nelligan (Attley) accompanying us. Our
route being for Kilmelchedor; and our first
object being –
     Killeenten or Killfountain
     It lies at nearly the same distance from
Dingle as Ballymorreagh and in the same
Valley, that is between the Dingle Mountain
and that behind Ventry and nearly ½-a mile
to the east of the road to Smerwick.
     The place is a cealluragh adjoining a
boggy heath, It is uninclosed and contains
the remains of a cell, quite ruinous, angular in
form and evidently of the same character as
that at Ballymorreagh. The measurement of this
building is 16 feet broad & 21 f 4 inches long not
more than 3 or 4 feet of its height remain.
     Near its S E angle but a few feet from it, is

(Windele 12.C.11, p. 417):
a small upright pillar (sand)stone four feet in
height 3½ inches thick & varying in breadth
from 9 inches near the top to 5 lower down
On its broad face is a kind of Maltese Cross
Within a circle With Scroll Work under and
Beneath that in Romanesque Letters the word
     INTEN
with the letters shown as in the drawing on p. 419
and on the side nearly at equal distances from
either angle are two groups of scores, one
containing 5 and the second 4. To which angle
they belong - the right or the left - there is
no telling. Certainly this is curious & remarkable
the finding of Inscriptions in two differing
characters on the same stone. It is of Unique
occurrence as we Know of no other Similar
instance. The Oghams would appear to be
Mere initials or forming part of some lost
Stenographic inscription. The Roman letters
form the name of Intin or Fintan from
whom the place has been called. Colgan has
a life of Fintan at 3rd January. He was called
Fintan of Dun Bleische & was of the noble family

(Windele 12.C.11, p. 418):
of Ara Cliach in the now County of Tipperary
He studied under Comgall of Bangor where he
became acquainted with Finian of Magh bile
We find him afterwards (says Lannigan) at a
place called from his name Kill fintan
somewhere in Munster, probably Killfinan in
the County of Limerick! This was a sorry
guess inasmuch as Killfinan would not
express the name of Killfintan.
    In the little cemetery which surrounds
the ruined cell no burial takes place save of
unbaptised children.

The remainder of page 418 is blank

Windele 12.C.11, p. 419:
Drawing of Kilfountan, unlabelled, showing face of stone with the cross and the text
— INTEN

Windele 12.C.11, p. 427:
Following some other material
    Our Visit to Kilmelchedar church was
Merely one of reinspection and cursory. The
Style of the Sculpture of the soffit of the chancel
Arch once more baffled my power of pencil. I
had to abandon the attempt after trying this
unfinished bit
two drawings follow, one unlabelled, the other labelled:
This head projects from the inner
face of the tympanum of the door
in the Western gable.

Windele 12.C.11, p. 435:
    Riesk we revisited. It is a Cealuragh or
ancient and now neglected burial place; but that
it was once of importance, the pains taken in
christianizing its monuments evince. Those omitted
by me on my former inspection I now sketched -
    I conjecture that the letters on the back of one of the
stones were intended for DNI the usual abbreviation [for *crossed out*] of
<u>Domini</u> as on the alphabet stone at Kilmelchedor.
*The remainder of the page contains drawings of the two inscribed faces of Reask 2 and
a drawing of the uninscribed stone now in the National Museum, Dublin. The latter
is labelled* badly done

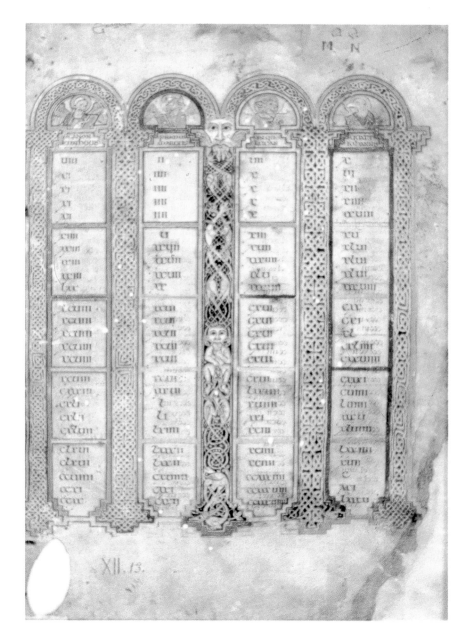

Plate 1. Canon Table, Barberini Gospels. Vatican City, Biblioteca Apostolica Vaticana, MS Barb. lat. 570, fol. 1ʳ. © The Biblioteca Apostolica Vaticana. By kind permission of the Prefect of the Biblioteca Apostolica Vaticana.

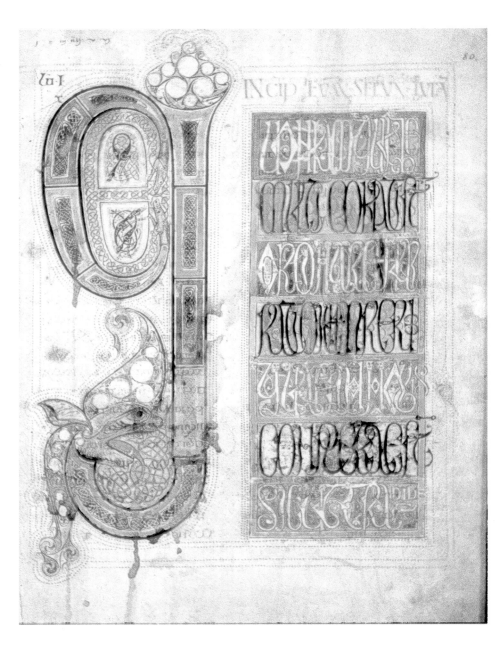

Plate 2. Incipit of St Luke's Gospel, Barberini Gospels. Vatican City, Biblioteca Apostolica Vaticana, MS Barb. lat. 570, fol. 80ʳ. © The Biblioteca Apostolica Vaticana. By kind permission of the Prefect of the Biblioteca Apostolica Vaticana.

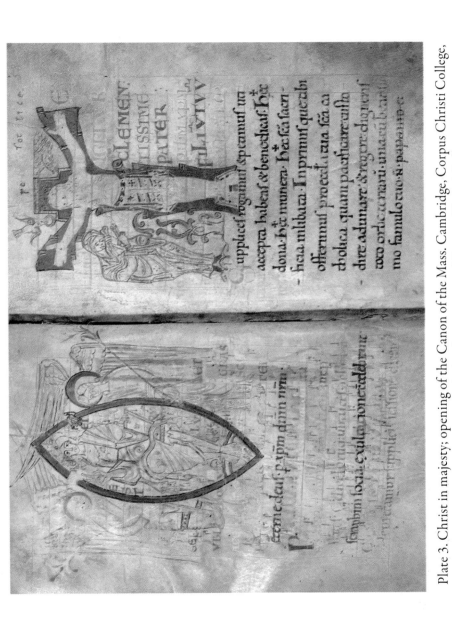

Plate 3. Christ in majesty; opening of the Canon of the Mass. Cambridge, Corpus Christi College, MS 422, pp. 52–53. By kind permission of Corpus Christi College.

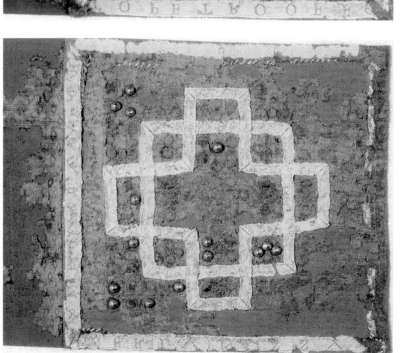

Plate 4a (left). End square 1 from the 'velamen' of St Harlindis, from St Catherine's Church, Maaseik. © IRPA-KIK, Brussels.
Plate 4b (right). End square 2 from the 'velamen' of St Harlindis, from St Catherine's Church, Maaseik. © IRPA-KIK, Brussels.
The reverse of the woven braid is shown in both cases.

Plate 5. The Alexander Flag. © Mainfränkisches Museum, Würzburg, Germany.

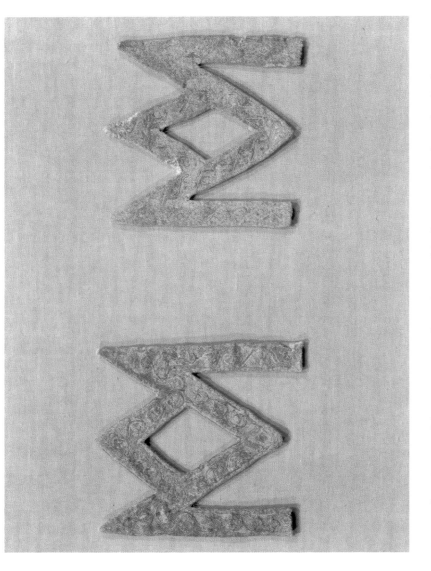

Plate 6. Two of the monograms from the 'casula' of Saints Harlindis and Relindis from St Catherine's church, Maaseik. © IRPA-KIK, Brussels.

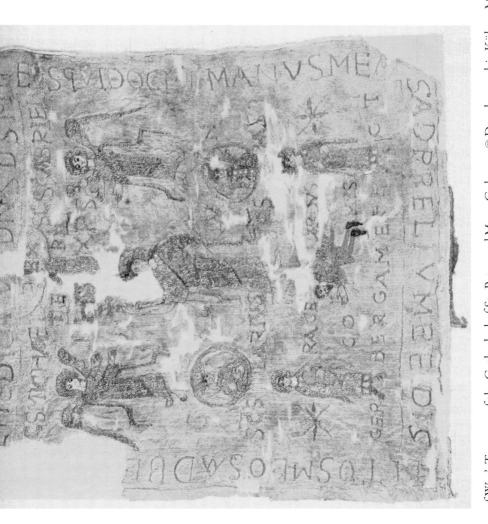

Plate 7. The 'Flag of War', Treasury of the Cathedral of Sts Peter and Mary, Cologne. © Dombauarchiv Kölnm Matz und Schenk.

Plate 8. Apse mosaic, the Aula Leonina, Piazza di San Giovanni in Laterano, Rome. © George Henderson.

Plate 13a (above). Leacht with cross-inscribed vertically set slab, near Reilig na mBan, Inishmurray, Co. Sligo. Photo: Tomás Ó Carragáin.
Plate 13b (below). Leachta within the principal enclosure, Inishmurray, Co. Sligo. Photo: Michael Ryan.

Plate 14. Open-air tomb shrine, Slane, Co. Meath. Photo: Michael Ryan.

Plate 15. *Tech Molaise* probable *memoria*, Inishmurray, Co. Sligo. Photo: Michael Ryan.

Plate 16. Tomb shrine (one of two) flanking the church, Teampuill Cronán, Co. Clare. Photo: Michael Ryan.

ÉAMONN Ó CARRAGÁIN: A BIBLIOGRAPHY

Compiled by Tomás Ó Carragáin

'The Sectional Divisions and the Structure of *Beowulf*' (unpublished master's dissertation, National University of Ireland, University College, Dublin, 1965).

'Structure and Thematic Development in *Beowulf*', *Proceedings of the Royal Irish Academy*, 66C (1967), 1–51.

'The Vercelli Book as an Ascetic Florilegium' (unpublished doctoral dissertation, The Queen's University of Belfast, 1975).

'Liturgical Innovations Associated with Pope Sergius and the Iconography of the Ruthwell and Bewcastle Crosses', in *Bede and Anglo-Saxon England*, ed. by Robert Farrell, British Archaeological Reports, 46 (London, 1978), pp. 131–47.

'Christ over the Beasts and the *Agnus Dei*: Two Multivalent Panels on the Ruthwell and Bewcastle Crosses', in *Sources of Anglo-Saxon Culture*, ed. by Paul E. Szarmach, Studies in Medieval Culture, 20 (Kalamazoo, 1981), pp. 377–403.

'How Did the Vercelli Collector Interpret *The Dream of the Rood*?', in *Studies in Language and Literature in Honour of Paul Christophersen*, ed. by Philip Tilling, New University of Ulster, Department of English, Occasional Papers in Linguistics and Language Learning, 8 (Coleraine, 1981), pp. 63–104.

'Crucifixion as Annunciation: The Relation of *The Dream of the Rood* to the Liturgy Reconsidered', *English Studies*, 63 (1982), 487–505.

'*Vidi Aquam*: The Liturgical Context of *The Dream of the Rood* 20a, "Swætan on þa swiðran healfe"', *Notes and Queries*, n.s., 30 (1983), 8–15.

'A Liturgical Interpretation of the Bewcastle Cross', in *Medieval Literature and Antiquities: Studies in Honour of Basil Cottle*, ed. by Myra Stokes and Tom Burton (Cambridge, 1987), pp. 15–42.

'The Ruthwell Cross and Irish High Crosses: Some Points of Comparison and Contrast', in *Irish and Insular Art, 500–1200: Proceedings of a Conference at University College Cork, 31 October–3 November 1985,* ed. by Michael Ryan (Dublin, 1987), pp. 118–28.

'The Ruthwell Crucifixion Poem in its Iconographic and Liturgical Contexts', *Peritia*, 6–7 (1987–88), 1–71.

'The Meeting of St. Paul and St. Anthony: Visual and Literary Uses of a Eucharistic Motif', in *Keimelia: Studies in Archaeology and History in Honour of Tom Delaney*, ed. by Gearóid MacNiocaill and Patrick Wallace (Galway, 1988), pp. 1–58.

'Seeing, Reading, Singing the Ruthwell Cross: Vernacular Poetry, Old Roman Liturgy, Implied Audience', in *Medieval Europe 1992: A Conference on Medieval Archaeology in Europe, 21st–24th September 1992 at the University of York, Organised by The Society for Medieval Archaeology, York Archaeological Trust, and The Department of Archaeology, University of York: Pre-printed Papers*, 8 vols (York, 1992), VII, 91–96.

The City of Rome and the World of Bede (Jarrow Lecture, 1994).

'*Traditio Evangeliorum* and *Sustentatio*: The Relevance of Liturgical Ceremonies to the Book of Kells', in *The Book of Kells: Proceedings of a Conference at Trinity College Dublin 6–9 September 1992,* ed. by Felicity O'Mahony (Aldershot, 1994), pp. 398–436.

Review of *The Ruthwell Cross: Papers from the Colloquium Sponsored by the Index of Christian Art, Princeton University, 8 December 1989*, ed. by Brendan Cassidy, *Medium Aevum*, 63 (1994), 317–19.

'Rome Pilgrimage, Roman Liturgy and the Ruthwell Cross', in *Akten des XII. internationalen Kongresses für christliche Archäologie, Bonn, 22. bis 28. September 1991*, ed. by Ernst Dassmann and Josef Engemann, 2 vols, Jahrbuch für Antike und Christentum, Ergänzungsband, 20, parts 1 and 2 (Aschendorff, 1995), II, 630–39.

(ed., with Anna Maria Luiselli Fadda), *Le Isole Britanniche e Roma in Età Romanobarbarica*, Biblioteca di Cultura Romanobarbarica, 1 (Herder, 1998).

'The Necessary Distance: *Imitatio Romae* and the Ruthwell Cross', in *Northumbria's Golden Age*, ed. by Jane Hawkes and Susan Mills (Stroud, 1999), pp. 191–203.

'Rome, Ruthwell, Vercelli: *The Dream of the Rood* and the Italian Connection', in *Vercelli tra Oriente ed Occidente, tra tarda antichità e medioevo*, ed. by Vittoria Dolcetti Corazza (Alessandria, 1999), pp. 59–100.

'The Terms *Porticus* and *Imitatio Romae* in Early Anglo-Saxon England', in *Text and Gloss: Studies in Insular Learning and Literature Presented to Joseph Donovan Pheifer*, ed. by Helen Conrad O'Briain, Anne Marie D'Arcy, and John Scattergood (Dublin, 1999), pp. 13–34.

'The Annunciation of the Lord and his Passion: A Liturgical Topos from St Peter's on the Vatican in *The Dream of the Rood*, Thomas Cranmer and John Donne', in *Essays in Anglo-Saxon and Related Themes in Memory of Dr Lynne Grundy*, ed. by Jane Roberts and Janet Nelson, King's College, London, Medieval Studies, 17 (London, 2000), pp. 339–81.

'Cynewulf's Epilogue to *Elene* and the Tastes of the Vercelli Compiler: A Paradigm of Meditative Reading', in *Lexis and Texts in Early English: Studies Presented to Jane Roberts*, ed. by Christian J. Kay and Louise M. Sylvester, Costerus New Series, 133 (Amsterdam, 2001), pp. 187–201.

'*Ut Poesis Pictura*: The Transformation of the Roman Landscape in Bottichelli's Punishment of Korah', in *New Offerings, Ancient Treasures: Studies in Medieval Art for George Henderson*, ed. by Paul Binski and Will Noel (Stroud, 2001), pp. 492–518.

(with Jane Hawkes and Ross Trench-Jellicoe), 'John the Baptist and the *Agnus Dei*: Ruthwell (and Bewcastle) Revisited', *Antiquaries Journal*, 81 (2001), 131–53.

'Between Annunciation and Visitation: Spiritual Birth and the Cycles of the Sun on the Ruthwell Cross: A Response to Fred Orton', in *Theorizing Anglo-Saxon Stone Sculpture*, ed. by Catherine Karkov and Fred Orton (Morgantown, WV, 2003), pp. 131–87.

Ritual and the Rood: Liturgical Images and the Old English Poems of the 'Dream of the Rood' Tradition (London, 2005).

'At Once Elitist and Popular: The Audiences of the Bewcastle and Ruthwell Crosses', in *Elite and Popular Religion: Papers Read at the 2004 Summer Meeting and the 2005 Winter Meeting of the Ecclesiastical History Society*, ed. by Kate Cooper and Jeremy Gregory (Woodbridge, 2006), pp. 18–40.

'Ruthwell and Iona: The Meeting of St Paul and St Anthony Revisited', in *The Modern Traveller to our Past: Studies in Honour of Ann Hamlin*, ed. by Marion Meek (Gretton, Northants, 2006), pp. 138–44.

'Rome Pilgrimage', 'The Roman Stational System', and 'Anglo-Saxon Sculpture', in *Pilgrims and Pilgrimage: Journey, Spirituality and Daily Life Through the Centuries*, ed. by Dee Dyas, Interactive CD-ROM, Christianity and Culture Project (York, 2007).

(with Richard North), '*The Dream of the Rood* and Anglo-Saxon Northumbria', in *Beowulf and Other Stories: An Introduction to Old English, Old Icelandic, and Anglo-Norman Literature*, ed. by Richard North and Joe Allard (London, 2007), pp. 160–88.

Forthcoming

'Chosen Arrows, First Hidden Then Revealed: The Archer Panel on the Ruthwell Cross as a Key to the Coherence of the Upper Stone and to the Unity of the Monument', to appear in a festschrift in honour of Patrick Wormald.

The Mind of the Anglo-Saxon Reader: The Vercelli Book as a Context for 'The Dream of the Rood' (Dublin).

'Sacralised Secular Images: The Archer Panel on the Ruthwell Cross and "mith strelum giwundad" in *The Dream of the Rood*', to appear in a festschrift for Anna Maria Luiselli Fadda (Rome).

'The Vercelli Book as a Pilgrim Manuscript', in *Peregrinatio: Pilgrimage in the Medieval World*, ed. by Damian Bracken and others (Turnhout).

'Who Then Read the Ruthwell Poem in the Eighth Century?', in *Aedificia Nova: Studies in Honor of Rosemary Cramp*, ed. by Catherine E. Karkov and Helen Damico (Kalamazoo).

(ed., with Carol Neuman de Vegvar), *Roma Felix: Formation and Reflections of Medieval Rome* (Aldershot).

TABULA GRATULATORIA

Richard N. Bailey
Janet Bately
Frederick M. Biggs
Brenda M. Bolton
George Hardin Brown
Michelle P. Brown
Howell Chickering
Mary Clayton
Elizabeth Coatsworth
H. Conrad-O'Briain
Rosemary Cramp
George Cunningham
Franco De Vivo
Marguerite-Marie Dubois
Nancy Edwards
Anna Maria Luiselli Fadda
Carol A. Farr
Anna Gannon
David Ganz
Jodi-Anne George
Gertie Goodhue
James Graham-Campbell
Mark A. Hall
Stephen Harris
Thomas E. Hart
Jane Hawkes

George Henderson
Maire Herbert
John Hines
Shaun F. D. Hughes
Nicolas Jacobs
Catherine E. Karkov
Colbert Kearney
Roy M. Liuzza
Rosemary C. Lord
Gearóid Mac Eoin
Hugh Magennis
Gilbert Márkus
Alastair Minnis
Carol Neuman de Vegvar
Richard North
The Medieval Institute, University of
    Notre Dame
Elizabeth O'Brien
Tomás Ó Carragáin
Jennifer O'Reilly
Elisabeth Okasha
Andy Orchard
M. B. Parkes
Cristina Raffaghello
Jane Roberts
Peter Roberts

Elizabeth Robinson
Kenneth Rooney
Michael Ryan
Diarmuid Scully
Richard Sharpe
John Sheehan
Eric Stanley
Paul E. Szarmach
Alan Thacker
Charles Thomas

M. J. Toswell
Elaine Treharne
Elizabeth Tyler
Kees Veelenturf
Leonie Viljoen
Eibhear Walshe
Jeffrey West
Niamh Whitfield
Charles D. Wright

STUDIES IN THE EARLY MIDDLE AGES

All volumes in this series are evaluated by an Editorial Board, strictly on academic grounds, based on reports prepared by referees who have been commissioned by virtue of their specialism in the appropriate field. The Board ensures that the screening is done independently and without conflicts of interest. The definitive texts supplied by authors are also subject to review by the Board before being approved for publication. Further, the volumes are copyedited to conform to the publisher's stylebook and to the best international academic standards in the field.

Titles in Series

Cultures in Contact: Scandinavian Settlement in England in the Ninth and Tenth Centuries, ed. by D. Hadley and J. Richards (2000)

On Barbarian Identity: Critical Approaches to Ethnicity in the Early Middle Ages, ed. by Andrew Gillett (2002)

Matthew Townend, *Language and History in Viking Age England: Linguistic Relations between Speakers of Old Norse and Old English* (2002)

Contact, Continuity, and Collapse: The Norse Colonization of the North Atlantic, ed. by J. H. Barrett (2003)

Court Culture in the Early Middle Ages: The Proceedings of the First Alcuin Conference, ed. by C. Cubitt (2003)

Political Assemblies in the Earlier Middle Ages, ed. by P. S. Barnwell and M. Mostert (2003)

Wulfstan, Archbishop of York: The Proceedings of the Second Alcuin Conference, ed. by Matthew Townend (2004)

Borders, Barriers, and Ethnogenesis: Frontiers in Late Antiquity and the Middle Ages, ed. by Florin Curta (2006)

John D. Niles, *Old English Enigmatic Poems and the Play of the Texts* (2006)

Teaching and Learning in Northern Europe, 1000–1200, ed. by Sally N. Vaughn and Jay Rubenstein (2006)

Narrative and History in the Early Medieval West, ed. by Elizabeth M. Tyler and Ross Balzaretti (2006)

People and Space in the Middle Ages, 300–1300, ed. by Wendy Davies, Guy Halsall, and Andrew Reynolds (2006)

John D. Niles, *Old English Poetry and the Social Life of Texts* (2007)

The Crisis of the Oikoumene: *The Three Chapters and the Failed Quest for Unity in the Sixth-Century Mediterranean*, ed. by Celia Chazelle and Catherine Cubitt (2007)

In Preparation

Precedent, Practice, and Appropriation: The Old English Homily, ed. by Aaron J Kleist